Exploring
IDAHO'S
Mountains

A Guide for Climbers, Scramblers & Hikers

TOM LOPEZ

THE
MOUNTAINEERS

The Mountaineers: Organized 1906 "... to explore, study, preserve, and enjoy the natural beauty of the Northwest."

Some aspects of mountaineering and related activities, including, but not limited to, the activities covered in this book, are potentially hazardous and dangerous. Any person using this book in any manner is personally responsible for learning the proper techniques involved, and assumes all risks and responsibility for any and all damages or injury from any use of this book as a guidebook. Guidebooks, like this book, are no substitute for personal instruction by a qualified person well versed in all appropriate safety techniques.

7 6 5
5 4 3

Published by The Mountaineers
1001 S.W. Klickitat Way, Suite 201, Seattle, Washington 98134

Published simultaneously in Canada by Douglas & McIntyre, Ltd.,
1615 Venables Street, Vancouver, B.C. V5L 2H1

Manufactured in the United States of America

Edited by Richard May
Maps by Nick Gregoric
Cover photographs: Top to bottom — Tangee Peak, Henrys Lake Range; Lost River Range; Ramskull Peak; The Sawtooths
All photographs by the author unless otherwise credited
Cover design by Barbara Bash
Book design and layout by Nick Gregoric

Library of Congress Cataloging-in-Publication Data

Lopez, Tom, 1951-
    Exploring Idaho's mountains: a guide for climbers, scramblers & hikers / Tom Lopez.
    p.   cm.
    Includes bibliographical references.
    ISBN 0-89886-235-3
    1. Mountaineering—Idaho—Guide-books. 2. Idaho—Description and travel—1981- —Guide-books. I. Title.
GV199.42.I2L67   1990
796.5'22'09796—dc20
                                                    90-6679
                                                        CIP

The southern end of the Tango Peaks is anchored by inspiring Cabin Creek Peak (right of center) and the Black Towers, which rise precipitously above Crimson Lake.

N

0   40 Miles

2.
1.
3.
Sandpoint

4.
5. 90 7.
Saint Joe River
SECTION
I
River
Lochsa
Selway
6.
River

Salmon
Riggins
River
Salmon
1.
4.
2. SECTION
II
7.
6.
5.
Stanley
River
6.
Payette
1.
SECTION
III
15
9.
8.
Boise 5.
Boise River
2.
7. Ketchum
Idaho Falls
10.
84
Snake
8.
3.
1.
River
9.
12.
Pocatello
86
11.
5. 7.
SECTION
IV
3.
6.
8.
2.
4.
10.

CONTENTS

INTRODUCTION

SECTION I NORTHERN IDAHO

From the Canadian Border South to
the Salmon River; From the Washington &
Oregon Border East to the Montana Border

SECTION II WESTERN IDAHO

From the Salmon River South to
the Snake River; From the Oregon
Border East to Idaho-75 and US-93

SECTION III EASTERN IDAHO

From Idaho-75 and US-93 East to
the Wyoming Border; From Montana
South to the Snake River

SECTION IV SOUTHERN IDAHO

From the Snake River South to
the Utah & Nevada Borders

APPENDIX

ACKNOWLEDGMENTS

No one could write a book like *Exploring Idaho's Mountains* without the help and input of many people. Since 1978, like a packrat, I have collected random bits of information gathered from numerous people, in addition to formal library research. Although I never learned the names of many of those who provided this information, their contributions are as important as any in adding to the total sum of information contained in this book.

Donna DeShazo and her staff at The Mountaineers Books are responsible for the final shape of the book. They provided useful input for the book's development over a three-year period. Others at The Mountaineers Books who made this book what it is include Steve Whitney, Rick May, and Marge Mueller.

There would be no guidebook without my wife, Dana. She has not only edited and re-edited drafts of the book, she has also been my climbing partner for over ten years and on hundreds of peaks. Without her encouragement and leadership, I would not have completed the book nor made it to the tops of many mountains.

Lyman Dye collaborated with me to write the section on the Sawtooths. The vast majority of the route information for Sawtooth peaks came from Lyman, who painstakingly collected it over the many years he spent as a climbing guide there. His firsthand knowledge of the Sawtooths and the great Sawtooth climbers goes far beyond anything I could have personally discovered.

Paul Bellamy, of Palouse, Washington, has served as my volunteer research librarian for the last six years, as well as leading Dana and me on the first ascent of Cabin Creek Peak and the third ascent of Cougar Rock. Paul's never ending encouragement helped see this project to its end.

Terry Maley, the author of *Exploring Idaho Geology*, provided professional editing for the geology section. Mark Mollner of the National Weather Service edited the weather section and taught me just how much I do not know about Idaho's weather. Alan Virta, Archivist of the Boise State University Library, is curator of the Robert Limbert Collection. His assistance in reviewing Limbert's documents and photographs allowed me to tell Limbert's story. Sandy Myers served as a research assistant, reviewing unindexed periodicals for information on Idaho.

Basil Service deserves special recognition as the most prolific contributor to this book, after Lyman Dye. Dana and I met Basil one day in the Boulder Mountains while we were climbing Ryan Peak. Basil, an extremely enthusiastic peakbagger, provided a lot of detailed information on climbs in the Pioneer, Boulder, White Cloud, Bannock and Portneuf ranges.

John Ebert of the Iowa Mountaineers provided me with access to the club's journals, which detailed their many encounters with the Sawtooths. The Iowa Mountaineers created and documented a big chunk of Idaho mountaineering history; their dedication greatly aided my research.

The members and journal editors of the Mountaineers, the Mazamas, the Appalachian Mountain Club and the American Alpine Club are responsible for recording and preserving the vast majority of Idaho mountaineering history. Without their efforts, much of the historical and route information would have disappeared forever.

Along these same lines, the publishers and editors of *Summit, Climbing, Rock and Ice* and the now-defunct *Off Belay* have also contributed to this book's contents by printing articles on Idaho climbing.

Thanks also go out to Merle W. King, Cyril Slanski, Bill Echo and Bob Hammer of the Idaho Alpine Club, which is centered in Idaho Falls. The club and its members have explored eastern Idaho for many years and are still, for the most part, an untapped source of information on Idaho's mountains.

Sheldon Bluestein provided me with advice and counseling on how to get this book published. More importantly, his hiking guides paved the way in the Idaho marketplace and demonstrated that such books would sell. Ron Watters, another Idaho author, provided me with both encouragement and route information.

Others who have contributed in one way or another to this book include: Buck Drew, who was especially helpful with Beaverhead peaks; Fred Beckey, Sawtooth pioneer; Dave Bingham, guidebook chronicler of the City of Rock; Glen DeVoe of Idaho Falls; Randall Green, guidebook chronicler of northern Idaho rock climbing; Steve Jennings of Boise; Ralph Maughan of Pocatello; Neil McAvoy of Kellogg; Mike Panting of Soda Springs; Gary Quigley of Boise; the late Louis Stur; McCall attorney Jim Weaver; Bing Young, who generously provided me with access to historical research on the fire lookouts of the Salmon National Forest; the staff of the Idaho Historical Museum in Boise; and the staff of the Idaho Falls Public

Library who, nine years ago, put up with me day after day as I reviewed every Idaho USGS quadrangle in their collection to begin my research. The Bureau of Land Management has also contributed to this book in a number of ways. From 1978 to 1982, the bureau employed me in Salmon, Shoshone and Idaho Falls, giving me the opportunity to work in and extensively explore the Lost River country and, to a lesser extent, southern Idaho. Furthermore, BLM personnel, both permanent and part time, were storehouses of information on Idaho's empty acres. Of special note are Chris Ketchum, John Christiansen and Curt Conner, who provided me with invaluable information on the mountains under their management.

Finally, my thanks go out to the United States Forest Service and its employees. Their "on the ground" knowledge, although a little difficult to collect, is second to none. The vast majority of the Forest Service people who helped me are unnamed. They provided detailed information on road and trail conditions, anonymously authored brochures, updated maps and built and maintained trails. Those Forest Service employees whose names I know are: Jo Barnier, William M. Heitler, Judy Schutza, Mike Wilson and Bob Oset of the Bitterroot National Forest; Earl LaOrange of the Caribou National Forest; Jim H. Smith and Howard Rosenkrance of the Challis National Forest; Duane Annis of the Clearwater National Forest; Ellen Mckenzie and Michael Cook of the Nez Perce National Forest; James E. Guest and James R. Morehead of the Salmon National Forest; Steve Lupus of the Sawtooth National Forest; John Kidd, Kim Marshall, Terry Brattian, Linda Magelone, Scott Bates, Robert C. Hammon, Marina Boulter and Keith Birch of the Targhee National Forest; Clyde D. Blake of the Idaho Pandhandle National Forest.

A Word About Safety

Climbing involves unavoidable risks that every climber assumes. The fact that a route is described in this book is not a representation that it will be safe for you. Routes vary greatly in difficulty and in the amount and kind of experience and preparation needed to enjoy them safely. Some routes may have changed or deteriorated since this book was written. Also, of course, climbing conditions can change from day to day, due to weather and other factors. A route that is safe in good weather or for a highly conditioned, properly equipped climber, may be completely unsafe for someone else or under adverse conditions.

You can minimize your risks by being knowledgeable, prepared and alert. There is not space in this book for a general discussion on climbing, but there are a number of good books and public courses on the subject, and you should take advantage of them to increase your knowledge. Just as important, you should always be aware of your own limitations and conditions existing when and where you are climbing. If conditions are dangerous, or if you are not prepared to deal with them safely, change your plans. It is better to have wasted a few hours or days than to be the subject of a bad fall or rescue.

Climb safely and have fun!

INTRODUCTION

This guidebook is an idea book. The opportunities for those who enjoy the mountains are unlimited in Idaho. The climbs listed in this guidebook represent a multitude of climbing opportunities throughout the state, which range from short trail walks to extremely difficult technical ascents far from roads and trails. No matter what need drives one to a mountain summit, Idaho can fulfill it. Most important, the adventurous will find that Idaho is far from "climbed out"— there is still room to explore, still time to create your own climbing history.

Hikers will discover that many Idaho mountain summits are reached by trail and that many of Idaho's most "chic" hiking destinations are not listed in hiking guidebooks. Trails lead to over a hundred Idaho summits, ranging from craggy 7,009-foot Scotchman Peak in the Cabinet Mountains and nearly 10,000-foot Trinity Mountain in the Boise Mountains to tiny Three Tree Butte (3,330 feet) in the Hoodoo Mountains. Peakbaggers and scramblers will find at least a thousand Idaho peaks well suited to those inclined to get to the top without ropes and $5,000 worth of equipment. Those who climb to collect summits will find a wealth of ideas to stimulate their psyches, starting with Idaho's nine 12,000-foot summits and, perhaps, ending with the highest peak in each Idaho mountain range. Mountaineers will find no shortage of challenging routes on granite, basalt and limestone. The Bighorn Crags, Lost River Range, Sawtooths, Selkirks, Seven Devils and a host of individual peaks scattered throughout Idaho's remaining mountain ranges provide high-quality Class 5 and Class 6 climbing. Numerous other peaks not suitable for technical climbing (because of rotten rock) offer exceptionally good Class 3 and Class 4 climbing on exposed ridges and incredible broken walls.

A Geographic Monstrosity

Captain Meriwether Lewis and Captain William Clark were the first white men to enter Idaho, crossing over the Beaverhead Range from Montana at Lemhi Pass. Unbeknownst to them as they enjoyed the view to the west, the land that lay ahead would one day become the state of Idaho. The two explorers probably did realize that before them stretched the most mountainous land they would cross on the journey to the west coast. Idaho is a virtual sea of mountains.

Over 65 percent of the state's 83,557 square miles is comprised of mountain terrain. Elevations range from 12,662 feet on Mount Borah in the Lost River Range to only 736 feet above sea level at Lewiston, Idaho. The land is up and down, with few truly level acres anywhere. More than 200 summits reach over 10,000 feet, and valley-to-summit elevation differences often exceed 4,000 feet, even when maximum elevations do not exceed 8,000 feet. The predominance of mountains is Idaho's most common characteristic and the one factor that keeps the state from developing into a homogeneous community. Due to its formidable mountain barriers, Idaho has always consisted of parts—north, west, east and south.

The difficulty of Idaho's terrain is underscored by the fact that, until 1920, not even a dirt road connected northern and southern Idaho; and it was not until 1938 that the road, US-95, was completely paved for its entire length. The first attempt to define and catalogue Idaho's geologic features and geographic parts took place in the 1930s. This depression-era effort resulted in the publishing of *The Idaho Encyclopedia*, which was compiled by the Federal Writers' Project of the Works Progress Administration. In those days the writers were without high-quality maps and few people were familiar with a state that was almost entirely a roadless wilderness. Idaho's diversity and regionalism proved to be the nemesis for the writers. They said of the state:

> Idaho is a geographic monstrosity. Its shape and size were determined with no regard to what they should have been, but as a leftover area after the limits had been fixed in the states around it. In consequence, of all States in the Union, it has perhaps the least geographic logic and integrity within its borders.
>
> Its long narrow Panhandle is bounded on the north by Canada, on the west by Washington, and on the east by Montana. The Bitterroot Range between it and Montana is a natural and logical boundary, and so is Canada on the north; but the western limit was fixed arbitrarily. South of the Salmon River, the State is bounded on the west by Oregon, with the Snake River

serving as a natural boundary for more than half the distance. On the south are Nevada and Utah, with no natural demarcation between Idaho and those States. On the east is Wyoming, with a high mountain range as a logical division. On the north and northeast is Montana, with the Bitterroot Range of the Continental Divide logically separating the two States.

Today, with the aid of an extensive road system and high-quality topographic maps, we know much more about the land the writers of the *Idaho Encyclopedia* found to be a "geographic monstrosity." Yet, the ever-present mountains still divide the state into numerous regions whose people have their own economies, needs and desires. People in northern Idaho still talk about forming their own state, and possessing an Ada County (Boise) license plate is more than likely to get you the cold shoulder almost any place you go in Idaho. Nevertheless, this book takes a unifying approach to Idaho's mountain world. They are, after all, the one unifying factor the whole state shares.

Mountaineering History

Undoubtedly, Indians, prospectors and United States Geological Survey crews were the first humans to visit the summits of many Idaho peaks. Few of these early explorers left tangible records of their adventures, so the beginnings of Idaho mountaineering are poorly documented. Gathering information on first ascents—outside of those of the Sawtooths and Chimney Rock—often involves sifting through the climbing stories of climbers who never gave the concept of "first ascent" a second thought. The following is a thumbnail sketch of Idaho's mountaineering history, which is filled with unavoidable gaps.

The earliest known written account (that the author has uncovered) of mountain climbing in Idaho was a 1926 article in the *Idaho Statesman* titled "Trailing Through the Land of Tomorrow" by Robert Limbert. The article, which recounted Limbert's 158-day pack trip through the Boise and Sawtooth Mountains, included an account of his climb of Snowyside Peak in the Sawtooths with a party consisting of his son, John Ewald, F. S. Barber and Ted Williams. According to Limbert, Ewald, an Idaho native, had climbed many of Idaho's peaks by the mid-1920s. In 1927, in a second article in the *Statesman*, "The Crown of the Sawtooths," Limbert provided a detailed route description of both of Snowyside Peak's main ridges, including the Class 4 north ridge. Although Limbert's articles fail to provide exacting details of what Idaho's early climbers were accom-

Self-portrait, Robert Limbert (photo courtesy of the Robert Limbert Collection of the Boise State University Library)

plishing in the 1920s, it is clear from the articles that a number of local people had taken an interest in climbing Idaho's peaks long before the outside world knew much about the state.

Bob "Two Gun" Limbert, a.k.a. "The Man from the Sawtooths," was a naturalist, explorer, guide, humorist, author, photographer, mountaineer, poet, painter, trick-shot artist, taxidermist, sculptor, big game hunter and bird and animal imitator. Limbert knew Idaho perhaps better than any of his contemporaries and, unlike others, wrote about what he saw on his many journeys throughout the state. He spent a great deal of his short life (he died at 48) promoting Idaho's scenic attractions and is credited with inspiring President Calvin Coolidge to create the Craters of the Moon National Monument.

Limbert turned his attention to the Sawtooths, where he constructed the Redfish Lake Lodge below Mount Heyburn and extensively explored and photographed the range. Limbert did not fill the stereotype of a true mountaineer, but he was the prototype for the Idaho Mountaineer—part woodsman, part explorer, part thrill-seeker. Although Two Gun Bob was probably the first person to reach the top of a number of Idaho peaks, we will never know the extent of his Idaho ramblings.

Today, most people are aware that Mount Borah is Idaho's highest peak, but for many years the popular belief was that Hyndman Peak in the Pioneers was the highest summit. Although not everyone was happy with this situation, it was the official view of the USGS. In the early 1920s the *Idaho Statesman* ran an article that proclaimed Hyndman Peak Idaho's highest peak and, soon after, the paper received protests declaring Patterson Peak in the White Cloud Peaks as the highest. The protesters even pinned a height of 13,000 feet on their choice. The fact is that in the early 1920s, the USGS had only started to map the state and no one knew with absolute certainty which peak was the highest.

The discovery of Idaho's highest peak was an accident. In 1929, Lee Morrison of the USGS was conducting a mapping survey of the terrain west of Challis, Idaho when he trained his instruments to the east on a far-off group of unnamed peaks that seemed a little bit too high to him. His ensuing calculations put the height of the highest peak at 12,650 feet and soon after the *Statesman* declared "Unnamed Peaks in Pahsimeroi Range Steal Hyndman's Glory." It was not until 1935 that the USGS actually surveyed the Borah Peak area, but the peak's new-found status as Idaho's highest attracted the public's interest. A year after Morrison's discovery, the peak was named for Idaho's late Senator, William E. Borah, who served in the U.S. Senate for 34 years.

Most of what we know of Borah's early history is due to the efforts of Robert Fulton, a free-spirited author, ranch hand and explorer who published two articles about the peak. Fulton, along with Ray Odle, placed the first register on the summit in 1930. Their climb was probably the first ascent made after the peak was declared Idaho's highest. In his 1935 article in the *Statesman*, Fulton stated that, before Borah's height was established, at least three people had summited. These were Clyde Jennings of Twin Falls, Norman Wilson from California and Will Bascom of Mackay. In 1938, Fulton published the first climbing guide to Mount Borah in the magazine *Seeing Idaho*. By that year, over 30 people had signed their names in the summit register and Fulton had climbed the peak three times.

The birth of modern mountaineering in Idaho took place in 1934, when experienced mountain-

eers first tested and subdued a number of the state's most demanding peaks. In northern Idaho, Chimney Rock, dubbed Idaho's "lightning rod," was first climbed by mountaineers with their roots in the Seattle area; and the Sawtooths saw the first visit of dedicated east coast mountaineers, who were also writers: Robert and Miriam Underhill. After the 1934 climbing season, Idaho would no longer be a sanctuary for local climbers and the "word" would slowly begin to trickle out.

Chimney Rock is a fantastic granite shaft that sits square on top of the crest of the Selkirk Range, east of Priest Lake. It is so visible and so close to Spokane, it is difficult to believe that the first recorded attempt on its tiny summit was not made until 1933. Nevertheless, the growing contingent of U.S. mountaineers remained oblivious to Chimney Rock's fine lines and the first attempt was left to a local, Byron Ward and his friend John Carey. Ward and Carey's first attempt was valiant, inadequately equipped and almost successful. Nearly at the top of the west face, the two finally turned back in foul weather. After having the following winter to think about their near-miss, the pair returned to the rock in 1934 with Mart Chamberlain and Fred Thieme and completed their route on the west face. The exploits of Ward and Carey are retold in some detail in Ron Klimko's 1972 article in *Off Belay* (See December 1972, #6.)

In 1934, when Boston mountaineers Robert and Miriam Underhill came to the Stanley Basin, the Sawtooths were well known for their spectacular scenery but were still an unknown quantity to mountaineers. Unlike Bob Limbert, John Ewald and other local climbers, the Underhills were established climbers. Robert Underhill had established difficult routes in the Tetons, climbed in the Alps and Himalayas and his wife was not far behind him in skill and determination. While climbing in the Tetons, Robert heard stories of the Sawtooths and set out to confirm rumors of "sharp granite peaks." When the husband-and-wife team arrived in Stanley they hooked up with local rancher Dave Williams, a superb woodsman who knew the Sawtooth country well, having spent many years hunting goats along the high ridges and guiding fishermen into the high lakes. The Underhills contributed the technical expertise and Williams the woodsman's knowledge, and the perfect Idaho climbing team went to work.

With Williams proclaiming "You folks pick out the mountain you want to climb, and ... I'll take you to it," the climbers wandered up their first canyon, and set their eyes on Snowyside Peak. When they reached the top they discovered others had preceded them, but whatever disappointment this revelation might have caused them was probably eased by the summit view, which was filled with dozens of stunning and most probably unclimbed summits. As Miriam Underhill explained, "It was from the top of Snowyside that we first discovered 'Red Finger Peak,' [known today as the North Raker] quite far to the northwest but so striking in its vertical lines that we set our hearts on it at once." While few peaks were difficult enough to turn the Underhills back, Red Finger's smooth walls were too much for them. Recognizing the peak would not be surmounted without some form of direct aid, they scampered up the lower south peak and planned their next climb.

The outside mountaineering world's first glimpse of the Sawtooths was from an article published by Miriam in *Appalachia* titled "Leading a Cat by Its Tail." Apparently their first Sawtooth fling left the Underhills with an appetite for more Sawtooth climbing and, not surprisingly, the article, while enthusiastic, was not too informative as it recounted the couple's 1934 experiences in the Sawtooths.

With the outside world still in the dark as to the extent of Sawtooth first ascents still available, 1935 saw the Underhills return to once again team up with Williams. This second time around, they finished off climbing everything that was within their abilities. During their two climbing seasons in the Sawtooths they racked up an impressive list of nearly 20 first ascents including the difficult, crumbling west summit of Mount Heyburn, Mount Regan, Williams Peak and Thompson Peak. More importantly, Robert published a second article in *Appalachia* in 1935 titled "The Sawtooth Mountains of Idaho," which would serve as a lure to many mountaineers—who, after reading the article, would be unable to resist visiting the Sawtooths.

During the late 1930s and early 1940s, a solitary man named A. H. Marshall was writing the initial climbing history of the Seven Devils mountains during a number of lonely expeditions in what was then extremely remote country. Marshall, who may have been the first person to reach the highest point in each of the 48 contiguous states, was a true Idaho mountaineer. As the editor of the *Mazama Journal* explained:

Since few men are willing to live solely on dates, peanuts and dehydrated soup for days at a time, carry heavy packs for miles through wild mountain terrain, go a whole day without water, sleep out in snow storms, ford foaming mountain torrents and tackle unscaled cliffs miles from any sign of civilization, he has seldom had companions on his journeys into the wilderness.

Marshall's Seven Devils exploits were published in the 1947 *Mazama Journal*, Vol. 29, #13.

When Marshall began his explorations in 1934, the Seven Devil country was not only difficult, it was also roadless—and his journeys to the alpine summits began 7,000 feet below, along the desert-like shores of the Salmon River. Despite the arduous nature of trips into the high country, between 1934 and 1943 Marshall recorded the first ascents of almost all of the major Seven Devils' summits. Today, Marshall's solo routes, which often verged on Class 5, are among the most rewarding climbs found in Idaho—a little wilderness, a little rotten rock, a little exposure and a little history. Like the Underhills' articles on the Sawtooths, Marshall's article would eventually bring well equipped and highly skilled climbers to the Seven Devils.

The establishment of Sun Valley in 1936 as the nation's first major destination ski resort had the unexpected result of advancing the state of Idaho mountaineering and providing the sport with a high degree of acceptance in most circles. The stimulus was provided when the resort hired a number of European ski guide/instructors who were at home in the mountains, winter and summer. Before the development of ski lifts, the traditional method of skiing involved climbing up the mountain and then skiing down it. Although the ski lift was invented at Sun Valley, the European guides led numerous ski trips into the Boulder and Pioneer Mountains and brought winter mountaineering to the state. In 1937 in an attempt to make the resort resemble the European standard, Sun Valley built the Pioneer Cabin on an incredibly picturesque, high saddle directly south of Handwerk Peak in the Pioneer Mountains. Florian Haemmerle, who managed Pioneer Cabin for many years, made the first ski ascents of a number of Pioneer Peaks and named a number of the peaks. One of Haemmerle's fellow guides, Andy Henning went on to publish a guidebook on winter ski routes in the Pioneer and Boulder Mountains.

After World War II, a new generation of Idaho mountaineering began with the arrival of the Iowa Mountaineers in the Stanley Basin. Enticed to the Sawtooths by the Underhills' articles, they brought with them guides, skill, group organization and a "let's do it" attitude. Led by various guides, including Paul Petzoldt, these flatlanders would write Sawtooth history for the next 25 years. They racked up a set of impressive first ascents and named many of the Sawtooth peaks. Among the Iowa Mountaineers first ascents in the 1940s were Chockstone Peak, The Goat Perch, Redfish Peak, Mount Carter, Ede Peak, Schwartz Pinnacle, Mount Bush, Mount Ebert, Mount Iowa and Warbonnet Peak.

The Iowa Mountaineers' finest accomplishment was their 1947 ascent of Warbonnet Peak. Unlike Mount Heyburn, which stuns people as it stands above the approach to Redfish Lake, the equally impressive Warbonnet is well hidden, invisible from roads and difficult to find. The peak had acquired a reputation as a difficult climbing problem from the time it was named in the 1920s by Arval Anderson, a USGS employee who conducted the initial survey of the range. Twenty years after Anderson named the peak, Bob Merriam, John Speck, Cal Wilcox, Bruce Adams, Cole Fisher and Paul Petzolt approached the peak's northwest face and pioneered the standard route to the summit.

Other groups came to the Sawtooths after the war. Fred Beckey arrived on the scene in the late 1940s and, over the next 25 years (along with a number of different partners), he pitoned and bolted his way up the most treacherous of the Sawtooths spires. Also making stops in the Sawtooths in the 1940s were the Harvard Mountaineers, Dartmouth Mountaineers and Seattle Mountaineers. Among the accomplishments of these diverse groups were the first ascent of the West Peak of Mount Heyburn (called unclimbable by the Underhills) and the Grand Aiguille by Joe Hieb, Wes Grande, Graham Matthews and Ralph Widrig; Splinter Tower by Jack Schwabland and Art Hoblen; the Thimble by Fred Beckey and Harry King; Big Baron Spire and El Pima by Fred Beckey, Pete Schoening and Jack Schwabland. Finally, Beckey and Schoening bagged the North Raker via a difficult aid route on the peak's north face.

An article in the Idaho Statesman in 1948 by Jack Anderson, titled "Here's a Club for You to Join, But it's a Rough Organization," indicated that, by the end of the 1940s most, if not all, of the named, highly visible Idaho peaks had been climbed. Also of note in the article was a reference to a climbing fatality on Leatherman Peak. Although no details were provided, this was probably Idaho's first mountaineering fatality.

In 1951, Louis Stur came to Sun Valley to act as a ski instructor. The Hungarian immigrant was destined to become the most prolific climber among the European guides who worked at Sun Valley. Stur, occasionally with Beckey and often with Jerry Fuller, raised the standards of Idaho mountaineering as he explored every nook and corner of the Sawtooths and established classic routes on many of the peaks. Stur specialized in climbing Warbonnet Peak and Mount Heyburn, both of which he ringed with routes. Stur and his companions tended to find lines of attack that others had missed. He pioneered three routes on Warbonnet: the south face in 1957 with Ring, Bennet and Franke; the west ridge in 1958 with Jerry Fuller; and the east face in 1960. He also established the west face route on Mount Heyburn in 1958.

Mount Heyburn, a conglomeration of spectacular shattered towers, attracted climbers to its slopes at least as early as the 1920s, when the east summit was probably first climbed. After making the first ascent of the slightly higher west peak, Robert Underhill described the peak's granite as "some of the worst stuff I have ever seen." Although many had tested the notoriously rotten granite, in 1958 none of the established routes were considered enjoyable and getting to the top was strictly a "because it was there" proposition. Stur, along with Jim Ball and Jerry Fuller, changed the mountain's reputation when they climbed the obvious but untried chimney on the peak's west face, which today is known as the Stur Chimney. The route, of moderate difficulty, avoided the "ball-bearing" granite encountered on other Heyburn routes by following a classic line grooved in solid granite for its entire distance.

While climbers were familiar with the Sawtooths, Seven Devils and Chimney Rock, little exploration had taken place outside of these three spots. This changed in the mid-1950s when Lincoln Hales and Pete Schoening, two Northwest-based mountaineers, discovered the Bighorn Crags. Although Hales' painfully brief article in the 1955 edition of the *Mountaineers Journal* titled "Climbing the Big Horn Crags of Idaho," raised more questions than it answered, it is clear that the pair were the first to test the granite in the Bighorn Crags. Hales and Schoening made a number of first ascents, including their ascent of shark-tooth-shaped Knuckle Peak, the major climbing prize in the Crags. More importantly, Hales' article served as a stimulus for Idaho mountaineers to travel to the Crags and make some climbing history before outsiders once again seized the day. Beginning in 1957, a group of climbers centered in Idaho Falls adopted the Crags granite and knocked off all but one of the major rock formations that dot the Bighorn Crags. These climbers, who were members of the Idaho Alpine Club included Bill Echo, Dean Millsap and Bob Hammer.

The 1960s began with the Iowa Mountaineers making the first ascent of a large, twin-humped peak in the Sawtooths known variously as Saddleback Peak, Sawtooth Dome and the Elephants Perch. Although the peak is located close to both Redfish Lake and many of the Iowans' earlier climbs, it was bypassed many times in favor of other sharper and more enticing peaks. Despite its size, the mountain has no walkup route and its west face is arguably Idaho's finest and most difficult granite wall.

Robert Limbert was the first person to systematically explore and photograph the Sawtooths (photo courtesy of the Robert Limbert Collection of the Boise State University Library).

The Iowa Mountaineers pioneered the original route up the moderate northwest shoulder and left the wall to others. The others were Fred Beckey, Steve Marts and Herb Swedlund, who climbed the 1,200-foot wall in 1963 utilizing fixed ropes, 110 pitons and 5 bolts. Their climb was, perhaps, the most technically difficult Idaho route yet climbed.

In 1963, a Mazama club outing led by Don Eastman arrived in the Seven Devils hoping to follow in A. H. Marshall's footsteps. In the process of retracing Marshall's steps they added a new chapter to the range's climbing history by establishing new routes on several peaks and by making the first ascents of the North Imp and the Devils Tooth. The Mazamas' success was categorized in two articles in the *Mazama Journal*, "We Climbed Nine of the Seven Devils" by Don Eastman and "North Tower of Devil's Tooth—First Ascent" by Jim Angell.

The late 1950s and early 1960s also saw further refinements and first ascents in the Selkirks, with Ed Cooper and Don Bergman climbing the northeast face of Chimney Rock, Neil McAvoy leading the first ascent of West Lionhead, Ed Cooper and D. Hiser climbing the east face of Chimney Rock

and Don Bergman and J. Miller making the first ascent of Gunsight Peak's north face. From 1968 and into the 1970s, Chris Copczynski and John Roskelley and a host of other climbers established numerous routes on Chimney Rock, which was quickly becoming the best-known rock-climbing peak in Idaho.

The 1960s also saw considerable activity in the Lost River and Lemhi Ranges by members of the Idaho Alpine club and others. Lyman Dye, a Ucon, Idaho, native who learned to climb in the nearby Tetons, turned his attention to his home state in the early 1960s and went on to establish himself as one of Idaho's premier climbers during the 1960s and 1970s, climbing successfully in the Sawtooths and in Idaho's crumbling Lost River Range. Dye's routes on the broken rock of the Lost River and Lemhi Ranges defy logic and have seldom, if ever, been repeated. Among his accomplishments are the first ascents of Diamond Peak's west face, Mount McCaleb's east face, Mount Borah's east face and Bell Mountain's north face and the treacherous north face of Mount Borah. Only those who have climbed in the Lost River Range can appreciate the beauty and difficulty of these climbs.

Lyman Dye also contributed to developing the Sawtooth mountaineering tradition. In the 1970s, he established the first climbing guide service in the Sawtooths and acted as a guide for Mazama and Iowa Mountaineers climbing parties. Both on his own and while leading his clients, Dye discovered new ways up many Sawtooth summits and set the stage for the less-than-experienced mountaineer to challenge the range.

During the 1970s, the great wall on the Elephants Perch quickly became riddled with routes as the wall's reputation attracted climbers from the northwest, Yosemite, the south and from the Shawangunks in the east. The major lines on the face were climbed one by one: In 1968, Gordon Webster and Steve Roper left Yosemite long enough to climb the East Face, a Grade V, Class 6 route up a five hundred foot dihedral; in 1972, Jeff and Greg Lowe climbed a variation of Beckey's original line without placing bolts; Bill March and Jeff Splittgerber knocked off the northwest face in 1975; and Reid Dowdle and Don Hough climbed the line that divides the west face from the south face in 1977. Between these major lines, many impressive routes have been worked up almost all of the nonconformities in the rock.

The late 1970s and 1980s saw further refinements take place in Idaho mountaineering, as rock climbing became very popular. Southern Idaho rock climbers followed the lead of Greg Lowe and many others and began to congregate at a land of beautiful granite formations tucked away in a small valley at the south end of the Albion Range in southcentral Idaho known as the "City of Rocks." No doubt numerous Idahoans and Idaho transplants learned to rock climb at City of Rock; the friendly competition at the City undoubtedly advanced the abilities of many local climbers and acted as a drawing card to bring others to the state. Spending Memorial day weekends at the City became especially popular during the 1970s; the invasions of rock climbers, four-wheel-drive enthusiasts, campers and sightseers often resembled a scene out of a 1960s love-in. Climbers in these gypsy groups pushed the route difficulty higher and higher; and as the routes proliferated, it was inevitable that, in 1985, Dave Bingham would publish *City of Rocks: A Climbers Guide*, the first rock-climbing guide to the City.

Although it is the rock climber who is advancing the state of Idaho mountaineering as this century draws to an end, there are many mountaineering problems that remain as challenges to those willing to get away from the crowds and find new ground. Since climbing activity has traditionally gravitated to a few well-defined areas, most of Idaho's endless mountains remain untested. As late as 1988, a major Idaho peak (9,968-foot Cabin Creek Peak) was climbed for the first time. The peak, as picturesque and difficult as any in the state, suffered from one disability—it was hidden in an out-of-the-way neighborhood where no mountaineer would have expected to find it. In all likelihood, there are still a few Idaho summits and an assortment of towers and pinnacles that have never seen a human footprint. Many other peaks offer high-quality route problems. Likewise, winter mountaineering has been concentrated in only a few areas, with Mount Borah, the Sawtooths and the Pioneers seeing the most winter activity. This book is only the beginning of the story.

More historical information can be found throughout this book and in Appendix B, which contains a list of first ascents for Idaho peaks. The history and the list are published with no guarantee of their accuracy, because too little is documented in print and too many Idaho climbers have yet to speak up.

Geology

The present-day surface of Idaho is a composite of bits and pieces of literally thousands of ancient landscapes. This puzzle holds the story of Idaho's geologic history in its strata and formations.

The oldest known pieces of the Idaho jigsaw puzzle are Precambrian rocks 2.7 billion years old. These ancient rocks can be found in the Salmon River Mountains of central Idaho, the Albion Range, south of the Snake River, and other locations. The origins of these rocks are little known because they have been subjected repeatedly to metamorphism (restructuring due to exposure to heat and pressure) and are drastically altered from their original condition.

Idaho's most common Precambrian rocks are found in the area that is now northern Idaho, southern Alberta and western Montana. These rocks, known as the "Belt Supergroup," are 850 million to 1.5 billion years old. They were originally sedimentary rocks, but in many instances are lightly metamorphosed. From observation of the physical features present in these sedimentary and metamorphic rocks (such as ripple marks, fossil algae and mud cracks) geologists have pieced together the ancient landscape and now know that it was an extremely shallow sea on the edge of an ancient continental plate. The sea received sediments from the many rivers that emptied into it and this sediment eventually formed into the very old rock visible in the Purcell, Cabinet and Coeur d'Alene mountains of northern Idaho.

The next oldest Idaho rocks were formed much later, during the Paleozoic Era, in what was then an ancient sea. From 570 million to 245 million years ago over 30,000 feet of sedimentary deposits

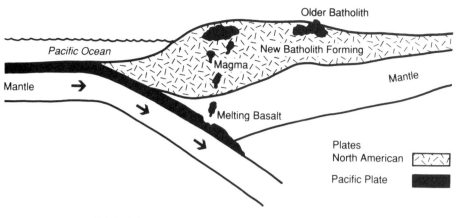

PACIFIC PLATE—NORTH AMERICAN PLATE
SUBDUCTION ZONE

formed in this Paleozoic sea which was much deeper than the Precambrian sea. These Paleozoic rocks include limestones, shales, sandstones (some of which later metamorphosed into quartzites), conglomerates and phosphorites and are found in the Lost River, Lemhi, Beaverhead, Centennial, Big Hole, Caribou, Peale and Bear River mountains.

Four hundred million years ago, all of the earth's continental crustal plates formed one massive continent, most of which was located in the southern hemisphere. This "super continent" began to break up around 300 million years ago, and the resulting pieces began to go their own separate ways. Moving at roughly one inch per year, the crustal plates have traveled many miles over 3.8 billion years, constantly forming and reforming. At times, the plates have joined together to form super continents; at other times, separated to create new oceans. From Idaho's point of view, the most significant event in this sojourn began around 100 million years ago, when the North American plate began to move west, overrriding the Oceanic Pacific plate.

When a continental plate overrides an oceanic plate, the denser oceanic plate is forced under the lighter continental plate. As the oceanic plate is forced down, pressure and friction liquify the oceanic rocks, forming magma. Because magma is lighter than rock, it rises toward the earths's surface, where it either forms massive bodies of granite rock known as batholiths, or magma chambers, which fuel volcanic activity. As is plainly evident in Idaho, the collison of the plates results in the uplifting of the earth's surface and the formation of mountains. Today, the process continues as the North American plate moves imper-

ceptibly westward over the Pacific plate, which is also moving slowly to the northwest.

During the late Mesozoic Era, the North American/Pacific plate subduction zone was responsible for the intrusion of large amounts of granite into the area that is now Idaho. The Idaho Batholith is the largest and most interesting of these Mesozoic intrusions. This incredible batholith took over 30 million years to form and covers roughly 15,000 square miles of land, stretching almost 300 miles from north to south and 100 miles east to west. Saint Maries marks the batholith's northwest corner; Missoula, Montana, the northeast corner; Challis, the southeast corner; and Boise, the southwest corner. The batholith was actually formed by many granitic intrusions, the oldest of which are on its western edges and are 90 million years old. The youngest intrusions are on the eastern edge of the batholith and are roughly 60 million years old.

Intrusion of the Idaho Batholith lifted central Idaho into a high tableland, which has since eroded into the present-day mountain terrain. Topographically, the lowest corner of the batholith is its northwest corner where the peaks are low, seldom exceeding 6,000 feet; the highest corner is the southeast, where Mount McGuire reaches over 10,000 feet. As the mountains fan out toward the northeast and southwest corners, elevations gradually change to roughly 8,000 feet. Much of the batholith is still covered by older sedimentary and metamorphic rocks, which have not yet eroded away.

Because of the extensive amounts of exposed sedimentary and metamorphic rock and the many different granitic intrusions that formed the batholith, there is great variety in the types and quality

0   50 Miles

THE BOUNDARIES
OF THE IDAHO BATHOLITH

of rocks found on the surface in this region. In fact, Idaho Batholith granite varies considerably in texture and form and at least a half dozen different types of granitic rock are present in the batholith. In addition to the Idaho batholith, a number of other batholiths formed during the Mesozoic era. These included the Kanisku Batholith (the foundation of the Selkirk Mountains) and the Owyhee

Batholith (the foundation of the Owyhee Mountains).

Two hundred million years ago the Pacific coast formed a line between present-day Boise and Riggins; far out to sea, there was a remote island chain. Although seemingly unrelated, the continent and the islands were destined to unite as the subduction of the Pacific plate continued to draw the islands slowly but inexorably toward the coastline. Between 150 and 75 million years ago, the islands and the North American plate collided to form the western edge of Idaho. The process that "accreted" the chain of islands to the continent is responsible for the complex geologic terranes of the Craigs, Seven Devil, West, Cuddy and Hitt Mountains. These ranges are highlighted by a wild variety of oceanic and continental rock types including, among many others, granite, metamorphosed chert, argillite, tuff, andesite, limestone, basalt, metamorphosed basalt, dacite and rhyolite.

At the same time the Idaho Batholith was being intruded into central Idaho and the island arcs were being accreted to the batholith's western edge, the land east of the batholith was folded up and pushed eastward. Perhaps this was a result of the forces associated with the collision of the island arc with North America, or those associated with the creation of the batholith. At any rate, this massive eastward movement of rock, known as the "overthrust belt," effectively shortened or compressed the earth's crust. In places, older rock formations actually moved 30 to 40 miles over the top of younger rock formations.

The overthrust belt forms a broad arc beginning in Alberta and extending south through eastern Idaho into Utah; it is known primarily for the oil and gas deposits trapped within its rock layers. (Oil and gas tend to accumulate in areas where a porous rock layer is located below non-porous

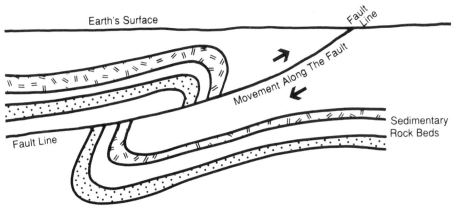

DIAGRAM OF A THRUST FAULT

Earth's Surface Before Crustal Extension

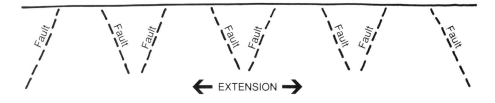

← EXTENSION →

Earth's Surface After Crustal Extension

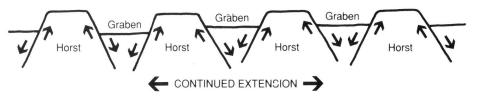

← CONTINUED EXTENSION →

THE DEVELOPMENT of BLOCK FAULTING

rock, such as where sandstone is covered by shale.) The Caribou and Snake River Mountains are the most likely spots in Idaho for oil discovery.

Fifty-one million years ago, a volcanic episode began in the area around present-day Challis. During the next 10 million years, this volcanic activity spread like a cancer to cover over half of the state with volcanic debris. Repeated eruptions formed accumulations of lava and ash over 10,000 feet deep, and buried older Precambrian, Paleozoic and Mesozoic rocks. These rocks (known as the Challis Volcanics), even after 40 million years of erosion, still cover nearly 2,000 square miles of Idaho.

Challis Volcanics form the eastern edges of the Salmon River Mountains and cover much of the area south and west of Challis, where they form the highly colored and barren slopes of the northern Lost River Range and the multicolored summits of the Boulder Mountains. Just west of Challis are numerous ash flows and tuffs which are associated with the Twin Peaks Caldera that was left when a massive volcano collapsed (the same type of event formed Crater Lake in Oregon) some 45 million years ago. Today, the caldera and its rim form the geologic backbone of the many ridge lines along the eastern edge of the Salmon River Mountains.

After ten million years of volcanic activity, when change could be abrupt and catastrophic, Idaho settled into a period of less dramatic change. In central Idaho more granite was injected into the Idaho Batholith. Between 46 and 42 million years

ago, 40 plutons (smaller and younger granitic intrusions, which are injected into an older granite batholith) were injected into the main Idaho Batholith. Pluton granite differs from the older Idaho Batholith granite in three ways. First, the original batholith granites are gray in color; the pluton granites possess a slightly different chemical makeup and are pink in color. Second, these plutons were implanted closer to the earth's surface and as the older rock overburden erodes away, it is more often pluton granite that is exposed at the surface. Finally, pluton granite is characterized by vertical jointing (cracking in vertical lines), which is responsible for the granite eroding into jagged edges rather than rounded domes. Hence, the pinkish granite we see forming high jagged granite mountains, like the those in the Sawtooths and the Bighorn Crags, is pluton granite, while the older batholith granite is most often found in canyon bottoms.

At approximately the same time that the plutons were implanted into the Idaho Batholith, changes were also taking place farther south. The forces that created the overthrust belt reversed and now the earth's crust was stretched apart and lengthened from east to west. As the crust was stretched apart, long linear cracks or faults developed. This faulting, known as block faulting, formed narrow bands of crust that moved vertically in relation to each other.

Block faulting is the process that formed the Great Basin, which encompasses all of Nevada as well as parts of Arizona, California, Oregon, Utah and Idaho. The basin is characterized by hundreds of north-south-trending mountain ranges separated by long narrow valleys. The Lost River, Lemhi, Beaverhead, Albion, Black Pine, Deep Creek, Bannock and Portneuf mountains are among the most prominent Idaho mountains formed at this time. While block faulting is most evident in southern Idaho, there are many other examples of this type of faulting visible throughout the state. The most prominent of these graben valleys are the Wood River Valley (home of Ketchum and Sun Valley) and the Purcell Trench in northernmost Idaho, which forms a broad valley between the Selkirk and Cabinet Mountains.

Fifteen million years ago volcanic activity on a massive scale began once again in Idaho. This activity created the expansive Snake River Plain and is still continuing, with the last eruptions occurring only two thousand years ago. Geologists are still formulating the theoretical explanation of the forces that formed the Snake River Plain. Some hold to the theory that the plain was formed by a massive subsidence of the earth's crust; there is evidence to support this theory. More recently, it has been theorized that the volcanic plain is the result of the North American Plate crossing over a "hot spot" in the mantle similar to the one that is credited with the formation of the Hawaiian Islands. According to this theory, the hot spot is now under the Yellowstone Plateau—where evidence of volcanic activity is certainly apparent. The age of the rocks in the Snake River Plain supports this theory; the youngest rocks are in the vicinity of Yellowstone, with the rocks getting progressively older to the west.

Whatever the explanation behind its formation, the Snake River Plain is a veritable museum exhibit of volcanic activity, with both volcanic cones and large fissures (where the earth simply opened up and lava poured out) on display. Many of the lava flows are so fresh that vegetation has barely taken hold. The features found in this region include massive calderas, shield volcanoes, symmetrical cinder cones, spatter cones, lava flows, lava tubes, ice caves and numerous rift systems.

The Great Rift runs from Craters of the Moon National Monument southeast and south for 50 miles and is up to 5 miles wide. An aerial view of the Great Rift reveals more about how the Snake River plain formed than words might ever express. From the air you see the rift as a huge crack which runs for miles. On either side of the crack, dark lava flows have poured out like blood from a cut and then hardened like crusty scabs.

At the same time that the Snake River Plain was forming, volcanic activity was occurring to the west on the Columbia Plateau. Some of this activity spilled into Idaho in the form of massive lava flows. These flows, which originated in Oregon, have built up, one over another, to a depth of over 11,000 feet and are known as the Saint Maries, Clearwater and Weiser Embayments. The Hitt, Cuddy, Seven Devils and Craigs Mountains are formed in part by this activity. The flows were added to the island arc terrain which had accreted to the continent millions of years earlier.

Finally, the last pieces of the present-day Idaho jigsaw puzzle were cut by glacial ice in conjunction with the great Pleistocene Ice Age. Although the Pleistocene Ice Age began 2.5 million years ago, it was not until the last one hundred thousand years that the ice moved south out of British Columbia and invaded Idaho. The ice sheet that crept into northern Idaho consisted of massive lobes from the peerless continental ice fields which formed in western Canada. This ice flowed south over northern Idaho, completely covering the Selkirks and the Purcell and Cabinet mountains. The weight of the ice, estimated to have been four thousand feet deep, cut and shaped the mountains, dug out the deep beds of Priest, Pend Orielle and Coeur d'Alene lakes, and forever altered the primeval terrain of northernmost Idaho.

South of the Saint Joe River, glaciation was less catastrophic and limited to mountain glaciers that carved and sculpted the high peaks, leaving numerous alpine cirques. The southern alpine glaciation was most intense from 25,000 to 7,000 years ago, while a second series of glaciers were present around four thousand years ago on the highest mountain summits. A few of the larger alpine glaciers extended down into adjacent valleys, leaving lakes such as Redfish Lake in the Sawtooths, in their aftermath. Throughout central Idaho, there are many stunning examples of U-shaped valleys, moraines, and alpine lake basins. A less obvious, yet equally significant effect of the glacial period was the increased volume of water carried by Idaho rivers when the glaciers melted. The glacial melt water dramatically increased stream flow, adding to the cutting power of rivers, which in turn allowed the rivers to rapidly cut the deep, narrow canyons found in central Idaho.

Weather

As a result of prevailing westerly winds carrying moist maritime storms inland from the Pacific, Idaho annually receives 100 million acre feet of precipitation, with eighty percent of this total falling as winter snows. This is enough water to irrigate more than 250,000 acres of crop land, raise 21.6 million acres of forest, fill the immense Snake River Aquifer and drive the Snake, Boise, Payette, Weiser, Salmon, Clearwater Spokane, Clark Fork and Kootenai river drainages. Idaho's pre-

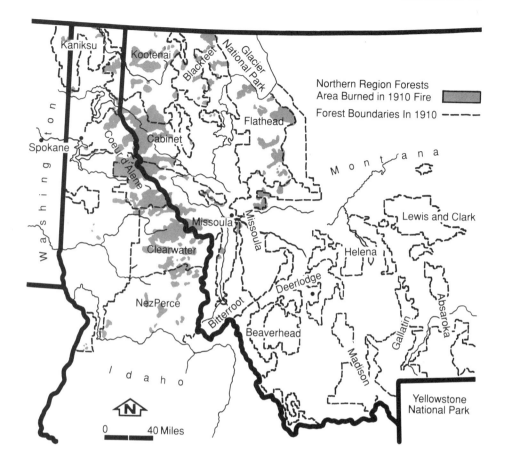

Northern Region Forests
Area Burned in 1910 Fire
Forest Boundaries In 1910 -----

AREAS AFFECTED BY FOREST FIRES (1910)

cipitation varies significantly from year to year, depending largely on the position of the jet stream, which shifts with the season. During the summer, the jet stream runs north through Canada shunting major Pacific storms north of Idaho. The result is dry, mostly clear weather. In winter the jet stream sags southward, carrying Pacific storms across Oregon and Washington into Idaho. Some winters, for reasons not entirely clear, the jet stream shifts farther to the south than usual, carrying storms across California and Nevada. When this pattern develops, Idaho experiences its coldest weather.

Idaho's mountains play a significant role in modifying these broad weather patterns. When prevailing winds push air eastward across the state's mountains, it rises and cools, causing moisture in the air to condense and fall as precipitation on the windward (western) slopes. Once over the mountain tops, the air sinks and grows warmer;

moisture evaporates and precipitation on the leeward (eastern) slopes tapers off or ceases. The resulting areas of increased aridity are said to lie in the rain shadows of the mountain ranges upwind.

Air temperature, like precipitation, is directly affected by latitude and elevation, decreasing as both increase. The hottest areas in Idaho are low-elevation canyons of the major rivers. Swan Falls Dam, deep in the Snake River Canyon, has the highest annual mean temperature in the state, at 55 degrees F. The highest recorded temperature—118 degrees F—was recorded along the Clearwater River at Orofino. The deep river canyons form desertlike environments where, with irrigation, melons, apples, peaches and apricots can be grown a few short miles from snow-covered mountain summits. Idaho's coldest temperatures are found at higher elevations. At 6,780 feet, Obsidian in the Stanley Valley has the lowest annual average at 35.4 degrees F. The state's record low temperature is −60 degrees F, recorded at Island Park in 1943.

The land north of the Columbia River receives much of its moisture from the Pacific Ocean. Because moist air can travel up the Columbia River Gorge without crossing the Cascades, northern Idaho feels the effects of the Pacific Ocean more than the central and southern parts of the state. This air is normally moister than that over southern Idaho. As a result, north of the Salmon River, mean annual precipitation levels range between 12 and 24 inches for the western valleys and 24 and 80 inches for the mountains. Because of its higher elevation and position at the head of an east/west mountain valley Wallace, Idaho receives the heaviest annual precipitation for any city in the state, 41.64 inches. Furthermore, the proximity of northern Idaho to the Pacific serves to moderate the Panhandle's winter weather, compared to equivalent areas in Montana, North Dakota, Minnesota and Maine. This moderation comes with a price: Northern Idaho receives only about 50 percent of the possible sunshine during any given year and less than 30 percent during the winter months.

The region between the Salmon River and the Snake River Plain contains the most mountainous terrain in the state and, because of its high elevations, receives massive amounts of winter snow. Precipitation in the region ranges between 12 and 80 inches, the totals generally increasing with elevation. Precipitation is rare in summer, particularly late in the season, when strong high-pressure systems often develop over this region, weakening or pushing aside incoming Pacific storms. The rain shadow of the Salmon River Mountains extends to the Challis, Big Lost, Little Lost and Lemhi valleys, all of which receive less than 12 inches of precipitation per year. This region receives nearly 70 percent of the annual average of available sunshine, more than 80 percent of which comes in July and August.

South of the central mountains, Idaho experiences somewhat greater extremes of climate over relatively short distances. The entire Snake River Plain, for example, which receives less than 12 inches of precipitation during the average year is classified as a high desert, while the Owyhee Mountains and the other southern mountain ranges rising out of the plain annually receive between 12 and 24 inches. A few of the higher peaks receive between 24 and 48 inches per year. In addition to the storms that hit central Idaho, the southeast corner of the state often receives the brunt of winter storm systems that originally cross inland in southern and central California. During a winter in which the Sierra Nevada has an above-average snowfall, the Albion Range and its eastern neighbors can receive incredible snowfalls for mountains that are essentially part of a semi-desert environment.

The maritime influence of Idaho's climate is weakest in the easternmost portions of the state, where the climate exhibits greater extremes in seasonal temperatures and a shift in precipitation to a predominantly wet summer/dry winter weather pattern. Many eastern Idaho weather stations record over 50 percent of their annual precipitation between April and September. The source of this summertime moisture is high-level, moisture-laden air that originates in the Gulfs of Mexico and California and migrates north to produce thunderstorm activity.

In years when high pressure over the continent fails to weaken, and winter or spring precipitation is shunted to the north, Idaho suffers drought. At such times, large wildfires affect many areas. The year 1988 was one of the worst ever for drought and forest fires, but in comparison to 1910, it was only moderately bad. In 1910, 90 major and some 3,000 minor fires killed 85 people and burned 3 million acres of timber.

Using This Book

Organization

This book divides Idaho into four sections. Section I covers northern Idaho and includes all of Idaho north of the Main Fork of the Salmon River. Section II covers western Idaho and includes an area bounded by the Snake River on the south and west, the Salmon River on the north and the Salmon and Big Wood rivers on the east. Section III covers eastern Idaho and includes an area bounded by the Salmon and Big Wood rivers in the west, Montana in the north, Wyoming in the east and the Snake River to the south. Section IV covers the remainder of the state and is bounded by the Snake River in the north, Oregon in the west, Nevada and Utah in the south and Wyoming in the east.

Each section includes individual write-ups that cover the major mountain ranges within that section. Many Idaho ranges are so large that they have, over the years, acquired more than one name. For example, the mountains that comprise the Lost River Range are known as the Pahsimeroi Mountains in the north and the Lost Rivers to the south; an eastern Lost River ridge line is known as the Hawley Mountains. Since this group is one distinct mountain range, it is treated as a whole; but the subranges are identified and discussed within each part.

Each mountain range write-up includes specific information on that range, individual peak listings and an approach section. The peaks are listed geographically from north to south and include information on location, mountaineering history (if any) and climbing routes. Approach directions for peaks are listed by bracketed entries that look like this: [Approach (A)(1)(b)]. (See next paragraph for explanation.) Finally, the peak listing includes the name of the United States Geological Survey (USGS) quadrangle on which the peak is located, and a keyed reference to a designated Wilderness Area, if the peak is located within one (e.g., USGS Chimney Peak / SBW, with the last item standing for the Selway-Bitterroot Wilderness).

Using the Bracketed Approach Entries

The "Approaches to" section at the end of each chapter is in an outline form. Bracketed entries ("character strings") in the text refer to that chapter's approach section. The capital letter designates a major approach point or highway. The next character, a number, refers to a "minor" road (which can be anything from a good paved road to a primitive jeep trail) that leaves from the major approach point. (A number with a decimal point indicates a dead-end side road branching off from a "minor" road.) The last character, a lower-case letter, refers to a trail accessed from that road. Additionally, roads and trails are identified by their Forest Service number designation and by name.

Abbreviations

In the interest of economy of space, this guidebook uses several abbreviations.

BLM	Bureau of Land Management
CG	Campground
FS-###	Designates a numbered Forest Service road, as identified on a national forest map
FH-##	Designates a numbered Forest Service highway, as identified on a national forest map
FST-###	Designates a numbered Forest Service trail, as identified on a national forest map
4WD	Four-wheel Drive, high-clearance vehicle
GS	Forest Service Guard Station
GHW	Gospel Hump Wilderness
HCW	Hells Canyon Wilderness
ID-##	Designates an Idaho State Highway
I-##	Designates an Interstate Highway
MLPA	Mallard-Larkins Pioneer Area
RNRW	River of No Return Wilderness
SBW	Selway-Bitterroot Wilderness
USGS	United States Geological Survey
US-##	Designates a U.S. Highway

Roads and Trails

A few words regarding Idaho's roads will help one expect the unexpected. Historically, recreational use of Idaho's mountains has taken a back seat to logging, mining and grazing. As a result of this tradition, access in Idaho is poor; but as recreational use increases, access is slowly improving. Almost all of Idaho's mountain roads (paved, gravel or dirt) will, depending on weather conditions, require the use of a four-wheel drive vehicle (4WD) at one time or another. In many places, you will find that the approach to a climb can only be accomplished on foot or with a 4WD. Some roads are so poor that they not only require 4WD, but also the ability to use the vehicle safely. This book will attempt to identify all roads that require something more rugged than a passenger sedan. However, keep in mind that as conditions change from season to season or year to year, the roads may become impassable. Be prepared for the worst on every trip because trees fall across roads, mud holes come and go and vehicles break down. Carry extra water and a good jack. Make sure there is air in your spare tire. Consider taking tire chains, a shovel and an axe if you're going to one of the state's many remote trailheads. Most of all, be prepared to take your time and drive slowly.

This advice also applies to trail conditions. Remember that, just because a trail is shown on a map, this does not necessarily mean that there is a well-worn path on the ground. Many of the trails listed in this book are too difficult for novice hikers and some will test the route-finding skills of intermediate and expert hikers. Although trail maintenance is on the upswing, route-finding skills and common sense are essential tools for venturing into much of Idaho's backcountry. Keep your goals within your skill levels. To paraphrase Clint Eastwood's movie character Dirty Harry, "A hiker has just got to know his limitations."

Maps

Maps form the essential foundation for almost every climb in this book. You should not consider attempting a trip without the necessary maps—and the know-how to use them. Idaho is an big state and, in some places, getting lost is easier than you might ever imagine. If you are a novice, read up on map use (*Mountaineering: The Freedom of the Hills*, by the Mountaineers, contains an excellent discussion on how to use topographic maps) and learn the basics from an experienced wilderness navigator before you start out on a climb. As a final note, remember that although maps are essential equipment, no map is perfect or absolutely complete and maps near more-developed areas become outdated with surprising speed. The climbing route descriptions include references to the USGS 7.5-minute and/or 15-minute quadrangles that contain that peak. Keep in mind that occasionally you will need two, three or even four USGS quads to complete a climb. Road and trail numbers are taken from Forest Service maps, and information on land ownership is based on Bureau of Land Management land status maps. Depending on where you are going, you may need to use all three formats to reach your goal.

USGS Topographic Maps

The USGS publishes two series of maps covering the United States that are useful for on-the-ground use. These are the 15-minute series (with a scale of 1:62,500 or nearly 1 inch to a mile) and the newer 7.5-minute series (with a scale of 1:24,000 or nearly 2.5 inches to a mile). The 15-minute series is gradually being phased out as the newer, more detailed 7.5-minute maps are published. A 15-minute quad covers an area of 12 miles by 18 miles, which is equal to the area covered by four 7.5-minute quads. No one is a complete mountaineer or backpacker without a good working ability to use these maps.

While the USGS quads are as accurate as can be in displaying physical features, they can be very inaccurate with regards to roads, trails and other human developments. The older 15-minute quads were often formulated when Idaho was unpopulated and undeveloped and, as such, often do not show a majority of the roads and other developments that exist today. Nor do they show land ownership, which is essential in areas where public and private lands are intertwined.

You can acquire an Idaho index to the USGS quads by writing the U.S. Geological Survey, Federal Center, Denver, Colorado 80225. The USGS hopes to have all of Idaho mapped in either the 7.5-minute or 15-minute format by 1990. USGS topo maps cost from $2.00 to $3.50, depending on where you buy them. Most outdoor shops carry these maps, and many government land management agencies also sell them.

Forest Service Maps

Forest Service maps vary greatly in quality, size, format and practicality. These maps are much smaller in scale than USGS quads (generally, 0.5 inch equals a mile) and do not show topography. However, these maps include numbered roads and trails, and many of the newer maps now include land status (ownership) for non-forest land. (Recently, all of the Idaho national forests published new versions of their maps, although the newness of these maps does not guarantee their accuracy.) Your first map acquisitions should include a complete set of national forest maps. Of special note are the Forest Service maps of the Selway-Bitterroot and River of No Return wildernesses; both maps are comprehensive, up-to-date and include topographic lines. Forest Service maps cost from $1.00 to $2.00 each, depending on the map.

Bureau of Land Management (BLM) Land Surface Management Status Maps

Bureau of Land Management maps are among the newest government maps. They depict drainages, roads and trails, and land ownership. These are large-scale maps (1:100,000) and are very helpful for orientation purposes, for large-scale coverage and for determining who owns the land. These maps are sold by the bureau's many offices throughout the state.

Mountain Names

In the route descriptions, peaks listed by unofficial (that is, non-USGS) names are marked by an asterisk: *Knuckle Peak**. This book uses many unofficial names, which are taken from mountaineering literature, Forest Service maps, commercial publications and local usage. Suggested names for peaks are printed in parentheses; for example, *Peak 9101 (Shoban Peak)*. Finally, unnamed peaks are named as they appear on the USGS quads; for example, *Peak 12063*.

Throughout history, the names for geologic features have evolved as part of the collective consciousness. Through word of mouth, a mountain became known as Diamond Peak or Sleeping Deer and then, when the first maps were published, some of this oral tradition became quasi-official and legitimized. Over the years many names have disappeared, including some that have appeared on maps at one time or another.

Today, the naming of geologic features has become systematized and integrated into the government's bureaucracy. In 1947, Congress passed Public Law 242, which created a central authority for standardizing geographic names. The new law's goal was to eliminate duplication of names attached to geologic features in the United States. The law places the authority to name unnamed features, and to standardize the names of features with multiple names, with the Secretary of Interior acting jointly with the Board of Geographic Names.

When new names are suggested or when conflicts arise, the USGS documents the conflict and turns it over to the Board of Geographic Names.

Citizens can make recommendations for names, but the Board has established such an incredible number of requirements that a proponent of a new name must be very serious and have lots of patience. This bureaucratic scheme has ignored (through inertia) many well-established names, leaving hundreds of Idaho peaks unnamed on USGS quads.

The Board attempts to adhere to a number of principles when naming geographic features. These principles are to (1) retain local names; (2) retain euphonious and suitable names of Indians; or foreign origin; (3) use names suggested by peculiarities of topographic features; (4) name features only after deceased persons; (5) not use names with derogatory implications; (6) avoid the multiplication of names for different parts of the same geologic feature; (7) replace existing names only to eliminate a duplication or an inappropriate name and (8) adopt new names for geographic features in federally designated wilderness areas only when an overriding need is identified. Additionally, climbers generally require a 300-foot drop in a connecting ridge line before two points will be considered separate mountain peaks.

The Climbing Routes

The climbing routes compiled in this book have been gathered from numerous sources including my own climbs, climbing journals and magazines (including the *American Alpine Journal*, the *Mountaineers Journal*, the *Mazamas Journal*, the *Iowa Mountaineers Journal, Summit, Off Belay, Rock and Ice* and *Climbing*), USGS maps and geology textbooks, records left in summit registers, information supplied by other climbers and Lyman Dye, who collaborated with me on the Sawtooths material.

While I have attempted to assure the accuracy of every entry in this book, it is impossible for one person to climb every mountain by every route. Route descriptions can be frustrating. Many guidebooks list detailed descriptions of every twist and turn of a complex route—yet, when you attempt to follow the route on the rock you come to believe you are on the wrong mountain. Other guidebooks tell you to "follow the easy slopes to the summit" and you find a near vertical "slope" capped by overhanging cliffs. Of course, these discrepancies are not due to any duplicity on the author's part, but rather from the inability of both the reader and the writer to translate a constantly changing natural environment into words.

The Ratings Game

The ratings attached to climbing routes are designed to inform a person of the difficulty of the climb. While the numbers appear to be objective, there is a great deal of subjectivity built into them. Both the person rating the climb and the person following the route are human and what may be difficult to one may be "a piece of cake" to another.

This book uses the Yosemite Decimal System (YDS), which was introduced in the U.S. by the Sierra Club in 1937. This system rates climbing routes by their most difficult (crux) move, and by length of commitment needed to complete a climb (the grade). (For complete descriptions and a comparison chart of the various rating systems, see *Mountaineering: The Freedom of the Hills*, 4th edition, published by the Mountaineers.)

The YDS climbing ratings are often broken into one of six grades based on the interplay of the route's length, average difficulty, exposure, quality of the rock and any other factors that might enter into the climb. Because most of the routes in this book fall into the minimum- to average-commitment category, only a few of the routes have been graded. Routes are further divided into one of six general classes.

CLASS 1   Hiking. There is a trail (or pseudo-trail) the entire way to the summit.

CLASS 2   Off-trail scrambling. These routes are more rugged and although you can probably walk to the summit, you may occasionally have to use your hands to climb.

CLASS 3   Climbing. These routes involve actual climbing.

CLASS 4   Belayed climbing. These routes involve climbing which may be no more difficult than Class 3 climbing, but do subject the climber to increased exposure.

CLASS 5   Belayed climbing with leader placing protection. This is "technical" rock climbing, pure and simple.

CLASS 6   Involves artificial aid climbing, which utilizes pitons, bolts or any other hardware placed in the rock to serve as a hold or for support.

Class 5 climbing is further broken down into degrees of difficulty under the Yosemite Decimal System. The fourth edition of *Mountaineering: The Freedom of the Hills* attempted, somewhat tongue-in-cheek, to put objective criteria to what has often been a very subjective set of numbers. Although not all climbers will agree with this breakdown, it does provide some objectivity to what has tended to be an extremely subjective set of numbers.

5.0 – 5.4 There are good handholds and foot holds for each move. The size of the handholds determines the degree of difficulty.

5.5 – 5.6 Handholds and footholds exist but are not obvious to the untrained.

5.7 Either one handhold or foothold is missing.

5.8 Two holds out of four are missing.

5.9 Only one hold exists for each move.

5.10 There are no holds at all.

5.11 Such routes are impossible to climb, but someone has done it.

5.12 The rock is smooth and flawless.

5.13 The rock is both smooth and flawless and overhanging.

Class 6 climbing is also broken down into six sub-categories. Although this book is not directed toward this type of climbing, a few of the routes described do involve aid climbing, so the following breakdown is provided. It should be noted that rock climbers are now climbing what were originally aid routes without artificial aids.

A0 Placement is used as a hold or to allow a resting spot.

A1 Etriers (aid slings for your feet) are utilized. Placements are solid and safe.

A2 Placements are harder to locate and are less secure.

A3 Placements are not likely to hold a significant fall.

A4 Placements are downright shaky and cannot be expected to hold a fall.

A5 Continuous use of A4 placements.

Addresses

Bitterroot National Forest
316 North Third St.
Hamilton, MT 59840
(406) 363-3131
    Bitterroot Mountains
    Clearwater Mountains

Boise District Office
Bureau of Land Management
3948 Development Ave.
Boise, ID 83705
(208) 334-1582
    Boise Mountains
    Owyhee Mountains

Boise National Forest
1075 Park Blvd.
Boise, ID 83706
(208) 334-1516
    Boise Mountains
    Salmon River Mountains
    West Mountains
    Danskin Mountains

Burley District Office
Bureau of Land Management
Route 3, Box 1
Burley, ID 83318
(208) 678-5514
    Albion Range
    Deep Creek Mountains
    Malta Range
    North Hansel Mountains
    Samaria Mountains

Caribou National Forest
Suite 294
Federal Bldg.
Pocatello, ID 83201
(208) 236-6700
    Bannock Range
    Caribou Range
    Malad Range
    Peale Mountains
    Portneuf Range

Cottonwood Area Office
Bureau of Land Management
Cottonwood, ID 83522
    Craigs Mountains

Challis National Forest
P.O. Box 404
Challis, ID 83226
(208) 879-2285
    Boulder Mountains
    Lost River Range
    White Cloud Mountains
    Salmon River Mountains

Clearwater National Forest
12730 Highway 12
Orofino, ID 83544
(208) 476-4541
    Clearwater Mountains

Hells Canyon National Recreation Area
P.O. Box 832
Riggins, ID 83549
(208) 628-3916
    Seven Devils Mountains

Idaho Department of Lands
Route 1 Box 284
Coolin, ID 83821
(208) 443-2516
    Selkirk Mountains

Idaho Falls District Office
Bureau of Land Management
940 Lincoln Rd.
Idaho Falls, ID 83401
Phone (208) 529-1020
 Blackfoot Mountains
 Beaverhead Range
 Hawley Mountains
 Lemhi Range
 Lost River Range
 Peale Mountains
 Pioneer Mountains
 Portneuf Range
 White Knob Mountains

Lolo National Forest
Fort Missoula, Bldg. 24
Missoula, MT 59801
(406) 329-3750
 Bitterroot Mountains

Nez Perce National Forest
319 E. Main
Grangeville, ID 83530
(208) 983-1950
 Clearwater Mountains
 Seven Devils Mountains

Panhandle National Forest
P.O. Box 310
Coeur D'Alene, ID 83544
(208) 667-2561
 Bitterroot Mountains
 Cabinet Mountains
 Chilco Mountains
 Coeur d'Alene Mountains
 Purcell Mountains
 Saint Joe Mountains
 Selkirk Mountains

Payette National Forest
P.O. Box 1026
McCall, ID 83638
(208) 634-2255
 Cuddy Mountains
 Hitt Mountains
 Lick Creek Range
 Salmon River Mountains
 Seven Devils Mountains
 West Mountains

Salmon District
Bureau of Land Management
P.O. Box 430
Salmon, ID 83467
(208) 756-2201
 Beaverhead Range
 Boulder Mountains
 Lemhi Range
 Lost River Range

Salmon National Forest
Highway 93 N.
P.O. Box 729
Salmon, ID 83467
(208) 756-2215
 Beaverhead Range
 Bitterroot Mountains
 Lemhi Range
 Salmon River Mountains
 Yellowjacket Mountains

Sawtooth National Forest
1525 Addison Ave. E.
Twin Falls, ID 83301
(208) 737-3200
 Albion Range
 Black Pine Mountains
 Boulder Mountains
 Goose Creek Mountains
 Pioneer Mountains
 Smoky Mountains
 Soldier Mountains
 Sublette Mountains

Sawtooth National Recreation
Area Headquarters Office
Star Route
Ketchum, ID 83340
(208) 726-8291
 Boulder Mountains
 Sawtooth Range
 Smoky Mountains
 White Cloud Mountains

Targhee National Forest
P.O. Box 208
Saint Anthony, ID 83445
(208) 624-3135
 Beaverhead Range
 Centennial Range
 Henrys Lake Range
 Lemhi Range

The west face of Scotchman Peak

NORTHERN IDAHO
From the Canadian Border
South to the Salmon River;
From the Washington
& Oregon Border
East to the Montana Border

1. The Selkirk Mountains

The Selkirk range begins on Mica Peak west of Coeur d'Alene, and runs north, paralleling the Idaho/Washington border for over 100 miles. The range, which is up to 30 miles wide in places, surrounds the Priest Lake basin. The Selkirk peaks are formed of granite from the Kaniksu Batholith and Precambrian rocks from the Belt Supergroup series. The name "Kaniksu Range" is sometimes used to identify the mountains west of the Priest Lakes; the central crest is sometimes known as the "Priest Range."

While the highest point of the Selkirk range reaches only 7,670 feet (on Parker Peak), valley-to-summit elevation differences are nearly 5,000 feet in places and the terrain is extremely rugged. During the Pleistocene Era, the Selkirk range was scraped clean by massive continental glaciers, which removed much of the Precambrian rock that covered the Kaniksu Batholith and carved the underlying granite into an appealing collection of alpine peaks. In addition to shaping the high peaks, the glaciers also gouged out Upper and (lower) Priest Lakes.

Land ownership in the Selkirks is a hodge-podge, with the state of Idaho and the Panhandle National Forest being the two largest landowners. (The state's land holdings include most of the scenic Priest Lake basin.) The Bureau of Land Management manages a few small borderline areas, and several large timber companies own a good portion of range. Due to the priorities of the various landowners—and the Selkirk's rich forest cover—much of the range is managed almost exclusively for logging. Recreation use, while having a very high potential, has a low priority with Selkirk land managers.

Under the Idaho Constitution, state lands must be managed to maximize a continuing rate of return. To meet this mandate, the Idaho Department of Lands has chosen to subject this area to a maximized timber management program. But, despite the heavy emphasis on logging, there is

some good news. In 1971 the State of Idaho and the Forest Service established the Selkirk Crest Management Area, which protects the highest Selkirk peaks and ridges. While it is safe to say that the roughly 26,000 acres the management area protects are high enough and rocky enough to be safe from the chainsaw, assuring protection for even a little of this granite hinterland is better than nothing.

Two other areas have drawn attention and are being considered as possible additions to the National Wilderness System. These areas are the Long Canyon area (west of Bonners Ferry) and the Salmo-Priest proposed Wilderness (near the Canadian/Washington/Idaho borders). Both areas are still pristine and worthy of protection on scenic, recreational and wildlife management grounds. Perhaps the strongest argument for protecting sections of the Selkirk wilderness is the range's status as the home of two highly threatened big game animals—the grizzly bear and the rare mountain caribou, both of which will be lost if development continues to encroach on their habitats.

Selkirk peaks offer a wide variety of climbing and hiking opportunities. True wilderness terrain still hides delightful and remote summits, roads lead nearly to the bottoms of imposing rock walls, and dozens of summits are excellent day-hiking destinations from valley camps. Rock climbers will find "super" granite in many spots. Randall Green's *Idaho Rock*, published by the Mountaineers, is an excellent climbing guide to Selkirk rock climbing routes; Sheldon Bluestein's *North Idaho Hiking Trails* provides information on several good hikes for beginning and intermediate hikers.

Snowy Top Mountain *7,572 feet (Class 2)*
Snowy Top is a big hulking mountain and the highest point in this northernmost corner of Idaho. The summit is barren, windswept and very enticing. To reach the top, scramble up the peak's south slopes from the saddle between it and Little Snowy Top Mountain. The saddle is reached by trail [Approach: (B)(1)(a)]. USGS Continental Mountain

Little Snowy Top *6,829 feet (Class 2)*
As the name infers, this peak is the little brother of Snowy Top Mountain. Together they stand guard along the U.S./Canadian border. The summit is an easy climb from the saddle (which is reached by trail [Approach: (B)(1)(a)]) connecting it to Snowy Top Mountain. USGS Salmo Mountain

Parker Peak *7,670 feet (Class 2)*
Parker Peak is located 8.5 miles south of the

27

Canadian border, on the eastern edge of the Selkirk Range. The highest Selkirk Peak in Idaho is an easy walk-up via its south ridge from FST-221 [Approach: (D)(2)(b)]. Although technically easy, the walk is long—7.0 miles—and steep—5,500 feet—when approached from the Parker Ridge trailhead (even farther if you choose to do the approach from Long Canyon). This area is especially alpine in nature in early summer, before the snow has completely disappeared from the glacially sculpted peaks. USGS Pyramid Peak

Fisher Peak *7,580 feet (Class 2)*
Pyramid-shaped Fisher Peak is located 2.5 miles east of Parker Peak. It features a precipitous north face, which drops almost a thousand feet to a swampy area. The summit is a short scramble from FST-27 [Approach: (D)(2)(b)], which crosses the ridge line south of the peak. At one time, a trail led to the top of the summit from the main trail; this route is still visible in places. USGS Pyramid Peak

Peak 7445 *7,445 feet (Class 2)*
This unnamed peak is a continuation of the Long Mountain/Parker Peak ridge that parallels the east side of Long Canyon. The summit is 1.0 mile north of Long Mountain and 2.0 miles southwest of Parker Peak. FST-221 [Approach: (D)(2)(b)] nearly reaches the summit, which is a hop, skip and a jump from the trail. USGS Pyramid Peak

Long Mountain *7,265 feet (Class 1)*
Long Mountain has a distinctive 0.5-mile-long summit ridge that forms part of the divide between Long Canyon and Parker Creek. Its summit is 3.0 miles southwest of Parker Peak. The summit is accessed by taking FST-221 [Approach: (D)(2)(b)] either south from Parker Peak or north from Trout Creek. USGS Pyramid Peak

West Fork Mountain *6,416 feet (Class 2)*
West Fork Mountain, the big mountain that looms above West Fork Lake, is located 3.0 miles west of Long Mountain. The summit is an easy 600-foot climb from the lake. Getting to the lake is the difficult part of the journey, as the trail in from West Fork Creek is in need of maintenance [Approach: (D)(3)(a)]. From the lake, gain the north ridge and follow it to the summit. The northeast face is quite an impressive wall. USGS Smith Peak

Smith Peak *7,653 feet (Class 3)*
Smith Peak is among the remotest of the Selkirk peaks. The peak's 800-foot north face is one of the steepest in the Selkirks. The shortest ap-

proach is from Smith Creek [Approach: (D)(3)]. From Smith Creek, climb to the northwest ridge and then climb directly to the summit. The longest approach is from Long Canyon [Approach: (D)(2)(a)]. Climbing the peak from Long Canyon involves a backpacking trip up that spectacular and very lengthy glacial valley. Hike up Long Canyon to the point where the outlet from Smith Lake empties into Long Canyon Creek and follow the drainage up to the lake. Above the lake is a steep granite wall which must be bypassed by climbing Point 7303. Once on the ridge line, follow the ridge south and then southeast to the summit. USGS Smith Peak

Abandon Mountain *7,022 feet (Class 2)*
Abandon Mountain is located 1.5 miles south of West Fork Mountain. The peak is best accessed via Smith Creek and the northeast ridge, but may be climbed by any one of its three ridges [Approach: (D)(3)(a)]. USGS Smith Peak

Pyramid Peak *7,355 feet (Class 2)*
Pyramid Peak is located 1.25 miles south of Long Mountain. The summit is climbed directly from FST-7 [Approach: (D)(2)(b)]. Take the trail north from Trout Creek to Pyramid Pass on the peak's northeast side and climb directly to the summit from the pass. USGS Pyramid Peak

The Lions Head *7,288 feet*
The Lions Head stands high above Abandon, Smith and Lion Creek 1.5 miles south of Abandon Mountain. This delightful peak exhibits twin summits, which are known as East Lions Head and West Lions Head. In 1964, Neil McAvoy of Kellogg led first ascents of both summits and left summit registers on the tops. According to Neil, a group of Spokane Mountaineers climbed the two peaks one week later and a first-ascent controversy has existed ever since. Because the peaks are not easily accessed, little technical climbing has been noted on the peaks in recent years. The shortest approach to the peak is from Lion Creek [Approach: (A)(5)]. Access is also possible from Smith Creek [Approach: (D)(3)] and Lookout Mountain [Approach: (A)(6)(a)]. USGS Smith Peak

West Lions Head (Class 4)
The lower of the two summits does not have a walk-up route. The standard route climbs the southwest face on a series of slabs with good holds and belay spots.

East Lions Head (Class 3)
The highest summit is climbed by its north ridge from the saddle just north of the peak. The climb involves a friction scamper on slanting slabs.

Lookout Mountain 6,727 feet (Class 1)

Lookout Mountain is located 2.0 miles west of The Lions Head. This fire lookout site can be accessed from Lookout Lake to the northwest via a short 2.0-mile trail. The lake is accessed via a state timber road [Approach: (A)(6)(a)] that runs up Caribou Creek from the top of Priest Lake to a point near Lookout Lake. From the trailhead hike to the lake and then on to the summit in 2.0 miles. USGS Caribou Creek

Kent Peak 7,243 feet (Class 2)

Kent Peak sits on a high ridge line between Kent Creek and Lion Creek 1.8 miles northeast of the Wigwams. Climb from either Kent Creek or Kent Lake to the saddle south of the peak and then follow the south ridge to the summit. Access to the peak is reportedly best via the Lion Creek road [Approach: (A)(5)], but most of this route is cross country and difficult. USGS Wigwams

The Wigwams 7,033 feet (Class 1)

The Wigwams are located 5.5 miles east of Squaw Bay at the north end of Priest Lake. A trail leads to the west summit of this twin-summited peak from the Two Mouth Creek drainage [Approach: (A)(4)(a)]. From the saddle between the two peaks, the east summit is an easy scramble. USGS Wigwams

Harrison Peak 7,292 feet (Class 3)

Harrison Peak is located 0.5 mile north of Harrison Lake. Harrison is a rugged mountain with spectacular south, west and north walls and only one non-technical route to its summit, that being via the eastern side of the mountain. Randall Green has described nine routes on the mountain, all rated at YDS 5.7 or higher. To reach the south face of the peak take FST-271 [Approach: (C)(4)] to Harrison Lake and then climb the ridge east of the lake (past Point 6558 on the USGS map). Traverse east over the talus slope at the base of the face until it is possible to work your way up to the peak's eastern slopes. Once on these easier slopes, climb due west to the summit. USGS Wigwams

Twin Peaks 7,599 and 7,374 feet (Class 2-3)

These peaks are 2.5 miles north of Chimney Rock and are quite impressive when viewed from the summit of Chimney Rock. Although both summits are accessed from the saddle that connects them, it is best to climb the north summit first from the southernmost Beehive Lake and then follow the ridge south to the second summit [Approach: (C)(1)(a)]. USGS Wigwams

Chimney Rock from the east

Silver Dollar Peak 7,181 feet (Class 2-3)

This nearly symmetrical peak has four ridges and three lofty faces. It is located 1.5 miles northeast of Chimney Rock and is most easily accessed from the east [Approach: (C)(3)]. The summit is an easy scramble from the southeast. Numerous technical climbing opportunities exist on the various faces and on the west ridge. USGS Wigwams

Roman Nose 7,260 feet (Class 1)

Roman Nose is located 4.0 miles east of Silver Dollar Peak (and the main Selkirk Crest) on a subsidiary ridge that divides the Pack River and Kootenai River valleys. The summit, which contains a Forest Service Lookout, can be reached by FST-1 [Approach: (C)(5)(a)]. The rock faces below Roman Nose provide many challenging climbing opportunities but are mostly untested. C. Michael Holt and Mark Guthrie made the first ascent of the north face of what they identified as Little Roman Nose in 1975. This climb evidently took place on Point 6943, which is actually the eastern summit of Roman Nose. The two rated the climb as Grade II, 5.8 A2. USGS Roman Nose

Chimney Rock *7,124 feet*

North Idaho's most imposing summit sits at the top of the Selkirk crest just north of Mount Roothaan. The rock is a vertical column of granite that provides a variety of technical rock climbing opportunities. Vertical cracks and small, often blocked chimneys make up the three faces of the wedged-shaped spire. The first ascent was in 1934 by John Carey, Mart Chamberlain, Fred Thieme and Byron Ward. The first winter ascent was by Spokane climber Chris Kopczynski and W. Parks. Today, there are over 26 major routes and variations on the spire's three major faces. Randall Green has detailed many of these highly technical rock climbing routes on the peak in his book *Idaho Rock*. I have included only the standard ascent route up the west face. Chimney Rock is accessed from the old Horton Ridge Lookout site [Approach: (A)(3)(a)]; or from the east via FST-256 [Approach: (C)(3)]. USGS Mount Roothaan

West Face. *(Grade II, 5.3)*

This is the original and still most popular route. From the ridge line just south of the face, climb out onto the face on an easy ledge system. The route begins in the middle of the face at the highest point accessible by foot, where there is a fixed pin. From this point, the route veers up and slightly to the left, utilizing several fairly obvious cracks toward

the western edge of the mountain where there is a broad step about 50 feet below the summit. The route to the step involves two moderate-length pitches where the exposure is much more noticeable than the degree of difficulty. The middle belay point is a very small ledge two thirds of the way up. (Some climbers use a double rope to avoid the intermediate belay point.) From the broad step, the route steps to the north around a bulging rock and finishes in an easy chimney. The descent is via a double-rope rappel from the broad step.

Mount Roothann *7,326 feet (Class 2-3)*

Mount Roothaan is located just south of Chimney Rock and is nearly as rugged as its more famous counterpart. The summit can be reached by the west ridge, which is accessed via the trail from the Horton Ridge parking lot [Approach: (A)(3)(a)]. The ridge walk to base of the peak and the easy scramble on the ridge are as rewarding as the view of Chimney Rock to the north. The peak can also be reached from the east side over the Pack River road to FS-2653 which leads up into Chimney Creek area [Approach: (C)(3)]. USGS Mount Roothaan

Gunsight Peak *7,352 feet (Class 2)*

This massive peak with a hulking northeast face is located 2.0 miles south of Mount Roothaan. It can be climbed from the Horton Ridge area. Climb either the north or east ridges for easy access to the summit [Approach: (A)(3)(a)]. See

Gunsight Peak from Mount Roothaan

Green's *Idaho Rock* for route information on two exceptional rock climbs on the north face. USGS Mount Roothaan

Hunt Peak *7,058 feet (Class 2-3)*

This is the last peak at the southern end of the Selkirks to reach 7,000 feet. The peak, which was caught in the great Sundance Fire, is a rugged piece of real estate with two large cirques on its northern and eastern slopes. The peak is a Class 2 climb via its southern slopes, and a Class 3 climb via its north and east ridges [Approach: (A)(2)(a)]. USGS Mount Roothaan

APPROACHES TO
THE SELKIRKS

Approach routes for this section are identified in the text by bracketed entries [Approach:], which include appropriate letter and number references.

Due to the extensive logging activity that has taken place in the Selkirks, road access is plentiful. Both primary highways and numerous forest roads (of varying condition) provide access to almost every nook and cranny within the range.

(A) Priest Lake Access Points.

ID-57 is the primary approach route into the Priest Lake section of the range. For much of its distance, this is a good paved road. The state highway designation ends on the west side of Priest Lake north of Nordman, where a number of Forest Service roads continue to the north.

(1) East Side Road. This road leaves ID-57 south of Priest Lake, runs east and north to Coolin and then continues along the east side of the lake. The road, paved for several miles past Coolin, then good gravel, follows the lake to Lionhead State Park at the north end of the lake. All of the land from the lake's edge to the Selkirk Crest is controlled either by the State of Idaho or by private timber companies. Almost every drainage contains a road that leads up toward the crest. Signing is almost nonexistent and it is difficult to get the state employees to give you any information on road conditions.

(2) Hunt Creek Road System. From the East Side Road, two rough roads lead east up Hunt Creek and the South Fork of Hunt Creek to the area below Hunt and Gunsight peaks. Drive north from Coolin for roughly 8.0 miles and turn east.

(a) Hunt Lake/Hunt Peak Trail. A very poor trail system leads to these two destinations from the end of the Hunt Creek Road. Hunters

are primarily responsible for keeping this area open at all.

(3) Horton Ridge Road. The Horton Ridge Lookout site is reached by road from Priest Lake; it provides quick access to the Chimney Rock area. Turn east onto a logging road about 9.5 miles north of Coolin. In 1984, the road was in poor but passable condition.

(a) Cross country to Chimney Rock. From the lookout site parking area, a trail leads to the ridge below Mount Roothaan, where climbers will get their first sighting of the Rock. The route from this point is cross country and involves either dropping off the ridge into the drainage below Chimney Rock, or crossing the saddle north of Mount Roothaan and traversing the east side of the ridge to the saddle north of Chimney Rock.

(4) Two Mouth Creek Road. This road leaves the main road at Hurricane Bay and ascends toward the crest. About 3.0 miles from the lake, a side road departs to the north and climbs toward The Wigwams.

(a) Lookout Mountain Trail. When the Two Mouth Creek Road dies out, a jeep/foot trail ascends the remaining distance to the summit, which at one time was a fire lookout. From the lookout, the trail continues east to Two Mouth Lakes and the Snow Creek Area on the east side of the divide. (See [Approach: (C)(1)].)

(5) Lion Creek Road. This road is accessed from the East Side Road just south of Lionhead State Park. The road follows Lion Creek east to a point due south of The Lion Head. A sketchy trail can be followed from the road's end to Kent Lake by following the stream bed.

(6) Caribou Creek Roads. Access this road, which runs northeast up the Caribou Creek drainage, just west of Lionhead State Park. Roughly 3.5 miles from the lake, the road forks. Follow the right hand fork southeast, over a number of switchbacks, toward Lookout Lake.

(a) FST-36, Lookout Lake Trail. Leaves the end of the Caribou Creek Road and climbs to Lookout Lake in 0.4 mile and to Lookout Mountain in 1.0 mile.

(B) Washington State Access Points.

Reaching the northern- and westernmost corner of Idaho is no easy task, and involves a drive into Washington State. From I-90 (either in Spokane or from the ID-41 exit) go north to WA-20 at Newport, Washington, and then drive north on WA-20 for 46.0 miles to its junction with WA-31. Continue north on WA-31 for another 16.8 miles to the Sullivan Lake Road.

(1) Sullivan Creek Road. This road leads east from WA-31. Follow it for almost 5.0 miles to a junction. Turn left at the junction and drive up

Sullivan Creek to Salmo Pass. Two trails leave from the pass.

(a) **Salmo River Cutoff/Salmo River Trails.** These trails leave from Salmo Pass and descend to the Salmo River in just under 4.0 miles, then climb up the Salmo River to the area south of Snowy Top Mountain in 7.0 miles.

(C) Pack River Access Points.
The Pack River drains a large area of the Selkirk Range between Roman Nose in the east, Harrison Peak in the north and Chimney Rock in the west. The Pack River Road, described below, provides alternative approach routes to most southern Selkirk peaks.

(1) **FS-231, Pack River Road.** This road leaves US-2/US-95 at Walsh Lake and proceeds north for almost 20 miles to a point just south of Harrison Peak. The land it traverses is controlled by the Forest Service, with interspersed sections of private and state land.

(a) **FST-279, Beehive Lake Trail.** This trail leaves FS-231 1.5 miles before that road ends. The trail runs northwest to the Beehive Lakes in 2.2 miles.

(2) **Hunt and Gunsight Peaks Access.** Drive on FS-231 11.5 miles and turn east onto the McCormick Creek Road. The road ends shortly and FS-059 continues on to Fault Lake.

(3) **Chimney Rock Access.** From the junction of US-2/US-95 and FS-231, drive north on the Pack River Road for roughly 16.0 miles to FS-2653. Turn west on FS-2653 and follow this road (staying on the most worn route) for about 2.5 miles until it becomes too difficult to traverse. Hike up the road for about 0.5 mile, cross Chimney Creek on a log bridge and then follow the old logging road up to the top of the ridge that divides the Chimney Creek and West Fork drainages. From this point, it is an additional 2.0 miles to the crest. Follow the path, which is marked with blazes on the trees and rock cairns along the ridge crest, into the cirque on a bench at the base of Mount Roothaan.

(4) **Harrison Peak Access.** The trailhead for Harrison Lake is located 0.25 mile south of the end of FS-231. The trail to the lake, FST-271, ends at the lake, but it is possible to go cross country to the ridge line from this point.

(5) **Roman Nose Access.** FS-2605 leaves FS-231 and climbs to the east, eventually reaching the ridge line near Dodge Peak. At this point, the road becomes FS-291. This road drops off the ridge and heads north until it connects with the extensive road system which leads into the range from Bonners Ferry.

(a) **FST-1, Roman Nose Trail.** This trail climbs to the top of Apache Ridge and continues on to the summit of Roman Nose in 4.5 miles.

(D) East Side Access Points.
Primary access to the eastern side of the Selkirk Range is from US-2/US-95, which runs from Sandpoint north to the Canadian border. At various points, good secondary highways leave this road and stay on the west side of the Kootenai River.

(1) **Bonners Ferry Area Access Points.** West of Bonners Ferry, a major Forest Service road system loops through the Snow Creek and Myrtle Creek drainages, almost reaching the Selkirk Crest at one point. From Bonners Ferry, follow the river road west to the Kootenai National Wildlife Refuge. When the road ends, turn north and drive to the refuge headquarters to access Myrtle Creek (FS-661), or turn south to access Snow Creek (FS-402).

(a) **FST-286, Myrtle Peak Trail.** Near the top of Myrtle Creek, turn from FS-633 onto FS-2406 and follow it to its end. The trail begins at this point and leads to the peak, which is only a couple of miles to the north.

(b) **FST-6, Harrison Lake Trail.** To reach this trail, leave the Myrtle Creek Road just after the road crosses Myrtle Creek and loops back to the east. Turn right (south) onto FS-2409 and follow it to its end, where there is an unmarked trailhead. The trail begins at this point and runs for 2.0 miles to the lake.

(2) **Long Canyon Access.** Take ID-1 north from its junction with US-95 and follow it for 1.0 mile to the Copeland turn. Drive through Copeland and cross the Kootenai River. Continue on to the West Side Road and then turn north. Drive another 6.7 miles north to the trailhead.

(a) **FST-16, Long Canyon Trail.** Long Canyon is the best example of primeval Selkirk wilderness still remaining. The trail is well maintained (partly due to volunteer efforts) and covers such spectacular scenery that it is recommended no matter how far one must drive to see it. FST-16 follows Long Canyon to Long Canyon Pass, a 12.0-mile trip.

(b) **Parker Creek and Parker Ridge Loop Trail.** Access to these trails is located on the West Side Road, 3.75 miles south of the Long Canyon Trailhead. From the trailhead, FST-221 crosses the Parker Peak ridge to Pyramid Peak; FST-14 traverses the Parker Creek drainage to just below Pyramid Pass, where it joins FST-221. FST-7 connects the following trails: FST-16, FST-221 and FST-14. Additionally, FST-27, the Fisher Creek Trail, leaves FST-14 2.5 miles from its trailhead on the West Side Road and crosses south to the Trout Creek Drainage.

(3) **FS-281 and FST-2464, Smith Creek Roads.** This road is best accessed from US-1 at Porthill on

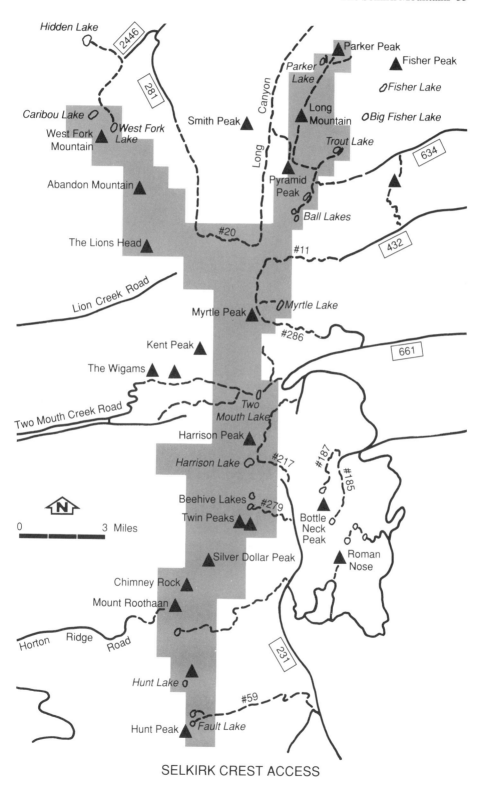

SELKIRK CREST ACCESS

the Idaho/Canada border. From Porthill, follow the road west along the border and then south to the Smith Creek turn in 4.0 miles. Turn west and follow the road up Smith Creek for 7.0 miles until it forks. Take the south fork, which forks again in 1.5 miles. The right fork goes on for another 4.0 miles and ends west of Smith Peak. The left fork ends in 2.0 miles near the trailhead for FST-21.

(a) FST-21, West Fork Lake to Hidden Lake Trail. This trail extends roughly 4.0 miles between Hidden Lake and West Fork Lake. The trail is accessed from the end of FS-2464, which joins the trail halfway between the two lakes.

2. The Purcell Mountains

The Purcell Mountains, primarily a Canadian range, extend south across the border into Idaho and Montana. The range is located northeast of Bonners Ferry and is bounded by US-95 and US-1 on the west and the Kootenai River and US-2 to the south. The Montana and Canadian borders form the eastern and northern boundaries, respectively.

The highest point in the Idaho section of the Purcells is an unnamed peak that reaches 6,779 feet. The range was completely inundated by Pleistocene era glaciers, which scraped away much of the range's Precambrian rock. The Moyie River Canyon splits the Idaho section of the Purcell Mountains; it is the most spectacular geologic feature within the range.

The Purcells are managed by the Panhandle National Forest, which primarily manages the range for timber harvesting. As a result, the range has an extensive road system and a very small and broken trail system. Only short day hikes are available for hikers. The few mountain lakes are reached by roads. Climbing opportunities are limited to non-technical Class 1 and Class 2 ascents.

Mission Mountain *6,206 feet*
Harvey Mountain* *6,402 feet (Class 2)*
These two peaks are located just south of the Idaho/Canadian border and are short climbs from either FST-156 or FST-409 [Approach: (A)(2)(a)]. USGS Hall Mountain

Bussard Mountain *5,968 feet (Class 1)*
Bussard Mountain is located 1.0 mile north of Queen Mountain. The summit is accessed via FST-52 [Approach: (A)(1)(a)], which leads west from the Moyie River past Bussard Lake to the summit in 3.5 miles. USGS Eastport

Queen Mountain *6,112 feet (Class 1)*
Queen Mountain is located 0.8 mile west of Queen Lake on the high ridge that divides the Moyie River and Kootenai River. The peak is approached either via FST-152 [Approach: (A)(3)(b)], which begins on the Moyie River; or from FS-2542, which intersects FST-152 1.0 mile below the summit. USGS Eastport

Goat Mountain *6,641 feet (Class 2)*
Goat Mountain is the highest named peak in the Idaho section of the Purcells. It is located northeast of Perkins Lake and 0.5 mile west of the Idaho/Montana border. The summit can be approached from Montana via FST-44 [Approach: (A)(5)(a)], which traverses a north/south ridge line from Keno Mountain in Montana to Line Point and Goat Mountain. The summit can no doubt be reached from Skin Creek, via the peak's northern slopes, but I have yet to find anyone who has taken this route. USGS Line Point

Peak 6779 *6,779 feet (Class 2)*
This unnamed summit is the highest Idaho Purcell peak. It is located 0.5 mile south of Goat Mountain; its summit can be reached from the ridge between the two peaks [Approach: (A)(5)(a)]. USGS Line Point

---

APPROACHES TO THE PURCELL MOUNTAINS

Approach routes for this section are identified in the text by bracketed entries [Approach:], which contain appropriate letter and number references.

(A) Purcell Mountain Access Points.
Access by road to these mountains is good—perhaps too good. Primary approach is from US-2 in the south and US-95 and ID-1 along the range's western fringes. In addition, US-95 cuts across the range's northwest corner, and the Moyie River Road and the Deer Creek Road (both major secondary roads) cut through the central sections of the range from north to south. Needless to say, due to the large number of logging roads, no area within the Idaho sections of the Purcells was recommended for wilderness designation.

(1) US-95 From US-1 to Eastport. US-95 leaves its junction with US-1 14.7 miles north of Bonners Ferry and runs northeast to the Canadian border at Eastport in 16.0 miles.

(a) FST-34, Bussard Mountain Trail. FST-34 leaves US-95 just west of Robinson Lake and climbs up to the north/south ridge line, which runs to Bussard Mountain in 6.5 miles. On the summit of Bussard, this trail joins FST-152, FST-32 and FST-225.

(2) FS-272 and FS-2481, Mission Creek Road. FS-272 leaves US-95 4.4 miles east of US-1 and runs north to the Canadian border. A mile from the border FS-2481 forks off to the east, up the East Fork of Mission Creek, and then meanders to the Miller Creek drainage, where it is closed by a gate.

(a) FST-156 and FST-409, Mission Mountain Trail. These trails combine to form a travel route between the Mission Creek Road and Gillion Creek. The eastern end of the trail can be accessed from the Mission Creek Road. In the west, the trail leaves FS-2481 at the divide between Mission Creek and Miller Creek, and then follows the ridge line north to Mission Mountain in a little over 1.0 mile. At Mission Mountain, the trail turns due east and descends a ridge line past Harvey Mountain to Gillion Creek. The trail's east end connects with FS-273 and Gillion Creek 1.4 miles north of US-95.

(3) FS-211, Moyie River Road. FS-211 is accessed from US-2 10.0 miles from Bonners Ferry. Turn north off US-2 on the first road west of the Moyie River bridge. This good gravel road runs north along the river for 20.0 miles to a junction with US-95 just south of the Canadian border.

(a) FST-32, Bussard Mountain Trail. FST-32 leaves FS-211 just north of Bussard Lake and climbs to the summit of Bussard Mountain in 3.5 miles, where it joins with FST-34 and 152.

(b) FST-152, Queen Mountain Trail. This trail leaves FS-211 at Twin Bridges and climbs to the summit of Queens Mountain in 3.5 miles, and then continues on to the summit of Bussard Mountain in another 1.2 miles.

(4) FS-453, Deer Creek Road. This road leaves US-95 1.4 miles east of the Moyie River bridge and runs north along Deer Creek and into Montana near Cannuck Peak.

(5) FS-627, Skin Creek Road. FS-627 leaves FS-453 where it crosses Skin Creek, and then works its way east and north to cross the Idaho/Montana border just north of Goat Mountain.

3. The Cabinet Mountains

The Cabinet Mountains are primarily a Montana range that extends into Idaho. The range is located southeast of Bonners Ferry and is bounded on the north by US-2 and the Kootenai River, on the west by US-2 and US-95, on the southeast by Lake Pend Oreille and to the south by ID-200 and the Clark Fork River.

The Cabinet range shares many similarities with the Purcell and Selkirk ranges. The basic foundation of the Cabinet Mountains are Precambrian Belt Supergroup rocks, which were carved and shaped by Pleistocene glaciation. Many of the peaks are high dome-shaped mountains, while a few, like Scotchman Peak, are sharp, sheer-edged summits reminiscent of the North Cascades. Summit elevations range between 6,000 and 7,000 feet; 7,009-foot Scotchman Peak is the highest summit in the Idaho Cabinets. East of the border, the Montana Cabinet Mountain peaks are considerably higher than their Idaho counterparts.

The Panhandle National Forest administers the Cabinet Mountains and, although much of the range has been logged in the past, a lot of high-quality country still exists for hikers and climbers. There are many miles of inviting, well-maintained hiking trails which traverse high treeless ridge lines and a few stream bottoms. Most Cabinet peaks are rated Class 1, but do not let this prejudice your judgment. These are big, beautiful mountains, and are more challenging than you might think.

Clifty Mountain 6,705 feet (Class 2)

Clifty Mountain is located in the northern section of the range, 6.0 miles southeast of Bonners Ferry. The peak is accessed from the Black Mountain Lookout Road, FS-274 [Approach: (A)(3)(a)]. Take FST-162, which leaves FS-274 at the road's last major switchback, and proceed east to this peak, which is only about 1.0 mile from the trailhead. When the trail enters the large clearing below the summit, ascend the south slopes to the summit. USGS Clifty Mountain

Iron Mountain 6,426 feet (Class 1)

Iron Mountain is located 3.5 miles south of Clifty Mountain. The peak is accessed from Boulder Creek and the Boulder Mountain trail system [Approach: (A)(3)(a)]. FST-179 leads directly to the summit. USGS Clifty Mountain

Boulder Mountain 6,298 feet (Class 2)

Boulder Mountain sits 3.0 miles south of Iron Mountain on the high ridge line that runs from Iron Mountain in the north to Lunch Peak in the south. FST-179 [Approach: (A)(3)(a)] reaches to within 300 feet of the summit. From the trail, follow either the north or south ridge up to the summit. USGS Clifty Mountain

Middle Mountain 6,220 feet (Class 2)

This peak is 1.5 miles southeast of Boulder

Mountain and can be reached by the same trail [Approach: (A)(3)(a)] that crosses near the summit of Boulder Mountain. USGS Clifty Mountain

Calder Mountain* *5,699 feet*
Purdy Mountain *6,062 feet*
Mount Willard *6,536 feet*
(Class 2)
These three summits stand on the main Cabinet ridge line between Boulder Mountain and Mount Pend Oreille. The summits are all climbed by following FST-67, either from Lunch Peak in the south or from Boulder Mountain in the north. Each summit is an easy walk from the ridge trail as it passes nearby [Approach: (A)(2.1)(a)]. USGS Mount Pend Oreille 15-minute

Mount Pend Oreille *6,755 (Class 1)*
The highest Cabinet Peak in Idaho is a big dome-shaped mountain with an extraordinary grass-covered summit, which features astonishing views in all directions. The summit is reached from either Lightning Creek or Lunch Peak [Approach: (A)(1)(a) or (A)(4)(a)]. USGS Mount Pend Oreille 15-minute

Smith Mountain *6,510 feet (Class 2)*
Smith Mountain, an old fire lookout site, sits above Smith Lake. The peak is located 3.5 miles east of Mount Pend Oreille. The summit is approached from either Idaho or Montana. The Montana route is Class 1 via a short walk from the end of a logging road. Idaho access is from the end of the Lightning Creek Road. Hike north on FST-52 [Approach: (A)(1)(a)] to a junction just below Lake Darling. From this junction, take FST-54 to South Callahan Creek. Leave the trail and ascend the steep southwest slope of the peak to the ridge and walk to the summit. USGS Mount Pend Oreille 15-minute

Lunch Peak *6,414 feet (Class 1)*
Lunch Peak is the southernmost peak on the main north/south ridge line that forms the northern section of the Idaho Cabinet Mountains. The mountain serves as a fire lookout site and is reached by road [Approach: (A)(2.1)]. Even with the road to its summit, the peak is an excellent goal because of its tremendous view. Hike to this summit from Darling Lake or Mount Pend Oreille (avoid the road). USGS Mount Pend Oreille 15-minute

Trestle Peak *6,320 feet*
Round Top Mountain *6,149 feet (Class 1)*
These two peaks are located along a major north/south ridge line that divides the Lightning Creek drainage from Lake Pend Oreille in the

southern section of the Cabinets. FST-120 traverses this ridge line for almost its entire distance [Approach: (A)(2)(a)]. Both peaks have striking summits with lofty views. The best route begins from FS-275 at the divide between Trestle Creek and Quartz Creek. From the saddle in the north, it is 3.0 miles to Trestle Peak and 6.0 miles to Round Top. USGS Mount Pend Oreille 15-minute

Bee Top Mountain *6,212 feet (Class 1)*
This former lookout site stands above the entrance to Lightning Creek 7.0 miles north of Clark Fork. Access the summit from the Alpine Way Trail and FST-63 [Approach: (A)(2)(a)], which leads to the summit. USGS Clark Fork 15-minute

Moose Mountain *6,543 feet (Class 1)*
Moose Mountain is situated 1.0 mile southwest of Moose Lake. To reach the summit, take FST-213 from the Rattle Creek Road [Approach: (A)(1.3)(b)]. Follow the trail north toward Moose Lake to the divide above the lake. From the divide follow the old trail up the ridge line to the peak. The peak can also be approached from Moose and Deer Creeks. USGS Mount Pend Oreille 15-minute

Scotchman No. 2 *6,989 feet (Class 3)*
This beautiful and rugged summit is located 2.0 miles northeast of Scotchman Peak, almost directly on the Idaho/Montana border. Although the summit can probably be reached from the west via either Morris or Savage creeks, the only route information available was from a climber who made the long, tedious traverse of the rugged ridge line between Scotchman Peak and Scotchman No. 2. This route involves considerable climbing just to descend Scotchman Peak's north ridge. Allow plenty of time for this trip. USGS Clark Fork 15-minute

Black Top Mountain *6,517 feet (Class 2)*
This peak is located midway between the two Scotchman peaks. To reach the summit, climb directly from Morris Creek on the west or traverse the ridge line north from Scotchman Peak. USGS Clark Fork 15-minute

Scotchman Peak *7,009 feet (Class 1)*
This summit, probably the hardest Class 1 peak in the state, is a craggy monster built of tilting metamorphic rocks that seem ready to slip down into Montana at any minute. The views of the "big" Cabinet peaks in Montana are awesome. To reach the highest point in the Cabinet Range, take FST-65 to the summit [Approach: (A)(1.2)(a)]. The trail is steep and rocky, and roughly 5.0 miles

and 3,500 feet in elevation gain from the start to the summit. USGS Clark Fork 15-minute

Goat Mountain *6,390 feet (Class 2)*

Goat Mountain is minor, nondescript summit located due west of Scotchman Peak. Climb this peak from the east where FST-65 [Approach: (A)(1.2)(a)] leaves the saddle between Goat Mountain and Scotchman Peak. Leave the trail at this point and follow the easy ridge line west to the summit. Although a minor summit, the view of Scotchman from the summit makes the walk worthwhile. USGS Clark Fork 15-minute

APPROACHES TO THE CABINET MOUNTAINS

Approach routes for this section are identified in the text by bracketed entries [Approach:], which include appropriate letter and number references.

(A) Cabinet Mountain Access Points.

Primary approach is via US-95 from Sandpoint to Bonners Ferry. This road travels along the western edge of the Cabinet Mountains. ID-200 provides access along the south edge; a combination of county and forest roads are the primary approach routes in the north. From all of these roads, visitors will find a number of roads leading into the inner range.

(1) FS-419, Lightning Creek Road. This is the major vehicular entrance into the southern sections of the range. The road departs from the center of the town of Clark Fork and goes north. A number of trails and side roads are accessible from this road.

(a) FST-52, Lake Darling/Mount Pend Oreille Trail. Roughly 18.0 miles from Clark Fork, the road up Lightning Creek ends. At this point, FST-52 continues up the drainage to Lake Darling in 2.0 miles and to the top of Mount Pend Oreille in 5.0 miles.

(1.2) FS-1058, Mosquito Creek Road. This road is accessed from the Lightning Creek Road 0.75 mile north of ID-200. Turn east onto the road and follow it for almost 4.0 miles to the Scotchman Peak trailhead.

(a) FST-65, Scotchman Peak Trail. This steep (repeat steep) trail is 5.0 miles long and ends at the ruins of a fire lookout on the summit of Scotchman Peak. As the trail nears the summit, you will not believe that it traverses the final treacherous ridge line. It does!

(1.3) FS-473, Rattle Creek Road. This road leaves FS-419 roughly 14.0 miles north of Clark Fork, and traverses eastward into Montana.

(a) FST-134, Lightning Peak Trail. Access this trail 4.0 miles from the Lightning Creek/Rattle Creek junction. The trail gives access to Lightning Peak's east slopes.

(b) FST-213, Moose Lake Trail. Leaves FST-134 3.5 miles east of Lightning Creek and runs due north to Moose Lake and Moose Creek in 4.25 miles.

(2) FS-275, Trestle Creek Road. The junction for this road is 17.0 miles from Clark Fork on the Lightning Creek Road. The road climbs to a pass north of Trestle Peak and then descends to ID-200 in 13.0 miles. This rough road has been traversed by sedans, but is quite rugged on the western side of the saddle where it detours up and around a section that is constantly being washed away by Trestle Creek.

(a) FST-120, Alpine Trail. This trail is designated as a National Recreational Trail. Hopefully, that means its route will not be violated by any more roads. The trail begins at the top of Trestle Creek (the trailhead is directly on the saddle). From the saddle, the trail quickly climbs to the ridge top and follows the divide south for roughly 14.0 miles to its end on Lightning Creek (just north of Clark Fork). The trail climbs over numerous peaks. The route is divided into two sections by FS-489. The walk is highly recommended for those who can shuttle the high end and walk to the low end.

(2.1) FST-1091, Lunch Peak Road. From the saddle at the top of Trestle Creek on FS-275, drive north on a good gravel road almost to the top of Lunch Peak. A lookout tower stands on the summit.

(a) FST-67, Lunch Peak Trail. From Lunch Peak, FST-67 follows the undulating ridge line north toward Mount Pend Oreille. It is 3.5 miles to that summit, another 1.3 miles to Purdy Mountain, another 2.1 miles to Calder Mountain and 3.0 more miles to Boulder Mountain. The trail, which stays on the ridge line for the entire distance, is a premier alpine hike.

(3) County Road 9, FS-408, Twentymile Creek Road. This road is accessed just north of Naples on US-95. The road proceeds up Twentymile Creek into the area surrounding Boulder Mountain. Follow this road east for 12.0 miles over a pass and onto the Boulder Creek Road. The Boulder Creek Road can be followed south toward the creek's headwaters or west toward the Kootenai River. Either choice will lead to trailheads that access the Boulder Mountain area.

(a) Boulder Mountain Trails. The country surrounding Boulder Mountain contains many fine trails which follow long winding ridge lines. At the top of Boulder Creek, FST-51 climbs up the slope to Divide Lake. At this point it joins FST-67, which goes south to Lunch Peak, and FST-179, which goes north over Boulder Mountain and on to Iron Mountain and eventually to Boulder Creek, far to the north. Additionally, FST-136 and FST-176 are both accessed from FST-179. FST-51 continues to the east, crossing over three peaks and ending near the Boulder City ghost town.

number of relics from the mining period can be found along the way.

The range, although scenic, has little to offer climbers. (The exception to the rule is Steamboat Rocks, located 10.0 miles north of Kingston on the Couer d'Alene River Road. A number of technical rock climbing routes have been established along their walls.) Because of the extensive road system, there is little of interest within the range, even for the dedicated peakbagger. Grizzly Peak, the highest point, is accessible by road. Of the 45 named peaks, only a couple are reached by trail.

4. The Coeur d'Alene Mountains

The Coeur d'Alene range is a triangular group of mountains stretching from Lake Pend Oreille in the north to Lake Coeur d'Alene in the south, to Kellogg, Idaho in the east and then back to Lake Pend Oreille. The range is bounded by the Bitterroot Mountains in the east, the Coeur d'Alene River in the south and Coeur d'Alene Lake and the Purcell Trench in the west.

The topography of the Coeur d'Alene Mountains suggests a broad plateau that has been shaped by streams into numerous canyons. Grizzly Mountain, at 5,950 feet, is the highest point in the range, which is formed by twisted layers of Precambrian sedimentary and metamorphic rocks that have been extensively faulted by the Osborn Fault system. During its history, the fault has moved Coeur d'Alene rock almost 16 miles. This faulting caused massive cracks to develop within the Coeur d'Alene rockbeds; these cracks filled with superheated, mineral-laden water, which precipitated the rich ore bodies that have made this region a famous mining district.

The Panhandle National Forest administers the majority of the area. Some private land is interspersed throughout the mountains as a result of patented mining claims. The range has an extensive road system to serve logging and mining interests. Little of the early trail system has survived the bulldozer.

Despite the overabundance of roads, there are still good hiking opportunities available in these mountains. The Coeur d'Alene River trail and the Independence Creek area are two popular destinations for area hikers. The Forest Service has set the Independence Creek Trail System aside as a roadless area with a variety of hiking trails. The area has historic as well as natural significance. The main trail down Independence Creek was originally a wagon road used to supply mining camps until the early 1930s, when the mining industry suffered a general collapse. A

CHILCO MOUNTAINS

The Chilco name identifies a small subrange of the Coeur d'Alene Mountains located on the western fringes of the main range, between Lake Pend Oreille and Lake Coeur d'Alene. The highest mountain in this subrange is Chilco Mountain, which reaches an elevation of 5,685 feet.

Chilco Mountain *5,685 feet*
South Chilco Mountain *5,634 feet*
(Class 1)
The only two named summits in the Chilco subrange of the Coeur d'Alene Mountains rise up due south of Lake Pend Oreille. Both peaks are reached by FST-14, which climbs to the summit of Chilco Mountain and continues south to South Chilco in another 1.5 miles [Approach: (A)(1)(a)]. USGS Athol 15-minute

---

Grizzly Mountain *5,950 feet*
To reach the highest Coeur d'Alene summit, take the Coeur d'Alene River Road north. Roughly 16.0 miles north of I-90, FS-260 runs up Grizzly Creek and eventually to the summit of Grizzly Mountain. It is about 8.0 miles up FS-260 to the summit. USGS Kellogg 15-minute

Graham Mountain *5,727 feet (Class 1)*
Graham Mountain is located 4.0 miles north of Kellogg. To reach the peak, drive 1.5 miles east from Kellogg on the road that parallels the Interstate. Turn north on FS-930 and follow it uphill toward Moon Saddle [Approach: (A)(3)(a)]. The trailhead is on the west side of the road. Hike FST-17 southwest and then northwest across the ridge top to the summit. The trail is not open to trail bikes and, therefore, gets little maintenance. If you get a chance, ask the Forest Service to put more emphasis on the trail. USGS Kellogg 15-minute

APPROACHES TO THE COEUR D'ALENE MOUNTAINS

Approach routes for this section are identified in the text by bracketed entries [Approach:], which contain appropriate letter and number references.

(A) Coeur d'Alene Mountain Access Points.

(1) Chilco Mountain Access. The only relevant approach point is FS-290, which gives access to the range's two named peaks. Take US-95 north from Hayden Lake. Turn east onto FS-290 1.5 miles south of Athol and follow this road 10.5 miles until the well-marked Chilco Mountain trailhead is reached.

(a) FST-14, Chilco Mountain Trail. This trail leaves FS-290 10.5 miles from US-95 and runs to the summit of Chilco Mountain in 2.0 miles and South Chilco Mountain in another 1.5 miles.

(2) Coeur d'Alene River Road. Access this road from I-90 at the Kingston exit. The road follows the river north into the heart of the range. Dozens of Forest Service roads depart from it to penetrate every corner of the range.

(3) FS-930, Moon Saddle Road. FS-930 is accessed from I-90 east of Kellogg. Take the first exit after Kellogg, drive to the north side of the freeway and then drive west along the freeway to Moon Creek. Follow this good road north to the ridge line above it in about 7.5 miles. At the T-intersection here, go left to Moon Saddle.

(a) FST-17, Graham Mountain Trail. FST-17 is accessed at Moon Saddle. The trail follows the ridge line west to Graham Mountain in roughly 5.5 miles.

(4) Independence Creek Trail System. This trail system is located in the northernmost sections of the Coeur D'Alene Mountains. Access to this area is possible from several directions. Probably the most direct route begins at the Coeur d'Alene River Road. From Prichard, drive north to the river's headwaters (the point where Independence Creek and Tepee Creek join). The Forest Service maintains six trails totalling 34.0 miles within this area.

5. The Saint Joe Mountains

The Saint Joe Mountains form a high ridge line that runs 45 miles east to west between the Saint Joe and the Coeur d'Alene rivers.

The range reaches its highest and most rugged heights northeast of Saint Maries, on a ridge anchored by Reeds Baldy and Latour Peak, the latter mountain being the highest Saint Joe summit at 6,408 feet. Geologically, the Saint Joe Mountains are made up of Belt Series sedimentary rocks, as are the nearby Coeur d'Alene Mountains. Much of the Saint Joes' contorted and complicated crest line is barren of trees due to both elevation and a great forest fire in 1910. The crest zig-zags east and west, north and south as it makes its way from the Bitterroots to its terminus at Lake Coeur d'Alene.

The Panhandle National Forest, the Idaho Department of Lands, and the Coeur d'Alene District of the Bureau of Land Management administer the public portions of this mountain group. The Coeur d'Alene Indian Reservation contains much of the western end of the range, while the Forest Service land is mostly grouped at the east end of the range; the BLM land is in the middle. While numerous roads penetrate much of the Saint Joes, there still are some roadless areas.

The Saint Joe Mountains offer excellent opportunities for hiking, peakbagging and cross-country skiing. The range's high open ridges are reminiscent of the Smoky Mountains of Tennessee and North Carolina. It is really a shame that more hikers are not aware of the quality of these mountains. If there were more public use, the Forest Service would surely take more interest in maintaining a good trail system. The best hiking is found between Latour Baldy and Reeds Baldy and in the Big Creek drainages.

The Saint Joes are a great place to find unsurpassed spring cross-country skiing. The area around Saint Joe Baldy and Reeds Baldy provides particularly good skiing in March and April (and sometimes even in May). The Phillips Draw and Rochat Divide roads, which begin at the Saint Joe River, melt out long before the snow-covered ridges above. Drive up either of these roads until you reach snow line, and then ski the roads to the high country above. In stable snow conditions, miles of open, rolling ridges can be traversed. The ridge between Reeds Baldy and Latour Peak is particularly enticing.

Climbing opportunities in the Saint Joes are limited to Class 1 and Class 2 excursions. Although the peaks are not technically difficult, trail conditions often warrant expert route-finding abilities and lots of endurance. Saint Joe vistas, however, are as good as any in the state.

It should be noted that the USGS maps for the Saint Joe Mountains are hopelessly out of date with regards to showing roads. (For example, the Saint Joe 15-minute quad was published in 1957.) Many roads have been constructed in this area

Saint Joe Baldy to Latour Peak; this crest is anchored by Latour Peak in the north (right) and Saint Joe Baldy in the south.

since the map was composed. The most important addition is the connection between the road along Latour Creek and the roads leading to Saint Joe Baldy. The present road crosses the crest just west of Rochat Peak, skirts that peak and the Pearson triangulation station and joins up with the mapped roadways just north of Saint Joe Baldy.

Latour Baldy *6,232 feet (Class 2)*
Latour Baldy is located at the north end of a major north/south ridge line which stretches for over 8.0 miles between the Coeur d'Alene River and the Saint Joe River. The peak is a short hike from the road that runs to the top of Frost Peak [Approach: (A)(2)]. USGS Saint Joe 15-minute

Latour Peak *6,408 feet (Class 2)*
The highest point in the Saint Joe Mountains is reached by the Pine Creek Road [Approach: (A)(2)]. The summit can also be reached by hiking north cross country from Reeds Baldy. This route follows the wide, open ridge between Latour Peak and Reeds Baldy. Total distance is 6.0 miles one way. USGS Saint Joe 15-minute

Iron Mast Mountain* *6,160 feet (Class 2)*
Iron Mast is unnamed on the Saint Joe USGS quad, but named on a Forest Service map. The summit is located 1.5 miles south of Latour Peak on the ridge that connects Latour and Reeds Baldy. To reach the top of this peak, follow the rolling, grass-covered ridge from either of the named peaks to the summit. USGS Saint Joe 15-minute

Reeds Baldy *6,153 feet (Class 1)*
Reeds Baldy is a big dirigible-shaped peak located 2.0 miles northeast of Saint Joe Baldy. From the roadway north of Saint Joe Baldy [Approach: (B)(2)(a)], follow the unmaintained ridge trail to the summit. At one time, this trail was maintained all the way to Latour Peak. USGS Saint Joe 15-minute

Saint Joe Baldy *5,825 feet (Class 1)*
This beautiful cone-shaped peak is visible from Saint Maries as well as other more distant locations. Although a road reaches the summit, the peak offers an excellent winter or early spring ski ascent. Follow either the Phillips Draw Road [Approach: (B)(1)] or the Rochat Divide Road [Approach: (B)(2)] to the saddle north of the peak, and then ski up the northeast ridge. An Idaho Department of Lands fire lookout is on top. USGS Saint Joe 15-minute

Wardner Peak *6,198 feet*
Kellogg Peak *6,397 feet (Class 1)*
These two peaks are located just south of Kellogg, Idaho. The city of Kellogg is planning to build a tram from the town to the top of the Kellogg Peak to stimulate tourism. If people knew how nice the hike to the top actually is, there would already be more tourists in Kellogg! To reach the summits, drive 4.0 miles east of Kellogg on I-90. Take the Big Creek Road, FS-264 south into the mountains. Follow FS-264 south to the FST-111 trailhead. Hike FST-111 south along Big

Creek and then turn west and follow the trail to the divide and FST-16, which leads northwest over Silver Hill to Wardner Peak. To reach Kellogg Peak, take a side trail from FST-16 to the summit. USGS Calder 15-minute

Lemonade Peak *5,651 feet (Class 1)*
This summit is located on the divide between Big Creek and Trout Creek. The peak offers a fine destination with a 360-degree view. A classically designed old lookout crowns the summit. Unfortunately, vandals have trashed the building, and it is no longer fit for human habitation. From the end of the Big Creek Road, take the Pierce Ridge FST-563, which begins with a very wet crossing of Big Creek [Approach: (B)(3)(a)]. At last report, portions of all Big Creek Trails were brushy and difficult to follow, so allow extra time for a trip into this area. USGS Calder 15-minute

Elsie Peak *5,257 feet (Class 2)*
Elsie Peak is the high point on the ridge line that divides the West Fork of Big Creek from the Middle Fork of Big Creek. The trail is climbed from FST-568 [Approach: (B)(3)(a)], which climbs the ridge to a point within 80 vertical feet of the summit before descending to Kellogg saddle. Scramble to the top from the trail. USGS Calder 15-minute

Placer Peak *5,240 feet*
Bad Tom Peak *5,587 feet*
Striped Peak *6,316 feet (Class 1)*
These three minor summits are located due south of Wallace. All three are Class 1 and are accessed via FST-16 from Slate Creek Saddle [Approach: (A)(3)(a)]. Although not as impressive as many other Saint Joe peaks, the ridge walk to these summits is enjoyable. USGS Wallace 15-minute

APPROACHES TO THE SAINT JOE MOUNTAINS

Approach routes for this section are identified in the text by bracketed entries [Approach:], which contain appropriate letter and number references.

(A) Northside Approaches.
I-90, which runs along the north side of the Saint Joe Mountains between Coeur d'Alene and the Montana border, is the primary approach in the north.
(1) Cataldo Exit. From the Cataldo exit on I-

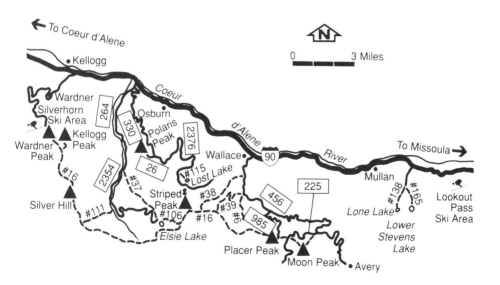

NORTH CENTRAL SAINT JOE MOUNTAINS
ROAD AND TRAIL ACCESS

CENTRAL SAINT JOE MOUNTAINS
ROAD & TRAIL ACCESS

90, the Latour Creek/Rochat Divide Road runs south along Latour Creek and crosses the Saint Joe range near Rochat Peak. The road·is often passable for passenger autos, but very rough.

(2) Pine Creek Road. This unnumbered road follows Pine Creek south from I-90 at Pinehurst. From this road, two feeder roads lead to the tops of two Saint Joe peaks, Frost and Latour.

(3) FS-456/FS-225, Slate Creek Saddle Road. From the Wallace area, this road crosses the Saint Joe range and leads to Hoyt Flats on the Saint Joe River. To access this road, drive south from Wallace on the Placer Creek Road, which eventually climbs to Slate Creek Saddle high above Wallace, and then descends to Hoyt Flats via Slate Creek.

(a) FST-16, Striped Peak Trail. This trail leaves Slate Creek Saddle and runs west to Striped Peak in 6.0 miles, crossing Placer Peak and Bad Tom Mountain on the way.

(b) South Fork of the Coeur d'Alene River Trails. The Forest Service maintains a number of trails along the Saint Joe divide. The trails traverse the higher Saint Joe ridges between the Silverhorn Ski Area and Placer Peak south of the towns of Kellogg, Osborn and Wallace. This true high-country trail is called the Saint Joe Divide Trail. The system is closed to motorcycles.

(B) South Side Approaches.
The Saint Joe River Road is the primary approach route in the south. The road leaves ID-97 on the west edge of Saint Maries.

(1) Phillips Draw Road. Turn onto this road 10.0 miles east of Saint Maries. The road climbs the divide and joins with the Rochat Divide Road.

The summit of Saint Joe Baldy is accessed via a feeder road, which makes a good spring cross-country ski route.

(2) Rochat Divide Road. This is the major approach road in the west end of the Saint Joes. The road is located 14.0 miles east of Saint Maries. It connects with the I-90 Cataldo exit in the north.

(a) Crystal Lake Trail. The trailhead is located on the saddle north of Saint Joe Baldy. This busy little trail is 2.0 miles in length and leads to a small but picturesque lake below Reeds Baldy.

(3) Calder Area Roads. Turn north from the Saint Joe River Road and drive into the village of Calder. From Calder, turn east and follow the gravel road that parallels the north shore of the Saint Joe River for 5.0 miles to join with the Big Creek Road, FS-537. This road, FS-537, leads to a number of scenic trails deep in the heart of the range.

(a) Big Creek Drainage Trails. The Big Creek drainage covers a lot of ground. At one time, it contained stately stands of white pine and small mining operations. Today, it is mostly unforested as a result of the great 1910 forest fire. The present trail system is surprisingly good (considering the low emphasis put on recreation in this ranger district). These trails intersect with the trails above Wallace to provide miles of exceptionally good hiking.

6. The Clearwater Mountains

The Clearwater Mountains are the largest of the Idaho Batholith mountain ranges and are located in northcentral Idaho. This massive group of mountains stretches 125 miles north to south and from 40 to 75 miles east to west. The Saint Joe River forms the range's northern boundary, the Bitterroot Mountains form the eastern boundary and the main fork of the Salmon River forms the southern boundary. The western boundary is not a definite geographic line, but roughly extends between Saint Maries, Moscow, Orofino, Grangeville and Riggins.

The Clearwaters are formed mostly of Idaho Batholith granite, covered in places by scattered deposits of older sedimentary and metamorphic rocks which have yet to erode away. During the Pleistocene ice age numerous alpine glaciers carved cirques and lake basins into the sides of many Clearwater peaks. The effects of the glaciers are most readily visible in the Mallard-Larkins and Selway Crags area of the range. Although the

Clearwater terrain is somewhat uniform in its overall appearance, several distinct ridges within the range have been singled out as subranges. These include the Selway Crags, the Moose Mountains, the Sheep Mountain Range, and the Little Goat Mountains.

Clearwater peaks are seldom over 6,500 feet high in the north, but gradually gain elevation as one moves to the south. The highest peaks are found just north of the Salmon River, where Buffalo Hump, Gospel Peak and Center Mountain rise abruptly from the Salmon's deep canyon. Stripe Mountain, at 9,001 feet, is the highest Clearwater Peak. It is located north of the Salmon along the very indefinite line which divides the Clearwater Mountains and the Bitterroot Mountains. There is no logical, or clearly defined dividing point between the Clearwater and Bitterroot mountains. In fact, they are physically the same set of mountains.

The Forest Service administers the vast majority of the range, although it takes several national forests to accomplish this monumental task. In the north, the Panhandle National Forest is in charge, followed by the Clearwater, Bitterroot, and Nez Perce, respectively, from north to south. Much of the land in the northwest Clearwater Mountains is owned by large private timber companies. This land, which was once owned by all Americans, fell into private ownership in the last century when Congress gave private corporations huge tracts of land in the American west as an incentive to build transcontinental railroad lines.

The Congressional scheme to stimulate development of the west entitled the railroads to receive (free of charge) their right-of-ways and alternating square-mile sections of land adjacent to their right-of-ways. This created the checkerboard pattern of alternating sections of federal land and private land which are readily visible on the Clearwater National Forest map. Eventually over 90 million acres of valuable public lands were given to the railroads under various pieces of legislation. In a few cases, rail lines were constructed just to secure the vast tracks of land.

Although Congress intended that the railroads raise investment capital by selling the "gift lands" to settlers, the railroads simply used it as collateral and exploited the timber reserves that were found on it. In the end, the railroads were built, but the U.S. Treasury saw little return on this incredible investment and the land passed out of the public's hands. The only good news is that for the most part, these lands are still open to the public without a permit. However, the land is private and its access may be restricted at any time.

Opportunities for hiking and climbing in the Clearwater Mountains are as unlimited as the

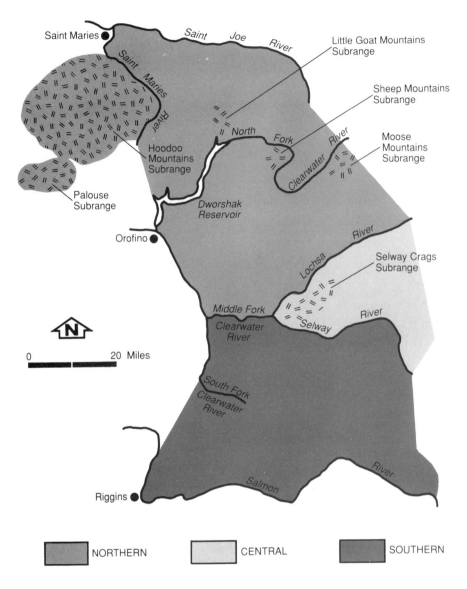

CLEARWATER MOUNTAINS AND SUBRANGES

mountains themselves. Although climbing opportunities in the Clearwater Mountains primarily fall into the Class 1 to Class 3 categories, a number of technical route possibilities exist throughout the range. The west face of Chimney Peak in the Selway Crags possesses one of the most notable walls in Idaho but, as of yet, it has not attracted any climber's interest. Clearwater Peaks come in an infinite variety and any hiker or peakbagger who ventures into the range will find a wonderful variety of challenges and—above all—solitude.

The variety of hikes available is impressive, ranging from short forested hikes to long alpine adventures. Three great officially designated wilderness areas, the Selway-Bitterroot, the Gospel Hump and the River of No Return, protect much of the Clearwater country. In addition, there are numerous other roadless areas that are worthy of wilderness designation and, with lots of hard work by environmentalists, they might someday be protected. These de facto wilderness areas include, but are not limited to, the Mallard-Larkins, Kelly Creek, Great Burn and Pot Mountain areas.

The Mallard-Larkins Pioneer Area is the largest and most important of the Clearwater's *de facto* wilderness areas. It is administered jointly by the Panhandle and Clearwater national forests and encompasses 30,500 acres; another 200,000 acres adjoining it are roadless and worthy of wilderness designation. The "pioneer" status, according to the Forest Service, "recognizes Mallard-Larkins' unique natural beauty and recreation values and gives special consideration to wildlife and fisheries." It is likely that, eventually, this area will receive wilderness designation because it is an extremely important habitat for big game animals that bring the state many hunter dollars each fall.

Much of the Mallard-Larkins country is alpine in nature, with high mountain lakes and glacial cirques. Elevation changes are quite extreme, ranging from 2,600 feet to over 7,000 feet at Black Mountain. This precipitous terrain is responsible for the area's diverse flora. The high alpine areas are characterized by grasses and wildflowers. Along the lower slopes, the hiker can find incredible stands of cedars that were spared by the 1910 fire.

The Gospel Hump Wilderness Area encompasses 206,000 acres in the southern Clearwater Mountains, down to the Salmon River's south side. This area is a home of beautiful forest, open meadows, mountain lakes and several notable summits. Many of the trails follow ridge tops and cross mountain tops, providing spectacular views of the surrounding wilderness. Buffalo Hump, at 8,924 feet, is the preeminent peak in the wilderness area and one of the highest points in the Clearwaters.

Because of the abundance of moose and elk, the Gospel Hump area was a favorite hunting ground of the Nez Perce tribe, which occupied this area as early as 6000 B.C. In 1861, gold was discovered in Florence Basin; by 1889, over 5,000 miners poured into the area, forced the Indians out, and temporarily ended the wilderness quality of the environment. In the early 1900s, the mining boom subsided and this high plateau returned to a wild, remote hinterland.

The 1.2 million-acre Selway-Bitterroot Wilderness Area lies in northcentral Idaho and western Montana, in a triangle formed by the Lochsa, Selway and Bitterroot rivers. Lowell, Idaho, Missoula, Montana, and Darby, Montana, roughly form the corners of this impressive mountain environment. The Selway-Bitterroot Wilderness, the first of Idaho's great wilderness areas to be recognized by the federal government, is an immense area which encompasses large sections of the Bitterroot and Clearwater mountains.

In addition to the cutting forces of the many rivers that drain the Selway-Bitterroot country, the natural history of the wilderness is affected by two factors. First, glacial action gouged out immense quantities of overburden in this area, which has exposed a monumental amount of batholith granite, especially on the eastern fringes. Second, the great fires of 1910 cauterized many of the slopes to such an extent that trees have yet to repopulate the sterile soil. Thus, even though the maximum elevations range only from 7,000 to 9,000 feet, much of the wilderness is open, treeless and alpine in nature.

A: THE NORTHERN CLEARWATER PEAKS
From the Saint Joe River South to the Clearwater and Lochsa Rivers

---

PALOUSE RANGE

This small subrange is the westernmost extension of the Clearwater Mountains. It rises up north of Moscow to form a divide 18 miles long and 10 miles wide, with a rolling forested crest containing a few granite outcroppings near the crest. Moscow Mountain, 4,983 feet, is the tallest peak in the range.

The majority of the Palouse range is privately owned. The Forest Service and Potlatch Company each own only small sections of the range, and the University of Idaho operates an experimental forest on roughly 6,000 acres. The remaining land is held by a variety of small landowners. The University of Idaho land is open to the public, but much of the private land is posted with No Trespassing signs. East Moscow Mountain is the only summit on public land and it is reached by a road. Winter use of the range for cross-country skiing is the recommended use.

Moscow Mountain *4,983 feet (Class 2)*
Moscow Mountain is located northeast of Moscow on the eastern end of the Palouse crest. Its summit, which is on private land, is easily reached by the major ridge road that traverses the range. From the saddle east of the peak, an unnumbered side road leads nearly to the summit

[Approach: (D)(1) and (2)]. Permission should be acquired from the landowner before attempting the peak (check at the Latah County Courthouse regarding the current owner). USGS Potlatch

East Moscow Mountain 4,511 feet (Class 1)

East Moscow Mountain is located east of Moscow Mountain on public land and is an excellent cross-country skiing destination in the winter. Approach the ski route via the Tamarack Ski Area Road [Approach: (D)(1) and (2)]. Once on the Tamarack Ski Area Road, drive toward the mountains until the road is no longer plowed. Park and ski the road past the ski area. From this point, it is possible to climb up old ski runs toward the summit and then climb the mostly open slopes above to the summit. This is a steep, difficult ski route which requires expert skill, good equipment and sufficient snow. The easier route is to follow the road north from the ski area, past a spring flowing into a cement trough (the water seldom freezes) to a major signed road junction roughly 1.0 mile north of the ski area. Turn left (west) at this point and ski west up the ridge. At the next major junction, turn left (east, this time) to go to the top of the mountain. Total distance is 3.0 miles one way. USGS Potlatch

HOODOO MOUNTAINS

This minor group of Clearwater summits is separated from the main body of Clearwater peaks to the east by the Saint Maries River. The range is oval-shaped and runs from the river west to the Washington/Idaho border, north to Lake Coeur d'Alene and south to Potlatch.

Hoodoo summits are low and rounded and for the most part forested. The highest point is Bald Mountain at 5,334 feet. A great deal of logging has taken place throughout the area and roads are replacing trails at a staggering rate. Hiking and climbing is minimal in this subrange. A few summits are reached by seldom-used hiking trails. Some summits have been clearcut and an expanding road system has left most trails abbreviated or broken and nearly useless. At the Giant White Pine Campground along ID-6, the Forest Service has made efforts to establish and preserve a series of short loop trails which are recommended for day hiking. Be aware that the two 15-minute USGS quads that cover this country are hopelessly out of date. The corresponding Forest Service maps are not much more accurate.

East Dennis 4,626 feet (Class 1)

This peak is an old fire lookout site with a view which is quickly disappearing as the forest grows

up around the summit. A road leads to the top from North South Pass on ID-6 [Approach: (C)(3)]. Although the road makes the summit uninteresting in the summer, it is a good place to visit on skis during the winter. From North South Pass, ski up the road for 3.0 miles to the signed side road that leads to the summit. From this point, it is another 0.5 mile to the summit. USGS Emida 15-minute

Bald Mountain 5,334 feet (Class 1)

Bald Mountain is the highest peak in the Hoodoos. Its summit is reached by dirt road from ID-6 [Approach: (C)(3)] or via a trail from Giant White Pines CG on ID-6 [Approach: (C)(2)(a)]. Although the trail's corridor is violated several times by roadways, the hike to the summit from the campground is a good early season conditioning hike for the diehard hiker. It is 9.0 miles one way. The dirt road to the summit from North South Pass is closed in winter and offers a good, long ski trip to the top. USGS Emida 15-minute

Three Tree Butte 3,330 feet (Class 1)

This is the lowest summit listed in this guidebook. The summit is reached by trail from ID-6 and Giant White Pine CG [Approach: (C)(2)]. The view from the top is limited, but the walk through the woods is quite nice. USGS Deary

Sand Mountain 4,960+ feet (Class 1)

Sand Mountain is an abandoned lookout site. All that remains of the lookout are four steel braces that stick out of the ground and remnants of an old phone line. The summit is now overgrown and the view is no longer a reason to hike to the top. However, even without a view the Sand Mountain Trail traverses beautiful cedar stands on its way to the summit (which is owned by the Burlington Northern Railroad) [Approach: (C)(1)(a)]. USGS Deary 15-minute

---

Grandfather Mountain 6,306 feet (Class 1)

Grandfather Mountain is located on BLM land 9.0 miles northeast of Clarkia. This Class 1 peak is accessed by hiking northwest for 4.0 miles on FST-275 from Freezeout Saddle [Approach: (B)(2)(a)]. USGS Grandmother Mountain

Grandmother Mountain 6,369 feet (Class 1)

Grandmother Mountain is located 1.5 miles southeast of Grandfather Mountain. Although the peak itself is not much more than a large hump, the hike to the peak offers an excellent introduction to the Clearwater Mountains, and the views from the trail are vast all along the grassy ridge top. From FS-301 at Freezeout Saddle, follow the signed and well-maintained trail to the summit, which is 2.0 miles from the road [Approach: (B)(2)(a)]. USGS Grandmother Mountain

Marks Butte *6,297 feet (Class 2)*
Marks Butte is located next to FS-301 just west of Freezeout Saddle. This peak (which is of little interest in the summer) is a good destination for cross-country skiers throughout the winter. During the winter, FS-301 is kept open to within a few miles of Freezeout Saddle for logging operations. Drive until the road is no longer plowed and ski in the remaining distance. There are several good locations in which to build snow caves and many open slopes to ski [Approach: (B)(2)]. USGS Grandmother Mountain

Lookout Mountain *6,789 feet (Class 1)*
Lookout Mountain is located east of the Grandfather/Grandmother Mountain ridge line on a parallel north/south ridge composed of Lookout and Widow mountains. This peak is 2.0 miles north of Widow Mountain and is reached by the same trail [Approach: (B)(2)(b)]. USGS Widow Mountain

Widow Mountain *6,828 feet (Class 1)*
Widow Mountain has a long, ridgelike summit over a mile long. The summit is reached by hiking north 1.5 miles via FST-52 [Approach: (B)(2)(b)]. USGS Widow Mountain

Snow Peak *6,760 feet (Class 1)*
Snow Peak is located 14.0 miles west of Red Ives GS on the Saint Joe River and 4.0 miles north of the Mallard-Larkins Pioneer Area in an area where public and private land are in a checkerboard pattern. The upper reaches of Snow Peak are pyramid shaped and quite picturesque. The summit, which contains a fire lookout, can be reached by trail. Reportedly, mountain goats are sometimes visible on the peak's rocky east ridge. The peak is reached by taking FST-55 for 5.0 miles from its start at FS-201 [Approach: (A)(4)(a)]. Camping is available in the meadows below the summit, where there is a small spring that flows year round (treat the water to avoid Giardia). USGS Montana Peak

LITTLE GOAT MOUNTAINS

The Little Goat Mountains are a petite subrange of the Clearwater Mountains. The range is located north of Dworshak Reservoir and it is roughly seven miles by four miles in size. These granite-based peaks have a northwest-to-south-

east orientation and reach their highest point at Blackdome Peak, 6,412 feet. The range has one mountain lake, which is located on the east side of the crest.

Blackdome Peak *6,412 feet (Class 2)*
Blackdome Peak is located north of the Little North Fork of the Clearwater River, just a short distance north of FS-457 [Approach: (B)(3)]. The summit is a short walk from the road.

Larkins Peak *6,661 feet (Class 1)*
Larkins Peak is located 7.0 miles due south of Snow Peak and is the westernmost of the Mallard-Larkins Pioneer Area peaks. The summit sits south of Larkins Lake on the main east/west ridge line that divides the Little North Fork and North Fork of the Clearwater drainages. To reach the summit hike either FST-240 [Approach: (E)(3)(a)], which leads to the summit, or hike up Isabella Creek until meeting FST-96 [Approach: (E)(3.1)(a)], which goes up Elmer Creek via FST-96 to meet FST-240 south of the peak. USGS Mallard Peak/MLPA

Crag Peak *6,879 feet*
Heart Peak *6,870 feet (Class 2)*
Both of these tree-covered peaks stand above the southwest edge of Heart Lake, a little over 1.0 mile east of Larkins Peak. FST-65 crosses a saddle between these two peaks [Approach: (E)(3)(b)]. Climb both peaks from the saddle. USGS Mallard Peak/MLPA

Mallard Peak *6,870 feet (Class 1)*
This old lookout site, the easternmost peak on the Mallard Larkins divide, is located 3.0 miles east of Heart Peak. The summit can be gained by a ridge trail from the south. From FS-705, hike up Isabella Creek (FST-95) until the ridge trail (FS-91) is gained in about 5.0 miles [Approach: (E)(3.1)(a)]. USGS Mallard Peak/MLPA

Black Mountain *7,077 feet (Class 1)*
Black Mountain is located south of the main Mallard-Larkins divide and east of Isabella Creek. The peak has a precipitous north face; its summit (an old lookout site) is reached by the trail that runs from Black Lake to the peak's south slopes [Approach: (E)(4)(a)]. USGS Mallard Peak / MLPA

SHEEP MOUNTAIN RANGE

The Sheep Mountain Range is located northeast of the town of Headquarters and is situated inside a major bend in the North Fork of the

Clearwater River. This minor Clearwater subrange is eight miles long and four miles wide. Eagle Point, at 5,709 feet, is the highest point in this heavily roaded and logged area.

Sheep Mountain *5,708 feet (Class 1)*
Sheep Mountain is located south of the Mallard-Larkins Pioneer Area near the Sousie Creek CG. To reach its summit, hike FST-93, which is a ridge trail, west from FS-682 for roughly 2.0 miles [Approach: (E)(2.1)(a)]. USGS Sheep Mountain.

Eagle Point *5,709 feet (Class 1)*
Eagle Point is located 3.0 miles northeast of Sheep Mountain. To reach its summit, take FST-93 northwest from FS-682 for less than 1.0 mile [Approach: (E)(2.1)(a)]. USGS Sheep Mountain

---

Pot Mountain *7,139 feet (Class 1)*
Pot Mountain is situated within a large bend in the North Fork of the Clearwater River east of Headquarters. The highest Clearwater peak in the region, it is the center of an unofficial wilderness area complete with a surprising number of mountain lakes and scenic vistas of the surrounding country. To hike to the summit of Pot Mountain, follow FS-711 to a side road designated FS-5259. Follow this road to its end. From here, FST-144 leads 3.0 miles to the summit [Approach: (E) (5.1)(a)]. USGS Pot Mountain

Cold Springs Peak *6,731 feet (Class 1)*
Cold Springs Peak is surrounded by high mountain lakes and is located 5.0 miles northwest of the Kelly Forks GS. The Class 1 summit is reached from the GS via FST-176 and FST-169 [Approach: (E)(5)(a)]. The summit can also be reached from FST-445, which runs between Cold Springs Peak and Elizabeth Mountain [Approach: (E)(5)(b)] or via FST-440 [Approach: (E)(5)(c)]. USGS Pot Mountain

Elizabeth Mountain *6,464 feet (Class 1)*
This picturesque summit is located 2.5 miles due east of Cold Springs Peak. The shortest route to the summit is FST-445, which climbs steeply from FS-250 to the summit in 2.5 miles [Approach: (E)(5)(b)]. USGS Elizabeth Lake

Flat Mountain *6,606 feet (Class 1)*
Flat Mountain is located 2.0 miles northwest of Kelly Forks GS and is the southernmost summit on the ridge that divides Cold Springs Creek from Kelly Creek. The summit is reached by FST-176 [Approach: (E)(5)(a)]. USGS Elizabeth Lake

MOOSE MOUNTAINS

The Moose Mountains were named after the mining town of Moose, which sat on the range's eastern slopes. These mountains are located roughly 30 miles east of Pierce in the Y formed by the North Fork of the Clearwater and Kelly Creek. This small group runs approximately 10 miles east to west, and is 4 miles in width. Moose Creek Butte is the highest point at 6,937 feet. Although the Forest Service recommended the Moose Mountains for wilderness protection in the late 1970s, Congress has yet to act on the recommendation.

Sheldon Bluestein, in his book *North Idaho Hiking Trails,* states that "the Moose Creek Buttes rank among Idaho's most rugged mountains." He goes on to say, "They have an inspirational value that makes them worthy of preservation... the Buttes' north sides dazzle you with a three-tiered display of blue sky, tan rock, and green meadows." While the scenery is spectacular, use of the area is low. The Moose Mountains offer a large roadless area that is seldom visited because it is located a long way from anywhere.

Moose Mountain *6,603 feet (Class 1)*
Moose Mountain sits at the Head of Moose Creek. Its western slopes descend steeply in 2.0 miles to the deep Black Canyon of the North Fork of the Clearwater River. The summit is accessed by trail from both the east and the north [Approach: (E)(6)(a) and (b)]. USGS Moose Mountain

Moose Creek Butte *6,937 (Class 2)*
Although no trail leads to the Buttes, scramblers can follow the ridge line from Moose Mountain to the summits. The Buttes are rugged—a good knowledge of cross-country travel is essential [Approach: (E)(6)(a) and (b)]. USGS Scurvy Mountain

---

B: THE CENTRAL CLEARWATER PEAKS
Between the Lochsa and Selway Rivers and west of the Bitterroot Mountains

---

SELWAY CRAGS

The Selway Crags are located at the western edge of the Selway-Bitterroot Wilderness Area, where the Selway and Lochsa rivers join at Lowell, and are the best known of the Clearwater subranges. The name Selway Crags attaches to a prominent ridge system that parallels the Lochsa River for 40 miles. The Selway Crags country is a rugged area, composed of sharp vertical granite summits and high mountain lakes. The trails are difficult because they are poorly maintained and because elevations range from 2,000 feet along the Lochsa and Selway Rivers to over 8,000 feet on Fenn Mountain. /SBW

Cantaloupe Peak *6,133 feet (Class 1)*
Cantaloupe Peak is really just a high point on the ridge line that leads to Huckleberry Butte, 1.5 miles to the north. The Class 1 summit is crossed by FST-220 [Approach: (E)(7)(c)]. USGS Huckleberry Butte/SBW

Huckleberry Butte *6,710 feet (Class 1)*
This bald summit is located 1.5 miles north of Cantaloupe Peak. It is reached in 6.0 miles from the Wilderness Gateway trailhead via FST-220 [Approach: (E)(7)(c)]. USGS Huckleberry Butte / SBW

Ghost Mountain *6,861 feet (Class 1)*
Ghost Mountain is the westernmost Selway Crags area peak listed in this guidebook. It is located 12.0 miles east of Lowell. FST-3 leads to the summit [Approach: (E)(9.1)(a)]. USGS Chimney Peak / SBW

Chimney Peak *7,840 feet*
Chimney Peak is the preeminent Selway Crag peak. An extremely rugged mountain for this part of the Idaho Batholith, it resembles a soot-stained chimney. The peak is located at the heads of Chimney and Old Man creeks, a little over 1.0 mile west of Old Man Lake. Although Chimney Peak's east and west faces present more interesting challenges, the peak has apparently only been climbed from the pass to the southeast via the south ridge. FST-3 provides access to the peak with the shortest route beginning from the Big Fog Saddle Road [Approach: (E)(9.2)(a)]. USGS Chimney Peak / SBW

South Ridge. *(Grade II, Class 3)*
From FST-3 at the saddle southeast of the summit, a long slanting gully is visible slicing up through the dark rock of the south ridge. This gully leads to the east side of Chimney's lower south peak. To reach the gully, drop off the saddle near the base of the east ridge by down-climbing a steep rocky step, through a thick stand of small firs. (This section of the route would be nearly impossible in wet conditions.) Once down the step, traverse west into a small boulder field and drop down through the boulders to a grassy bench. Traverse north along the narrow bench to the

Chimney Peak is the most vertical summit in the Selway Crags. This view is from the ridge top just southeast of the summit.

bottom of the slanting gully. Climb the gully to its top and then traverse around the south summit to the ridge line between the south and main summits. Follow the ridge north to the base of the main summit. At this point, the route drops off the ridge top to the west, through thick t. nber to a gully filled with "whitish" rock. Climb this Class 2-3 gully until it ends at the base of a large block. Traverse around this block on the west and climb the next large summit block to the ridge top. From this point, the route follows the knife-edged ridge line north to the true summit across 100 feet of slanting blocks.

Gedney Mountain *7,360+ feet (Class 1)*
Gedney Mountain is a fin-shaped summit located just west of Cove Lakes. The summit is a short walk from FST-708 [Approach: (E)(9)(a)] or [Approach: (E)(9.2)(c)]. USGS Chimney Peak / SBW

49

Stanley Butte *7,362 feet (Class 1)*

Stanley Butte is a hump-shaped peak located 5.0 miles north of Fenn Mountain, just west of Shasta Lake. FST-220 comes within 200 feet of the summit; it is an easy scramble to the top from the trail [Approach: (E)(7)(c)]. USGS Fenn Mountain / SBW

Fenn Mountain *8,021 feet*

Fenn Mountain is named after Major Frank Fenn, who served three terms in the Idaho Territorial Legislature and was the first supervisor of the Sawtooth National Forest. The mountain chosen to honor Fenn is the culmination of a large craggy northeast-trending ridge with numerous summits, which reaches its highest point at its northern end. The highest point in the Selway Crags, it offers lots of route possibilities, but is seldom climbed. Access the peak from Jesse Pass [Approach: (E)(9.2)(b)]. USGS Fenn Mountain / SBW

Jesse Pass Route. *(Grade III, Class 3)*

From Jesse Pass, it is difficult to pick out the summit of Fenn Mountain because the foreground melds into the background. Three major summits are clearly distinguishable from the pass. From Jesse Pass follow the trail off the pass to the boulder field in roughly 0.3 mile. Climb up the boulder field to a grass-filled gully on the east side of the third peak. At the top of the gully, head north, crossing another boulder field, to the ridge top and then continue on toward a rock fin that sits squarely on the ridge line. From this point to the peak's southern slopes, route-finding is difficult. As a general rule, when faced with an option to go up, or go down—go down and around. Bypass the first fin on the west side and then cross back to the east side of the ridge to bypass the next fin. Cross again to the west side of the ridge to bypass the last fin. Once past the last fin, cross back to the east side of the ridge and climb out onto the south slopes of the true summit. Climb up and north, past a window in the peak's south ridge, to the true summit.

Lower Three Links Lake Route. *(Grade II, Class 2-3)*

This route climbs the large gully that runs from the Lower Three Links Lake directly to the summit. The gully is filled with almost 2,000 feet of loose rock, but presents no real difficulties.

East Peak *7,852 feet (GR II, Class 2)*

East Peak towers over the largest of the Lizard Lakes, climbing over 1,500 feet in 0.25 mile. From the lake, climb to the saddle north of the peak and follow the ridge to the summit [Approach: (E)(9.2)(e)]. USGS Fenn Mountain / SBW

Fenn Mountain, viewed from the ridge line above Cove Lake; the saddle is Jesse Pass.

Lizard Peak *7,104 feet (Class 2-3)*
The peak is located north of Lizard Lakes and northeast of East Peak. From the second-largest Lizard Lake, climb to the saddle west of the peak and scramble up the ridge to the summit [Approach: (E)(9.2)(e)]. USGS Fenn Mountain/SBW

Big Fog Mountain *7,122 feet* (**Class1**)
Big Fog Mountain contains a massive summit field which was burned off in the 1910 fires. The view of the peaks to the north is one of the finest views in Idaho. FST-343 leads to the summit from the Big Fog Mountain Road [Approach: (E)(9.2)(d)]. USGS Fenn Mountain / SBW

Sponge Mountain *7,349 feet (Class 1)*
Sponge Mountain is located north of Boulder Pass and east of Long Lake. FST-206 crosses the summit 1.6 miles north of Boulder Pass [Approach: (E)(7)(d)]. USGS Fish Lake / SBW

Eagle Mountain *7,427 feet (Class 2)*
Eagle Peak is 0.5 mile south of Sponge Mountain. To reach the peak, take FST-206[Approach: (E)(7)(c)] from Boulder Pass to Eagle peak's south ridge. Leave the trail, which continues along the peak's west slopes, and climb up the south ridge to the summit. USGS Fish Lake/SBW

Greystone Butte *6,545 feet (Class 1)*
Greystone Butte is located south of the Lochsa River and just west of Greystone Lake. FST-206 crosses the summit [Approach: (E)(7)(d)]. USGS Greystone Butte/SBW

Flytrap Butte *6,338 feet (Class 1)*
Flytrap Butte is located 2.0 miles norhteast of Greystone Butte. FST-208 crosses its summit [Approach: (E)(7)(e)]. USGS Greystone Butte/SBW

Freezeout Mountain *5,986 feet (Class 2)*
Freezeout Mountain is located3.5 miles east of Flytrap Butte. The summit is accessed via FST-209 [Approach: (E)(7)(e)], which crosses over the peak's northern slopes to the summit. (The trail is accessed from the Mocus Point trailhead.) USGS Bear Mountain/SBW

Bear Mountain *7,184 feet (Class 1)*
Bear Mountain is located at the head of Kinnikkinnick, Mountain, Colgate and Queen creeks, 3.0 miles south of the Lochsa River. Take FST-209 to FST-21, which leads to this lookout site [Approach: (E)(7)(e)] or [Approach: (E)(7)(f)]. The quickest approach is via the Warm Springs Pack Bridge trailhead. USGS Bear Mountain/SBW

McConnel Mountain *7,424 feet (Class 1)*
McConnel Mountain is a remote summit that divides four drainages—Pedro, Wag, Chain and Moose creeks. FST-213 leads to the summit [Approach: (E)(7)(b)]. USGS McConnel Mountain/SBW

Tom Beal Peak *7,568 feet (Class 2)*
This peak is located 5.5 miles southeast of the Powell GS. Climb to the peak's upper slopes via either FST-37 [Approach: (E)(7)(e)] or FST-44 [Approach: (E)(7)(f)]. FST-44 provides the shortest approach, while FST-37 offers an excellent ridge walk to the summit. USGS Tom Beal Peak / SBW

Grave Peak *8,282 feet (Class 1)*
Surrounded by lakes, Grave Peak sits 4.0 miles south of Tom Beal Peak. The summit is reached via an old unmaintained trail up the south ridge from Friday Pass, which is reached via FST-45 [Approach: (E)(8)(a)]. From FS-358, it is 4.5 miles to the summit. USGS Grave Peak / SBW

Big Rock Mountain *7,109 feet (Class 2-3)*
Big Rock Mountain is located at the head of Sixtytwo Ridge, east of the Selway Crags. Climb from FS-423 [Approach: (E)(9)(b.1)]. USGS Big Rock Mountain / SBW

Shissler Peak *6,375 feet (Class 1)*
Shissler Peak is located north of the Moose Creek GS at the head of Whistling Pig Creek. The summit can be accessed via trails from the south or north. From the GS, FST-613 and FST-450 provide the most direct approach to the summit [Approach: (E)(9)(b.3)]. USGS Shissler Peak / SBW

Bailey Mountain *7,386 feet (Class 1)*
Bailey Mountain is located between the north and east forks of Moose Creek and just west of May Lake. This lookout site is reached by two trails from the north or south. The shortest route from a road is to approach the peak from the Selway River Road via the Moose GS by taking FST-619 to the summit [Approach: (E)(9)(c)]. USGS Hungry Rock / SBW

Goat Heaven Peaks *7,254 feet*
Gateway Peak *6,283 feet (Class 2-3)*
These peaks are located above Goat Lakes, many miles due south of Powell and US-12. While there are no trails to the lakes, FST-491 [Approach: (E)(8)(b)] (see also [Approach: (E)(9)(c)]) leads to within a short distance of Gateway Peak's summit and then proceeds southeast along the south side of the Goat Heaven Peaks. Both sum-

mits are accessible from the trail. Goat Lakes can be accessed from FST-42 along the East Fork of Moose Creek by hiking cross country up the outlet stream. To climb the Goat Heaven Peaks from the lakes, gain the ridge and follow it to the various summits. USGS Cedar Ridge / SBW

Freeman Peak *7,294 feet (Class 1)*
Freeman Peak is located 7.0 miles east of the Moose Creek GS between Moose Creek and the Selway River. The shortest route to the summit from the GS is via FST-430 [Approach: (E)(9)(d)]. USGS Freeman Peak / SBW

Wahoo Peak *7,682 feet (Class 1)*
Wahoo Peak is located 7.5 miles east of Freeman Peak and 6.0 miles south of Goat Heaven Peaks. The summit is reached by five different trails. The shortest approach is from Montana via FST-430 and FST-432 to the summit. (See the section for Approaches to the Bitterroot Mountains, [Approach: (D)(4)(a)].) The most enjoyable approach would probably be from Freeman Peak via FST-430, which begins at the Moose Creek GS many miles to the west [Approach: (E)(9)(d)]. USGS Wahoo Peak / SBW

Nick Wynn Peak *5,780 feet (Class 1)*
Nick Wynn was a prospector, trapper and friend of Beaver Jack. The peak is located 6.0 miles south of the Paradise GS, which sits at the end of the Selway River Road. Take FS-13 to a point just south of the summit and walk to the top [Approach: (F)(5)(b)]. USGS Spot Mountain / SBW

Beaver Jack Mountain *7,068 feet*
Cayuse Mountain *6,579 feet (Class 1)*
Beaver Jack was an early trapper in the area who secured some of the earliest logging contracts in the Bitterroot National Forest. Both peaks are climbed from FS-13, which crosses near the summit of both [Approach: (F)(5)(b)]. USGS Beaver Jack Mountain / SBW

C: THE SOUTHERN CLEARWATER PEAKS
From the Clearwater and Selway Rivers south to the Salmon River

---

Mink Peak *7,054 feet (Class 1)*
Mink Peak is located south of the Selway River, roughly 12.5 miles east of the Selway Falls

GS. The summit, which can be approached by trail from all four compass points, is crossed by FST-438 [Approach: (E)(9)(b.2)]. The shortest approach from the Selway Falls GS is via FST-4 and FST-438. Before leaving for this summit, note that the Mink Peak summit is a very long way from anywhere. USGS Mink Peak / SBW

Grave Meadow Peak *7,373 feet (Class 2)*
Grave Meadow Peak is located 5.5 miles south of Mink Peak. The summit is a relatively easy scramble from FST-602, which passes over the saddle just west of the peak [Approach: (E)(9)(b.2)]. USGS Running Lake / SBW

Indian Peak *7,728 feet (Class 2)*
Indian Peak is 2.0 miles southwest of Grave Meadow Peak and sits directly on the boundary of the Selway-Bitterroot Wilderness. To climb the peak, hike on FST-602 to the saddle west of Grave Meadow Peak and follow the snaking ridge southwest to the summit [Approach: (E)(9)(b.2)]. USGS Running Lake / SBW

Rocky Peak *7,640 feet (Class 3)*
Rocky Peak is located 1.0 mile due south of Indian Peak. This peak can be climbed by traversing the ridge line between it and Indian Peak. USGS Running Lake

Vermilion Butte *7,575 feet*
Disgrace Butte *6,589 feet (Class 1)*
From Fenn Ranger Station, drive up the Selway River Road, FS-223, to Slim's CG. Take FST-726 to FST-609, which is located 0.5 mile east of the Meadow Creek Guard Station [Approach: (E)(9.3)(b)]. FST-609 climbs a ridge, crosses Disgrace Butte and then comes within a short distance of the summit. It is 19.0 miles from the campground to the summit. USGS Vermilion Peak

Elk Mountain *7,826 feet*
Bilk Mountain *7,610 feet (Class 2)*
Take FST-517 [Approach: (F)(4.1)(a)] to north side of the peak and scramble to the top. The trail then continues on to Bilk Mountain. Total distance is 7.0 miles. USGS Running Lake

Wylies Peak *7,799 feet (Class 1)*
This summit was named for an old prospector who originally blazed some of the trails in this section of the Selway-Bitterroot Wilderness. FST-526 leads to the summit. It can be accessed from FST-602 [Approach: (E)(9)(b.2)], or from FST-4 [Approach: (F)(5)(d) and (d.3)]. USGS Wylies Peak / SBW

Box Car Mountain 7,589 feet (Class 2)
Box Car Mountain is located 4.0 miles south of Wylies Peak. FST-529 crosses the peak's south slopes. Leave the trail and scramble to the top along the peak's south ridge [Approach: (F)(5)(d.2)]. USGS Wylies Peak / SBW

Archer Mountain 7,492 feet (Class 2)
This peak is named for George Archer, a trapper who died after skiing off a cliff on this peak in 1909. The peak is located 2.0 miles east of Box Car Mountain. FST-529 crosses Archer Saddle west of the summit and then traverses the peak's north side to a point near the summit. Leave the trail at this point and hike to the peak's highest point [Approach: (F)(5)(d.2)]. USGS Wylies Peak / SBW

Pyramid Peak 8,369 feet (Class 2)
Pyramid Peak is located in the Gospel Hump Wilderness Area 1.0 miles north of Gospel Peak and east of Gospel Lakes. The summit is easily reached from Gospel Lakes, which in turn are reached by a short cross-country hike from FS-444 [Approach: (F)(7)]. USGS Sawyer Ridge / GHW

Gospel Peak 8,345 feet (Class 2)
The peak gained its name because of a man named Billie Knox, a district court clerk in Grangeville in the 1890s, who preached Sunday sermons as a hobby. One Sunday, while on a horseback trip through the country south of Grangeville, he came upon a road gang and gave them one of his favorite sermons. Evidently moved by the sermon, as payment in kind for Knox's spiritual blessings, the road gang named the nearest mountain Gospel Peak. Gospel Peak is located on the western edge of the Gospel Hump Wilderness above Gospel Lakes. The summit is a short, easy walk from FS-444 [Approach: (F)(7)]. USGS Hanover Mountain / GHW

Round Top 7,842 feet
Little Round Top 7,495 feet (Class 2)
These twin peaks are located across Slate Creek, 2.0 miles southwest of Gospel Peak. The peaks can be climbed from FST-313 [Approach: (F)(7)(a)]. From either the western or eastern trailhead, hike until you reach the small drainage that descends to Slate Creek from the saddle between the two summits. Follow this drainage to the saddle and climb the peaks from this point. USGS Hanover Mountain / GHW

Hanover Mountain 7,966 feet (Class 1)
Hanover Mountain is located 5.0 miles due south of Gospel Peak. Take FST-125 south from FS-444 to this summit [Approach: (F)(7)(b)]. USGS Hanover Mountain / GHW

Baking Powder Mountain 7,593 feet (Class 2)
Baking Powder Mountain is located along the northern boundary of the Gospel Hump Wilderness, southeast of Sourdough Fire Lookout. This peak is an easy cross-country walk from FST-300 [Approach: (F)(8)(b)], which leaves the Sourdough road just below the summit of Sourdough Peak. USGS Sourdough Peak / GHW

North Pole 8,818 feet (Class 1)
North Pole anchors a north/south ridge line that connects with Buffalo Hump to the south. The ridge forms the eastern border of the Gospel Hump Wilderness. The region east and south of the ridge is not included in the wilderness because of the extensive mining activity which took place in the area during the late 1800s and early 1900s. Take FST-299 [Approach: (F)(9)(b)] west from Wildhorse Campground to the summit area, which is less than 2.0 miles away. From this trail, just north of the summit a side trail climbs the peak's north ridge 0.25 mile to the top. USGS North Pole / GHW

Buffalo Hump 8,938 feet (Class 2)
This is the highest peak in the Gospel Hump Wilderness area. It is located 2.0 miles south of North Pole and is surrounded by four mountain lakes. The summit is a (you guessed it) hump-shaped ridge that reaches its high point at dead center. Take either FST-299 [Approach: (F)(9)(b)] from Wildhorse Campground over North Pole and on to Crystal Lake and Hump Lake, or FST-313 to Hump Lake [Approach: (F)(9)(c)]. From Hump Lake, the remnants of an old jeep road may be found running due west from the lake and over the ridge line just south of the Buffalo Hump summit. Follow this route from the lake and then climb the ridge due north to the summit. USGS Buffalo Hump /GHW

Oregon Butte 8,464 feet
Quartzite Butte 8,371 feet (Class 2)
These two peaks are located south of Buffalo Hump in the southeastern section of the Gospel Hump Wilderness. Both of these peaks are reached by trail and both are a long way from any road. There are three potential starting points. The first two begin at Orogrande Summit where FST-313 [Approach: (F)(9)(c)] and FST-204 [Approach: (F)(9)(a)] lead south. Follow either trail south to FST-230 and then follow FST-230 until it forks, past the Del Rio mine. FST-202 and 225 lead to Oregon Butte. FST-221 and 226 lead to Quartzite Butte. The third way into the area around Oregon and Quartzite Buttes is from Dixie via FST-215 [Approach: (F)(2.2)(a)]. USGS Buffalo Hump / GHW

Nipple Mountain *7,098 feet (Class 1)*

Nipple Mountain is located on the northeast boundary of the Gospel Hump Wilderness. From Orogrande CG, take FST-801 for 3.6 miles until it joins FST-800, which leads to the summit [Approach: (F)(9)(d)]. USGS Orogrande / GHW

Porters Mountain* *6,421 feet (Class 1)*

Porters Mountain is located 4.0 miles north of Moose Butte, on the same ridge line. FST-508 [Approach: (F)(2)(a)] leads to the summit in 8.0 miles. USGS Moose Butte

Moose Butte *7,121 feet (Class 1)*

Moose Butte, located south of Elk City, is the highest point on a major north/south ridge line that divides Big Creek from the South Fork of the Red River. The summit is accessed via FST-207 from either the north or south [Approach: (F)(2)(a.1)]. USGS Moose Butte

Burpee Mountain *6,848 feet (Class 1)*

Burpee Mountain is located southwest of Dixie Summit on the same ridge line that contains Moose Butte. FST-209 and FST-207 [Approach: (F)(2)(b)] lead 3.0 miles to the summit from FS-222. USGS Moose Butte

Blue Ribbon Mountain *6,055 feet (Class 1)*

Blue Ribbon Mountain is located 4.0 miles due east of downtown Elk City. From Elk City, drive FS-1818 south to FS-1807. Turn east onto FS-1807 and follow it to the trailhead, which is 2.3 miles from town [Approach: (F)(2.1)(a)]. From the trailhead, follow FST-833, an old jeep road, to the summit in about 2.0 miles. USGS Black Hawk Mountain

Black Hawk Mountain *6,091 feet (Class 1)*

Black Hawk Mountain sits 4.5 miles east of Blue Ribbon Mountain. Take FS-423 north from the Red River Road to within a mile of the summit, where the road is closed. Follow the road to the top and a terrific view [Approach: (F)(3.1)]. For those with lots of time, the area north of Black Hawk's summit is an undesignated wilderness encompassing the Meadow Creek drainages which stretches north to the Selway River. The hiking reportedly is excellent in this area. USGS Black Hawk Mountain

Granite Peak *7,232 feet (Class 1)*

Granite Peak is located 3.5 miles south of Bilk Mountain on a high ridge line that divides Three Prong Creek and the East Fork of Meadow Creek. FST-647 leads to the summit from the Windy

Saddle Road [Approach: (F)(4)(c)]. The trailhead area has seen considerable mining activity in the past, and the trail begins by following a mining road to the ridge top. It is 6.0 miles to the summit, with many good vistas along the way. USGS Green Mountain

Green Mountain *7,227 feet*
Little Green Mountain *6,980 feet (Class 1)*

These two summits are located 5.0 miles east of Red River Hot Springs. A Forest Service road leads to the summit of Green Mountain and its lookout site. FST-541 gives quick access to the smaller peak in 1.2 miles [Approach: (F)(4.1)(a)] or [Approach: (F)(3)(a)]. USGS Green Mountain

Three Prong Mountain *8,182 feet (Class 2)*

Three Prong Mountain is located in a rugged area on the western boundary of the Selway-Bitterroot Wilderness. Take FST-539 [Approach: (F)(4.2)(a)] north from Burnt Knob Lookout; it follows a ridge line to a saddle on the south slopes of the peak in 5.0 miles. Scramble to the top from the saddle. USGS Three Prong Mountain

White Top Mountain *7,886 feet (Class 2)*

White Top Mountain is 2.0 miles northwest of Burnt Knob Lookout. To climb the peak from Burnt Knob Lookout, follow FST-539 north for 1.5 miles and then take the intersecting ridge line due east for 0.5 mile [Approach: (F)(4.2)(a)]. USGS Sabe Mountain / SBW

Sabe Mountain *8,245 feet (Class 1)*

This peak is located southeast of Burnt Knob Lookout. The summit of Sabe Mountain is located just north of the Nez Perce Trail Road and is accessed by FST-61, which leads from the road to the summit in under 1.0 mile [Approach: (F)(4)(c)]. USGS Sabe Mountain / SBW

Magruder Mountain *7,421 feet (Class 1)*

Lloyd MaGruder was a packer who operated pack trains between Lewiston, Idaho and Virginia City, Montana. In 1863, while he was returning to Lewiston from selling goods to miners in Montana, he and several of his packers were murdered for the $25,000 MaGruder was carrying. (The gang who murdered the packers was eventually caught in San Francisco, and hanged in Lewiston.) FST-7 and FST-13 provide an easy approach to MaGruder summit from the Nez Perce Trail Road. It is 3.0 miles to the top [Approach: (F)(4)(f)]. USGS Magruder Mountain / SBW

Boston Mountain *7,648 feet (Class 1)*

Boston Mountain is located south of the Old Nez Perce Trail Road on a north/south ridge line that divides Mallard Creek from Bargain Creek. Its summit is located on the edge of the River of No Return Wilderness and has a large tree on its grassy summit. The old ladder attached to the tree was used in the 1930s by a fire lookout who climbed the tree for an even better view. Although trails reach the summit from all compass directions, the best route is from the Nez Perce Road via FST-580 [Approach: (F)(4)(a)]. USGS Boston Mountain

Churchill Mountain *6,687 feet (Class 1)*
Churchill Mountain is located 3.25 miles west of Dixie and is the highest point on Blue Ridge. The trailhead for FST-210 is found in Dixie, at the south end of town [Approach: (F)(2)(c)]. It is 4.3 miles to the summit. USGS Dixie

Blowout Mountain *6,629 feet (Class 1)*
Blowout Mountain is situated east of the Dixie GS. The Class 1 summit is a 3.5-mile walk from the GS [Approach: (F)(2)(d)]. The summit can also be reached from the northeast by turning off FS-222 onto FS-222D just south of Dixie and following FS-222D for 2.5 miles to the FST-233 trailhead. The condition of this route is unknown, but it is only 2.0 miles to the summit from the end of the road. USGS Dixie

Center Mountain *8,260 feet (Class 2)*
Center Mountain is located north of the Salmon River in the River of No Return Wilderness, 8.0 miles south of Burnt Knob Lookout and the Old Nez Perce Trail Road. The summit, which has three mountain lakes on its eastern flanks, is a moderate scramble up the peak's east ridge from where FST-578 crosses the ridge [Approach: (F)(4)(b)]. USGS Sheep Hill / RNRW

Harrington Mountain *8,186 feet (Class 1)*
Harrington Mountain is 6.0 miles southeast of Center Mountain and 6.0 miles north of the Salmon River. FST-28 and FST-9 lead to the summit from the Nez Perce Trail Road after 15.0 very long miles [Approach: (F)(4)(d)]. USGS Dennis Mountain

Salmon Mountain *8,943 feet (Class 1)*
Salmon Mountain is located just south of the Nez Perce Trail Road and is reached via a short trail leading from the road. The summit contains a fire lookout tower and an exceptional view [Approach: (F)(4.3)]. USGS Stripe Mountain

Thirteen Mountain *8,973 feet (Class 2)*
Thirteen Mountain is located directly north of Stripe Mountain. The peak has a horseshoe-shaped summit, which surrounds a beautiful lake. The peak should be climbed in conjunction with a climb of Stripe Mountain by simply crossing the connecting ridge between the two peaks. USGS Stripe Mountain/RNRW

Stripe Mountain *9,001 feet (Class 2)*
This peak, the tallest Clearwater Mountain summit, sits atop the headwaters of the Selway River near the boundary between the Clearwater Mountains and the Bitterroot Range. The peak is climbed via its east ridge from FST-069. The route presents no difficulties [Approach: (F)(4)(e)] or [Approach: (F)(4)(g.1)]. USGS Stripe Mountain / RNRW

Waugh Mountain *8,887 feet (Class 1)*
This peak is located southwest of Stripe Mountain. The summit is reached by trail from the north, south and east. The recommended approach is from the Old Nez Perce Trail Road to the north via FST-019 [Approach: (F)(4)(e)]. USGS Waugh Mountain / RNRW

APPROACHES TO THE CLEARWATER MOUNTAINS

Approach routes for this section are identified in the text by bracketed entries [Approach], which contain appropriate letter and number references.

The Clearwater Mountains are nearly as big as some states and, consequently, the combination of federal, state, county and Forest Service roads that crisscross the range is as complex as any state's highway system. Almost by definition, such a road system contains all types of road surfaces, and drivers must be prepared for all contingencies. For clarity's sake, this section describes the Clearwater road system as it exists in relation to the major "gateway towns" which are (A) Saint Maries, (B) Clarkia, (C) Potlatch (D) Moscow, (E) Orofino and (F) Grangeville. Each of these towns forms a major hub, from which the majority of Clearwater journeys will begin.

(A) Saint Maries Approaches.
Saint Maries, a town of 3,000, is located on the northeast corner of the Clearwater Range and offers all essential services.
(1) FH-50/FS-218, Saint Joe River Road. This road leaves ID-3 on the west edge of Saint Maries and stretches east and then south for 74.0 miles to Red Ives GS. This road can also be accessed from Saint Regous, Montana via I-90. Leave the freeway 1.0 west of Saint Regous and drive south from the exit on the Little Joe River road, cross the

Idaho/Montana border at Roland Summit and drive down the North Fork of the Saint Joe River to the Saint Joe River at Avery. These roads are usually open to passenger cars (weather permitting).

(2) FS-321, Marble Creek Road. This road leaves the Saint Joe River Road 34.5 miles east of Saint Maries. The road, which is well signed, makes a 31.0-mile journey over 4,500-foot Hobo Pass on its way to Clarkia. This road is open to passenger autos, but can have a rough surface.

(3) FS-301, Fishhook Creek Road/ Freezeout Saddle Road. This road leaves the Saint Joe River Road just east of Avery, 43.0 miles east of Saint Maries, and heads south. The road, which requires a high-clearance vehicle for much of its distance, leads south and then west to Clarkia, crossing some of the more remote northern Clearwaters on the way. Also see [Approach: (B)(2)], below.

(4) FS-201, Sisters Creek Road. This road begins 9.75 miles south of Avery at FS-301 and runs east for nearly 40.0 miles to the summit of Granite Peak and a junction with FS-395, which leads south to the Mallard-Larkins area. The route traverses checkerboard patterns of public and private land where a great deal of road construction and logging has taken place; consequently, route-finding will require a map. Fortunately, most major junctions are signed.

(a) FST-55, Snow Peak Trail. FST-55 leaves FS-201 26.6 miles east of its junction with FS-301. The trailhead is signed and has room for several vehicles. The trail traverses an undulating ridge for 5.0 miles to the base of Snow Peak, where there is some camping and a small spring for water (treat for Giardia). After the meadow, the trail forks. The right fork continues west toward Spotted Louie Point and the left fork climbs to the top of Snow Peak.

(5) FS-395, Surveyors Ridge Road. This road leaves FS-201 and proceeds to Sawtooth Saddle in roughly 10.0 miles. This is a rough road and passenger cars are not recommended.

(a) FS-111, Northbound Creek Trail. This trail provides the longest and most difficult approach route into the Mallard-Larkins Pioneer area. The trail begins at the end of FS-395 at Sawtooth Saddle and then steeply descends to Sawtooth Creek, where it climbs up Northbound Creek to join FST-65 on the Mallard-Larkins crest. See [Approach: (E)(3)(b) and (c)], below.

(6) FS-303, Beaver Creek Road. This road is a connector between the Saint Joe River Road and FS-201. The road is accessed 1.7 miles north of Red Ives, and is a better alternative for those going to the north end of the Mallard-Larkins Pioneer Area.

(B) Clarkia Area Access Points.
Clarkia is a wide spot in ID-3 32.0 miles south of Saint Maries and 51.0 miles east of Moscow. Although this village is a heavily used gateway into the northern Clearwaters, it provides few traveler services. During regular business hours, it is possible to get gas and food in the town.

(1) FS-321, Hobo Pass/Marble Creek Road. This road heads due east out of Clarkia and proceeds east and then north to the Saint Joe River in 31.0 miles. See [Approach: (A)(2)] above. At 1.0 from Clarkia, this road junctions with FS-301.

(2) FS-301, Freezeout Saddle Road/Fishhook Creek Road. Take FS-312 east from Clarkia 1.0 mile and turn right onto this road which leads to Gold Center CG in 4.5 miles. Turn left at Gold Center and follow the road for about 12.0 bumpy and twisty miles to Freezeout Saddle and FST-275. The Widow Mountain trailhead is another 5.0 miles down FS-301. This road is good gravel, a bit narrow, and is open to autos when the weather is good. Note that during the winter FS-301 is often plowed to within a few miles of Freezeout Saddle to allow loggers to remove logs. This allows cross-country skiers to use the road on November and December weekends to reach relatively high terrain and good snow. Also note that while FS-301 can be utilized to reach Snow Peak, the better route to this mountain leaves the Saint Joe River Road. See [Approach: (A)(4)(a)], above.

(a) FST-275, Grandmother Mountain Trail. This popular trail leaves Freezeout Saddle and leads to Grandmother Mountain in 2.0 miles and Grandfather Mountain in 4.0 miles; it is well maintained.

(b) FST-52, Widow Mountain Trail. This trail leaves FS-301 21.0 miles east of Clarkia and traverses a ridge east for 6.0 miles to Widow Mountain. The trail is on BLM land and is seldom, if ever, maintained.

(3) FS-457, Little Goat Mountain Road. From Clarkia, take FS-301 over Freezeout Saddle to FS-457, which climbs up to the Little Goat divide and Goat Mountain. This road eventually traverses along the crest of this minor Clearwater subrange and provides access to all of its peaks. A 4WD is recommended.

(C) Potlatch Area Access Points.
During good economic times, Potlatch contains 1,000 people and provides all major services. From Potlatch, working clockwise, the Hoodoo Mountains are circled by US-95, ID-5, ID-3, ID-9 and ID-6. ID-6 traverses the range from Harvard to Sanders, through the remnants of a great western white pine forest.

(1) Laird Park Access Points. Take ID-6 east from Potlatch for 12.0 miles to the signed turn for

Laird Park, where there is a Forest Service CG. Beyond the campground, the road splits into three roads at the beginning of a maze of roads that crisscross this section of the Hoodoo Mountains. Take the right fork to reach the Sand Mountain Trail.

(a) FST-330, Sand Mountain Trail. This trail, which was recently rebuilt along Sypah Creek, climbs 3.0 miles through a beautiful forest to the summit of Sand Mountain.

(2) Giant White Pine Campground Trail System. This campground is located 16.0 miles northeast of Potlatch, along ID-6. The Forest Service has constructed a series of short loop trails in the area. All provide beautiful forest hikes.

(a) FST-228, Bald Mountain Trail. The old Bald Mountain Trail "ain't what it used to be." Although it is well signed, has a good tread, and traverses exciting scenery, the Bald Mountain Trail crosses two major roads (which do not show up on the map board in the CG) as it climbs 9.5 miles to the summit of Bald Mountain. Nevertheless, the trail provides a good, long hike and melts out early in the hiking season.

(3) North South Pass Access Points. ID-3 crosses this pass 19.0 miles from Potlatch. From the pass, gravel roads lead both east and west along the Hoodoo Mountains divide. The east road ends on Bald Mountain and the west road eventually leads to US-95. During the winter these roads are closed, and regularly groomed, serving as a state-run Park n' Ski area.

(D) Moscow Access Points.
Moscow is a college town of 16,000, with all of the essential services plus outdoor equipment suppliers. The town is the primary approach point for the Palouse Range, which is surrounded by federal and state highways. US-95 forms the west boundary of the range, ID-8 the south, ID-9 the east and ID-6 the north.

(1) Tamarack Ski Area Road. To reach this road, take Sixth Street east from the Moscow Business District until the road ends; turn right and drive 0.25 mile, then turn left and follow the good paved road 4.0 miles to the Robinson Lake Park (note: there is no longer a lake at the park). Turn right and cross the old dam and follow the gravel road for another 5.0 miles to the Tamarack Road. Turn left onto this road, which leads to the old ski area (closed) in 4.0 miles, and the Palouse Crest road in 5.5 miles. The road is usually passable to autos during the summer. In the winter the road is usually plowed to within 2.0 miles of the ski area (and sometimes all the way to the ski area).

(2) Palouse Crest Road. This road follows the crest of the Palouse Range, traversing state, federal and private land along the way. It is often passable to autos, weather permitting. The road is a favorite cross-country ski route of University of Idaho students during the winter.

(E) Orofino Access.
Orofino is a town of 4,000 located along the Clearwater River on US-12, 42.0 miles east of Lewiston. The town provides all essential services.

(1) ID-11, Orofino to Headquarters. From Orofino, drive east on US-12 for 7.0 miles and turn left onto ID-11, which leads east to Headquarters in 42.4 miles. This good paved road climbs out of the Clearwater canyon and crosses the Weippe Prairie before eventually returning to the mountains and arriving at Headquarters, population 300, which is owned by the Potlatch Corporation.

(2) FS-247, Beaver Creek Road. This paved road continues the route from Headquarters to the North Fork of the Clearwater River over Beaver Creek Divide in 24.0 miles.

(2.1) FS-248, Sheep Mountains Access. This road leaves FS-247 about 3.0 miles south of the North Fork of the Clearwater River and leads east into the Sheep Mountain Range. FS-248 almost completely circles this group and the areas it does not reach can be accessed by FS-682, which crosses the range from north to south. Eagle Point is reached by a side road (numbered FS-6050) off FS-248, or by trail from FS-682.

(a) FST-93, Sheep Mountain Trail. This route leaves FS-682 at its high point and proceeds west to summit of Sheep Mountain in 2.0 short miles from the trailhead.

(b) FST-93 to Eagle Point. Eagle point is a short 1.0-mile walk to the east from the trailhead and FS-682.

(3) FS-700, Smith Ridge Road. From Headquarters, take the Beaver Creek Road (FS-247) north for 24.0 miles to the North Fork of the Clearwater River. At this junction, go left on FS-700, which follows the North Fork of the Clearwater River for 0.6 mile before turning up Isabella Creek. Follow this road for roughly 3.0 miles up Isabella Creek to a junction. At this point, FS-705 continues up the Isabella drainage to a trailhead, while FS-700 runs east to Smith Ridge and the main Mallard-Larkins trailhead in about 10.0 miles.

(a) FST-240, Goat Ridge Trail. FST-240 leaves the trailhead on FS-700 and connects with FST-65 in 8.0 miles, following the ridge top over Goat Ridge Peak.

(b) FST-65, Mallard Divide Trail. This trail follows the Mallard-Larkins divide, staying near the crest of the ridge, and provides access to a number of peaks, which the trail contours around. Access to this trail is available from many different points including [Approach: (E)(2)(a)] and [Approach: (a)(5)(a)].

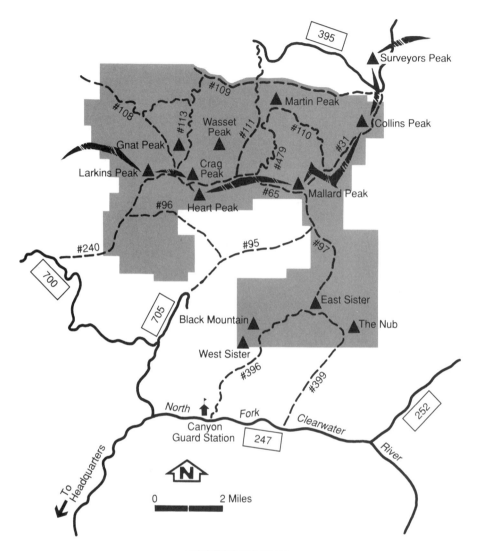

ACCESS TO THE
MALLARD–LARKINS PIONEER AREA
OF THE CLEARWATER MOUNTAINS

(c) **FST-111, Northbound Trail.** This trail leaves FST-65 1.0 mile east of Heart Peak, descends to the north to Northbound Lake and then continues on to Martin Creek and Sawtooth Creek. At Sawtooth Creek, the trail immediately climbs up steep north slopes to Sawtooth Saddle where it joins FS-395/FS-102, which connects with FS-201 near Snow Peak. See [Approach: (A)(5)(a)], above. Total distance from FST-65 to Sawtooth Saddle is roughly 5.0 miles.

(d) **FST-475, Martin Creek Trail.** This trail leaves FST-65 0.5 mile east of its junction with FST-111 and descends along Martin Creek to Sawtooth Creek in 1.5 miles. See [Approach: (A)(5)(a)], above.

(e) **FST-97, Mallard Peak/East Sister Trail.** This trail leads south from FST-65 and Mallard Peak to a trail junction east of East Sister, where it joins FST-685 and FST-399 in 4.0 miles. Midway, it junctions with FST-95, which descends to Isabella Creek.

(3.1) FS-705, Isabella Creek Road. This road leaves FS-700 at 1.4 miles up Isabella Creek and then crosses the creek. Shortly after the crossing, the trailhead for FST-95 is reached.

(a) FST-95, Isabella Creek Trail. FST-95 leaves FS-705 and runs northeast to join FST-97 in 5.0 miles. FST-96 forks off of this trail 1.9 miles from the trailhead.

(b) FST-96, Elmer Creek Trail. This trail begins where FST-97 passes Elmer Creek, and then climbs up the drainage to the northwest for 4.0 miles to junction with FST-65 on Goat Ridge.

(4) FS-249, North Fork Clearwater River Road. This road begins where FS-247 ends, and follows the meandering river east to Orogrande Creek, where it joins FS-250, which runs south to Pierce and northeast to Kelly Forks GS. The road is passable for autos.

(a) FST-396, East Sister Trail. Access this trail at the Canyon GS, 1.5 miles east of the FS-247/FS-249 junction. The trail leads to Black Lake and FS-97 in 7.0 long, steep miles.

(b) FST-399, The Nub Trail. FST-399 follows Upper Twin Creek, past the steep walls of the North Fork canyon, to the vicinity of the Nub and a junction with FS-97. This trail is accessed east of the Canyon GS.

(5) FS-250, Pierce, Idaho to Montana Road. This road is accessed from ID-11, just south of Pierce. FS-250, known as the French Mountain Road, climbs over French Saddle, follows French Creek and then descends along Orogrande Creek to the North Fork of the Clearwater River and FS-249. See [Approach: (E)(4)], above. Once the road meets the North Fork, it proceeds east to Kelly Forks GS and then north to Hoodoo Pass on the Idaho/Montana border.

(a) FST-176/FST-169, Cold Springs Mountain Trail. This trail leaves FS-250 at the Kelly Forks GS and climbs north up a ridge that divides the Cold Springs drainage from the North Fork of the Clearwater drainage. Flat Mountain is 3.0 switchback-filled miles from the road, and Cold Springs Mountain is 6.0 miles from the road. Beyond Cold Springs Mountain, the trail designation becomes FST-169 and the trail continues north along a ridge line for many miles to Fly Hill and FS-715.

(b) FST-445, Elizabeth Mountain Trail. FST-445 leaves FS-250 4.0 twisting miles north of Kelly Forks GS and climbs out of the North Fork's canyon toward Elizabeth Mountain, which is reached in 2.5 miles. From this summit, the trail turns due west to meet FST-176 just south of Cold Springs Mountain in another 3.0 miles.

(c) FST-440, Elizabeth Creek Trail. FST-440 leaves FS-250 3.0 miles past the FST-445 trailhead and climbs the drainage to the lake basin east of Cold Springs Peak in 4.0 miles. One mile from the trailhead, a cutoff trail leaves FST-440 and runs to the summit of Elizabeth Mountain in 1.25 miles.

(5.1) FS-253/FST-711, Pot Mountain Cutoff Road. These two roads form a short-cut across a large bend in the North Fork of the Clearwater River between the outlet of Quartz Creek and the Cold Springs GS. FS-253, the western entrance to the cutoff, can be accessed from FS-249 7.0 miles east of the Canyon GS. FS-711, at the Cold Springs Ranger Station, is the eastern entrance to the cutoff. Mush Saddle, the high point along the cutoff, is located 8.5 miles from the GS and 12.0 miles from the outlet of Quartz Creek.

(a) FST-144 and other Pot Mountain Trails. Access for FST-144 is gained 1.5 miles west of Mush Saddle. Turn south onto FST-5259 (an old logging road) which wiggles on for 1.5 miles to where the road becomes too rough for all but 4WDs. The road eventually turns into a trail, which runs to the summit of Pot Mountain in 3.0 miles and eventually descends to the North Fork of the Clearwater River in another 11.0 miles. All of the other trails in the area south of Pot Mountain can be accessed from FST-144.

(b) FST-169, Mush Saddle Trail. This trail leaves Mush Saddle and follows a ridge northeast to Cold Springs Mountain in 4.0 miles.

(6) FS-255, Kelly Creek Road. This road leaves the North Fork of the Clearwater at the Kelly Fork GS and follows Kelly Creek north until it eventually turns off at Ruby Creek and runs north to Moose City. Several trailheads are available from this road; all of the trails eventually lead to the top of Moose Mountain.

(a) FST-690, Moose Mountain Trail. From FS-255 2.0 miles north of Ruby Creek CG, drive on FS-5440 up Moose Creek for 2.0 miles. Pick up the trail and follow it 3.0 miles to the summit of Moose Mountain. A 4WD is recommended.

(b) Other Moose Mountain Trails. From the summit of Moose Mountain FST-690 continues on north to Deadwood Ridge. From this point, a cross-country route can be followed from the trail onto the northern slopes of the Moose Creek Buttes.

(7) US-12 Access Points. US-12 runs between Lewiston, Idaho and Lolo, Montana by first following the Clearwater River and then the Lochsa River to Lolo Pass. A number of trailheads which furnish access to the Selway-Bitterroot Wilderness Area are located along US-12. US-12 is a long, narrow, twisting two-lane road that requires a lot of patience to drive, so leave extra time in your schedule to get to the trailhead.

(a) FST-133, Split Creek Trail. This trailhead is 10.0 miles east of Wilderness Gateway.

After crossing the river on a suspension bridge, the trail goes east along the river to Split Creek and then, almost immediately, climbs up Split Creek Ridge, eventually reaching Chimney Peak in roughly 12.0 very steep miles. Although there is only limited parking available at the trailhead, it's no problem because this trail receives little use except during hunting season.

(b) FST-211/FST-213, Boulder Creek Trail and beyond. This trail leaves from the Wilderness Gateway Trailhead and CG, which are located 26.0 miles east of Lowell. The Boulder Creek Trail provides direct access to the north end of the Selway Crags and the entire Selway-Bitterroot Wilderness. It is roughly 15.0 miles to Boulder Pass from the trailhead. East of the pass the trail continues on to Fish Lake and its GS and then down Fish Creek, where it junctions with FST-213 and FST-60. FST-213 runs north and south and provides access to McConnel Mountain to the south and Bear Mountain to the north. FST-60 crosses two drainages and then follows a ridge line east before joining the Warm Springs Creek Trail. Numerous side trails lead from these trails to provide access to almost every corner of the Crags.

(c) FST-220. This trail leaves the Wilderness Gateway trailhead, climbs up and crosses Cantaloupe Peak, Huckleberry Butte and Stanley Butte before reaching Old Man Lake and the Chimney Peak area after 20.0 miles. Although this is the longest approach into the Selway Crags, it is considered the most enjoyable route for those who have the time and endurance.

(d) FST-206, Selway Crag Divide Trail. This trail is the main east/west approach route in the Selway Crags. It begins along US-12 15.0 miles east of Wilderness Gateway, at the Eagle Mountain Pack Bridge, climbs up to the Selway Crags divide north of Greystone Butte and then proceeds southwest, roughly following the divide (on the ridge/off the ridge) to Chimney Peak. From where the trail reaches the divide, it is 1.0 mile to Greystone Butte, 8.0 miles to Boulder Pass and FST-211, 19.0 miles to Shasta Lake and 26.0 miles to Chimney Peak. See [Approach: (E)(7)(d)] below for more information.

(e) FST-469, Mocus Point Pack Bridge. This trailhead is located 25.0 miles east of Wilderness Gateway, along US-12. FST-469 leads to FST-209, which is a principal wilderness trail. From this trail, FST-21 provides quick access to the summit of Bear Mountain.

(f) FST-49 and FST-44, the Warm Springs Pack Bridge Trails. These trails are located 36.0 miles east of Wilderness Gateway along US-12 (52.0 miles east of Lowell). FST-49 and FST-44 lead into the wilderness by making the long climb from the river to the ridge top. Jerry Johnson Hot

Springs is located 2.0 miles up FST-49, so the first part of this trail system sees considerable use from day hikers.

(g) Powell Area Trails. Powell is the proverbial wide spot in the road. There is a lodge and ranger station and a road to Elk Summit. FST-37 leads up a ridge to a point near Tom Beal Peak.

(8) FS-111, Elk Summit Road. This road provides one of the highest approach points in the Selway-Bitterroot Wilderness. Its roughly 18.0 miles from Powell to Hoodoo Lake. The road also provides access to a number of trails that lead east into the Bitterroot Range. Those trails are discussed in the Bitterroot approach section.

(a) FST-45 to Grave Peak. To reach this trail, drive up FS-111 to its junction with FS-358. Follow this road east to its end where the trail begins. Its 3.0 miles to Friday Pass, 4.0 miles to Wind Lakes and 4.5 miles to the peak via an unmaintained side trail.

(b) FST-486 to the Moose Creek Drainage. This trail leaves the end of FS-111 and proceeds south to the upper reaches of the East Fork of Moose Creek in 6.0 miles, where it joins FST-421. FST-421 follows the East Fork of Moose Creek between the Moose Creek GS (to the west) [Approach: (E)(9)(c)] and Twin Lakes (which are in Montana).

(9) FS-223, Selway River Road. This road leaves US-12 at Lowell, 26.0 miles east of Kooskia, and follows the Selway River for 19.0 miles to Selway Falls. Although paved for much of its distance, it is exceedingly narrow in places and should be driven slowly.

(a) FST-708, Gedney Mountain Trail. The trailhead is located 17.0 miles up the Selway River from Lowell on US-12. Take FST-708, first up Gedney Creek and then up Gedney Mountain's long south ridge to the summit in 10.5 miles and 5,100 feet of elevation gain. The trail is no longer maintained on a regular basis and, according to the Forest Service, the lower portions of the trail along the ridge are hard to find.

(b) FST-4, Selway River Trail. The westernmost section of the Selway River Trail begins at the end of FS-223. This trail follows the Selway River upstream through the entire Selway-Bitterroot Wilderness to the Paradise GS. See [Approach: (F)(5)] below.

(b.1) FST-606, Sixtytwo Ridge Trail. FST-606 leaves FST-4 and proceeds north for 9.0 miles to a junction with FST-693, which leads west to Big Fog Saddle [Approach: (E)(9.2)(e)] and east to Shissler Peak and the Moose Creek GS. Big Rock Mountain is located 1.0 mile north of the junction.

(b.2) FST-438/FST-602, Mink Peak/Bilk Mountain Trail. This trail leaves FST-4 opposite of the Sixtytwo Ridge Trail and runs south to

Mink Peak in 6.0 miles and Bilk Mountain in 16.0 miles. From Bilk Mountain, FST-602 can be followed northeast toward Wylies Peak; FST-517 leads south to FS-285 [Approach: (F)(4.1)(a)]. This very rugged trail requires near-expert abilities and good conditioning.

(b.3) FST-693/FST-450, Shissler Peak Trail. This trail leaves FS-4 west of the confluence of Moose Creek and climbs steeply up the ridge line to Shissler Peak.

(c) FST-421, Moose Creek Trail. This trail is the major east/west travel route in the Selway-Bitterroot Wilderness. The trail runs for approximately 42.0 miles between Moose Creek GS and Twin Lakes, which are on the Montana side of the Bitterroot divide.

(c.1) FST-619, Bailey Mountain Trail. FST-619 leaves FS-421 5.0 miles north of the Selway River and climbs to Bailey Mountain in 9.5 steep miles.

(d) FST-430, Freeman Peak/Wahoo Pass Trail. This trail gives hikers another way to hike between the Moose Creek GS and Montana. Although shorter than FST-421, it involves considerable up-and-down travel. The trail leaves the GS and climbs to Freeman Peak in 10.0 miles, continues on to the southern slopes of Wahoo Peak in another 10.0 miles and to Wahoo Pass on the Idaho/Montana border in another 9.0 miles. FST-631 and FST-432 both lead to the summit of Wahoo Peak from this trail.

(9.1) FS-317, Coolwater Ridge Road. FS-317 leaves the Selway River Road less than 1.0 mile south of Lowell and climbs to the summit of Round Top Mountain. A 4WD is recommended, but not required.

(a) FST-3, Chimney Peak Trail. Leaves FS-317 roughly 1.0 mile short of the summit of Round Top Mountain and heads northeast toward Ghost Mountain and then continues along a ridge over Louse Point and on to the Chimney Peak area in a total of 10.0 miles.

(9.2) FS-319, Big Fog Saddle Road. This road is the prime southern approach point into the Selway Crags. The Fog Mountain Road is steep and usually graded, but contains literally hundreds of deep water bars that force one to drive very slowly. Although a passenger auto can use this road, it is not recommended for cars with automatic transmissions because their brakes are destined to overheat on the descent. The trailhead is 12.0 miles from the river. Three trails leave the road at its end.

(a) FST-3, Cove Lake Trail. This trail leaves Big Fog Saddle and drops down into the Canteen Creek drainage, climbs up to a saddle west of Cove Lakes and east of Gedney Mountain, descends to the lakes and then continues on to Chimney Peak

for a total of in 10.0 miles. Even though the trail begins right on Big Fog Saddle, it is hard to find its starting point because an old road that leads off to the north is distracting. The trail begins in the trees, just north of where the road drops off the saddle. Although this trail has a well-worn tread (to the extent of being seriously eroded), it is very brushy in places and completely overgrown in other spots. Expert route-finding abilities are required beyond Cove Lakes.

(b) Jesse Pass Trail. This trail is not an official Forest Service route and does not show up on their maps. However, the trail, which is accurately shown on the Fenn Mountain USGS quad, actually exists and is in no worse condition than the Cove Lake Trail. The junction for this trail is located 0.7 mile north of Cove Lake, exactly as shown on the USGS quad. Look for the junction in a clump of trees, where a somewhat obvious tread leaves the main trail and climbs uphill. From the junction to Jesse Pass is 0.8 miles. A spring below the pass is the last water before the pass (treat the water for Giardia). From the pass, the trail descends into the Three Links drainage and eventually connects with FST-693.

(c) FST-708, Gedney Mountain Trail. This trail leaves FST-3 just west and above Cove Lakes, climbs over Gedney Mountain and then descends down to the Selway River. (See [Approach: (E)(9)(a)] in this section.) The trail is no longer maintained but can easily be followed to the top of Gedney Mountain.

(d) FST-343 and 363, Big Fog Mountain and Big Fog Lake Trails. Although these trails are no longer maintained by the Forest Service, they are still passable. From Big Fog Saddle, the unsigned FST-343 is hard to find. From the obvious trailhead (complete with large sign) for FST-693, walk north along the edge of the trees until you see the trail heading uphill. Once on the trail, it is easy to follow it to the top of Big Fog Mountain. From Big Fog's summit, the tread of FST-363 is no longer visible; but the ridge line to the north is visible and easy to follow. Keep on the ridge line and, as it narrows, the trail will show up. Although a fairly good tread leads down to the lake from the ridge top, cross-country expertise is essential. For those wishing for quick access to the Fenn Mountain area, the ridge line can be followed north to Three Links Lake and Jesse Pass with a minimum of Class 2 climbing. It should be noted that this route is difficult and only for those with lots of energy.

(e) FST-693, Big Fog Saddle to Moose Creek GS Trail. This trail is the only clearly visible trail to leave Big Fog Saddle. It runs east for many miles along the higher ridges before descending to the Moose Creek GS, providing access to many

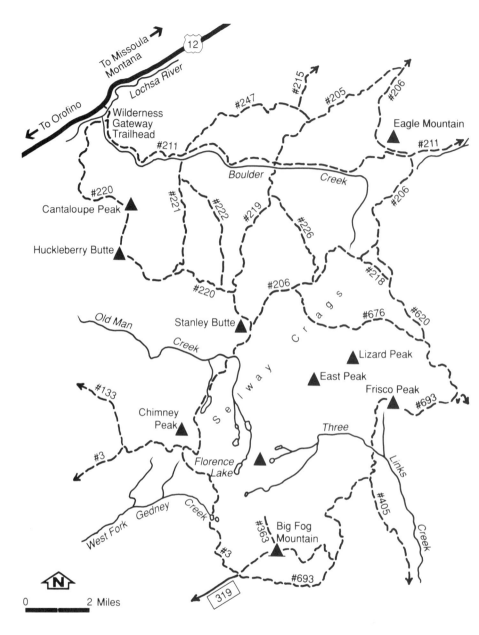

SELWAY CRAGS WILDERNESS GATEWAY AND BIG FOG MOUNTAIN
TRAILHEADS AND TRAILS

Selway-Bitterroot trails.

(9.3) Meadow Creek Road. This road leaves the Selway River Road 18.75 miles from Lowell. Cross the Selway Falls Bridge and drive up Meadow Creek to the trailhead, which is at the Slims CG.

(a) FST-726, Meadow Creek Trail. FST-726 leaves the trailhead and follows Meadow Creek south and then east to FS-285 [Approach: (G)(4.1)] near Windy Saddle. Meadow Creek is centered in an extremely beautiful roadless area just west of the Selway-Bitterroot Wilderness and, although some logging is taking place in its upper reaches, most of this very large drainage is still in a wilderness condition.

(b) FST-609, Vermilion Creek Trail. This trail leaves FST-726 at the Meadow Creek GS and proceeds northeast to FST-438. On the way, the trail crosses Disgrace Butte and Vermilion Peak.

(F) Grangeville Access.

Grangeville is a "pretty nice burg" according to one longtime resident. The town of 4,000 offers all necessary services and is the headquarters of the Nez Perce National Forest.

(1) ID-14, The Elk City Road. This good paved road is reached from Grangeville by following ID-13 east out of town for 10.0 miles to its junction. This road follows the South Fork of the Clearwater River to Elk City in 49.6 miles.

(2) FS-222, Red River/Dixie Road. This paved road leaves ID-14 2.7 miles west of Elk City. It is 14.0 miles to the Red River GS and 30.0 miles to Dixie. South of Dixie, the road turns to gravel and eventually leads to MacKay Bar on the main Salmon River.

(a) FST-508, Porters Mountain Trail. Drive 21.0 miles south of Elk City on FS-222 to the Porter Mountain trailhead. Follow FST-508 up the West Fork Red River for 4.5 miles to FST-207, which leads to the summit in 1.0 mile.

(a.1) FST-207, Moose Butte Trail. This trail stretches between FST-508 in the West Fork of the Red River and Burpee Mountain, a distance of 7.0 miles. The trail can also be accessed on its south end from FS-222 on Dixie Summit via FST-209, which is described in the next entry.

(b) FST-209, Dixie Summit Trail. This trail leaves Dixie summit and runs west along a ridge line for 1.8 miles to a junction with FST-207 north of Burpee Mountain.

(c) FST-210, Churchill Mountain Trail. FST-210 is accessed from Dixie. The trail runs due east over Churchill Mountain and on to the Salmon River.

(d) FST-211/FST-212, Blowout Mountain Trail. This trail leaves FS-222 at the Dixie GS and runs east and then south to the top of Blowout Mountain. From the top of the mountain, the trail can be followed southeast to the Salmon River.

(2.1) FS-1818/FS-1807. This road leaves downtown Elk City and proceeds southeast to Wigwam Creek, which is full of dredge tailings, in about 3.0 miles. When the road reaches Wigwam Creek, it forks. The right fork connects with FS-222 in less than 0.5 mile; the left fork turns east and follows Wigwam Creek for several miles.

(a) FST-833, Blue Ribbon Mountain Trail. FST-833 was formerly a mining road which left

FS-1807 and led to the top of Blue Ribbon Mountain. Today, it is a foot trail which continues eastward from Blue Ribbon Mountain along a ridge to Black Hawk Mountain. This route receives a lot of motorcycle use.

(2.2) FS-2221, Halfway House CG Road. Access this road at the Dixie GS at the south end of the runway. Follow it to the CG, where the Halfway House Trailhead is located.

(a) FST-215/FST-204/FST-215, Southeast Gospel Hump Trails. The entire southeast corner of the Gospel Hump Wilderness is accessed from the Halfway House Trailhead. Follow FST-215 west for 3.0 miles to where it joins the other trails. FST-204 leads north to Orogrande Summit, and FST-215 leads south to Salmon River and FST-203, which leads west to Oregon Butte.

(b) FST-204, Lake Creek Trail. See [Approach: (F)(9)(a)], below.

(3) FS-234, Red River Hot Springs Road. This road leaves FS-222 at the Red River GS and reaches the resort after 11.0 miles.

(a) FST-541, Green Mountain Trail. Leaves the Red River Hot Springs area and proceeds east to Green Mountain and FS-285 in 8.0 miles.

(3.1) FS-423, Black Hawk Mountain Road. This road leaves FS-234 roughly 6.0 miles from the GS and proceeds north toward Black Hawk Mountain. The road is closed 1.0 mile from the summit. From the summit a number of trails are accessible, including FST-833 [Approach: (F)(2.1)(a)], which leads to Blue Ribbon Mountain. A 4WD is required.

(4) FS-468, Nez Perce Trail Road. This road stretches 113.0 miles between Red River GS and Darby, Montana. This twisty dirt road, the only "non-wilderness" break between the massive Selway-Bitterroot and Frank Church River of No Return wilderness areas, offers a wonderful combination of scenery, history and washboard road that makes for a slow crossing of the once-impenetrable Clearwater Mountains. There are no services along the road, and it takes hours and hours to drive it—even when it's dry and graded. The road has numerous trailheads which are of interest to those who are wilderness bound. To reach the road from the Montana side, turn west off of US-93 4.0 miles south of Darby and follow paved road till it splits at the West Fork Guard Station. Take the right fork to Nez Perce Pass.

(a) FST-580, Boston Mountain Trail. FST-580 leaves FS-468 10.25 miles east of Red River and reaches Boston Mountain in 4.0 miles. From the peak, trails leave in all directions, while FS-580 proceeds southeast to Barganin Creek.

(b) FST-575/FST-578, Center Mountain Trail. This trail leaves FS-468 at Dry Saddle, 26.0

miles east of Red River. The Center Mountain Trail follows a high ridge, which has numerous lakes on its flanks, south toward Sheep Hill Lookout and Center Mountain. Five miles from the trailhead, the trail forks. The right fork, FST-576, goes to Sheep Hill Lookout; the left fork goes toward Center Mountain. After roughly 2.0 miles, the left fork trail passes Center Mountain's western slopes. Once the trail passes by the summit and is on the peak's south side, FST-578 forks off and proceeds east out onto Center Mountain's east ridge, where it eventually ends. South of the FST-578 junction, the Center Mountain Trail connects with FST-577, which descends to the Salmon River.

(c) FST-61, Sabe Mountain Trail. The Sabe Mountain Trailhead is located 2.0 miles south of Sabe Saddle. From the road, the trail quickly climbs to the summit of Sabe Mountain in less than 1.0 mile.

(d) FST-28/FST-29, Harrington Mountain Trail. This trail leaves FS-468 at the Horse Heaven Saddle Trailhead and heads south toward Harrington Mountain, which is reached after approximately 15.0 long up-and-down miles.

(e) FST-019, Waugh Mountain Trail. FST-019 is another long ridge trail that eventually leads from the Nez Perce Trail Road to the Salmon River. Waugh Mountain is located 14.0 miles south of the trailhead.

(f) FST-7/FST-13, Magruder Mountain Trail. This trail leaves FS-468 10.5 miles south of the Selway River and leads to Magruder Mountain in 2.0 miles.

(g) FST-004, Selway River Trail. This portion of the Selway River Trail follows the river south from the Magruder GS to the river's headwaters below Stripe Mountain, a distance of nearly 20.0 miles. Numerous side trails are accessed from the main travel route, the most important being FST-069, which leads to Waugh Mountain.

(g.1) FST-069, Stripe Mountain Trail. FST-069 leaves FST-004 at Stripe Creek and proceeds southwest to FST-019 in 6.0 miles.

(4.1) FS-285, Windy Saddle Road. This road leaves Nez Perce Trail Road 20.0 miles east of Red River and proceeds north along a ridge to the south slopes of Elk Mountain in 15.0 miles. This road can be quite rough and a 4WD might come in handy if it rains.

(a) FST-517, Elk Mountain/Bilk Mountain Trail. FST-517 leaves FS-285 at the road's end, climbs to the top of Elk Mountain in less than 1.0 mile, and then continues on to Bilk Mountain on the Selway-Bitterroot Wilderness Boundary. North of Bilk Mountain, the trail joins FST-602 [Approach: (E)(9)(b.2)], which leads north to-

ward the Selway River.

(b) FST-529, Windy Saddle/ Archer Mountain Trail. This trail leaves FS-285 at Windy Saddle (2.0 miles from the road's end) and runs northeast to Archer Mountain and then the Selway River, which it meets north of the Paradise GS.

(c) FST-647, Granite Mountain Trail. This trail leaves FS-285 9.5 miles from its beginning, and follows the ridge to the summit in 4.0 miles.

(4.11) Green Mountain Road. This road is accessed 3.0 miles from the beginning of FS-285. The summit of Green Mountain is less than 1.0 mile from the main road.

(a) FST-541, Green Mountain Trail. This trail leaves from the top of Green Mountain and proceeds west to Red River Hot Springs. See [Approach: (F)(3)(a)], above.

(4.2) Burnt Knob Lookout Road. This road leaves the Nez Perce Trail Road just north of Dry Saddle and climbs up to the lookout site in 1.0 mile.

(a) FST-539, Three Prong Mountain Trail. This trail traverses the ridge between Burnt Knob Lookout and Three Prong Mountain in 6.0 miles.

(b) FST-3, Spot Mountain Trail. FST-3 leaves FST-539 just south of Three Prong Mountain and follows a ridge east to Spot Mountain in 4.0 miles. From Spot Mountain, the trail descends to the Selway River. See [Approach: (F)(5)(a)], below.

(4.3) FS-765, Salmon Mountain Lookout Road. This road is now closed and maintained as a trail. It begins along FS-468, at a signed trailhead 14.0 miles from the Selway River.

(5) FS-6223, Paradise Road. This road is the most important southern approach point into the Selway-Bitterroot Wilderness. From Magruder GS on FS-468, FS-6223 runs 12.0 miles up a non-Wilderness corridor into the heart of the Selway-Bitterroot Wilderness to the Paradise GS. Five major trails leave from the road's end, and three major trails leave the road between the two guard stations.

(a) FS-3 to Spot Mountain. The trailhead is 1.0 mile north of Raven Creek CG. The trail climbs a ridge to Spot Mountain in 4.5 miles. FS-40 follows a ridge north over Mount Aura and then drops down to the Selway River just above Paradise GS. See [Approach: (F)(4.2)(b)].

(b) FS-13/east and west. This trail is one of Idaho's premier ridge trails. The trailhead is located on FS-6223, just below Raven Creek CG. The west fork goes up Magruder Ridge to Magruder Mountain [Approach: (F)(4)(f)]; the east fork of the trail climbs a ridge that leads to Nick Wynn Mountain, Beaver Jack Mountain, Cayuse Mountain and Nez Perce Peak. The trail eventually ends at Nez Perce Pass.

(c) FST-10, Indian Ridge Trail. The trailhead is at Indian Creek CG. The trail switchbacks up to the ridge line, which it follows to Green Mountain and Burnt Strip Mountain.

(d) FS-4, Selway River Trail. This trail traverses the unroaded sections of the Selway River, eventually ending at the Selway River Road. (See [Approach: (E)(9)(b)].) Although this area is more attractive to river runners and kyakers than to hikers, it offers the quickest approach available to many Selway-Bitterroot peaks and lake basins.

(d.1) FST-517, Gardiner Peak Trail. This trail leaves FS-4 opposite the Running Creek Ranch and climbs up Gardiner Creek to Gardiner Peak in 6.0 miles.

(d.2) FST-529, Archer Mountain Trail. FST-529 leaves FS-4 2.0 miles south of the Shearer GS and climbs southeast to Archer Mountain in 7.0 miles. From the peak, the trail continues on to Windy Saddle and FS-285. See [Approach: (F)(4.1)].

(d.3) FST-526, Wylies Peak Trail. This trail leaves FST-4 at the Shearer GS and follows Goat Ridge west to Wylies Peak. West of Wylies Peak, the trail junctions with FST-602 [Approach: (E)(9)(b.2)], FST-436 and FST-562.

(6) FS-221, Grangeville/Salmon Road. This road leaves Grangeville from the east edge of town and proceeds south toward the Fish Creek Recreation Area.

(7) FS-444, Moores Station Road. This road leaves FS-221 30.0 miles south of Grangeville and runs east into the Gospel Peak Wilderness and Moores GS. The last 12.0 miles are rugged and require a 4WD, especially when the road is wet. This ridge road has remained open as a compromise between the Forest Service and the people claiming mining rights in the area.

(a) FST-313, Slate Creek Trail. This trail, which leaves FS-444 just east of its starting point, climbs up Slate Creek for 5.0 miles to Slate Lakes. At this point, a side road leads east back to FS-444.

(b) FST-125, Hanover Mountain Trail. FST-125 begins at Slate Lakes and runs due south to the Salmon River in 11.0 miles.

(c) FST-312, Marble Butte Trail. This trail begins at the Moores GS and traverses the Gospel Hump central sections, running south along ridges for over 12.0 miles. Marble Butte is 9.0 miles from the trailhead.

(8) FS-492, Sourdough Road. Thirty miles east of the ID-13/ID-14 junction, turn south off of ID-14 onto this recently rebuilt road, which ends on the summit of Sourdough Peak.

(a) FST-415, Tenmile Creek Trail. This trail begins 12.0 miles south of ID-14 and leads directly into the northeast corner of the Gospel Hump Wilderness, where it connects with numerous other wilderness trails.

(b) FST-300, Baking Powder Mountain Trail. FST-300 leaves FS-492 just short of the road's end and provides access to the entire northern section of the Gospel Hump. The south flanks of Baking Powder Mountain are 3.0 miles from the trailhead.

(9) FS-233, Crooked River/ Orogrande Road. This road leaves ID-14 8.0 miles west of Elk City, and runs for 21.0 miles through Orogrande and on to Orogrande Summit, where the road splits. The right fork leads to Wildhorse Campground in 3.0 miles; the left fork goes to a trailhead on Lake Creek in 2.5 miles. The Lake Creek extension is generally too rough for passenger cars.

(a) FST-204, Fish Lake/Jumbo Canyon Trail. This trail leaves the Lake Creek trailhead and extends 13.0 miles across the southeast corner of the Gospel Hump Wilderness to the Halfway House campground, just south of Dixie. See [Approach: (F)(2.11)(a)], above.

(b) FST-299, North Pole Trail. FST-299 leaves from Wildhorse CG, heads west and then south over North Pole, and then onto the east slopes of Buffalo Hump.

(c) FST-313, Orogrande Trail. From Orogrande Summit, a road descends south into the basin below. The road is exceedingly rough (4WD only); it is advisable to park on the summit and walk 2.0 miles to the road's end, where FST-313 begins. The trail runs across private land (public access on the trail only) to Hump Lake in 2.5 miles, where it joins FST-299. This area south of Orogrande is crisscrossed by trails that provide excellent hiking.

(d) FST-801/FST-800, Wilderness Boundary Trail. This trail is accessed from the Orogrande CG on FS-233. From the trailhead, it is 3.0 miles on FST-801 to FST-800, which can be followed south to Wildhorse CG, or north to Nipple Mountain.

7. The Bitterroot Mountains

Nevin M. Fenneman, in his book the *Physiography of The Western United States*, described the Bitterroot Mountains as follows: "These mountains, while not remarkable for great height, are among the most characteristically alpine of the United States. Everywhere the effects of glacia-

The Bitterroot Mountains, which form the Idaho/Montana border, are a rugged mix of granite and talus that was sharply carved by glaciers. This view of the crest was shot from Trapper Peak, which is located on the Montana side of the border.

tion are prominent." The range Fenneman described is a long narrow mountain chain that forms roughly 150 miles of the Idaho/Montana border between Lost Trail Pass north of Salmon and the Clark Fork River east of Lake Pend Oreille.

The Bitterroots are a collection of sharp peaks, forested ridges, glacial cirques, alpine lakes and everlasting granite. Physically the range forms, for the most part, the eastern edge of the Idaho Batholith in the south, and a high divide in the Coeur d'Alene Mountains in the north. Other than its political designation—as the Idaho/Montana border—the range's boundaries are mostly speculative, as it merges with the Clearwater Mountains in the south and the Coeur d'Alene Mountains in the north. As with most Idaho ranges, the Bitterroot gains elevation from north to south, with 10,131-foot Trapper Peak (which is actually located in Montana) its highest point. The highest point in the Idaho portion of the range is an unnamed 9,439-foot peak which is located along the main divide forming the state boundary.

The range is administered in the north by the Panhandle National Forest (in Idaho) and the Lolo National Forest (in Montana). Further south, the Bitterroot and Clearwater national forests assume management responsibilities. In the Lolo Pass Area, numerous sections of land are held by private landowners.

Hiking and climbing opportunities are abundant throughout the Bitterroots. Although the most technically challenging summits are located wholly within Montana[1], many of the peaks that form the border are worthwhile goals for both hikers and climbers. Between Lolo Pass and Nez Perce Pass, the vast majority of the range is within the Selway-Bitterroot Wilderness Area. Between Lolo Pass and Hoodoo Pass, much of the divide remains roadless and offers excellent wilderness terrain to those willing to explore remote country. North of Hoodoo Pass, a number of Bitterroot peaks sit at the centers of tiny pocket wilderness areas and serve as excellent destinations for overnight and day trips. Foremost among these are Packsaddle Mountain and Binocular Peak.

Packsaddle Mountain   6,402 feet (Class 1)

Packsaddle Mountain anchors the northern end of the Bitterroot Mountains in a grand fashion. The peak towers over the surrounding peaks by nearly 1,000 feet. It rises 4,400 feet above Lake Pend Oreille, providing an enormous view of Idaho and Montana. The peak can be reached from the west by hiking up the Fall Creek, Minerva Ridge [Approach: (A)(1)(a)], or Granite Creek trails. However, the recommended route begins on the peak's east side, where a steep 2.0-mile trail leads to the summit from the saddle at the head of Granite Creek [Approach: (A)(2)(a)]. Because of the many logging roads in the area, a recent Panhandle National Forest map is essential for finding the trailheads. USGS Packsaddle Mountain 15-minute

Divide Peak   5,205 feet (Class 2)

Divide Peak is the northernmost Bitterroot Peak directly on the Idaho/Montana border. The summit is a short walk from FS-430 [Approach: (A)(3)], which traverses the Bitterroot divide to

within a short distance of the summit. USGS Jordan Creek

Ulm Peak   6,444 feet (Class 2)

Ulm Peak is located 5.0 miles southeast of Divide Peak. Like Divide Peak, its summit is easily accessed from FS-430, which continues to traverse the divide. This road provides quick access to the summit [Approach: (A)(3)]. USGS Gem Peak

SHOSHONE RANGE

The Shoshone Range is a small subrange which is tucked into the west side of the Bitterroot Mountains northeast of Kellogg. This small, north-to-south trending range is roughly 12 miles long and 5 miles in width. It is separated from the Coeur d'Alene Mountains on the west by the Coeur d'Alene River and from the Bitterroot by Big Creek and Shoshone Creek. This tree-covered range reaches its highest point at Bennett Peak, 6,209 feet.

Bennett Peak   6,209 feet (Class 1)

Bennett Peak is the only Shoshone Range peak listed in this guidebook. It is located 10.0 miles due south of Divide Peak. Its Class 1 summit can be reached via FST-81 from both the north and the south. The north approach is via Shoshone Creek Road [Approach: (A)(4.2)] and the Hemlock Creek Road [Approach: (A)(4.21)]. The southern approach is from the Shoshone Crest Road [Approach: (A)(4.3)(a)]. FST-81 traverses the ridge between these two roads and provides easy access to the highest Shoshone Range summit. USGS Taylor Peak

---

Black Peak   6,548 feet (Class 1)

Black Peak is the prominent summit which sits at the heads of the East Fork of Eagle Creek (on the Idaho side of the border) and White Pine Creek (on the Montana side). The peak's Class 1 summit is easily accessed from both states, as FST-7 traverses the border in this region. To reach the peak from the Idaho side of the border, drive up FS-152 and then hike up FST-148 to FST-7 [Approach: (A)(4.1)(a) and (b)]. USGS Copper Gulch

Granite Peak   6,815 feet (Class 1)

Granite Peak sits east of the Idaho/Montana border above Revett Lake, 7.0 miles north of Mullan. The summit is accessed via FST-137 from Sunset Mountain, which is a Coeur d'Alene

---

[1]Bitterroot peaks which are located totally inside the State of Montana are not included in this guidebook. For information on those peaks, see *Climbers Guide To Montana* by Pat Caffrey, published by Mountain Press Publishing Company, Missoula, Montana.

Mountains peak. From Sunset Peak, follow FST-137 [Approach: (A)(5)(a)] east along a connecting ridge line to the Granite Peak summit. USGS Burke 15-minute

Stevens Peak *6,838 feet (Class 2-3)*

Stevens Peak is located west of the main Bitterroot divide and 2.5 miles south of Mullan and I-90. It is a rugged alpine summit which is attractive to hikers and climbers. The Spokane Mountaineers used this peak for their snow-climbing school for years. According to Neil McAvoy, "the likes of John Roskelley, Chris Kopscinsky, and hundreds more learned to use ice axes and crampons on this pleasant little hill." The Forest Service has designated the area around the summit as the Stevens Peak Alpine Lakes Area (for whatever that is worth). The peak can be accessed from a number of directions. The two most popular routes are from I-90 via either the Willow Creek Road [Approach: (B)(2)(a)] and one of the trails that lead up to Stevens Lakes and Long Lake, or from the Lookout Pass Ski resort [Approach: (B)(1)]. A third approach route from Mullan leads up Boulder Creek on FST-128 to the peak's west shoulder [Approach: (B)(3)(a)].

The precipitous summit has been climbed from almost every direction and is a popular destination for cross-country skiers. The most direct route to the summit is from Mullan via FST-128. Hike the trail south to the divide and then follow the divide due east to the western slopes of the peak. Leave the trail and hike the moderate slopes to the summit. The total distance is about 4.5 miles, with a 3,600-foot elevation gain. A winter ski ascent of the peak is best accomplished in mid-winter from the Lookout Pass ski resort. It should be noted that the route from the resort involves traversing a long 6.0+-mile ridge with considerable ups and downs. Only extremely experienced skiers should consider this route. USGS Wallace 15-minute

Bald Mountain *6,033 feet*
Dominion Peak *6,032 feet*
Crittenden Peak *6,416 feet (Class 2)*

Following the Bitterroot divide south from Stevens Peak, one encounters these three minor summits. They are easily scaled from FS-391 [Approach: (B)(6)]. The best approach begins in Montana. Take the Saltese, Montana exit from I-90 and then follow the road which parallels the freeway west to Rainy Creek and FS-506, which leads up the divide to FS-391. Because of the near proximity of the road, these peaks offer good goals for a long winter ski trip. USGS Saltese 15-minute

Quarles Peak *6,560+ feet (Class 1)*

Quarles Peak is located 2.5 miles south of Crittenden Peak. An old jeep road leads to the summit of this long narrow peak from FS-391 [Approach: (B)(6)]. There is a lookout site located on the Idaho side of the border. USGS Saltese 15-minute

Ward Peak *7,312 feet (Class 2)*

Ward Peak is the northernmost Bitterroot Peak over 7,000 feet in height. The summit is easily reached from FS-391, which crosses the peak's southern slopes. From FS-391, FST-250 leaves the road south of the peak [Approach: (B)(6)(a)]. Hike the trail northwest to the border and then climb the west slope from the trail. USGS Haugan 15-minute

Eagle Cliff *7,543 feet (Class 2)*

Eagle Cliff sits high above Cliff Lake, 11.0 miles southwest of St. Regis, Montana. FST-738 follows the border in this area and passes along the peak's western slopes [Approach: (B)(7)(a)]. The summit is a short scramble from the trail at almost any point along the western slopes. USGS Illinois Peak 15-minute

Binocular Peak *7,266 feet (Class 2)*

Binocular Peak is the large impressive peak with a treeless summit that is located 2.5 miles south of Eagle Cliff. Binocular's north face drops almost 900 feet to Heart Lake in less than 0.25 mile. The peak is accessed from FST-738 [Approach: (B)(7)(a)]. This trail traverses around the peak by swinging south around its southern slopes. Climb the peak from the point where the trail crosses the 6,800-foot contour line on the USGS map. USGS Illinois Peak 15-minute

Illinois Peak *7,690 feet*
Graves Peak *7,200 feet (Class 1)*

The Saint Joe River begins in a scenic alpine cirque which is nestled in the western slopes of these peaks. Both peaks are climbed from Saint Joe Lake via FST-49 [Approach: (B)(8)(a)]. The trail leaves the north side of the lake and climbs to the divide above, where it meets FST-738 [Approach: (B)(7)(a)], which follows the border from north to south. From this point, the trail continues on to cross over the top of Illinois Peak, and then drops down the peak's east ridge into Montana. To climb Graves Peak, follow FST-738 south from its junction with FST-49 to the peak's west ridge and then climb the ridge to the summit. USGS Illinois Peak 15-minute

Admiral Peak *7,323 feet (Class 2)*

Admiral Peak is located at the head of the South Fork of Kelly Creek, 2.0 miles east of Fish Lake. Fish Lake can be accessed via Lake Creek and FST-419/FST-478 [Approach: (C)(1.1)(b)] or FST-478 [Approach: (C)(2)(a)] or via the State Divide Trail, FST-738 [Approach: (C)(1)(a)]. The summit is climbed from FST-738 [Approach: (B)(7)(a)] by following the trail east from Fish Lake to its highest point on the peak's southeast ridge. Leave the trail at this point and follow the ridge to the summit. USGS Straight Peak 15-minute

Shale Mountain *7,612 feet (Class 3)*

This is one of the more rugged peaks in the area. Climb it from the point where FST-508 [Approach: (C)(3)(a)] crosses the Bitterroot divide at Cache Saddle and leads into Montana. The saddle can be accessed from FS-581 via FST-508 or from Granite Pass via FST-46 [Approach: (C)(5)(a)]. Leave the trail at the divide and follow the ridge line north to the summit in 1.0 mile. USGS Rhodes Peak

Rhodes Peak *7,930 feet (Class 2)*

Rhodes Peak is located 3.0 miles south of Shale Mountain. The peak sits on a subsidiary ridge south of the Idaho/Montana border. Climb the peak from FST-508, which passes along its western slopes [Approach: (C)(3)(a)]. (See the directions for Williams Peak below.) USGS Rhodes Peak

Granite Peak *7,551 feet (Class 2)*

Although this is the second Bitterroot Peak to bear this name, there is little danger of confusing the two peaks since they are separated by many miles. This Granite Peak sits 3.5 miles directly east of Shale Mountain. The summit is reached by climbing either the peak's western or northern ridge from FST-46 [Approach: (C)(5)(a)]. USGS Granite Pass

WILLIAMS RANGE

The Williams Range, located south of Rhodes Peak and west of Lolo Pass, is a subrange of the Bitterroot Range. This range is composed of a major subsidiary ridge that runs south from the main Bitterroot crest for 9 miles and has a width of 4 miles. Williams Peak, 7,501 feet, is the highest peak in the range.

Williams Peak *7,501 feet (Class 1-2)*

The highest point in the Williams subrange is located high above Williams and Goat Lakes. To reach the summit of this peak, follow FST-248

[Approach: (C)(3)(a)] up Silver Creek to where it joins FST-508, which leads to Goat Lake. From the lake, follow the trail eastward toward the summit. Although the top is only a short scramble from the trail, the trail is difficult to follow in places and physically demanding. USGS Cayuse Junction

Old Stormy *8,203 feet (Class 2)*

Old Stormy is located south of US-12 and Lolo Pass and just west of Stormy Pass, in the Selway-Bitterroot Wilderness Area. The peak is easily climbed from FST-307 [Approach: (D)(1)(a)] at Stormy Pass via its east ridge. USGS Ranger Peak / SBW

Ranger Peak *8,817 feet (Class 3)*

Ranger Peak sits 1.0 mile due west of Old Stormy. Although the peak can be climbed from the Idaho side of the border, approach considerations dictate that the easiest route to the summit is from the Big Creek Lakes on the Montana side of the border. Follow FST-11 [Approach: (D)(1)(a)] around the largest Big Creek Lake to its west side and the first inlet stream. Follow this stream up to the high basin on the peak's southeast slopes. From the basin, climb to Ranger Peak's south ridge line and then follow the ridge to the summit. USGS Ranger Peak / SBW

Sky Pilot Peak *8,792 feet (Class 3)*

Sky Pilot Peak is located 4.5 miles south of Old Stormy, at the head of the North Fork of Bear Creek. The peak is best accessed from the Montana side of the border by hiking up FST-5 [Approach: (D)(2)(a)] to Bear Creek Pass (note: this trail is designated FST-43 on the Idaho side of the border). From the pass, follow the ridge line east to the summit. USGS Cash Point / SBW

Frog Peak *8,078 feet (Class 2)*

Frog Mountain sits east of the main Bitterroot divide, on a subsidiary ridge that runs north from the border near Mill Lake to Hidden Peak in 5.0 miles. Climb to the summit via the peak's western slopes from FST-906 [Approach: (D)(6)(a)]. The trails in this area are reportedly difficult to follow due to brush and many downed trees. USGS Blodgett Mountain / SBW

Blodgett Mountain *8,647 feet (Class 3)*

Blodgett Mountain was named after Joseph Blodgett, who was an early packer in the Bitterroot valley. The peak is located 15.0 miles due west of Hamilton, Montana and sits directly on the Idaho/Montana border. Climb the east ridge from Blodgett Pass [Approach: (D)(3)(a)]. USGS Blodgett Mountain / SBW

Saddle Mountain *8,258 feet (Class 2)*

Twin-summited Saddle Mountain is located west of the main divide, near Twin Lakes. To reach the summit, follow FST-430 [Approach: (D)(4)(a)] west from the Twin Lakes trailhead to the divide at Wahoo Pass in about 1.0 mile. Leave the trail and climb due north to the ridge top west of Lost Horse Pass. At this point the ridge forks. Take the western fork and follow the ridge for 2.25 miles to the Saddle Mountain Summit. USGS Saddle Mountain / SBW

Hunter Peak *8,472 feet (Class 2-3)*

Hunter Peak is a triangular summit located 1.0 mile west of the divide near Bell Lake. To reach this isolated summit, start in Montana at Lake Como and hike west on FST-580 [Approach: (D)(5)(a)] to the border. From the border, descend FST-522 past Bell Lake to the first stream crossing. Turn south and follow this stream to the ridge top above. Once on the ridge, turn west and follow the ridge to the summit. USGS Hunter Peak / SBW

Mount Paloma *8,371 feet (Class 2)*

Mount Paloma is located west of the Idaho/Montana border on a major subsidiary ridge that runs from the border to the Selway River at Elevator Mountain in 17.0 long miles. Paloma is the highest point along this ridge. To reach the summit, take FST-24 [Approach: (E)(1.4)(a)] up White Cap Creek from Paradise GS to FST-717 [Approach: (E)(1.4)(b)], which leads to Cedar Saddle, Mount George and Mount Paloma. This is a long, mostly dry hike along ridge lines. The trail deteriorates after Cedar Saddle. Keep on the ridge line. Please note that the quadrangle does not display the present-day trail system. The cirques below the peak offer good overnight destinations. USGS Mount Paloma / SBW

Mount George *7,714 feet (Class 1)*

Named after Ben George, a trapper and Forest Service employee, this peak is located 3.5 miles south of Mount Paloma. Follow the route described for Mount Paloma above. USGS Mount George / SBW

Nipple Knob *8,505 feet (Rating Unknown)*

This peak is located northeast of Mount Paloma and is part of the same subsidiary ridge that includes Paloma. Nipple Knob is included in this book because it is one of Idaho's unknown peaks. It has impressive dimensions on the maps, but no one has ever reported climbing it. Because there are no maintained trails within a reasonable distance of this peak, it is possible that its granite summit has never seen a human foot. At any rate, the peak's north face is as steep as you will find anywhere. While you are in the area, Peak 8474 (0.5 mile east of Nipple Knob) is also worth a look. USGS Mount Paloma / SBW

Vance Mountain *8,793 feet (Class 2)*

Vance Mountain is a high vantage point named for James Vance, a Forest Service ranger. The peak is located west of the border near White Cap Lakes. Climb this peak via its northwest ridge, which is reached from either FST-45 or FST-46 [Approach: (E)(1.4)(c)]. USGS Tin Cup Lake / SBW

Peak 9439 *9,439 feet (Class 2-3)*

This unnamed summit is located 0.5 mile northwest of Bare Peak and is the highest point in the Idaho section of the Bitterroot Mountains. The summit can be climbed from the southwest via Soda Springs Creek, which is traversed by FST-250 [Approach: (E)(1.2)(a)]. Little is known about this rugged summit because it does not have a name and is largely ignored by climbers. The peak can also be approached from Boulder Lake to the north via FST-617 [Approach: (E)(1.1)(a)]. Although a route up the peak's northern slopes looks feasible, no one has reported climbing the peak from this direction. USGS Mount Jerusalem

Watchtower Peak *8,790 feet (Class 3)*

Watchtower Peak is located 8.0 miles north of Nez Perce Pass and is the last major summit within the Selway-Bitterroot Wilderness along the Bitterroot divide. The peak is climbed via its southeast ridge, which is accessed from FST-699 [Approach: (E)(1.3)(a)]. USGS Watchtower Peak / SBW

Nez Perce Peak *7,531 feet (Class 1)*

Nez Perce Peak is located 2.5 miles east of the Idaho/Montana border and Nez Perce Pass. The summit is crossed by FST-13. To climb to the summit start either on Nez Perce Pass and follow FST-16 to FST-13 [Approach: (E)(1)(a)] or take FST-14 from the Old Nez Perce Trail to FST-13 [Approach: (E)(1)(b)]. USGS Nez Perce Peak

APPROACHES TO THE BITTERROOT MOUNTAINS

Approach routes for this section are identified in the text by bracketed entries [Approach:], which include appropriate letter and number references.

As would be expected for a mountain range that runs almost 175 miles from north to south, there are many approach points to the range's many valleys. The vast majority of Bitterroot vehicular access points begin on the Montana side of the border because much of the Idaho side is contained within the Selway-Bitterroot Wilderness. The approach section is divided into four sections, which are listed from north to south.

(A) ID-200 South to Lookout Pass (I-90).
The northernmost stretch of the Bitterroots is served by two major east/west highways: ID-200, which runs between Sandpoint, Idaho and Noxon, Montana in the north; and I-90, which stretches between Wallace, Idaho and Missoula, Montana in the south.

(1) FS-278, Pend Oreille Shore Road. Access this road at Clark Fork, Idaho, which is 26.0 miles east of the junction of ID-200 and US-2/US-95. From ID-200, turn south at the National Forest access sign, cross the Clark Fork bridge and follow the river west several miles before it swings south and climbs up into the mountains. This road parallels the entire east shore of Lake Pend Oreille before connecting with FS-209, far to the south.

(a) FST-610, Minerva Ridge Trail. This trail is accessed from FS-278. The trailhead is unsigned and difficult to locate—take a Forest Service map. To reach the trailhead, turn off FS-278 onto the Fall Creek Road and drive up Fall Creek Road for 0.1 mile, and then turn left (northeast) onto a rough road. The trailhead is 0.25 mile ahead. The trail quickly climbs to the top of Minerva Ridge and follows the ridge line up to the base of Packsaddle Mountain in 7.0 miles.

(2) FS-332, Pend Oreille Divide Road. This road is accessed from FS-278 [Approach: (A)(1)] by taking FS-1060 across Monarch Ridge. This road, like FS-278, parallels the east shore of Lake Pend Oreille, but, unlike FS-278, its route is near the top of the mountains. From its junction with FS-1060, the road runs east and then southeast to the Idaho/Montana border. Although this road is narrow and steep in places, in good weather much of it is generally passable to autos. The eastern end of the road is primitive in nature and a 4WD could be required.

(a) FS-611, Packsaddle Mountain Trail. This trail begins in the saddle southeast of the summit of Packsaddle Mountain and climbs to that peak's summit in 2.0 miles, gaining 1,900 feet in elevation.

(3) FS-430, State Divide Road. This road begins where FS-332 ends at the Idaho/Montana border and follows the border south. It runs on or near the crest for many miles, providing access to many summits. Check with the Forest Service for current driving conditions before using this road.

(4) Coeur D'Alene River Road. This road is accessed from the Kingston exit on I-90. The road follows the meandering river east and north.

(4.1) FS-152, East Fork Eagle Creek Road. This road is accessed from the Coeur d'Alene River Road at Prichard. From Prichard, drive east for 2.6 miles to Eagle Creek, turn north up Eagle Creek and then, after 1.3 miles, turn east.

(a) FST-148, Casper Creek Trail. FST-148 leaves FS-152 at a signed trailhead and climbs up Casper Creek in just over 2.0 steep miles, where it joins FST-7.

(b) FST-7, State Divide Trail. At one time, this trail followed the Bitterroot crest along the Idaho/Montana border for much of its distance. Currently much of the trail has been replaced by roads (such as FS-430); also, mining and logging operations are creeping closer to the remaining sections of trail. The trail section between Bloom Peak and Black Peak is long and unbroken, however, and can be accessed from FST-148.

(4.2) FS-151/FS-412, Shoshone Creek Road. This road leaves the Coeur d'Alene River Road at the Shoshone Creek GS and follows Shoshone Creek north for roughly 17.0 miles to Hemlock Creek and FS-992. From Hemlock Creek, the road makes a half circle to the west, where it again joins the Coeur d'Alene River Road. Numerous logging roads of varying quality climb up into the Bitterroot and Shoshone ranges from this road.

(4.21) Hemlock Creek Road. This road leaves FS-412 and climbs up Hemlock Creek to the Shoshone Range divide. Once on the divide, the road runs south along the crest to Pond Peak and FST-81. This is a rough road and a 4WD is recommended.

(a) FST-81, Shoshone Crest Trail. See [Approach: (A)(4.3)(a)], below.

(4.3) FS-502, Shoshone Crest Road. This road leaves the Coeur d'Alene River Road near the Shoshone Creek GS and climbs 10.0 miles up a ridge (passing several side roads along the way) to a point on the crest of the Shoshone Range below Downey Peak. From this point, the road continues on to Little Guard Peak; this section is closed to motorized vehicles.

(a) FST-81, Shoshone Crest Trail. This trail leaves FS-502 and runs north along the Shoshone Range Crest to Pond Peak and FS-992 in just over 3.0 miles, crossing over Bennett, Little Sentinel and Sentinel peaks along the way.

(5) FST-456 and FS-261.1, Sunset Peak Road. These two roads lead to the summit of Sunset Peak from Wallace. It is roughly 8.0 miles to the summit.

(a) FST-137, Granite Peak Trail. This trail follows the ridge line eastward from Sunset Peak for 3.5 miles to Granite Peak.

(B) Lookout Pass South To Hoodoo Pass.
Primary access to this section of the Bitterroots is provided by I-90 and many secondary and Forest Service roads. Much of the Bitterroot divide between Lookout and Hoodoo passes is roaded.

(1) Lookout Ski Area Road. This road is accessed from the Lookout Pass exit on I-90. The road runs a short distance to the south and leads to the Lookout Pass Ski Area.

(2) Willow Creek Road. This road leaves I-90 at the east end of Mullan and follows Willow Creek south for 1.3 miles. This is the primary approach road for the Stevens Peak Alpine Lakes Area, which is administered by the Forest Service.

(a) FST-165, Stevens Lake Trail. FST-165 leaves the Willow Creek Road and runs 1.1 miles to Stevens Lake at the base of Stevens Peak.

(3) Boulder Creek Road. This road is accessed from Mullan by following Boulder Creek south from town for less than 1.0 mile to the National Forest boundary.

(a) FST-128, Boulder Creek Trail. FST-128 begins at the end of the Boulder Creek Road at the National Forest boundary. The poorly maintained trail climbs 2.75 miles up Boulder Creek to the ridge line above, where it joins the ridge trail that leads due east to the Stevens Peak area and FST-278.

(4) Saint Joe River Road. This road leaves ID-3 on the west edge of Saint Maries and stretches east and then south for 74.0 miles to Red Ives. It can also be accessed from Montana and I-90 as described in [Approach (B)(5)], below. The road is paved from Saint Maries to Marble Creek, just west of Avery.

(5) FS-456/FS-388, Rolland Summit Road. This road connects I-90 with the Saint Joe River Road. It is accessed from I-90 1.0 mile west of Saint Regis, Montana. From the I-90 exit, drive south up the North Fork of Little Joe Creek to Rolland Summit in 12.8 miles and then descend to the Saint Joe River Road and eventually to Saint Maries. The road is gravel for much of its distance and is suitable for passenger autos during good weather.

(6) FS-391, State Divide Road. FS-391 begins on Rolland Summit and follows the Bitterroot crest and the Idaho/Montana border south for over 40.0 miles to a point south of Little Joe Mountain. This primitive road can be accessed from numerous points on both sides of the border.

(a) FST-250, Eagle Peak Trail. This trail leaves FS-391 directly south of Ward Peak and runs due north across the border and into Montana in 0.5 mile. From the border, the trail traverses Eagle Peak and Gold Peak before joining FS-3816 near Up Up Mountain.

(7) FS-389, East Fork Gold Creek Road. This road leaves FS-388 1.75 miles east of the Saint Joe River Road and climbs to the Bitterroot divide in 14.6 miles.

(a) FST-738, State Divide Trail. This section of the State Divide Trail is one of Idaho's least known and most outstanding trails. It begins south of Little Joe Mountain and follows the Bitterroot crest south for over 20.0 miles to Hoodoo Pass.

(8) FS-320, Red Ives Creek Road. This road leaves the Saint Joe River Road just south of Red Ives GS, and then climbs up to Simmons Ridge and a junction with FS-346. From this point, the road drops down to the upper reaches of the Saint Joe River. A 4WD is recommended.

(a) FS-49, Saint Joe Lake Trail. This trail follows the Saint Joe River 5.0 miles to Saint Joe Lake. From the lake the trail climbs up and joins FST-738 [Approach: (B)(8)(a)] just below Illinois Peak. Access the trail from FS-320 16.0 miles east of the Red Ives GS.

(9) FS-346, Simmons Ridge Road. This road leaves FS-320 9.3 miles from the Red Ives GS and follows the ridge line to the north. A 4WD is recommended.

(a) FST-74, Heller Ridge Trail. FST-74 leaves FS-346 0.5 miles north of its junction with FS-320 [Approach: (B)(7)(a)] and runs to FST-738, the State Divide Trail, between Eagle Cliff and Binocular Peak.

(b) FST-78, Simmons Ridge Trail. FST-78 leaves FS-346 and proceeds northwest past Simmons Peak to Midget Peak before, eventually, descending to the Saint Joe River.

(10) FS-715/FS-720, Saint Joe/North Fork Road. This road connects the Saint Joe River drainage with the North Fork of the Clearwater drainage. It is accessed from FS-320 [Approach: (B)(8)] roughly 3.25 miles south of Heller Creek CG and runs south to join FS-250 [Approach: (C)(1)] in 24.0 miles. Although this is a good gravel road, it is about the longest and slowest 24.0 miles you will ever drive.

(C) Hoodoo Pass South To Lolo Pass.
Primary approach to this section is provided by FS-250, which crosses the Bitterroot divide at Hoodoo Pass as it runs between Pierce, Idaho and Superior, Montana.

(1) FS-250, North Fork Clearwater River Road. This road begins at Pierce, Idaho and then runs east along French Creek and Orogrande Creek until it eventually meets the North Fork of the Clearwater. Once it meets the river, it follows the river east to the confluence of the North Fork and Kelly Creek. (The right-hand fork, FS-255 [Approach: (C)(2)] is discussed below.) From this junction, FS-250 continues up the North Fork of the Clearwater River through Black Canyon to

Hoodoo Pass. Many people prefer to take the longer FS-255 because it is a better road, while some prefer the shorter, but much more primitive, stretch of FS-250 which runs through Black Canyon. From Hoodoo Pass, the road continues on to Superior, Montana.

(a) FST-738/FST-46, State Divide Trail. From Hoodoo Pass, this most pristine section of the State Divide Trail runs south for over 40.0 miles to Kelly Creek Saddle (above the Middle Fork of Kelly Creek), following the Bitterroot divide as it forms the Idaho/Montana border. Further south, at Cache Saddle, the State Divide Trail continues as FST-46 and proceeds along the crest to Granite Pass. (See [Approach: (C)(5)(a)] below.) Numerous feeder trails provide access to this trail from both the Montana and Idaho sides of the border.

(1.1) FS-295, Lake Creek Road. This road leaves FS-250 roughly 10.0 miles south of Hoodoo Pass and follows Lake Creek east until it forks in about 4.0 miles. The left fork leads up Goose Creek for 1.0 mile to where it is gated shut. The right fork continues along Lake Creek for another 1.0 mile until it is also gated shut.

(a) FST-414, Goose Lake Trail. From the gate on the Goose Creek Road, follow the road for nearly 0.5 mile to the trailhead. It is 4.0 miles up Goose Creek to Goose Lake and the State Divide Trail.

(b) FST-419/FST-478, Fish Lake Trail. From the gate on FS-295, continue along Lake Creek on the closed road, which soon turns into a trail. It is roughly 5.0 miles to Fish Lake and the State Divide Trail.

(2) FS-255, Kelly Creek/Moose Road. This road leaves FS-250 and the North Fork of the Clearwater and follows Kelly Creek north to the Kelly Creek GS, where Moose Creek flows into Kelly Creek. At this point, the road turns up Moose Creek toward Moose and then eventually rejoins FS-250 north of Deception Saddle.

(a) FST-478, Pollock Ridge Trail. This trail leaves FS-255 roughly 2.0 miles north of the Kelly Creek GS. The trail quickly forks twice—keep to the right at both junctions. After the trail leaves Swamp Creek, it climbs steeply up to the top of Pollock Ridge and follows the ridge for 8.0 long miles to the northern slopes of Wapito Peak. The trail bypasses the peak and drops down to Fish Lake in another 2.0 miles.

(b) FST-567, Kelly Creek Trail. This trail is accessed just east of the Kelly Creek GS, where FS-581 crosses Kelly Creek. Kelly Creek, a large drainage, is still in a wilderness condition and could be included in the proposed Big Burn Wilderness. This well-maintained trail follows Kelly Creek for 10.0 miles to a point past Hanson

Meadows, where it quickly divides into three trails, two of which are listed below.

(b.1) FST-493, North Fork Kelly Creek Trail. This trail continues up Kelly Creek and then the North Fork of Kelly Creek for another 9.0 miles to join with the State Divide Trail between Fish Lake and Admiral Peak.

(b.2) FST-503, Middle Fork Kelly Creek Trail. FST-503 leaves FST-493 and quickly climbs up the Middle Fork of Kelly Creek to the State Divide Trail in 5.0 miles.

(3) FS-581, Toboggan Ridge Road. This road leaves FS-255 just east of the Kelly Creek GS, crosses the Kelly Creek, climbs the ridge to the south and drops into the Cayuse Creek valley. The road crosses Cayuse Creek and then wiggles and worms its way east for many miles to FS-500, the Lewis and Clark Road. (See [Approach: (C)(4)], below.)

(a) FST-248/FST-508, Williams Peak/Cache Saddle Trail. This trail leaves FS-581 1.5 miles north of Cayuse Junction, where FS-581 and FS-500 meet.

(4) FS-500, Lewis and Clark Road. FS-500 is designated as the route followed by Lewis and Clark. It parallels US-12, running from north to south, and can be accessed from a number of points which connect with US-12. The quickest way to use FS-500 for Bitterroot access is via FS-569, the Parachute Hill Road, which is located 72.0 miles east of Lowell on US-12. Turn north off US-12 and follow FS-569 2.5 miles to FS-500. Turn left and follow this good gravel road to Cayuse junction and FS-581, which drops off the ridge and crosses Cayuse Creek.

(5) FS-595, Granite Pass Road. This road leaves US-12 at Lolo Pass and follows the divide north through Granite Pass. Two miles north of the pass, the road ends and FST-738/FST-46, the State Divide Trail, begins.

(a) FST-46, State Divide Trail. The southernmost portion of the State Divide Trail is accessed from Granite Pass by taking the gravel road that leads from the pass north along the border. Follow the road for about 1.0 mile until it drops off the ridge to the east. At this point, the trail continues along the ridge line toward Rocky Peak and Cache Saddle. (See [Approach: (C)(3)(a)].)

(D) Lolo Pass South to Nez Perce Pass.
   Primary access to this section of the Bitterroots is via US-12 and US-93. US-12 crosses Lolo Pass as it runs between Lewiston, Idaho and Lolo, Montana. US-93 runs along the eastern front of the Bitterroots between Lolo and Darby, Montana.

(1) FS-1321, Big Creek Road. Turn off US-93 1.5 miles north of Victor and follow the road to Big Creek Campground and trailhead.

(a) FST-11, Big Creek Trail. From FS-1321, it is roughly 9.0 miles to Big Creek Lake. From the lake, FST-11 continues along the western shore of the lake and south over Packbox Pass and into Idaho. Also, FST-307/99 leaves the lake and travels due north to nearby Stormy Pass and then drops down in the South Fork of Storm Creek on the Idaho side of the border. The Idaho portion of the trail is in poor condition.

(2) FS-737, Bear Creek Road. Take the paved road which leaves Victor and runs west and follow the signs to Bear Creek Campground and trailhead.

(a) FST-5, Bear Creek Pass Trail. From the trailhead, follow FST-5 for 10.0 miles northwest to Bear Creek Pass and the Idaho border. Once at the pass, the trail designation changes to FST-43 on the Idaho side. FST-43 descends to Garmet Creek, and then joins FST-50, which follows White Sandy Creek north and south. FST-50 can be followed south to access the Frog Peak Trail, FST-906 [Approach: (D)(6)(b)] or north over Packbox Pass to Big Creek Lake and FST-11 [Approach: (D)(1)(a)].

(3) Blodgett Creek Road. This road leaves US-93 at Hamilton and proceeds west to Blodgett Canyon Campground and the Blodgett Pass trail.

(a) FST-19, Blodgett Pass Trail. This trail leads over Blodgett Pass and into Idaho in 14.0 miles. At the divide, the trail climbs steeply to the pass on a series of switchbacks and then drops north into Idaho and Big Sand Creek, where it is designated FST-4. FST-4 then leads to FS-111, the Big Elk Road, in Idaho. (See [Approach: (D)(6)(a)] below.)

(4) FS-429, Lost Horse Creek Road. This road system penetrates the Bitterroot divide clear to its crest. Drive 3.6 miles north of Darby, turn west onto FS-429, and follow it to the point where it splits. FS-5605 ends at Twin Lakes and FS-429 ends on the divide at Bear Creek Pass. A number of peaks and high mountain lakes are accessible from the three trails that leave this road's trailheads.

(a) FST-430, Wahoo Pass/ Freeman Peak Trail. This trail leaves Lost Horse Pass, crosses Wahoo Pass and runs due west to the Moose GS on the Selway River. (See [Approach: (E)(9)(d)] in the Clearway Access Section.)

(5) FS-550, Lake Como Road. Access this road from US-93, at a signed junction 6.0 miles north of Darby, Montana. The signed road quickly leads to Lake Como, which has trailheads on both sides of its dam.

(a) FST-580/FST-522, Elk Lake Trail. This trail leaves from the south side of the Lake Como dam and runs directly west up Rock Creek to Elk Lake, crosses the Idaho/Montana border, and descends into Idaho to reach Bell Lake in about 16.5 miles. West of Bell Lake, the trail is poorly maintained and difficult to follow in places.

(6) FS-111, Elk Summit Road. This is one of the few western vehicular approach points for the Idaho side of the Bitterroots in the Selway-Bitterroot Wilderness Area. Access the road at Powell on US-12 and follow it north to the Elk Summit GS trailhead for FST-4.

(a) FST-4, Big Soda Creek Trail. This trail leaves from the Elk Summit GS and proceeds due east to Big Sand Creek in 4.0 miles. One mile from the trailhead, FST-18 forks off and climbs to Diablo Mountain. Once at Big Sand Creek, FST-1 follows the creek south and FST-4 continues along the creek to the east to eventually arrive at Blodgett Pass in 11.0 more miles. FST-906 is accessed at Big Sand Lake.

(b) FST-906, Frog Peak Trail. This trail leaves FST-4 at Big Sand Lake and proceeds up a ridge line to the northeast. Once up the ridge, the trail drops into the Frog Lake basin and then once again climbs, this time to Frog Lake, which is just 1.0 mile north of Big Sand Lake. This area was recently burned by a forest fire and the trail is hard to follow in places.

(E) Nez Perce Pass Area Access.

Primary access to this section of the Bitterroots is provided by FS-468, the Old Nez Perce Trail Road and US-93.

(1) FS-468, Old Nez Perce Trail Road. This road leaves US-93 7.0 miles south of Darby, Montana and crosses Nez Perce Pass, 6,587 feet. The road eventually traverses the entire state of Idaho, cutting between the Selway-Bitterroot and River of No Return Wilderness areas. (See [Approach: (E)(8)] in the Approaches to the Clearwater Mountains section for additional information on trails that are accessed from this road.)

(a) FST-16, Indian Hill Trail. This trail leaves FS-468 at Nez Perce Pass and follows the Bitterroot divide both north and south. The northern section of the trail ends at a pass on the western slopes of Indian Hill 9.0 miles from Nez Perce Pass. Several trails fork off here, including FST-35, which follows a ridge line west to Cayuse and Beaver Jack Mountains (which are Clearwater peaks); and FST-14, which is discussed below.

(b) FST-14, Nez Perce Peak Trail. This trail runs between FS-468 and FST-16 over Nez Perce Peak for a distance of approximately 6.5 miles. From FST-16, access this trail 3.0 miles northwest of Nez Perce Pass; from FS-468, access the trail just west of Schumaker Creek.

(1.1) Boulder Creek. Turn off FS-468 just east of the West Fork GS and drive 1.0 mile to Boulder

Creek Campground and trailhead.

(a) FST-617, Boulder Creek Trail. This trail leads into a remote section of Idaho (near Vance Mountain) from the end of the Boulder Creek Road and eventually reaches the Idaho/Montana border in 10.5 miles. The trail is deeply rutted in places, but also well-marked and easy to follow. At a small pond just east of the border, FST-249 leads south to Boulder Lake in about 1.0 mile.

(1.2) FST-5635, Soda Springs Creek Road. FST-5635 leaves FST-468 5.0 miles west of the West Fork GS. Follow FS-5635 north to the trailhead in a little over 1.0 mile.

(a) FST-250, Soda Springs Creek Trail. This trail leaves the FS-5635 trailhead and follows the creek up its drainage for 7.0 miles to a small unnamed lake at the base of Bare Peak.

(1.3) Watchtower Creek Trailhead. This trailhead for FST-699 is accessed from FS-468 1.5 miles east of Fales Flat CG by turning north onto a short access road and driving a short distance north to the road's end.

(a) FST-699, Watchtower Creek Trail. This trail runs up Watchtower Creek for 7.5 miles to a point on the border of the Bitterroot divide southwest of Watchtower Peak.

(1.4) FS-6223, Paradise Road. This road is the most important southern access point into the Selway-Bitterroot Wilderness Area. From Magruder GS on FS-468, FS-6223 runs 12.0 miles up a non-Wilderness peninsula into the heart of the Wilderness, to the Paradise GS. Five major trails leave from the road's end, and three major trails leave the road between the two guard stations.

(a) FST-24, White Cap Creek Trail. FST-24 leaves the Paradise GS and follows White Cap Creek eastward to the Bitterroot divide in 26.0 miles.

(b) FST-717, Mount Paloma Trail. This trail is accessed from FST-24 3.75 miles east of the Paradise GS. The trail leaves White Cap Creek and immediately climbs a ridge line which leads north to Cedar Saddle in 2.5 miles. From the saddle, the trail turns east and climbs almost to the summit of Mount George in another 1.0 mile and then once again turns north and leads to Mount Paloma in 4.0 additional miles. (Note that FST-711 also runs between White Cap Creek and Mount George. This trail leaves White Cap Creek 6.0 miles east of the Paradise GS and follows Barefoot Creek to Mount George in roughly 3.0 miles. The Forest Service no longer maintains this trail on a regular basis, and it will be difficult to follow in places.)

(c) FST-45/FST-46, Vance Mountain Trail. This loop trail leads from White Cap Creek to the cirque below the western slopes of Vance Mountain, and then returns to White Cap Creek. Access FST-46 at Cooper Flat 7.0 miles east of the Paradise GS by crossing the bridge and heading southeast along Canyon Creek for a short distance, until the trail forks. Take the right-hand fork and follow the trail up the ridge line that divides White Cap Creek and Canyon Creek. The trail runs east for about 7.0 miles to the base of Vance Mountain, where it joins FST-45, which descends along Fall Creek to White Cap Creek in 3.0 miles.

He Devil, viewed from Sheep Lake

II
WESTERN IDAHO

From the Salmon River
South to the Snake River;
From the Oregon Border East
to Idaho-75 and US-93

1. The Seven Devils Mountains

The Seven Devils Mountains extend along the Idaho/Oregon border for roughly 40 miles between the Idaho towns of Whitebird and Council and are bounded by the Snake River on the west and the Salmon and Little Salmon rivers on the east. The range ranks high among Idaho's mountain chains in terms of ruggedness and scenic quality; it is the state's most precipitous range, with elevations varying from just above 1,000 feet at the Snake River to 9,393 feet on the summit of He Devil.

The range was formed by block faulting of the region's very complicated rock layers, which contain a little of everything, from oceanic sedimentary rocks to intrusive igneous rock and limestone caves, all within short walking distance of each other. In the past, mining activity has taken place in this range; old digs can still be found, mostly at the lower elevations. While the Seven Devils block was uplifting, the Salmon River cut an immense trench on the east side of the range, and the Snake River cut an even deeper canyon along the western side. Between the two river canyons is a high 3-mile-wide bench which forms the Seven Devils high country. This range runs north to south and is most pronounced on its east side, where all of the major peaks are found. The western slope of the range, while at first more moderate than the eastern side, eventually descends rapidly into the Hells Canyon of the Snake River. The effects of Pleistocene Era glaciers are evident everywhere in the upper regions of the range, where there are dozens of prominent cirques and some thirty mountain lakes. From the central portion of the range, the Seven Devils crest loses elevation as it runs north and south.

In 1975, Congress established the Hells Canyon National Recreation Area, which includes sections of both Idaho and Washington. This rela-

tively new pseudo-national park includes most of the Seven Devils Mountains; 190,000 acres (including the entire high peak area of the central range) are designated as the Hells Canyon Wilderness. The southern section of the range is managed by the Payette National Forest, and the eastern foothills are managed by the Nez Perce National Forest.

The range is readily accessible, with the most popular route beginning in Riggins, Idaho, and allowing passenger autos to reach over 8,000 feet in elevation at Windy Gap. While the southern and northern approach routes are more primitive, they do offer quick approaches to most of the Seven Devils' most important summits. Hiking and climbing opportunities are above average. Due to the large elevation differentials, the Seven Devils have the longest hiking season of any Idaho mountain range, with hiking beginning along the Snake River in early March. While the best known trails are located within the Wilderness boundaries, many excellent trails are located in the southern Seven Devils, west of Council.

Because the peaks are conglomerations of hard and deteriorated rock strata, shattered towers, massive talus slopes and slanted rock bedding, climbing opportunities run the gamut from Class 1 hikes to Class 5 climbs on the Devils Tooth. Seven Devils peaks have a deceptive quality that often puts route-finding abilities to the test. Ledges appear and end in the most unlikely places, and chimneys that look very prominent are generally traps for the unwary. Climbing is a combination of slushing in talus, boulder-hopping, and climbing short, broken ledges. Technical climbing opportunities are limited by the loose rock that clutters every ledge, shelf, or ridge top. Using a rope for protection would, in most instances, invite rockfall which would more than likely destroy the rope or injure the climber.

Although there is no record of winter ascents in the Seven Devils, several groups have skied from snowline to Windy Saddle in March. The snowbound road is closed to snowmobiles, making this a relatively peaceful area, and the snow in the vicinity of the saddle is reported to be excellent. Winter access to the major peaks would be entirely dependent on snow conditions.

CRAIGS MOUNTAINS

This minor subrange is the northernmost extension of the Seven Devils Mountains. It is located west of Grangeville, where the Salmon and Snake Rivers join on the Idaho and Oregon border. The subrange, which is separated from the Seven Devils proper by the Salmon River, is named after Colonel William Craig. This country is more akin to a high plateau than a mountain range and contains only five named peaks, the highest of which is Craig Mountain at 5,341 feet. Much of the range is in private ownership, with the public lands administered by the Bureau of Land Management [Approach (A)(1)]. USGS Frye Point

Devils Tooth   7,760+ feet

This imposing andesite spire is located north of Sheep Lake in the Sheep Creek Drainage. Actually, there are two teeth (summits) separated by a narrow gap, the northernmost being the most formidable. The Tooth rises over 200 feet vertically on three sides, with the south face measuring about 100 feet. The southernmost summit is easily reached from the south via a short pitch of Class 3 climbing. The northern and highest summit is a technical climb. The peak is accessed from the

The Devils Tooth, as seen from the east

Seven Devils Loop Trail [Approach: (A)(3)(a)] or from Sheep Lake, which can be accessed via [Approach: (A)(3)(a.12)] or cross country from Windy Gap [Approach: (A)(3)(b)]. USGS He Devil 15-minute/HCW

North Face Route. *(Class 5)*

The Devils Tooth is almost 2,000 feet shorter than the neighboring peaks. However, what it lacks in altitude it makes up for by the perpendicular nature of its walls. The first ascent was made in 1963 by a group of Mazamas. After circling the tower and exploring a number of alternatives, the group attacked the north face, which they believed was the "easy way" up. Although they eventually encountered smooth hard andesite ranging from 65 degrees to overhanging in places, after five pitches and four terraces they reached the summit. First ascent by D. Eastman and J. Angell.

Tower of Babel   9,269 feet

This formidable peak is located 0.5 mile east of Sheep Lake. It is visible from Windy Gap, from which point it resembles the witche's castle in the Wizard of Oz. The first ascent was in June, 1939 by A. H. Marshall. According to Marshall, the route followed ledges which "made a complete spiral to reach the top." This spiral ramp reminded him of a picture of the Tower of Babel he had seen as a child; hence the name. Marshall called the climb the "most interesting climb I had ever made, bar none." Access the peak from Sheep Lake [Approach: (A)(3)(a.12)] or [Approach: (A)(3)(b)]. USGS He Devil 15-minute/HCW

The Marshall Ledges Route. *(Class 3)*

This route is not obvious. According to Marshall, the route begins at the southwest base of the peak and then circles around the peak, becoming steeper as it crosses the east face and climbs across a ledge to the north face, where it narrows, eventually reaching a rubble slope that leads to the summit. The Mazamas climbed the route in 1963 and described it as a broad 30-degree slope, covered with loose rock on the lower sections and with more solid rock above. According to the Mazamas, the route begins on the west face, then curves onto the south face, crosses the south ridge and moves on to the northeast face. At this point, the ridge narrows to one foot in width. From here, climb up on solid rock to a boulder field and then continue to the top.

South Ridge. *(Class 3)*

Climb to the col between Mount Baal and She Devil and traverse the east slopes of Baal toward the summit. The col can be reached from Sheep Lake or from Windy Saddle via the east side of the Loop Trail. Between Mount Baal and the Tower of Babel, you will encounter four towers as you approach the main summit along the ridge. Pass the first two towers on the east and then drop down about 100 feet on the west side of the third and fourth towers. Cross the talus to what appears, from a distance, to be a dead end corner. From this point, good ledges lead up the steep wall to the knife-edged notch above. Climb the boulder leaning against the north wall of the notch to reach the slanting slabs above. Follow the slabs up to and under the large overhanging roof to the talus slopes above. Climb loose rock from here to the summit.

Other Routes.
There are many routes on this peak. Three others include the North Ridge, the Northwest Chimney, and the West Face. These routes can be reached from either Sheep Lake or Mirror Lake by climbing up to the north ridge and gaining access to the upper tower walls from this point. All three of these routes involve difficult routefinding, loose rock, and the possibility of no retreat without rappelling.

Broken Column*
This unusual feature is located under an overhanging block on the south wall of the Tower of Babel. The 30-foot pillar is precariously perched under the overhang and on the edge of a cliff. It is unknown if this formation has ever been climbed, but it is worth a look.

Mount Baal* *9,040+ feet (Class 2)*
This peak, unnamed on the He Devil USGS quad, is located midway between She Devil and the Tower of Babel on the intervening ridge. A register in an old metal film container dates back to 1960. The date of the first ascent is unknown. The peak strikes an imposing west face above Sheep Lake, while its eastern slopes are far less impressive. The east and south slopes are easy scrambles and are accessed from Sheep Lake [Approach: (A)(3)(a.12)] or [Approach: (A)(3)(b)]. From Sheep Lake, climb the 1,200-foot scree gully which leads to the ridge between Mount Baal and She Devil, and then scramble up the south ridge to the summit. The west face is

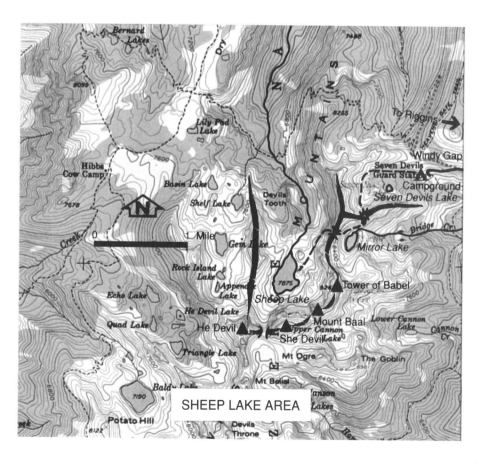

She Devil (left) and Mount Ogre, viewed from the summit of He Devil

probably unclimbed. USGS He Devil 15-minute/ HCW

She Devil *9,280+ feet*

She Devil is located 0.6 mile southwest of the Tower of Babel. It was first climbed by A. H. Marshall in June of 1940. Marshall named the peak Lucifer, as he had already attached the name She Devil to a peak farther to the south which was later named the Devils Throne by the USGS. Many routes have been tried on this peak; the two most popular routes are described here. Access the peak from Sheep Lake [Approach: (A)(3)(a.12)] or [Approach: (A)(3)(b)]. USGS He Devil 15-minute/HCW

Northeast Ridge Route. *(Class 2)*

This is the original route used by Marshall. Climb from Sheep Lake to the saddle northeast of the peak and then follow the northeast ridge to the summit. Stay high up on the northwest side of the ridge. This is a long but easy walk.

West Ridge. *(Class 3)*

This routes climbs up from the col between She Devil and He Devil. From the col, move up the south side of the west ridge to a large talus-filled gully which leads up to a point near the ridge crest where a number of rock walls of varying difficulty are encountered. Choose a route around or over the walls best suited to your ability and climb to the summit ridge, which you can follow to the top.

He Devil *9,393 feet*

He Devil, the highest Seven Devils summit, is located due west of She Devil and southwest of Sheep Lake. A. H. Marshall reached the summit in June, 1938. He found a piece of wood at the top with the following names carved on it: B. Savage, C. Brown, H. Barton and J. W. Ratcliff. (There was no date.) He Devil is an impressive dark tower with steep walls on all sides of its three summits. The north summit is the highest. Access the peak from FST-123 [Approach: (A)(3)(a.12)] or from Sheep Lake [Approach: (A)(3)(b)]. USGS He Devil 15-minute/HCW

Northwest Ridge Route. *(Class 2)*
The summit can be reached from the northwest ridge from either He Devil Lake or Gem Lake, or from the saddle above Sheep Lake. From either the saddle or the lakes, follow the relatively gentle slopes up to the ridge top; from there, hike to the summit along the ridge which splits the north and west faces of the peak. Although this route looks difficult from below, it is nothing more than a simple scramble.

East Ridge Route. *(Class 3)*
A more difficult route than the northwest ridge, this route leads up from the col between He Devil and She Devil. From the col, the route works across the ledges on the south side of the ridge to the base of the mountain. The route from here is somewhat obscure, but follows two connecting gullies to the summit. Be careful on the very rotten talus that fills these gullies.

Southeast Face. *(Class 4)*
The first ascent was made by the Mazamas in 1963. Climb the lower scree slopes to the lowest point on the face. Climb the face to the summit. The Mazamas used pitons for protection.

Mount Ogre   *9,200+ feet*

Mount Ogre is located 0.5 mile southeast of She Devil, east of the main Seven Devils crest. When Marshall reached the summit of She Devil in 1940, he spotted a large cairn on the top of the then-unnamed Mount Ogre. When he finally climbed the peak three years later by its west ridge, he found no record of who had made the first ascent and named the peak Mount Appollyon (a name not adopted by the USGS). The peak presents a massive 1200-foot northeast face to tiny Upper Canyon Lake. The peak is accessed from the Boise Trail section of the Seven Devils Loop Trail by hiking south from Windy Gap to either Cannon Creek (2.0 miles) or Hanson Creek (almost 4.0 miles) and then following one of these drainages to the base of the peak [Approach: (A)(3)(a.3)]. USGS He Devil 15-minute/HCW

West Ridge. *(Class 2)*
This ridge is accessed from the low saddle between Mount Ogre and She Devil. It is easily followed to the summit.

East Ridge. *(Class 3)*
From the saddle between the Orge and the Goblin, traverse to the southwest until a feasible route to the ridge top is visible. Climb to the ridge and follow it to the top.

North Face. *(Class 4)*
First ascent by the Mazamas. The route climbs the large central couloir and chimney system. The chimney is roofed by a chockstone. The route

begins by climbing a series of steps to reach the west wall of the couloir. Then a Class 4 crack is climbed to a sloping ledge which runs under an overhanging wall. From here, the route leads to a triangular snowfield in the couloir one third of the way up the face. Look for a smooth V-shaped crack with a tree at its top. The Mazamas climbed toward the tree until the leader could escape the crack, moving out onto the face where he found a "sheltered cleft." From this point, a number of options will lead to the top.

The Goblin   *8,981 feet (Class 2-3)*

The summit of this companion of Mount Ogre is located due east of Ogre on the same ridge line. The Goblin was first climbed from the Boise Trail section of the Seven Devils Loop Trail via its eastern slopes by A. H. Marshall and Ed Hughes in August 1935. Marshall gave the peak its name, attempting to stay with the original devilish theme

The Devils Throne, viewed from the summit of Mount Belial

given the range by local Native Americans. Views of the main crest to the west are spectacular. Although the peak may be approached from a number of directions, the recommended route to the summit is from Hanson Lake [Approach: (A)(3)(a.3)]. From the lake, climb southeast directly to the summit. USGS He Devil 15-minute/HCW

Mount Belial   *8,880 feet (Class 2)*
Mount Belial is located midway between He Devil and the Devils Throne on the main Seven Devils crest. The first ascent of this tri-summited peak probably belongs to A. H. Marshall, who in 1943 tentatively named the peak after Belial, a fallen rebel angel in Milton's *Paradise Lost*. The peak, while not imposing from a distance, possesses three very rugged summits and offers a multitude of mostly untested route possibilities. It is unknown whether the middle and north summits have been climbed.

Access the peak from either Hanson Creek in the east or via Triangle Lake in the west. Both of these approaches are accessed from the Seven Devils Loop Trail [Approach: (A)(3)(a)]. The south summit is the highest point, and is climbed via its southwest ridge (from the saddle between it and the Devils Throne), or via its east ridge. USGS He Devil 15-minute

Painted Peak*   *8,160+ feet (Class 3)*
Painted Peak is unnamed on the He Devil USGS quad. It is the crumbling summit located on a subsidiary ridge 1.0 mile west of Mount Belial and directly south and above Triangle Lake. The first reported ascent was by the Mazamas, who climbed it in 1963. Access the peak from the Seven Devils Loop Trail and Baldy Lake [Approach: (A)(3)(a.2)]. USGS He Devil 15-minute/HCW

Devils Throne   *9,280+ feet*
Relying on the advice of an old miner, A. H. Marshall climbed this peak in June of 1938, believing it to be She Devil—which it may have been called in 1938, before the USGS printed the official maps. The peak is located 1.0 mile due south of He Devil on the main crest and has an impressive summit buttressed by three ridges. Marshall climbed the west ridge and left a register on the summit. Access is from the Seven Devils Loop Trail and Baldy Lake in the west [Approach: (A)(3)(a.2)] or via the cirque on the peak's northeast side [Approach: (A)(3)(a.3)]. USGS He Devil 15-minute/HCW

West Ridge.   *(Rating Unknown)*
The details of Marshall's original route are unknown. The ridge is a ragged conglomeration of towers and blocks, which will present some route-finding difficulties. It looks to be difficult Class 3 terrain.

Northeast Face.   *(Class 4)*
The route follows a steep gully on the right side of the face. This gully runs 500 feet to the top of the north ridge. The Mazamas climbed the gully for 300 feet, where they discovered a second gully heading up to the left to the east ridge. The Mazamas took this gully to the east ridge, which led to the summit. The first ascent was led by D. Eastman in 1963.

Southwest Boulder Field.   *(Class 3)*
This reportedly is the easiest way to the summit (if you like loose rock). From Baldy Lake, hike into the cirque on the peak's southwest side and climb southeast until the slope steepens noticeably. From this point, turn northeast and climb to the ridge top just south of the summit and follow the ridge to the top.

Twin Imps   *9,240+ feet*
This twin-summited peak is located 0.7 mile south of the Devils Throne. The first ascent of the higher north summit was by a Mazama group in 1963. The first ascent of the southern summit was by (who else?) A. H. Marshall on June 20, 1938, the same day he made the first ascent of Devils Throne. The peak's base can be reached from the west [Approach: (A)(3)(a.2)] and probably from Dog Lake on the range's east side. To reach Dog Lake, follow the Boise section of the Seven Devils Loop Trail south from Windy Gap for 5.2 miles to where it crosses Dog Creek. Leave the trail and hike up the drainage for 1.0 mile to the lake [Approach: (A)(3)(a.3)]. USGS He Devil 15-minute/HCW

South Peak.   *(Class 3)*
Climb from the saddle between the two summits. Approach from the east via a ledge system.

North Peak.   *(Class 5)*
The Mazamas climbed this summit via its northeast arete. Approach from the northeast across a mostly-talus slope (through scattered trees) to the wall above. Follow a ledge that leads onto the north face. At the beginning of the ledge, take a crack system which leads 100 feet up to a second ledge which is on the crest of the arete. At this point, the crest is blocked by a large tower and it is necessary to descend 30 feet down a gully on the south side of the arete. Move out onto the arete's south face and slide around a "bulging rock." A V-shaped gully should be visible—climb this gully to the crest above the tower. The route from here follows the crest, switching from side to side.

Granite Mountain *8,015 feet (Class 2)*
This tree-covered peak is located 1.75 miles directly west of Horse Heaven Lookout. The summit is easily reached by following the connecting ridge west from the lookout to the summit. Access the lookout from the north via the Seven Devils Loop Trail [Approach: (A)(3)(a.2)] or [Approach: (A)(3)(a.3)] and from the south via the Horse Heaven Lookout Trail [Approach: (A)(5)(a)]. USGS He Devil 15-minute

Cliff Mountain *7,384 feet (Class 2)*
Cliff Mountain is situated 1.5 miles southwest of Granite Peak. This peak has little appeal other than the fact that it is an outstanding and remote location to view spectacular Hells Canyon as few people ever see it. Approach from Black Lake CG via FST-218/FST-216 by hiking to Oxbow Saddle. From the saddle, hike FST-311 north to Oxbow Spring and then continue north to the summit ridge and follow it to the top [Approach: (A)(5)(a.1)]. USGS He Devil 15-minute

Jackley Mountain *8,747 feet (Class 2)*
Jackley Mountain is located 3.0 miles southeast of Horse Heaven Lookout and is a former lookout site itself. The summit is reached by an easy scramble up the peak's south ridge from Holbrook Saddle which is crossed by FST-191 [Approach: (A)(5)(b)]. USGS Cuprum 15-minute

Monument Peak *8,957 feet (Class 2)*
Monument Peak sits 2.0 miles southwest of Jackley Peak and directly north of Crystal Lake. The peak is the most formidable summit in the southern Seven Devils and route-finding on its slopes can be tricky. Reach this peak from FST-214 which passes by its western side [Approach: (A)(5)(a)]. Leave the trail 1.0 mile north of Emerald Lake and climb into the gully that leads to the saddle south of the summit. Once in the gully, you will eventually arrive at a headwall. Turn due north at this point and climb up, aiming for a point just west of and 100 feet below the summit. Look for a chute that leads to the summit. USGS Cuprum 15-minute

Smith Mountain *8,005 feet (Class 1)*
Smith Mountain is located 3.5 miles south of Black Lake and just east of FS-112, which passes within 300 vertical feet of the summit. This mountain was named after an early prospector, Crazyhorse Smith. The summit is reached by a short trail from the road [Approach: (A)(5)]. USGS Cuprum 15-minute

APPROACHES TO THE SEVEN DEVILS MOUNTAINS

Approach routes for this section are identified in the text by bracketed entries [Approach:], which include appropriate letter and number references.

(A) US-95 Access Points.
US-95 provides primary access to much of the Seven Devils as it runs between the Idaho towns of Council, New Meadows, Riggins and Cottonwood. (All of these towns can provide gas, food and lodging.) The entries below are listed from north to south.

(1) Craigs Mountains Access. Access is via backroads from either Cottonwood or Lewiston. A secondary road connects these two towns with Soldier Meadow Reservoir, which is located roughly midway along the route. In the north, leave Lewiston on County Road P2 and drive east to the Waha Road, which runs south through Waha to Cottonwood. From US-95 at Cottonwood, drive west from town toward Waha. From the Waha road, several feeder roads provide access to the heart of the Craigs Mountains. Check with the Bureau of Land Management's Cottonwood Office regarding current road conditions before making a trip into this area. There are no designated trails in the Craigs Mountains.

(2) FST-493, Pittsburg Landing Road. This approach point is used by those wishing to approach the range from the west. It is the longest and most difficult access route in the Seven Devils country. From the White Bird junction on US-95, drive south for 1.5 miles and then turn west on the road (signed Hammer Creek Recreation Area) that follows the Salmon River downstream. At 1.5 miles, a bridge crosses the river. Cross the bridge and turn left on the Deer Creek Road. From this point on, there are a lot of minor feeder roads, but the main road was well marked in 1988 and is scheduled for improvement in 1990. This road climbs over a high saddle, but is often passable throughout the winter to 4WDs.

(a) FST-102, Snake River Trail. This trail leaves Pittsburg Landing and follows the Snake River south for 29.0 miles to the Hells Canyon Dam. The trail provides important early season access to the western slopes of the Seven Devils. FST-57 and FST-112 lead from the river to the Seven Devils high country.

(3) FST-517, Windy Gap and Heavens Gate Lookout Road. This is the major approach point to the high peaks. Take US-95 1.0 mile south of Riggins and turn west onto the Squaw Creek

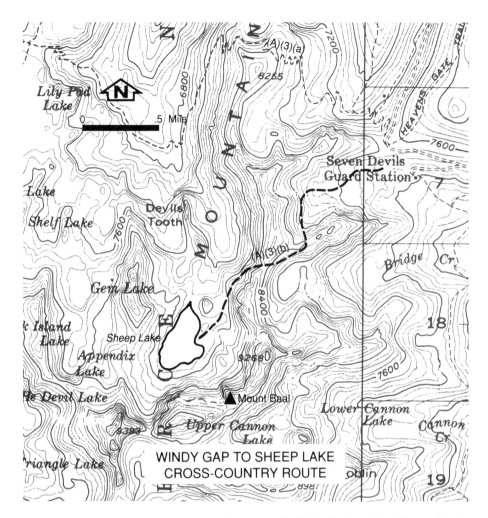

WINDY GAP TO SHEEP LAKE
CROSS-COUNTRY ROUTE

Road. The steep gravel road winds for 17.0 miles until it reaches Windy Gap; Heavens Gate is another 2.0 miles farther along the road. There are camping sites and some trail information at Windy Gap.

(a) FST-112/FST-56/FST-101, Seven Devils Loop Trail. A loop trail leaves from the saddle and circles the major peaks in 27.0 miles of hiking. Side and feeder trails lead to many of the high mountain lakes and provide access to the bases of most peaks. The trail is broken into three main sections, which are listed below under (a.1), (a.2) and (a.3).

(a.1) FST-112, Windy Gap to Snake River Trail. This trail, in part, forms the northern section of the Seven Devils Loop Trail as it traverses around the high peaks section of the range, leading 7.2 miles from Windy Gap to Hibbs Cow Camp. From Hibbs Cow Camp, the trail descends

a total of 13.5 miles along Little Granite Creek to the Snake River and FST-102 [Approach: (A)(2)(a)].

(a.11) FST-57, Dry Diggins Trail. This trail leads west from FST-112 to Dry Diggins Lookout, which is a total of 8.2 miles from Windy Gap.

(a.12) FST-123, Sheep Lake Trail. Sheep Lake is the primary destination for mountaineers. It is is accessed by following the Seven Devils Loop Trail west from Windy Gap to Dry Diggins Ridge. Turn south on the ridge and hike about 0.5 mile to the FST-123 junction. From Windy Gap, it is a little over 8.9 very long miles to Sheep Lake. Note that this trail is shown on the Nez Perce National Forest map, but not on the He Devil USGS quad. The route can be shortened by leaving the main trail at 3.5 miles from Windy Gap (where the trail crosses Sheep Creek) and hiking cross country up the west side of the Devils Tooth to Sheep Lake. This is a strenuous route that most will find difficult.

(a.2) FST-56, West Side Trail. This trail begins along the Snake River, climbs steeply to Dry Diggins Lookout, and then turns south to junction with FST-112. From this junction, the trail becomes part of the Seven Devils Loop Trail as it runs from Dry Diggins 6.5 miles south to Horse Heaven Lookout.

(a.3) FST-101, Boise Trail. This is the final 12.2-mile link in the Seven Devils Loop Trail, connecting Horse Heaven Lookout to Windy Gap. This trail provides access to all of the major east-facing valleys along the Seven Devils high country, from Tower of Babel south to the Twin Imps. Fishermen's trails lead to both Hanson and Dog Lakes. To reach Hanson Lakes from the Boise Trail, leave the trail where it crosses Hanson Creek and then stay on the creek's north side. Watch your footing and look for a poorly defined trail. The trail to Dog Lake leaves the Boise Trail on the south side of Dog Creek, but soon crosses back to the north side. This trail is sketchy in places, but passable.

(a.31) Lower Cannon Lake Trail. This trail is not shown on the Nez Perce National Forest map, but is nevertheless well marked where it leaves the Boise Trail at Cannon Creek. The trail quickly climbs to the lake at the base of The Goblin. Total distance from Windy Gap is 4.0 miles.

(b) Goat Pass Cross-country Route. Goat Pass is the second way into Sheep Lake from Windy Gap. This route is not marked on the USGS He Devil quad. In just 2.0 short miles you will traverse from Windy Gap to Sheep Lake across two high saddles and a spectacular ledge. From the trailhead parking lot, follow the gravel road south to the lower campground. Keep right where the road forks in the campground and follow this fork to the first campsite after the second set of restrooms. The cross-country trail starts from here. A short way into the trees, there is a bulletin board marking the beginning of the trail. The trail is in good condition and easy to follow for the most part.

The trail climbs out of the trees and up to the saddle on the ridge separating the Seven Devils Lake basin and the Mirror Lake basin. There are two spots along this section of the route that are steep and somewhat exposed, which will cause some people to pause and think about the wisdom of going on. After crossing the first saddle, the trail traverses to Goat Pass (0.25 mile west of Mirror Lake) along fairly stable slopes. From Goat Pass, the route drops to the west side of the ridge, where it traverses down to Sheep Lake, passing several spectacular viewpoints of the Devils Tooth. The last section of the trail descends along an exciting

ledge which clings to a vertical cliff. The route, while generally easy to follow, is a cross-country route—it can be dangerous and should only be used by the experienced.

Goat Pass is unnamed on the He Devil USGS quad, but apparently it, and this route, were identified on older Forest Service maps. The trail has occasionally been subject to trail maintenance efforts in the past, but today the management policy is apparently to leave the route for the adventurous only.

(4) FS-2114, Rapid River Road. The central portion of the range can be reached from the Rapid River Trail system. Take US-95 south of Riggins for 3.5 miles to the Rapid River Road and turn west. Follow the Rapid River road for 3.0 miles to its end at a fish hatchery.

(a) Rapid River Trails. From the end of the Rapid River Road, an extensive trail system follows the drainage's many twists and turns. These trails begin at 2,200 feet and can be accessed as early in the year as March. These trails also approach the Seven Devils high country, for those who want to climb the peaks the old fashioned way—from the valley floor.

(5) Southern Seven Devils Access. The south end of the range is heavily roaded due to extensive mining activity in the past. Access to this area begins at Council, Idaho via FS-002, the Hornet Creek Road. Turn west at the city park in Council (where US-93 makes a 90-degree turn) and follow the signs to the village of Bear. (Bear junction is 31.0 miles from Council.) At Bear, the road forks. FS-002 is the left fork, which leads west toward Hells Canyon. Continue on the right fork, FS-105, through Bear for 4.9 miles and turn right onto the Black Lake Road (which, of course, leads to Black Lake). A Forest Service map is essential in reaching this destination; also, be advised that this road is usually not clear of snow until the middle of July. A 4WD is recommended.

(a) FST-214, Horse Heaven Trail. FST-214 is the most important of the trails which are accessed from the Black Lake area. It can be followed north past Emerald Lake to Horse Heaven Lookout where it joins the Seven Devils Loop Trail in 8.0 miles. See [Approach: (A)(3)(a)], above.

(a.1) FST-218/FST-216, Oxbow Saddle Trail. These two trails form a loop on the west side of FST-214. FST-218 leaves FST-214 in Horse Pasture Basin and runs west to Six Lake Basin in 5.0 miles. The trail continues west, past the lakes, and joins FST-216 and FST-217. FST-217 descends to Deep Creek and the Snake River. FST-216 runs northeast to Oxbow Saddle and then continues west to rejoin FST-214.

(b) FST-191, Holbrook Saddle Trail. FST-

191 leaves FS-002 just east of Black Lake and follows an indirect course north to Holbrook Saddle in about 4.0 miles. From the saddle, the trail drops into the West Fork of the Rapid River, where it junctions with FST-113. FST-113 descends along Rapid River and meets FST-192 and FST-194, both of which connect with FST-214 [Approach: (A)(5)(a)] to the west.

> **(b.1) FST-189, Ruth Lake Trail.** This trail runs between FST-191 and FST-214 in 4.0 miles. Midway along the trail, a short feeder trail provides access to Ruth Lake.

2. The West Mountains

The West Mountains are separated from the Salmon River Mountains by the Little Salmon River and the North Fork of the Payette River. The range forms a long narrow chain of mountains, which run from New Meadows in the north 75 miles to a southern terminus near Horseshoe Bend. The range varies in width from 10 to 15 miles. The towns of New Meadows, McCall, Cascade and Banks are found along the range's eastern edge; Council is located in the west.

Geologically, the West Mountains form a meeting ground between the Idaho Batholith and the Island Arc structures of the Seven Devils, Cuddy and Hitt mountains to the west. Fault blocking has lifted the range to 8,322 feet on Snowbank Mountain and has formed a crest which consistently stays above 7,000 feet. While the range is heavily forested along its lower slopes, the highest peaks are above timberline and large meadows dot the crest.

The range is managed by the Payette National Forest in the north and the Boise National Forest in the south. The State of Idaho controls a number of sections throughout the range; there are also a few major private holdings within the national forest boundaries. The FAA operates a large radar facility on Snowbank Mountain.

Though the West Mountains are not well known and see little use by hikers and climbers, the exceptionally good Snowbank Mountain Road (which is maintained to provide access to the FAA radar facility) provides quick access to a beautiful high country. Along the crest, several West Mountains peaks and several high-altitude lakes provide interesting destinations for hikers. Climbing is limited to Class 1 and Class 2 walks, with Council and Tripod peaks the most popular destinations. Additionally, between Tripod and Snowbank Mountain a number of small granite faces are available for rock climbers.

Council Mountain *8,126 feet (Class 2)*
Council Mountain is located 8.0 miles east of Council, Idaho, at the north end of the range. At one time, a lookout stood near the summit of this bald-headed summit. Today, the old lookout site can be reached by a number of trails of varying lengths and conditions. Approach the summit from FST-198 [Approach: (A)(2)(e)] as it traverses the northern and eastern slopes of the peak. It is an easy scramble to the top from almost any point along this trail. USGS Council 15-minute

Lookout Peak *7,813 feet (Class 2)*
Lookout Peak is located directly east of Cascade, Idaho, and roughly 6.0 miles north of Snowbank Mountain along the main West Mountains crest. The peak is reached by trail via FST-133, which is accessed from either the Snowbank Mountain Road in the south [Approach: (A)(5)(f)] or the Big Flat Road in the north [Approach: (A)(4)(a)]. The trail across the crest is listed as a jeep trail on the USGS quad, but is now closed to vehicles. Follow the trail to its highest point on the peak's western slopes and then scramble to the top. USGS Cascade 15-minute

Wilson Peak *7,865 feet (Class 2)*
Wilson Peak is a minor summit located 1.5 miles northwest of Snowbank Mountain and west of the main West Mountains divide. Hike to the peak from the Snowbank Mountain Road via trail FST-135 [Approach: (A)(5)(e)], which crosses over the peak's southern shoulder. Once on the peak, climb up its gentle south slopes. USGS Smiths Ferry 15-minute

Snowbank Mountain *8,322 feet*
The summit of this, the highest peak in the West Mountains, is occupied by a large FAA radar dome which is clearly visible from ID-55 south of Cascade. The summit of Snowbank forms a large flat plateau with east and west high points. The western summit is crowned by the radar dome; the eastern summit (also reached by road) has a small radio transmission facility. The summit is reached by FS-446 [Approach: (A)(5)]. It is roughly 8.0 miles to the summit from ID-55. USGS Smiths Ferry 15-minute

Gabes Peak *7,655 feet (Class 2)*
Gabes Peak is located 2.0 miles south of Wilson Peak and almost due west of Granite Peak. The summit is clearly visible from the Snowbank Mountain Road, since it sits to the west of the road, across a large meadow. A small lake known as Gabe's Bathtub sits northwest of the summit. Climb Gabes Peak from the Snowbank Mountain Road via trail FST-136, which leads nearly to the

Tripod Peak is the most dominant peak in the southern stretches of the West Mountains.

summit [Approach: (A)(5)(b)]. USGS Smiths Ferry 15-minute

Granite Peak *8,273 feet (Class 2)*
Granite Peak sits on the West Mountains crest 1.0 mile due south of Snowbank Mountain. This summit is a five-minute walk from FS-446 [Approach: (A)(5)], the Snowbank Mountain Road. Park on the pass just south of the summit and walk up the south ridge to the summit. USGS Smiths Ferry 15-minute

Tripod Peak *8,086 feet (Class 2)*
This is the premier summit in the southern section of the range. The view from the lookout tower is expansive and the walk to the summit threads through a beautiful mix of forest and meadow. The summit is reached by FST-131 from the Snowbank Mountain Road [Approach: (A)(5)(d)]. The hike to the summit takes in about 5.0 miles of the West Mountains crest. USGS Smiths Ferry 15-minute

APPROACHES TO THE WEST MOUNTAINS

Approach routes for this section are identified in the text by bracketed entries [Approach:], which include appropriate letter and number references.

(A) East Side Access.
Primary approach to the east side of the West Mountains is via ID-55, which runs between Banks and New Meadows.
(1) FS-422, Cascade Reservoir Road. This road follows the west shore of Cascade Reservoir from north to south. Access the road from ID-55 at either Donnelly or Cascade. From Cascade, drive west at a signed junction at the north end of town to the reservoir, and then follow the road around the south end of the reservoir to FS-422. From Donnelly, drive due west for 1.6 miles, turn south and drive 1.0 mile, then turn west and drive to FS-422 in about 1.5 miles.

(2) FS-186, Middle Fork Weiser River Road. This road leaves FS-422 from the north end of Cascade Reservoir and runs north, then west, then south and finally west to US-93 5.0 miles south of Council.

(a) FST-206, Crest Trail. FST-206 leaves FS-186 at No Business Saddle and follows the West Mountains crest south to FS-435.

(b) FST-210, Granite Creek Trail. This trail is accessed from FS-186 just south of its junction with FS-245. The trail leads due east toward the ridge north of Council Mountain, reaching FST-201 in 3.75 miles.

(c) FST-205, Crystal Creek Trail. FST-205 follows the Crystal Creek drainage east to the southern slopes of Council Mountain, where it joins FST-198, which continues on to the northwest, where it joins FST-201 and FST-203. To reach the trail, follow FS-186 south from No Business Saddle for about 5.25 miles.

(d) FST-203, Warm Springs Creek Trail. This trail is accessed from FS-186 1.5 miles east of Cabin Creek CG. The trail begins by following Warm Springs Creek north and then climbs a ridge line and proceeds due north to a junction with FS-198 in roughly 8.5 miles.

(e) FST-198, Council Crest Trail. This trail runs along the top of the Council Mountain crest for roughly 6.0 miles. It connects the five trails which approach Council Mountain from the north, south and east.

(3) FS-245/FS-172, East Fork Weiser River Road. This road is accessed from FS-186 west of No Business Saddle, where No Business Creek meets the Middle Fork of the Weiser River. Turn north on FS-245 and follow it for 5.0 miles to a junction; turn left onto FS-185, which cuts west to the East Fork and FS-172. (This cutoff section is not advised in wet weather.)

(a) FST-201, East Fork Trail. This trail leaves FS-172 where it switchbacks out of the East Fork drainage. Turn on the old logging road that follows the river south and take it until it becomes too rough for your vehicle (or ends—whichever comes first). The trail follows the river drainage south and eventually joins FST-198 [Approach: (A)(2)(e)] north of Council Mountain.

(3.1) FS-486, Dewey Creek Road. This road leaves FS-172 where Dewey Creek flows into the East Fork, and then follows the drainage south. After a couple of miles, the road turns west and leaves the drainage to follow a ridge to Cold Spring Summit.

(a) FST-213, Cold Spring Summit Trail. FST-213 is accessed where FS-487 crosses Cold Spring Summit. From the pass, the trail runs due south until it unites with FST-198 [Approach: (A)(2)(e)] and FST-201 [Approach: (A)(3)(a)]

about 2.0 miles north of Council Mountain.

(4) FST-435/FST-835/FST-206, Big Flat Road. This road leaves FS-422 on the west side of Cascade Reservoir just north of the Cambell Creek CG turn. The road climbs up to the West Mountains crest in 6.0 miles and then drops down to the west into Anderson Creek. The road follows Anderson Creek south to the Little Weiser River, and then follows the Little Weiser west to US-93.

(a) FST-206, Crest Trail South. This trail leaves the Big Flat Road at the top of the West Mountains crest. This trail runs both north and south from FS-206. Park at the pass. The trail runs north along the crest for 15.0 miles to FS-186 [Approach: (A)(1)] at No Business Saddle and south to the Snowbank Mountain Road [Approach: (A)(5)] in 11.0 miles.

(5) FS-446, Snowbank Mountain Road. This road provides quick access to the crest of the West Mountains and the summit of Snowbank Mountain. Turn west to Cabartron off ID-55 at the Clear Creek store 8.0 miles south of Cascade. Follow the paved road west until it abuts the base of the mountains. The paved road turns north, crosses a bridge and, shortly thereafter, FS-435 begins. This exceptional gravel road is steep, but passable to passenger autos.

(a) FST-119, Blue Lake Trail. This 1.0-mile trail leaves FS-446 just before that road crosses the crest and runs to Blue Lake. It is possible to go cross country from the lake to FST-131 by traversing around to the south side of the lake and climbing to the saddle 0.5 mile south of the lake. This route is rated at Class 2 and requires the use of a topo map.

(b) FST-136, Gabes Peak Trail. This trail leaves FS-446 after it crosses the West Mountains crest and turns north. The trail begins as an old road and runs due west across a large meadow toward Gabes Peak, which is less than 2.0 miles from the road. From the peak, the trail continues to the south, where it joins FS-653 north of Sage Hen Reservoir.

(d) FST-131, West Mountain Trail. This trail is accessed from the Gabes Creek Trail a short distance west of FS-446. It runs north and south between Squaw Creek and Little Sage Hen Basin (east of Sage Hen Reservoir). (See [Approach: (A)(6)(a)] below for more details.) Approximately 3.0 miles south of its junction with FST-136, a short side trail leaves FST-131 and climbs to the top of Tripod Peak in 0.25 mile. This side trail is faint in places, washed out in others, but still relatively easy to follow. When in doubt, just go up!

(e) FST-135, Wilson Peak Trail. This trail forks off of FST-131 about 1.0 mile north of that trail's junction with FST-136. From where it leaves

FST-131, the trail proceeds due north toward Wilson Peak and then descends to the southwest to Squaw Creek.

(f) FST-133, Crest Trail. This trail leaves FS-446 at Snowbank Mountain and proceeds north along the crest to FS-206 in 11.0 miles. The trail leaves FS-446 as an old roadway, which is only signed to say that it is closed to motor vehicles. Note also that this trail is misidentified as the Wilson Creek Trail on the Boise National Forest map.

(6) FS-644/FS-645/FS-626, Sage Hen Reservoir Road. Sage Hen Reservoir is accessed from ID-55 at Smiths Ferry. Leave ID-55, turning west, following FS-644 west and then north for roughly 3.5 miles to its junction with FS-626. Turn west on FS-626 and follow it to the reservoir. From the reservoir, a number of road options continue to the north, west and south and provide alternative access routes into the southern West Mountains.

(a) FST-131, Snowbank Mountain Trail. This trail leaves the Sage Hen Reservoir road west of Tripod Creek and runs north toward Tripod Peak. See [Approach: (A)(5)(d)] above for additional details.

(B) West Side Access.
Primary access is from US-93 between Cambridge and New Meadows.

(1) FS-172, East Fork Weiser River Road. This road leaves US-93 10.0 miles north of Council and follows the river into the mountains. See [Approach: (A)(3)] above for additional road and trail information.

(2) FS-186, Middle Fork Weiser River Road. This road leaves US-93 about 5.0 miles south of Council, just before the highway crosses the Middle Fork of the Weiser River. See [Approach: (A)(2)] above for road and trail information.

(3) FS-206/FS-435, Big Flat Road. This road is accessed from US-93 12.0 miles east of Cambridge. Turn off the highway onto the road which runs south through Indian Valley. Turn east onto FS-206 at the south end of Ben Ross Reservoir and follow this road to Big Flat CG. See [Approach: (A)(4)] above for more details.

3. The Cuddy and the Hitt Mountains

These two small mountain ranges are located north and west of US-93 as it runs between the Idaho towns of Weiser and Council. These ranges, which are physically connected, are geologically a continuation of the Seven Devils Mountains terrain and share that range's complex geologic history. The Cuddy Mountains, the northernmost

group, reach their highest point on Cuddy Mountain, which attains an elevation of 7,867 feet. The Hitt Mountains are located to the south and reach their highest point on Sturgill Peak, which is 7,589 feet.

Both ranges are managed by the Payette National Forest through its Council Ranger District. The State of Idaho owns large sections of land within the National Forest boundaries. Hiking and climbing opportunities are available, but seldom used. Climbing opportunities are limited to Class 1 and Class 2 walks.

Cuddy Mountain   *7,867 feet (Class 2)*
The highest point in the Cuddy Mountains is located 18.0 miles west of Council. Take ID-71 west from Cambridge to the Brownlee GS. From the GS, follow FS-044 until it splits. Continue up the creek bottom until the road ends and then follow the old trail for 3.5 miles to the summit [Approach: (A)(1.1)(a)]. USGS Copperfield 15-minute

Sturgill Peak   *7,589 feet*
The highest point in the Hitt Mountains is a fire lookout site with a road to the summit. The lookout and road were built in 1933 by the Civilian Conservation Corps. Currently the road has deteriorated and a 4WD is needed to reach the summit via the road. The road, which sees little use, makes a good hiking route to the summit [Approach: (B)(1)]. USGS Sturgill Peak 15-minute

Hitt Peak   *7,410 feet (Class 2)*
Hitt Peak is located 2.0 miles southeast of Sturgill Peak. The summit can be climbed from FST-276 [Approach: (B)(1.1)(a)], which crosses the saddle east of the peak. From the saddle, follow the ridge line north from the saddle to the summit.

APPROACHES TO THE CUDDY AND THE HITT MOUNTAINS

Approach routes for this section are identified in the text by bracketed entries [Approach:], which include appropriate letter and number references.

(A) Cuddy Mountain Access.
Primary access is via US-93. In addition to the roads listed in this guide, numerous other roads lead into the Cuddy Mountains.

(1) ID-71. This state highway leaves US-95 at Cambridge and crosses a pass between the Cuddy and Hitt mountains as it runs northwest to the Snake River and Oregon.

(1.1) FS-044, Brownlee Creek Road. This road leaves ID-71 where it crosses East Brownlee Creek and runs east to Brownlee CG. Just past the CG, the road forks. Follow the left hand fork until it ends.

(a) East Fork Brownlee Creek Trail. This trail leaves from the end of FS-044 and follows the drainage north to the ridge line north of Cuddy Mountain. Once on the ridge, the trail turns southeast and leads to the top of Cuddy Mountain. This trail is not well maintained.

(B) Hitt Mountain Access.
Primary access to this range is from US-95 and ID-71. In addition to the roads listed in this guide, numerous other roads lead into the Hitt Mountains.

(1) FS-009, Mann Creek Road. This road is accessed just north of Weiser. It leads north to the Mann Creek GS and eventually to the top of Sturgill Peak. Beyond Lower Spring Creek CG, the road requires a 4WD.

(1.1) FST-573, Hitt Creek Road. This road leaves FS-009 north of the Mann Creek GS and follows Hitt Creek north for 4.0 miles to FST-276.

(a) FST-276, Hitt Peak Trail. FST-276 leaves the end of the Hitt Creek Road and climbs to the eastern slopes of Hitt Peak in 3.25 miles. Beyond Hitt Peak, the road continues north to Sturgill Peak in another 2.0 miles.

4. The Salmon River Mountains

The Salmon River Mountains are the second largest of the Idaho Batholith mountain groups. They encompass an immense area in southcentral Idaho which includes two million acres of officially designated wilderness, hundreds of rugged summits, and scores of deep river canyons. These mountains are named for the Salmon River, which encircles nearly the entire range, forming its boundary from Riggins in the northwest, to Salmon in the northeast, to Challis in the southeast and finally to Stanley, halfway across the range's south boundary. From Stanley, the southern boundary is formed by the Sawtooth Mountains and then by the South Fork of the Payette River. The western margins are formed by the North Fork of the Payette and the Little Salmon rivers.

Salmon River terrain is characterized by its numerous drainage systems, which have formed a great natural maze in the Idaho Batholith. Elevations range from 1,400 feet at Riggins to over 10,400 feet on White Mountain. Abrupt 5,000-foot elevation changes are common throughout the range. Although the geology of this range is primarily the geology of the Idaho Batholith, the predominance of the batholith granite is spiced by a wide variety of overlying sedimentary and metamorphic strata and volcanic rocks. The oldest rocks in the area are found along Big Creek near Edwardsburg, where the quartzites, slates, and schists are of Precambrian age; the area west of Challis is composed of extensive deposits from the Challis Volcanics, which form the youngest Salmon River terrain. Five major ridge networks within the Salmon River Mountains have been singled out as subranges. They are the Bighorn Crags, the Yellow Jacket Mountains, the Lick Creek Range, the North Fork Range and the Grass Mountains.

Four national forests (Boise, Challis, Payette, and Salmon) administer sections of the Salmon River Mountains. The State of Idaho owns the majority of the North Fork subrange in the southwest corner of the Salmon River Mountains, as well as a number of scattered sections in other locations. The Forest Service manages nearly two million acres of these mountains as designated wilderness. In addition to the Frank Church-River of No Return Wilderness (RNRW), many more acres of the Salmon River country are currently under consideration for future wilderness designation.

Though it is never easy to have Congress declare an area a wilderness, the creation of the River of No Return is a casebook study of what can be accomplished when the right political ducks are lined up. The political history of the area started in 1930, when a group of prominent Idaho citizens led by former governor H.C. Baldridge encouraged the Forest Service to set the area aside and protect its natural and roadless condition. Remarkably, in April of 1931, the Idaho Primitive Area was established to protect over 1.2 million acres of public land. More remarkably, this "primitive area" status was maintained for many years—without strong environmental lobbying—against ever-growing pressures to open the area to logging and mining.

In the late 1970s, as mining and logging interests turned up the rhetoric, Congress (acting against all odds) established the present River of No Return Wilderness, not only protecting the original 1.2 million-acre "primitive area" but also tossing in another one million acres of surrounding mountains. This final victory in the battle required a Democratic congress, a senior U.S. Senator (Frank Church, who was a devout conservationist), a Secretary of Interior (Cecil Andrus, who was a former governor of Idaho and a staunch conservationist) and a Democratic president who just happened to have made a presidential float trip down the Middle Fork of the Salmon two years earlier. Beyond the luster of the big names, thousands of people worked to insure the establishment of a wilderness area that is almost too big to comprehend.

Access, hiking opportunities and climbing opportunities are almost unlimited in the Salmon River Mountains. In addition to an extensive road system, the Salmon River Mountains possess a number of public airstrips that allow quick access to many points—even within the RNRW. Though the River of No Return Wilderness is known throughout the nation, it is seldom crowded because the vastness of the wilderness can swallow up thousands of hikers. (Margaret Fuller's *Trails of the Frank Church-River of No Return Wilderness* is the definitive hiker's guide). Recreation opportunities beyond the RNRW are also virtually unlimited. While the region around McCall sees the most use from hikers and climbers, everywhere you go in the Salmon River Mountains you will find trails to hike and peaks to climb.

A. THE WESTERN SALMON RIVER MOUNTAINS

From the Salmon River south to the Payette River; from the Little Salmon and North Fork of the Payette rivers east to the South Fork of the Salmon and the Deadwood rivers

Patrick Butte   *8,841 feet (Class 2)*

Patrick Butte is located 8.5 miles southeast of Riggins, Idaho. Its summit is the highest peak in the northwest corner of the Salmon River Mountains and commands a stunning vista of the surrounding country. The summit is reached after a moderate scramble up the peak's southern slopes from FST-153 [Approach: (B)(1)(c.3)]. USGS Patrick Butte

Hershey Point   *8,232 feet (Class 1)*

This peak is located 4.0 miles due east of Patrick Butte, where it forms a high promontory above the Salmon River and serves as a lookout site for the Forest Service. The stunning view on the summit is reached after a Class 1 hike via FST-149 [Approach: (B)(1.1)(a)]. USGS Hershey Point

Sams Throne   *8,283 feet*
Lava Butte   *8,328 feet (Class 2)*

These twin summits are located in line due

south of Hershey Point on the same north/south ridge line. FST-152 is a poorly maintained trail which climbs to the saddle between the two peaks [Approach: (B)(1.1)(b)]. Climb Sams Throne from the saddle via its southern slopes; climb Lava Butte from the saddle via its northern slopes. USGS Hershey Point

Hard Butte   *8,695 feet (Class 1)*

Hard Butte is located almost 4.0 miles south of Patrick Butte above Rainbow Lake. The peak's rocky summit, which still holds the ruins of an abandoned fire lookout, is a Class 1 hike on a poorly maintained trail [Approach: (B)(1)(c.2)]. USGS Patrick Butte

Bruin Mountain   *8,767 feet (Class 2)*

Bruin Mountain sits directly east of the Hard Creek GS and above Upper Hazard Lake. The summit is easily reached by climbing its western slopes from the lake [Approach: (B)(1)(d)]. USGS Black Tip

Black Tip   *8,292 feet (Class 2)*

Black Tip sits at the head of eight drainages, northwest of Upper Payette Lake and 1.5 miles east of Fisher Creek Saddle. The peak is best accessed from either French Creek via FST-308 [Approach: (B)(2.1)(a)] or from Fisher Creek Saddle, which is reached by FS-281 [Approach: (B)(1.2)]. From Fisher Creek Saddle, the route traverses the ridge line east to the summit in roughly 1.5 miles. Though FST-308 leads to the summit, it is not well maintained—the ridge traverse from Fisher Creek Saddle is recommended because it is much shorter. USGS Black Tip

THE GRASS MOUNTAINS

The Grass Mountains are located northeast of New Meadows and east of US-93. They form the divide that parallels the highway from Goose Lake to Hazard Creek. This Salmon River Mountains subrange, which has no definite borders, encompasses a number of mountain lakes and bald ridge lines that offer scenic vistas and good hiking. Granite Mountain is this small subrange's highest peak at 8,478 feet.

Granite Peak   *8,478 feet (Class 1)*

The highest point in the Grass Mountains is located high above Twin Lakes and 2.0 miles west of Goose Lake. The summit is accessed by FST-165 from the east or the west [Approach: (B)(1)(a)]. USGS Brundage Mountain

THE LICK CREEK RANGE

Although the Lick Creek Range is the largest of the Salmon River Mountains subranges, its name is found on few maps and has not been adopted by the USGS. Nevertheless, this group of mountains forms a very impressive divide between the North Fork of the Payette and the South Fork of the Salmon rivers, running about 40 miles north to south. The highest Lick Creek peaks are clustered at the range's northern end; North Loon Peak, at 9,322 feet, takes the honors as the highest of the bunch. Of special interest is an area known as the Needles, which is a group of granite spires in the Gold Fork River drainage. Much of the Lick Creek Range is roadless and is recommended for wilderness designation. The southern section of the range is administered by the Boise National Forest. In the north, the Payette National Forest runs the show.

This area is better known for its hiking than its climbing opportunities. Although the climbing is not well publicized, it is also highly rated. While Nick Peak and Jughandle Mountain are the best known peaks in the range, another dozen peaks offer good goals for peakbaggers, and the Needles spires and Slick Rock offer technical climbing opportunities. Access is plentiful, but often requires high-clearance or 4WD vehicles.

Storm Peak   9,080+ feet (Class 2-3)

Storm Peak is located 4.5 miles east of Upper Payette Lake and 6.0 miles north of Lick Creek Summit (which is crossed by FH-21) [Approach: (B)(2)]. Although tree-covered, the peak features much exposed granite; a number of cliffs can block your way. The summit view of North and South Loon peaks is great. The mountain can be approached from either the lake or Lick Creek Summit. The shortest approach is from the lake via FST-085/315, which leads east to the Twenty-mile Lake basin [Approach: (B)(2)(a)]. Hike east on FST-315 to North Twentymile Lake. From the lake, climb northeast to the ridge line just east of the peak and then follow the ridge northwest to the summit. USGS Victor Peak

Victor Peak   8,718 feet (Class 2)

Victor Peak is located 2.0 miles northeast of Storm Peak on a very rugged connecting ridge line. No one has reported traversing the ridge between the two summits, but it should be possible, given enough time. Climb to the summit from Loon Lake [Approach: (B)(2)(b)] or [Approach: (B)(4)(c)] by leaving the trail at the center of the lake's western shore and climbing due west to the small, poorly defined ridge line above. Once on the ridge, turn south and climb to Point 6773 on the USGS map. From this point, the route

turns due west and climbs up a steep timbered slope to the summit, which is another 1.5 miles away and 2,000 feet above. USGS Victor Peak

North Loon Mountain   9,322 feet (Class 2)

The remote North Loon Mountain summit is situated 3.0 miles southeast of Storm Peak and northwest of Enos Lake, which is a popular destination for fishermen. The summit is most easily reached via the mountain's east ridge. Enos Lake is remote and not approached by trail, making the hike to the lake the most difficult part of the journey. To reach the lake, hike south from Loon Lake on FST-081 [Approach: (B)(2)(b)] or north from FH-21 on FST-081 [Approach: (B)(4)(c)] to the point where the trail crosses Enos Creek, and then follow the drainage southwest to the lake. From Enos Lake, at Point 7800 on the USGS quad, climb directly north to the top of the ridge and then follow the ridge west to the summit. USGS Enos Lake

South Loon Mountain   9,287 feet (Class 2)

South Loon Mountain is located directly south of North Loon Mountain and is by far the most impressive of the two peaks. While this peak can, like North Loon Mountain, be climbed from Enos Lake, the shortest approach is from FH-21 via FST-083 and 082 [Approach: (B)(4)(b.1)]. Hike from the road to Hum Lake. Just west of the lake, FST-083 switchbacks its way north to the ridge line above and then traverses northeast to Point 8056 on the southwest ridge of South Loon Mountain. Leave the trail at this point and climb the ridge line directly to the summit. USGS Box Lake

Beaverdam Peak   8,653 feet (Class 2-3)

This pyramid-shaped peak has a sharp north face and is composed of a light-colored granite. The peak is best approached from FH-48 [Approach: (B)(4)] by parking 1.5 miles above the FST-104 Snowslide Lake Trailhead. From this point, work your way cross country from the road and climb the southeast ridge to the summit. USGS Box Lake

Sawtooth Peak   8,875 feet

Sawtooth Peak is located 1.2 miles north of Snowslide Lake. Despite Sawtooth Peak's somewhat innocuous-looking south side, its north face is among the most impressive granite walls in Idaho, rising vertically for 600 feet. There are no reports of climbing attempts on the north face. USGS Fitsum Summit

South Ridge.   (Class 3)

The ridge begins at Snowslide Pass and rises 900 feet in 1.0 mile to the summit of Sawtooth

Peak. Take FST-104 from Snowslide Lake to reach the pass above and the base of the ridge [Approach: (B)(4)(a)]. The ridge is easy to follow at first, but eventually it narrows and the route is blocked in several spots by rock walls and pinnacles. Generally, bypass the first obstacles on the west side of the ridge and the later obstacles on the east side of the ridge. At times it is necessary to drop well below the ridge line to make the route go.

Snowslide Peak 8,522 feet

Snowslide Peak is located 3.0 miles southeast of Beaverdam Peak. While its vertical north face is clearly visible from FH-48 (as one descends from Lick Creek Summit towards McCall), it is one of Idaho's least-known summits. The view from the road is of Snowslide's extreme north face, which rises abruptly above Snowslide Lake, climbing over 1,400 feet in less than 0.5 mile. The last 700 feet of face are nearly vertical. USGS Fitsum Summit

Northwest Ridge. *(Class 3)*
Traverse around the east end of Snowslide Lake and climb up to the small pond above. (This involves traveling over very brushy terrain, but presents no real obstacles.) From the pond, go due south to the base of a prominent gully which cuts slightly southwest. Climb the gully until it ends at the base of several short, broken, tree-covered cliffs. Look for a steep shelf that cuts to the left (east) and use this to bypass the cliffs. Work around the cliffs to a small gully and then climb directly up to the ridge line above. Once on the ridge, it is possible to follow it northeast to the summit without too much difficulty. Obviously, route finding is the most difficult part of this climb. In all likelihood, a number of options besides the one described here exist. Whatever you do, keep off the cliffs directly below the summit, unless you are experienced with, and equipped for, high-angle rock climbing. Snowslide Lake is reached by following FST-104 east from FH-48 for 2.0 miles [Approach: (B)(4)(a)].

Northeast Ridge. *(Class 3)*
From Snowslide Lake, hike FST-104 to the pass above [Approach: (B)(4)(a)]. From the pass, follow the southeast side of the ridge line southwest to the summit. The route is straightforward for the first two thirds of its distance. The final third of the route involves a little more difficult route-finding and steeper climbing. Stay on the ridge line, if your skill level will allow it. Otherwise, traverse out onto the southeast slopes until you find a gully (several options exist) which appeals to you. Follow the gully to the ridge top.

Nick Peak 9,064 feet (Class 3)

Nick Peak is located 11.0 miles east of McCall and is one of the highest points in the Lick Creek Range. Though Nick Peak has attracted some interest from peakbaggers because its summit is visible from downtown McCall, the peak is not easily approached from any direction. The shortest approach to the summit is from Lake Fork CG on the peak's west side via FST-104 [Approach: (B)(4)(a)]. Follow this trail north until it crosses Idler Creek. This point is located directly below Fitsum Summit (Pass). Leave the trail and climb the steep, loose slope up to the pass. A second approach is via the peak's northwest side via FST-087 [Approach: (C)(2)(a)], which follows Fitsum Creek to Fitsum Summit. This route provides the easiest route to Fitsum Summit, but it too involves a very long hike. Once on Fitsum Summit, it is a relatively easy task to follow the ridge to the summit, which is 1.0 mile to the south and 800 feet higher. USGS Fitsum Peak

Boulder Mountain 8,377 feet (Class 1-2)

Boulder Peak is located 7.0 miles due east of the McCall Airport. At one time, the Forest Service maintained a short trail to the summit of this peak from FST-103, which crosses Boulder Pass just east of the peak. Although the summit trail is no longer an official trail, its remnants can be easily followed from Boulder Summit [Approach: (B)(7)(b)]. USGS Fitsum Summit

Twin Peaks 7,960+ feet (Class 2)

The small, rounded Twin Peak's summits are located between Boulder Lake and Jughandle Mountain. The south summit is the highest. The mountain, which is only 1.0 mile south of Boulder Lake, can be climbed from almost any direction, but is most often approached from Boulder Lake [Approach: (B)(7)(c)] via the old trail that crosses the peak's east slopes and south ridge on its way to Louie Lake. USGS Paddy Flat

Jughandle Mountain 8,340 feet

Jughandle is the big peak with a long north/south summit ridge that sits south of Boulder Lake. The peak's north face, like many Lick Creek Range mountains, is nearly vertical as it plunges down into Louie Lake. The mountain is a popular winter destination for McCall area cross-country skiers when snow conditions are good. USGS Paddy Flat

Louie Lake Route. *(Class 2)*
A jeep trail leads to Louie Lake from FS-403 [Approach: (B)(7)(a)]. Follow this trail to the lake, go around the west shoreline to the peak's northwest ridge and follow the ridge to the summit.

The west face of Buckhorn Peak, as seen from Boulder Lake

Northeast Ridge. *(Class 2)*
Approach this ridge from either Louie Lake or Boulder Lake [Approach: (B)(7)(a) or (c)]. The ridge provides a straightforward route to the summit.

Buckhorn Mountain *8,457 feet (Class 2)*
Buckhorn Mountain is located 1.7 miles due east of Boulder Lake. The pyramid-shaped peak is flanked by small lakes on its north, east and south sides. The peak is easily climbed from Buckhorn Summit and FST-96 [Approach: (B)(7)(b)] via its southeast ridge. From Buckhorn Summit (Pass), climb the tree-covered slopes to the north until the top of the ridge is reached. From this point, work along the mostly treeless ridge to the summit 0.5 mile to the northwest. USGS Paddy Flat

Rapid Peak *8,264 feet (Class 2)*
Rapid Peak is located 0.5 mile south of Buckhorn Mountain. Its summit sits just south and a little over 400 feet above Buckhorn Pass [Approach: (B)(7)(b)]. Leave the trail at the summit and climb the peak's north ridge to the summit. USGS Paddy Flat

Blackmare Peak *8,724 feet (Class 1)*
This lookout site is located 4.0 miles north of Square Top Mountain. FST-303 leads to the summit from the Cougar Creek Summit (Pass) which is accessed via FST-099 [Approach: (B)(8)(a)]. USGS Blackmare Peak

Square Top Mountain *8,681 feet (Class 2)*
Square Top Mountain is the distinctive summit located 2.25 miles northeast of the Needles. Access the peak from Kennally Creek CG and FST-101 [Approach: (B)(8)(b)], which leads to Needles Summit (Pass), which is located just north of the Needles. From the pass, follow seldom-maintained FST-303 north along the ridge to the second saddle above Blackmare Lake. From this point, climb over the high point just south of Square Top to reach the saddle due south of the peak. It is an easy walk from this saddle to the mountains's prominent top. This route is 7.0 miles from trailhead to summit. The peak can also be reached via a long scramble from Blackmare Lake. USGS Blackmare Peak

Needles Peak* *8,302 feet*
Needles Peak is located 2.25 miles south of Square Top Mountain and just south of Needles Summit (Pass) along the main Lick Creek crest. The peak is identified as "The Needles" on the Gold Fork USGS quad. This mountain would just be another hump-shaped mountain except that its summit is crowned by three impressive granite formations. The northernmost formation is a tepee-

Needles Peak Class 4 Route

The highest point on Needles Peak is climbed via an easy Class 4 route.

shaped spire, which is the peak's highest point, while the southern and middle formations are fin-shaped and slightly lower in elevation. Additionally, several other granite formations are found on Needles Peak's lower slopes. The most impressive of these is found 0.25 mile west of the summit. Apparently little or no technical climbing has taken place on Needle's granite, so there is only one route included in this guidebook. This should not deter rock climbers from investigating this area's potential. The granite, for the most part, is solid and clean and possesses a number of good faces and cracks which promise high quality one- or two-pitch climbing opportunities.

Access to the summit area is from either the north via Kennally Creek or the south from the Gold Fork trailhead. From the north, take FST-101 [Approach: (B)(8)(b)] to Needles Summit and then follow the western side of the Lick Creek divide to the south until the ridge crest can be reached. Follow the ridge to the summit area. From the south, near the Gold Fork trailhead

[Approach: (B)(9)(a)], it is possible to climb directly to the summit area via the peak's south ridge. USGS Gold Fork 15-minute

North Summit. *(Class 4)*
The north tepee-shaped spire rises+ 100 to 150 feet above the surrounding terrain and is climbed on its north side. Hike around the spire's east face to the small saddle on the spire's northeast corner. This saddle is located between the summit spire and a small granite formation 100 feet to the northeast. From this point, one can view the entire route as it follows a prominent crack system to the small notch on the summit's north side. From the base of the spire, scramble up the northeast corner until a wall blocks your way. Climb this wall on its left side, where it forms a 10-foot step with good holds. Once above the step, climb up a steep diagonal shelf to the northwest (to your right) to the base of a second wall (8 or 10 feet high), which is capped by a small pine tree. (Because this tree blocks the route, the move over this wall is more difficult than it might be.) Climb this wall directly up through the tree to the shelf above. From this point, follow the shelf back to the east for 10 feet and then climb over a boulder and into the diagonal gully that leads to the summit notch. Follow the gully up to the notch on constantly deteriorating rock. From the notch, climb around to the west side of the peak and stem up for 10 feet between the northernmost and middle summit blocks.

Stolle Peak* *7,563 feet (Class 1-2)*
Stolle Peak is located 5.0 miles southwest of Warm Lake and directly east of Stolle Meadows on the divide that separates the Middle Fork of the Payette River and the South Fork of the Salmon River. This peak is identified as the Cougar triangulation station on the Gold Fork USGS quad. The summit is formed by a granite outcropping that is adorned with the remains of an ancient fire lookout which once used the peak's commanding viewpoint to good advantage. The summit is nominally accessed by a very poor trail, FST-109, which according to the Forest Service map begins at the Stolle Meadows GS. Do not be fooled by the map—see the approach section below [Approach: (C)(2)(f)]. USGS Warm Lake 15-minute

Cougar Rock *(Grade I, YDS 5.8)*
Cougar Rock is the impressive granite dome that is located 1.0 mile north of Stolle Peak. The rock is accessed from the South Fork of the Salmon River near Stolle Meadows [Approach: (C)(2)(f)]. While little is known of the formation's climbing history, it is certain that the rock has been climbed at least three times. Although a walk around the base of the formation will provide views of many possible climbing lines, all three prior ascents

have apparently climbed the west face of the rock.
The two-pitch route, which leads up the west face, begins at the notch between Cougar Rock and a smaller formation on its west side. From the Cougar Rock trail, climb a 10-foot pitch into the notch and set up your belay. (You may also circle around the base of the smaller formation and approach the notch from the south.) From the notch, the route climbs the vertical west wall, following an obvious line up a thin flake and alongside a left-facing open book which overhangs slightly at its top. From the top of the flake, the route moves south (or to your right) into a narrow crack in the overhanging open book's wall. Jam up the crack and climb up onto the ledge above. Stand up on the narrow ledge and move left to its most exposed point. From this point, you must take one giant airy step to your left across the lower portion of the route to a good bucket-sized ledge, six to eight feet away. Once on the ledge, traverse out and around toward the north face for 10 to 15 feet to a small pine tree. (Note: do not drop down onto the more prominent ledge which is just below you.) Go by the tree to the base of a wide crack which leads directly up to a shelf in about 25 feet. The first pitch ends on this shelf.
The second pitch is shorter and less exposed. From the shelf, the route climbs due east, with good holds, for 25 feet up and over the wall that faces the shelf. Above this wall, the technical climbing ends at a medium-sized pine tree (a good rappel anchor for the descent). The final summit block is and easy scramble. The rappel from the tree to the notch will require two 165-foot ropes and a large sling for an anchor. USGS Gold Fork 15-minute

Rice Mountain *8,696 feet (Class 1)*
The long north/south summit of Rice Mountain was once a fire lookout site. The peak sits on a high ridge which separates the South Fork of the Salmon River from the Deadwood River 12.0 miles north of Deadwood Reservoir. The summit, which offers a good view of this region, is easily reached by three different trails. The preferred route utilizes the Switchback Trail, FST-009/102, to reach the summit from the Deadwood Reservoir Road [Approach: (C)(3)(a)]. USGS Warm Lake 15-minute

THE NORTH FORK RANGE
This minor Salmon River Mountains subrange is located in the extreme southwest corner of the Salmon River Mountains, above the confluence of the North Fork of the Payette River and the Payette River. ID-55 and the North Fork of the Payette River form the range's western boundary, while the Middle Fork of the Payette forms the

eastern boundary. The North Fork Range reaches 30 miles from north to south between Banks and Cascade. The maximum width of the range is 8 miles. The only named summits in the range are East Mountain, 7,752 feet (which is the highest point) and Packer John Mountain, 7,055 feet.

East Mountain *7,752 feet (Class 1)*
Located southeast of Cascade, the highest peak in the North Fork Range is accessed by both road and trail. The recommended route to the top (for truly addicted peakbaggers) is via FST-033/FST-100 [Approach: (D)(2)(a)], which begins at Boiling Springs GS and eventually reaches the summit after 10.0 long miles.

B. THE CENTRAL SALMON RIVER MOUNTAINS
From the South Fork of the Salmon River and the Deadwood River East to the Middle Fork of the Salmon River

---

Sheepeater Mountain *8,486 feet (Class 1)*
Sheepeater Mountain is located 7.0 miles south of the Salmon River and 7.0 miles west of Chamberlain Meadows in the northern section of the River of No Return Wilderness. This large peak, which sits above and west of Sheepeater Lake, is one of the most isolated mountains in the entire state. Reaching its summit will take most people several days of hiking. The peak is accessed from FST-003 [Approach: (B)(6.1)(g)], which crosses its summit. USGS Sheepeater / RNRW

Chicken Peak *8,600 feet (Class 1)*
Chicken Peak is located 7.0 miles southwest of Sheepeater Mountain. Its summit is the culmination of three long ridges (Mosquito Ridge, Horse Ridge and Sheepeater Ridge) and provides a fine view of the wilderness country to the northeast. Several Forest Service trails converge on the summit. The shortest approach is from the Werdenhoff Mine trailhead via FST-003 [Approach: (B)(6.1)(g)]. It is roughly 6.0 miles to the summit from the trailhead. USGS Chicken Peak / RNRW

Mosquito Peak *8,774 feet (Class 2)*
Mosquito Peak is a seldom-visited summit located 2.0 miles southeast of Chicken Peak and above Mosquito Lake. The peak can be accessed from FST-003 [Approach: (B)(6.1)(g)]. Leave the trail where it crosses the peak's southwest ridge

and follow the ridge line to the summit, which is about 1.0 mile to the northeast. USGS Mosquito Peak/ RNRW

Camel Peak *9,225 feet (Class 2)*
Camel Peak is located in the northeast corner of the RNRW and 5.5 miles southwest of Corn Creek CG on the main Salmon River. It is the first high summit along FST-168, the Black Peak Trail [Approach: (H)(3)(b)] and sits high over Basin Creek to the north. The summit is a short walk from trail. USGS Cottonwood Butte / RNRW

Cottonwood Butte *9,349 feet (Class 2)*
The peak is located 1.75 miles southwest of Camel Peak and east of Cold Meadows GS. FST-168 [Approach: (H)(3)(b)] provides access directly to the mountain's summit. USGS Cottonwood Butte

Farrow Mountain *8,992 feet (Class 2)*
Farrow is located 2.25 miles southwest of Cottonwood Butte along the route of FST-168 [Approach: (H)(3)(b)], which crosses its eastern slopes. Because the trail stays relatively high along the mountain's slopes, the summit is easily reached. USGS Cottonwood Butte / RNRW

Cold Mountain *8,084 feet (Class 1)*
This peak, with a lookout, is located north of Big Creek and directly north of Cold Meadows in the northern section of the River of No Return Wilderness. The Class 1 summit is reached by FST-043 [Approach: (B)(6.1)(e)]. USGS Vinegar Hill / RNRW

Wolf Fang Peak *9,007 feet (Class 2)*
Wolf Fang Peak is a rugged, triangular mountain located 2.0 miles north of Elk Summit (Pass) on FS-340 [Approach: (B)(6)]. The rocky summit juts out from a group of pinnacles and crags, called the Wolf's Fangs, on its east side. Although the name conjures up thoughts of steep, pointed spires, the Fangs are less impressive than you might imagine and only one of the metamorphic fangs might be of some interest to rock climbers.

Climb the peak from Elk Summit. From the highest point on the pass, a road leaves FS-340 and leads to the top of the 9,000-foot unnamed peak just north of the pass. Follow this road until it forks, on the north side of the unnamed peak. Take the left fork and park on the ridge top 100 yards ahead. From this point, follow the undulating ridge north for 1.5 miles to the summit. The ridge is broad and offers a decent tread for most of its distance. Once on the peak's south ridge, pick your route around a few small obstacles and keep to the center of the slope as much as possible.

Wolf Fang Peak, viewed from the south

USGS Wolf Fang Peak / RNRW

Mount Eldridge   *9,207 feet (Class 2)*
This is the prominent peak that sits directly southeast of Elk Summit (Pass) and FS-340 [Approach: (B)(6)]. Mount Eldridge is 3.0 miles due south of Wolf Fang Peak and 1.0 mile southeast of Elk Summit. Climb the peak from the pass via the connecting ridge. A good, but hard to find, game trail leads from Elk Summit directly to the low spot in the ridge due south of Elk Summit. If you cannot find this trail in the timber, climb to the high point southwest of the ridge over loose talus and then follow the connecting ridge to the Eldridge summit. USGS Wolf Fang Peak

Bismark Mountain   *8,128 feet (Class 2-3)*
This peak is situated 2.2 miles north of Big Creek. The mountain is accessed after a long hike from FST-009 [Approach: (B)(6.1)(a),(c) and (d)], which crosses its southeast and northeast ridge lines. Although the information is sketchy, the best route to the top utilizes the northeast ridge and may or may not involve Class 3 climbing. USGS Bismark Mountain / RNRW

Black Butte   *8,711 feet (Class 1-2)*
Black Butte is located 5.5 miles south of Farrow Mountain and 5.0 miles north of Big Creek.

At one time, a maintained Forest Service trail led to the top of this isolated mountain from near the junction of FST-168 and FS-044 [Approach: (H)(3)(b)]. Reportedly, the old trail can still be followed, but hikers should be prepared to follow the ridge line without the aid of a trail. USGS Papoose Peak / RNRW

Horse Mountain   *8,184 feet (Class 1)*
Horse Mountain is located 4.75 miles southwest of Black Butte. Its summit, which served as a fire lookout site at one time, rises steeply above Big Creek (gaining over 4,000 feet in less than 1.5 miles). The summit is accessible by FST-044 [Approach: (B)(6.1)(f)]. Like many peaks in the RNRW, its summit is a very long walk from anywhere. USGS Vinegar Hill / RNRW

Tail Holt Peak*   *7,769 feet (Class 1)*
Although not officially named by the USGS, this peak, which sits on the long north/south ridge line that divides the Secesh and South Fork Salmon River drainages, has been named Tail Holt by the Forest Service. The summit is accessed by a trail which begins near Ponderosa CG on FH-48, the Lick Creek Road [Approach: (B)(4)(d)]. It is roughly a 5.0-mile walk to the summit. USGS Williams Peak

Williams Peak   6,826 (Class 1)

The summit of Williams Peak is located east of the confluence of the South Fork of the Salmon River and the East Fork of the South Fork of the Salmon River. Though the summit is relatively low, its position commands an exceptional view, making it a perfect location for its Forest Service fire lookout. The summit is reached by trails from the north, east and south. The recommended route follows FST-073 from FH-48 [Approach: (B)(4)(e)] for 3.0 steep miles. USGS Williams Peak

Parks Peak   8,833 feet (Class 1)

This beautiful rocky summit anchors the western end of the Hidden Divide and forms the culmination of Rainbow Ridge. Because the summit once was the sight of a fire lookout, it can be reached by trail from the South Fork of the Salmon River. Take FST-069, the Parks Peak Trail, to the summit [Approach: (B)(4)(g)]. USGS Parks Peak

Profile Peak   8,965 feet

Profile Peak is a sharp, steep-walled peak at the top of the Logan Creek drainage east of Profile Gap. The peak, as well as Profile Gap and Wilson Peak, are named after Profile Sam Wilson, who prospected in the area during the early part of this century.

Profile Peak is not easily approached from any direction—climbing the peak will involve long, strenuous cross-country travel. USGS Profile Gap

Profile Gap Route. (Class 2)

Profile Peak may be climbed from Profile Gap in conjunction with Crater Peak, Wilson Peak and Big Creek Point. This route involves a long (4.0 miles one way) ridge walk with considerable ups and downs. Park on Profile Gap [Approach: (B)(6)] and climb to Point 8325 on the ridge line due west of the road. From this point, follow the ridge line south to the summit of Crater Peak, then turn west and follow the ridge over Point 8856. From the top of this unnamed peak, the ridge line swings northwest and leads over the summits of Wilson Peak, Big Creek Point and finally to the top of Profile Peak. Leave early and carry plenty of water.

Profile Lake Route. (Class 2-3)

Profile Lake sits 0.5 mile north of the summit of Profile Peak. FST-284 leads up the South Fork of Elk Creek to within 1.0 mile of the lake [Approach: (B)(6)(e)]. The last portions of the drainage are steep and not easily crossed. If you reach the lake, climb the slopes directly to the south towards the ridge line just west of the cliffs that form the final summit block. Once on the ridge, stay on the south side and hike to the top.

Big Creek Point   8,893 feet (Class 2)

This big rectangular summit sits west of Profile Gap between Profile Peak and Wilson Peak. The peak is climbed from Profile Gap. See the Profile Gap Route, listed under Profile Peak, for directions. The summit is 3.0 miles from Profile Gap. USGS Profile Gap

Wilson Peak   8,955 feet (Class 2)

Wilson Peak is located southeast of Profile Peak on the same ridge line. To reach the summit, which is a 2.0-mile ridge walk from Profile Gap, see the Profile Gap Route, listed under Profile Peak. USGS Profile Gap

Crater Peak   8,800+ feet (Class 2)

Crater Peak is a pointed, tree-covered summit located just west of Profile Gap and directly north of Crater Lake. The summit is 1.0 mile from Profile Gap. See the Profile Gap Route, listed under Profile Peak. USGS Profile Gap

Coin Mountain   8,994 feet (Class 2)

Coin Mountain forms the eastern wall of Profile Gap. The summit is located 1.5 miles southeast of Profile Gap and is reached via the tree-covered connecting ridge [Approach: (B)(6)]. USGS Profile Gap

Marble Mountain   9,128 feet (Class 2)

Marble Mountain is the big bulky mountain that sits east of the Big Creek GS. The summit is reached by a long but easy climb from the Cougar Basin Trail [Approach: (B)(6)(c)]. USGS Edwardsburg / RNRW

Cougar Peak   9,120 feet (Class 2)

Cougar Peak is located 5.0 miles east of Coin Mountain and sits up above pristine Cougar Basin in the Frank Church-River of No Return Wilderness Area. The peak is an easy scramble from the basin, which is reached from FS-340 [Approach: (B)(6)(c)]. (FS-340 begins just south of the Big Creek Work Center.) USGS Edwardsburg / RNRW

Pinnacles Peak*   9,273 feet (Class 3)

Pinnacles Peak is located northeast of Yellow Pine at the highest point of the Missouri Ridge above Profile Creek. This peak is identified as the "The Pinnacles" on the Edwardsburg USGS quad. Although the mountain is slightly less precipitous than its name implies, it is still the most rugged Salmon River Mountain in the entire area. The peak, which towers over the upper portion of the Missouri Creek drainage, consists of three rock towers. The middle tower is the highest and the northernmost is the most rugged. The peak can be climbed from either the unofficial Missouri Ridge Trail or from the small lake at the top of the Missouri Creek drainage. Both routes are long and at times steep. USGS Edwardsburg / RNRW

Missouri Ridge. *(Class 3)*
Take the Missouri Ridge Trail [Approach: (B)(6)(a)] to the top of the Missouri Ridge and follow the ridge line north to the summit, passing all obstacles on the east side of the ridge. At the final summit block, cross over onto the west side of the ridge to bypass the small tower that blocks the ridge and climb to the notch between the tower and the summit. Cross through the notch and traverse out onto the east face for 25 feet on the obvious ledge, and then climb straight up on good rock to the summit.

Missouri Creek Route. *(Class 3)*
Follow the Missouri Ridge Trail [Approach: (B)(6)(a)] until you reach a cabin where the trail crosses the creek. Leave the trail and, staying on the west side of the drainage, follow the creek up to the small lake below the west face of the peak. The forested terrain is difficult to pass through at first, but quickly opens up to allow fast progress to the upper basin. From the small lake, climb the gully that runs directly up to the notch on the south side of the summit. From this point, follow the directions for the final portion of the Missouri Ridge route.

Center Mountain *9,323 feet*
Snowslide Peak *9,104 feet (Class 2)*
Both of these summits are located northeast of Cougar Peak on the same ridge line. Both peaks are accessed from Cougar Basin and FST-065 [Approach: (B)(6)(c) and (d)], which is not signed and no longer receives regular maintenance. Follow the trail north from FST-004 where it crosses the pass northeast of Cougar Peak. The trail stays high above Snowslide and Little Marble Creek drainages as it climbs nearly to the top of Snowslide Peak in 3.3 miles and then continues on to the summit of Center Mountain in another 2.2 miles. USGS Center Mountain / RNRW

Lookout Mountain *8,680 feet (Class 1)*
Lookout Mountain is located 14.0 miles east of Pinnacles Peak and sits high above Monumental Creek. The mountain is the highest point on Lookout Mountain Ridge, which begins at the end of the Monumental Creek Road and runs north for many miles. Access to the top is via an 8.0-mile hike along FST-061 [Approach: (B)(5)(b)] from the nearest trailhead to the southeast. Although trails approach the summit from every direction,

only FST-061 provides a relatively short approach to the summit. USGS Monument / RNRW

Dave Lewis Peak *9,252 feet (Class 2)*
Dave Lewis Peak is located 7.0 miles northwest of the Bernard Creek GS on the Middle Fork of the Salmon River. This peak anchors the northeast end of the long divide which runs southwest to Shellrock Peak in a little over 8.0 miles and includes Mormon Mountain, Two Point Peak and Shell Rock Peak. The summit is reached by making an easy scramble from the saddle to the southwest, which is reached by FST-061 [Approach: (B)(5)(b)]. USGS Dave Lewis Peak / RNRW

Mormon Mountain *9,545 feet (Class 1)*
This domineering peak is located 3.25 miles southwest of Dave Lewis Peak. It overlooks the Middle Fork of the Salmon River and forms one of the highest and most remote uplands in the entire Frank Church-River of No Return Wilderness Area. The summit is accessed via FST-061 [Approach: (B)(5)(b)], a seldom-maintained trail that climbs out of Brush Creek to Two Point Mountain before turning north to cross Mormon Mountain. From Mormon Mountain, the trail follows the ridge line north to the saddle west of Dave Lewis Peak. USGS Mormon Mountain / RNRW

Two Point Mountain *9,426 feet (Class 2)*
Two Point Mountain is the rocky twin-summited peak located on the ridge that connects Shellrock Peak to Mormon Mountain. In the early 1920s, the peak served as a fire lookout site; but in the 1930s, it was replaced by a superior site located to the southwest on Shellrock Peak. Its summit is an easy scramble from the point where FST-061 crosses Bush Creek Summit [Approach: (B)(5)(b)]. USGS Shellrock Peak / RNRW

Shellrock Peak *9,435 feet (Class 2)*
Shellrock Peak served as a fire lookout for many years beginning in the 1930s; its summit still holds the ruins of the old lookout. When the lookout was in use, a trail was maintained to the top via the ridge line that runs north to Two Point Mountain. Since the lookout was abandoned, the trail has deteriorated, but the ridge line is passable and provides easy access to the summit [Approach: (B)(5)(b)]. USGS Shellrock Peak / RNRW

Rainbow Peak *9,325 feet (Class 2-3)*
Rainbow Peak is located 13.0 miles due east of Yellow Pine, Idaho. According to the miners who first visited this country in the 1800s, the peak's slopes are composed of many strata of rock that sparkle like a rainbow when the sun strikes them—hence the name. Climb Rainbow Peak from the

Monumental Creek Road FS-375, then follow Rainbow Creek to its upper reaches and climb the steep southeast slopes to the summit [Approach: (B)(5)]. USGS Rainbow Peak / RNRW

Log Mountain *9,179 feet (Class 1-2)*
Log Mountain, which sits midway between Yellow Pine and Warm Lake, is the highest point on the major north/south ridge that separates the South Fork of the Salmon River from Johnson Creek. The peak's summit once served as a fire lookout site and its tiny summit block still contains wood planks and rusty nails, remnants of the primitive hut that once served as a lookout tower. Log Mountain is reached via trail after hiking nearly 10.0 miles and gaining 5,000 feet in elevation from where Fourmile Creek dumps into the South Fork. The last portion of the trail is seldom maintained and consequently requires Class 2 skills [Approach: (C)(2)(c.1)]. USGS Log Mountain

Thunderbolt Mountain *8,652 feet (Class 1)*
This fire lookout site is located on a beautiful chunk of white granite on the high divide between the South Fork of the Salmon River and Johnson Creek, 6.0 miles south of Log Mountain. The summit can be accessed by trail from either Johnson Creek (the longer route) [Approach: (C)(4)(a)], or Cabin Creek [Approach: (C)(1.1)(a)]. The Johnson Creek route is recommended because it crosses more interesting terrain. USGS Warm Lake 15-minute

Morehead Mountain *8,506 feet (Class 1)*
Morehead Peak is located 11.0 miles southeast of Landmark in the Frank Church—River of No Return Wilderness. This peak, a fire lookout site which overlooks the Middle Fork, offers rewarding views into the wonderful Middle Fork canyon. The summit is reached by trails from three different directions [Approach: (C)(3.1)(a)]. USGS Chinook Mountain 15-minute/ RNRW

Cape Horn Mountain *9,526 feet (Class 2)*
This peak's long narrow summit is located high above the headwaters of the Middle Fork of the Salmon River. The summit provides excellent views of the entire region—so good, in fact, that the mountain was used in 1922 as a triangulation station for the initial USGS mapping of the area.
The summit is reached after a beautiful ridge walk from the south. Approach the summit by hiking FST-024 from Cape Horn Summit on the Landmark-Lowman Road [Approach: (C)(3)(c)]. The trail climbs over 2,500 feet in 3.5 miles to the ridge line, and then follows the ridge north for 1.0

mile to a point above the Lolo Creek drainage. The trail is faint on the ridge top and, although the map shows it making a descent into the Lolo Creek drainage, the route is not readily apparent. From the ridge above Lolo Lake, follow the ridge line cross country to the summit. USGS Cape Horn Lakes / RNRW

Red Mountain *8,733 feet (Class 1)*
Red Mountain is a somewhat isolated peak which is located 15.0 miles northeast of Lowman and ID-21. The former lookout site, which is reached by trail, is a popular destination for day hikers. Take FST-145 (which eventually leads to the many small lakes east of the summit) to its junction with FST-083, which climbs to the mountain's summit [Approach: (E)(1.1)(a)]. The summit can also be reached via a Class 2 scramble from the lakes east of the peak. USGS Cache Creek

---

C. THE EASTERN SALMON RIVER MOUNTAINS
From the Middle Fork of the Salmon East to the main Salmon River

---

THE BIGHORN CRAGS

The Bighorn Crags form a high granite divide 20 miles long and up to 10 miles wide. It stands on the east side of the Middle Fork of the Salmon River, nearly 1,000 feet above the surrounding mountains. Although these peaks are part of the Salmon River Mountains, they are unique in their physical shape and geologic makeup because Crags granite was formed by a younger granitic intrusion, called a pluton, which was interjected into the older Idaho Batholith granite roughly 40 million years ago. This chemically different, younger granite is characterized by vertical jointing, which has eroded it into spires and sharp walls.

The Bighorn Crags offer many excellent challenges to mountaineers and a surprising amount of good rock to challenge rock climbers. The quality of the Crags granite is much like Sawtooth granite: hard and clean in some places, soft and deteriorated in others. Many of the best walls and rock are located down in the canyons rather than on the peaks, which in some cases are still covered by metamorphic overburden. Climbers who come to the Crags should expect to find little in the way of company, or conveniences such as established bolts for rappelling. (See the Introduction for a brief climbing history of the Crags.)

There are two major rock-climbing areas within the Crags. The first is the "Cathedral's Cemetery" which begins 2.0 miles from Crags Campground and occupies an area along the main trail for almost 2.0 miles to the base of Cathedral Rock. (The domes and spires resemble giant tombstones; Cathedral Rock resembles, of course, a cathedral.) Climbing in this area is limited to one- and two-pitch routes, in almost any degree of difficulty. The Cemetery includes 14 spires and domes, which vary considerably in size and shape and offer simple bouldering problems as well as more complicated rock-climbing projects. The second area of interest to climbers is a tangled collection of spires, faces and cliffs located at the west end of Ship Island Lake called the Litner Group. Because it is over 10 miles from the nearest trailhead, little climbing activity has taken place in the Litner Group. But rest assured—the area has high potential for serious rock climbers.

Dome Mountain *9,316 feet (Class 2)*
This peak's tree-covered summit, the northernmost of the Bighorn Crags summits, is located 1.0 mile north of Goat Lake. The summit is reached after a short scramble up the south ridge from the Crags Trail [Approach: (H)(4.12)(a)]; leave the trail just above the switchbacks that climb out of the Goat Lake basin. USGS Mount McGuire / RNRW

Beehive *9,610 feet (Class 2)*
This rugged peak is located at the north end of the range, 1.5 miles southwest of Dome Mountain. The summit is most easily approached via the southwest ridge where it is crossed by the Crags Trail [Approach: (H)(4.12)(a)]. USGS Mount McGuire / RNRW

Goat Mountain *9,607 feet (Class 2)*
This peak, which is located 3.0 miles north of Mount McGuire, is the most remote Bighorn Crag peak. It can be reached only after a long cross-country march from either Ship Island Lake or Goat Lake. If you really want to go "where no one has gone before," this is the place. The summit is an easy scramble from either its east or south ridges [Approach: (H)(4.12)(c) and (d)]. USGS Mount McGuire / RNRW

Litner Peak* *8,837 feet (Class 5)*
Litner Peak is the highest point in the Litner Group; it is located at the west end of Ship Island Lake [Approach: (H)(4.12)(c) and (d)]. Little is known about the route; the first ascent was by L. Hales and P. Schoening, in 1955. USGS Aggipah Mountain / RNRW

The Chisel* *8,920+ feet (Class 4)*
This descriptively named formation is located west of Ship Island Lakes [Approach: (H)(4.12)(c) and (d)]. The peak is the highest point on the northwest ridge of Aggipah Mountain. It was first climbed by Hales and Schoening in 1955. USGS Aggipah Mountain / RNRW

Mount McGuire *10,082 feet (Class 2)*
The highest peak in the Bighorn Crags is located directly north of Airplane Lake and is composed of a huge pile of broken metamorphic overburden on a granite base. The pyramid-shaped peak has a steep, but rotten, north face and offers no technical climbing.
The most economical route to the summit is from the south via the stream that runs into Airplane Lake from the north. From the trail to Ship Island Lake [Approach: (H)(4.12)(c) and (d)], follow the stream up until you reach its source, a small pond at 9,150 feet. From the pond, continue up to the saddle over increasingly broken ground for another 250 feet, then turn west and climb directly up the southeast ridge, skirting a couple of granite towers partway up on their south side. The summit is a double, with the east summit being the highest. USGS Mount McGuire / RNRW

Aggipah Mountain *9,920 feet (Class 3)*
This large peak rises just to the southwest of Ship Island Lake to form a massive flat-topped mountain that presents a bold face to the lake. Aggipah, which means salmon in the Chinook Indian dialect, is located on the west end of a subsidiary ridge that connects with the main Bighorn Crag crest at Knuckle Peak.
The peak is (probably) most easily climbed from Ship Island Lake. This route begins at the unnamed lake just south of Ship Island Lake and climbs the scree slope to a col on Aggipah's southeast ridge, then follows the steep ridge to the summit [Approach: (H)(4.12)(a),(c) and (d)]. Although many other route possibilities exist, all of these would involve much longer and more difficult approaches. USGS Aggipah Mountain / RNRW

Sheepeater Mountain* *9,920 feet (Class 2-3)*
This is the large peak that rises up due north of Terrace Lakes. The view of Ship Island Lake from the summit is beautiful. Climb from the southeast ridge (Class 3) or the south ridge (Class 2) [Approach: (H)(4.12)(a) and (c)]. USGS Mount McGuire / RNRW

Mount McGuire, the highest point in the Bighorn Crags, viewed from the summit of Knuckle Peak

FISHFIN RIDGE

The USGS Mount McGuire quad lists the Bighorn Crags' most complex feature simply as Fishfin Ridge. Climbers, on the other hand, have recognized the complexity of this exceptional ridge, which contains four major formations, all of which are unofficially named. The highest and western-most point is known as Knuckle Peak; to the east, in order of appearance, are the Rusty Nail, Pinnacle #3 and Pinnacle #4.

Knuckle Peak* *9,700 feet*

Knuckle Peak, perhaps the most impressive feature in the Bighorn Crags, is the highest point on the Fishfin Ridge. It was named by Lincoln Hales and Pete Schoening, who made the first ascent in 1955. The three-sided mountain has no simple route to its top, which is a jumble of small jagged spires and blocks. Although the peak's granite is generally hard, climbers should be aware that its quality can vary a great deal in a short distance.

The peak has three faces. On its west side, the peak presents an 800-foot face to Wilson Lake. This face is a conglomeration of smooth slabs, without any major cracks. There is a wide variety of overhanging obstacles to block many possible

routes, sometimes repeatedly. The north face rises impressively above Birdbill Lake and is 300 feet higher than the west face. On this side, the face can be reached from the upper portion of the Beaver Tail trail [Approach: (H)(4.12)(c)], where the trail hits the crest above the Birdbill Lake. The east face is the least impressive of the three faces—but is still imposing. It rises above the Crags trail, which provides easy access to its lower slopes. The route of the first ascent, described by Hales in the Mountaineers Journal, is unclear. USGS Mount McGuire / RNRW

East Face/South Ridge. *(Grade I, 5.2)*
From the Crags Trail [Approach: (H)(4.12)(a)], climb the easy ledges up to the base of the face. From the top of the easy ledges, locate a narrow ramp which leaves the upper ledges and cuts diagonally to the south. Follow this ramp until it ends. From this point, a series of moderately difficult steps lead almost directly up to the south ridge with one small section of 5.2 climbing (and moderate exposure). Once on the ridge, the route follows the ridge to the summit, encountering only Class 3-4 climbing. The south ridge has also been climbed directly from the notch between Knuckle Peak and the Rusty Nail; the move out of the notch has been rated 5.7.

The Rusty Nail, as seen from Wilson Lake

The Rusty Nail*

This spire is located next to Knuckle Peak, near its southeast corner. Lincoln Hales, who named this spire, was unable to reach its summit. In the late 1950s and early 1960s several members of the Idaho Alpine Club made attempts on the formation, but without success. Someone eventually did climb the spire, but there is no information available on who did it or what route they took [Approach: (H)(4.12)(a)]. USGS Mount McGuire / RNRW

Pinnacle #3* *(Class 3)*

This stubby, obelisk-shaped spire is the second peak from the south end of Fishfin Ridge. The route utilizes the numerous ledges that form the west side [Approach: (H)(4.12)(a)]. The first ascent was by Bob Hammer and a group of Idaho Alpine Club members in 1963. USGS Mount McGuire / RNRW

Pinnacle #4* *(Class 4)*

The easternmost of the Fishfin Ridge formations is climbed by way of a thin crack system on the spire's north side [Approach: (H)(4.12)(a)]. The first ascent was by Bob Hammer and a group of Idaho Alpine Club members in 1963. USGS Mount McGuire / RNRW

Bighorn Peak* *9,821 feet (Class 2)*

This peak, located west of and above Harbor Lake, has a broad summit ridge and a rough broken face which is half metamorphic rock and half loose debris. From Harbor Lake, the peak can be climbed by either its north or south ridges. Class 3 climbing could be encountered climbing to the north ridge, depending on the route chosen. From Harbor Lake, climb the scree slopes to one of the ridge tops and then follow the chosen ridge to the summit [Approach: (H)(4.12)(a) and (c)]. USGS Mount McGuire / RNRW

Ramskull Peak* *9,460 feet (Class 4)*

This peak was named by Pete Schoening and Lincoln Hales in 1955, after they made the first ascent. It dominates its surroundings, presenting an almost unbroken 1,000-foot face to Wilson Creek. From Wilson Lake, it resembles a two-pronged granite spire. The summit can only be reached by climbing on very poor quality granite. The route begins at Harbor Lake [Approach: (H)(4.12)(a) and (c)]. From the lake, scramble up to the ridge line west of the peak and then follow the ridge to the base of the summit block. From this point, drop down the south side of the ridge for roughly 40 feet, keeping to the base of the summit block, until you are at the base of a large gully which leads up to the summit in one relatively easy Class 4 pitch. The crux of the climb is the descent, because the summit is composed of deteriorated granite and it is impossible to place an adequate rappel anchor. USGS Mount McGuire / RNRW

Heart Peak* *9,573 feet (Class 2)*

This is a pointed peak that rises to the south of Heart Lake. Its lofty summit can be reached via its relatively gentle east ridge. Technical climbing opportunities exist on this peak, including a major snow gully on the northeast face [Approach: (H)(4.12)(b)]. USGS Mount McGuire / RNRW

Cathedral Rock *9,400+ feet*

This impressive peak is located 2.0 miles east of Fishfin Ridge and directly above its namesake Cathedral Lake. From the lake, it is an impressive collection of granite cliffs and slabs that quickly rise up 800 feet. The Rock is composed of three major summits. The north summit had been climbed by the year 1924, when a Forest Service marker was cemented to its summit. The more difficult (and highest) south summit was first climbed by Hales and Schoening in 1955. The middle summit evidently has not been climbed; nor has the Rock's imposing east face [Approach: (H)(4.12)(a)]. USGS Mount McGuire / RNRW

North Summit. *(Class 3)*
From the trail, work your way through the tree-covered slopes to the highest point on the west face, next to the northernmost summit. Climb the small north summit block from the west side via a 25-foot scramble from a boulder field which reaches nearly to the summit.

South Summit. *(Grade I, 5.4)*
The middle and south summits are separated by a steep gully on their western side. Climb the gully (on bomb-proof holds) in one short pitch, and then traverse south to the summit.

Puddin Mountain *9,684 feet (Class 2)*
This peak is located 1.5 miles south of Harbor Peak. It is named after Puddin River Wilson who was the Saloon keeper at Yellowjacket during that mining town's heyday. Climb via the southeast ridge from Turquoise Lake, by keeping on the south side of the ridge near its crest [Approach: (H)(4.12)(e)]. USGS Puddin Mountain / RNRW

Wilson Mountain *9,520 feet (Class 3)*
Wilson is the other Bighorn Crags peak named for Puddin River Wilson. It is located 1.5 miles south of Puddin Mountain. Climb the peak from either Ramshorn or Paragon Lakes to the east via the east ridge [Approach: (H)(4.12)(e)]. USGS Hoodoo Meadows / RNRW

YELLOWJACKET MOUNTAINS

This subrange of the Salmon River Mountains was named by miners after the now abandoned town of Yellowjacket. The range runs 24 miles from southwest to northeast and is located due east of the Bighorn Crags. These mountains are almost indistinguishable from the surrounding Salmon River peaks. The highest point is located in the south on Middle Fork Peak at 9,127 feet. This book includes four Yellowjacket summits: Gant Mountain, Sugar Loaf, Mount McEleny and Middle Fork Peak.

Gant Mountain *8,276 feet (Class 1)*
Gant Mountain anchors the north end of the Yellowjacket Mountains. It is located on massive Gant Ridge 6.0 miles north of the point where Panther Creek flows into the main Salmon River. One of the earliest fire lookouts in the Salmon National Forest was placed on the summit in 1933

Sugar Loaf in the Yellowjacket Mountains, viewed from the Crags Trail in the Bighorn Crags

or 1934 and was used for several years and then abandoned. To reach the summit from the Panther Creek Road, take the Birch Trail, FST-023, to the summit [Approach: (H)(4)(a)]. The trail gains over 4,500 feet from start to finish and teaches people an excellent lesson about how vertical the Salmon River country actually is. USGS Blackbird Mountain 15-minute/ RNRW

Sugar Loaf *9,045 feet (Class 2)*
Sugar Loaf, located directly west of Yellowjacket Lake [Approach: (H)(4.11)], is a half-dome-shaped peak which presents an 800-foot vertical east wall. Rock climbers who have approached the granite wall with great anticipation have been disappointed by the deteriorated condition of the wall. I do not know of any attempt to climb it. The Sugar Loaf summit can be reached

by a short cross-country walk from the Yellowjacket Lake Campground via either its south or north sides. USGS Hoodoo Meadows

McEleny Mountain *8,938 feet (Class 1)*
McEleny Mountain is located 3.0 miles southeast of Sugar Loaf. This peak is reached via a 3.0-mile walk up FST-039 from Hoodoo Meadows and the end of FS-113 [Approach: (H)(4.11)(a)]. The trail leads almost the entire distance to the summit, which it passes on the peak's west side. From the trail, it is a short stroll to the top. USGS Hoodoo Meadows

Middle Fork Peak *9,127 feet*
Middle Fork Peak, the highest Yellowjacket Mountain peak, has been a lookout site since the early 1920s. Unfortunately, the peak is reached by both a road and a trail. (The road is not suited for low-slung cars.) The trail (FST-047) climbs up Warm Springs Creek from the Middle Fork of the Salmon river, gaining over 5,000 feet in the process [Approach: (H)(4.1)]. USGS Aparejo Point

Taylor Mountain *9,960 feet (Class 2)*
This peak is located 26.0 miles north of Challis and north of Morgan Creek summit in a small roadless area that is accessible from either the north or the south. Eleven mountain lakes are visible from the summit of Taylor Mountain. The recommended approach is from Morgan Creek Summit [Approach: (G)(3)]. From this point, a road turns off to the northeast. Follow it until it ends and then find FST-093, which enters the lake basin southeast of the peak. The summit is reached after a long scramble on moderate slopes from the lake basin. USGS Taylor Mountain

Martin Mountain *9,406 feet (Class 1)*
Martin Mountain is located west of Challis and north of Sleeping Deer Mountain. From Sleeping Deer, follow FST-103 [Approach: (G)(2)(b)] north for 5.0 miles to the summit. Both peaks are on the boundary of the River of No Return Wilderness. USGS Sleeping Deer Mountain / RNRW

Sleeping Deer Mountain *9,881 feet (Class 1)*
This large mountain, which is located 28.0 miles northwest of Challis, shows signs of past alpine glaciation in its many cirques, a number of which contain beautiful lakes. The trail to the summit is accessed from FS-086 [Approach: (G)(2)(a)] at a trailhead at 9,100 feet elevation on the peak's east side. From the trailhead, it is a short walk to the summit. USGS Sleeping Deer Mountain / RNRW

Greyhound Mountain *8,995 feet (Class 1)*
Greyhound Mountain's bald summit is located 4.5 miles northwest of the Seafoam GS, which in turn is located northwest of Stanley. Approach the peak from the south on FS-011 [Approach: (F)(1)(e)], which leads to the Greyhound Mine. Drive or walk to the end of the road and then take FST-006 north to the summit. USGS Greyhound Ridge / RNRW

Big Soldier Mountain *8,984 feet (Class 1)*
This fire lookout site is located southwest of Greyhound Mountain and directly east of the Middle Fork of the Salmon River. Because the peak is a fire lookout site, it is approached by four different trails. The best approach is from the Josephus Lake CG [Approach: (F)(1)(d)] via FST-019, passing by Soldier and Cutthroat Lakes and then on to the summit. USGS Chinook Mountain / RNRW

Mount Mills *9,185 feet (Class 2)*
Mount Mills is located southeast of Big Soldier Mountain and just south of Lost Lake. The summit is an easy scramble from FST-014. From the Josephus Lake CG, take FST-019 and then FST-014 to the peak's northwest ridge [Approach: (F)(1)(d) and (a)]. Climb the easy ridge to the summit. The peak can also be reached from the Langer Peak area. USGS Greyhound Ridge / RNRW

Langer Peak *9,315 feet (Class 2)*
Langer Peak is a minor summit located 3.0 miles southeast of Mount Mills, above Rocky Lake. Its summit is a simple scramble from the lake. Take FST-014 [Approach: (F)(1)(a)] to Langer Lake and then hike cross country to Rocky Lake. From this lake, climb to the saddle due north of the summit and then follow the ridge south to the summit. USGS Langer Peak / RNRW

Roughneck Peak *9,419 feet (Class 1)*
Roughneck Peak, an active fire lookout site, sits 2 miles southwest of Langer Peak. The peak is nearly surrounded by mountain lakes and is a popular destination during the summer. Because of the fire lookout, its summit is reached by a well-maintained trail from Island Lake. The trail makes an easy, but long, Class 1 ascent [Approach: (F)(1)(a)]. USGS Langer Peak

THE TANGO PEAKS

The name Tango Peaks evidently originated with the miners who first explored the area in the mid-1800s. Later, the Forest Service's RARE II study of roadless areas adopted the name and

Roughneck Peak, 9,419 feet, as seen from Langer Lake

attached it to the prominent north/south ridge anchored by 10,000-foot Mount Loening in the north and by brightly colored Red Mountain in the south. Chisel-shaped Cabin Creek Peak and Last Tango Peak are the other named Tango Peaks.

Mount Loening* 10,012 feet (Class 3)

This peak, located at the north end of the Tango ridge, is identified on the Knapp Lake quad as the Knapp triangulation station. Loening, a prodigious jumble of shattered rock towers, is named for a bush pilot who spent many years flying the Salmon River backcountry. The peak can be climbed via its south face by utilizing a system of gullies and ribs that carve up the broken face. Approach the face from Crimson Lake [Approach: (F)(3.1)(a)] by climbing to the main ridge north of Cabin Creek Peak and then follow this ridge to the north over Last Tango Peak to the base of the south face. Although the ridge line is narrow in places, it is easily followed.

At the base of the peak, the route is blocked by a tower. Drop down on the west side of the peak to a ledge and traverse to the northwest until you reach the base of a steep, rotten couloir. Follow this couloir up until it dead ends and then cross over to the east, enter the next couloir and follow it up to the summit blocks. The final summit blocks are climbed on the west side. USGS Knapp Lakes

Last Tango Peak* 9,647 feet (Class 2)

Last Tango is a minor summit on the main ridge between Cabin Creek Peak and Mount Loening. It is easily bagged as part of an ascent of Mount Loening. See the entry above for information [Approach: (F)(3.1)(a)]. USGS Knapp Lakes

Cabin Creek Peak 9,968 feet

This is one of the most rugged peaks in the entire state. Its first ascent was apparently not made until 1988. The knife-edged summit, formed by a fine-grained granite, stands nearly 400 feet high on its east face and almost 1,200 feet high on its west face. The summit is broken into two major sections by a deep, narrow notch. The highest point is located on the south side of the notch. North of the notch, the summit ridge is razor-thin.

Although Cabin Creek Peak is a spectacular summit and made up of somewhat solid granite, it was unknown to climbers because of its remote location and the fact that it is not readily visible from the nearby Stanley Basin. It is unlikely that a non-climber would have stumbled all the way to the summit because of the difficulty of the terrain.

In 1984, the author and his wife made two aborted attempts on the peak, which they had stumbled upon by accident. Research during the next four years failed to turn up anyone with knowledge of the peak or any written accounts which mentioned the peak. They returned in 1988, accompanied by Paul Bellamy, and climbed to the summit via the east face, uncovering no evidence that the peak had been previously climbed. USGS Knapp Lakes

East Face. *(Grade I, 5.3)*
To reach the east face from Crimson Lake [Approach: (F)(3.1)(a)], climb to the saddle due south of the lake (between the twin dark towers that are visible from the lake). Descend the saddle below the north tower and then climb up to the saddle on its west side. To reach the face from south, take the Basin Butte Road [Approach: (F)(2)] for 18.0 miles to the locked gate and then hike the road to the point where it crosses the creek that drains the east side of the peak. Follow the creek up to the east face.

The east face is cut by three gullies. The northernmost gully is vertical, the middle meanders back and forth across the face and the southernmost (which is the widest) is highlighted by a cave at its base. The route begins just to the right of the southernmost gully (the one with the cave), and follows the small buttress up and to the left for two and one half pitches. The fine-grained granite that forms the summit block is highly fractured, so wear a helmet. The first ascent, lead by Paul Bellamy with Dana Lopez and T. Lopez, was made in August of 1988.

Red Mountain *9,387 feet (Class 2)*
Red Mountain is located 2.0 miles east of Cabin Creek Peak. The eastern and northern talus slopes of this mountain display a bright red tint as they rise up steeply above the surrounding drainages. The summit can be climbed from almost any direction, but the most direct approach is from West Fork of the Yankee Fork [Approach: (F)(3.1)(a)]. Those with a 4WD may approach by taking the Basin Butte Road to the point where it

is closed by a locked gate, and then following the mining road to the peak's west ridge [Approach: (F)(2)]. USGS Mount Jordan

The General* *10,329 feet (Class 2)*
The General is an attractive summit that rises sharply above Mystery Lake just 1.5 miles northwest of Mount Jordan. The mountain's two summits both reach above 10,000 feet. The south summit is the highest point. It is recommended that the peak be climbed by traversing the ridge line from the Mount Jordan summit, although the peak is approachable from most directions [Approach: (F)(3.3)]. USGS Mount Jordan

Mount Jordan *10,063 feet (Class 2)*
Mount Jordan is named after Sylvester Jordan, who discovered gold in this area in 1870. The peak is located north of the town of Bonanza and due west of Loon Creek Summit. It is climbed via its south ridge from the jeep trail that runs up Jordan Creek from just below Loon Creek Summit [Approach: (F)(3.3)]. Follow the old roadway to the south ridge and then scamper up the ridge. USGS Mount Jordan

Custer Peak *9,753 feet (Class 1)*
Custer Peak is located 5.0 miles east of the Bonanza GS and the Yankee Fork of the Salmon River. The summit is identified on the Challis National Forest map as the Custer fire lookout. The lookout (no longer used) is open for public use on a first-come, first-use basis. Custer Peak, the culmination of a number of rugged ridges, stands in the heart of a small slice of de facto wilderness that is seldom visited. From the top, Mount Borah and Mount McCaleb in the Lost River Range, Cabin Creek Peak and Twin Peaks in the Salmon River Mountains, and the Sawtooths are clearly observable. Trails lead to the summit from north, east, south and west. The 6.0-mile-long north route, which utilizes FST-161 [Approach: (F)(3)(a)], is recommended because of its scenic qualities.

The Twin Peaks
South Twin Peak *10,340 feet*
North Twin Peak *10,196 feet*
The area just west of Challis was the heart of the Challis Volcanics (see the Introduction); the area features the highest real estate in the Salmon River Mountains, rising over 5,000 feet above the Salmon River in just 5 miles. Many of the surrounding peaks sit on the rim of a huge caldera that was left when a massive volcano (much like Mount Rainier) collapsed millions of years ago. The summits identified as Twin Peaks are actually two separate mountains that form part of the rim of the Twin Peaks Caldera. South Twin Peak, the

second highest mountain in the Salmon River Mountains, contains a fire lookout reached by road. USGS Twin Peaks 15-minute

North Twin Peak Route. *(Class 2)*
Climb this peak via its southern ridge from the saddle between it and South Twin Peak. It is 1.0 mile and 1,000 feet of elevation gain to the summit over moderate slopes. Leave FS-086 [Approach: (G)(2)] and walk due north up through the forest and barren upper slopes to the ridge top. From this point, stay on the ridge as it curves northeast to the summit.

South Twin Peak Route. *(Class 1)*
FS-090 [Approach: (G)(2.2)] leads directly to the summit, and is taken by 99 percent of those who visit the summit. The road requires a 4WD and thus does not see much traffic—for those interested in walking to the top.

White Mountain *10,400+ feet (Class 2)*
The highest summit in the Salmon River Mountains is located 1.5 miles southwest of Twin Peaks. The name "White Mountain" is derived from the peak's western ridge, which is composed of a brilliant white rock visible from all of the major summits to the west. Nevertheless, there is some confusion about this peak because the USGS attached the name "White Mountain" to a lower subsidiary point on the peak's shoulder, rather than to the actual highest point, which is 0.5 mile to the west. However, there is nothing "white" about this point. Perhaps this error will be corrected when the new 7.5-minute quads are published for this area. USGS Twin Peaks 15-minute

North Ridge Route. *(Class 3)*
Access the north ridge from South Twin Peak and FS-090 [Approach: (G)(2.2)]. Turn onto FS-090 and follow it to the second switchback, at 1.5 miles. There is a large turnout and a sign that proclaims "Twin Creek Lakes Trail" at this point. This trail, which is not on any map, leads down South Twin Peak's south ridge to the saddle just below White Mountain. Leave the trail at this point and follow the ridge up, on mostly stable rock (the last 400 vertical feet cross extremely broken and loose rock), to the base of the summit. Pass the first fin on the ridge by staying low and traversing its west side. From this point, it is possible to stay mostly on the top or the east side of the ridge for the remaining distance. Some may find it easier to detour down onto the lower eastern slopes of this ridge in order to avoid a tricky notch about midway along the ridge.

Southwest Ridge Route.
This route begins at Challis Creek [Approach: (G)(2.1)]. To reach the lakes, take the Challis Creek road out of Challis and follow it to its end at Mosquito Flat Reservoir. From the reservoir,

The north face of White Mountain, the highest summit in the vast Salmon River Mountains

follow the jeep trail west and then north up Challis Creek to the lakes. (It is best to walk the jeep trail.) The ascent to the summit presents no objective difficulties until the base of the summit pyramid, where some easy Class 3 climbing is encountered.

Ramshorn Mountain *9,895 feet (Class 2-3)*

Rocky Ramshorn Mountain is located west of Challis and north of Bayhorse Creek. The peak's lower slopes have been the site of an extensive mining operation in the past and are strewn with debris from this activity, including the ruins of a tramway that used to lead up to the mine shafts on the upper slopes. The peak is climbed from lower Bayhorse Lake [Approach: (G)(1)]. From the lake, there is a faint trail that leads off toward the summit. Although the route is not physically difficult, finding the correct route can be a problem. USGS Bayhorse

The east face of Ramskull Peak, viewed from Boulder Lake

Bald Mountain *10,313 feet (Class 2)*

This peak is the third-highest point in the Salmon River Mountains. It rises over 5,000 feet in just 3.2 miles, making it one of the steepest peaks in the state. The best route up the peak is from the north. Drive up the Bayhorse Creek Road, FS-051 [Approach: (G)(1)(a)], to the forest boundary. Take the jeep trail that leads to the south until it ends, and then follow the unnamed drainage to the summit.

APPROACHES TO THE SALMON RIVER MOUNTAINS

Approach routes for this section are identified in the text by bracketed entries [Approach:], which include appropriate letter and number references.

Second in size only to the Clearwater Mountains, the Salmon River Mountains include a massive and diverse chunk of Idaho within their circumference. Literally hundreds of roads and trails crisscross the land, creating a complex and varied approach system. This section describes the Salmon River road system as it exists in relation to the major "gateway towns," which are (A) Riggins, (B) McCall, (C) Cascade, (D) Banks, (E) Lowman, (F) Stanley, (G) Challis and (H) Salmon.

(A) Riggins Approaches.

Riggins, a village of 527 people, is located on US-95 at the extreme northwest corner of the Salmon River Mountains. The town provides all essential services.

(1) FS-1614, Salmon River Road. This road leaves US-95 at the south end of Riggins and runs up the main fork of the Salmon River for 27.2 miles.

(1.1) FS-246, French Creek/ Burgdorf Road. This road leaves FS-1614 and the Salmon River 20.0 miles east of Riggins, climbs to Burgdorf in 23.0 miles, and connects with FH-21, the Warren Wagon Road, in 2.0 more miles. See [Approach: (B)(2)] below.

(B) McCall Approaches.

McCall, a growing resort town on the shores of Payette Lake, has a population of over 2,000. Primary access to the town is via ID-55. Food, gas, lodging and even some outdoor equipment is available from the town's merchants.

(1) FS-257, Goose Creek Road. This road is reached from McCall by driving northwest on ID-55 for 6.0 miles to the Brundage Mountain Ski Area turnoff. From the highway, this road leads north for over 25.0 miles, ending north of Hazard

Lake. The road is paved to the junction for the ski area.

(a) FST-165, Granite Mountain Trail. To reach this trail, follow FS-257 north for 12.0 miles to the FST-165 trailhead. The trail climbs west to the summit of Granite Mountain in just under 3.0 miles. Once over the summit, the trail descends to FS-294, which connects with US-95 near New Meadows. To reach the trail from New Meadows, drive north on US-95 for 4.0 miles and turn right onto FS-294, which parallels the edge of the mountains for a number of miles before reaching the trailhead along Browns Creek.

(b) FST-163, Grass Mountain Divide Trail. This trail leaves FS-257 just south of the Hard Creek GS, which is 18.0 miles north of ID-55. FST-163 leads into the heart of the Grass Mountains and provides access to several mountain lakes along its course.

(c) FST-347, Hard Butte Trail System. FST-347 leaves from the end of FS-257 7.0 miles north of the Hard Creek GS and leads northwest to Warm Springs Saddle, where it accesses the extensive Hard Butte trail system, which crisscrosses this roadless area. Trail conditions vary from trail to trail and generally require at least intermediate skills.

(c.1) FST-344. This trail leaves FST-347 at Warm Springs Saddle and makes a half-circle around the eastern, southern and northern ends of Hard Butte in roughly 6.0 miles.

(c.2) FST-508, Hard Butte Trail. FST-508 runs due west from Warm Springs Saddle, crosses over Hard Butte and then descends to join FST-344 west of the Butte.

(c.3) FST-152/FST-151/FST-153/ FST371, Paradise Lake Loop. This route leaves Warm Springs Saddle and loops north between Hard Butte and Patrick Butte, providing access to Paradise Lake. From the loop, FST-152 runs east down Partridge Creek and then climbs west to join FST-149 near Sams Throne and Lava Butte [Approach: (B)(1.1)(a) and (b)].

(d) FST-169, Upper Hazard Lake Trail. This trail loops into the country south of FS-257. The trail can be accessed at either the Hard Creek GS or the Hazard Lake CG.

(1.1) FS-308, Lava Butte Road. This road leaves FS-257 5.5 miles north of the Hard Creek GS and proceeds many tortuous miles north to provide access to the area east of Lava Butte.

(a) FST-149, Lava Butte Trail. This trail follows the major north/south divide which makes up the Lava Butte area. The trail begins where FS-308 crosses Big Dave Creek. FST-149 can also be accessed from several feeder trails including FST-347, which is the shortest route into the Lava Butte area.

(b) FST-152, Partridge Creek Trail. FST-152 leaves FST-149 southeast of Sams Throne and climbs westward over a saddle before descending into Partridge Creek. The trail is not well maintained and, in places, is only marked by sporadic blazes on trees. See [Approach: (B)(1)(c.3)].

(1.2) FS-281, Fisher Creek Trail. This road leaves FS-257 just below Brundage Reservoir, eventually crosses into the Fisher Creek drainage, and ends on Fisher Creek Saddle after 10.5 miles. The road can be quite rough in its upper reaches.

(2) FH-21, Warren Wagon Road. This is one of the major Salmon River Mountains roads. The road begins in McCall on the west side of Payette Lake and runs up the North Fork of the Payette River to Secesh Summit, then crosses eastward to the Warren GS, where it ends. It is paved for 31.5 miles to the Burgdorf junction, and then gravel for 14.2 miles to Warren.

(a) FST-085/FST-315, Twentymile Lakes Trail. This trail leaves FH-21 at the north end of Upper Payette Lake and leads 6.0 miles east to north Twentymile Lake.

(b) FST-080/FST-084 and FST-081, Loon Lake Trails. These trails are accessed from the Chinook GG just south of FH-21 and lead to Loon Lake at the north end of the Lick Creek Range. To reach the trailhead take FH-21 north from McCall for 35.1 miles and turn onto the CG which is 1.2 miles from the main road. FST-080 follows the Secesh River to Loon Creek, where it becomes FST-084 and climbs up Loon Creek to Loon Lake in a total of 5.0 miles. FST-081 leads directly from the CG to the lake by following the slopes above the river. From Loon Lake, FST-084 continues south for 12.0 miles to Duck Lake, Foolhen Meadows and FH-48 (see [Approach (B)(4)(b)], below).

(2.1) FS-260, Squaw Meadows Road. This road forks off of FH-21 just north of Upper Payette Lake and follows the North Fork of the Payette River north for nearly 4.0 miles.

(a) FST-504/FST-308, Black Tip Route. From the end of FS-260, FST-504 proceeds west and then northwest to French Creek in 4.0 miles. At French Creek, FST-504 junctions with FST-308, which follows French Creek both north and south. To reach Black Tip, turn left (south) onto FST-308 and hike 6.0 miles to the summit. This trail sees little use and is difficult to follow in many places.

(3) FS-340, Warren to South Fork Salmon River. This gravel road leads from Warren to the South Fork of the Salmon River and the South Fork GS. It crosses the river on a new bridge and continues onto Big Creek. See [Approach: (B)(6)] below for more information on this narrow and steep road.

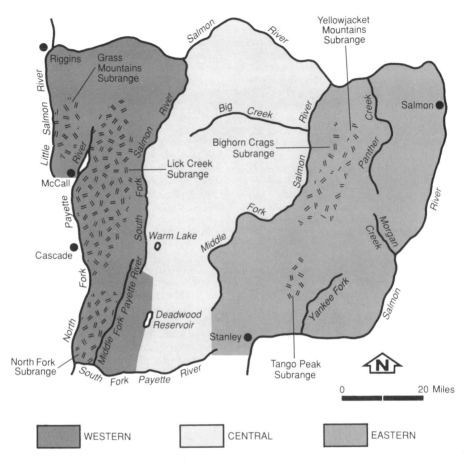

SALMON RIVER MOUNTAINS AND SUBRANGES

(4) FH-48, Yellow Pine Road. This road leaves McCall at the only traffic light in town and proceeds along the east shore of Payette Lake to Little Payette Lake, Lick Creek Summit and the town of Yellow Pine.

(a) FST-104, East Fork of Lake Fork/Snowslide Lake Loop Trail. This trail has two trailheads along FH-48. The first is at Lake Fork CG 10.0 miles northeast of McCall and the second is located 6.0 miles north of the Lake Fork CG.

Lake Fork CG Trailhead. From the CG, the trail follows the Lake Fork Creek east to a trail junction in roughly 1.0 mile. At this junction, FST-103 [Approach: (B)(7)(b)] runs south to Boulder Summit (Pass); FST-104 continues east a short distance and then turns north to follow the East Fork of Lake Fork drainage north for 5.0 miles to a second junction. At this second junction, FST-

104 meets FST-086 [Approach: (B)(4)(a.1)] and then turns west, crosses the Lick Creek Range crest between Snowslide and Sawtooth peaks and then descends to rejoin FH-48 in another 4.0 miles.

Snowslide Lake Trailhead. The northern trailhead is identified by a sign on FH-48. There is parking for only two or three vehicles at this trailhead. From this trailhead, the trail immediately crosses the North Fork of Lake Fork (which will be difficult in high water) and almost immediately begins to climb to Snowslide Lake in 2.0 very steep miles. From the lake, the trail takes an even steeper route to the saddle between Snowslide Peak and Sawtooth Peak, which is 1.0 mile farther on.

(a.1) FST-086, North Fitsum Summit Trail. This trail leaves FST-104 6.0 miles north of Lake

Fork campground and provides access to the North Fork of Fitsum Creek.

(b) FST-084, Duck Lake/Loon Lake Trail. This trail is accessed just north of Lick Creek Summit. From FH-48, the trail runs north to Duck Lake in about 1.0 mile and then continues northeast over a divide and into the upper section of the Loon Creek drainage, eventually reaching Loon Lake after 12.0 miles. See [Approach: (B)(2)(b)], above.

(b.1) FST-083/FST-082, Hum Lake/North Fork Lick Creek Trail. This trail forks off of FST-084 at Duck Lake and runs northeast to Hum Lake. At Hum Lake the route divides. FST-083 descends Hum Creek to meet FH-48, while FST-082 climbs up to the top of the divide north of the lake and then traverses northeast to the southern slopes of South Loon Mountain in 2.0 miles. From the high point on South Loon Mountain, FST-082 descends along the North Fork of Lick Creek to a junction with FST-081 in 5.0 miles.

(c) FST-081, Loon Lake Trail. This trail is accessed from FH-48 where the North Fork of Lick Creek crosses the road just west of Ponderosa CG and the Secesh River. The trail runs north from FH-48 to Loon Lake in 10.0 miles. Also see [Approach: (B)(2)(b)] above.

(d) FST-079, Tail Holt Peak Trail. The lower portion of this trail is not shown on the Payette National Forest map; nevertheless, FST-079 leaves FH-48 at a signed trailhead west of the point where the Secesh flows into the South Fork of the Salmon River. The trail climbs steeply to Tail Holt Peak in roughly 6.0 miles and then follows a ridge line north to Bear Lake in another 7.0 miles.

(e) FST-073, Williams Peak Lookout Trail. This trail leaves FH-48 where that road crosses Williams Creek. It makes a short but steep 3.0-mile ascent of Williams Peak.

(f) FST-070, Rainbow Ridge Trail. FST-070 begins at a signed junction just past the Williams Peak summit and runs east (as the crow flies) to a point below Parks Peak, where it joins FST-069. This rugged and poorly maintained trail is roughly 12.0 miles long.

(g) FST-069, Parks Peak Trail. This trail leaves FH-48 where Parks Creek flows into the South Fork. Turn onto the 4WD road, park and then follow the road to the trailhead. This route reaches the summit in about 6.5 miles, after gaining 4,000 feet in elevation. The trail is sketchy and difficult to follow in its upper reaches.

(5) FS-412/FS-375, Yellow Pine to Monumental Creek. From Yellow Pine, FS-412 continues east. In 5.0 miles it junctions with FS-340 [Approach: (B)(6)], which leads to Big Creek. From this junction, the road continues east over Monu-

mental Summit to Monumental Creek. After 25.0 miles the road reaches the Upper Monumental Creek Trailhead. From this trailhead, FS-375 leaves Monumental Creek and climbs up Coon Creek to the Lookout Mountain Ridge Trailhead and FST-061. Leave plenty of time in your schedule to reach these trailheads. Also, be warned that these roads receive heavy traffic from mining-related vehicles. Watch out!

(a) FST-005, Monumental Creek Trail. This trail leaves FS-375 at Coon Creek and follows Monumental Creek north to the trailless sections of Big Creek in the RNRW, a distance of over 20.0 miles [Approach: (B)(6.1)(a)].

(b) FST-061, Lookout Mountain Ridge Trail. This trail leaves the end of FS-375 and crosses Lookout Mountain Ridge to Lookout Mountain in 8.0 miles.

(6) FS-340, Yellow Pine to Big Creek to Warren. This road leaves FS-412 5.0 miles east of Yellow Pine and runs north, climbing over Profile Gap, 7,605 feet, in 14.0 miles and then descending to the Big Creek Work Center at mile 24.0. Just south of the Work Center, the road turns west and runs over Elk Summit, 8,670 feet, in another 9.3 miles. From Elk Summit, the road descends to the South Fork of the Salmon River and eventually continues to Warren (and eventually FS-21) in a total of 75.3 miles. See [Approach: (B)(3)] for further details.

(a) Missouri Ridge Trail. This trail leaves FS-340 4.4 miles north of its junction with FS-412. The trail is actually an old mining road that leads up the Missouri Creek drainage for 3.0 miles. Park at the beginning of the roadway because it is impassable to all vehicles a short distance from FS-340. The trail follows the stream bottom for 2.0 miles to a cabin, and then crosses the creek and begins to switchback up the Missouri Ridge. After many switchbacks, the roadway narrows and becomes a trail for the last 1.0 mile to the top of Missouri Ridge, where it ends. Although the trail is moderately easy to follow at this time, it is not a maintained Forest Service route and could become impassable in the future. At this time, it provides an excellent approach route to Pinnacles Peak.

(b) FST-066, Missouri Ridge Lookout Trail. FST-066 forks off the Missouri Ridge Trail 0.5 mile east of FS-340 and ends at a viewpoint on the western end of the ridge.

(c) FST-004, Cougar Basin Trail. This trail leaves FS-340 22.0 miles north of its junction with FS-412, 1.5 miles south of the Edwardsburg/Big Creek junction. The trail runs southeast over Cougar Saddle into Cougar Basin, and then meets FST-005 and Monumental Creek [Approach: (B)(5)]. Total distance is about 17.0 miles.

(d) FST-065, Center Mountain Trail. This is a primitive trail that leaves FST-004 north of Cougar Basin and climbs over Snowslide Peak and Center Mountain in 5.5 miles and then descends to Big Creek in 12.5 miles.

(e) FST-120/FST-284, South Fork Elk Creek Trail. This trail leaves FS-340 roughly 8.0 miles west of Elk Summit and climbs the South Fork of Elk Creek toward Profile Lake at the base of Profile Peak. The 6.0-mile-long trail is maintained to within 1.0 mile of the lake.

(6.1) FS-371/FST-373, Smith Creek Road/Werdenhoff Mine Road. FS-371 begins at the Edwardsburg/Big Creek junction on FS-340 [Approach: (B)(6)] and follows Big Creek north, past the Forest Service Big Creek Work Center, to its junction with Smith Creek and the Big Creek Trailhead in 3.0 miles. The road then turns northwest and follows Smith Creek for 5.0 miles to a signed junction. From this junction, FS-371 continues up Smith Creek and is either impassable or nearly impassable (A sign states: Mining Access Road/Not Recommended for Public Use. The sign is accurate.) FS-373, the Werdenhoff Mine Road, is rough and a 4WD is highly recommended (perhaps necessary) to reach these trailheads. From the junction, FS-373 leads to the Mosquito Ridge Trailhead in 2.3 miles and the Pueblo Summit Trailhead in 4.0 miles.

(a) FST-196, Big Creek Trail. This is one of the major east/west routes through the Frank Church-River of No Return Wilderness. The trail covers over 40.0 miles as it follows Big Creek east to the Middle Fork of the Salmon River.

(b) FST-001, Beaver Creek/Chamberlain GS Trail. This trail leaves Big Creek and FST-196 4.5 miles east of FS-371 and runs north through Chamberlain Basin to the Main Salmon in 39.0 miles.

(c) FST-002, Crooked Creek/Cold Meadows GS/ Chamberlain Basin GS Trail. This trail is a primary north/south route through the northern portion of the RNRW known as the Chamberlain Basin. It leaves Big Creek and FST-196 at Crooked Creek and proceeds northeast to Cold Meadows GS in 16.0 miles, then turns northwest and follows a ridge line to Chamberlain Basin in another 20.0 miles.

(d) FST-009, Bismark Mountain Trail. This trail leaves FST-002 2.8 miles above Big Creek and climbs up to Bismark Saddle in 4.0 miles.

(e) FST-043, Cold Mountain Trail. FST-043 leaves FST-002 0.5 mile south of Cold Springs GS and climbs up to the summit of Cold Mountain in 2.5 miles.

(f) FST-044, Horse Mountain/Black Butte Trail. This trail leaves Big Creek at Cabin Creek and then climbs up to the summit of Horse Mountain in 6.0 miles. From this point, it continues northeast to Black Butte and a junction with FST-168 [Approach: (H)(3)(b)] in another 5.5 miles.

(g) FST-003, Mosquito Ridge Trail. FST-003 leaves FS-371/FST-373 7.3 miles above Big Creek and climbs steeply up to the top of Mosquito Ridge. The trail then follows the ridge top north to Mosquito Peak in 12.0 miles and Sheepeater Mountain in another 9.0 miles. From Sheepeater Mountain, the trail turns east and proceeds to Chamberlain Basin GS in another 11.0 miles. Chicken Springs and Mosquito Springs provide adequate water (remember to boil or use a filter) even in the driest years.

(7) FS-403, Boulder Creek Road. Turn east off ID-55 just south of the McCall airport at highway milepost #142. (A new Mormon church is located just east of ID-55 at this turn.) Follow this paved road east as it makes several 90-degree turns and eventually junctions with FS-403 at a signed intersection. Turn onto FS-403, which is paved, and follow it east. In 1.0 mile the pavement ends and at 1.8 miles the road crosses a cattle guard. Just after the cattle guard there is a major junction—proceed straight ahead here, and at all other minor junctions. FS-403 dead ends after 4.8 miles, at the base of the Boulder Meadows Reservoir dam. There are two trailheads at the end of the road.

(a) Louie Lake Trail. This trail begins at a signed trailhead 100 yards west of the Boulder Meadows Reservoir dam and runs for 2.0 miles to Louie Lake at the base of Jughandle Mountain's picturesque north face. The last 1.0 mile of the trail is along a jeep trail which can also be accessed from the west.

(b) FST-105/FST-103/FST-096, Boulder Creek Trail System. From the end of FS-403 at the north end of the Boulder Meadows Reservoir, this trail system leads to Boulder Lake and beyond and gives access to many of the Lick Creek Range's most interesting peaks. FST-105 runs due east from the trailhead for 3.0 miles past Boulder Lake to a trail junction. From this junction, FST-103 runs north and south. Taking FST-103 north will lead to Boulder Summit in just over 1.0 mile and eventually to Lake Fork CG on FH-48 [Approach: (B)(4)(a)] in another 4.0 miles. Traveling south on FST-103 leads to the Paddy Flat GS in 7.0 miles. Also, from this junction FST-096 runs due east over Buckhorn Summit and eventually to the South Fork of the Salmon River at Poverty Flat [Approach: (C)(2)(d)].

(c) Boulder Lake to Louie Lake Trail. The Paddy Flat USGS quad shows a trail leaving FST-105 just east of Boulder Lake and proceeding south to the pass between Jughandle Mountain and Twin Peaks, where it descends to Louie Lake.

Even though this trail is not shown on the newest Payette National Forest maps, it does exist as indicated on the USGS map. An old vandalized sign on a tree (visible only to those walking west on FST-105) marks the beginning of the trail. Although the tread is difficult to follow at first (and disappears occasionally), following this very scenic trail is well worth the effort. The USGS map will prove invaluable in following this route. (Some maintenance work was done by volunteers in 1989.)

(8) FS-388, Kennally Creek Road. This road leaves ID-55 3.0 miles north of Donnelly. Turn east onto a county road which becomes FS-388. This road leads to Kennally Creek campground. From the road's end, FST-099, FST-101 and FST-102 lead deep into the range's roadless country and provide access to many peaks. The road is passable to passenger cars. Access to the Jughandle Mountain area is also possible from FS-388, but you will need a 4WD.

(a) FST-099/FST-306, East Fork to Blackmare Lookout Trail. This trail leaves the Kennally Creek trailhead and proceeds up Kennally Creek to Cougar Creek Summit in 5.5 miles, where it junctions with several other trails including FST-306, which leads to the top of Blackmare Peak in another 0.8 mile.

(b) FST-101, Needles Trail. FST-101 leaves FST-099 just east of the Kennally Creek trailhead and climbs steeply to Needles Summit (Pass) in 4.0 steep miles. At the summit, the trail enters the Boise National Forest and junctions with FST-115, which runs south into the Gold Fork drainage and FST-303 [Approach: (C)(2)(e)], which supposedly follows a ridge top east toward White Rock Peak and then northeast to the South Fork of the Salmon River. In 1987, FST-303's tread was almost impossible to find east of Needles Summit.

(9) FS-498/ FS-402, Gold Fork Access. From the Cascade, Idaho Post Office, drive north on ID-55 for 12.9 miles to a point just south of where the highway crosses the Gold Fork River. Turn east and drive 0.2 mile, turn right again and drive south for 0.3 miles and then turn left onto FS-498. Follow FS-498 east for 9.3 miles to the first FS-498/FS-402 junction. (Note that FS-402 loops east and then rejoins FS-498 further north.) Continue straight ahead for another 2.7 miles and turn left at the second FS-402 junction. Turn right and follow FS-402 for 7.2 miles to the Gold Fork Trailhead. From this trailhead, FST-114 and then FST-115 give access to the southern Lick Creek divide. (Note: FS-498 continues north from its junction with FS-402 and eventually leads to Kennally Creek CG [Approach: (B)(8)].) A 4WD is recommended.

(a) Needles Peak Access. This approach point is located 100 yards west of the Gold Fork Trailhead, where an old skid road numbered FS-402D (and not shown on the Forest Service map) runs off to the northeast. The old skid road requires a 4WD—it may be best to park on FS-402 and walk it as it cuts around a hillside to a clearcut. Once in the clearcut, leave the road, climb west up to the ridge top and then hike the ridge north cross country up to the top of Needles Peak. The first part of the ridge is very brushy.

(C) Cascade Approaches.
Cascade is a small resort/logging town located on ID-55. The town of 1,000 provides food, gas and lodging.

(1) FS-22, Warm Lake Highway/Landmark. This road leaves Cascade and ID-55 at the north edge of town and proceeds 26.0 miles to Warm Lake, another 11.0 miles to Landmark and to Stanley in 108.0 miles. The road is paved to Landmark and has recently been plowed in the winter to Warm Lake. Whether this plowing will continue every winter is unknown.

(1.1) FS-467, Cabin Creek Road. This road leaves the Warm Lake Road north of Warm Lake and follows Cabin Creek north for 5.0 miles. A 4WD is recommended.

(a) FST-086, Thunderbolt Mountain Trail. FST-086 leaves FS-467 at its end and proceeds to the top of Thunderbolt Mountain in 1.2 miles.

(2) FS-474/FS-674, South Fork Salmon River Road. This road follows the South Fork of the Salmon River from near its headwaters (south of Stolle Meadows) to its confluence with the East Fork of the South Fork of the Salmon River (east of Yellow Pine), a distance of 45.0 miles. The section of the road between the Warm Lake Road and FH-21 is often plowed in the winter to provide access to Yellow Pine. Recently the Forest Service proposed closing sections of the road to protect the river from erosion; due to the subsequent public protest it is not known at this time whether the road will be closed, paved or left the way it is.

(a) FST-087, Fitsum Creek Trail. This trail leaves the South Fork Road just south of its junction with FH-21, the Lick Creek Summit/Yellow Pine Road. The trail runs southwest up Fitsum Creek for 12.0 miles to Fitsum Summit northwest of Nick Peak. Though brushy, the trail has a good tread. Stream crossing will be difficult early in the season.

(b) FST-090, Indian Ridge Trail. FST-090 leaves the South Fork Road at the Krassel Work Center and follows Indian Ridge southeast to Indian Peak in 8.0 miles, and on to Eagle Rock in an additional 3.0 miles. In the vicinity of Eagle Rock, the trail junctions with several other trails, including FST-091 to Caton Lake, FST-092, which

The unclimbed east face of Cougar Rock

leads south to Log Mountain and FST-093, which is discussed directly below.

(c) FST-093, Fourmile Creek Trail. This trail leaves the South Fork Road 17.4 miles south of the Warm Lake Road and climbs up to Fourmile Summit (just south of Eagle Rock) in 7.0 miles, where it joins with the Indian Ridge trail system.

(c.1) FST-092, Log Mountain Trail. FST-092 leaves FST-093 just south of Fourmile Summit and follows a ridge line south to Log Mountain in 5.0 miles. The tread of this trail varies from good to nonexistent. For the most part, when the trail is in the trees it is easy to follow and when it goes through meadows it is hard to find. Keep your eyes open.

(d) FST-100, Blackmare Creek Trail. This trail leaves FS-674 and the South Fork at the Poverty Flat trailhead, which is 14.4 miles north of the Warm Lake/Landmark Road. There is camping available at the trailhead and a good steel bridge across the river. FST-100 reaches Blackmare Summit after 8.0 miles. From Blackmare Summit, FST-306 runs northeast to Blackmare Peak, FST-098 leads north to Cougar Creek and FST-099 leads west to the Boulder Lake area. See [Approach: (B)(7)(b)] above.

(e) FST-303, White Rock Peak Trail. This trail leaves the South Fork Road at the same point as FST-100 described above and climbs southwest to White Rock Peak in 5.0 miles and Needles Summit in about 9.0 sometimes obscure miles [Approach: (B)(8)(b)].

(f) FST-109, Cougar Rock Trail. This trail is located south of the Warm Lake/Landmark Road. On the latest edition of the Payette National Forest map and on the USGS Warm Lake quad, this trail is clearly shown leaving the South Fork Road at the Stolle Meadows GS. Though both maps are out of date and inaccurate, as of 1989, a sign just north of the GS identifies an old road as the trailhead. At the trailhead, one discovers that the trail no longer exists in a usable form and that it is very difficult to cross the South Fork at this point. If you cross the river and find your way around the swamp on the other side, it is possible to find the old trail—cluttered with downed timber—and eventually reach Cougar Rock and Stolle Peak.

However, there is a better way. Take FS-474 south from FS-22 for 4.7 miles and then turn west onto FS-483, which is signed "Logging Road—Dead End." (FS-483 is partially shown on the Payette National Forest map, but is not shown on the Warm Lake quad.) Drive across the river on a good bridge, turn left when the road forks and follow it up to a saddle 1.0 mile southeast of Cougar Rock, at 5,640 feet. At this saddle, the road turns sharply and drops steeply downhill to the south; there is some room to park here. Look carefully, and the trail can be found running uphill. The route is vague in places, but sharp eyes can find blazes on trees for the entire distance. Cougar Rock is reached in 1.0 mile; Stolle Peak is 2.0 miles from the start of the trail. A 4WD is required to drive FS-483, and expert skills are required to hike the trail.

(3) FS-579, Landmark/Stanley Road. This high-quality gravel road runs from Landmark to ID-21 west of Stanley. Using this road, ID-21 and the Warm Lake Road, it is 108.0 miles between Cascade and Stanley.

(a) FST-009/FST-102, Rice Peak Trail. The route to Rice Peak begins 3.0 miles south of Deadwood Summit and climbs up to a ridge top in 4.0 miles. From the top of the ridge, FST-102 runs north and south. Rice Peak is 2.0 miles south of the junction. This trail receives little use or maintenance.

(b) FST-013, Blue Bunch Mountain Trail. This trail leaves the Landmark/Stanley Road 5.0 miles northwest of Cape Horn Summit at Fir Creek CG and climbs to the top of Blue Bunch

Mountain in a long 4.5 miles.

(c) FST-024, Lolo Lakes Trail. FST-024 begins at Cape Horn Summit on the Stanley/Landmark Road and climbs up to the base of Cape Horn Mountain before dropping down into Lolo Creek. In 1988, the trail along the top of the ridge and down the ridge into Lolo Creek was not in the best of condition. However, the open nature of the terrain allows for easy cross-country travel.

(3.1) FS-568, Dagger Falls Road. This road leaves the Landmark/Stanley Road in Bruce Meadows and runs north to the Middle Fork of the Salmon River in 11.0 miles.

(a) FST-068/FST-082, Morehead Mountain Trail. These two trails provide the best access to the summit of Morehead Mountain. FST-068 is the main trail down the Middle Fork. Follow it for 3.0 miles and then, just past the Morgan Airstrip, turn west and follow FST-082 up Prospect Creek to the summit.

(4) FS-413, Johnson Creek Road. This road begins at Landmark and follows Johnson Creek north for 23.0 miles to Yellow Pine. This road is graded and suitable for autos.

(a) FST-091, Trout Creek Trail. Access this road by turning west off of the Johnson Creek Road 7.2 miles north of Landmark. Follow the dirt road to its end, where the trail begins. It is roughly 3.0 miles to the top of Thunderbolt Mountain.

(4.1) FS-410, Shell Rock Road. This road leaves the Johnson Creek Road at Coffee Creek and then wiggles its way northwest to a trailhead east of Shell Rock Peak in about 12.0 miles.

(a) FST-094/FST-093/FST-096, Caton Lake Trail. The Caton Lake Trail leaves the Shell Rock Road trailhead and proceeds north to Caton Lake in 6.0 miles and then joins up with the FST-090 on Indian Ridge in 9.0 miles. See [Approach: (C)(2)(b)] above.

(D) Banks Approaches.

Banks is located 36 miles north of Boise on ID-55, at the point where the North Fork and main Fork of the Payette River converge. Banks is the proverbial "wide spot in the road" and offers only gas and food as services.

(1) Payette River Road. This road leaves ID-21 at Banks and follows the South Fork of the Payette River east through Garden Valley to Lowman in 33.0 miles. The road is paved to Garden Valley.

(1.2) FS-698, Middle Fork Payette River Road. This road leaves the Payette River Road at Crouch (8.1 miles east of ID-55) and runs north to Boiling Springs GS.

(2) FS-555, Deadwood Reservoir Road. This road leaves the Payette River Road 23.1 miles east of ID-55 (and 9.0 miles west of Lowman) at Big Pine Creek and runs north to Deadwood Reservoir and FS-579, the Landmark/Stanley Road. It is 26.0 long, narrow miles to Deadwood Reservoir and a total of 36.0 miles to the Landmark/Stanley Road.

(a) FST-033/FST-100, East Mountain Trail. This trail leaves the Boiling Springs GS and follows Middle Fork of the Payette River north for many miles to Clear Creek Summit. At mile 6.0, FST-100 runs up Fool Creek Ridge to reach East Mountain in another 5.0 miles.

(3) FS-670, Smiths Ferry Road. This road leaves ID-55 north of Banks at Smiths Ferry and connects with FST-698 and the Middle Fork of the Payette River south of Boiling Springs GS.

(4) FS-689, Packer John Road. This road accesses the North Fork Range from ID-55 and Smiths Ferry. Leave ID-55, cross the river, and then turn right and follow the river south until the road turns sharply and begins a climb up to the crest of the range on Packer John Mountain. A 4WD is recommended.

(E) Lowman Approaches.

Lowman is a small village situated on the South Fork of the Payette River. Primary access is via ID-21. Lowman is 72.0 miles northeast of Boise and 57.0 miles southwest of Stanley. The village is connected with Banks by the South Fork of the Payette River Road [Approach: (D)(1)]. Lowman has a few year-round residents and offers gas, food and lodging.

(1) FS-582, Clear Creek Road. This road leaves ID-21 at Lowman and proceeds north to FST-579, the Landmark/Stanley Road, in 21.0 miles.

(1.1) FS-515, Red Mountain Road. This road leaves FS-582 12.0 miles north of Lowman and runs northeast for 5.0 miles to the Red Mountain trailhead.

(a) FST-143 and FST-145, Red Mountain Area Trails. FST-143 leads to the top of Red Mountain in 2.5 miles; FST-145 leads to Red Mountain and Cat Creek Lakes, which are 3.5 to 4.5 miles away from the trailhead.

(2) ID-21. From Lowman to Banner Summit west of Stanley, ID-21 is (by Idaho standards) a wide, fast road with only a few sharp turns. This stretch of state highway accesses only one trailhead of note.

(a) FST-148, Eightmile Mountain Trail. This well-marked trailhead is located east of Lowman, where the highway crosses Warm Springs Creek. Turn at the National Forest trailhead sign and follow the road to its end. The trail climbs up to the Eightmile Mountain Ridge and then continues on to the north and the area east of Red Mountain.

(F) Stanley Approaches.

Stanley was once just a small ranching town at the base of the Sawtooth, Salmon River and White Cloud mountains. With the creation of the Sawtooth National Recreation Area, Stanley's economy is changing from running cattle to running people. ID-21 reaches Stanley from Boise after 129.0 miles; ID-75 reaches Stanley from both Ketchum and Challis. Gas, food and lodging are available.

(1) FS-008, Seafoam Road. This road leaves ID-21 19.0 miles west of Stanley at a well-signed junction. The road forks immediately after it leaves ID-21. Take the right fork and then, in 0.5 mile, take the left hand fork toward Seafoam GS. This road runs north and then west for 21.0 miles to the Josephus Lake CG.

(a) FST-014, Langer Lake Trail. This trail leaves FS-008 6.8 miles north of ID-21. The trail runs west to Langer lake in 2.6 miles and connects with the trail to Ruffneck Peak fire lookout in 3.75 miles; here, FST-014 turns north and leads to FST-013 and Helldiver Lake in 6.0 miles.

(b) FST-007, Rapid River Trail. To reach this trail, follow FS-008 1.2 miles north from the Seafoam GS and then turn onto a dirt road, which runs north up Rapid River for a short distance to the trailhead. This trail connects with FST-207 in 10.0 miles and reaches the Middle Fork of the Salmon River in 14.0 miles.

(c) FST-207, Cabin Creek Trail. This trail leaves FST-007 10.0 miles north of its trailhead, and then follows Cabin Creek north to the base of Little Soldier Mountain and a junction with the short trail that leads to its summit in 4.0 miles. From the summit, the trail descends to the Middle Fork of the Salmon near the Pistol Creek Ranch landing strip in another 4.0 miles.

(d) FST-013, Big Shoulder Mountain Trail. This trail begins at the end of FS-008 at Josephus Lake and runs to the Middle Fork of the Salmon River. Big Soldier Mountain is 10.0 miles from the trailhead along a beautiful route which passes numerous lakes and crosses a long, scenic ridge.

(e) FS-011/FST-008, Greyhound Mountain Trail. This route leaves FS-008 roughly 2.0 miles before the Josephus CG. The road was originally built to service the Greyhound Mine. A 4WD is recommended.

(2) FS-032, Basin Butte Road. This road leaves ID-21 5.0 miles west of Stanley and climbs up to Basin Butte Lookout in 9.0 miles. From a junction just south of the lookout, the road continues on to Hindman Lake and then to a locked gate at 18.0 miles. The last 9.0 miles to the gate require a 4WD. Beyond the gate, the mining access road continues almost to the summt of Red Mountain and provides access to the east side of Cabin Creek Peak.

almost to the summit of Red Mountain and provides access to the east side of Cabin Creek Peak.

(3) FS-013, Yankee Fork Road. To reach this road, drive east on ID-75 toward Challis for 14.0 miles to Sunbeam (42.0 miles west of Challis). At this wide spot in the highway, turn north on the Yankee Fork Road, FS-013, and proceed 9.0 miles to Bonanza.

(a) FST-161/FST-163, Custer Peak Trail. This route is accessed where FS-013 crosses Five Mile Creek, 4.5 miles northeast of Bonanza. The trail runs to the top of Custer Peak in 6.0 long miles. The route is easy to follow and well maintained. The only confusing spot is around a large meadow at 3.0 miles in. At this point, an obvious trail leads uphill; take the less obvious trail (actually the main trail) around the meadow.

(3.1) FS-074, West Fork Road. This road leaves Bonanza at the GS. Drive west to the spot where the road is gated. This is a rough road, but autos should be able to make it to the gate.

(a) FST-155, West Fork Trail. FST-155 leaves from the end of FS-074 and works its way up the West Fork of the Yankee Fork for 5.5 miles to the confluence of Cabin Creek. From this point, follow FST-113 up Cabin Creek until the turn for Crimson Lake is reached. The Crimson Lake trail is not shown on either the Forest Service or USGS maps, but it is signed and in passable condition. Camping is excellent at the lake, and all three named Tango Peaks can be climbed from this base camp.

(3.2) FS-172, Loon Creek Summit Road. This road begins 0.75 mile north of Bonanza (just past the old Yankee Fork Dredge sitting by the road). The road climbs to Loon Creek Summit in 10.0 miles, and then descends to Loon Creek GS deep inside the Frank Church-River of No Return Wilderness in another 13.0 miles. From the GS, roads lead north, west and south to provide access to a number of hiking trails which penetrate the southern portion of the RNRW.

(3.3) FS-356, Jordan Creek Road. This 4WD road leaves FS-172, the Loon Creek Summit Road, 6.1 miles north of its beginning. Turn west off of FS-172 onto this road, which ends in 2.5 miles, at roughly 9,300 feet in elevation. Beyond the road's end, a sketchy trail continues west and crosses the slopes of Mount Jordan and then drops into the Lightning Creek drainage.

(G) Challis Approaches.

Challis is a boom-or-bust town, dependent on the price of cattle and molybdenum. Gas, food and lodging are available at the present time. US-93 and ID-75 run north and west, respectively, from Challis and provide primary access to the eastern end of the range.

(1) FS-051, Bayhorse Creek Road. This road leaves ID-75 10.0 miles west of its junction with US-93 and climbs steeply up to Bayhorse Lake CG in 10.0 miles. Along the way, the road passes the mining town of Bayhorse.

(a) FST-206, Juliette Creek Trail. FST-206 leaves FS-051 1.3 miles above the ghost town of Bayhorse and runs due south to Kinnikinic Creek. A saddle on the west flanks of Bald Mountain is crossed 5.0 miles from Bayhorse Creek. This saddle is the best access point to the peak.

(2) FS-086, Challis Creek/Sleeping Deer Mountain Road. This road leaves downtown Challis and proceeds west for 43.1 miles to the base of Sleeping Deer Mountain. To reach this road, turn west off US-93 onto the Challis main street and then, in 0.5 mile, turn right onto the signed Challis Creek Road and follow it north and then west. The road is paved at first, then gravel. It eventually becomes very narrow and quite steep. FS-080 [Approach: (G)(2.2)] is reached in 10.5 miles, FS-090 (which leads to the South Twin Peak lookout [Approach: (G)(2.1)]) in 18.5 miles and the saddle between Twin Peaks in 19.0 miles. From the saddle, the road follows winding ridge lines west for another 23.9 miles to its end high above Rock Lakes. A 4WD is recommended.

(a) FST-112, Sleeping Deer Mountain Trail. This trail leaves from the end of FS-086 and climbs to the top of the mountain in 2.0 miles. It is an easy-to-follow trail which gains 760 feet along the way.

(b) FST-103, Woodtick Summit Trail. This superb ridge walk leaves FST-112 about 1.0 mile below the summit of Sleeping Deer Mountain. The trail reaches Woodtick Summit in 4.0 miles, and the base of Martin Mountain in another 2.5 miles.

(2.1) FS-080/FST-091, Challis Creek Lakes Road. This road leaves FS-086 10.5 miles west of Challis and runs to Mosquito Reservoir and Challis Creek Lakes in 18.0 miles. Beyond the reservoir a 4WD is recommended.

(2.2) FS-090, South Twin Peak Road. This road leaves FS-086 18.5 miles west of Challis (0.5 mile east of the Twin Peaks saddle). The road climbs to South Twin Peak's 10,340-foot summit in just over 1.0 mile. A 4WD is recommended.

(3) FS-055, Morgan Creek Road. This road leaves ID-93 10.0 miles north of Challis and climbs to Morgan Creek Summit in 24.0 miles, and then descends to Panther Creek, where it becomes the Panther Creek Road [Approach: (H)(4)], which eventually reaches the Main Fork of the Salmon [Approach: (H)(3)] east of US-93.

(3.1) FS-057, West Fork Road. The West Fork Road leaves FS-055 1.0 mile north of the BLM's Morgan Creek CG. This rough road runs north-

west for 7.0 miles to the Blowfly CG and trailhead.

(a) FS-143, White Goat Mountain Trail. This poorly maintained trail follows the West Fork of Morgan Creek west for 5.0 miles to the ridge line south of White Goat Mountain, where it joins FST-138, which runs north and south and crosses the summit of White Goat.

(H) Salmon Approaches.

Salmon is, perhaps, Idaho's nicest mountain retreat. The town of 3,400 is reached via US-93 from Missoula and Challis, and via ID-28 from eastern Idaho. Food, gas, lodging and some outdoor equipment shops can be found in town.

(1) FS-021, Williams Creek Road. This road is accessed from US-93 5.1 miles south of Salmon. Turn west off the highway and cross the Salmon River. Follow the road west for 0.5 miles and then follow it south along the Salmon River to Williams Creek. It is roughly 16.2 miles from this point to Williams Creek Summit, and another 10.0 miles to Panther Creek and FS-055.

(2) FS-020, Salmon River Mountain Road. This road runs along the eastern crest of the Salmon River for 42.0 miles between Iron Lake CG in the south and Napoleon Hill in the north. The road is accessed by many roads, including FS-021 as discussed above. A 4WD is advisable for much of the road.

(a) FST-093, Hat Creek Lakes Trail. FST-093 leaves FS-020 at its southern terminus at Iron Lake CG and runs due south 2.5 miles to Hat Creek Lakes. It meets FS-055 [Approach: (G)(3)] 6.0 miles beyond the lakes.

(3) FS-030, Salmon River Road. This road leaves US-93 at North Fork, 21.0 miles north of Salmon, and follows the Salmon River west for 26.0 miles to Corn Creek CG. The road is paved at first, then gravel, and provides access to FS-055, the Panther Creek Road [Approach: (H)(4)], and the Middle Fork canyon.

(a) FST-162, Salmon River Trail. From the end of FS-030, this trail follows the Main Fork west and provides access to many trails that make the long climb out of the canyon and up to Chamberlain Basin. The trail eventually connects with FS-1614 [Approach: (A)(1)], which leads to Riggins and US-95.

(b) FST-202/FST-168, Black Butte Trail. This trail leaves FS-30 at Corn Creek CG and climbs steeply to Butts Creek Point. From the point, the trail soon joins FST-168, which leads south to Black Butte in 16.0. miles. Southeast of the butte, the trail joins FST-169 which is discussed below. Also see [Approach: (B)(6.1)(f)].

(c) FST-169, Stoddard Trail. This trail leaves the end of FS-030, crosses a bridge and almost immediately climbs up toward Chamber-

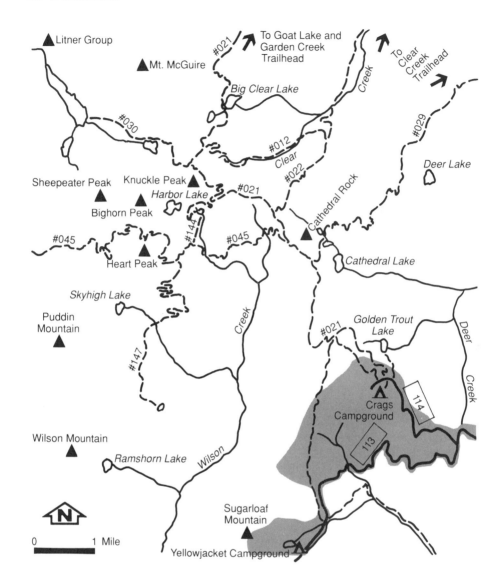

BIGHORN CRAGS TRAILS

lin Basin. It is the most direct approach into the basin from the east—direct, but also long and difficult.

(d) FST-172, Dome Mountain Trail. This trail leaves FS-30 just west of Panther Creek and then climbs to Dome Mountain in 11.0 steep miles. At Dome Mountain, the trail joins FST-021 [Approach: (H)(4.12)(a)] and then turns northeast, crosses Horse Heaven Peak and makes a steep descent to the Salmon River, which can be crossed with the aid of a cable cart.

(4) FS-055, Panther Creek Road. This road leaves FS-030 and the Main Salmon 26.0 miles west of North Fork. It runs north to Morgan Creek Summit, where it becomes the Morgan Creek Road [Approach: (G)(3)] and leads south to US-93 at a point 10.0 miles north of Challis. This road is a major avenue in the eastern Salmon River Mountains and is well maintained.

(a) FST-023, Birch Trail. This trail leaves FS-055 roughly 7.0 miles south of the Main Salmon River and climbs to Gant Peak and FST-026 in 6.0

long miles.

(4.1) FS-112, Yellowjacket Road. This road leaves the Panther Creek Road at Porphyry Creek. In 6.0 miles, the road crosses a saddle where FS-114 [Approach: (H)(4.12)] forks off to the north. FS-112 continues on to the summit of Middle Fork Peak. Yellowjacket CG is located along the way at Yellowjacket Lake, which is at the base of Sugar Loaf Peak.

(4.11) FS-113, Yellowjacket Lake Road. Turn off FS-112 onto FS-113, which leads to a junction with FS-114 in roughly 10.0 miles. Continuing straight ahead leads to Yellowjacket Lake in 4.0 miles, and the road's end in 5.0 miles.

(a) FST-039, McEleny Mountain Trail. This trail begins at the end of FS-113 and climbs to the top of McEleny Mountain in 3.0 miles, then descends to FS-112 at the old Yellowjacket town site.

(4.12) FS-114, Bighorn Crags Road. This road leaves FS-113 and proceeds north to Crags CG in 1.8 miles. The road is usually washboard-rough, but passable to autos.

(a) FST-021, The Crags Trail. This is the longest of the Bighorn Crag Trails. It starts at Crags CG and ends at Panther Creek, 31.0 miles later. Wilson Lake is about 7.0 miles from the CG and Dome Mountain is 15.0 miles in. For most of its distance, the trail follows a major ridge system and passes the following landmarks in this order: trail junction for Frog Meadows, view of Golden Trout Lake, the "tombstone" area (of the Cemetery, below), trail junction for Gant Ridge Trail, trail junction for the Water Fall Trail and Clear Creek Trails, the Cemetery, Cathedral Rock, Fishfn Ridge, Wilson Lake, Dome Mountain and Sagebrush Lookout. FST-029 leads to Cathedral Lake, where there is good camping for those interested in rock climbing in the Cemetery.

(b) FST-045, Waterfall Trail. Starting at the Crags Trail just west of Cathedral Rock, this long trail goes for 16.0 miles across the Crags and down to the Middle Fork of the Salmon.

(c) FST-144, Beaver Tail Trail. This trail connects Welcome and Birdbill Lakes. At its midpoint, just east of Wilson Lake, it connects with the Crags trail. The short north section of the trail runs from this junction to Birdbill Lake in 1.7 miles. (This trail is often covered by snow until late in the summer.) The equally short (also 1.7 miles) south section connects with the Waterfall Trail and the South End Trail.

(d) FST-030, Ship Island Lake Trail. This trail leads from Birdbill Lake to Airplane Lake, crosses a saddle and then descends to Ship Island Lake in 3.9 miles. Aggipah Mountain and the Litner group can be easily reached from the lake. It is 12.0 miles from Crags CG to the lake.

(e) FST-147, South End Trail. It is 6.1 miles

from Welcome Lake to Buck Lake. The trail provides access to several lakes and a number of named and unnamed peaks.

5. The Boise Mountains

The Boise Mountains form the southernmost portion of the Idaho Batholith. The range is bounded by the South Fork of the Payette River in the north, the Sawtooth, Smoky and Soldier mountains in the east and the Snake River plain in the south. The range's western boundary is roughly formed by ID-55, which runs between Boise, Horseshoe Bend and Banks.

The Boise Mountain topography holds over 20 mountain lakes and 35 named summits. Its terrain runs the gamut from gentle and rolling to rocky and vertical. Two Point Mountain, which reaches 10,124 feet, is the highest point. The Boise Mountains are hotter and drier than the northern Idaho Batholith mountains, with relatively short winter seasons, due to their low elevation and southern location.

The Boise Mountains are the main component of the Boise National Forest, which manages the vast majority of the range. The Sawtooth National Forest manages the eastern edge of the range, the State of Idaho manages a large track of land near Danskin Peak and the BLM manages some of the range's southern foothills.

Though mining and logging activities have long dominated the region's economy, several large tracks of roadless mountains still offer good opportunities for hiking and exploring. The largest roadless areas are the Trinity Mountain region and the upper reaches of the South Fork of the Boise River drainage. Besides these spots, hikers will find many other seldom-used trails worthy of their consideration.

The Boise Mountains, as a general rule, are less rugged than the Batholith's other mountain ranges. Still, there are a number of Boise peaks which provide worthwhile goals in the Class 1, Class 2 and Class 3 categories. Serious explorers can probably turn up numerous rock walls and formations which will provide adequate testing grounds for rock climbers. Most of the summits listed below provide great panoramic views, at a minimum. Many are rarely visited because they are unknown to the general public, and most offer choice opportunities for quality mountain experiences.

Wilson Peak *7,837 feet (Class 1-2)*
Wilson Peak is located 11.0 miles northeast of

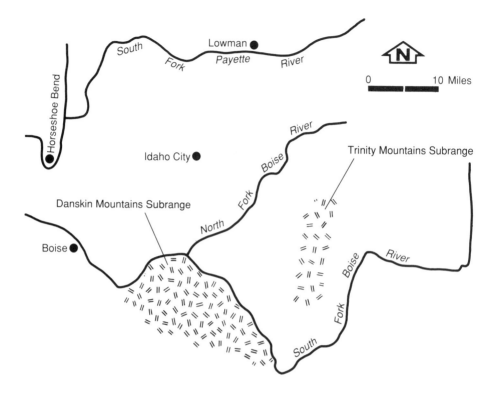

BOISE MOUNTAINS AND SUBRANGES

Idaho City and 3.5 miles west of Pilot Peak. From the road between Pilot and Freeman Peaks, an old Forest Service trail leads to the summit of this peak. The trail was included on the 1977 version of the Boise National Forest map, but is missing on the 1987 version. It is unknown if the trail will be maintained in the future, but because it follows a ridge line for its entire distance, the route can be followed with a map [Approach: (B)(3)(a)]. USGS Sunset Mountain

Freeman Peak* *8,096 feet (Class 2)*
This peak is located just 1.25 miles southwest of Pilot Peak and is identified on the Boise National Forest map. Drive or ski to the saddle between the two peaks and then hike or ski up the peak's eastern slopes to the summit [Approach: (B)(3)]. USGS Sunset Mountain

Pilot Peak *8,128 feet (Class 1)*
Pilot Peak is located 2.0 miles north of ID-21, where it crosses Mores Creek Summit. This former lookout site, the present site of a radio communications station, is reached by FS-380 [Approach: (B)(3)]. On winter weekends, dozens of cross-country skiers ascend the peak via the snow-bound road. The skiers either descend the road or the peak's broad south ridge. Note that there is some potential for avalanches at various points along the road and the ridge. USGS Sunset Mountain

Sunset Mountain *7,869 feet (Class 1)*
Sunset is located 5.0 miles south of Pilot Peak. It is an active fire lookout site during the summer, and is reached by FST-380 [Approach: (B)(3)], which leaves ID-21 at the top of Mores Creek Summit. Because of the road, the peak is of little interest in the summer months; but in the winter it is a popular ski touring route. It is 5.0 miles to the summit from Mores Creek Summit and ID-21. USGS Sunset Mountain

Wolf Mountain *8,876 feet (Class 2)*
Wolf Mountain is one of the more noteworthy Boise Mountain summits. It is composed of numerous cliffs and faces, which culminate in an impressive granite summit block. The peak is located 12.0 miles southeast of Lowman, where it sits at the headwaters of the Crooked and Bear rivers.

The peak is climbed from FST-312 [Approach: (B)(4.1)] by driving to Shonip Creek, which is roughly 3.0 miles east of the road's junction with the Jackson Peak Road. A side road leads south from the main road just past the "Shonip Creek" sign. Turn onto this road and park after 100 yards. From this point, the route involves difficult cross-country travel. Start the ascent by crossing the Crooked River (difficult in high water) and then continue on by slogging through a swamp of beaver ponds and mud. Once past the swamp, the route climbs up and to the south, paralleling Shonip Creek through thick timber for 1.0 mile. The timber eventually begins to thin out, and a view of the summit opens up to the south. Continue on to the large meadow at 8,000 feet. From this point, it is possible to access both the peak's north and west ridges. Either route will go with little difficulty, with the west ridge the easier one. To climb to the north ridge, follow the spur ridge just north of the meadow over easy but steep ground to the ridge line above. To avoid several obstacles, stay on the east side of the north ridge as it climbs to the summit. To climb to the west ridge, hike due south from the meadow through a short stretch of timber to the peak's open north slopes. Set a course that will bring you to the top of the ridge line at roughly the 8,500-foot level. Once on the west ridge, the route is open to the summit block. To avoid technical climbing, climb the summit block

from the south. USGS Jackson Peak

Tyee Mountain   8,753 feet (Class 2)

Tyee Mountain is situated 4.25 miles due east of Wolf Mountain and just a little more than 1.0 mile east of FS-312 [Approach: (B)(4.1)]. Climb to the summit from FS-312 via the connecting ridge that leads from the road east to the peak's summit. USGS Tyee Mountain

Shepard Peak   8,833 feet
Silver Mountain   8,573 feet (Class 2-3)

These two peaks are located 3.5 and 4.0 miles south of Tyee Mountain; both are accessed from FS-312 [Approach: (B)(4.1)]. Park where the road crosses the saddle northwest of the peaks, at the head of Big Silver Creek. From that saddle, contour southeast to another saddle, which is located northeast and directly below Shepard Peak's northwest ridge. From here, climb the ridge directly to the summit in a total of 1.5 miles of Class 2 climbing.

Silver Peak sits 0.75 mile southeast of Shepard Peak and is actually the southern summit of Shepard Peak. Even though it is 250 feet lower than its neighbor, it is a much more impressive-looking peak. Silver's north face is a broken 400+-foot vertical wall that has never been tested by climbers. Climb this peak from Shepard Peak and the connecting ridge line. The route is straightforward

The west face of remote Wolf Mountain

Goat Mountain forms the highest point on a long north–south ridge line that hides a number of seldom-visited lakes.

until the last 200 vertical feet. Keep on the southwest side of the summit ridge and follow it to the summit. USGS Swanholm Peak

Goat Mountain *8,915 feet (Class 3)*
Goat Mountain is isolated from the nearest roads by very difficult terrain. The peak sits 1.75 miles southwest of Shepard Peak at the southern end of a very rugged north/south ridge line. On the Swanholm Peak USGS quad, the name Goat Mountain is attached to the wrong point. The true summit is 0.4 mile due south of the named point. Two routes lead to the summit. The most direct (and most practical) route to the summit begins from FS-248 [Approach: (B)(1.3)] where it crosses Hunter Creek. Park at the crossing and follow the drainage east to the saddle just north of the peak and then climb the north ridge to the summit. The second route leaves FS-312 at the saddle at the head of Big Silver Creek and follows the ridge line for 1.5 miles to the summit [Approach: (B)(4.1)]. USGS Swanholm Peak

Swanholm Peak *8,727 feet (Class 1)*
Swanholm Peak is 5.5 miles south of Goat Mountain and 2.0 miles north of the North Fork of the Boise River. A number of trails lead to this lookout site. The recommended route follows FST-050 to the summit from FS-327 [Approach: (B)(2)(b)]. Hike up FST-050 along Horse Creek

for roughly 2.0 miles to a side trail that runs south to the summit via a ridge top. USGS Swanholm Peak

West Warrior Peak *8,930 feet (Class 2)*
West Warrior sits 1.5 miles southeast of Swanholm Peak and directly above Warrior Lakes, which are located in a broad cirque on the peak's northeast side. The summit is a Class 2 climb along the peak's north ridge from the point where it is crossed by FST-051 [Approach: (B)(2)(b)]. USGS Swanholm Peak

Grand Mountain *7,264 feet*
Granite Mountain *7,084 feet (Class 1-2)*
These peaks are located 5.0 miles southwest of Swanholm Peak on a high divide which separates the Middle Fork and North Forks of the Boise River. Both peaks can be climbed by either FST-049 [Approach: (B)(2)(a)] or FST-048 [Approach: (B)(1)(b)]. These trails are poorly marked and seldom used—make sure you take a USGS quad. The recommended route utilizes FST-49. Along this trail, it is roughly 2.0 miles to Granite Mountain and 3.0 miles to Grand Mountain. USGS Grand Mountain

Mores Peak *7,237 feet (Class 1)*
Mores Peak is located along the extreme western edge of the Boise Mountains 12.0 miles north

of Boise. The summit is reached from the Shaffer Butte picnic area, which is located in a saddle between Mores Peak and Shaffer Butte, via a 2.0-mile-long nature trail. Follow the trail around the peak until you are on its western side. Leave the trail at this point and walk the short distance to the broad summit. The picnic area is 20.0 road miles from Boise and can be reached via the Bogus Basin Road [Approach: (A)(1)(a)]. On a clear day, the views of the Sawtooths from the summit are striking. USGS Shaffer Butte

Shaw Mountain 5,908 feet (Class 1)
This peak is located 5.0 miles due east of Boise and 5.0 miles north of the Lucky Peak Reservoir dam. The summit area is reached by a rugged 4WD road [Approach: (A)(3)] from Boise. The road is seldom used by trucks and is becoming a favorite route for mountain bike enthusiasts. This is a good spring conditioning hike. USGS Lucky Peak

Sheep Mountain 8,148 feet (Class 2)
Sheep Mountain sits 12.0 miles south of Grand Mountain and 10.0 southwest of Steele Mountain. FST-124 traverses the north/south ridge line which contains Sheep Mountain. The shortest approach to this trail begins in the south from the Roaring River Road and FST-124 [Approach: (B)(1.2)(a)], or in the east from the same road and FST-045 [Approach: (B)(1.2)(b)]. The longest approach route begins where Sheep Creek empties into the Middle Fork of the Boise River and follows Sheep Creek east to a junction with FST-124 [Approach: (B)(1)(a)]. Once on FST-124, take it to the peak's eastern side and then scramble to the summit. USGS Little Trinity Lake

Rattlesnake Mountain 8,177 feet (Class 1)
This summit is situated 6.5 miles southwest of Sheep Mountain and is approached by trails from a number of different directions. The shortest walk is from Tipton Flat CG via FST-128 [Approach: (B)(1.11)(a)], which leads almost to the summit. Other approach routes to consider are FST-128 [Approach: (B)(1)(a)], which reaches the peak from Sheep Creek in the north, and FST-126/125 [Approach: (D)(3.1)(a) and (b)], which reaches the peak from the Trinity Mountain area to the east. USGS Prairie

Lava Mountain* 7,882 feet (Class 1)
Lava Mountain is located 3.5 miles due south of Rattlesnake Mountain and sits almost directly north of Prairie. Drive FS-222B to FST-125 [Approach: (B)(1.12)(a)], which leads to within a short distance of the summit. Scramble to the top

from the trail. As a longer alternative, the peak can be approached from the Trinity Mountain region. See [Approach: (D)(3.1)(a)] below. USGS Prairie

THE TRINITY MOUNTAINS
The long, high north/south ridge line that runs from Dog Mountain (just above Anderson Ranch Reservoir) to Sheep Mountain (just north of the Middle Fork of the Boise River) was known to prospectors as the Trinity Mountains. However, the USGS failed to adopt this name on its most recent maps, and the name is disappearing from the collective consciousness. Much of what was once known as the Trinity Mountains reaches above treeline and contains scattered mountain lakes in glacially carved cirques. The biggest of these cirques is located on the northeast side of Trinity Mountain (the highest point in this Boise Mountain subrange) and contains eight lakes.

Trinity Mountain 9,451 feet (Class 1)
Trinity Mountain is the very rugged culmination of the Trinity Mountains. Its steep northeast facade harbors a number of mountain lakes and numerous cliffs. The peak is located 8.5 miles west of Featherville and has a fire lookout on its summit. A service road, which is closed to private motor vehicles, provides a good route for a walk to the summit [Approach: (D)(3.1)(c)]. USGS Trinity Mountain

Peak 9037 9,037 feet (Class 2)
This unnamed summit sits 1.25 miles northeast of Trinity Mountain. From FS-129 [Approach: (D)(3.1)], ascend the peak's west ridge to the summit, a vertical distance of a little more than 500 feet. The view of Trinity Mountain from the top is as good a reason as any to climb this peak. USGS Trinity Mountain

---

Steele Mountain 9,730 feet
Steele Mountain is a jagged, steep granite peak that rises quickly out of the surrounding drainages to its ragged summit. It is located 10.0 miles north of Featherville. This twin-summited peak possesses steep walls and has several rotten needles on its lower ridges. The Forest Service has airlifted a small radio transmission facility to the summit, which is the highest point in the entire area. USGS Rocky Bar

Elk Creek Route. (Class 3)
This peak is most often climbed from Elk Creek. From Featherville, take FS-156 to Rocky Bar. Turn right onto FST-126, the James Creek

Road [Approach: (D)(6)], which runs northeast to Atlanta. In 4.0 miles, this road crosses Elk Creek where an unmarked trail leads up Elk Creek. Follow the trail up the drainage until it ends, and then continue up the eastern slopes of Steele Mountain's north peak. Pass the north peak on its southeastern side and climb the higher southern summit via the notch between the two peaks.

West Slope Route. *(Class 2)*
The summit can be reached from the west via the short but steep west side. From Rocky Bar, take FS-156 [Approach: (D)(5)] to the saddle just west of the peak. Park on the saddle and head up. The route begins in thick timber and later breaks out into the more open upper slopes. The broad slopes above the saddle eventually narrow down and the route becomes more obvious.

North Summit. *(Class 3)*
This 9,680+-foot peak is located slightly northeast of the main summit and is noteworthy because it is so rugged and enticing when viewed from the top of Steele. Climb via the saddle between the two peaks.

Two Point Mountain *10,124 feet*
Two Point Mountain is the highest point in the Boise Mountains. It is located 28.0 miles northwest of Fairfield, along the extreme eastern edge of the range, in a spectacular and little-visited area above the upper reaches of the South Fork of the Boise. Both summits (which are 0.5 mile apart) reach above 10,000 feet—the only two points in the Boise Mountains above that elevation. The higher south summit stands only 64 feet above the north summit, which is 10,060 feet tall. USGS Newman Peak

West Ridge Route. *(Class 3)*
From the South Fork and FS-012 follow FS-080 [Approach: (D)(7.11)(a)] up Bear Creek (4WD only) for 4.0 miles to Goat Creek. A jeep road leads up Goat Creek to an old mine. Park here and hike up this road until you reach the 8,400-foot contour line on the USGS quad, and then gain the ridge top, which leads up and around the cirque on the peak's west side. The ridge eventually reaches the lower (but very rugged) north summit without much difficulty. From this summit, follow the ridge to the main summit, staying mostly on the west side. Pass the difficult middle tower by winding around a rubble-filled ledge on its eastern side.

South Ridge Route. *(Class 2)*
Use the same approach directions as those provided for the West Ridge Route, but leave the road at the first stream crossing and follow a broad tree-covered ridge north for 1.5 steep miles to the summit.

Ross Peak *9,773 feet (Class 2-3)*
Ross Peak is located 2.0 miles southwest of Two Top Mountain. Two approach routes to the peak's western side have been suggested: (1) From the south, drive up FS-227 and get on FST-019 [Approach: (D)(7)(a)], which follows Willow Creek, and hike north for 10.0 miles to the saddle that divides Willow Creek from the South Fork of the Boise. (2) Take the shorter approach route from Bear Creek and FS-080. From the end of the road, find FST-197 [Approach: (D)(7.11)(b)] and follow it west across the nearby divide and then down into Willow Creek, where it joins FST-019. Though this peak can undoubtedly be climbed from its east side, the only reported climb was accomplished from the saddle northwest of the peak. From this saddle, the ridge line is passable to the summit, which is about 0.5 mile away. USGS Ross Peak

Newman Peak *9,603 feet (Class 2)*
This is a very picturesque and somewhat isolated summit. Take FS-012 from Big Smoky GS into the upper section of the South Fork drainage. Access the peak from FS-012 [Approach: (D)(7.1)(a)] at the Boise Corrals, which are located 1.25 miles after FS-012 crosses the South Fork. From this point, FST-069 departs and climbs up High Creek, crossing the southeastern slopes of the peak to the south ridge in 3.5 miles. Scramble up the south ridge. USGS Newman Peak

Gunsight Peak *9,527 feet (Class 2)*
Gunsight Peak is situated in the Willow Creek drainage, 3.25 miles southwest of Ross Peak. The peak is accessed from FST-019 [Approach: (D)(7)(a)], which traverses Willow Creek. One person reported that while deer hunting, they left the trail at Fern Gulch, climbed up the gulch, crossed over the summit and then descended down Gunsight Creek to the trail. Though the account of this journey was sketchy, it probably is a reasonable route. USGS Ross Peak

Jumbo Mountain *8,216 feet (Class 2)*
Jumbo is located 6.0 miles south of Gunsight Peak and 2.0 miles north of the South Fork of the Boise River. Follow FST-027 to the saddle north of the peak, leave the trail and climb up the north ridge to the summit [Approach: (D)(7)(b)]. USGS Ross Peak

THE DANSKIN MOUNTAINS

This small Boise Mountain subrange is 15 miles long, 3 to 5 miles in width and encompasses

Two Point Mountain, the highest point in the Boise Mountains, is a ragged collection of shattered towers and steep faces when viewed from the mountain's lower northern summit.

all of the Boise Mountains south of the South Fork of the Boise River. The highest summit in the range is Danskin Peak at 6,694 feet. Because of their relatively low elevation and proximity to the Snake River plain, the Danskins thaw out earlier than most Idaho mountains and are sometimes accessible as early as March. Although the range does not reach 7,000 feet in elevation, it rises over 2,500 feet from the South Fork to the summit of Danskin Peak in just 3 miles. The terrain is mostly open, with a few small stands of pine and firs on the wetter slopes. Many primitive roads penetrate the range and provide access to much of the range's terrain. The hiking is off-trail, but because this area is open, it is easy for experienced hikers to find their way. Numerous ridges and unnamed summits provide excellent hiking destinations.

Kerpos Mountain   5,428 feet (Class 1-2)

Kerpos offers a good early season hike. Its summit is located west of Lucky Peak Reservoir and 3.5 miles north of Three Point Mountain. Access the peak from FS-189 [Approach: (C)(1)(a)] and Three Point Mountain. From Three Point Mountain (using a USGS map), follow the connecting ridge lines north to the summit. USGS Arrowrock Dam

Three Point Mountain   5,300+ feet (Class 1-2)

This is the obvious, tri-summited mountain

visible from I-84 at the Black Creek Road Exit. Because of its low elevation and proximity to the Snake River plain, this summit is probably the first summit to melt out in Idaho. To reach the summit from Blacks Creek Pass, which is crossed by FS-189 [Approach: (C)(1)(a)], hike west up the jeep trail that leads to the ridge line just north of the north summit, and then follow the ridgeline south over the middle summit to the southernmost summit, which is the highest. A USGS survey marker is found on the summit, along with a terrific view of the Snake River plain. USGS Arrowrock Dam

Danskin Peak   6,694 feet (Class 1)

Danskin Peak is a worthy goal, not only because it is the highest point in the Danskin Mountains, but also because it is a beautiful, somewhat isolated summit with a terrific 360-degree view. The peak is located due north of Mountain Home and 7.0 miles southwest of Prairie. Most years, snowdrifts will keep the summit access road closed until late July, allowing hikers to visit the summit without being bothered by motor vehicles.

Throughout the spring, the shortest route to the summit follows FS-167 [Approach: (D)(1)] from where it crosses the Danskin Mountain crest east to the summit. The peak can also be approached from the southeast via FS-143, but this would involve a long hike over trailless terrain. USGS Danskin Peak 15-minute

127

Cathedral Rocks *5,280+ feet*

These vertical granite formations tower above the South Fork of the Boise River and are clearly visible from the area around Prairie, Idaho. They are included because they have an untested potential for rock climbing. The best approach to the rocks is to drive almost to the summit of Danskin Peak and hike down to the formations [Approach: (D)(1)]. USGS Danskin Peak 15-minute

APPROACHES TO THE BOISE MOUNTAINS

Approach routes for this section are identified in the text by bracketed entries [Approach:], which include appropriate letter and number references.

(A) Boise Access Approaches.

(1) FS-297, Bogus Basin Road. This road begins as part of Harrison Boulevard in Boise. From the corner of Main and 15th in downtown Boise, drive north on 15th (one-way) to West Hays. Turn left (west) on Hays and drive one block to the beginning of Harrison Boulevard. Turn right (north) on Harrison and follow it north into the Boise Mountains. It is 19.0 miles to the Shaffer Butte CG, which is located between Shaffer Butte and Mores Mountain. The road is paved almost to the Bogus Basin Ski Resort.

(a) Mores Mountain Trail. This is a short loop trail which circles the summit of Mores Mountain in roughly 2.0 miles. The trail leaves from the Shaffer Butte CG.

(2) Shaw Mountain Road/Rocky Canyon Road. From downtown Boise, take State Street east to Fort Street. Follow Fort east for one block and turn left on Reserve (at the corner of the park) and follow Reserve north. Reserve becomes Shaw Mountain Road and curves its way up through the Foothills East subdivision. At the top of the subdivision, the road forks. Table Rock Road is the right fork and Rocky Canyon is the left fork. Go left. It is 8.0 miles to the top of Aldape Summit and another 6.0 miles from the summit to ID-21.

(3) Table Rock/Lucky Peak Road. This road (now trail) leaves the Shaw Mountain Road at the top of the Foothills East subdivision and climbs to the top of Table Rock in just under 3.0 miles. The Lucky Peak Road forks off just before the summit of Table Rock and proceeds north, under the power lines, to the top of Lucky Peak in 5.5 miles. The road was closed to motor vehicles in early 1989.

(B) ID-21 Approaches.

ID-21 leaves Boise via Warm Springs Avenue.

Exit I-84 at the Broadway Exit and drive north on Broadway to the corner of Warm Springs and Broadway. Turn right and proceed east on Warm Springs (a continuation of Boise's Main Street) toward Lucky Peak Reservoir and Stanley. From Boise, ID-21 cuts through the heart of the Boise Mountains as it passes through Idaho City and Lowman. From Lowman to Grandjean, the highway follows the South Fork of the Payette River, which divides the Boise and Salmon River mountains. This highway provides access to numerous roads that penetrate the Boise Mountains. It is narrow and twisty, and often congested on summer weekends. Leave extra time in your travel schedule for those busy days.

(1) FS-269, Middle Fork Boise River Road. This road leaves ID-21 at the upper end of Lucky Peak Reservoir and follows the Middle Fork of the Boise east to Atlanta in 72.0 miles. It begins by following the edges of Lucky Peak and Arrowrock reservoirs for many tortuous miles before following the river east to Atlanta.

(a) FST-122, Sheep Creek Trails. FST-122 begins 30.1 miles east of ID-21. The Sheep Creek drainage runs to the base of Trinity Mountain and encompasses a number of trails which follow the drainage's tributaries and ridges. Two of these side trails are of particular interest. FST-128 leaves FST-122 4.5 miles east of the trailhead and leads south to Rattlesnake Mountain in another 6.0 miles of "now you see it, now you don't" trail. FST-124 leads to Sheep Mountain. Take FST-122 east for 11.0 miles and then follow FST-124 northwest for 1.0 mile to Sheep Mountain. Because the Sheep Creek trailhead is located at 3,400 feet in elevation, it melts out as early as the end of March—good for spring hiking.

(b) FST-048, Browns Creek Trail. This trail leaves FS-269 east of the Ninemyer CG and runs north to FS-049 in 7.5 miles. The trail is hard to follow in its upper end; also, its numerous stream crossings will be difficult in periods of high water.

(1.1) FS-113, Slide Gulch/Long Gulch GS Road. This road connects FS-269 (near the Middle Fork of the Boise River) with FS-189 (near the South Fork of the Boise River). The road is accessed from FS-269 just east of Willow Creek CG; from FS-189, 3.0 miles east of Prairie. Long Gulch GS is located midway between the road's two ends.

(1.11) FS-217, Tipton Flat Road. This road leaves FS-113 where the road crosses Rattlesnake Creek. The road follows the creek east to Tipton Flat CG in about 4.5 miles.

(a) FST-128, Rattlesnake Mountain Trail. FST-128 begins at the Tipton Flat CG and proceeds north over Rattlesnake Mountain in 3.0 miles and then descends along Devils Creek to meet Sheep Creek and FST-122 [Approach: (B)(1)(a)]. North of Rattlesnake Mountain, the trail junctions with FST-127, which also provides access to Sheep Creek.

(1.12) FS-222, Lava Mountain Access Road. This road leaves FS-113 where it crosses Spring Creek, then runs northeast toward Lava Mountain. In about 1.0 mile, the junction with FS-222b is reached. Follow this road, which is rough and sometimes impassable, to its end in 3.5 miles.

(a) FST-125, Smith Creek Lake Trail. FST-125 begins near the end of FS-222B, just west of the summit of Lava Mountain, and then leads to the summit area before running northeast to Smith Creek Lake, and eventually to the Trinity Mountain Area [Approach: (D)(3.1)(a)].

(1.2) FS-255, Roaring River Road. This route begins several miles west of the Dutch Creek GS, runs south up Roaring River and then east to FS-129 [Approach: (D)(3.1)] in roughly 15.0 miles.

(a) FST-124, Sheep Mountain Trail. FST-124 leaves FS-255 3.0 miles south of that road's beginning at the Middle Fork of the Boise River. This trail climbs due west to the ridge line that includes Sheep Mountain, and then runs due south to Sheep Mountain in about 5.0 miles. South of the mountain, it joins with FST-122 [Approach: (B)(1)(a)].

(b) FST-045, Roaring River Trail. This trail leaves FS-225 at its southernmost crossing of the Roaring River and begins the long climb out of the drainage to run due south to the Trinity Mountain area. It junctions with FST-122 [Approach: (B)(1)(a)] 2.0 miles from where it begins.

(1.3) FS-248, Bear River Road. This road begins at the Deer Park GS and runs north past Steamboat Creek, the Bear River and then into the Crooked River drainage before junctioning with FS-384 [Approach: (B)(4)] near the Willow Creek CG. This road was constructed to provide access to logging sites and its condition is far from ideal.

(2) FS-327, Granite Creek/North Fork Boise River Road. This road leaves ID-21 just east of Idaho City, climbs up Granite Creek, crosses over to Rabbit Creek and then descends to the North Fork of the Boise River, which it follows east to the Deer Park GS. From the GS, the road runs south over a divide to meet FS-269 along the Middle Fork of the Boise River.

(a) FST-049, The Grand Mountain Trail. FST-049 follows the high ridge line that divides the North and Middle Forks of the Boise River. The trail leaves FS-327 near the Barber Flat GS and runs northeast for 12.0 miles to Swanholm Creek Summit, where it once again joins FS-327. Along the way the trail junctions with FST-048 [Approach: (B)(1)(b)] just east of Grand Mountain.

(b) FST-050/FST-051/FST-052, Horse Heaven Creek/Swanholm Peak Trails. These trails are accessed from FS-327 1.8 miles south of Deer Park. Follow the old logging road up the Horse Heaven Creek drainage until it crosses the creek for the second time. At this point, the trail leaves the road and climbs up the drainage to the northeast to eventually cross Blue Jay and Lodgepole creeks. FST-052 runs up Lodgepole Creek and connects with FST-051 on the ridge at the top of the drainage. FST-051 runs from Swanholm Peak east into Warrior Lakes basin and then continues east to junction with FST-053 along the banks of Black Warrior Creek.

(3) FS-380, Sunset Peak/Pilot Peak Road. This road leaves ID-21 at Mores Creek Summit and runs both north and south from the highway. South of the highway, the road runs to the fire lookout on top of Sunset Peak in 5.0 miles. North of the highway, the road runs to a saddle north of Pilot Peak and then continues on to Pioneerville. From the saddle, a rough gravel road leads to the top of Pilot Peak.

(a) Wilson Peak Trail. This trail is no longer maintained by the Forest Service. The route, which is identified on the USGS quads and older Boise National Forest maps, begins as an old road between Freeman and Pilot Peaks, and then continues northwest along a ridge line for 1.5 miles, before turning due west along another ridge line and running to Wilson Peak in another 1.5 miles. This trail has not been maintained or signed in some time, and its current condition is questionable.

(4) FS-384, Willow Creek Road. This road is accessed from ID-21 just east of Mores Creek Summit. It leads south to FS-327 and the North Fork of the Boise River, and is the best approach available to the upper drainages of the North and Middle Forks of the Boise. The road opens up late in the summer and is often congested with logging trucks.

(4.1) FS-312, Graham GS Road. This road is accessed from ID-21 via FST-384. It usually requires a 4WD and the ability to use it in a safe manner. Turn off ID-21 and follow FS-384 for 4.0 miles, then turn east onto this road, which eventually leads to the Graham GS on the edge of the Sawtooths. It begins by following Banner Creek and then quickly turns onto Pikes Fork Creek, which it follows northeast to a high ridge line just south of Jackson Peak. East of the junction for Jackson Peak, the road drops into the Crooked River drainage, which it follows east, eventually climbing out of the drainage between Tyee Mountain and Wolf Mountain. For the next few miles, the road runs south along a ridge line and then drops into Big Silver Creek, which leads to the

North Fork of the Boise River.

(C) I-84 Approaches.
This Interstate Highway is the major east/west connector in Idaho.

(1) FS-189, Upper Blacks Creek Road. This road leaves I-84 at Exit #64, 10.0 miles east of Boise. The good gravel road extends north from the exit to Blacks Creek Pass in 9.0 miles. Keep left at the only major fork. From the pass, the road descends to the South Fork of the Boise River, which is located in a spectacular gorge cut out of lava rock. The road crosses the river and works its way east for 24.0 miles to Prairie, Idaho.

(a) Arrowrock Ridge Tracks. At the top of Blacks Creek Pass, there is a mining operation located on private property. On the north side of the pass cattle guard, a jeep track traverses Forest Service land and heads west up the ridge line to a point just north of Three Point Mountain. Once the ridge line is surmounted, the jeep tracks can be followed along the ridge line north to Kerpos Mountain and beyond. These tracks provide excellent early-season hiking.

(1.1) FS-113, Long Gulch/Slide Gulch Road. See [Approach: (B)(1.1)].

(D) Mountain Home Approaches.
Mountain Home is located 45.0 miles east of Boise and 89.0 miles west of Twin Falls, along I-84. The town of 8,000+ inhabitants offers all services.

(1) FS-167, Canyon Creek/Danskin Peak Road. This road is accessed from Mountain Home. From I-84, take Exit 90 and follow the old highway east toward town for 3.1 miles. Turn north on Canyon Creek Road and follow it through town and into the desert. In 8.2 miles, the pavement ends and a well-graded gravel road begins. The road forks at this point—keep left. Follow the gravel road to the northwest across a drainage for another 5.9 miles, to a point where the main gravel road veers sharply to the west. From this point, FS-167 begins and climbs directly uphill to the north. From this point on, the road is dirt—steep, rutted and almost impassable when wet—and a 4WD is highly recommended. Numerous side roads lead off the main road and will cause some confusion for those following the road without a map. Keep on the most-used road at each junction until a small reservoir is reached after 8.8 miles. Drive just past the reservoir and turn north up Case Creek. In another 4.5 miles, the road reaches the crest of the Danskin Mountains, west of Danskin Peak. From this point, a road descends to the South Fork of the Boise River, where it ends at a closed gate at a private property boundary. FS-167 continues on to the summit of Danskin Peak in 3.0 steep miles.

(2) ID-20. This state highway leaves I-84 at Exit 95 in Mountain Home and runs north and east to Fairfield. A major approach route, it is one of the best-constructed highways in Idaho. On Friday evenings, expect lots of trailer and recreational vehicle traffic.

(2.1) FS-131, Pony Creek Road. This road leaves ID-20 15.5 miles north of Mountain Home (3.7 miles past the Tollgate Cafe). Turn north on a distinct gravel road which runs north to the South Fork of the Boise River, where it connects with FS-113.

(2.2) FS-134, Anderson Ranch Dam Road. This road leaves ID-20 20.8 miles north of Mountain Home and runs north to the dam, where it connects with FS-113. The road is paved to within 1.0 mile of the dam.

(3) FS-113, South Fork Boise River Road. This road begins at the north end of Anderson Ranch Reservoir and follows the reservoir, and then the South Fork of the Boise River, west to the site of the old Danskin GS. From this point, the road climbs north out of the canyon and goes to the village of Prairie and FS-189 [Approach: (C)(1)] in 8.2 miles.

(3.1) FS-123/FS-129, Trinity Mountain Road. This road leaves Anderson Ranch Reservoir 8.8 miles east of the dam at Fall Creek. The road follows Fall Creek north to the top of the Trinity Mountain divide in 16.5 miles. From the high point, the road follows a ridge line north and joins up with FS-156 [Approach: (D)(5)] just west of Steele Mountain. Though a major thoroughfare, this route is narrow, steep and rough in places.

(a) FST-125, Smith Creek Lake Trail. This trail leaves FS-129 and runs west to Smith Creek Lake in 1.5 miles, and then continues on to Lava Mountain in another 5.5 miles.

(b) FST-126, Bear Gulch Cutoff Trail. FST-126 leaves FST-125 3.0 miles west of Smith Creek Lake and runs north to join with the Sheep Creek Trail system east of Rattlesnake Mountain. See [Approach: (B)(1)(a)] above.

(c) FS-129A, Trinity Mountain Road. This road leaves FS-129 and runs east. It is open for about 0.5 mile and then gated shut. From the gate, it is 1.5 miles to the summit of Trinity Mountain.

(4) FH-61, Featherville Road. This road leaves ID-20 31.9 miles northeast of I-84 at Exit 95 and runs north to Featherville. The road is gravel to the north end of Anderson Ranch Reservoir, and then paved to Featherville.

(5) FS-156, South Fork/Middle Fork Road. This road begins in Featherville and runs northwest to Rocky Bar in 8.0 miles, to FS-129 in about 6.0 more miles and then eventually the Middle Fork of the Boise River and FS-268 [Approach: (B)(1)]. Just north of its junction with FS-129, the road crosses a saddle on the western flanks of

Steele Mountain. This is the starting point for a climb of that peak.

(6) FS-126, James Creek Road. This road is an alternative route to Atlanta. It begins at the Rocky Bar ghost town and runs north to Atlanta. It is steep in places and a 4WD would be useful, but not required.

(7) FS-227, South Fork Road. This excellent gravel road begins in Featherville and proceeds east along the South Fork of the Boise River to Big Smoky GS. Note that this road can also be accessed from both Fairfield and Ketchum via Forest Service roads. See [Approach: (A)(1)] in the Soldier Mountain Access section and [Approach: (A)(7)] in the Smoky Mountain Access section.

(a) FST-019, Willow Creek Trail. This trail leaves FS-227 at the Willow Creek CG and follows Willow Creek northeast for nearly 10.0 miles to a pass northeast of Ross Peak, where it joins FST-227 [Approach: (D)(7.1)(b)].

(b) FST-027, Jumbo Creek Trail. This trail leaves FS-227 just east of the Baumgartner CG. and follows Jumbo Creek northeast to a ridge line north of Jumbo Mountain.

(7.1) FS-012/FS-079, Upper South Fork Road. This road is accessed from FS-227 at the Big Smoky GS. It runs northwest from the Big Smoky area, crosses a small divide and drops into the upper reaches of the South Fork drainage. The road follows the river north, nearly to the Sawtooth Wilderness boundary. Be advised that the upper stretches of this road require a 4WD.

(a) FST-069, Newman Peak Trail. This route begins at the South Boise Corral. From FS-012, the trail climbs along High Creek for almost 2.0 miles, and then runs south and west to the upper reaches of the Bridge Creek drainage. At this point, the trail is situated on the high slopes of Newman Peak. It continues west across the southern slopes of that peak, then continues on further to the west, where it joins an extensive trail system not covered by this book.

(b) FST-227, South Fork Trail. This trail begins at the end of FS-012 and proceeds south to Ross Pass, northwest of Ross Peak. At the pass, the trail joins FST-019, which traverses Willow Creek [Approach: (D)(7)(a)].

(7.11) FS-080, Bear Creek Road. This road leaves FS-012 near the South Fork CG. It is a rough, rutted primitive road that requires a 4WD. It begins with a stream crossing, then proceeds due west from the South Fork to the old Red Horse Mine in about 6.0 miles.

(a) FST-061, Goat Creek Trail. FST-061 leaves FS-080 where Goat Creek flows into Bear Creek, then climbs north to the Tip Top Mine and Goat Lake. Although not shown on the Forest Service map, the trail continues over the divide to

the north and drops down into Bass Creek, where it is designated FST-061. This trail is actually a 4WD road for most of its distance.

(b) FST-197, Bear Divide Trail. This trail begins at the end of FS-080, runs west, climbs almost immediately over a divide and then drops down into Willow Creek, where it joins FST-019 [Approach: (D)(7)(a)].

6. The Sawtooth Range
by Lyman Dye and Tom Lopez

The Sawtooth Range is located completely within the Sawtooth National Recreation Area (SNRA), just west of Stanley and the Stanley Valley. This oval-shaped group of mountains is bounded by the Stanley Valley on the east and by ID-21 in the north and west. The Boise and Smoky mountains form the less well-defined southern boundary of the Sawtooth Range, which ends on the slopes of Greylock Mountain north of Atlanta.

The Sawtooths are the home of Idaho mountaineering and are the best-known of Idaho's many mountain ranges. The range is an extremely rugged collection of granite peaks and alpine lakes with an eastern escarpment which is perhaps Idaho's most impressive mountain wall. Scattered throughout the range are 33 peaks that exceed 10,000 feet, as well as numerous spires and formations crowding the high Sawtooth ridges. The Sawtooth crest runs over 32 miles from north to south and measures 20 miles across its widest point. The main crest begins on McGown Peak and snakes south to Snowyside Peak. Along this route, a number of impressive subsidiary ridges spread out from the crest and include some of the range's most challenging summits: Thompson Peak, the highest Sawtooth peak at 10,751 feet; Mount Heyburn, the most unusual-looking Sawtooth peak; and Warbonnet Peak, the most difficult Sawtooth peak.

Geologically, granite and glaciation are the main characters in the story of the Sawtooths. The Sawtooth pluton was injected into the larger Idaho Batholith 40 million years ago, at a depth of only 3 to 4 miles. Its granite is pinker than Idaho Batholith granite because it contains more feldspar. Sawtooth granite is also extensively fractured by vertical jointing, which has caused the range to erode into jagged edges and towers rather than keeping the hump-shaped appearance characteristic of much of the Idaho Batholith mountains. Sawtooth glaciation was both merciless and artistic as it cut away millions of tons of rock and created the state's largest alpine lake basins—and a climbing environment second to none.

The Forest Service, through the SNRA, manages the Sawtooth Range. From almost the beginning of this century, there have been numerous unsuccessful proposals to include the Sawtooth Range in the National Park System. Finally, in 1972, with the aid of a favorable political climate, the Sawtooth National Recreation Area was created by Congress as a compromise between environmentalists and resource developers. In effect, the SNRA is a de facto national park which has provided the Sawtooths with protection without creating a Yosemite-like (i.e. carnival-like) atmosphere. The concept, which emphasizes recreation, protection of 200,000 acres of wilderness and preservation of the ranching economy, is working well and has gained wide acceptance within the state.

The SNRA offers limited services by national park standards, but more than adequate services by Idaho standards. There are numerous developed campgrounds, and camping is generally allowed along most roads. Stanley is a unique small town that provides visitors with food, lodging and gasoline—as long as you do not need them too late at night.

Because of the "knock your socks off" scenery and the National Recreation Area designation, the Sawtooths are Idaho's busiest location for hiking and climbing. Although hikers tend to cluster around the major Stanley area destinations, the entire Sawtooth backcountry is worthy of consideration. (Consult Margaret Fuller's *Trails of the Sawtooths and White Cloud Mountains* for additional hiking information.)

The Forest Service is slowly upgrading the roads, trailheads and trails within the SNRA. Some roads are still unforgiving destroyers of automobiles, but most are surprisingly nice. The trail system is almost too good—most trails have been rebuilt over the last 20 years and are in near-perfect condition. No permits are required to enter the backcountry unless you have an unusually big group, or are using horses.

The Sawtooths' granite offers climbers the largest number of climbing opportunities in Idaho, as well as the most variety, with routes ranging from Class 1 to Class 6 in difficulty. Although the majority of the technical routes are clustered around Redfish Lake, the challenges provided by the entire range are unlimited and the climbing is seldom crowded. The climbing potential of the Sawtooths will only be realized, when climbers expand their horizons beyond the Heyburn/Warbonnet area.

Mount Zumwalt   *8,816 feet (Class 2)*

Trees grow right to the summit of this Sawtooth peak, which is located 4.0 miles northwest of the Grandjean CG. Yet, it is a worthwhile climb because it offers a good view of the Sawtooth Crest to the east. Park your car 0.25 miles east of where the Grandjean Road [Approach: (B)(3)] crosses Canyon Creek. From this point, climb due north up the steep, broad ridge which rises above the road. The ridge narrows down after a 1,000-foot climb. Stay on its crest as much as possible and work your way to Point 7175. Catch your breath, and then continue up the ridge until it connects with Mount Zumwalt's west ridge at roughly 8,200 feet. Turn east and follow the ridge the last 600 feet to the summit. Total distance of this route is about 3.0 miles, with a 3,800-foot elevation gain. USGS Grandjean

McGown Peak   *9,860 feet*

This spectacular summit rises serenely 2.0 miles south of Stanley Lake. Except for Mount Regan, it is the most picturesque of the Sawtooth peaks. The first ascent was by R. Underhill, M. Underhill and D. Williams, in 1934. USGS Stanley Lake / SW

Northeast Diagonal Route. *(Grade II, Class 4)*

Cross the south shoreline of Stanley Lake [Approach: (B)(2)(b)] and proceed across the northern slopes of the peak to the base of a large diagonal couloir which cuts from southwest to northeast. Start climbing at the top of the moraine just north of the stream. (This will avoid some of the thick underbrush but does cross lots of downed timber.) The couloir rises to the peak's south ridge. Gain the ridge and climb to the north, staying on the west side of the ridge. You will reach a saddle with a long, high, smooth cliff on the right. The summit, which is not in view at the top of this cliff, is not the broad peak directly to the north. To reach the true summit, cross the entire base of the cliff on snow patches and ledges, then double back and climb to the southeast up to the northeast rim. From this point, the 300-foot summit pinnacle is visible. The route continues up the pinnacle and makes a nearly-complete spiral to the summit.

Other Routes.

At least two other routes have been climbed. No ratings are available for either of these routes. The first follows FST-640 [Approach: (B)(2)(a)] to the point above Lady Face Falls where the trail crosses Stanley Lake Creek. Climb the forested west buttress to Point 9248, and then follow the ridge to the summit. The second route follows FST-528 [Approach: (B)(2)(b)] along the peak's east side. Leave the trail at the 7,400-foot contour, drop down to the creek and then follow the creek to Lake 8609. Climb to the saddle due west of the lake, then climb to the north along the ridge to the summit.

Observation Peak *9,151 feet (Class 1)*

Observation peak sits 3.0 miles south of McGown Peak and west of the main Sawtooth crest. The peak's summit is reached by a good trail, which can be accessed from the north, south and east. The most direct route utilizes FST-640 [Approach: (B)(2)(a)], which it follows south up Stanley Creek for 6.0 miles to a well-marked junction with FST-024 [Approach: (B)(2)(a.1)], which leads to the summit. USGS Stanley Lake

Alpine Peak *9,861 feet (Class 2)*

This peak rises up directly east of Sawtooth Lake and provides excellent vistas of the lake and of Mount Regan as well. From FST-478 [Approach: (B)(1)(c)], at the south end of Sawtooth Lake, follow one of the numerous gullies to the easy slopes above. Gain the summit ridge east of the summit and follow it to the top. Other than loose scree, the route is straightforward. USGS Stanley Lake / SW

Mount Regan *10,190 feet*

Mount Regan is the most photographed of all Sawtooth peaks. Its northwest face has graced numerous calendars and book covers. The peak is located at the south end of Sawtooth Lake and 1.0 mile southwest of Alpine Peak. The first recorded ascent was by R. Underhill, M. Underhill and D. Williams, in 1934. To approach the peak for all of the routes listed below, hike to Sawtooth Lake [Approach: (B)(1)(b)]. USGS Stanley Lake / SW

Southeast Ridge. *(Class 3)*

First ascent by R. Underhill, M. Underhill and D. Williams, in 1934. From Sawtooth Lake, take the trail south across the broad saddle and drop down to Lake 8271. From the lake, contour around the base of the southeast ridge and enter a large (and rotten) gully. Follow the west side of the gully up until it is nearly vertical, and then exit to the west onto a steep tree-covered slope that leads to the top of the ridge. Follow the ridge up until it deadends at the base of the summit dome. From this point, the route follows an exposed ledge out onto the east face for 50 feet to a concave pocket. There are two obvious lines up the pocket's walls to the ridge above. Climb up to the summit ridge, and then weave in and out of the large blocks to reach the summit.

Lower East Face. *(Grade II, YDS 5.2)*

From Lake 8489, just south of Sawtooth Lake, climb toward the steep couloir that cuts up toward the southeast ridge. Above the lake, a ledge system leads to the base of the couloir. Climb the couloir to the southeast ridge (see above) and follow it to the summit. This couloir is a steep snow climb in the early summer, but becomes an ex-

tremely loose rock chute in late summer.

North Ridge. *(Class 5)*

Climb the steep slabs at the south end of Sawtooth Lake. Follow the ridge toward the summit to the highest point directly above the prominent notch which separates the ridge from the mountain. Rappel down into the notch until it narrows enough so that you can safely anchor yourself on the opposite wall. Climb up the notch wall to the ridge and follow it to the summit.

Other Routes.

The summit register contains a number of references to ascents by other ridges. None of the write-ups were detailed enough to be included in this book.

Merritt Peak* *10,312 feet*

This peak is located 1.9 miles east of Mount Regan and 0.5 mile south of Goat Lake. The peak's name is taken from the latest copy of the Sawtooth National Forest map. The summit is barred by near-vertical walls on almost every side. Access the peak from Goat Lake [Approach: (B)(1)(a.1)]. USGS Stanley Lake / SW

Snowfield Route. *(Class 4)*

Climb via the snowfield system above Goat Lake and on the peak's northeast side (this system is clearly shown on the Stanley Lake USGS quad). Although few details are available, the route is reportedly straightforward when good snow conditions exist.

Williams Peak *10,635 feet (Class 3)*

This peak is named after Dave Williams, the Stanley Valley rancher who teamed up with Robert and Miriam Underhill to make many of the early first ascents in the range. The first ascent was made by D. Williams, R. Underhill and M. Underhill, in 1934. Williams Peak is located 5.5 miles southwest of Stanley. Climb via the southwest ridge from the saddle between Williams and Thompson Peak. Access this route from FST-528 [Approach: (A)(4)(e)] or [Approach: (B)(1)(a)]. (See Thompson Peak, below, for route directions to the saddle.) The peak can also be climbed from Goat Lake via its northwest ridge. Access the lake from Iron Creek [Approach: (B)(1)(a.1)]. USGS Stanley Peak / SW

Thompson Peak *10,751 feet*

This is the highest summit in the Sawtooth Range and is clearly visible from both ID-21 and ID-75. The peak, which is 0.8 mile south of Williams Peak, is composed of metasedimentary rocks which are believed to be Precambrian in age. Although the peak is visible from the valley, it is remote by Sawtooth standards, with no easy ac-

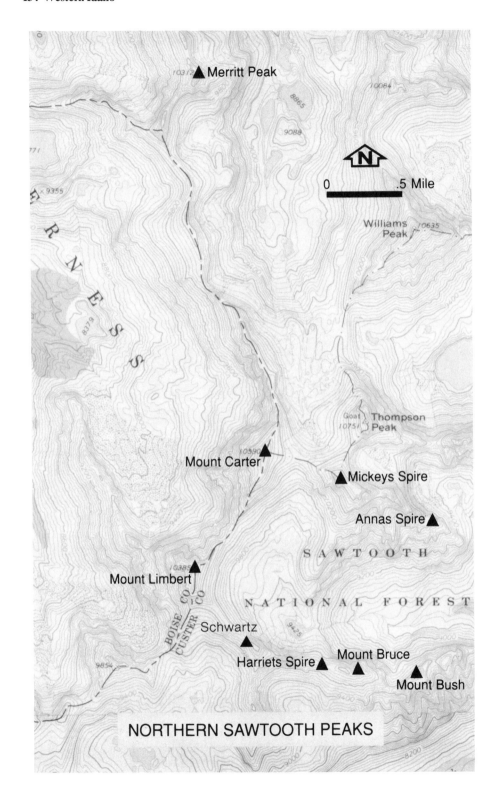

NORTHERN SAWTOOTH PEAKS

cess points. The first known ascent was by R. Underhill, M. Underhill and D. Williams, in 1934. The most advantageous approach route is from the Alpine Way Trail [Approach: (A)(4)(e)]. Leave the trail at its highest point on east ridge of Williams Peak. Turn south and traverse into the basin that holds a large unnamed lake at roughly 9,000 feet. (This lake is known as Goat Lake by the valley dwellers.) From a point just below the north face of Thompson Peak, scramble up the terraces to the saddle between Thompson and Williams or to the saddle between Thompson and Mickeys Spire. USGS Stanley Peak / SW

South Couloir. *(Class 3)*
North of the saddle between Thompson Peak and Mickeys Spire is a broad couloir. The couloir, which contains lots of loose rock, rises directly up to the notch between the peak's east and west summits. Climb to the notch, and then scramble to the west over solid rock to the summit.

Southwest Couloir. *(Grade II, Class 5)*
The route begins on the saddle between Thompson and Mickeys Spire. From the saddle, traverse across the west face toward the southwest couloir. The couloir is fairly open and lies west of the South Couloir route described above. The couloir is entered about 150 feet below the saddle; it is relatively free of loose rock. There are two alternatives that lead to the summit. The first leaves the couloir where it narrows below the notch in the west ridge, and climbs out onto the southwest face following easy Class 5 ledges to the summit. The second alternative climbs the couloir directly to the notch in the west ridge. (This point is roughly 60 feet west of the summit block.) From the ridge crest, climb a short 30-foot section of 5.2 rock and then scramble to the summit.

Northeast Face. *(Class 5)*
First ascent by T. Gathe and J. Kahn, in 1968. This route climbs to the large couloir which splits the face, and eventually summits on the north ridge. The climb is described as following the right side of the couloir for several leads, then entering a chimney, which is partially climbed to an "alcove." From the alcove, the climbers turned right and followed a crack system to the north ridge. Gathe and Kahn rated the climb as moderate to difficult Class 5 climbing.

West Crack. *(Grade II, YDS 5.2)*
Located to the east of the saddle between Thompson Peak and Williams Peak is a prominent notch with an associated couloir. In early summer, this couloir is entirely filled with snow at approximately a 50-degree angle. In late summer, the upper portions of the couloir are filled with hazardous loose rock—care should be exercised.

Thompson Peak (photo by Lyman Dye)

This couloir ends at the north ridge notch some 200 feet above the saddle. About 100 feet above this notch, on the northwest face, is a large crack that cuts directly up the northwest face.

The first lead is directly up the crack to an overhang and a pile of loose rock. The second lead requires a touchy move up and over the overhang. Above the overhang, scramble out across the west wall to the southwest on an easy ledge. The third lead takes you back to the notch directly above the notch which overlooks the north face. (This point is directly west of the first tower on the west ridge.) The fourth lead is a traverse across an easy ledge on the north face to the notch between the first and second tower. When conditions are icy, it might be advisable to climb the first tower and descend into the notch from its top. The fifth lead climbs directly out of the notch and onto the north face for about 60 feet, then climbs up to the ridge once again. From this point, climb to the summit of the second tower and then descend into the notch between the second tower and the summit

Mickeys Spire   Thompson Peak

Annas Pinnacle

Left to right: Mickeys Spire, Annas Pinnacle and Thompson Peak

pinnacle. From this point, the route joins the Southwest Couloir route. Climb a short 30-foot step out of the notch and then scramble up the ridge to the summit.

Mickeys Spire* *10,680+ feet*

This peak is, in essence, the south summit of Thompson Peak; its present (unofficial) name was given to it by the Iowa Mountaineers in 1948. The peak is not a spire, but rather a flat-topped summit. The first ascent by R. Underhill, in 1934. USGS Stanley Peak / SW

North Slope. *(Grade II, Class 4)*

Take the Fishhook Trail [Approach: (A)(4)(f)] to its end. Follow the sparsely timbered bench up the west side of the canyon wall as long as it is passable. Near the mouth of south Thompson Canyon there is a heavy growth of underbrush. Skirt this barrier on its upper west side. As you enter the canyon opening, you will see a cliff formation with a visible dark concave rock structure dividing the canyon. Take the right fork and continue up over three terraces to the headwall between Thompson Peak and Mickeys Spire. Climb the headwall on the Thompson side (this is actually the east face of that peak) to the saddle between the two peaks. The route from the saddle is a scramble up broken scree to the summit.

West Ridge. *(Class 3)*

To reach this route, follow the directions in the North Slope description above. However, instead of taking the right fork, take the left fork of the upper Fishhook Creek drainage and ascend into the upper basin past Lake 9425. To reach the upper basin, you must climb the lower headwall (below the lake) on the north side of the stream. Once in the upper basin, turn north and hike to the saddle between Mount Carter and Mickeys Spire. Follow the easy ridge to the summit.

East Ridge. *(Grade II, Class 5)*

First ascent by L. Dye, A. Barnes and W. Boyer in 1972. The approach is the same as the North Slope and West Ridge routes. The east ridge forms the north wall of this canyon. The spire near the east end of the ridge is known as Annas Pinnacle. To climb the east ridge, locate the large couloir that leads from the lower meadow to a large notch. From the notch, there are three alternatives. The first continues through the notch and crosses out onto the north face. From this point, follow the steep ledges (which are often filled with snow) west to the summit. The second alternative attacks the east ridge directly. This route involves climbing or bypassing many small gendarmes on the way to the summit. The third alternative leaves the notch and climbs the southeast face toward the south ridge spur. The route then climbs up this spur to the east ridge.

South Ridge Headwall. *(Grade II, Class 5)*
First ascent by L. Dye and the Iowa Mountaineers in 1972. From the upper basin near Lake 9425, climb toward the prominent diagonal crack that ascends the headwall to the north. (This crack is about halfway up the headwall. It is somewhat broken and contains some loose rock. Climbing within the crack considerably moderates the exposure.) Near the top of the crack is a small saddle. Cross the saddle to the spur on the peak's southwest face. The spur is climbed with two 60-foot leads separated by a short traverse. At the top of the second lead, scramble back to the west to the summit ridge.

Mount Carter* *10,590 feet (Class 2)*
This peak is located 0.25 mile due east of Mickeys Spire. The first reported ascent was by the Iowa Mountaineers in 1948. They named the peak after the current President of the University of Iowa. Climb to the saddle just east of the peak from either the Goat Creek [Approach: (B)(1)(a.1)] or Fishhook drainage [Approach: (A)(4)(f)] and climb to the summit. USGS Stanley Lake / SW

Peak 10385 (Mount Limbert*)
10,385 feet (Class 3)
This peak is located 0.5 mile south of Mount Carter. The Iowa Mountaineers were the first to record a climb of this peak. Though the Iowa Mountaineers named it after Ede Ebert, who was the wife of their leader, Mount Limbert seems a more appropriate name. Climb from Lake 9425 in the upper Fishhook drainage [Approach: (A)(4)(f)] via the easy eastern slopes. USGS Stanley Lake / SW

Schwartz Pinnacle* *10,000+ feet*
This formation is located on the ridge between Mount Limbert and Mount Bush. It was originally called Pattys Pinnacle by the Iowa Mountaineers and has more recently been known as Schwartz Pinnacle in honor of Hans Schwartz, a professional mountain guide from Canada who climbed in the Sawtooths in the 1940s. The first ascent was by the Iowa Mountaineers in 1948. USGS Stanley Lake / SW

East Ridge. *(Grade I, Class 4)*
Access this route from the Fishhook drainage and Lake 9425 [Approach: (A)(4)(f)]. Climb to the prominent notch in the east ridge and follow the ridge to the summit. The route occasionally moves out onto the broken south slopes. The route is obvious until about 100 feet below the summit, where a low-angle slab forms the crux. There are ample holds leading up a short crack, which quickly places you on the summit.

Southwest Crack. *(Grade II, YDS 5.4)*
From the west side of Lake 9425 [Approach: (A)(4)(f)] climb the obvious couloir to the notch between Mount Limbert and Schwartz Pinnacle. Snow remains in the lower sections of the couloir through most of the summer. From the notch, traverse around the west shoulder of the pinnacle, bypassing a minor crack, to the first large crack that opens to the south. The route now follows the crack up for 140 feet to a cove in the face. Climb above the cove for 30 feet to a thin ledge, which allows a tricky traverse across the face and onto the ridge. Follow the ridge to the summit. The traverse is the crux of the climb. The first ascent was by L. Dye, Springer, Howard, Taylor and Bravence in 1973.

South Couloir. *(Grade II, Class 4)*
From Lake 9425 in the Fishhook drainage [Approach: (A)(4)(f)], climb to the saddle east of the pinnacle and south of the lake. Traverse out onto the south face until this major couloir is reached. Follow the couloir across very loose rock to the ridge spur and then follow the spur to the summit on sound but broken rock. First ascent by Lyman Dye in 1973.

Mount Bush* *9,600+ feet*
Mount Bush is located 1.0 mile east of Mount Limbert, on a ridge which extends east from the main crest. It is the highest point on this ridge, east of Schwartz Pinnacle, and directly east of the first major notch in this ridge as it rises out of Fishhook Creek. While Mount Bush is much lower than the surrounding peaks, it attracted the attention of the Iowa Mountaineers because of its impressively thin, pointed shape. The first ascent was by the Iowa Mountaineers in 1948. Access the peak from the Fishhook drainage [Approach: (A)(4)(f)]. USGS Stanley Lake / SW

East Ridge. *(Grade II, Class 4)*
This is probably the route used by the Iowa Mountaineers in 1948. Approach via the Fishhook Trail and the bench west of the creek until you are well beyond the eastern end of the east ridge. Directly north of the prominent snow couloir on Horstmann Peak is a couloir which ascends the south side of Mount Bush's east ridge. This couloir leads to the first notch west of the ridge's eastern end. Climb the couloir three quarters of the way to the notch. At this point, turn west and climb up the ledges and a crack system to the summit.

North Face. *(Grade I, YDS 5.6)*

The climb starts at the base of a crack that descends to the valley floor from the notch west of the summit. To reach the crack you must cross some low-angle slabs which lead to the base of crack. Climb up the crack, keeping mostly on its east side, to an overhang. To avoid the overhang, traverse out onto the east wall, toward a small ledge with a twisted tree. (There are ample holds along the way.) This tree serves as an excellent rappel anchor for the descent. From the tree, follow a ledge back to the crack. Climb the crack directly to the notch. From the notch, take a small ledge system to the east. The ledges end against the peak's northwest face. A small break in the face is climbed back to the west toward a step, which is located about 40 feet above the notch. Continue up the face for 80 feet using small, but beautiful, holds. Descent is by two rappels down the north face. The first ascent was by L. Dye and K. Morrison in 1972.

Southwest Face. *(Grade I, YDS 5.4)*

This route follows the North Face route to the notch. Move directly out of the notch and up the west ridge for about 40 feet to a step. From the step, the route moves out onto the west face, ascending a ledge system to a bowl halfway across the face. The most difficult pitch is the one getting out of a pocket located below the bowl. From the bowl, the summit is a short scramble. The first ascent was by L. Dye in 1972.

Harrietts Pinnacle* *(YDS 5.4)*

This pinnacle is located due east of Schwartz Pinnacle. It is a scramble from the east, south or west. A short technical climb leads up the west face, but little is known about this route. USGS Stanley Lake / SW

Mount Bruce* *9,800+ feet (YDS 5.2)*

This minor summit is located 0.25 miles due west of Mount Bush. From the Fishhook drainage [Approach: (A)(4)(f)], climb to the saddle west of the peak and then follow the west ridge to the summit. The route alternates between the ridge and the ridge's north face. USGS Stanley Lake / SW

Grandjean Peak *9,160+ feet*

This peak was named after Emil Grandjean, who was a Danish-trained forester and the first supervisor of the Sawtooth and Payette National Forests back in 1905. Grandjean came to the United States from Denmark in 1883 and mined, trapped and explored in central Idaho before beginning his forestry career. The peak is located at the western end of the Verita Ridge. Its four summits are as ragged as the entire ridge line.

Little is known about this peak because it is off the beaten path. USGS Warbonnet Peak / SW

West Face. *(Class 4-5)*

The following route is offered with the caveat that the information may not be reliable. From FS-452 [Approach: (B)(3)(b)], make a long and unappealing climb toward Point 9105 on the USGS quad. The lower portion of the route through the forest is uneventful. Once at the base of the peak, the angle increases dramatically. Reportedly, a route exists from the trees to Point 9105, which is in the range of hard Class 3. From Point 9105 to the summit, the route is steeper and more exposed, and is rated Class 4.

Baron Peak *10,297 feet (Class 3)*

First ascent by R. Underhill, M. Underhill and D. Williams in 1934. Climb via the south ridge, which can be accessed from either the east or the west [Approach: (A)(4)(f) or [Approach: (B)(3)(c)]. USGS Warbonnet Peak / SW

Mount Ebert* *9,880+ feet*

This complex peak is located on the ridge that runs between Baron Peak and Braxon Peak 1.5 miles southeast of Baron. The peak was named for John Ebert, president of the Iowa Mountaineers. The first ascent was made by the Iowa Mountaineers in 1957. USGS Warbonnet Peak / SW

West Ridge. *(Grade II, Class 5)*

The route begins in the Fishhook drainage [Approach: (A)(4)(f)] on the north side of the peak, at the base of the main couloir. The couloir leads to a notch in the west ridge. The climb up the couloir crosses plush meadows and easy slabs to a landing formed by a shallow cliff band. Just above this landing, climb up the east side of the wall to a scree delta at the base of the couloir. The climb up the couloir is straightforward. From the notch, the route continues up the west ridge (with an occasional traverse onto the southwest face) to the summit. This is the route of the Iowa Mountaineers first ascent. The first ascent was by the Iowa Mountaineers in 1957.

East Face Dike. *(Grade II, YDS 5.2)*

Access this route from the Stephens Lakes in the upper sections of the Fishhook drainage [Approach: (A)(4)(f)]. The route climbs the prominent dike and then traverses the face. First ascent by L. Dye, Springer, Howard, Taylor and Bravence in 1973. Approach the peak from Stephens Lakes. The east face contains a prominent black dike. This dike ends to the right of a large notch south of the summit. The climb up the dike to the notch is straightforward. From the notch, traverse to the north to the top of an easy ledge that leads to a crack system which leads to the next notch up the face. Climb this crack, utilizing a small ledge on the face, to a solid belay point. Continue on to the notch. Descend the east face for 40 feet to a ledge system which crosses the face to the north. Take this ledge system across the face and up to the spur ridge, which is located near the third notch. Two leads up this spur puts you in yet another notch. Climb out of this notch for another 80 feet to the summit. To descend, follow the spur directly down from the summit until you are above the main cliffs. Cross the face to the black dike and follow it back down.

Ed-Da-How Spire *9,333 feet (Grade II, YDS 5.2)*

This pinnacle resembles a big thumb. It is located southeast of Mount Ebert. The pinnacle is part of the Ebert ridge, but is separated from the main ridge by a large notch. The first ascent was by L. Dye, Springer, Howard, Taylor and Bravence in 1973 via the north ridge. Descend from the notch above the dike on Mount Ebert's east face to the saddle slab. The north side of the pinnacle is attacked directly from the saddle. The ridge becomes increasingly difficult as it climbs toward the summit. USGS Warbonnet Peak / SW

Rothorn Spire *9,440+ feet (Grade II, YDS 5.7)*

Located southeast of Ed-da-how. It was first climbed by L. Dye and Brodie in 1973. This spire is the largest pinnacle in this area. Its rock is reddish in color and sound in consistency. The only known ascent route climbs up the north face. From the saddle north of the spire, descend out across the north face to a large crack near the

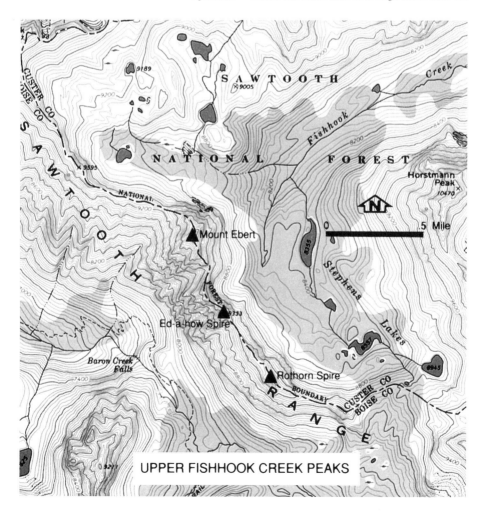

UPPER FISHHOOK CREEK PEAKS

Horstmann Peak, 10,470 feet, dominates the Fishhook Creek drainage.

northwest corner of the spire. This crack has a large chockstone wedged in it about 60 feet up the wall. Climb the crack to the chockstone. There is a second chockstone above the first. Bypass both on the left. Above the second chockstone, the route moves out onto the wall on thin holds and climbs up to a slightly overhanging slab. A 30-foot layback up another crack system takes you to a point above this slab. From here, the route moves to the west and reaches an open shelf about 100 feet below the summit block. Climb from here to the summit. USGS Warbonnet Peak / SW

Stephens Spire* 9,440+ feet (Grade I, YDS 5.1)

This picturesque pinnacle is directly west of Rothorn Spire. This minor spire rises about 100 feet above the ridge crest. Climb the spire from Stephens lake via its north couloir. Scramble up the loose scree and talus occupying the lower slopes. From the ridge crest, the spire can be climbed from east, west or south, with about the same degree of difficulty. The actual climb is only about 60 feet. USGS Warbonnet Peak / SW

Horstmann Peak 10,470 feet

This peak was originally called Mount Hancher by the Iowa Mountaineers, but was later officially named after an early Stanley Basin homesteader and friend of Dave Williams. The peak is located 1.4 miles due east of Mount Ebert and is a spectacular conglomeration of ridges, couloirs and gendarmes, which encompasses several rewarding routes. The first ascent was by R. Underhill, M. Underhill and D. Williams in 1934. Access for all routes listed below begins at various locations in the Fishhook drainage [Approach: (A)(4)(f)]. USGS Warbonnet Peak / SW

North Face. (Grade II, YDS 5.2)
This route was first climbed by the Iowa Mountaineers in 1957. A variety of routes are available on the face—none of which present any great difficulty. Access is from the Fishhook drainage.

Northeast Ridge. (Grade II, YDS 5.2)
Follow the Fishhook Creek Trail to its conclusion. From this point, there is a small aspen grove visible just beyond the stream. Follow the fairly open bench associated with this grove to the northeast shoulder of the peak. Cross the creek and proceed up through the timber to the ridge shoulder. Continue past this shoulder, across the terraced platforms, to the point where the ridge swings to the west. Climb the gentle couloir that leads to the ridge crest. Follow the ridge, occasionally moving out onto the north face, to the summit. The last 50 feet is climbed on the north

face. First ascent by L. Dye, A. Barnes and W. Boyer in 1965.

North Ridge Spur. *(Grade II, YDS 5.2)*

From the end of the Fishhook Creek Trail, follow the aspen-covered bench to a crossing of the creek near the large snowfield at the base of the north couloir. There is a small pinnacle near this snowfield, and just beyond it is a subsidiary ridge which descends from the main north ridge. This is the north ridge spur. It is composed of rather shattered downsloping granitic rock. The entire climb is on this unsettling rock. The first ascent was by M. Howard and D. Walters in 1971.

East Face. *(Grade II, Class 4)*

This was probably the route used by the Underhills and Dave Williams in 1934. The route, which moves directly up the face with no route-finding difficulties, begins in the south fork of the Fishhook drainage. Climb to the bowl below the face and then choose one of several routes that climb the ledge network to the summit. This is a good spring route when snow conditions are right.

South Ridge. *(Class 3)*

Climb to the saddle south of the peak. The route from the saddle follows the crest of the ridge on broken rock, bypassing various pinnacles along the way. The summit is visible for the entire distance.

Fishhook Spire*

This fantastic spire is located between Mount Iowa and Horstmann Peak. Its history provides a good example of how confusing names can become. The "original" Fishhook Spire was located in the Baron Creek drainage. That formation, which is now called El Pima, was called Fishhook Spire by Beckey and others because (of course) it looked like a fishhook. However, to the northeast, in the Fishhook Creek drainage, there were other spires that could be mistaken for the "original" Fishhook Spire. Thus, to avoid confusion, the name of the Baron Creek area spire was changed to El Pima(it also looked like a cat claw). The Iowa Mountaineers then dubbed the Fishhook Creek area formation "Fishhook Spire" not so much for its appearance, but because it is at the top of the Fishhook drainage. Access is from, of course, the Fishhook drainage [Approach: (A)(4)(f)]. USGS Warbonnet Peak / SW

Southwest Couloir. *(YDS 5.5)*

The route follows this couloir on the formation's southwest side up over very broken rock. The first ascent was by R. Maynard and F. Chappel.

Mount Iowa* *10,327 feet*

Guess who named this peak? This summit is located midway between Braxon Peak and Horstmann Peak on the connecting ridge. USGS Mount Cramer / SW

Northwest Ridge. *(Class 3-4)*

First ascent by the Iowa Mountaineers in 1947. This route begins in the saddle between Horstmann and Mount Iowa. Follow the ridge up, bypassing Fishhook Spire on its south side, and then scramble up the remaining ridge, keeping on the east side of the crest.

Southeast Ridge. *(Class 4)*

This route follows the ridge west of Braxon to the crest east of the summit. The ridge can be accessed from Stephens Lakes or the basin between Heyburn and Horstmann.

Mount Heyburn *10,200+ feet*

This beautiful peak is situated just west of Redfish Lake. It is the best-known Sawtooth peak and possibly Idaho's most majestic mountain. As seen from the highway near Stanley, the peak has three major summits. The two highest summits are separated by a deep snow couloir known as the Silver Saddle. The westernmost of these two summits is the highest by 1 or 2 feet. It was first climbed by Robert and Miriam Underhill in 1935. The east peak was probably first climbed by Robert Limbert in 1927. Since the first ascent, the peak has been a focal point for Sawtooth climbers. A third summit, the West Pinnacle, is located southwest of the Heyburn's two main summits. USGS Mount Cramer / SW

West Summit Routes.

The west summit is composed of some of the Sawtooth's most deteriorated granite. This rock, which is soft beyond belief in places, can make climbing to the summit much more of a tedious chore than an adventure. The one exception to the deteriorated rock syndrome is the Stur Chimney Route on the west face.

Southwest Ridge. *(Grade II, Class 4)*

First climbed by the Underhills and Dave Williams. The route begins on the saddle between the west summit and the West Pinnacle. The saddle is attained from the trail above Redfish Lake by following a small drainage up toward the northwest. In the upper sections of the drainage, a couloir leads to the saddle. From the saddle, the ridge is blocked by a pinnacle. Bypass this pinnacle by descending its west side, and then ascend the crack that leads to the notch above. The lead out of the notch is the most difficult move on the route as it climbs to the ridge line. It is reported that the lower ridge is somewhat solid, but the upper ridge, according to Underhill, is a crumbling mess. The remaining ridge is moderate in difficulty but on extremely decomposed granite. An alternate route to the southwest ridge, which avoids the rotten move out of the notch, begins in the couloir which separates the east and west summits. From this couloir, a series of rotten slabs can be followed to the notch on the southwest ridge. The exposure is minimal, but the rock is something else.

Yet another variation on this route was climbed by the Iowa Mountaineers in 1947. This route is rated YDS 5.2 and was first climbed by K. Jones, B. Adams, J. Ebert, G. Goodrich and J. Speck. About halfway up the couloir followed by the Underhills, the Iowa Mountaineers followed a smaller crack to the notch at the base of the southwest ridge. This bypassed the difficult move below the notch.

East Face/Snow Couloir. *(Grade II, YDS 5.3 A1)*

From the upper Bench Lake area, a prominent but rotten couloir leads to the notch separating the two summits. Follow this steep couloir up past the north face cliffs to the Silver Saddle. From the saddle, the west summit is a vertical wall. The only technical difficulty encountered on this route is a 40-foot section on this wall. Paul Petzoldt first climbed the wall with a group of Iowa Mountaineers (E. Carter, C. Fisher, B. Merriam and C. Wilcox) in 1947, using a double-rope tension technique. Above this pitch, the summit is easily reached. (The route has since been climbed free).

The normal descent route utilizes two rappels down the wall to the saddle. The final rappel is set up just above the tension pitch, in a crack located on the south cliff wall.

Northwest Ridge. *(Class 4-5)*

Climb across the scree slopes directly above and west of the highest Bench Lake to the west corner of Heyburn and then enter the steep, "goat-traveled" couloir. Climb halfway up the couloir and then traverse sharply to the left onto the west wall. Traverse for three pitches to the west ridge. Follow the ridge to the summit. The first ascent was by the Iowa Mountaineers in 1948.

Northwest Ridge/North Face. *(Grade II, YDS 5.6)*

This multi-pitch route climbs the northwest ridge and north face. It is a long and demanding route, few details of which have been recorded. The climb begins by following the northwest ridge to a shelf. One strenuous layback move is required to reach the shelf. The route is then blocked by a tower. Instead of scaling this monolith, rappel down to a ledge on its east side. From here, two pitches will lead you up to the foot of the final section of the northwest ridge, some 500 feet below the summit. The most exhausting section of the ridge crosses a vertical wall using a crack system, micro footholds and intermixed jams and laybacks. This crack eventually moderates and leads to a platform. From here, the platform gives access to the north face, where the route enters a steep, exposed crack system that leads to the summit region. The first ascent was by F. Beckey and J. Fuller in 1961.

Northwest Ridge Direct. *(Grade II, YDS 5.6)*

This route completes the Beckey and Fuller route on the northwest ridge and avoids the north face. From the upper Bench Lake, climb to the base of the northwest ridge. Follow the ridge to the false summit that dominates the skyline when viewed from the lake. Rappel onto the wide terrace, which is at the same level as the wide V notch on the ridge. From here, a thin ledge leads out onto the exposed west face. Follow this ledge to a chimney, which climbs back to the ridge and quickly turns into the west face. Traverse around the exposed corner and climb a chimney to the summit. The first ascent was by L. Stur and J. Ball, in 1961.

Stur Chimney. *(Grade II, YDS 5.2)*

From the saddle above the uppermost Bench Lake, traverse across scree slopes to the base of the west face. From this point, an almost-vertical chimney becomes visible in the face. The chimney, unlike the rest of Heyburn, is composed of solid rock which provides bomb proof belay points. Begin by following the couloir that climbs up to the notch on the southwest ridge, until it is possible to cross a ledge to the base of the chimney. Climb 40 feet up the chimney, cross a chockstone and then continue on to a cave. (The cave is actually just a large opening in the wall.) Climb out of the cave on its west wall, over the roof and into a small pocket above. From this point, there are two alternatives: climb out of the chimney, on the right, on ice cracks to the open pocket 30 feet below the summit; or continue to climb the chimney directly. The second alternative requires a move out and over the larger chockstone in the crack. The move involves maintaining one hand jam under the chockstone while the other hand searches for a hold above the stone. The last pitch from the pocket is an easy lead on a fracture line that cuts to the south. The first ascent was by L. Stur, J. Fuller and J. Ball in 1958. The first winter ascent was by W. Cove and L. Adkins 2/25/75—or by L. Stur and F. Beckey 4/3/61, depending on when you consider winter to end.

East Summit Routes.

Once the west summit of Heyburn was unofficially declared the peak's highest point (by two Iowa Mountaineers with a spirit level), much of the appeal of the equally beautiful east summit was lost. The east summit should not be overlooked. It offers good climbing, a good view and what difference does a couple of feet make, anyway?

The east summit is hard to distinguish because of the enormous number of pinnacles which comprise it. The east summit's granite block, the most picturesque of Heyburn's summits, is formed by a shaft of rock rising 30 feet from a ledge. When the Underhills and Dave Williams reached the east summit in 1934, they found evidence of a previous ascent. It is likely that Bob Limbert or one of his contemporaries made the first ascent of this summit in the 1920s.

South Rib. *(Grade II, YDS 5.2)*

This route climbs to the Silver Saddle via the main south couloir. (The saddle can also be reached from the Bench Lake area.) From the saddle, climb to the east onto the peak's the west wall until you reach a crack that leads up the west face of the summit pinnacle. The crack angles up to the south and finally exits on the south wall. From this point, follow the ledge to the east and the south rib. Climb directly up the exposed rib.

Northeast Ridge. *(Grade II, Class 4)*

This pinnacle-studded ridge rises out of the lateral moraine that divides the Redfish drainage from the Bench Lake drainage. The ridge can be accessed from the Bench Lake trail, or by climbing the prominent couloir that appears directly above the Redfish Inlet Campground. Gain the ridge above the trees and climb onto the ledge system. A pinnacle that looks like a person wearing a robe (Saint Peters Pinnacle) is visible up the ridge. Climb the ridge, meandering from east to west to avoid various assorted towers, to the summit block. The summit block can be climbed from the north or east sides. Route finding around the many pinnacles on the ridge can be time consuming.

North Buttress. *(Grade III, YDS 5.9 A1)*

This obscure route was first climbed by F. Beckey and J. Fuller, who used no less than 35 pitons, in 1965. (This route is listed here for historical purposes only.)

West Pinnacle Route. *(Grade III, Class 6)*

Heyburn's West Pinnacle has seen little climbing activity over the years. The only reported route begins on the saddle between the west summit and the West Pinnacle. From the saddle, hike to the base of the pinnacle and look on the north side of the tower for a long, narrow tunnel behind an enormous flake. The tunnel leads to a large platform. From the platform, scramble down to the northern side of the base of the pinnacle. This wall contains two piton-sized cracks, which eventually join. The first ascent climbed this wall by using a double rope tension technique. There is a small rock projection on the wall. Pass a sling over it and use two pitons to overcome the first 10 feet. The next 20 feet are overhanging. Use four pitons for direct aid to get over this obstacle to the ledge above. The moves involved in getting to the ledge are awkward and difficult. Six feet above the ledge is a large rock projection. Place another sling over it to provide direct aid. Climb up the next high-angle flake and past a 20-foot slab to reach the summit. The first ascent was by R. Widrig, J. Hieb, W. Grande and G. Matthews, in 1948.

Rotten Monolith*

This formation, which is visible from Stanley Basin, is located on the north side of Braxon Peak. Some consider it the lower north summit of Braxon. The east side of the tower is 500 feet high and the west side is 150 feet high. USGS Mount Cramer / SW

West Face. *(Class 6)*

This formation was first climbed by F. Beckey and L. Stur, in 1961. Stur reports that the rock was "unbelievably rotten." Twelve pitons and one bolt were used on the ascent. In several spots, the pitons were hammered directly into the granite wall (sans cracks).

Braxon Peak *10,353 feet*

This twin-summited peak is located 1.1 miles southwest of Mount Heyburn. The peak's summit, a moderate scramble from several directions, is an enormous pile of decomposed granite. The ascent is often best done in early spring, when the snow covers the talus. Details of the first ascent are unknown. USGS Mount Cramer / SW

East Slope. *(Class 3)*

Climb from the saddle to the east of the peak. The saddle can be reached from the two small lakes just south of the peak.

West Side. *(Grade II, Class 4)*

From the saddle west of the peak (between Braxon and Horstmann), climb up the snowfields and steep scree and talus to the summit. Pass the horn-shaped formation on its north side. Once above the tower, scramble up the loose scree to the base of the east wall. From this point, the route follow the base of the wall to a notch which separates the horns south of the summit from the summit itself.

REDFISH LAKE CREEK COMPLEX

On the slopes that rise directly north of the Elephants Perch and northwest of Redfish Lake Creek are five extraordinary granite formations that were first described by Robert Underhill.

The Grand Aiguille above Redfish Lake Creek
(photo by Lyman Dye)

These formations occupy the rugged ridge system which connects Braxon Peak and Mount Heyburn. To approach these formations leave Redfish Lake Creek [Approach: (A)(4)(b)] near to where it crosses the 7,200-foot contour and climb the large slide area on Mount Heyburn until it narrows to a slot. Then turn to the southwest, climb into the cirque and then gain the ridge line. The five formations are described below.

Grand Aiguille*

This formation is clearly visible from the south end of Redfish Lake. It appears as a shallow fishtail summit with an overhanging north face. The first ascent was in 1946, by Hieb, W. Grande, R. Widrig and W. V. Graham Mathews. USGS Mount Cramer / SW

Northwest Side. *(Grade II, YDS 5.4)*

This was the line of the first ascent. The climb begins from the notch on the west side of the formation, where it joins with the Split Tooth. The

route to the notch is relatively easy. However, early in the season, climbing the snow-filled couloir and crossing the bergschrund might present some problems. The route above the notch consists of four or five pitches of moderate but exposed climbing. The first pitch leads up the northwest face past several trees and ends behind a large flake. The second lead runs from the flake to a second notch out on the southeast face by crossing a deep pit and squeezing up a 40-foot chimney. From the notch, the third pitch leads (using a layback) to some large granite flakes out on the face. (These flakes are shaky when pulled outwards but are secure when pressure is placed directly down on them.) From the flakes, the final lead traverses back to the southeast on the crest of the summit block.

South Face. *(Grade II, Class 5)*

This face was first climbed by F. Beckey and J. Fuller, in 1962. The route climbs up a rotten southwest gully to more solid rock above. From the top of the gully, Beckey made a pendulum traverse around a blind corner to a platform. From this spot, he followed a crack up for 250 feet to a tree. The route follows the original crack above the tree until a more prominent crack system can be entered. The new crack is followed for two and one half pitches to where it joins the original crack, which is then followed to the summit.

Small Aiguille*

Located east of the Grande Aiguille and next to the Black Aiguille, this formation is much less impressive than its neighbors and contains spots of rotten rock. The first ascent was made by H. King and A. Holben, in 1948. USGS Mount Cramer / SW

North Face. *(Grade II, YDS 5.3)*

The route begins on the col to the west. The first pitch climbs to the left up a roughly horizontal dike on the north face. From the dike, a tricky diagonal traverse on unsound rock leads to a chimney. The next lead climbs this chimney to a large block, and then moves out onto the face to climb a short vertical pitch, then moves back into the chimney, which leads to the summit. Two long rappels can be used to return to the col. The first ascent was by H. King and A. Holben, in 1948.

South Face. *(Grade II, YDS 5.4)*

From the Redfish Lake Trail, several chimneys are visible in the east wall. All of the chimneys offer alternative routes to the knife-edged summit ridge. Climb up and across a boulder field just east of the tower to the base of the south face. Scramble from this point to the west to the base of a smooth wall. The first ascent route followed a

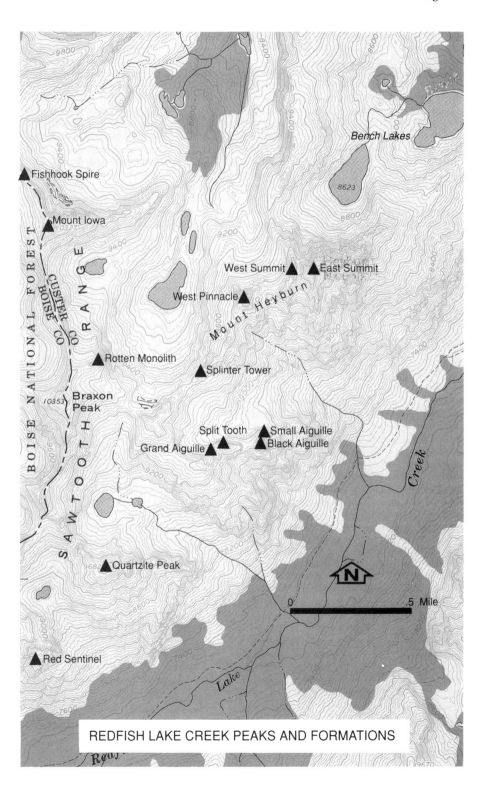

REDFISH LAKE CREEK PEAKS AND FORMATIONS

chimney just southwest of this wall. Climb this chimney to its top, where a second chimney is accessed. (It is located above and to the right of the first chimney.) The second chimney is broken by a homey ledge and several trees as it leads straight up to the east end of the summit ridge. A shoulder stand was used to reach the final few feet to the summit. The summit ridge is exposed and composed of extremely poor rock. The first ascent was by L. Stur and J. Fuller, in 1960.

Black Aiguille*

This spire is south of the Small Aiguille. The summit, which appears rounded and has a definite black color when compared to the other summits in the area, is free of cracks and covered by friable granitic rock. The rock is so rotten that the first ascent party easily carved a saddlehorn-like fixture into the rock to use as a rappel anchor. The first ascent was by Hans Gmosser and Rod Harris. The formation was named by the Iowa Mountaineers. USGS Mount Cramer / SW

East Couloir. *(Grade II, YDS 5.2)*
Scramble up the main couloir on the east face. This couloir contains two very sharp spires. Relatively easy ledges and chimneys lead out of the couloir and up the east face to the summit.

South Side. *(Rating and route unknown.)*
First climbed by the Iowa Mountaineers, who were lead by Idaho Falls native Bill Echo, in 1960.

Split Tooth*

This spectacular tower is located immediately west of the Grand Aiguille. The tower is split by a massive crack, which divides the formation into two summits. The lower summit is the easier of the two. The first ascent was made by B. Echo and a group from the Idaho Falls Alpine Club in 1960. USGS Mount Cramer / SW

Northeast Tower. *(Grade I, Class 6)*
This route climbs the lower summit from the notch on the formation's west side and then utilizes a tyrolean traverse to reach the summit. The route, about 110 feet in length, is on exposed, rotten rock.

Northeast Crack. *(Grade I, YDS 5.7)*
From the notch between Split Tooth and the Grand Aiguille, climb the fissure as far as possible by stemming and then move onto the northeast side of the south pinnacle. Follow this face to the top. An old piton is visible, marking Fred Beckey's 1963 first-ascent route.

Southwest Ridge. *(Grade II, YDS 5.6 A1)*
Climb into the cirque to the southwest of the formation and approach the cirque's southeast wall. Take the first major crack in this wall to the

ridge above. From this point, you are above and to the west of the formation. Descend the ridge to the northeast and climb to the summit of the lower spire. Make a Tyrolean traverse to the higher spire.

SPLINTER TOWERS*

The main ridge between Mount Heyburn and Braxton Peak is infested with numerous towers and spires. Three of the spires are named—Splinter, Steeple and Thimble. All three towers were first climbed in 1948. Splinter was climbed in 1948 by Holden and Schwabland via eight Class 4 pitches up the south face. Steeple was first climbed by King and Beckey via the west ridge. Thimble was first climbed by King and Beckey, who used direct aid on the summit block. USGS Mount Cramer / SW

Quartzite Peak* *9,682 feet*

Quartzite Peak is located due south of Split Tooth and Braxon Peak. The first ascent was by H. Gmosser, W. Joura and the Iowa Mountaineers. The exact line of this ascent is unknown, as are any details on the route. USGS Mount Cramer / SW

Red Sentinel* *(Grade II, YDS 5.4 A1)*

Also known as Flatrock Needle, this is a sheer, orange-colored wall which is visible from the Redfish Lake Creek Trail near its junction with the trail to Alpine Lake. It can be climbed from the point where the trail forks by ascending a narrow couloir which eventually leads to the ridge top. Approach the needle from this point [Approach: (A)(4)(b)]. The first ascent was by H. Gmosser, B. Echo, D. Millsap and C. Brown. USGS Mount Cramer / SW

The route starts up the main south couloir and is blocked by a boulder about one quarter of the way up. A chimney and a delicate ledge system on the left wall provide a bypass of the boulder that leads into the upper couloir. Once on the needle proper, the route traverses the south side to the corner. The route moves onto east face; direct aid is needed to reach a platform just below the summit. The final move to the summit is short and exposed.

Le Bec D'Aigle* *9,727 feet*

This peak is situated directly north of Airplane Lake and northeast of Baron Pass. The pointed summit is composed of extremely smooth rock on the west side and broken ledges and cracks on the east side. The first ascent was up the east face, but the peak contains lots of solid untried cracks and

Splinter Tower (photo by Lyman Dye)

walls. Access this formation from FST-101 [Approach: (A)(4)(c)]. USGS Warbonnet Peak / SW

East Face. *(Grade I, YDS 5.3)*

The route begins at the small lakes north of Alpine Lake. Scramble up the hardpan scree and talus slope northeast of the uppermost lake. South of the summit buttress there is a fairly level spot in the south ridge. Cross one of the cracks in this area and move onto the peak's east side. There is an obvious ledge leading out onto the face which becomes broken near a tree halfway across. From the tree, a friction step up leads to a broken terrace. Follow this terrace to a fragmented crack at its far northeast end. Climb this crack to the platform above. From the platform, a long diagonal crack ascends to the base of the summit block to a step about 15 feet below the actual summit. Climb the crack to the step. Above the step, follow a horizontal flake (which moves when you touch it) to the summit. First ascent by H. Adams Carter and G. Constan, in 1957.

North Buttress. *(Grade I, YDS 5.2)*

Take the trail from Alpine Lake toward Baron Pass. Just below the pass, leave the trail and contour northeast to the saddle just west of the summit and south of Braxon Lake. From the saddle, scramble up to the base of the buttress. (Note: From this point, you can access the East Face route by traversing south across the west face

to the south ridge. Cross the ridge via one of its many chimneys.) At the base of the North Buttress, there is a large crack that leads up a hump to the top of the buttress. The buttress itself provides a fine line that leads from the hump to the summit in a 120-foot lead. The final 30 feet are exposed and made up of rotten rock. First ascent by L. Dye, M. Howard and the Mazamas.

Old Smoothie* *9,211 (Class 6)*

This splendid granite spire is topped by a summit block which overhangs on all sides. The spire is located in the Baron Creek drainage above Baron Lakes, to the north of Warbonnet Peak. The first ascent was made via the west face by Fred Beckey, Jack Schwabland and Pete Schoening, in 1949. The spire is also known as Big Baron Spire. Access is via FST-101, which begins either at Redfish Lake [Approach: (A)(4)(c)] or Grandjean [Approach: (B)(3)(c)]. USGS Warbonnet Peak / SW

The Beckey/Schoening/Schwabland route begins from Little Baron Lake and works its way up to the south ridge, beginning on the spur ridge that comes directly off the south ridge (from an obvious hump on the south ridge) toward the lake. Near the top, a wide dirt ramp leads to the north, toward the notch which separates the "hump" from the main tower. The ramp ends at a ledge and crack system. Climb through this system to

147

Big Baron Spire and El Pima (photo by Lyman Dye)

reach a narrow V-shaped gully, which leads up to the notch. From the notch, the route moves out onto the west face and climbs a series of steps and chimneys to the base of a smooth vertical chimney. Climb the chimney to an overhang, which is bypassed on the left using, according to Jack Schwabland, a "tricky finger traverse." The crack above the overhang runs up to the south ridge just below the overhanging summit block. The route then traverses, via a narrow ledge, onto the west face in search of easier terrain. When the ledge ends, climb up the steep, broken wall on good holds to a boulder field at the base of the summit block.

From the base of the overhanging summit block, the route moves up a narrowing ledge and over a corner to the north shoulder of the spire. From this point, the first ascent team began placing bolts. They used fourteen bolts to get above the overhang and into a small bowl. Above the bowl, the corner steepens to near vertical and the first-ascent route required four more bolts before the climbers could make the summit. The climb took three days because of unstable weather— and the time required to place twenty bolts.

El Pima* 9,837 feet

El Pima is located midway between Old Smoothie and Warbonnet Peak, just west of Baron Lake. Beckey and his partners originally dubbed

this formation Fishhook Spire, a name now attached to a spire in the Fishhook drainage. El Pima signifies that the summit block resembles a great cat claw. The first ascent was by F. Beckey, P. Schoening and J. Schwabland, in 1949. Access is via FST-101, which begins either at Redfish Lake [Approach: (A)(4)(c)] or Grandjean [Approach: (B)(3)(c)]. USGS Warbonnet Peak / SW

East Face. *(Grade II, Class 6)*
The route begins on the east face and climbs a dirt-filled chimney to a shelf below the overhanging summit block. From here, Beckey and his crew climbed toward a "monster chockstone" wedged against the summit block. From the chockstone, the party used pitons for direct aid to reach the sloping ledge that leads to the summit.

West Face. *(Class 6)*
The first ascent was made via a rather confusing route that began on the west face. The pioneer climbers used twenty bolts and three days to overcome the many obstacles. The account is chronicled in the 1950 American Alpine Journal, in an article by Jack Schwabland.

Tohobit Peak 10,046 feet *(Class 3-4)*
This peak is the northernmost named formation on the Verita Ridge. It is located 1.1 miles northwest of Warbonnet Peak. (Tohobit means black in the dialect of a west coast Indian tribe).

CENTRAL SAWTOOTH PEAKS AND FORMATIONS

Little is known about this peak. Apparently, the peak is climbed from the lower reaches of Baron Creek. Leave the Baron Creek trail [Approach: (B)(3)(c)] when it is due north of the large drainage that runs steeply up Tohobit's northwest face. Climb high into this drainage and directly to the snowfields below the summit (these are shown on the USGS quad). At the base of the first snowfield, turn due west and climb to Point 9389. Once at this point, climb the ridge southeast to the summit, staying on the southern side of the ridge as much as possible. USGS Warbonnet Peak / SW

Warbonnet Peak *10,200+ feet*

Warbonnet is part of the Verita Ridge Complex. The peak has been called the "Grand Teton of Idaho" by some. No matter what you call it, Warbonnet is an impressive peak from any direction. All routes to the top involve Class 5 climbing. In the Off Belay magazine article "Sawtooth Mountaineering" (February 1975), Louis Stur said of the peak:

> The sheer walls on both sides of the 'rooftop' overhang menacingly into nothingness down below; holds are a bare minimum and piton cracks zero ... the view from the top ... is exceptionally breathtaking. Quite understandably so since a stone dropped from this point will fall for nine seconds before disintegrating on the boulder fields below.

The peak is distinctive because of the massive fin-shaped summit block that caps it. The fin is split by a large fissure that splits the block into two massive blocks. At the south end of the summit block is a prominent notch, which is the focus of most routes on the mountain.

The original reconnaissance and first ascent was led by Bob Merriam and Paul Petzoldt during the Iowa Mountaineers 1947 Sawtooth outing. Louis Stur made the first ascents of the peak's south, west and east faces in the late 1950s. More recently, Jeff Lowe and Kevin Swigert brought their rock-climbing expertise to Warbonnet. They established a route up the north face which they named the "Black Crystal Route." This route, which involved the most difficult climbing yet done on the peak, included 5.10 and 5.11 pitches. Primary approach is via FST-101, which begins either at Redfish Lake [Approach: (A)(4)(c)] or Grandjean [Approach: (B)(3)(c)]. USGS Warbonnet Peak / SW

West Face. *(Grade II, YDS 5.7)*

Climb up to the saddle directly west of the summit. From this point, traverse first to the southeast and then back toward the west, gaining elevation on moderate terrain. Climb to a spot just below the sheer west wall and two-thirds of the way across the face. The route now climbs up a difficult crack which eventually dies out. At this point, a tension swing is necessary to cross over to an adjoining crack in a fairly large debris-filled pocket. Follow a crack and chimney system out of

the pocket to a platform, which is 40 feet below the summit. From the platform, a solid fissure leads to the notch in the summit block. (The view of the summit from the notch is breathtaking.) From the notch, step across the fissure onto a narrow ledge and start up the summit block. The holds are moderately large at first, but progressively become smaller near the top. There is a bolt just over the lip of the fin which provides protection for the move up to the broken ledge near the apex. The first 40 feet of the summit block offer little opportunity for placing protection other than bolts. In 1971, bolts were placed on the upper stretches of the block. The first ascent was by the Iowa Mountaineers in 1947; the party included B. Merriam, J. Speck, C. Wilcox, B. Adams, C. Fisher and P. Petzoldt.

South Face. *(Grade II, YDS 5.7; summit block is 5.4).*

This route climbs the face from the saddle on the southeast side of the peak by following a series of connecting chimneys. To reach the chimneys, scramble up the scree slopes above Feather Lake to the saddle, and then climb up the east face an additional 40 or 50 feet to a ledge system that runs diagonally out to the peak's southeast corner. The access to this ledge system is somewhat flaky, but sound. The ledge system terminates behind a large detached slab. Climb over or below this slab to the west side of the ridge. From this point, there are three alternative chimney routes, all of which lead to a shelf below the "staircase" (a talus-filled crack which leads up to the "friction highway"): the far left chimney, which is rated at YDS 5.4 and involves considerable exposure; the center chimney, also rated at YDS 5.4, contains a chockstone and is shaped like an hourglass (one climber—despite having only a 31-inch waist—became wedged into the narrow section of the chimney); and the far right chimney, which is the most difficult of the three and is rated YDS 5.6. This last chimney is directly above the detached slab and contains a chockstone which should be avoided. Exiting this chimney requires stemming up under the crack roof and then doing a twisting pull-up (mantel) on a thin handhold. From the top of the chimney, climb up the "staircase" to the "friction highway," which leads to the west on a ledge which connects with the notch at the base of the summit block. Follow the West Face route to the top from this point. The first ascent was by L. Stur, B. Ring, N. Bennet and S. Franke, in 1957.

Southwest Ridge. *(Grade II, YDS 5.4)*

This route climbs a large ravine that parallels the west side of the southwest ridge. Louis Stur describes the route as "tremendously wide and extremely steep." The route crosses four rock

The north face of Warbonnet Peak (photo by Lyman Dye)

walls, which are separated by talus and grass slopes, before eventually joining the original Iowa Mountaineers route near the summit block. The climbing gets more difficult as each wall is climbed. The platform at the top of the fourth wall is the 40-foot fissure in the summit block. Climb the fissure to the notch at the top and follow the West Face route to the summit. The first ascent was by L. Stur and J. Fuller, in 1958.

Northeast Face. *(Grade II, Class 6)*
Start at the southeast notch and traverse on ledges across the north face to the east until the ledges end. Climb a chimney with a chockstone (by bypassing the steep lower section to the right on a steep slab) to a ledge. Follow the ledge back into the chimney above the slab. The chimney opens up on the ridge crest at a vertical headwall. (The first-ascent team overcame the vertical wall with the aid of seven bolts.) From the top of the wall, a steep slab leads to the summit. The first ascent was by D. Davis, S. Marts and F. Beckey, in 1962.

Black Crystal Route. *(Grade II, 5.11+)*
This route climbs the north face 1,200 feet to the summit. It covers 5.10 terrain on its lower sections and then joins the northeast face route for the final pitch. The first ascent was by Kevin Swigert and Jeff Lowe, in 1981; they climbed final

pitch without resorting to a bolt ladder, rating it at 5.11+.

East Face. *(Grade II, YDS 5.1)*
This route begins at the base of the main vertical chimney on the east face. This chimney is usually filled with ice and dripping water. The route moves up on solid slabs and ledges on the left side of the crack to a notch about 60 feet below the summit fin. Follow the West Face route from the notch to the summit. The first ascent was by L. Stur and J. Fuller, in 1960.

Cirque Lake Peak* *10,210 feet*
This peak is located directly east of Warbonnet, above the uppermost Baron Lake. Despite some rotten and broken rock, the views of the surrounding peaks make this summit well worth the climb. The first ascent was originally credited to H. Adams Carter and G. Constan, in 1954. However, during a 1973 ascent, a register was located on the summit. The register was left by the (Seattle) Mountaineers in 1949, and incorrectly identified the summit as Warbonnet. Access is via FST-101 which begins either at Redfish Lake [Approach: (A)(4)(c)] or Grandjean [Approach: (B)(3)(c)]. USGS Warbonnet Peak / SW

East Face. *(Grade II, YDS 5.1)*
Scramble up the moraine debris south of the

middle Baron Lake until you reach the cirque lake above. Climb the gentle friction slabs on the west side of the lake to the upper debris-filled ledges. From here, a crack is visible in the face. Follow the crack on good rock through the cliff bands to the upper, decomposed face.

West Slope. *(Grade I, Class 3-4)*
Climb from the saddle between Warbonnet and Cirque Lake Peak. From the saddle, scramble up the talus-covered slopes past several large blocks. The only obstacle involves crossing several large slabs near the base of the Lions Head. From above these slabs, the route is nothing more than a scramble over large blocks and slabs, which are relatively stable.

North Ridge. *(Grade II, YDS 5.2)*
The first ascent was by H. Adams Carter and G. Constan, in 1954. No details are known.

Southwest Spur. *(Grade II, YDS 5.9, A1)*
The route begins at Warbonnet Lakes and then ascends toward the col west of the peak's west buttress. About 300 feet below the col, the route crosses diagonally to the right, to a headwall between the west and southwest spurs of the peak and 100 feet to the right of a large cleft. From this point, the route continues diagonally to a platform and then diagonally left to a dihedral and large flake. The first-ascent party then pushed up the flake until they found a ledge which led to the crest of the southwest spur. From the ridge top, it was one pitch to the west ridge and two pitches along the west ridge to the summit tower. A chimney on the tower's south face was then followed to the summit. The first ascent was by Helmcke, Schmidt and Errington, in 1972.

VERITA RIDGE COMPLEX

Between Warbonnet Peak and the main Sawtooth crest is a ridge line cluttered with granite formations that runs from southeast to northwest between Baron and Goat Creeks. These formations have received more attention by mountaineers than any other single place in Idaho. This is understandable when you first see it. The ridge is a complex rampart of summits and towers composed of solid granite. The ridge's southern exposure, toward Goat Creek, is a steep mass of scree, talus and hardpan. The northern side of the ridge, which rises above Baron Creek, is generally composed of lovely, solid, high-angle slabs. Access all of the formations listed below from FST-101, which begins either at Redfish Lake [Approach: (A)(4)(c)] or Grandjean [Approach: (B)(3)(c)]. USGS Warbonnet Peak / SW

Silicon Tower* *9,680+ feet (Class 6)*
This pinnacle is located at the lowest point in the Verita Ridge. The first ascent was made by H. Adams Carter, in 1961. The route climbs the northeast corner via a chimney system. The earliest climbs used direct aid. More recent climbs have evidently been done free. USGS Warbonnet Peak / SW

Tilted Slab Pinnacle* *10,000+ feet (YDS 5.3)*
This pinnacle is located on the west side of the Verita Ridge, just east of the major saddle which separates the Warbonnet group from the Monte Verita Group. This pinnacle is capped by a tilted slab which looks like it was balanced on the formation's shaft. The first ascent was by L. Dye, in 1971. USGS Warbonnet Peak / SW
Climb to the saddle in the Verita Ridge just northwest of this formation. Descend from the saddle for 20 feet to a fragile ledge on the southwest slope. Traverse east over several spur ridges until you are on the east side of the formation. A large crack rises to the talus pocket at the base of the pinnacles above. A chockstone is located about halfway up this crack. Climb behind the stone and out through an attic door. Scramble out of the crack to the west over easy ledges to the north face of the pinnacle. Follow easy ledges to the base of the summit block, approaching the block from the west. The summit slab is tilted to the north at about 50 degrees. Use a mantle move to get onto the shelf at the base of the block and then friction climb to the summit.

Leaning Tower of Pisa* *10,040+ feet (Class 6)*
This is the massive leaning granite tower on the ridge crest just west of Monte Verita. The first ascent was done via the northwest side. It was made by F. Beckey, D. Davis and S. Marts, in 1961. The climb involved continuous direct aid. USGS Warbonnet Peak / SW

Damocles* *9,800+ feet (Class 5)*
The various written accounts which mention this formation are conflicting as to the exact location of this pinnacle. It is located below the ridge crest and to the south of the Leaning Tower. The first ascent was made by F. Beckey and S. Marts, in 1961. Their route, called the "Merry Go Round," begins at the northeast base of the pinnacle. From this point, the route goes diagonally to the right on a ledge system and makes about a two-thirds circle of the tower to a belay spot. From the belay spot, turn back to the left on a finger traverse to a roomy ledge. From this ledge, a short chimney leads to the summit. USGS Warbonnet Peak / SW

Peak   Warbonnet Peak

Lions Head

Cirque Lake Peak

The Verita Ridge (photo by Lyman Dye)

Monte Verita *10,080+ feet (Class 4)*

This peak is on the southeastern section of the Warbonnet Peak ridge complex. The exact location of this peak is a hotly contested issue. This guide will accept the USGS designation on the Warbonnet Peak quad, which depicts a twin-summited peak just below the printed name. The southernmost high point is the summit of Monte Verita; the northernmost summit (which is slightly lower in elevation) is known as the Perforated Pinnacle. Monte Verita is visible from the Alpine/Baron Lakes divide; it appears as a collection of spires.

Access to the summit is via a scramble up the northeast ridge. This ridge begins at the western shore of the Upper Baron Lake and is composed of low-angle polished ledges. These ledges are severely broken on the crest. The ridge's east face is loose talus and scree. The ridge's west face steepens and becomes a beautiful sheer wall above Baron Lake. Follow the ridge up to the summit blocks. From the north, the summit blocks are climbed by a short obvious pitch. USGS Warbonnet Peak / SW

Peforated Pinnacle* *10,080+ feet (Class 4)*

This is actually Monte Verita's lower northern summit. The granite summit block is broken (or perforated), and flat on top. Once you are at its base, the summit block is an easy climb from any side and involves only one lead. (See the Monte Verita description for more details.) USGS Warbonnet Peak / SW

Mikes Pinnacle* *9,900+ feet (Class 5)*

This formation is located southwest of the Perforated Pinnacle, below the ridge crest. It forms a sharp shaft which rises out of broken talus. The route climbs up the north edge of the shaft. USGS Warbonnet Peak / SW

Cirque Lake Tower* *9,600+ feet (Class 5)*

This pinnacle is located on Monte Verita's north ridge. The top of the formation is reached by a 40-foot lead up the south face. USGS Warbonnet Peak / SW

Dinner Tower* *9,900+ feet (Class 5)*

This is the westernmost "meal" tower. The route climbs the southeast face, up an easy Class 5 crack system. The first ascent was by F. Beckey, E. Bjornstad, D. Davis and S. Marts, in 1961. USGS Warbonnet Peak / SW

Lunch Tower* *9,900+ feet (Class 4)*

This tower is east of Dinner Tower, below the ridge crest to the southwest. The route follows a chimney on the tower's northwest side. The major difficulty is the traverse into the chimney at the start. The first ascent was by E. Bjornstad and D. Davis, in 1961. USGS Warbonnet Peak / SW

Breakfast Tower* *9,700+ feet (Class 6)*
This is the third tower in the line, looking from from west to east. The first ascent was by E. Bjornstad and D. Davis, in 1961. They climbed up the south rib. The first pitch leads to the top of the rib and is easy Class 5 climbing. The second pitch follows a poor crack system; it required five pitons, which were used for direct aid. USGS Warbonnet Peak / SW

Dessert Tower* *9,500+ feet (Class 4)*
This is the fourth tower from west to east. It is the first tower above the saddle which is directly west of Peak 9769. The first ascent was by D. Davis, in 1961. Davis followed a crack system on the southeast face. The rock is crumbly, and the cracks are rounded on their corners. USGS Warbonnet Peak / SW

Peak 9769 *9,769 feet (Class 3)*
This peak is located on the main Sawtooth crest 0.5 mile southwest of Alpine Lake. It has been referred to as Monte Verita in the climbing literature. However, the USGS placed that name on a peak further west. The peak is an easy scramble from the saddle to the west [Approach: (A)(4)(c)]. USGS Warbonnet Peak / SW

Mount Alpen* *9,680+ feet (Class 3)*
This twin-summited peak is located 0.5 mile southwest of Alpine Peak and 1.0 mile southwest of Alpine Lake. It is plainly visible from the lake. It is erroneously identified as Packrat Peak by the USGS. From Alpine Lake, follow the stream to the west and then turn south and climb the gully to the saddle west of the peak. There is a permanent snowfield in the upper stretches of the gully. From the saddle, it is a short scramble to the summit. USGS Warbonnet Peak / SW

Packrat Peak *10,240+ feet*
The USGS has misnamed Packrat Peak on the Warbonnet Quad. The peak that mountaineers know as Packrat is actually located 0.5 mile southwest of the summit marked on the quad. The true Packrat Peak is a notable mountain distinguished by two towers on its northern side that resemble the ears of a giant rat when viewed from the distance. The actual summit of this peak is formed by an impressive leaning fin of granite. The peak offers several hundred feet of technical climbing from all directions. The first ascent was by R. Underhill, M. Underhill and D. Williams, in 1934. USGS Warbonnet Peak / SW

Northeast Ridge. *(Grade II, YDS 5.1)*
The climb begins at the saddle between Alpen Peak and Packrat, which is accessed from the upper Redfish Lakes. Hike to the lakes cross country from FST-154 [Approach: (A)(4)(b)]. Follow the ridge toward Packrat's summit. The ridge crest is climbed directly to the main notch below the first buttress. From the notch, climb to the base of the north towers. From this point, two alternatives are available.

One possible route is to climb to the north for 25 feet across an angled slab, turn the corner and continue up the north face, climbing between the north towers to the upper saddle.

The other alternative is to follow a thin horizontal crack out to the south, below the tower cliffs and across the face. From this crack, the upper saddle (which is south of the north tower) can be reached by making a delicate YDS 5.6 move up and over the lip of the saddle.

The summit block is visible from the upper saddle. Climb the summit block via a 30-foot layback. The first ascent was by L. Dye, M. Howard and the Mazamas, in 1971.

North Face. *(Grade II, Class 5)*
First ascent by D. Davis, S. Marts and F. Beckey, in 1962. Access the base of the North Face from either Upper Baron Lake or Redfish Lake Creek. From Upper Baron Lake [Approach: (A)(4)(c) or (B)(3)(c)], hike southwest and cross the saddle due south of the lake and just west of Peak 9769 and drop into the Warbonnet Lake cirque. From Redfish Lake Creek and FST-154 [Approach: (A)(4)(b)], hike cross country to Upper Redfish Lakes, and then cross the saddle between Packrat and Mount Alpen.

The North Face route starts at the base of the face, near its center. Ledges lead at an angle from here to the largest slab. Avoid the slab by climbing a chimney on its left side. From the top of the chimney, the route follows diagonal ledges to the right. This ledge system eventually intersects a left-trending ledge, which is followed for 200 feet to a grassy ledge that intersects with a second ledge. From the second ledge, a gully leads up to a point near the summit. This route is rated Class 3, with occasional Class 4 and Class 5 pitches. Dan Davis writes in the 1963 American Alpine Journal that the major problem was route-finding.

East Face. *(Grade II, YDS 5.1)*
Access from upper Redfish Lake (see directions above). The moderate ledges of the eastern cirque wall become more difficult as you approach the main buttress. It may be difficult to find a route up through the lower ledges. Once the upper ledges are reached, the best route to the summit block is just to the left of the peak's center point.

Follow an angled crack which tilts to the south, and then turn back to the north on the ledge which forms the summit base. Climb the tilted summit block up the exposed south rib. The first ascent was by R. Underhill, M. Underhill and D. Williams, in 1934.

South Couloir. *(Grade II, YDS 5.3)*
From the west, climb to the saddle between Packrat and Mount Underhill. This is an easy scramble. From the saddle, the route enters the south couloir and then follows easy ledges to the base of the buttress. Turn the corner on the buttress and gain a broken ledge. Follow this ledge to the north and onto the face. From here, an angled crack, which is tilted to the south at its upper end, leads to a higher ledge. Move to the north end of this ledge and climb one of the many cracks that infest this spot. The cracks lead to the saddle north of the summit. Walk back to the south on the saddle ledge to the summit block.

La Fiamma* *9,900+ feet*
This beautiful formation is located near the end of, and just south of, the ridge leading west from Packrat Peak. The shortest approach is from Baron Creek and FST-101 (which begins either at Redfish Lake [Approach: (A)(4)(c)] or Grandjean [Approach: (B)(3)(c)].) Cross the saddle due south of Upper Baron Lake and drop into the Warbonnet Lake cirque and then climb to the saddle between Packrat Peak and the Mayan Temple. USGS Warbonnet Peak / SW

East Face. *(Grade II, YDS 5.6)*
The route starts at the notch where the tower meets the main ridge and then angles up the broken face toward the north side to a second notch. From this point, traverse across to the west face and a chimney that splits the lower tower. Climb the chimney. At the top of the chimney, the route goes up the upper west face. The first ascent was made using direct aid, but later climbers have done the route without aid. The first ascent was by F. Beckey, S. Marts and D. Davis, in 1962.

Mayan Temple* *10,080 feet*
This peak is located directly west of Packrat Peak on the subsidiary ridge that runs west from the main divide. It is also referred to as Japan Peak. See the approach write-up for La Fiamma. USGS Warbonnet Peak / SW

East Ridge. *(Class 4)*
The climb begins in the saddle just west of Packrat and beyond La Fiamma. To reach the saddle, skirt the Temple's north face (normally accomplished on snow) or come around Packrat from the south. The east ridge is easy terrain to the summit block, which is Class 4.

Northeast Couloir. *(Class 5)*
This route begins in the Goat Creek Basin at Feather Lakes. (There are two couloirs on the ridge wall—this couloir is the narrower one, to the east.) Except in low snow years, the route in the couloir is a moderate-angle snow climb. Climb the couloir to the notch just west of the first tower on the ridge crest and continue to the summit from this point. The couloir contains a buttress about two thirds of the way up, which can be bypassed on the west wall.

Cony Peak *9,606 feet (Class 2)*
Cony Peak is situated 2.25 miles due west of Mount Underhill and 2.0 miles southwest of Warbonnet Peak. From the South Fork of the Payette River and FST-452 [Approach: (B)(3)(b)], follow Garden Creek to its upper reaches (a steep, direct slog) and then climb through the trees to the southeast ridge and follow this ridge to the summit. USGS Warbonnet Peak/SW

Mount Underhill* *10,160+ feet*
This stunning and complex peak is unnamed on the USGS quad. It is the next summit south of Packrat Peak. Climbers have incorrectly identified this peak as Reward Peak. Journals and magazine articles that have talked about climbs on Reward Peak were referring to this summit, not the less interesting summit to the south, which was named Reward Peak by Arval Anderson in 1927. It is suggested that the peak should be named after Sawtooth pioneers Robert and Merriam Underhill, who, along with Dave Williams, first climbed it in 1935. The west side of the peak can be accessed from the South Fork of the Payette River and FST-452 [Approach: (B)(3)(b)] via a long cross country walk up Goat Creek, or from Baron Creek cross country into Warbonnet Lake. The east side of the peak is accessed from Upper Redfish Lakes [Approach: (A)(4)(e)]. USGS Warbonnet Peak / SW

Southwest Couloir. *(Grade II, Class 4)*
The first half of the couloir is a scramble. The second half is dominated by harder and steeper rock, which is composed of multiple ledges. The crux is in the last 40 feet—but even here, the holds are good and the exposure is minimal. The first ascent was by R. Underhill, M. Underhill and Dave Williams, in 1935.

Northwest Ridge. *(Grade I, Class 4)*
The route starts at the saddle between Packrat and Mount Underhill and follows the ridge to the summit. Cross the saddle to the peak's northwest ridge, which rises sharply and is blocked by a tower. The climb starts at a prominent ledge which cuts diagonally across the north face of the tower

and provides access to the notch directly west of the tower. The climb continues above the notch on the ridge crest (occasionally moving onto the north or southwest faces to avoid obstacles). The first ascent was by L. Dye, M. Howard and the Mazamas, in 1971.

Mazama Couloir. *(Grade II, YDS 5.2)*
This couloir is reached from the northernmost Upper Redfish Lake. It is a large vertical couloir which rises the full length of the peak and ends at a notch just east of the summit. The couloir is a 55-degree snow climb in early spring. Once the snow has melted, the climb up the couloir encounters only one obstacle: a band of cliffs two thirds of the way up the couloir. The holds through this section are good. Above the cliffs, the couloir begins to open up and form a bowl in the north face. Climb up the broken ledges in the bowl to the northwest ridge, which is reached about 75 feet below the summit. The first ascent was by L. Dye, Howard and a Mazama Club group, in 1971.

Northwest Couloir. *(Grade II, YDS 5.6)*
This crack is the smaller of the two major couloirs on the north face of Mount Underhill. The crack ends at the notch east of the peak's main west tower. The entrance to the crack is easy and usually snow-covered. The first one third of the climb is the most difficult, technically, as the route crosses a horizontal band of cliffs. The couloir is plagued with chockstones, and its upper portion is filled with loose and broken rock. Occasionally, the route moves out onto the face to avoid chockstones. The climbing becomes easier as the route moves between the first and second set of cliffs. The crack dies out near the second set of cliffs, and then opens up again some 250 feet below the notch. From this point, the route joins the northwest ridge route. Rockfall is a constant danger on this route. The first ascent was by the Colorado Mountain Club, in 1972.

Other Routes.
The north and south ridges are reportedly rated easy Class 3; further details are unknown.

Mount Reward *10,074 feet (Class 2)*
This peak is located 1.25 miles due south of Mount Underhill. It was named in 1927 by Arval Anderson, who was surveying for the USGS. Anderson found a note on top which offered the finder a $25 reward for returning the note. (The note was originally left on the summit in 1925.) The peak is an easy scramble from the southernmost of the Upper Redfish Lakes [Approach: (A)(4)(e)]. From the lake, gain the top of the northeast ridge and follow it to the summit. USGS Warbonnet Peak / SW

Elk Peak *10,582 feet (Class 3)*
Elk Peak is located 0.75 mile south of Reward Peak, on the main Sawtooth Crest. The first ascent, which climbed the east ridge, was by R. Underhill and D. Williams, in 1934. (The east ridge is accessed from the upper sections of the Redfish Lake Creek drainage and FST-154 [Approach: (A)(4)(b)]. No details are available about their route.) The peak has also been climbed from the west. To approach from the west, leave FST-452 [Approach: (B)(3)(b)] roughly 2.0 miles above Elk Lake and climb northeast to treeline. From this point, angle up and north to the summit. It should also be possible to climb this peak via its west ridge. USGS Warbonnet Peak / SW

Pinchot Mountain *9,502 feet (Class 2)*
Pinchot Mountain is named after Gifford Pinchot, the father of American forestry. It is located 3.0 miles due west of Elk Peak. Climb from the Fern Falls area on the South Fork of the Payette River via the north ridge. Be aware that crossing the Payette River to reach the bottom of the ridge can be quite dangerous even in low water. Look for a safe crossing. USGS Warbonnet Peak / SW

Grand Mogul *9,733 feet*
This enticing peak is located at the south end of Redfish Lake, just south of Mount Heyburn. The peak, composed of sections of both hard and degenerated granite, which forms alternating walls and talus slopes. Little technical climbing has taken place on its slopes. USGS Mount Cramer / SW

Northeast Ridge. *(Class 3)*
From the Inlet Transfer Camp at the south end of Redfish Lake [Approach: (A)(4)(b)], take the trail along the end of the lake to the east. Hike to the base of the prominent treeless chute that cuts the lower portion of the ridge and follow the chute up toward the ridge top. At treeline, look for a small protrusion which resembles a serpent's head. There is a notch directly west of this formation. Scramble up to this notch. From the notch, the route generally follows the gendarme-studded ridge, with occasional visits to the east face to avoid the more difficult terrain. A more difficult alternative route moves from the notch directly to the east face, which is climbed diagonally below the east face cliff formations to a point just below the south cirque's imposing walls. Climb one of the numerous chimneys up this wall to the summit.

Tarn Route. *(Grade II, Class 4)*
Follow the Northeast Ridge route to treeline, and then traverse over to the tarn lake at 8,500 feet

Grand Mogul (photo by Lyman Dye)

in elevation. Climb up to the base of the east ridge on one of the numerous ascent lines.

North Face Snow Couloir. *(Grade II, Class 5)*
The north face of the Grand Mogul is split by a large couloir that gives the peak its distinctive look. (The couloir is usually filled with snow until late summer.) From the south end of Redfish Lake, a small stream descends out of the couloir; follow this drainage up into the couloir. Once in the couloir, the route rises quickly to a notch directly west of the summit. This route was first climbed by the Iowa Mountaineers, in 1957.

North Face/West Ridge. *(Grade II, YDS 5.7)*
This route was pioneered by R. Fisher. The route follows a long dihedral in the north face. No other details are known.

SADDLEBACK LAKES CIRQUE

This cirque, located south of the Elephants Perch, contains three lakes and is surrounded by six major summits—Elephants, Chipmunk, Goat and Eagle perches—as well as Decker Peak and Redfish Point. Each of these peaks is discussed below. In its own small way, the cirque resembles the Wind Rivers' Titcomb Basin, and is of major interest to mountaineers.

Elephants Perch* *9,670 feet*
This massive twin-summited peak is located directly southwest of the Grand Mogul. The early settlers in the Stanley area dubbed the peak Saddleback because of its shape; other early reports called it Sawtooth Dome. The Iowa Mountaineers gave the peak its present (unofficial) name in 1960, after making the first ascent. The Iowa Mountaineers reasoned that the two summits of the peak were elephant's ears. Others have said that the name is descriptive of the large saddle between the two summits—where the elephant perched. USGS Mount Cramer / SW

Northwest Face. *(Grade II, Class 4)*
Cross Redfish Lake Creek about 2.5 miles above the Inlet Campground [Approach (A)(4)(b)]. The trail comes very close to the creek at this point. From the trail, there are several very prominent granite slabs near the southwest face; these should be used as landmarks. Using the slabs to guide you, climb up to the southwest shoulder. From the shoulder, turn northeast and, using a zig-zag route, climb the many steps and ledges that lead to the saddle between the two summits of Elephants Perch. The first two steps are the most difficult. Once the route reaches the upper broken ledges, the climbing is rather easy.

Northwest Shoulder. *(Grade II, Class 5)*
This is the original ascent route of the Iowa Mountaineers. Hike up the unmaintained trail to the Saddleback Lakes [Approach: (A)(4)(d)] to the base of the shoulder. At this point, a sound chimney and crack system leads up the shoulder which is just north of the main west face. The

157

Elephants Perch

West Peak

West Face

The lower west summit and the west face of Elephants Perch (photo by Lyman Dye)

route stays between the west face and Northwest Face route described above. There are no major route-finding difficulties as long as you stay to the northeast of the shoulder.

Other Routes.

The west wall of Elephants Perch, the home of Idaho big-wall climbing, has three main facades. The first ascents of each of these facades, and of the peak's east face, are chronicled below. A complex description of the numerous routes on the faces would be beyond the scope of this book, but it is important to note that a lot of impressive rock climbing has taken place on the west face. Some of the climbers who have pioneered routes up the Perch's faces include Fred Beckey, Raymond Brooks, Jim Catlin, Reid Dowdle, Dick Foster, Jeff Gruenburg, Jeff Hall, Don Hough,

Jennifer Jones, Jeff Lowe, Greg Lowe, Bill March, Russel Oberg, Mike Paine, Steve Marts, Herb Schwabland, Gene Smith, Kevin Swigert, Steve Roper and Gordon Webster. (My apologies to all of those I have missed.) The face has been climbed in the winter and has seen at least one free solo ascent.

West Face. *(Grade III, Class 6)*
The first ascent of this giant wall came in 1963 and was made by F. Beckey, S. Marts and H. Schwabland. The route, which follows a line up the middle of the face, used 110 pitons and a number of bolts. J. Lowe and G. Lowe climbed a variation of the original route in 1972 and did not use bolts.

Southwest Face. *(Grade III, Class 6)*
This route climbs up the "prow" or point where the west face turns into the southwest face. The first ascent was in 1965, by R. Dowdle and D. Hough. For details on this route, see AAJ 1979.

Northwest Face. *(Grade III, Class 6)*
This route was pioneered by J. Splittgerber and B. March in 1975. The route involves six pitches of severe climbing. For details on this route see AAJ 1976.

East Face. *(Grade II, Class 6)*
This route ascends a 500-foot dihedral. The first ascent was by G. Webster and S. Roper.

Peak 9847 *9,847 feet (Class 4)*
On the 1963 version of the Mount Cramer quad, this peak was identified as Decker Peak. On the 1972 version of the map, that name had been shifted to another peak. This peak has occasionally been referred to as the Chipmunks Perch. This peak can be climbed from the Saddleback Lakes via the west face [Approach: (A)(4)(d)]. USGS Mount Cramer / SW

Eagle Perch* *10,200+ feet (Class 5)*
This peak is located southwest of the Elephants Perch and the Saddleback Lakes. The first ascent was by the Iowa Mountaineers, led by H. Adams Carter, in 1972. The route ascends the northwest buttress on an obvious line to the summit ridge. Follow the summit ridge to the top. USGS Mount Cramer / SW

Goat Perch* *10,080+ feet*
This is the lower northern summit of Goat Perch. The first ascent was made via the north ridge by the Iowa Mountaineers, led by Hans Gmosser, in 1960. USGS Mount Cramer / SW

North Ridge Route. *(Class 5)*
This very exposed route starts on the east face and then climbs up to the exposed ridge line. The

ridge line is then followed to the summit, with an occasional brief foray out onto the face. Hans Gmosser, who led the climb, compared it to a famous climb in the Alps on the Piz Badille [Approach: (A)(4)(d)].

Southwest Ridge. *(Grade II, Class 5)*
To reach this route, hike cross country up Chockstone Basin [Approach: (A)(4)(d)]. The route climbs the snow couloir on the west face and ascends to the notch on the southwest ridge (climbing difficulty is Class 4 to this point). From the notch, climb to the summit block. Climb the exposed block on the rib.

Chockstone Peak* *9,320 feet*
This peak is located on the south side of Redfish Lake Creek. The peak has two summits and a large boulder wedged in the col that divides the summits. The first ascent was by the Iowa Mountaineers in 1954. USGS Mount Cramer / SW

Iowa Couloir. *(Grade II, Class 4)*
Cross Redfish Lake Creek near Flatrock Junction [Approach: (A)(4)(b)] and follow the drainage (which is known as Chockstone Basin) up to the peak's east face. Follow the central gully to just below the chockstone and then skirt around to the lower summit. A large chimney separates the east face from the col between the two summits.

Climb this chimney two thirds of its distance to a point where it divides. At this point, the route toward the south summit eventually leads out onto the face. To reach the north summit, continue up the chimney to the chockstone and then go to the summit. The first ascent was by the Iowa Mountaineers, in 1954.

East Face. *(Grade II, YDS 5.3)*
Make a Class 3 scramble several hundred feet up the Iowa Couloir (described above) to a point which provides good access to the east face. Twelve pitches of Class 4 and Class 5 climbing leads to the notch just east of the true summit. Two more pitches, with small holds, lead across the exposed east face to the summit.

West Face. *(Grade II, YDS 5.6)*
This route follows the Iowa Couloir (described above) to the Chockstone. Climb out from underneath the chockstone to the west summit on easy, but rotten rock. From here, move to the west face of the higher eastern summit. The climb up the face begins on two ledges (both about three inches wide) and continues around the corner to the west face. At this point, the upper of the two ledges narrows to one inch and the lower ledge disappears. Two almost imperceptible, downsloping holds allow you to make a long step to a 20-foot vertical flake. Climb to the top of this flake and then contour upward to either an open book or a

Goat Perch to Chockstone Peak (photo by Lyman Dye)

Goat Perch — Eagle Perch — Chockstone Peak — Redfish Point

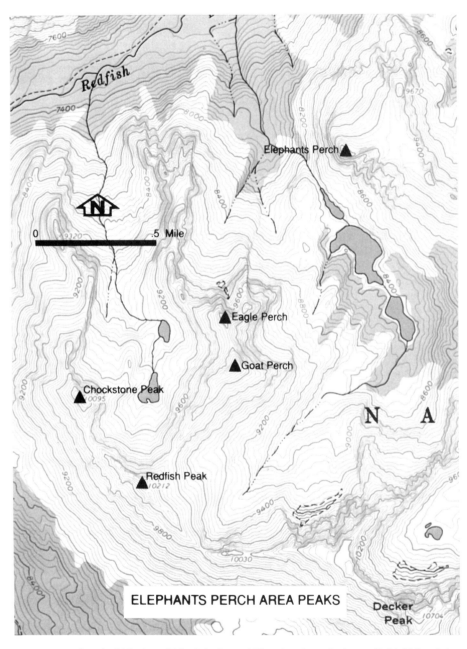

ELEPHANTS PERCH AREA PEAKS

narrow exposed crack. At the top of this pitch, the route finishes on a short friction pitch to the summit.

Redfish Point* *10,095 feet*

Point 10095, located between this Redfish Peak and Chockstone Peak, is known as Redfish Point.

Although not an actual summit, this high point on the ridge line has attracted considerable interest. The southeast slopes are a Class 3 scramble. The Iowa Mountaineers probably made the first ascent in 1948. It is unclear what route they followed. USGS Mount Cramer / SW

West Face. *(Grade I, Class 4)*
This route begins on the ledges south of Chockstone Peak and climbs into the diminutive upper bowl. Once in the bowl, the route follows a series of ledge and crack systems to the summit. Approach this route from the Redfish Lake Creek Trail [Approach: (A)(4)(b)] by leaving the trail south of Flatrock Junction.

East Face. *(Grade II, YDS 5.2)*
This route climbs out of the lake basin to the east of the summit [Approach: (A)(4)(b)]. Climb the Class 3 to Class 4 ridge that begins at the outlet of the upper lake to the face for the final 200 feet on easy Class 5 rock. The first ascent was by L. Dye and Barnes, in 1965.

Redfish Peak* *10,212 feet (Class 3)*
This peak is located 1.75 miles southwest of the Elephants Perch, at the junction of the ridges leading from Chockstone Peak and the Goat Perch. The first ascent was by the Iowa Mountaineers, in 1948. The summit is an easy scramble up either its northeast or southeast ridge. Both ridges can be accessed from the Saddleback Lakes basin [Approach: (A)(4)(d)]. The first ascent was by R. Underhill, D. Underhill and D. Williams, in 1934. USGS Mount Cramer / SW

Decker Peak *10,704 feet (Class 2-3)*
Although this peak is the third-highest summit in the range, it has received little attention from climbers. Decker Peak is located 2.0 miles due south (almost) of the Elephants Perch. Climb via the south ridge, which can be gained from either Decker Creek on the east or Redfish Lake Creek on the west [Approach: (A)(4)(b)]. USGS Mount Cramer / SW

Finger of Fate *9,760+ feet*
This is a striking tower that sits above Hell Roaring Lake. The soaring granite walls are easily visible from ID-75. The first ascent was made by Louis Stur and Jerry Fuller, in 1958. All routes are reached from Hell Roaring Lake [Approach: (A)(3)(b) and (c)]. USGS Mount Cramer / SW

Southeast Face. *(Grade II, Class 4)*
The route crosses the base of the tower from west to east. Climb up the ledges and chimneys in the southeast face toward the west ridge. The west ridge is reached midway between the notch and the summit. The summit block is then climbed via a V-shaped crack to a point near the summit where it is capped by a roof. Exit the crack, circle around to the south and climb the summit boulder on the southeast. The first ascent was by L. Stur and J. Fuller, in 1958.

Finger of Fate from Hell Roaring Lake

East Face. *(Grade III, YDS 5.6)*
This route begins in the right-facing open book leading up the face. Climb up the book on cracks and then up the face to an overhang. Bypass the overhang on the right to a small belay ledge. From here, climb up the book for two more leads to a broad flat area. The next lead involves chimneying up the right side of a large blocky area to a jam crack, which is followed up and to the right to a ledge. From this ledge, climb up into a prominent chimney just above. Climb this chimney to a shelf. Above the shelf, climb up and right to where another short chimney can be entered. This chimney ends near the summit block. Finish the climb on the Southeast Face route. The total climb is nearly 1,000 feet in length. First ascent was by J. Beaupre and G. Webster, in 1967.

Open Book Route. *(YDS 5.8)*
This route was first climbed by D. Dorworth and L. Poulsen, in 1972. The route is located 75 feet to the right of the southeast face route in an obvious open book. The first 75 feet are a scramble to a large ledge. From the ledge, the route continues to the left, around a corner and up a second open book, which becomes overhanging 100 feet

up. Avoid the overhang by moving to the left and climbing a jam crack to a spot 10 feet above the overhang. (Poulsen wrote in the *AAJ* that the overhang was climbable.) The next pitch follows a jam crack up for 25 feet to a another open book which leads to the top of a large flake 160 feet from the start of the pitch. The next pitch utilizes a crack which leads to a ramp. From the ramp, there are several choices of routes to the top.

West Face. *(Grade II, YDS 5.4)*
Climb up the talus slopes from a point beyond the bottom of the pinnacle's west face to a break in the southwest ridge. This notch separates the Finger from the flat-topped summit to the south. Climb up to the notch on the walls to the northwest, and then climb from the notch to the ridge crest. Follow the ridge northeast to the face of the tower. Located out on the southwest wall is a large rectangular concave indentation called "the locker." Climb up into the locker, and then out onto its right face by using a finger traverse. Climb up onto the open shelf and then cross the large crack to a ledge below and east of the summit block. Move up to the step about 30 feet below the summit, which provides a good belay stance. From here, climb the summit block on its north side.

Red Bluff* *10,272 feet*
This impressive formation, composed of reddish rock, sits on the Sawtooth crest just north of Mount Sevy. The small pinnacle due north of the Red Bluff is known as the Sentry; the large block north of the Sentry is called the Coffin. (This formation can be accessed from Upper Cramer Lake in the west [Approach: (A)(4)(b)] or via Hell Roaring Lake in the east [Approach: (A)(3)(b) or (c)]. The first ascent was by Gordon Vendor and Emily Vendor, in 1960.   USGS Mount Cramer / SW

East Face. *(Grade II, YDS 5.4)*
This was the route of the first ascent. Climb the conspicuous crack in the east face. Nothing else is known about the route.

Northeast Ridge. *(Grade II, YDS 5.3)*
From Hell Roaring Lake, follow the unmaintained trail [Approach: (A)(3)(c)] into the basin below the formation. Begin climbing up the east face to the north of the steep cliff buttress. The route up to the summit block varies from scrambling to easy Class 5. The first view of the summit block will knock your socks off. The summit block is split by an 80-foot-high crack, which narrows as it ascends. The first 30 feet of the crack are the most difficult. Despite the exposure, there are plenty of good holds. The first ascent was by M. Howard and V. Howard, in 1972.

West Couloir. *(Grade II, YDS 5.4)*
This route begins on the western side of the divide at the Upper Cramer Lake. Scramble up the scree and talus to the base of the north branch of the main west couloir, and then up the couloir to the notch separating the west tower from the face. (This is the junction point of the north and south branches of the couloir, about two-thirds of the distance up the face.) The rock is loose but not treacherous. Climb from this notch to the main notch in the northeast ridge. From the main notch, follow ledges out onto the northeast ridge. The summit block is clearly visible to the south. Climb up and over two small cliffs, following the obvious route. From here, the summit block can be surmounted with some difficulty. First ascent by L. Dye and M. Ranger, in 1972.

Mount Sevy* *10,480+ feet (Class 5)*
Mount Sevy is located on the main Sawtooth crest 0.6 miles west of the Finger of Fate and is misidentified as the Arrowhead on the USGS quad. This fang-shaped summit is climbed via its eastern ridge and south face. Sevy's summit block is a typical Sawtooth upright block surrounded by smaller broken blocks. Though this peak offers a number of challenging lines, few have tried its granite; there is only one reported route to its summit. USGS Mount Cramer / SW
From the west end of Hell Roaring Lake [Approach: (A) (3) (a)] climb directly toward the Finger of Fate and the unnamed lake at its eastern base. Pass under the Finger, close to its base, and continue on to the small ponds at the base of Mount Sevy's southern slopes. From the uppermost pond, climb directly north to Sevy's east ridge and then follow the ridge to a notch about 80 feet below the summit. (This section of the route involves about 400 feet of easy Class 4 climbing.) From this notch, the route moves out onto the south face and then up the face for another 40 to 50 feet of moderately difficult Class 4 climbing, to a small notch at the base of the upright summit block. The final moves up the summit block are on thin, airy holds and are rated low Class 5.

The Arrowhead *(Grade II, YDS 5.9)*
This formation is located on the Sawtooth crest, on the north slopes of Peak 10579. The rock looks exactly like a giant arrowhead. (Note: on the 1963 version of the Mount Cramer quad, the Arrowhead was erroneously located on the summit of Mount Sevy.)
Climb the west face from the ridge crest. This one-pitch climb first leads up to a small ledge. From the ledge, traverse about 15 feet to the left, to small right-facing open book (the 5.9 crux). Ascend the short open book via a jam crack to a

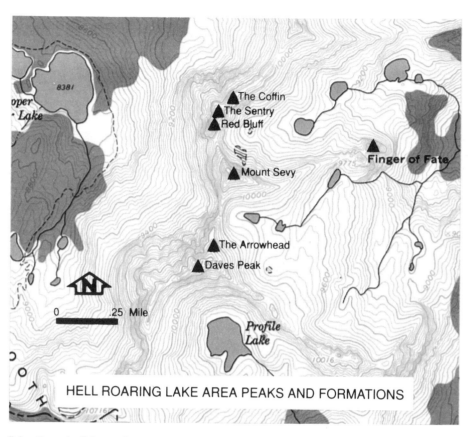

HELL ROARING LAKE AREA PEAKS AND FORMATIONS

flake. From the flake, moderate Class 5 climbing leads to the summit. The first ascent of the formation was made by Gordon Webster and John Beaupre (date unknown.) USGS Mount Cramer / SW

Mount Cramer *10,716 feet*

This is the dominant peak above the Cramer Lakes. The second-highest peak in the Sawtooth Range, its north face rises almost vertically for the last 1,000 feet to the summit. USGS Mount Cramer / SW

East Face. *(Class 3)*

This route follows the wide, prominent east ridge up to the east face, where it crosses a large boulder field just below the summit. From the Hell Roaring Lake area, follow the Imogene Lake trail [Approach: (A)(4)(b)] to within 1.0 mile of Imogene Lake. Hike cross country over relatively easy ground to the highest unnamed lake just south of the east ridge.

West Face. *(Grade II, YDS 5.3)*

This route climbs the main couloir on the face. (This vertical couloir is the first break north of the center of the west face.) The route, which begins at the bottom of the face, is relatively straightforward [Approach: (A)(4)(b)]. Exit the crack about 150 feet below the summit and climb into a pocket on the face. (The pocket will hold snow into early summer.) Climb one of the snow gullies out of the pocket to a point southeast of the summit. The rock is fairly solid. The first ascent was by L. Dye, M. Ranger and M. Herman.

Payette Peak 10,211 feet (Class 2)

Payette Peak is located on the main Sawtooth crest, 1.5 miles east of Imogene Lake. From Imogene Lake [Approach: (A)(3)(b)], hike cross country along the string of lakes up to the basin below the peak Scramble up to the saddle north of the summit and follow the ridge to the top. USGS Snowyside Peak / SW

Imogene Peak* *10,125 feet (Class 2-3)*

Imogene Peak is located 2.6 miles due east of Payette Peak, on the east side of Imogene Lake.

The west face of El Capitan, as seen from the Alice Lake basin

The peak is identified as the Imogene triangulation station on the USGS quad. The summit can be reached from Farley Lake [Approach: (A)(2)(a)]. Climb from the west end of the lake directly to the summit ridge and then follow the ridge east to the summit. USGS Snowyside Peak / SW

Parks Peak 10,280 feet (Class 3)

Parks Peak is located 2.0 miles due south of Imogene Peak. To climb this mountain, take the Alice Lake Trail, FST-095 [Approach: (A)(2)(a)], toward Alice Lake. Leave the trail at the 8,400-foot contour and hike due north to the base of an obtrusive buttress which trends southeast from the summit. Climb up the west side of the buttress to just above a granite point that overlooks the valley below. Cross over to the east side of the buttress at this point. Climb along the east side of the buttress toward the south face wall. Climb the low-angle wall on broken ledges to the summit. There is a register on the summit (left by D. Miller, T. Robertson and H. Wendling, in 1960).

This peak has also been climbed from Farley Lake via the prominent north couloir—but the route is not recommended because of the broken nature of the rock. (This route is rated Class 3.) USGS Snowyside Peak / SW

Glenns Peak 10,053 feet (Class 2)

Glenns Peak sits 2.25 miles west of Snowyside Peak, directly south of Ardeth Lake. Follow the west ridge from FST-463 [Approach: (B)(4)(a)] where that trail crosses the pass between Spangle and Ardeth lakes. USGS Mount Everly / SW

Snowyside Peak 10,651 feet

Because of its striking appearance and its proximity to the popular Alice/Toxaway hiking loop, this may be the most often climbed summit in the Sawtooths. The peak was a popular destination for Idahoans long before the Underhills climbed the peak in 1935. In 1926, Bob "Two Gun" Limbert wrote an article for The Statesman on the east and north ridge routes. (There is no record of who made the first ascent.) Both the north and east ridges are climbable from FST-095 [Approach: (A)(2)(a)] where it crosses the pass above Twin Lakes. USGS Snowyside Peak / SW

East Ridge. (Class 3)

Leave FST-095 at the pass and follow the east ridge to the summit, staying on the south side of the ridge until it turns north. Then stay near the ridge top and climb directly over short intervening walls.

North Ridge. (Grade I, Class 4)

Start up the east ridge route for 0.25 mile and then traverse north to the rugged shoulder of the north ridge. From the top of the shoulder, the route makes an airy crossing of the ridge to a wall just below the summit.

El Capitan 9,901 feet

This peak sits just east of Alice Lake, 1.7 miles south of Parks Peak. Its summit forms a dome with a large west facing wall reminiscent of the real El Cap in Yosemite. Access is from Pettit Lake [Approach: (A)(2)(a)]. USGS Snowyside Peak / SW

East Side. (Class 3)

From the two small lakes below Alice Lake, climb into the cirque northeast of the peak. Work your way to the east ridge, which leads to the summit. The first ascent was by R. Underhill, M. Underhill and D. Williams, in 1935.

Northeast Ridge. (Grade II, YDS 5.2)

This route begins on the bench north of Alice Lake. Leave the trail and climb up to the first terrace. A small headwall, which forms the south side of this terrace, extends clear to the east wall of the cirque. Several easy chimneys lead through this wall to a second terrace. From the second terrace, the climb continues above the south headwall in a westerly direction to the notch between the summit and the north tower. From the notch, climb up the ridge to the south and follow the crest to the summit. The first ascent was by L. Dye and B. Hansen, in 1972.

Upper North Face. (Grade II, YDS 5.2)

This route begins at the base of the south headwall near the east face of the peak's north tower. Follow the chimney that is situated just east of where the upper terrace base joins the north tower. Climb from the top of the chimney to the notch that separates the tower from the main peak, then continue through the notch and out onto the north face on a ledge system. Ascend the north face ledges to the summit. The first ascent was by L. Dye and B. Hansen, in 1972.

McDonald Peak 10,068 feet (Class 2)

McDonald Peak is located 2.0 miles south of the west end of Pettit Lake. The summit is the culmination of a long, high ridge line which rises up from Pettit Lake and runs due south. From FST-095 [Approach: (A)(2)(a)] at the upper end of Pettit Lake, climb directly up the steep forest slopes to Point 9681 and then follow the long ridge to the summit. USGS Snowyside Peak / SW

Perfect Peak* 10,269 feet (Class 3-4)

This interesting summit, located 1.7 miles southeast of Snowyside Peak, is unnamed on the

The north side of Perfect Peak, viewed from Snowyside Peak

USGS quad. The name is adopted from Sheldon Bluestein's *Hiking Trails of Southern Idaho.* Although it has undoubtedly been climbed, there are no reports available of any ascents of this peak. Access the peak from either Alpine Creek and FST-094 [Approach: (A)(1)(a)], or from Alice Lake to the north [Approach: (A)(2)(a)]. USGS Snowyside Peak / SW

THE RAKERS

These three imposing peaks are among the remotest peaks in the Sawtooths. They are located west of the South Fork of the Payette River above Fall and Pinchot Creeks. As delineated by the USGS on the Mount Everly quad, the North Raker (which was called Red Finger at one time) has two summits. The northern summit is 9,970 feet; the south, 9,880+ feet. Climbers have always referred to these two peaks as North and South Raker. However, the USGS identified a smaller

peak 1.0 mile to the south as South Raker. For our purposes (although it is a little confusing) we will stick with the original designations for the peaks. Because the Rakers are so remote, they have seen little climbing activity. As a matter of fact, as of 1986 only four parties had reached the summit of the very difficult North Raker.

The Rakers are visible for miles and are very enticing when seen from almost any other Sawtooth peak. Thus, it is not surprising that the first attempts on the Rakers were made by the Underhill and Williams party in 1934. Although the party made it to the top of the South Raker, they were unable to finish the final pitch on the North Raker. Robert Underhill declared the peak unclimbable, and it was not conquered until 1949. The first ascent was accomplished only after Fred Beckey and Pete Schoening used their "hard rock engineering techniques" (read direct aid) to overcome the peak's formidable difficulties. The register is located in a cigar box on the saddle between the north and south peaks.

Access to the peaks requires a long cross-country hike from the South Fork of the Payette River [Approach: (B)(3)(b)]. USGS Mount Everly / SW

North Raker *9,970 feet*
(Grade III, Class 6)
The route makes an exposed traverse out to the north corner of the peak from the saddle. From this corner, traverse 15 feet on a flake to the underside of an overhang. Using direct aid, climb the overhang up a crack which splits the rotten, decomposed granite. Above this, the face becomes smooth. Beckey and friends utilized a shoulder stand from the notch above the smooth section to reach a 12-foot jam crack, which gave them access to the summit. USGS Mount Everly / SW

South Raker *9,880+ feet (Class 3-4)*
The USGS has erroneously labeled the 9,600-foot peak to the south of the main Raker formation as the South Raker. The true South Raker is located right next to the North Raker and is an easy scramble from the saddle. The summit block is rated at either Class 3 or Class 4, depending upon who you ask. USGS Mount Everly / SW

Blacknose Mountain *9,802 feet (Class 2)*
Blacknose Mountain is located 1.5 miles south of the North Raker. Climb from FST-494 [Approach: (B)(5)(c)] and Pats Lake. From the lake, climb due east and directly to the summit on a relatively easy slope. USGS Mount Everly / SW

The Rakers

Mount Everly *9,852 feet (Class 3)*
Mount Everly is a gorgeous block-shaped summit that rises steeply on all sides. It is located 1.6 miles southeast of Blacknose Mountain. The best route is up the south slopes from Everly Lake [Approach: (B)(5)(a)]. Mount Everly contains several formidable walls that have high potential for interesting routes; it is well worth the long walk into its base. USGS Mount Everly / SW

Plummer Peak *9,978 feet (Class 3)*
Plummer Peak is located 1.25 miles southeast of Mount Everly. Access the peak from Three Island Lake on its northeast side, via a short side trail from FST-462 [Approach: (B)(6)(a.1)]. Begin at the lake and climb to the saddle on the peak's southeast side. From the saddle, it is a short scramble up the southeast ridge to the summit. USGS Mount Everly / SW

Browns Peak *9,705 feet (Class 2-3)*
Browns Peak is the northernmost summit on the impressive ridge that divides the Queens River and Little Queens River drainages. Browns Peak is located 3.0 miles southwest of Plummer Peak. Climb this pup-tent-shaped peak from Browns Lake on its western slopes. The lake is located 1.0 mile east of FST-454 [Approach: (B)(5)(b)] and is reached by a short side trail, FST-480. From the lake, climb directly west to the summit. USGS Nahneke Mountain / SW

Flat Top Mountain *9,665 feet (Class 3)*
Flat Top Mountain is located 1.2 miles south of Browns Peak. Climb the peak from Flat Top Lake (Lake 8850 on the USGS quad), which is reached by FST-456 [Approach: (B)(5)(b.1)]. From the lake, hike south to the unnamed lake 0.25 mile away. Once at this lake, turn east and climb to-

ward the peak's south ridge. Follow the ridge directly to the summit. USGS Nahneke Mountain / SW

Nahneke Mountain *9,582 feet (Class 3-4)*
Nahneke Mountain sits 1.6 miles due south of Flat Top Mountain. Climb the peak from the Scenic Lake drainage [Approach: (B)(5)(b.1)]. This peak has two summits of almost equal height. The easternmost summit, the highest and the most impressive of the two, is buttressed by four nice ridges. Although all four ridges are probably climbable, only the north ridge is reported to have been climbed. To access this ridge, hike to Lake 8676, which is 0.4 mile east of Scenic Lake. The north ridge begins just above as a rather broad rampart, but soon narrows down to create a more challenging problem. USGS Nahneke Mountain / SW

Greylock Mountain *9,363 feet (Class 2)*
The name Greylock Mountain reportedly originated with the Chinese, who prospected in the Atlanta area in the 1800s. As the story goes, the Chinese called the mountain "Greyrock" because of its grey color, but their accented pronunciation was taken literally and the mountain became Greylock instead. Occasionally climbed by campers from the Atlanta area campgrounds, Greylock can be a treacherous peak. In 1987, a group of amateur climbers got lost and hung up on a cliff while descending. One fell and was killed. Despite the number of easy scrambles to the summit, do not disregard the lesson of 1987. Use common sense. If you get off route, do not push ahead if the going becomes difficult or confusing. Access the peak from Atlanta [Approach: (B)(4)(a)]. USGS Atlanta East / SW

APPROACHES TO THE SAWTOOTH RANGE

Approach routes for this section are referenced in the text by bracketed entries [Approach:], which include appropriate letter and number references.

Overall, the Sawtooths are the most accessible of all of Idaho's mountains. The combination of a central location and the National Recreation Area designation have dictated that the Forest Service maintain relatively good access. The Sawtooth Range is flanked on three sides by two primary high-quality state highways. ID-75 flanks the east side of the range between Galena Summit and Stanley; ID-21 flanks the range's northern and

western sides between Stanley and Grandjean. A number of Forest Service roads provide access to the southern end of the range.

(A) Idaho 75 Approaches.
This good two-lane highway runs along the entire eastern side of the range from the headwaters of the Salmon River to Stanley. It is accessed from Challis and US-93 in the east or from Twin Falls and I-84 in the south.

(1) FS-205, Alturas Lake Road. This road leads from ID-75, past Alturas Lake for, 7.0 miles (5 miles paved and 2 miles gravel), and then continues on in the form of a rough jeep road. This road system provides access to the southeastern portion of the Sawtooths.

(a) FST-094, Alpine Creek Trail. FST-094 leaves FS-205 1.5 miles west of Alturas Lake (or roughly 7.0 miles from ID-75) just before the road fords Alpine Creek and then follows Alpine Creek northwest for 3.5 miles to Alpine Lake. The trailless portions of the upper Alpine Creek drainage, which contain over 50 lakes and ponds, are seldom visited. From this trail, there is good access to the south side of Perfect Peak.

(2) FS-208, Pettit Lake Road. This road begins 19.0 miles south of Stanley and runs west from ID-75 to Pettit Lake and the Tin Cup Transfer Camp trailhead in about 2.5 miles of good gravel road.

(a) FST-095, FST-092 and FST-096, Alice Lake/Toxaway Lake Loop Trail. This is one of the most popular and crowded trails in Idaho. The 19.0-mile loop leaves Pettit Lake and follows Pettit Creek to Alice Lake in 6.0 miles, to Twin Lakes in 7.0 miles and then crosses into the Toxaway Lake basin over Snowyside Pass in 11.0 miles. From Toxaway Lake, the trail drops down the drainage past Farley Lake. From here, you can stop at Yellowbelly Lake, or climb south over the intervening ridge to return to Pettit Lake. The loop provides access to Parks Peak, El Capitan and Snowyside Peak.

(b) Pettit Lake and beyond. From the high ridge just north of Toxaway Lake, two trails lead to the west and north. The first, FST-452, goes to Edna Lake and then to Grandjean via the South Fork of the Payette River [Approach: (B)(3)]. The second, FST-092, leads north to Imogene Lake and then out Hell Roaring Creek [Approach: (A)(3)(b)].

(3) FS-315, Hell Roaring Creek Road. Take ID-75 south from Stanley for 12.0 miles, turn west, cross the Salmon River and then drive 5.0 miles on a rugged dirt road, best suited for a 4WD, to the trailhead. Though the Forest Service plans to gradually improve this route, it is probably the roughest road in Idaho (actually, it is more like a rock garden than a road). A high-clearance vehicle is recommended, although passenger cars have made it to the parking lot.

(a) FST-092, Hell Roaring Lake Trail. From the end of the road, this short trail reaches Hell Roaring Lake, which is located directly below the Finger of Fate, in 1.8 miles. From the parking area at the end of the road, the trail begins by fording the creek, which (as you probably guessed from the name) carries a lot of water early in the summer. There is also access from the lake to a lot of trailless country, including the areas around Profile Lake, which is next to Mount Cramer and Red Bluff Peak.

(b) FST-092, Hell Roaring Lake to Toxaway Lake Trail. From Hell Roaring Lake, it is 3.0 miles to Imogene Lake and another 3.5 miles to Toxaway Lake [Approach: (A)(2)(a)]. Most of this trail is built to very high standards and sees a lot of use.

(c) Route to the upper basin. From the western end of Hell Roaring Lake, a fisherman/climber route of good quality leads up into the high basin to the north of the Arrowhead and the Finger of Fate. Although this trail is not maintained, it is passable and easy to follow. Leave the main trail and hike around Hell Roaring Lake to the second inlet stream and look for the trail in this area.

(4) FS-214, Redfish Lake Road. Turn west off ID-75 5.0 miles south of Stanley and drive 2.0 miles on a paved road to Redfish Lake. A large backpackers' parking lot is located just before the lake on the north side of the road. During the summer, a tourist boat will haul you the 5.0 miles up Redfish Lake (for a small price) and save you the long up-and-down hike around the lake.

(a) FST-155, Bench Lake Trail. This trail leaves the backpackers' parking lot and leads to the first two Bench Lakes at the base of Mount Heyburn in 4.5 miles and 1,300 feet of elevation gain. From the first lake, it is a 1.5-mile walk on a sketchy fisherman's trail to get to the uppermost Bench Lake and the starting point for several climbing routes on Heyburn.

(b) FST-101, FST-154, Redfish Lake Creek Trail. This trail begins at the top of Redfish Lake, 5.0 miles from the trailhead parking lot. There are two ways to reach the top of the lake: take the boat during the tourist season, or hike the first 2.0 miles of the Bench Lake trail and then descend a cutoff trail for 3.0 miles to the west end of Redfish Lake. (Take the boat when it is available.) The trail, which runs from the inlet on the west end of Redfish Lake to Cramer Lake, is the main approach route to the northeastern portion of the Sawtooths. The Saddleback Lakes cross country route begins 2.0 miles from the Inlet [Approach: (A)(4)(d)]. At 3.5 miles, the trail reaches Flat

Rock junction. At this junction, FST-101 leaves Redfish Lake Creek and runs toward Alpine Lake, Baron Pass and Baron Creek to the west [Approach: (B)(3)(c)]. The main trail (now designated FST-154) extends on to Cramer Lake, which is 11.0 miles from the lake (16.0 miles from the parking area). From Cramer Lake, the trail continues west over the Cramer Divide, drops down to Payette Lake and joins FST-452 [Approach: (B)(3)(b)] and [Approach: (A)(2)(b)].

(c) FST-101, Alpine Lake/ Baron Lakes Trail. This wide, switchbacking trail leaves the Redfish Lake Creek trail at Flat Rock Junction 3.5 miles above Redfish Lake and climbs 1,000 feet in roughly 2.0 miles to Alpine Lake. From Alpine Lake, the trail climbs over the Baron Divide and then drops down to the Baron Lakes in 2.5 miles [Approach: (B)(3)(c)].

(d) Saddleback Lakes Cross-country Route. This route leads into a rugged cirque surrounded by the four "perches": Elephants, Eagle, Goat and Chipmunk. The route is not signed and may take a little time to find. Two miles above Redfish Lake, the Redfish Lake Creek Trail crosses a stream coming down off the flanks of Mount Heyburn. Several hundred feet past this point, look for a path on the south side of the trail that drops down to Redfish Lake Creek. Find a safe place to cross, and then look for a path that leads along the creek. Follow this path upstream until it turns uphill toward the cirque.

(e) FST-528, Alpine Way Trail. This is a long trail that contours along the northeast and northern fronts of the Sawtooths between Redfish Lake, the Iron Creek trailhead and Stanley Lake. The trail varies in quality along its route; it is not regularly maintained between Iron Creek trailhead and Stanley Lake. Access the trail from the backpackers' parking lot at Redfish Lake by taking the signed route (which immediately crosses a paved road) out of the parking lot and following it 0.75 mile past the Bench Lake Trail junction to a second junction. At this junction, the left fork trail proceeds up Fishhook Creek [Approach: (A)(4)(f)]. Continue on the right fork, which is the Alpine Way Trail. Follow this trail for 4.0 miles to reach Marshall Lake, which is a good jumping-off point for climbing Williams and Thompson Peaks. From this lake, the trail leads on to the Iron Creek trailhead [Approach: (B)(1)(a)].

(f) FST-186, Fishhook Creek Trail. Follow the directions for FST-528 to reach this trail. From the junction with the Alpine Way Trail, this route runs up a spectacular valley for 2.0 miles toward Fishhook Spire and Horstmann Peak. The upper reaches of the Fishhook drainage cover a large area and are generally accessible via relatively easy cross country travel.

(B) Idaho 21 Approaches. This state highway connects Stanley and Boise. Historically, the road is closed during the winter months, but recently the highway department has attempted to keep it open year round. ID-21 leads northwest from Stanley (following the northern margins of the Sawtooths) and then swings sharply south (following the western edges of 'he Sawtooths). The highway eventually turns to the southwest and crosses through the heart of the Boise Mountains on its way to Boise.

(1) FS-619, Iron Creek Road. Drive 2.0 miles northwest from Stanley on ID-21. Turn onto this signed road and drive 4.0 miles to its end, where there is a campground and a large backpackers' parking lot.

(a) FST-528, Alpine Way Trail. The Alpine Way Trail is accessed 1.0 mile from the trailhead. It runs northwest and southeast from the trailhead. (See [Approach: (A)(4)(e)] and [Approach: (B)(2)(b)] for more details.)

(a.1) Goat Lake Trail. This trail is not shown on either the USGS quads or the Forest Service map. Nevertheless, you can access Goat Lake from the Alpine Way Trail by hiking 1.0 mile southwest from the Iron Creek trailhead to the Alpine Way junction and then following the Alpine Way Trail southeast for another 1.75 miles. Turn right on the Goat Lake Trail and follow it for another 0.75 mile. This route is not well marked and can be difficult to follow.

(b) FST-640, Sawtooth Lake/McGown Lake Trail. Sawtooth Lake is a 5.0-mile hike from the trailhead along a well-signed, maintained trail. The trail leaves the trailhead just past the large information sign, gradually ascends a tree-covered alluvial fan and intersects with the Alpine trail in 1.0 mile. From this junction, follow the trail's right fork for 0.75 mile and then turn left at the next junction. From the last junction, it is 2.25 miles to the Alpine Lake turnoff and 3.25 miles to Sawtooth Lake. Mount Regan and Alpine Peak can be climbed from the lake, but Sawtooth Lake is usually crowded and camping there is not recommended. From the north end of the lake, trails lead south and west. The trail to the south leads into the North Fork of Baron Creek drainage and out to the Grandjean entrance [Approach: (B)(3)]. The trail west leads 1.0 mile to McGown Lakes. From McGown Lakes, Observation Peak as well as the Grandjean and Stanley Lake trailheads can be reached by trail.

(c) FST-478, North Fork of Baron Creek Trail. FST-478 begins at the north end of Sawtooth Lake, proceeds south along the lake and then drops into the upper reaches of the North Fork of Baron Creek. The trail eventually joins the Baron Creek Trail, in about 5.0 miles.

(2) FS-455, Stanley Lake Road. This road leaves ID-21 5.0 miles west of Stanley at a well-signed junction. The trailhead is 3.8 miles from ID-21 at Inlet Campground.

(a) FST-640, Stanley Creek Trail. FST-640 leaves the Stanley Lake trailhead and follows the creek south for 7.25 miles to a saddle at its headwaters. From this saddle, it runs east to Sawtooth Lake and eventually the Iron Creek trailhead [Approach: (B)(1)(b)]. From the saddle, FST-024 [Approach: (B)(2)(a.1)] leads to Observation Peak, and FST-453 [Approach: (B)(3)(a)] leads to Grandjean.

(a.1) FST-024, Observation Peak Trail. This trail leaves FST-640 and climbs west to the top of Observation Peak in 1.5 steep miles.

(b) FST-528, Alpine Way Trail. FST-528 leaves FST-640 1.0 mile from Stanley Lake and traverses along the northern and eastern sides of Mount McGown, crossing through some of the most remote parts of the Sawtooths, before ultimately reaching the Iron Creek trailhead [Approach: (B)(1)(a)]. This portion of the Alpine Way Trail is not maintained on a regular basis.

(3) FS-524, Grandjean Entrance Road. This entrance is located 38.0 miles west of Stanley on ID-21. A good gravel road leads east from the signed turnoff for 7.0 miles to the trailhead, which is at an elevation of 5,200 feet.

(a) FST-453, Trail Creek Trail. This trail provides a steep and relatively long approach into the Observation Peak and Sawtooth Lake areas [Approach: (B)(2)(a)].

(b) FST-452, South Fork Payette River Trail. FST-452 starts from the end of FS-524 and follows the South Fork of the Payette south for several miles, providing access to the country on the west sides of Cony, Reward and Elk peaks. The trail reaches Fern Falls, and then, in 11.0 miles, Elk Lake, before crossing over the main Sawtooth crest and linking up with the Alice Lake/Toxaway Lake Loop Trail [Approach: (A)(2)(b)].

(c) FST-101, Baron Creek Trail. This trail provides good, but long, access to lots of good climbing, including Grandjean Peak, Baron Peak, Mount Ebert, Tohobit Peak, Big Baron Spire and the entire Verita Ridge Complex. From the trailhead to Baron Lakes, it is roughly 10.0 miles and 3,100 feet of elevation gain. The trail begins at the Grandjean trailhead, crosses Trail Creek and then forks. Take the right fork and go 1.5 miles to another fork at Baron Creek. Stay left and follow Baron Creek to the lakes. From the lakes, the trail crosses the Baron divide and drops into Alpine Lake [Approach: (A)(4)(c)].

(4) Atlanta Area Access. Atlanta is one of the most remote areas in Idaho. The village can be reached from a number of different directions on fair-to-primitive roads. All of these routes require lots of time and driving skill. Primary approach is from ID-21. It begins at a signed junction next to the Edna Creek CG, just east of Mores Creek Summit. From ID-21, it is 47.0 miles to Atlanta on a good gravel road. Be sure to take Boise and Sawtooth national forest maps with you in order to assure finding Atlanta (there are a lot of side roads).

Access to Atlanta can also be gained via the Middle Fork of the Boise River. This is the most direct and trouble-free route to Atlanta for those driving from the Boise area. (It is also the slowest route.) Drive 17.0 miles north from Boise on ID-21 to the top of Lucky Peak reservoir. Turn east on FS-168 and follow this gravel road 72.0 miles to Atlanta.

Access is also possible from I-84 at Mountain Home. Take Exit 95 at Mountain Home and drive north on ID-20 for 31.9 miles to the Featherville turn onto FH-61. Follow FH-61 north to Featherville. From this small village, take FS-156 to Rocky Bar and then the Middle Fork of the Boise River. (Note: FS-126 runs almost directly between Rocky Bar and Atlanta, but it is a primitive road not suited for most passenger cars.) Once FS-156 reaches the Middle Fork Road (FS-268), turn east onto this road and follow it to Atlanta.

(a) FST-460, Middle Fork Trail. The Powerhouse CG and trailhead are located 1.5 miles north of Atlanta. The Middle Fork trail heads generally north into the heart of the Sawtooths, where it links up with the Sawtooths' many other trails. It is roughly 15.0 miles from the trailhead to Spangle Lake, where the route junctions with FST-462/FST-463.

(b) FST-462/FST-463, Spangle Lake Trail. This trail loops from the South Fork of the Payette and FST-452 [Approach: (B)(3)(b)] south up Benedict Creek, junctions with FST-458 [Approach: (B)(5)(a)], then turns southwest and traverses past Robert Jackson Lake and Lake Ingeborg to Spangle Lake. At this lake the trail junctions with FST-460 [Approach: (B)(4)(a)]. From this point, the trail turns north and runs to Ardeth Lake and then descends along Tenlake Creek to rejoin the South Fork of the Payette and FS-452.

(5) FS-206, Queens River Road. The Queens River transfer camp is located northeast of Atlanta. From Atlanta, drive 4.5 miles west on FS-168 to the Queens River CG. Turn north on FS-206 and follow it to the trailhead. The trailhead is located at the point where the Little Queens River flows into the Queens River. Trails lead up both of these drainages.

(a) FST-458, Queens River Trail. FST-458 follows the Queens River north for 9.0 miles to its headwaters near Mount Everly. Eight miles from the trailhead, it junctions with FST-494 [Approach: (B)(6)(a.1)] which leads west over a divide, past Arrowhead and Pats lakes, to junction with FST-459 [Approach: (B)(6)(a)] and [Approach: (B)(5)(b)], which access the Little Queens River and Johnson Creek drainages, respectively. From this junction, FST-458 crosses a divide on the north slopes of Mount Everly and connects with FST-462 [Approach: (B)(4)(b)] in the Benedict Creek drainage. The trail then climbs south to cross a high pass and leads to the headwaters of the Little Queens River.

(b) FST-454, Little Queens River Trail. This trail follows the river for 9.0 miles to a junction with FST-459 [Approach: (B)(6)(a)] which leads west to Graham and also junctions with FST-494 [Approach: (B)(6)(a.1)], which leads east to the Queens River drainage.

(b.1) FST-456, Scenic Creek Trail. FST-456 is a side trail that leads into the country around Scenic and Flat Top Lakes. Access the trail 6.0 miles north of the Queens River Transfer Camp. Once on this trail, follow one fork 3.5 miles to Scenic Lakes; the other goes about 3.0 miles to Flat Top Lakes.

(6) Graham GS Road. Turn off ID-21 at Edna Creek CG and follow FS-384 for 4.0 miles to FS-312. Turn north on FS-312 and drive 23.0 miles on a rugged road to the Graham GS area. This trip requires a 4WD and some driving skill.

(a) FST-156, FST-459, Bayhorse Creek/Johnson Creek Trails. Access these trails from FS-312 just before it reaches the North Fork of the Boise River (north of the Graham GS). The trail leaves from this point, crosses Cow Creek and then parallels Bayhorse Creek to the southeast for 3.5 miles until it junctions with FST-459 and Johnson Creek at the boundary of the Sawtooth Wilderness. From this junction, it is 5.0 miles to a second junction where FST-459 turns south and crosses into the Little Queens River drainage and FST-494 [Approach: (B)(6)(a.1)], then runs east toward Pats Lake and Mount Everly.

(a.1) FST-494, Pats Lake Trail. This trail leaves FST-459 and runs east to join FST-458 in the Upper Queens River drainage. It is 2.6 miles to Pats Lake and 6.9 miles to the Queens River from the junction.

7. The Smoky Mountains

The Smoky Mountains are located on the west side of the Wood River Valley, the home of

Ketchum and Sun Valley. The range extends south from the Sawtooth Range 40 miles to the flats of the Camas Prairie. The Big Wood River and ID-75 form the eastern boundary of the range, while the South Fork of the Boise River and the Soldier Mountains flank the range on its western side.

Geologists believe that the Smokys were originally forced up by the implanting of the nearby Idaho Batholith 60 million to 90 million years ago. The peaks are composed of deteriorated metamorphic and granitelike rocks that reach a high point of 10,441 feet on Saviers Peak. More recently, block faulting has occurred, causing the Wood River Valley to sink in relation to the Smoky and Boulder Mountains. Consequently, the Smoky Mountains have developed a steep eastern facade that contrasts sharply with the range's western slopes, which merge almost invisibly into the Boise and Soldier Mountains.

In addition to the seven summits that exceed 10,000 feet, the range includes a number of exquisite mountain lakes and is the home of a large herd of mountain goats. The Smoky Mountains are administered by the Sawtooth National Forest in the south and the Sawtooth National Recreation Area in the north. Logging and grazing are the primary consumptive uses.

The quality of vehicle access points within this range is above average because of the economic power of the Ketchum/Sun Valley resort center. The Forest Service is regularly improving access points and for the most part maintains Smoky Mountain trails in tip-top shape. The major Smoky peaks of interest to climbers are located north of Ketchum between Baker Peak and Galena summit. All of these are reached by Class 2 or Class 3 routes. The southern end of the range contains a maze of hiking trails and minor peaks that offers excellent opportunities for solitude.

Titus Peak* *10,110 feet (Class 2)*

Titus Peak, which features a rugged north/south summit ridge, is the northernmost major summit on the Smoky Mountain skyline. It is located 2.5 miles south of Galena Summit, O.6 mile east of Bromaghin Peak. (The USGS has identified it as the Titus triangulation station on their quad.) The summit can be climbed from either Titus Lake or Galena Summit. The recommended route begins at Galena Summit and follows the connecting ridge line without much difficulty. There is an unmaintained trail for the first 1.5 miles of the ridge line from Galena Summit [Approach: (A)(1)(b)]. The trail ends at Point 10005, where there is a good view of Titus Peak to the south. The remaining sections of ridge to the top of Titus Peak are well defined and present no

objective problems to those experienced with cross-country travel. It is 2.6 miles from Galena Summit to the top of the peak. USGS Galena

Bromaghin Peak *10,225 feet (Class 3)*

This peak was named after a Captain Ralph Bromaghin, a former Sun Valley ski instructor and member of the 10th Mountain Division who lost his life in World War II. It is located 0.6 mile southwest of Titus Peak. The peak can be climbed from Owl Creek, or by traversing the ridge from Titus Peak. Following the ridge from Titus is Class 2, until the final short section up the east face, which is easy Class 3. The route stays on the south side of the broken face and then follows the obvious gully to the top. From Owl Creek [Approach: (A)(2)], follow the drainage up to the saddle between Titus and Bromaghin and climb the face to the summit as described above. USGS Galena

Savier Peak* *10,441 feet (Class 3)*

Many local people call this peak Silver Peak. However, because there is an officially named Silver Peak due east across the valley in the Boulder Mountains, it may be more appropriate to name the peak after Mr. and Mrs. George Saviers, who climbed the peak on their honeymoon in 1947 and left a register on the summit in a Band Aid can. The peak is located 0.5 mile south of Bromaghin Peak on the main Smoky Mountain crest. Both the north ridge from Bromaghin Peak and the east ridge from Owl Creek have been climbed.

From the summit of Bromaghin Peak (See Route description above) follow the ridge line south to the summit. Pass the rocky ribs that bar the top of the ridge line on the west side of the ridge and scramble up the final summit blocks on the west side. To climb the peak from Owl Creek [Approach: (A)(2)], most scramblers evidently utilize the east ridge to reach a point just south of the summit, but because of the open nature of the peak's east side, there are a number of suitable lines which can be followed to the summit. USGS Galena

Norton Peak *10,336 feet (Class 2)*

Norton Peak stands east of the main Smoky Mountain crest, forming a rugged island surrounded by forest. The summit is 9.0 miles southeast of Saviers Peak, directly east of Miner Lake. The rocky upper slopes, one of the best places in the state for viewing mountain goats, provide a super view of the Ketchum/Sun Valley area.

This summit is easily reached from the saddle between Miner Lake and upper Norton Lake and FST-135 [Approach: (A)(4)(b)]. From either of these lakes, follow the seldom-maintained trail that links the lakes with the saddle above. From the saddle, climb east up through a stand of pines to the rocky slopes above and then to the ridge top. From the top of the ridge, the route is obvious to the north along the summit ridge. Stay as close as possible to the ridge crest as you make the traverse. USGS Galena

Prairie Creek Peak* *10,138 feet (Class 2)*

Prairie Creek Peak is located 1.5 miles southwest of Norton Peak on the main crest of the Smoky Mountains. When viewed from Prairie Lakes, it forms a large pyramid directly to the south. Unnamed on the USGS quads, it is referred to by locals as Prairie Creek Peak. To reach its summit, hike to the saddle south of upper Prairie Lake on FST-134 [Approach: (A)(3)(a)]. From the saddle, gradually work your way to the east up the peak's west ridge, skirting a couple of small rock towers on the south side of the ridge. USGS Baker Peak

Peak 10099 *10,099 feet (Class 2-3)*

This peak, which provides the stunning backdrop for Baker Lake, is located 1.4 miles north of Baker Peak. Its north, south, and east ridges are easy scrambles. The most direct route is from Baker Lake [Approach: (A)(4)(a)]. USGS Baker Peak

Baker Peak *10,174 feet (Class 2)*

Baker is one of the more hidden Smoky Mountain peaks because it sits far back (over 10.0 miles from the Big Wood River) and views of its summit are obstructed by low ridges. It is located 6.5 miles southwest of Norton Peak on the range's main crest. Approach the peak by hiking to Baker Lake [Approach: (A)(4)(a)] and then hiking on FST-211 [Approach: (A)(4)(a.1)] to the saddle just north of Baker Peak. Leave the trail and follow the ridge to the summit. USGS Baker Peak

Peak 10137 *10,137 feet (Class 2)*

The southernmost 10,000-foot summit in the Smoky Mountains is located 0.8 mile southeast of Baker Peak, on the main crest. Although this mountain's relatively gentle slopes can be climbed from almost any direction, access considerations make a ridge traverse from Baker Peak the best choice. USGS Baker Peak

Big Peak *10,047 feet (Class 2)*

Big Peak, located 2.6 miles west of Baker Peak, is one of the more isolated 10,000-foot peaks in the state. The shortest route to the summit is to leave FST-211 [Approach: (A)(4)(a.1)] from the saddle north of Baker Peak and then follow the ridge north to Point 9956. From this point, take the subsidiary ridge due west for 2.0 miles to

where it turns south, and climb to the peak's summit. USGS Baker Peak

Bear Peak *9,525 feet (Class 2)*

Bear Peak is located 10.0 miles due west of Ketchum, 4.5 miles east of Baker Peak. From the Warm Springs Creek road, take FST-168 [Approach: (A)(7)(a)] up Barr Gulch to a point near the summit on the peak's southwest slopes. From this point, scramble to the top. It is roughly 3.0 miles one way. USGS Boyle Mountain

Griffin Butte *8,411 feet (Class 2)*

Griffin Butte is located just north of Ketchum, above Adams Gulch. Hiking this peak is a totally scenic experience with super vistas of Bald Mountain and the entire Ketchum Area. The ascent begins at the Adams Gulch trailhead [Approach: (A)(6)(a)]. From the trailhead, take FST-142 north and then northwest for roughly 1.0 mile to the Butte's south slope, where you can leave the trail and hike cross country to the summit. USGS Griffin Butte

Bald Mountain *9,151 feet (Class 1)*

This is the most famous of Idaho's many mountains that use the word "bald" for their names. It is the home of the Sun Valley Ski Resort's main downhill ski runs. To reach the summit in the summer, hike up one of the service roads (closed to private autos) that lead up the east and north sides of the mountain. Although not a wilderness experience, the climb provides unsurpassed views of this impressive area. USGS Griffin Butte

Dollarhide Mountain *9,301 feet (Class 2)*

Dollarhide Mountain is situated 4.0 miles due south of Baker peak. It is the first summit north of Dollarhide Summit on the Warm Springs Creek Road [Approach: (A)(7)]. From Ketchum, drive to the summit, park and then hike 1.25 miles on the ridge line north to the summit. USGS Dollarhide Mountain

Shaw Mountain *9,650 feet (Class 2)*

Shaw mountain is located 1.5 miles east of Dollarhide Mountain. The two mountains are connected by an arcing ridge line that is easily traversed from Dollarhide Mountain. USGS Dollarhide Mountain

Buttercup Mountain *9,075 feet (Class 2)*

Buttercup, the southernmost Smoky Mountain peak covered in this book, sits high above the Deer Creek drainage in an area that offers excellent hiking opportunities. From the end of the Deer Creek Road [Approach: (A)(9)(a)], take FST-158 for 1.0 mile and then FST-160 for 3.0

miles up Currant Gulch to the peak's south ridge. Leave the trail at this point and follow the ridge north to the summit. USGS Buttercup Mountain

APPROACHES TO THE SMOKY MOUNTAINS

Roads and trails listed in this section are referenced in the text by a bracketed entry [Approach:], which includes appropriate letter and number references.

(A) ID-75 Access Points.
This well-maintained state highway is the major north-south corridor between Shoshone and Challis. It provides access along the entire eastern slope of the Smoky Mountains. ID-75 access points are described from north to south.

(1) Galena Summit Area. ID-75 crosses this pass north of Ketchum and then descends into the Stanley Basin. (The pass is the point where the Smoky and Boulder Mountains meet).

(a) FST-190, Titus Lake Trail. Just before ID-75 reaches Galena Summit, on the last sharp switchback, an old jeep road leaves the pavement. Park across the road in the large turnout. The trail follows the jeep road a short distance and then contours around the ridges to 8,900-foot-high Titus Lake in just 2.0 miles.

(b) Galena Ridge. From the Titus Lake trailhead, continue following the old road (the beginning of FST-190) past the sign for that trail. This old road contours around the draw and ends up at the ridge top directly above the point where ID-75 passes over Galena Summit. From this point, a good but unofficial trail goes directly up the ridge. There are excellent views along the ridge of both the Wood River Valley and the Stanley Basin. The trail ends in about 1.5 miles on Point 10005.

(2) FS-181, Owl Creek Jeep Trail. Turn off ID-75 roughly 20.0 miles north of Ketchum. FS-181 immediately fords the Big Wood River and then runs up this drainage for 3.0 miles to the base of both Saviers and Bromaghin Peaks. It is best to park at ID-75 and walk this road, which requires a 4WD. This is a popular cross country ski route in the winter, but the upper sections of the canyon are often swept by avalanches.

(3) FS-179, Prairie Creek Road. This road leaves ID-75 approximately 18.0 miles north of Ketchum and runs west 2.5 miles into the Smokys to the Prairie Creek trailhead. This dirt road is often rutted and can cause problems for passenger cars.

(a) FST-134, Prairie Lakes. From the end of the Prairie Creek Road, a well-maintained trail leads to the shallow Prairie Lakes and then continues on, climbing over a pass just north of Prairie Creek Peak. The trail is roughly 5.0 miles long.

(b) FST-135, Miner Lake Trail. FST-135 leaves Prairie Creek Road 2.5 miles from ID-75. Miner Lake is a 4.0-mile hike. From the lake, the trail climbs over a subsidiary crest of the Smoky Mountains to Norton Lakes.

(4) FS-162, Baker Creek Road. This good gravel road leaves ID-75 15.8 miles north of the traffic light in Ketchum and leads 9.5 miles into the heart of the Smoky Mountains, to near the base of Baker Mountain.

(a) FST-138, Baker Lake Trail. FST-138 begins at the end of the Baker Creek Road. A steep 2.0-mile hike brings you to Baker Lake at the base of an unnamed peak. (The lake receives heavy use and is not a place to visit on weekends.) From Baker Lake, the trail runs due north and joins with FST-134 [Approach: (A)(4)(c)] at Norton Creek.

(a.1) FST-211, Baker Creek/West Fork Cutoff Trail. This trail runs between Baker Lake and West Fork Creek by crossing the Smoky Mountain divide just north of Baker Peak.

(b) FST-135, Norton Lake Trail. To reach the trailhead, drive 6.0 miles up the Baker Creek Road and then turn right on a signed road, which is rough but generally passable to autos. Follow this road 1.2 miles to the trailhead. The trail to Norton Lakes is well maintained and reaches the first lake in 3.5 miles and the second lake in another 0.5 mile. From the second lake, the trail climbs up to a saddle just north of Norton Peak and then drops down to Miner Lake and the Prairie Creek drainage [Approach: (A)(3)(b)].

(c) FST-134, Norton Creek/Bluff Creek Trail. This trail leaves from the Norton Lake Trailhead and climbs 3.0 miles over the Smoky crest, where it intersects with FST-138 [Approach: (A)(4)(a)] and FST-196. FST-138, which is not well-marked, leads south to Baker Lake. FST-196 drops over the crest and eventually gives access to the large roadless area of the upper Big Smoky Creek drainage. Neither of these trails receive much use.

(5) Lake Creek Trailhead. This trailhead is located on ID-75, roughly 2.5 miles north of Ketchum. It has a large parking lot complemented by a good bridge across the Wood River. Several different trails are accessible from this point. This is a popular area for day hikers, mountain bikers and runners in the summer and cross country skiers in the winter.

(6) FS-141, Adams Gulch Trailhead. This road leaves ID-75 1.6 miles north of Ketchum. Turn west onto the signed road, which serves as a trailhead for two important trails.

(a) FST-142, Adams Gulch High Trail. FST-142 leaves FS-141 just past the forest boundary. This is one of the best (and least known) high routes in Idaho. The trail climbs north toward Griffin Butte and then turns west to rejoin the Adams Gulch trail in 6.0 miles. From this point, the trail runs east along a high ridge line for another 7.0 miles to Lost Shirt Gulch, where it junctions with FST-212. FST-212 drops north down a gulch to Baker Creek and FS-162 [Approach: (A)(4)]. FST-145, FST-144 and FST-168 are all feeder trails that connect the High Trail with the Warm Springs Creek Road [Approach: (A)(7)].

(b) FST-177, Adams Gulch Trail. FST-177 leaves the end of FS-141 and runs up Adams Gulch for 4.0 miles, where it connects with FST-142.

(7) FS-227, Warm Springs Creek Road. This road leaves ID-75 in downtown Ketchum just north of the stoplight. Look for the road that forks off to the west just past the restaurant in a railcar. The road twists and turns for 19.0 miles to the Dollarhide Summit. From the summit, the road continues for another 16.0 miles to the Big Smoky Fire Camp on the South Fork of the Boise River.

(a) FST-168, Bear Gulch Trail. FST-168 leaves FS-227 as a two-track road 4.0 miles west of Warfield Hot Springs. The road soon ends and the trail continues up Bear Gulch and eventually past the west slopes of Bear Peak to join with FST-142 [Approach: (A)(6)(a)] in 4.5 miles.

(8) FS-117, Greenhorn Gulch Road Area. This road, which is a little over 4.0 miles long, leaves ID-75 5.0 miles south of Ketchum. FST-156 is at the road's end; a good loop hike with a number of side trails.

(9) FS-097, Deer Creek Road Area. This road begins at ID-75 8.0 miles south of Ketchum. The Deer Creek Road is part of an extensive road and trail system which sees little use by hikers despite the enjoyable nature of the area.

(a) FST-158 and 160, Curran Gulch Trails. From the end of FS-097, these trails combine to climb up to the ridge line just south of Buttercup Mountain in 3.0 miles. FST-160 then runs south along the Smoky Mountain Crest to Wolftone Creek.

8. The Soldier Mountains

The Soldier Mountains are located north of Fairfield, Idaho, at the southern edge of the cen-

tral Idaho mountains. They cover a roughly triangular piece of real estate 30 miles wide and 15 miles from north to south. The range is bordered by the Camas Prairie in the south, the South Fork of the Boise River in the north and west and the Smoky Mountains in the east.

Physically, the range is nearly indistinguishable from the surrounding Smoky and Boise mountains. Its topography is characterized by long winding ridges with only a few dominant summits. The 10,095-foot Smoky Dome is the range's highest summit. The Soldiers are relatively dry mountains with a few stands of really dense timber which tend to cluster on the north and eastern slopes and along the stream bottoms. The upper slopes of the highest ridges are alpine in nature. A few small ponds dot the slopes around Smoky Dome, but the range is without a large mountain lake.

The Sawtooth National Forest manages almost the entire range through its Fairfield Ranger District. The BLM and the state control a few sections of land in the southern foothills. Domestic sheep grazing apparently takes place in all but the highest points of these mountains. Despite heavy sheep grazing, the Soldiers are still inhabited by a large concentration of deer.

Access quality varies throughout this small range. Some roads are well signed and maintained, others are hard to locate. Because few hikers come to the Soldier Mountains, trail maintenance does not receive the highest priority. Hikers will find that, although these mountains are seldom used, they offer better-than-average hiking opportunities. Where the trails are not well maintained, the Soldier's open terrain is excellent for cross country hiking. Climbers will find that there are only nine named summits in the Soldier Mountains and only two of these—Smoky Dome and Iron Mountain—are of special interest.

Smoky Dome   *10,095 feet*
Smoky Dome dominates the Soldier Mountains. The big, crown-shaped mountain not only rises 5,000 feet above the Camas Prairie but also stands from 1,000 to 1,200 feet above every peak in the range except Iron Mountain. Views from the summit of Smoky Dome take in a huge chunk of Idaho from the Sawtooths in the north to the Camas Prairie and Mount Bennet Hills in the south. Trinity and Steele mountains are clearly visible in the distance to the west, and the main crest of the Pioneer Mountains dominates the view to the east. The peak is a massive mountain with a half a dozen points above 9,000 feet on subsidiary ridges. The north summit reaches 9,937 feet and sports massive, unstable rock cliffs. USGS Fairfield 15-minute

Iron Mountain, viewed from Smoky Dome

The Grand Tour Route. *(Class 2)*
In terms of nearby roads and trails, the highest peak in the Soldier Mountains is quite remote. Climbing Smoky Dome by this route involves a long, difficult approach hike. The route begins at the end of FS-093 [Approach: (A)(2)(a)]. From the road's end, follow the closed road up the South Fork of Soldier Creek for 2.0 miles until it ends just after crossing the creek. After crossing the creek where the road runs downhill and dies out, there is a small clearing where FST-087 vaguely runs off through the trees and up the creek to the west. Leave the road/trail and climb up to the ridge top to the south. Once on the ridge, the route follows the ridge line west for several miles. The majority of the ridge is traversed by an old sheepherder's trail and though it is brushy in places, it is not difficult to follow. The ridge eventually joins the eastern slopes of Smoky Dome below the north peak. From this point, traverse south across the meadows and talus to the saddle between the main and north peaks. It is a steep but easy scramble to the summit from this saddle. This route is roughly 5.5 miles in length and gains over 4,000 feet of elevation from start to finish. The Sydney and

Boardman Peak USGS quads will be helpful in following this route.

Other Routes.
The open nature of the Soldier Mountains makes it possible to approach the peak from almost any direction. Southern approaches would be shorter but private land will increase access problems. In stable snow conditions, Smoky Dome could offer excellent backcountry skiing. The north summit is an easy Class 2 ascent via its south ridge or east face.

Iron Mountain *9,694 feet (Class 1)*
Iron Mountain is located 7.0 miles northwest of Smoky Dome. A fire lookout sits on the summit of this impressive rockpile. Heart Lake, which is the largest of the Soldier Mountain ponds, can be found just northeast of the summit. You can approach the summit, which is reached by trail, from almost any direction. The shortest approach to the summit is from the north. It begins along the Middle Fork of the Boise River. Follow FST-052, FST-053 and FST-050 to the top [Approach: (B)(1)(a)]. USGS Jumbo Mountain

APPROACHES TO THE SOLDIER MOUNTAINS

Approach routes for this section are referenced in the text by bracketed entries [Approach:], which include appropriate letter and number references.

Road access to the Soldier Mountains begins at ID-20, which runs east to west past the range's southern flanks. The Forest Service maintains a good system of roads along the perimeter of the range and from Fairfield into the heart of the range. Numerous trails and old 4WD roads pierce almost every corner of the range. Trail maintenance varies in quality, but overall probably rates poorly.

(A) Fairfield Access Points.

Access through Fairfield leads into the central portion of the range and also to the southern portions of the Smoky mountains. Turn north off US-20 and drive through downtown Fairfield, following the signs for the Soldier Mountain Ski Area. In 2.0 miles, the road enters the village of Soldier, where it jogs to the east and becomes FS-094.

(1) FS-094, Couch Summit Road. This good gravel road is a continuation of the Soldier Mountain Road. It leads north and junctions with FS-093 in 5.0 miles. FS-094 continues north from this junction to Couch Summit and then drops down Little Smoky Creek to the South Fork of the Boise River.

(2) FS-093, Soldier Creek Road. This road forks off of FS-094 and, shortly after passing by the Soldier Mountain Ski Area, crosses a cattleguard and ends just past the mouth of the South Fork of Soldier Creek. There are several campsites here

and plenty of parking. The road up the South Fork is closed.

(a) Soldier Creek Trail System. From the end of FS-094, there is access to an extensive trail system that penetrates most of the higher elevations of the Soldier Mountains. An old road (which is not shown on the newest Forest Service map) runs up the South Fork of Soldier Creek. The road, which is closed to vehicles, connects with FST-087 and FST-185. Also, from the end of FS-093, FST-005 runs up the North Fork of Soldier Creek and eventually connects with FST-087.

(B) Anderson Ranch Reservoir Access Points.

This reservoir, located on the South Fork of the Boise River, divides the Soldier Mountains from the Boise Mountains. The US-20 turnoff is 31.9 miles from Mountain Home. Turn north off the highway and take the dirt road to Pine and Featherville. Featherville is a central hub for access into this entire area; services are available from early summer through hunting season.

(1) FS-227, South Fork of the Boise River Road. From Featherville, FS-227 winds along the South Fork of the Boise River to Little Smoky Creek, where it connects with FS-094 [Approach: (A)(1)], which goes south to Fairfield. Numerous trails lead into the Soldier Mountains from this road.

(a) FST-052, FST-053 and FST-050, Iron Mountain Trail. This trailhead is roughly 11.0 miles east of Featherville. The trail, a main thoroughfare into the western part of the Soldier Mountains, intersects with every trail in the area. From the Boise river, it is 9.5 miles to the summit of Iron Mountain. To reach the trailhead, turn south off FS-227 at the sign for Baumgartner CG. After the road crosses the river, it forks. Take the right fork, which parallels the south fork of river and runs west. Follow this road to its end at Kelly Creek in a little over 1.0 mile.

WCP-5 is the most interesting of the northern White Cloud Peaks. Its split summit and rotten, vertical slopes make it appear unapproachable.

SECTION

III

EASTERN IDAHO

From Idaho-75 and US-93
East to the Wyoming Border;
From Montana South
to the Snake River

1. The White Cloud Mountains

The White Cloud Mountains, located southeast of Stanley, lie totally within the boundaries of the SNRA. The range is about 20 miles long and 16 miles wide. The Salmon River flanks its western and northern boundaries, while the East Fork of the Salmon River flanks the range on its eastern side. In the south, the White Clouds and the Boulder Mountains merge together with no definite division between them.

The geologic history of the range is highlighted by the Pleistocene Era Ice Age. Glaciers extensively carved the peaks and canyons, scraping out beautiful lake basins, which now contain over 100 lakes, and slicing steep faces from the White Cloud limestone. The extensive deposits of the white limestone in the northwestern portion of the range looked like white cumulus clouds to early settlers, who named the range in the late 1800s. The highest elevation is 11,815 feet at the summit of Castle Peak. A group of fourteen peaks, all over 10,000 feet, is specifically known as the White Cloud Peaks.

The entire range is managed by the Sawtooth National Recreation Area with the exception of a number of private inholdings which evolved primarily from mining claims. The presence of gold and silver brought mining activity to these mountains as early as the 1880s. The remains of this activity can be found in the Fourth of July, Three Cabins, and Washington Basin areas. It is possible that mining activity may resume within the range—pressure from mining interests continues to block Congress from declaring the range a designated wilderness. Despite the mining problems, the Forest Service manages the range primarily for recreational pursuits—a perfect use for what is probably Idaho's most scenic mountain range. Much of the upper reaches of the White Clouds are a barren, treeless world of alpine meadow and rock, which contrasts sharply with the dense stands of Douglas fir and lodgepole pine that blanket the lower slopes. During the short summer seasons, the combinations of wildflowers, water and jagged rock are unbeatable.

Vehicle access points to the range's trailheads are plentiful, although many of the roads are too rough for passenger cars. The SNRA is slowly upgrading roadway conditions. The range contains many miles of trails, most in good to excellent shape. The Boulder Lake and Little Boulder Chain of Lakes areas, the busiest spots in the range, are the only areas that can be considered crowded. Climbing opportunities range from Class 1 through Class 3. Although there are a number of faces which are appealing, technical climbing is generally out of the question because of the shattered nature of the White Cloud rock.

Lookout Mountain   *9,954 feet   (Class 1)*
Lookout Mountain is located in the northeast corner of the White Cloud Mountains, 9.0 miles east of Stanley. This peak, a lookout site, is reached by taking either the Rough Creek or Casino Lake trails to the point where they join FST-647 [Approach: (A)(3)(a)] and then following FST-647 to the summit of Lookout Peak. The shortest approach (5.5 miles) is via Rough Creek. The lookout is no longer in use. The Forest Service leaves it open for public use—please help keep it clean. USGS Casino Lakes

WCP-1*   *10,353 feet   (Class 2)*
WCP-1 is the northernmost peak of the group designated as the White Cloud Peaks by the USGS. It is located 5.5 miles southeast of Lookout Mountain; its summit is just 0.75 mile west of Hoodoo Lake. Access to this peak is via FS-666 and the Hoodoo Lake Trail [Approach: (A)(5)(b)], which leads to Hoodoo Lake. From Hoodoo Lake, hike into the cirque southwest of the lake until the slope steepens, then turn due north and hike directly toward the summit. USGS Robinson Bar

WCP-2*   *10,271 feet   (Class 2)*
WCP-2 is located 1.2 miles southwest of WCP-1, just north of Swimm Lake. The peak can be climbed from Swimm Lake—the catch is that there is no trail to Swimm Lake. To reach the lake, hike cross country up Swimm Creek from FST-671 [Approach: (A)(2)(c)] or begin in Iron Basin [Approach: (A)(2)(d)] and climb into the Swimm Lake basin from the south over the saddle between WCP-4 and WCP-5 (a steep, grungy crossing). If you manage to get to the lake, climb from Swimm Lake to the saddle east of the summit and then follow the ridge to the summit. USGS Robinson Bar

179

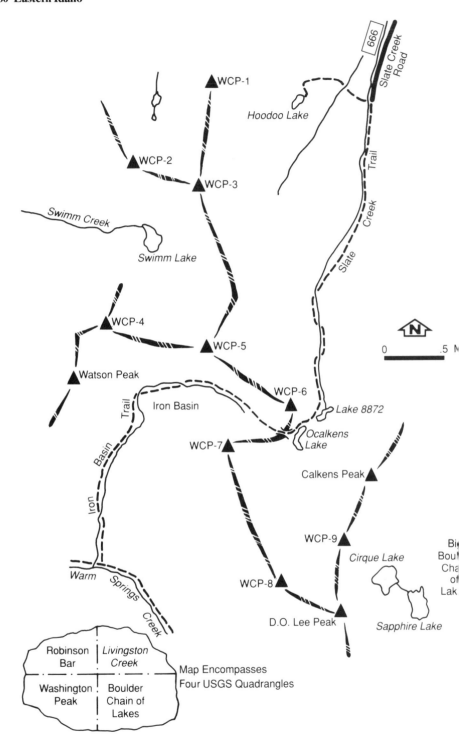

NORTHERN WHITE CLOUD PEAK GROUP

The south side of Caulkens Peak

WCP-3* *10,588 feet (Class 2)*
This pyramid-shaped summit is located 0.75 mile south of WCP-1, just north of Swimm Lake. (See the write-up for WCP-2 for approach information.) Climb from Swimm Lake via either the west or south ridges. Gaining either ridge involves crossing a considerable amount of loose scree, reportedly the hardest part of the climb. USGS Robinson Bar

WCP-4* *10,450 feet (Class 3)*
WCP-4 is located 0.6 mile north of Watson Peak and 1.5 miles southwest of WCP-3. The peak is accessed from Iron Basin [Approach: (A)(2)(d)]. From the general area where the trail crosses the 9,200-foot contour line on the USGS quad, climb northwest to the peak's east ridge, which leads to the summit. USGS Robinson Bar

WCP-5* *10,597 feet (Class 3)*
WCP-5 is a three-sided column that rises precipitously for its last 600 feet. It is situated 1.0 mile east of WCP-4, just north of Ocalkens Lake. The west ridge has been climbed from Iron Basin [Approach: (A)(2)(d)], but no details are available. USGS Robinson Bar

Watson Peak *10,453 feet (Class 2)*
Watson Peak sits west of the main White Cloud Peak divide and just south of WCP-4. Climb via the south ridge, which can be reached from the Iron Basin Trail [Approach: (A)(2)(d)]. Hike north toward Iron Basin from Warm Springs Creek until the trail crosses the area represented by the 8,800-foot contour on the USGS quad. At this point, it

is possible to climb up a large east-facing gully which ends just below the east ridge. At the top of the gully, traverse southwest to the ridge top and then follow the ridge to the summit. USGS Robinson Bar

WCP-6* *10,256 feet (Class 2)*
The summit of WCP-6 is located 0.6 mile southeast of WCP-5. Access to the peak is via the Iron Basin Trail [Approach: (A)(2)(d)] where it crosses Ocalkens Pass just south of the peak. Leave the trail at the pass and climb the south ridge, which rises 650 feet to the summit. USGS Robinson Bar

WCP-7* *10,777 feet (Class 3)*
WCP-7 presents a bold pyramid-shaped east face to Ocalkens Lake. It sits 0.7 mile due south of WCP-6 and Iron Basin. Access the peak's north ridge from the Iron Basin Trail [Approach: (A)(2)(d)]. The route climbs the north ridge and east face. The peak's north ridge is rugged and steep at first, but still Class 2. After it abuts the east face, the route becomes Class 3, with a little exposure in two places. Stay on the ridge top when possible. (It is possible to climb the peak from other directions, but this route provides the best access.) USGS Washington Peak/Robinson Bar

Caulkens Peak* *11,487 feet (Class 3)*
This peak is located 1.6 miles due east of WCP-7, just west of Tin Cup Lake. It is identified on the USGS quad as the Caulkens triangulation station. Access the peak from the Big Boulder Chain of Lakes Trail [Approach: (B)(2)(a.1)] by leaving the trail where it crosses Tin Cup Creek and hiking

181

The north ridge of D. O. Lee Peak, as seen from WCP-8

cross country to Tin Cup Lake (roughly 2.0 miles). Climb into the bowl southwest of Tin Cup Lake and work your way up the north side of the bowl until you can reach the summit ridge. Follow the ridge to the summit. USGS Boulder Chain of Lakes

WCP-10* *11,102 feet (Rating Unknown)*
WCP-10 is located 0.5 mile due east of Caulkens Peak. It is the steepest of all of the peaks designated as part of the White Cloud Peaks. Route information is unavailable. Access the peak from the Big Boulder Chain of Lakes Trail [Approach: (B)(2)(a.1)]. USGS Boulder Chain of Lakes

WCP-8* *10,557 feet (Class 3)*
WCP-8 is situated 1.4 miles south of WCP-7 and 0.9 mile east of D. O. Lee Peak. Access is from the Warm Springs Creek Trail [Approach: (A)(2)(c)]. Leave the trail at the point where the creek that drains the peak's southern slopes crosses the trail. Follow this creek upstream until you are at approximately the 9,000-foot level. At this point, turn west and climb to the south ridge and then follow this ridge to the summit. USGS Washington Peak

WCP-9* *11,263 feet*
WCP-9 is located 1.1 miles northeast of WCP-8 and 0.6 mile north of D. O. Lee Peak. The peak

has a gentle south ridge and a treacherous north ridge. The west face is cut by a spectacular gully. Both routes utilize the south ridge. USGS Washington Peak

Cirque Lake Route. *(Class 2)*
From Cirque Lake [Approach: (B)(2)(a.1)], hike southeast into the saddle south of the peak. At roughly 10,300 feet, turn northwest and climb directly to the peak's south ridge. Follow the north ridge to the summit.

West Buttress. *(Class 3)*
Access this buttress from Ocalkens Lake [Approach: (A)(5)(c)]. From the lake, hike south into the upper basin to the base of the buttress, at 9,800 feet elevation. This prominent formation is covered by mountain goat tracks and loose talus. The route generally stays on the buttress' north side and has only two short sections of Class 3 climbing.

D. O. Lee Peak *11,342 feet*
D. O. Lee is identified on newer Forest Service maps, but has yet to appear on the USGS quad. Dave Lee was the Wilderness Ranger for the SNRA and a relative of the Dave Williams of Sawtooths fame. The peak the Forest Service chose to honor Lee has two summits and an impressive east face. This peak is located at the west end of the Boulder Chain of Lakes basin, at the southern terminus of the peaks known as the

White Cloud Peaks. As you trek up its summits, you will pass igneous rocks near the Boulder Chain of Lakes, then metamorphic rocks, and finally, on the summit, brilliant white sedimentary limestones. USGS Washington Peak

South Ridge. *(Class 3)*
The route begins on the peak's east side at Cove Lake. From Cove Lake [Approach: (B)(2)(a.1)], hike to the small lake to the southeast and gain the saddle just southeast of that lake. Reaching the saddle is the most difficult part of the climb. Most years a snowfield exists below the saddle. Once on the ridge, follow it north to the summit. It may also be possible to climb this peak via its south ridge from Warm Springs Creek.

North Ridge. *(Class 3)*
From the saddle between D. O. Lee and WCP-9, the north ridge rises nearly 600 feet in 0.25 mile. The route stays on the west side of the ridge—and gets progressively steeper as you climb. The crux is located just below the summit, where a steep indentation in the ridge holds snow and ice into late summer. An ice axe is invaluable here, at least until the ice is gone. To access this route, use the West Buttress Route on WCP-9.

Blackman Peak *10,300 feet (Class 2)*
Blackman Peak is situated northwest of Fourth of July Lake, 3.0 miles south of D. O. Lee Peak.

The peak is named after George Washington Blackman, who mined in the area beginning in 1875. From the Fourth of July Lake trailhead, climb this peak from any of its three prominent ridges. FS-041 [Approach: (A)(2.1)] leaves the trailhead and contours around the peak's western slopes, providing good access to the southwest ridge; FST-219 [Approach: (A)(2)(b)] crosses the peak's east ridge. USGS Washington Peak

Patterson Peak *10,872 feet (Class 2)*
Patterson Peak is a prominent pyramid-shaped summit that sits 1.8 miles southeast of Blackman Peak. Climb this peak from FST-219 [Approach: (A)(2)(b)] by leaving the trail where it crosses the peak's west ridge and then following the ridge 1.0 mile to the summit. USGS Boulder Chain of Lakes

Merriam Peak* *10,920 feet (Class 3)*
Merriam Peak is named for Doctor John H. Merriam, founder and president of the Greater Sawtooth Preservation Council. The peak is named on the latest Forest Service map but not on the USGS quad. It is located at the east end of the Serrate Ridge, 0.8 mile north of Castle Peak. Climb from Lake 9419 [Approach: (B)(2)(c)] via easy slopes. USGS Boulder Chain of Lakes

Castle Peak *11,815 feet*
This is perhaps Idaho's most visible peak.

The north face of Castle Peak, with the Serrate Ridge in the foreground, viewed from Windy Devil Pass and FST-683

Because of its distinctive color and shape and because the peak conspicuously stands hundreds of feet above all surrounding peaks, it is easily distinguishable from almost all surrounding mountains. The few climbers that venture into the White Cloud Peaks come to climb Castle Peak. Although one hiking guide correctly points out that there are a number of routes up the peak, none of the routes up this crumbling mountain is an easy climb. The main problem encountered in climbing Castle Peak is loose rock combined with excessive steepness (an Idaho tradition). A scrambler can generally find at least one easy talus slope to the top of most White Cloud Peaks, but Castle Peak is in a class by itself. The wedge-shaped peak is a complex maze of rock walls, talus slopes and treacherous gullies, which culminates in four summit towers of almost equal height. The peak's shattered rock redefines the word "grungy." From the summit, 25 mountain lakes are visible, including Hell Roaring, Yellowbelly and Alturas.

Details of the first ascent are unknown, although Bob Limbert climbed the peak in the mid-1920s. The first winter ascent, which took place in December 1971, was made by R. Watters, I. Gayfield, J. Hokum, H. Hilbert, S. Schaffer and J. Elphanson. They made their approach up Little Boulder Creek and climbed the north face. USGS Boulder Chain of Lakes

North Side Routes. *(Class 3)*
The north side route begins at an isolated and unnamed lake located just northeast of the peak at 9,419 feet [Approach: (B)(2)(c)]. (See the Boulder Chain Lakes Quadrangle.) There is no trail to the lake, but there is a good cross-country route to the lake from a point near the junction of Chamberlain Basin and Wickiup Creek trails. There are several exceptional camping spots, as well as good fishing, at the lake.

From the lake, go due west and climb the headwall by following a winding route just next to the waterfall. At the top of this first obstacle, the route traverses the talus-filled basin surrounded by the Serrate Ridge to the north and west and Castle Peak to the south. Follow the talus slope to the south, staying close to the abrupt cliff that plunges toward the Lake 9419. When the angle steepens dramatically, the route cuts directly to the east, winding along just under several threatening towers, until the talus slope ends at the mouth of a prominent debris-filled gully.

This major gully separates the north buttress from the north face. The "big gully," a nightmare of loose rock, is no place for more than one party at a time. Climb the gully, making your own best guess about which side contains less loose rock. At the top of the gully is a small saddle. The route goes from this saddle onto the face, and then

contours around and up to the prominent notch between the peak's two eastern summit towers 200 feet above.

The easternmost summit is about 10 feet shorter than the other three summits, while the next summit to the west is arguably the highest of the four. From the notch, the route goes up for 40 feet along the second tower's edge and then drops down a narrow ledge and out onto the north face. The route squeaks out along the ledge, passing several climbable gullies on the way. The third gully will lead to the summit via a couple of airy moves.

From this summit (the second from east to west), it is possible to scramble over to both of the western summits. I climbed all four towers and I'm still not sure which one is highest. There are rock cairns on three of the four, and survey markers on the westernmost summit.

West Side Route. *(Class 3)*
This route begins at the western end of Chamberlain Basin [Approach: (A)(2)(a.1)] or [Approach: (A)(1.1)(c.1)] and climbs up the peak's southwest slopes on steep talus to the westernmost summit.

Chamberlain Basin Route. *(Class 3)*
From the east side of Lake 9179 in Chamberlain Basin [Approach: (A)(2)(a.1) or [Approach: (A)(1.1)(c.1)], head due north to the base of the peak. Look for the large gully that broadly cuts the south face directly below the summit and then narrows as it nears the base of the mountain. At the base of the peak, mount the small buttress on the right-hand side and climb up across crumbly white rock until the face becomes steeper. From this point, veer to the left and climb up into the large gully one third of the way up the face. As you climb up, the rock changes from crumbly talus to large boulders. Two thirds of the way up the face, you may either continue to follow the gully up across increasingly bigger boulders, or keep to the right on steep terrain (the most direct route to the summit.)

Washington Peak *10,519 feet (Class 2)*
Washington Peak (also named after George Washington Blackman) is located 3.5 miles south of Blackman Peak. From Champion Lakes [Approach: (A)(1.1)(a)], climb to the saddle south of the peak. The trail shown on the quad is mostly nonexistent, but the way is not difficult. From the saddle, follow the easy south ridge to the summit. The peak offers an exceptionally good view of Castle Peak. USGS Washington Peak

Croesus Peak* *10,322 feet (Class 2)*
This peak, which is named on the Sawtooth National Forest map but not on the Horton Peak Quad, is located 1.0 mile south of Washington

Peak. Access this peak from Washington Basin [Approach: (A)(1.1)(b)]. The peak can be easily climbed via its west ridge, which is reached by following the old mining trail out of Washington Basin to the saddle west of the peak. USGS Horton Peak

Horton Peak *9,954 feet (Class 1)*

Horton Peak is located 5.0 miles southwest of Croesus Peak on the western fringes of the White Cloud Mountains. This abandoned fire lookout site is reached by FST-106 [Approach: (A)(1)(a)], which leaves the Pole Valley Road and quickly climbs to the summit in 2.5 moderately steep miles. USGS Horton Peak

---

APPROACHES TO THE WHITE CLOUD MOUNTAINS

Approach routes for this section are referenced in the text by bracketed entries [Approach:], which include appropriate letter and number references.

There are two primary approach roads to the White Clouds. The first is ID-75, which traverses the west and north sides of the range; the second is the East Fork of the Salmon River Road, which flanks the range's east side from ID-75 south to the Bowery GS.

(A) Idaho 75 Approaches.

ID-75 leads north from Ketchum over Galena Summit to Stanley before turning east and running to Challis. This wide paved road accesses all of the major secondary roads leading into the western and northern stretches of the White Clouds.

(1) FS-194, Pole Valley Road. This road parallels ID-75 along the base of the White Cloud Mountains between Champion and Pole creeks. Access from ID-75, in the north, is 16.5 miles south of Stanley, where the highway crosses Champion Creek; in the south, 24.0 miles south of Stanley.

(a) FST-106, Horton Lookout Trail. This trail begins as a dirt road which leaves FS-194 just north of the point where FS-194 crosses Taylor Creek. Turn onto the dirt road and follow it until its end (about 0.75 mile). The trail runs to the summit of Horton Peak in 2.5 miles and 2,700 feet of elevation gain.

(1.1) FS-197, Pole Creek/Germania Creek Road. This road is accessed from ID-75 24.0 miles south of Stanley (and roughly 1.0 mile south of the lodge at Smiley Creek). The first section of road is the Pole Valley Road, which crosses the wide

valley to the base of the mountains and Pole Creek. The road up Pole Creek is rough at the start and its condition deteriorates as the miles go by. A 4WD is recommended to go as far as Pole Creek Pass because the road fords the creek several times. From the pass, the road drops into Germania Creek Basin and ends 3.5 miles from the summit at Three Cabins Creek. (Note: a jeep trail continues from this point into Washington Basin and gives access to Washington Peak. See [Approach: (A)(1.1)(b)] below.)

(a) FST-105, Champion Lakes Trail. This vague trail leaves the road 1.5 miles east of Pole Creek Summit and follows a stream for a short distance before climbing out of the drainage and crossing a ridge. From the top of the ridge, the trail descends to Champion Lakes in another 2.5 miles. From the first Champion Lake, the trail runs northwest down Champion Creek to the Stanley Valley. (Note that, although the trail eventually leads to the Stanley Valley, there is no public access to the trail's western end because it dead ends on private property.)

(a.1) FST-126, Washington Basin Trail. FST-126 begins at the southernmost of the Champion Lakes and proceeds to the east over a pass and into Washington Basin in 1.5 miles.

(b) FS-197, Washington Basin Jeep Trail. This road begins at the point where the Germania Creek Road reaches Three Cabins Creek. The road beyond this point is more of a trail than a road—do not attempt to drive to Washington Basin, which is 5.0 miles away. The basin itself is a narrow valley filled with the relics of the White Cloud mining era. Some of the land in the basin is privately owned.

(c) FST-047, East Side Trail. Access this trail from Germania Creek. From its trailhead on FS-197, follow FST-111 east down Germania Creek for 1.25 miles to a junction with FST-109 at the confluence of Washington Creek. Follow FST-109 north up Washington Creek for another mile to the junction that marks the start of FS-047 [Approach: (B)(2)(a)]. From this point, FST-047 can be followed north across the eastern front of the range to Boulder Creek.

(c.1) FST-110, Chamberlain Basin Trail. Access this trail where FST-047 crosses Chamberlain Creek. This short trail leads west to the uppermost of the Chamberlain Lakes.

(2) FS-209, Fourth of July Creek Road. To access this road, turn east off ID-75 just past the turnoff for the Forest Service Work Center on the east side of the highway. The road, which has recently been improved, crosses the broad alluvial fan formed over the eons by Fourth of July Creek to the base of the mountains, and runs a total of 9.0 miles to a trailhead. (Note: the Forest Service is debating whether to close the road at a point short of its present end, but work is not likely to begin anytime soon.)

(a) FST-109, Fourth of July Lake Trail. This trail runs 1.0 mile to Fourth of July Lake, which is at 9,300 feet in elevation. The lake, situated in the heart of the White Cloud high country, is representative of the many high basins in the range. Just below the lake, FST-219 takes off to the north into Ants Basin, and FST-671 leads into the Warm Springs Creek drainage. From Fourth of July Lake, FST-109 continues to the south to Washington Lake and a junction with FST-047 [Approach: (A)(1.1)(c)] in roughly 3.0 miles.

(a.1) Cross-country Route to Chamberlain Basin. By using a topo map, it is possible to make a cross-country hike across the Boulder crest and directly into Chamberlain basin at the base of Castle Peak. This route, although harder than the trails which lead into the basin, will save you many miles of walking. To reach the basin by trail, see [Approach: (A)(1.1)(c)].

(b) FST-219, Ant Basin Trail. This trail acts as a connector between the Fourth of July Creek drainage and the Warm Springs Creek drainage. The trail begins at Fourth of July Lake and runs over the ridge between Blackman and Patterson peaks to FST-671 in 2.0 miles.

(c) FST-671, Warm Springs Creek Trail. This trail follows Warm Springs Creek from its confluence with the Salmon River for 20.0 miles to a pass on the main White Cloud Mountain crest. At the pass, it joins FST-683 [Approach: (B)(2)(b)], which leads east to the Little Boulder Chain of Lakes area. Besides access from the Fourth of July Creek Area, you can access this trail from ID-75 near the Robinson Bar CG from the Casino Lake Trail [Approach: (A)(3)(a)] and from the Rough Creek Trail [Approach: (A)(4)(a)]. Because this trail crosses through Warm Springs Creek many times, its lower end is not easy to negotiate until the water level drops late in the summer.

(d) Iron Basin/Slate Creek Trail. This trail is no longer maintained. It leaves FST-671 and Warm Springs Creek due south of Watson Peak and works its way up to Iron Basin and Ocalkens Lake. From the lake, it descends along Slate Creek to FS-666 in 3.0 miles. Although no longer maintained, it is the primary approach to the many summits known specifically as the White Cloud Peaks. Snow often remains in Iron Basin and Slate Creek until late summer; consequently, high water makes travel in this area difficult. Do not attempt to traverse this route until late July at the earliest.

(2.1) FS-041, Strawberry Basin Road. This road begins at the end of the Fourth of July Creek

Road, runs north along the western side of Blackman Peak, and eventually ends after several miles on a ridge line between Warm Springs Creek and Mountain Home Canyon. A 4WD is required to drive this route; it is suggested that you hike this route instead.

(3) FS-212, Boundary Creek Road. This gravel road leaves ID-75 at a signed junction 6.0 miles south of Stanley. Once on it, you will encounter a fork; Take the left fork and follow it to the trailhead in about 1.0 mile.

(a) FST-103 and FST-616, Casino Lake Trail. FST-103 leaves the Boundary Creek trailhead and proceeds to Casino Lakes in 4.5 miles, crossing over a steep divide on the way. The Casino Lake area gives access to a remote section of the range including Big Casino Creek, Garland Lakes, Rough Lake and Lookout Mountain.

(4) FS-626, Rough Creek Road. Follow ID-75 from Stanley toward Challis for 6.0 miles and turn south. This steep road, which is 4.0 miles long, follows Rough Creek to a trailhead.

(a) FST-647, Rough Creek Trail. This well-maintained trail provides the best access to the region around Lookout Mountain. From its trailhead, it reaches FST-616 [Approach: (A)(3)(a)] in just under 4.0 miles.

(5) FS-666, Slate Creek Road. This road leaves ID-75 20.0 miles east of Stanley. There is a sign at the turnoff. The road follows the Salmon River west before turning up Slate Creek. It is 8.0 miles from the highway to the trailhead.

(a) Livingston Creek Trail. Livingston Creek flows into Slate Creek 6.0 miles up the Slate Creek Road. Just past this confluence, a sign for "Crater Lake" is posted. The Livingston Creek Trail leaves from this point and terminates at the lake in 4.0 miles.

(b) Hoodoo Lake Trail. This trail begins at the end of the Slate Creek Road and runs via a winding route to Hoodoo Lake in 1.5 miles. This route is an old mining road; it passes several "digs" along the way.

(c) Slate Creek/Iron Basin Trail. This trail is no longer maintained by the Forest Service. The road is gated shut at an old mine. Park at this point and follow the road through the mining works until it forks. Take the left fork and cross Hoodoo Creek. The beginning of the trail is difficult to find—look for it cutting up the hillside 25 yards from Hoodoo Creek. See [Approach: (A)(2)(d)] for further information.

(B) East Fork Salmon River Approaches.

The East Fork Salmon River Road, which leaves ID-75 38.6 miles east of Stanley (17.4 miles west of Challis), is paved for much of its distance, with the remaining portions consisting of good gravel. At the time of writing, a private landowner has closed the road near its end; the Forest Service has reportedly purchased an easement around this roadblock and plans to reopen the road by mid-1990.

(1) Jimmy Smith Lake. This foothill lake is located 1.0 mile west of the main road. Turn off the East Fork Road at a signed junction roughly 14.0 miles from ID-75. From the lake, two trails lead into the seldom-used northeast corner of the White Clouds.

(2) FS-667, Big Boulder Creek Road. Turn off the East Fork Road onto this road at the well-marked junction roughly 18.0 miles from ID-75. At 9.0 miles from the highway is Livingston Mill, a semi-active mining camp, and other private land. There is a large, well-marked trailhead with lots of parking just below the mill. There have been reports of hikers returning to find that their gas tanks have been siphoned dry or the air let out of their tires.

(a) FST-047, East Side Trail. This trail is the major north/south approach route on the east side of the White Cloud Mountains. From the trailhead, the trail proceeds over a divide to Frog Lake in 5.0 miles. From Frog Lake, it is 1.0 mile to FST-683, which leads to Boulder Chain of Lakes, another 1.0 mile to Little Boulder Creek, another divide crossing and an additional 3.5 miles to Chamberlain Creek and FST-110 [Approach: (A)(1.1)(c)]. It is a total of about 14.5 miles to Germania Creek. See [Approach: (A)(1)(c)].

(a.1) FST-680 and FST-601, Big Boulder Creek Trail. FST-680 leaves FST-047 roughly 1.5 miles south of the trailhead and leads to the Big Boulder Chain of Lakes. The trail forks in 2.0 miles, with FST-680 leading to Island Lake; FST-601 leading to Walker and the many other Boulder Lakes.

(b) FST-683, Little Boulder Creek Trail. The upper portions of this trail pass spectacular examples of glacially carved lakes. It then climbs over two passes (one is the main divide) and connects with FST-671 [Approach: (A)(2)(c)], which leads to Warm Springs Creek.

(c) Lake 9419 Cross-country Route. Leave FST-047 where it junctions with FST-684 and contour northeast through the trees. Once out of the trees, look for a path running north across a talus slope. Follow this trail to the lake.

(3) Little Boulder Creek Trailhead. Three miles south of the turn for the Big Boulder Creek road is a transfer camp and trailhead for Little Boulder Creek.

(a) FST-682, Little Boulder Creek Trail. This trail leaves the East Fork Road where it crosses Boulder Creek at a signed trailhead and follows the creek west to FST-047 [Approach: (B)(2)(b)] in 6.5 miles.

2. The Boulder Mountains

The Boulder Mountains are best known for their multi-colored southern escarpment, which rises abruptly along ID-75 just north of Ketchum. The range stretches north from Ketchum for over 50 miles to Challis. It is flanked in the west by ID-75 between Ketchum and Galena Summit, the White Cloud Mountains and the East Fork of the Salmon River; in the north by the main Salmon River; in the east by US-93 between Challis and Thousand Springs Valley; and by the Pioneer Mountains in the south.

The range is composed of granite, Challis Volcanics material and highly metamorphosed rocks that have been extensively shattered and faulted. The impressive southern front of the Boulder Mountains, which rises up above the Big Wood River Valley, is composed of three layers of material. The top layer is made up of andesite and dacite, which were deposited by the Challis Volcanics around 60 million years ago; the middle layer is pink granite, which was intruded roughly 50 million years ago. The bottom layer is the oldest and is mainly composed of light-colored limestones and quartzites. The intrusion of igneous rock into the Boulder's sedimentary rocks formed minerals, which were exploited in the late 1800s. At one time Boulder City, a small mining town in a 10,000-foot Boulder Mountain valley, was Idaho's highest town. Today it is only a ghost town.

The Boulder Mountains terrain varies considerably as one moves from Ketchum north to Challis. The southern stretches are higher and more rugged—the effects of Pleistocene glaciation are readily visible in the many cirques and glacially carved valleys. The range's highest point, 11,714-foot Ryan Peak, is found along the southern escarpment. Farther north, the Boulder Mountains are lower in elevation. Because these northern peaks sit in the rain shadow of the White Cloud and Salmon River mountains, there are very few trees. Only on the highest slopes of appropriately named Lone Pine Peak are there any significant stands of timber. The northern peaks, closer to the center of the Challis Volcanics, are composed of volcanic rock.

The Sawtooth National Recreation Area and the Sawtooth National Forest manage the southern sections of the Boulder Mountains. Both organizations emphasize recreational use of the mountains; they have developed and maintained a good trail system. The northern sections of the

Boulders are administered by the Salmon District of the Bureau of Land Management, which emphasizes cattle grazing as the primary use of the range and maintains no hiking trails.

Overall, vehicle access to the Boulder Mountains is adequate. While a 4WD will be invaluable in most places, it is not a necessity on the major roadways. Hiking within the range, both on- and off-trail, is rewarding and seldom crowded.

Although there is a lot of competition for the honor, the Boulder Mountains win the prize for being Idaho's most rotten mountains. Even rock that at first blush appears to be solid will crumble in your hands. (The mystery of how these peaks stand up to gravity is still unsolved.) Climbing is generally limited to Class 2 or Class 3 non-technical routes due to the poor condition of the rock. Even scrambling in the Boulders can be difficult because of the loose rock and impossible talus slopes. However, the views from these high peaks often are ample reward for the high price one must pay to reach a summit.

The growing popularity of cross-country and backcountry skiing (and the proximity to Ketchum) has brought many skiers to the Boulders in recent years. Track skiing is available in several places. The Galena Touring Center, located 30.0 miles north of Ketchum on ID-75, is a major ski-touring center. Those who prefer to break trail will find good access to the Boulders' open slopes. The area east of Galena Summit, with its many challenging open slopes, is the most popular area. Avalanche dangers can be extreme in this country.

Lone Pine Peak   *9,658 feet (Class 2)*

Lone Pine Peak is a big hulking mountain located just 11.0 miles due south of Challis. It forms the northern terminus of the Boulder Mountains. Access the peak from the Spar Canyon Road [Approach: (D)(1)] via a side road that leads to a saddle west of the peak. From the saddle, a jeep road leads toward the peak. Walk the jeep road to its end, and then climb east to the summit ridge and on to the summit. USGS Lone Pine Peak

Sheep Mountain   *10,915 feet (Class 1)*

Sheep Mountain is located 21.0 miles southeast of Lone Pine Peak and 1.0 mile north of Bowery Peak. FST-186 [Approach: (C)(2)(a)] at one time followed Pin Creek to the summit in roughly 7.0 miles. The trail, which is accessed from the road up the East Fork of the Salmon River, is no longer maintained the entire distance, but its route can be followed over open terrain to the summit. USGS Bowery Peak

Bowery Peak   *10,861 feet (Class 2)*

This peak is roughly 1.0 mile due south of Sheep Mountain. The only practical way to climb this peak is to traverse the connecting ridge line from Sheep Mountain. USGS Bowery Peak

Jerry Peak   *10,015 feet (Class 2)*

Jerry Peak is located 20.0 miles south of Lone Pine Peak and 12.0 miles east of Sheep Mountain. Access this peak from Herd Lake [Approach: (C)(1)], which is 3.5 miles northeast of the summit. Above the lake, Lake Creek flows down off the western slopes of Jerry Peak. Flanking the drainage are two ridge lines, both of which can hiked to the summit. The easiest route is to follow the closed road west from Herd Lake to a BLM campground located on a saddle just west of Point 9534 on the USGS map. From the CG, hike to Point 9534 and then follow the long connecting ridge line south to the summit, a total distance of about 6.0 miles. This is very open country; a multitude of variations will lead to the summit of Jerry Peak from almost any direction. USGS Jerry Peak

The Cross*   *9,225 feet (Class 2)*

The Cross is a small summit located 0.5 mile north of Galena Summit and ID-75. Unnamed on the quad, this peak was named for a wooden cross that once stood on its summit. (The peak is identified as the Galena triangulation station on the USGS map.) The summit is a short, easy walk from Galena Summit via the ridge line [Approach: (A)(1)], which is also a popular ski ascent. From the summit, several open slopes descend to ID-75. The short ski up, combined with the long ski down, makes this an excellent run. USGS Horton Peak

Avalanche Peak*   *9,433 feet (Class 2)*

Avalanche Peak, another unofficially named summit, is located 0.5 mile due north of The Cross. Access this peak from Galena Summit [Approach: (A)(1)]. It, like the Cross, is a popular ski destination when snow conditions are stable. USGS Horton Peak

Galena Peak   *11,153 feet (Class 2)*

Galena Peak, a big talus pile with a rotten northeast face, is the northernmost 11,000-foot Boulder Mountain Peak. It is located 3.0 miles east of the Galena Lodge on ID-75. Take the Senate Creek Road [Approach: (A)(3)] northeast from ID-75 and follow it to its end. Gain the west ridge and follow it to the summit. USGS Galena Peak

Cerro Ciento*   *11,046 feet (Class 2)*

Cerro Ciento is located 2.5 miles southeast of Galena Peak on the same connecting ridge line.

The climb is a very long hike from the end of the Spring Creek Road [Approach: (A)(4)]. Drive the Spring Creek Road to the high bench above and north of the creek. Once at the top of the bench, you will find a junction with a second road, which leads northeast. Park here (unless you have a 4WD) and hike this second road until it eventually veers sharply to the north. Leave the road at this point and hike east through the forest, paralleling Spring Creek. Continue hiking along the upper edge of the Spring Creek bench until you reach roughly 8,000 feet. From this point, it is possible to traverse (without losing much elevation) to Spring Creek. Once in the creek bottom, follow its steep course up to the pass just north of the peak and 2,600 feet above. The last 400 feet are on terribly loose talus. Once at the pass, follow the ridge line to the summit. (Note: you will need both the Galena and Easley Hot Springs quads and a Sawtooth National Forest map to complete this climb. The road system shown on the USGS maps is not accurate.) USGS Easley Hot Springs

Easley Peak *11,108 feet (Class 2)*
Easley Peak is located 0.5 mile south of Cerro Ciento. Climb the peak by traversing the ridge line from Cerro Ciento. The peak can also be climbed via its southwest ridge; start from ID-75 where it crosses Prairie Creek. This route involves an elevation gain of over 4,100 feet. (Note: the King Creek Road shown on the USGS quad is no longer open to vehicles.) USGS Easley Hot Springs

Silver Peak *11,112 feet (Class 3)*
Silver Peak is located 2.0 miles east of Easley Peak, directly west of Boulder City. The best route up this peak is from Silver Creek. Leave ID-75 on Silver Creek Road [Approach: (A)(5)(a)] and follow the road to its end. From the road's end, hike to the divide just west of the peak. Follow the west ridge to the summit. This route is reportedly very time-consuming, so get an early start. USGS Easley Hot Springs

Peak 11041 *11,041 feet (Class 2)*
This unnamed peak, located 0.5 mile north of Boulder Peak, has often been referred to as Silver Peak (which actually lies over a mile to the west). The summit is located directly west of Boulder City; it is an easy goal for those who can make the 4WD approach to that ghost town [Approach: (A)(6)(a)]. Where the Boulder City Road forks just east of Boulder City, take the right fork and hike due west toward the ridge top. Once out of the trees, this route climbs to the saddle between Point 10723 and Peak 11041. Climb northwest until the headwall steepens and then turn due west, working your way along the peak's north-

east slope until you are able to gain the peak's northwest ridge. Take the ridge to the summit. USGS Easley Hot Springs

Boulder Peak *10,981 feet*
Boulder Peak sits directly above the Wood River valley, 1.0 mile southeast of Silver Peak. It is one of the most decayed piles of rubble in the range. USGS Easley Hot Springs

North Couloir. *(Class 3)*
Directly above Boulder City [Approach: (A)(6)(a)], a steep couloir leads to the top of the peak's east ridge. The couloir is often filled with snow until late summer, which makes for good footing while the snow lasts. A number of people have made spring ski descents of this couloir. From the top of the couloir, follow the ridge west to the summit.

South Ridge. *(Class 3-4)*
Drive or walk the Boulder City Road [Approach: (A)(6)(a)] to the 7,400-foot contour on your topo map. The route reportedly traverses the creek and follows the ridge to the top; a long 3,500-foot climb. (Climbing this ridge will probably involve a lot of route-finding difficulties. Start early.)

Glassford Peak *11,602 feet (Class 3)*
Glassford, a beautiful peak of red rocks and crumbling ribs, is highly visible from Ryan Peak. It is located 5.5 miles northeast of Silver Peak, 3.5 miles west of Ryan Peak. Climb this peak from the saddle southwest of the summit. This route is extremely strenuous but avoids the rotten rock that plagues the peak's steeper walls. Access the saddle via the North Fork of the Big Wood River [Approach: (A)(7)(a)]. Follow the trail up the drainage until it ends, at around 8,000 feet. From this point, gain 3,000 feet by climbing due north to the high point just south of Glassford Peak. Once on the ridge top, traverse north to the saddle just south of the Glassford summit by staying on the west side of the ridge top. From the saddle, the route goes directly up the peak's south slopes. USGS Ryan Peak

Ryan Peak *11,714 feet*
The 23d highest named peak in Idaho is well hidden from the bottom of the Wood River Valley. The fragile pile of rock that forms this decaying summit is located 15.0 miles north of Ketchum. The mountain was named for Mike Ryan, an early Wood River Teamster. Primary approach to the pass is via Forest Service trails, which lead from the North Fork of the Big Wood River to West Pass [Approach: (A)(7)(a)(b)]. USGS Ryan Peak

The impressive north face of Kent Peak viewed from Ryan Peak

South Ridge. *(Class 2)*
From the pass southwest of the summit, the route climbs directly up to the top of the south ridge and then follows the ridge directly to the summit. From the trailhead, it is a 12.0-mile round trip that gains and then loses a total of nearly 10,000 feet.

East Ridge. *(Class 2)*
The summit can also be reached from North Fork Lake to the northeast[Approach:(B)(2)(a)]. Follow the trail up to the small lake above North Fork Lake. Turn south and climb to the ridge top between Ryan and Point 11415. Follow the east ridge to the summit.

Kent Peak *11,664 feet (Class 2)*
This summit is named for Kent Easton, a Wood River mountaineering enthusiast who died in 1959. Kent is an extremely rugged peak. Its north face possesses a permanent snowfield, complete with a burgschrund. The summit is located 0.8 mile southeast of Ryan Peak. USGS Ryan Peak

Northwest Ridge. *(Class 3-4)*
It is possible to traverse this ridge from the saddle south of Ryan Peak; access the route from FST-115 [Approach: (A)(7)(b)]. The route clambers up and down along the ridge crest and the southwest-facing slopes. Although you must avoid or climb over numerous towers of extremely rot-

ten rock, the route is feasible for those with good route-finding abilities.

South Ridge.
Take the same trail [Approach: (A)(7)(b)] as for Ryan Peak, but leave the trail at the 9200-foot contour and climb up to the peak's south ridge, which leads directly to the summit.

Peak 10680 *10,680 feet (Class 2)*
This unnamed but appealing peak forms a large cone-shaped summit 1.25 miles southwest of Kent Peak. The summit can be climbed from the saddle between it and Kent Peak, as well as by its northern side [Approach: (A)(7)(b)]. USGS Ryan Peak

Basils Peak* *10,414 feet (Class 2)*
Basils Peak is located 2.0 miles due east of Boulder Peak. It is unnamed on the USGS map. Drive 9.5 miles north from Ketchum on ID-75 and park at Wood River CG. Cross the highway and gain the ridge that meets the highway between Konrad Creek and Goat Creek. Follow the treeless ridge to Point 9829, then turn west and hike to Point 9935. The ridge plunging down to the west from Point 9829 is an alternative but less-appealing ascent route. From Point 9935, the route goes up the crumbling ridge to the northwest and the summit. Stay on the south side of the ridge to avoid

190

the numerous towers that block the way. The route is roughly 4.0 miles (one way) and 4,000 feet elevation gain. USGS Amber Lake

Rock Roll Peak* *10,458 feet (Class 2)*
Rock Roll Peak is located at the high point on the Trail Creek/Lake Creek divide, 8.0 miles southeast of Kent Peak. This peak has excellent views of the surrounding countryside and the Pioneer Mountains. Climb the south ridge from the saddle. Access to the south ridge is possible either from Trail Creek [Approach: (B)] or Lake Creek. From the only traffic light on Ketchum's main street, drive northeast for 5.4 miles up Trail Creek and turn left at the Antelope Creek sign. Park above Trail Creek and drop down to the creek, which you must wade across (difficult before late in the summer). A poorly maintained unofficial trail climbs up Antelope Creek toward Point 9557. From this point, drop down 500 feet into the saddle at the base of the south ridge. Access from Lake Creek follows a trail, built partly on an old mining road, which leads to a point below the saddle where you can leave the trail and climb to the south ridge. USGS Rock Roll Canyon

Meridian Peak *10,400+ feet (Class 2)*
Meridian Peak is a tri-summited mountain situated 5.5 miles northeast of Ryan Peak and just

north of the North Fork of the Big Lost River. The USGS has identified the lower middle summit as Meridian Peak; however, the true summit is the northernmost point, which is over 100 feet higher. Climb this peak from FS-128 [Approach: (B)(2)(a)] by hiking FST-050 from the road north for roughly 1.0 mile. Leave the trail and hike up a small drainage to the peak's southeast ridge. Once out of the trees, follow the ridge up to Point 10285 and then follow the connecting ridge to the north (true) summit. Total distance is 2.5 miles from the road's end. USGS Meridian Peak

APPROACHES TO THE BOULDER MOUNTAINS

Approach routes for this section are referenced in the text by bracketed entries [Approach:], which include appropriate letter and number references.

The Boulders are best accessed from the Ketchum area via ID-75 and Trail Creek Road. Access is also possible via the East Fork of the Salmon River Road, which leads into the areas around West Pass Creek and the South Fork of the upper East Fork drainage.

Kent Peak, the highest Boulder Mountain summit, from West Pass

(A) Idaho 75 Approaches.

The section of ID-75 traverses the southern edge of the Boulder Mountains between Ketchum and Galena Summit. It is a good paved highway that provides primary access to a number of the range's most important peaks.

(1) Galena Summit. Galena Summit is an 8,700-foot pass which separates the Boulder and Smoky Mountains. You can find good spots to park (which are plowed during the winter) on both sides of the pass. This area is little used for approach in the summer, but is a popular spot in the winter for cross-country ski tours and ascents of the Cross and Avalanche Peak.

(2) FS-189, Gladiator Creek Area. From the Galena Lodge, 30.0 miles north of Ketchum, a dirt road leads up Gladiator Creek. At the road's end, a steep and seldom-used trail, FST-108, leads up to the Boulder Mountain Divide between Peak 10243 and Peak 10185.

(3) FS-186, Senate Creek Road. This road leaves ID-75 150 yards south of the Galena Lodge and climbs up Senate Creek for 2.0 miles.

(4) FS-186, Spring Creek Road. This road leaves ID-75 20.0 miles north of Ketchum. Drive 0.8 mile along the creek bottom until the road turns sharply and climbs up the bench north of the creek. In another 0.8 mile, the road reaches a junction on top of the bench. The main road turns north and drops off the ridge toward Cherry Creek, while the Spring Creek Road runs north up the bench another 1.0 mile to a wide spot, where parking is possible.

(5) FS-174, Silver Creek Road. This road leaves ID-75 15.8 miles north of the stoplight in Ketchum. Turn right (northeast), and follow the road across the river on a good bridge. After crossing the Big Wood River, the road turns upriver for a short distance. Go right when the road forks and follow the Silver Creek drainage to a second major fork. Go right once again and follow the road, which quickly climbs high up onto the flanks of the Boulders and eventually ends at around 8,400 feet. The road is about 3.0 miles long, and a 4WD is recommended.

(a) Silver Creek Trail. From the end of the road, head uphill on game trails toward the obvious opening in the mountains. Silver Lake and several small ponds are located in the high cirque; Silver Peak towers over the top of the cirque.

(6) FS-158, Boulder Basin 4WD Road. This is an extremely rugged road, which leads 6.0 steep miles into Boulder Basin at 9,200 feet. Driving this road requires considerable 4WD driving experience and specialized 4WD equipment. Although the road gets a lot of vehicle use in the summer, many people hike the road rather than risk the drive. Boulder Basin, which contains the remains of an old mining camp, is surrounded by spectacular mountains and ridges. Take ID-75 north from Ketchum for 13.0 miles and follow the signed dirt road for 0.5 mile until it forks. Take the right fork, cross the creek and follow the road upstream and into the mountains. In roughly 2.0 miles, the road reaches a steep pitted grade that has stopped many off-roaders.

(a) FST-184 and FST-113, Boulder Basin to East Fork Trail. This poorly maintained trail climbs north out of Boulder Basin and then drops into the basin east of Silver Peak, where it follows the East Fork of the South Fork of the Salmon north.

(7) FS-146, North Fork Area. Turn off ID-75 at the SNRA headquarters building. A good dirt road leads from the headquarters for 5.5 miles to the road's end at a small camping area.

(a) FST-115 and FST-128, North Fork Big Wood River Trail. This trail proceeds up the drainage for 4.5 miles before crossing a pass west of Glassford Peak. The trail is continually swept by avalanches during the winter, receives little maintenance and can be hard (if not impossible) to follow at its upper end.

(b) FST-115, West Pass Trail. This trail leaves the North Fork trail 1.5 miles from the trailhead. The junction is in a small clearing and can be difficult to find. Look for small rock cairns in a sagebrush-filled clearing that marks the trail's start. If you are unable to find the start, hike 50 yards past the canyon opening and then hike northeast uphill until you find the trail. Despite the lack of a sign at its beginning, this is a good trail. It leads to the top of 10,400-foot West Pass, which is approximately 5.0 miles from the trailhead. From the pass, the trail makes its way down to the East Fork of the Salmon River.

(c) FST-129, West Fork of the Big Wood River Area. This trail leads up the West Fork to near Window Lake; a side trail leads up to Amber Lakes. This is a seldom-visited area near several unnamed peaks.

(B) Trail Creek Road Approaches.

Trail Creek Road leaves the center of Ketchum and continues east through Sun Valley, eventually crossing Trail Creek Summit in 12.2 miles and then dropping down into the Big Lost River drainage. Turn northeast off ID-75 at the stoplight in Ketchum. The road is paved up to the base of the pass.

(1) FS-140, Park Creek Road. This road is 14.0 miles east of Ketchum. It runs up the east flank of the Boulders and gives access to FST-124 and FST-126.

(2) FS-128, North Fork of the Big Lost River Road. This road leaves the Trail Creek Road roughly 9.0 miles northeast of Trail Creek Summit and heads west into the more remote sections of the Boulders. Several seldom-used trails and a number of high cirques can be reached from the road.

(a) FST-050, Hunter Creek Trail. This trail leaves the end of FS-128 and proceeds north up Hunter Creek, crosses a divide and drops down into East Pass Creek, where it is designated FST-188 [Approach: (C)(1)(a)].

(C) East Fork Salmon River Approaches.

For a complete discussion of this road, see the entry [Approach: (B)] in the White Cloud Mountains approach section. At this time, the road has been closed by a private landowner below the Bowery Guard Station and is no longer a practical way to approach the Ryan Peak section of the Boulders. The Forest Service hopes this problem will be remedied and the road reopened in 1990.

(1) FS-148, Herd Lake Road. Access this road from the East Fork Road at a signed junction 9.0 miles south of ID-75. Follow the road southeast for 9.5 miles, to a point where it is closed by the BLM. From this point, the road can be used as a trail. It continues to a saddle at 9,000 feet.

(a) FST-188, East Pass Creek Trail. FST-188 leaves the Herd Creek Road where East Pass Creek flows into Herd Creek and runs southwest until it connects with FST-050 [Approach: (B)(2)(a)], which leads to the North Fork of the Big Lost River.

(2) Pine Creek Road. This road leaves the East Fork Road 3.0 miles west of the Herd Lake Road turnoff. A short road, it serves as the trailhead for FST-186.

(a) FST-186, Sheep Mountain Trail. This trail follows Pine Creek south toward Sheep Mountain. At one time, the trail was maintained to the summit of the peak, and its tread can still be followed most of the distance. To follow the trail to the top of Sheep Mountain, stay in the main Pine Creek drainage (which arcs around the peak's western side) until the trail begins to climb the peak's northwestern slopes.

(D) Northern Boulder Mountain Approaches.

This area is of limited interest for hiking and climbing. ID-75 follows the northern section of the range between the East Fork of the Salmon River and Challis. US-93 follows the eastern side of the range from Challis south toward Mackay. Although the northern Boulder Mountains are both high and precipitous, they are crisscrossed by many roads which vary in quality from good gravel to almost impossible jeep trail. The primary approach road is the Spar Canyon Road, which runs across the range from the East Fork of the Salmon River road to US-93. This gravel road is passable to sedans when it is dry. From this road and the

two paved highways, almost every side canyon contains a road. Travel in this area requires a well-prepared vehicle and plenty of extra water.

(1) Lone Pine Peak Access.

In addition to USGS maps, you will need the newest edition of the Challis National Forest map to approach Lone Pine Peak. Follow the Spar Canyon Road from either US-93 or the East Fork of the Salmon until the road is crossed by a high-tension power line. At this point, a 4WD road heads off to the north. Follow this road north for about 4.0 miles until you are in the area indicated as Section 36 on the national forest map. Find a convenient place to park below the south ridge of the peak.

3. The Pioneer Mountains

The Pioneer Mountains, an oval-shaped range roughly 40 miles by 30 miles, are located southeast of Ketchum, Idaho. The range is bounded by the Big Wood River in the west, the Snake River Plain in the south, the Boulder Mountains in the north and the White Knob Mountains in the east.

The Pioneer Mountains consist of two lobes. The northwestern lobe runs from Trail Creek Summit to the area around Standhope Peak; the southeastern lobe from Standhope Peak toward Arco, Idaho. Geologically, the range has a granitic foundation, which was intruded into schists and quartzite at approximately the same time as the Idaho Batholith was forming farther north. The Pioneer granite covers roughly 25 square miles and is exposed on the eastern side of the range while the western slopes are covered with sedimentary and metamorphic overburden that is quite broken. The range's highest summit, 12,009-foot Hyndman Peak, is made up of a massive pile of quartzite on a granite base. As a substance for climbing, the Pioneer rock varies in quality. While the granite has formed some impressive walls and even a few domes on the eastern slopes, all of the major peaks are covered by highly shattered and weathered metamorphic rock that defies technical climbing.

The Pioneers held several large glaciers in the past; there are many spectacular cirques and mountain lakes. Wildhorse Canyon, on the east side of the range, is comprised of spectacularly vertical rock walls left by glacial action. Dozens of high mountain lakes dot the landscape, providing pleasant base camps for climbing trips into the range.

The Pioneer Mountains are managed by the Sawtooth and Challis national forests. The Forest Service has proposed Wilderness designation for

The Boulder Creek approach to the towering Devils Bedstead East, which dominates the drainage skyline (photo by Dana Lopez)

65,972 acres in the Pioneers. Although Congress has yet to act upon this proposal, the Pioneers stand a very good chance of being so designated if the Idaho Wilderness Bill is ever passed.

Hiking and climbing opportunities are extensive, but little known. While little technical climbing has taken place in the Pioneers, both the north face of Hyndman Peak and the north face of Old Hyndman Peak were climbed in the 1970s, and there are a number of relatively unknown granite formations that would attract rock climbers. During the 1950s and 1960s, the range saw extensive use by skiers, who used the Pioneer Cabin as a base camp for many winter ascents.

Phi Kappa Mountain   10,516 feet
Peak 10885   10,885 feet   (Class 2)

Phi Kappa Mountain is located 2.75 miles east of Trail Creek Pass; Peak 10885 is located 0.75 mile northwest of it. Climb these peaks from the Summit Creek Trail [Approach: (A)(2)(a)] via the southeast ridge of Phi Kappa Mountain. From the summit of Phi Kappa, follow the ridge to the northwest to Peak 10885. This is a good peak for those who seek a short trip to a high place. USGS Phi Kappa Mountain

Devils Bedstead West   11,051 feet

This peak is located 2.0 miles southeast of Phi Kappa Mountain. There is some confusion as to which Pioneer peak is really the Devils Bedstead. The USGS quad and the latest Forest Service maps for Challis National Forest mark this peak on the main divide, while the newest Sawtooth National Forest map shows Peak 11865, above Washington Lake, as the Devils Bedstead. For our purposes, the USGS-named peak will be known as the Devils Bedstead West; the peak identified by the Forest Service will be known as the Devils Bedstead East. USGS Phi Kappa Mountain

West Ridge. (Class 3)

The shortest approach is from Trail Creek Summit via FST-053 [Approach: (A)(2)(a)]. From the alpine saddle at the top of Summit Creek, traverse the ridge line over to the saddle just west of the peak. Although the climb is relatively steep, the presence of numerous goat trails makes it an easy walk. From the second saddle, the route works up the ridge on solid rock to the summit. The first winter ascent was by L. Stur, R. Kiesel, B. Gorton and B. Bachman.

Devils Bedstead East* *11,865 feet*

This spectacular peak is located 1.5 miles northeast of the Devils Bedstead West and 0.25 mile west of Washington Lake. It is truly a forbidding peak, with "sheer walls on two sides and really steep walls on the other two." The rock is rotten and the approach is long. USGS Phi Kappa Mountain

Northeast Ridge. *(Class 3-4)*

From the small unnamed lake between the 9,800- and 10,000-foot contours on the USGS quad [Approach: (C)(1)(a.1)], climb through the wall above the lake and onto the 10,600-foot saddle on the peak's northern ridge. The ridge above the saddle is steep, rugged, and in places, exposed. A sharp step just below a false summit is the crux of the climb.

Northwest Face. *(Class 3)*

From the saddle on the northeast ridge (see description above), contour across the mountain and onto the northwest face. Work your way into the major gully that cuts the face. Follow the gully to the ridge line above the false summit and then ascend the ridge to the top.

Salzburger Spitzl* *11,600+ feet (Class 2)*

This peak is positioned 1.5 miles southeast of the Devils Bedstead West and 1.0 mile due north of Handwerk Peak. It was named by Florian Haemmerle, who managed the Pioneer Cabin for

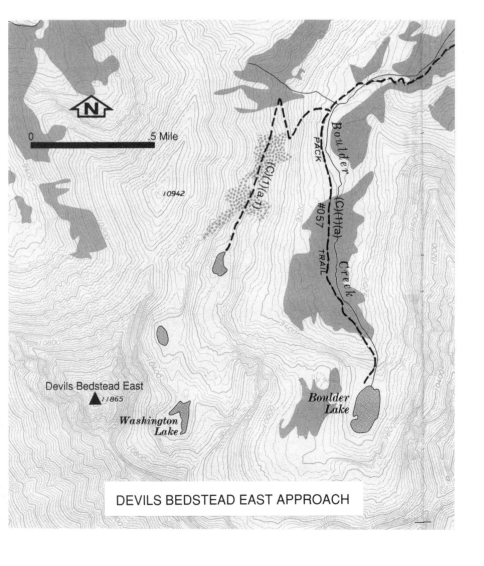

DEVILS BEDSTEAD EAST APPROACH

the Sun Valley Resort for many years. Climb from the North Fork Hyndman Creek via its southern slopes [Approach: (B)(2)(b)].

Goat Mountain* *11,913 feet*

This summit, the second highest Pioneer summit, is located 2.25 miles southeast of the Devils Bedstead West. For many years, a sign stood atop the Sun Valley ski runs identifying this peak and incorrectly giving its elevation at over 12,000 feet. The peak has twin summits; the north-ernmost summit is the highest. A few people have called the northern summit Kane Peak, but there is insufficient vertical relief between the two summits for them to constitute two mountains. USGS Phi Kappa Mountain

South Route. *(Class 3)*

The summit can be reached from the upper reaches of the North Fork of Hyndman Creek via its southeastern slopes [Approach: (B)(2)(b)]. Follow the unnamed drainage leading into the basin south of Handwerk Peak until its walls steepen considerably at about 10,000 feet. The route climbs the boulder field, heading directly toward the large, distinct granite fin (known as Florians Nudl) on Goat's south ridge to a shelf 400 feet above. Turn directly north at this point and climb to the lower south summit on relatively stable material. From the top of the south summit,

drop down the ridge line to the saddle between the south and north summits. Keep on the east side of the ridge as much as possible by working the ledges. Once in the saddle, climb the ridge directly to the summit. There is some exposure on the traverse between the two summits, making this a difficult Class 3 climb.

Peak 11516 *11,516 feet (Class 3)*

This peak is located 0.9 mile southeast of the Devils Bedstead West and 1.2 miles east of Kane Lake. Access the peak from Kane Lake [Approach: (A)(3)(a)]. The route from the lake proceeds up the boulder-strewn gully to the saddle south of the peak, and then climbs the south ridge to the summit. USGS Phi Kappa Mountain

Handwerk Peak *10,840 feet*

Handwerk Peak is located 1.0 mile south of Salzburger Spitzl, directly north of Pioneer Cabin. While not the highest peak in the range, this double-summited mountain is one of the most interesting peaks. Its unique "twin fangs" shape is plainly visible to the east from the Pioneer Cabin. The east summit is about 10 feet shorter than the more rugged east summit. There is no practical route between the two summits. The peak is named after Ted Handwerk, who was killed in Italy during World War II. USGS Phi Kappa Mountain

Salzburger Spitzl (left) and twin-summited Handwerk Peak

Johnstone Peak, as seen from the Pioneer Cabin Trail

West Peak Route. *(Class 2)*
From the 9200-foot contour in the unnamed basin [Approach: (B)(2)(b)] south of the peak, climb up to the west ridge through steep and loose talus. Once on the ridge, stay on its top and head east to the summit past two small cliffs located on the south side of the ridge. A Class 4 descent leads down into the saddle between the east and west summits, but there is no reliable way to cross the deep gully which divides the two summits

East Peak Route. *(Class 3-4)*
From the 9,800-foot contour in the unnamed basin south of the peak [Approach: (B)(2)(b)], climb up the ridge line just east of the east summit. From this point, the route climbs up to the summit in a fairly direct manner, keeping on the north side of the ridge in two difficult spots.

Johnstone Peak *9,949 feet (Class 2)*
Johnstone Peak is situated 7.0 miles east of Ketchum and 5.0 miles southwest of Handwerk Peak. One approach is via the Pioneer Cabin Trail, FST-122. Follow it to its junction with FST-121 [Approach: (A)(1)(a)], then take FST-121 until it crosses a saddle on the peak's east ridge. Follow this ridge for 1.25 miles to the summit.

Another possibility is to follow the Corral Creek Road [Approach: (A)(1)] for 1.5 miles, turn onto the dirt road that proceeds up Uncle Johns Gulch until it becomes too rough, then park.

Hike up the road until it ends, and then continue to the saddle at the top of the gulch. From the saddle, follow the southwest ridge to the summit. USGS Hyndman Peak

Duncans Peak* *11,755 feet (Class 3-4)*
This peak, which sits 1.1 miles due west of Handwerk Peak, is not officially named on the USGS map, but is instead identified as Duncan Ridge. The true summit is the highest point on the ridge line, although some locals have stated that the 11,491-foot western summit is the actual summit. The peak is named for former Sun Valley resident Jonathan Duncan, who died in World War II. The peak has reportedly been climbed from two, and possibly three, directions. The only route that sounds practical begins at the saddle between Duncan Peak and Goat Mountain and climbs the steep north ridge to the summit. The route is over steep, loose rock and reportedly is somewhat exposed. Access is from the North Fork of Hyndman Creek [Approach: (B)(2)(b)]. USGS Phi Kappa Mountain

Hyndman Peak *12,009 feet (Class 2)*
The ninth highest summit in the state is located 0.6 mile southeast of Duncan Peak. It was named after Major William Hyndman, a Civil War veteran. Access this peak from the west via Hyndman Creek or from the east via Wildhorse Creek.

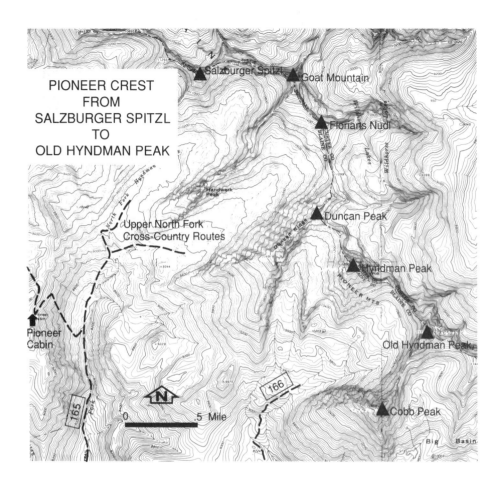

PIONEER CREST
FROM
SALZBURGER SPITZL
TO
OLD HYNDMAN PEAK

Details of the first ascent are unknown; the first winter ascent was made by L. Stur and others in the early 1960s. USGS Hyndman Peak

East Ridge. *(Class 2)*
Access this route from Hyndman Creek Road [Approach: (B)(2)(c)]. The east ridge is an easy scramble once you get to the saddle between Hyndman and Old Hyndman Peak, 5.0 miles from the end of the Hyndman Creek Road. From the saddle, follow the ridge to the summit, staying on the south side of the ridge.

North Ridge. *(Class 3-4)*
Access this ridge from Wildhorse Canyon [Approach: (C)(1)]. Avoid obstacles by dropping onto the west side of the ridge. The first known ascent was made by the Idaho Alpine Club (B. Echo, C. Caldwell and W. Sherman) in 1957.

Other Routes.
Hyndman has undoubtedly been climbed by other routes. Basil Service reports that a Califor-

nia group climbed the formidable north face in 1986, but no details are known about this climb.

Cobb Peak *11,650 feet*
Cobb Peak sits 1.25 miles south of Hyndman Peak. A big pyramid-shaped peak, it dominates the entire Hyndman Creek area. USGS Hyndman Peak

West Ridge. *(Class 3)*
Access the west ridge from the unnamed drainage that separates Hyndman Peak and Cobb Peak [Approach: (B)(2)(c)]. From the point where the creek crosses the 9,440-foot contour on the USGS quad, look for a talus-covered rib that leads to the ridge top. The ridge is a walkup except for the last 400 feet, where it turns into a series of rock walls and rotten gullies. A wide variety of routes lead over this portion of the ridge to the summit. Stay on the south side of the ridge and be prepared to drop as much as 100 feet below the ridge crest in order to avoid technical climbing.

East Face. *(Class 3)*
This route begins in Big Basin [Approach: (B)(2)(e)]. The face is composed of broken ledges and slabs. A number of routes are feasible. It is best to keep on the north side of the face.

Old Hyndman Peak *11,775 feet*

Old Hyndman is located on the main Pioneer crest, 1.0 mile southwest of Hyndman Peak. This is a very rugged and stunning peak, especially when viewed from the mouth of Wildhorse Canyon (from there, it resembles the Matterhorn). From all directions, it appears as a vertical shaft without an easy slope. USGS Grays Peak

East Ridge. *(Class 3)*
The only easy route on the peak climbs the peak from Big Basin [Approach: (B)(2)(e)] via the east ridge. Follow the Big Basin drainage to the peak's east ridge and then climb the south side of the ridge to the summit.

Northeast Face. *(Class 5)*
This route begins in Wildhorse Canyon [Approach: (C)(1)] and climbs an obvious southeast-slanting ice and snow couloir on 45- to 50-degree slopes for 900 feet. At this point, the route steepens to 60 degrees for a pitch that leads to a short, steep rock pitch at the top of the couloir.

The route then climbs north for 1,200 feet to a steep section of loose rock roughly 150 feet below the top. Climb directly to the top from here. First ascent by B. March, N. Fujita, J. Leitch and H. Hilbert, in 1975.

Angels Perch* *11,687 feet (Class 3)*

This remote summit lies north of the main Pioneer crest, 2.0 miles west of Standhope Peak and 0.75 mile west of Angel Lake. Climb the peak via the east ridge, from a point just south of the lake. Reportedly, the hardest part of the climb is getting to Angel Lake [Approach: (C)(2)]. USGS Standhope Peak

Peak 11305 *11,305 feet (Class 2-3)*

This unnamed peak is the junction point for a major north/south ridge line that extends south from the main Pioneer crest to Grays Peak. It is located 1.8 miles due east of Old Hyndman Peak. Two routes have been used to reach the peak's pointed summit. One follows the south ridge from Johnstone Pass—the most direct route, but one which involves climbing around several obstacles along the way [Approach: (B)(1)(a)]. Another way up is to climb the east ridge from Box Lake. This is a steep, short route with no serious obstacles [Approach: (B)(1)(a)]. USGS Grays Peak

The massive south face of Cobb Peak rises over 3,400 feet in just under 1 mile.

The heart of the Pioneer Mountains (left to right): Cobb Peak, Hyndman Peak, and Old Hyndman Peak

Grays Peak   *10,563 feet (Class 2)*

Grays peak is located almost 5.0 miles south of Old Hyndman and the main Pioneer crest. Climb via the west ridge from Federal Gulch CG or from the saddle south of the peak, which is crossed by the Federal Gulch Trail, FST-169 [Approach: (B)(1)(b)]. USGS Grays Peak

Standhope Peak   *11,878 feet*

This picturesque mountain is located at the head of Surprise Valley, 2.25 miles east of The Angels Perch. It offers enjoyable Class 3 climbing via several routes. Although there are no reports of winter ascents, it is evident that the north face would provide a exciting spring snow climb. USGS Standhope Peak

North Ridge. *(Class 3)*
Climb from the high lake in Surprise Valley [Approach: (C)(2)(a)]. From the lake, climb up to the saddle on the mountain's north ridge. Follow the ridge to the summit. The route occasionally crosses the ridge from side to side to avoid walls and to bypass the several notches along the way.

Southeast Ridge. *(Class 3)*
Follow the trail to the saddle between Betty and Baptie lakes [Approach: (C)(3)(a.3)]. From the saddle, the route goes up the ridge on rotten rock, passing occasional towers that add to the difficulty.

Southwest Ridge. *(Class 2)*
Begin the climb from the saddle between Betty

and Baptie lakes [Approach: (C)(3)(a.3)]. This is the easiest route to the summit. Climb to the saddle west of the peak and follow the ridge to the top.

Peak 11887   *11,887 feet (Class 3)*

This summit is located 0.75 mile directly south of Standhope Peak. Although unnamed, it is an impressive summit, shaped like a large fin, which rises up southwest of Goat Lake. Climb the peak via its north ridge from the saddle directly west of Goat Lake [Approach: (C)(3)(a.3)]. USGS Standhope Peak

Big Black Dome   *11,353 feet (Class 1-2)*

Big Black Dome is a hulking summit that dominates the view west from Copper Basin. The summit is located north of the main Pioneer crest, 1.75 miles north of Pyramid Peak. Follow FST-059 [Approach: (C)(3)(a.1)] west from FS-138 for about 2.0 miles to where the trail crosses the peak's east ridge. Leave the trail and climb the ridge to the summit. USGS Copper Basin 15-minute

Pyramid Peak   *11,628 feet (Class 2)*

Pyramid is a ragged summit located due north of Bellas Lakes. The summit is protected on three sides by very steep walls and is best climbed from Bellas Lakes via the east ridge. From the upper lake, climb directly north to the ridge line and then follow the ridge to the summit [Approach:

(C)(3)(a.2)]. USGS Copper Basin 15-minute

Glide Mountain 10,265 feet (Class 2)

Glide Mountain is located 7.0 miles south of Big Black Dome and 8.0 miles north of the Garfield GS. Climb from either Copper Basin via the Star Hope Creek Road and the east slopes [Approach: (C)(3)(a.4)], or from FST-176 and the mountain's west ridge [Approach: (D)(1)(a)]. USGS Muldoon Canyon 15-minute

Swede Peak 8,480 feet (Class 2)

Swede Peak, located 4.0 miles north of the Garfield GS, sits at the head of a number of small drainages. This peak is a short walk from the end of FS-130 via FST-179 [Approach: (D)(1)(a)]. USGS Muldoon Canyon 15-minute

Mandolin Peak 9,189 feet (Class 1)

Mandolin Peak is located 2.0 miles north of Swede Peak. Take FST-170 for 2.0 miles from its beginning at the end of FS-130 and then leave the trail and hike up the 200 feet to the summit [Approach: (D)(1)(a)]. USGS Muldoon Canyon 15-minute

Scorpion Peak 10,545 feet (Class)

Scorpion Peak is located 7.5 miles southeast of Glide Mountain, at the source of Garfield and Muldoon creeks. The best route to the summit follows Garfield Canyon north from Garfield GS to the mining scarps 2.0 miles up the road. Leave the old mining road and follow the drainage up to a spring located northwest of the summit. From this point, climb almost directly to the summit [Approach: (D)(1)]. USGS Muldoon Canyon 15-minute

Copper Basin Knob 10,784 feet (Class 2)

Located in the eastern lobe of the Pioneer Mountains, this peak is the first major summit south of Copper Basin Flat. Reach the summit from Lake Creek via the saddle on the west side of the peak. From where FS-138 crosses Lake Creek, follow the Lake Creek Trail [Approach: (C)(3)(b)] east for roughly 2.0 miles. At this point, leave the trail and bushwhack up the steep slope to the saddle between the summit and Point 10225, and then follow the ridge east to the summit. USGS Copper Basin 15-minute

Smiley Mountain 11,508 feet (Class 2)

Smiley Mountain, a large dome-shaped summit, dominates the entire eastern end of the range. It is located 4.0 miles southeast of Copper Basin Knob. USGS Muldoon Canyon 15-minute

North Ridge. (Class 2)

Climb this route from Lake Creek by going due east around Round Lake toward Point 10806. Follow the upper bowl to the south and gain the peak's broad north ridge. Follow the ridge to Point 11179 and then on to the summit [Approach: (C)(3)(b)].

South Ridge. (Class 2)

The south ridge is the most popular route on Smiley Mountain. Because of its southern exposure and the relatively low elevation of its approach, it is possible to climb the ridge in early May—even in heavy snow years. From the Antelope Creek Road (see [Approach: (A)(1)] under the White Knob Mountains), turn onto FST-221 just past Iron Bog CG. Follow FST-221 to a large, sagebrush-filled clearing, from which the upper slopes of Smiley Mountain are clearly visible. The elevation at this point is roughly 8,000 feet. Park here and climb due north up a gully for 400+ feet, to a large level clearing. From this clearing, a second gully leads up through the forest to the treeless slopes above. Stay on the east side of the gully, topping out on the peak's southeast ridge. Follow this ridge up to the top of the south ridge, which leads to the summit.

APPROACHES TO THE PIONEER MOUNTAINS

Approach routes for this section are referenced in the text by bracketed entries [Approach:], which include appropriate letter and number references.

There are many trailheads in the Pioneers. While good gravel roads lead to several, most are reached by roads only passable to 4WD vehicles. Although Forest Service maps show an extensive trail system within the range, actual trail conditions in the range vary from good to poor and, in a few cases, trails have disappeared altogether. Cross-country travel can be difficult because of numerous cliffs and walls.

(A) Trail Creek Access Points.

Trail Creek Road travels east from Ketchum over Trail Creek Summit (where the Boulder and Pioneer Mountains meet) and then drops down into the upper reaches of the Big Lost River drainage. The road is paved to the base of the pass and then is gravel for the remaining distance. Several good access points are available from this road, which is accessed either from ID-75 in the west or US-93 in the east.

(1) FS-137, Corral Creek Road. Drive 4.0 miles east of Ketchum on Trail Creek Road. Turn right onto the Corral Creek Road and drive 4.0 more

miles on a good gravel road to its end at a trailhead.

(a) FST-122, FST-121, Pioneer Cabin Trail. This 4.0-mile-long trail is well marked and maintained. The trail runs to Pioneer Cabin, which was built by the Sun Valley Company on an extremely scenic saddle. The view east from the cabin is one of the most beautiful alpine views in the state, featuring the entire Pioneer Crest from Salzburger Spiltz to Cobb Peak. From the cabin, the trail continues down into the North Fork of Hyndman Creek where it joins FST-165 [Approach: (B)(2)(a)]. (The cabin is open to the public on a first-come, first-served basis.)

(a.1) Pioneer Cabin/Corral Creek Trail. This trail runs from Pioneer Cabin north to Corral Creek, where it joins FST-123 [Approach: (A)(1)(b)]. The trail is very difficult to follow in places and is not shown on the Hyndman Peak USGS quad. Its beginning is marked by a sign at Pioneer Cabin.

(b) FST-123, Corral Creek Ridge Trail. This trail leaves the trailhead and climbs the ridge between Corral and Long Gulch canyons to the top of a small subsidiary peak just south of the main divide, and then drops down into seldom-visited Wilson Creek. The trail eventually joins up with the Trail Creek Road. About 1.5 miles from the trailhead, an old trail (without a designated number on the Forest Service maps) [Approach: (A)(1)(a.1)] heads east toward Pioneer Cabin. This trail can be difficult to follow.

(2) Trail Creek Summit Area. The summit is 12.0 miles east of Ketchum on the Trail Creek Road. Park on the south side of the road near a snow measurement marker.

(a) FST-053, Summit Creek Trail. This good trail follows tiny Summit Creek up from the pass to a high alpine valley with a large meadow. The route continues through the meadow to a saddle in 4.0 miles. From this point, it is possible to drop into the valley below via a seldom-used trail and join FST-066 [Approach: (A)(3)(a)].

(3) FS-134, Kane Creek Road. From Ketchum, take Trail Creek Road 21.0 miles to reach Kane Creek road. Turn right and drive up the creek for 3.5 miles to the Kane Lake trailhead.

(a) FST-066, Kane Lake Trail. This 4.0-mile trail takes you to the 9,300-foot lake at the foot of the Devils Bedstead West.

(B) ID-75 Access Points.

This highway is the primary approach to the Sun Valley/Ketchum area and the Sawtooth National Recreation Area. The highway connects Shoshone and Challis, Idaho.

(1) FS-118, East Fork of the Wood River Road. Turn east off ID-75 onto this road 4.0 miles

south of Ketchum and drive toward the mountains. The road is paved to the Triumph Mine site, then gravel and dirt for its remaining distance. One mile above the Triumph Mine, the road forks. The left fork goes to the North Fork of Hyndman Creek; the right fork ascends the East Fork of Big Wood River toward Johnstone Pass. Beyond this fork, both roads can be ugly and may require 4WD capability.

(a) FST-175, Johnstone Pass Trail. Keep right when the East Fork road forks above the Triumph Mine and follow this rugged road to its end at over 8,000 feet. There is enough parking for several vehicles at this point. The trail leaves the parking area and heads up the north side of the creek. After 2.0 miles, the trail crosses the creek and switchbacks up an unstable slope of deteriorated granite to the 10,000-foot pass in just over 3.5 miles. It is not uncommon for this trail to severely wash out during a thunderstorm. From the pass, the trail descends to Upper Box Canyon Lake and eventually all the way to the bottom of the Little Wood River canyon. By following a topo map, you can reach Windy Lakes via a cross-country traverse from Upper Box Canyon Lake. From the lake, traverse around the ridge to the east, cross the unnamed drainage and climb over the ridge to the west of Windy Lake, just north of Point 10695.

(b) FST-169, Federal Gulch Trail. FST-169 leaves FS-118 and climbs to a pass southwest of Greys Peak in 3.0 steep miles. From the pass, the trail continues east and descends into the Little Wood River canyon.

(2) FST-203, Hyndman Creek Road. Take the left fork where the East Fork road divides above the Triumph Mine. Three miles beyond the fork, the road crosses Hyndman Creek on a brand new bridge and then climbs up the hillside, continuing on for 2.0 more miles to meet the North Fork of Hyndman Creek and abruptly ending at a locked gate. Park here.

(a) FST-165, North Fork Hyndman Creek Trail. FST-165 provides access to Pioneer Cabin and the upper North Fork basin. The trail, recently improved, runs 4.0 miles to Pioneer Cabin.

(b) Upper North Fork Basin Cross-country Routes. The route into the upper basin begins where FST-165 turns sharply and begins its climb out of the North Fork of Hyndman Creek drainage. From this turn, follow a game trail that parallels the creek up the valley, keeping west of the creek, and heads to the white cliffs at the head of the drainage. Hike up through an obvious gully that splits the cliffs to a shelf above the cliffs, and then follow the creek upstream to a crossing near the base of Handwerk Peak. From this point, game trails lead into the basins south and north of

Handwerk Peak. Follow the unnamed drainage on the south side of Handwerk Peak to the east to reach Handwerk, Goat and Duncan peaks. To reach Salzberger Spiltz, follow the North Fork of Hyndman Creek into the basin north of Handwerk.

(c) FST-166, Hyndman Creek Trail. This trail starts at the end of FS-203, behind the locked gate. The trail follows an old road, fording the North Fork of Hyndman Creek, then continues on for 3.0 more miles to the base of Cobb Peak. From the road's end, an unofficial but surprisingly good sheepherder's trail follows the creek into the meadows below Hyndman Peak. Look for this trail where the creek traverses down a steep slope near the end of the old road.

(d) FST-165, Hyndman Cutoff Trail. This trail, which has not been maintained in many years, is difficult to follow for its entire distance between Hyndman Creek and the North Fork of Hyndman Creek.

(e) Big Basin Trails. Near the base of Cobb Peak, an old mining road departs the Hyndman Creek Trail (described above) and leads to the south. It quickly crosses the creek and then turns up the hillside to an old mine. Follow this road, which is designated as FST-166, to a point at which you can strike east and contour into the valley holding Cobb Lakes. The lakes are 3.0 miles from the beginning of FST-166, behind Cobb Mountain and Old Hyndman Peak.

(C) Copper Basin Access Points.

The Copper Basin Road leaves the Trail Creek Road 22.0 miles east of Ketchum and follows the East Fork of the Big Lost River into a magnificent windswept basin. From Copper Basin, several other roads break out to the south, east and north. FS-135 leads over Antelope Summit to the east and eventually reaches US-93 via Antelope Creek. Antelope Summit is the dividing point between the Pioneer and White Knob Mountains.

(1) FS-138, Wildhorse Creek Road. This road leaves the Copper Basin Road 2.0 miles south of its junction with Trail Creek Road and proceeds up dramatic Wildhorse Canyon. The road is in good condition to Wildhorse CG. A 4WD is recommended for the remaining sections of this road.

(a) FST-057, Boulder Lake Trail. This trail leaves the Wildhorse Creek Road just before the Wildhorse CG. The trail runs up Boulder Creek to the lake in 3.5 miles. There is no bridge and the stream crossing will be difficult during high water. Once across the creek and through the willows, look for a sign marking the beginning of the trail.

(a.1) Unnamed Lake Trail. This enigma of a trail leads to the unnamed lake 0.7 mile north-west of Boulder Lake. (Look for this lake between the 9,800- and 10,000-foot contour lines on the Phi Kappa Mountain USGS quad.) This Forest service trail is not shown on any recent map. While its beginning is unmarked, old signs can be found along its route, and some maintenance has taken place in recent years. Look for the trail in a sagebrush-filled clearing at the point where the Boulder Lake Trail crosses the 8,960-foot contour on the USGS quad. (In 1989, two rock cairns and a piece of blue flagging tape marked the start of the trail.) From its tenuous beginning, the trail switchbacks up the open slopes above and then turns due south to make a direct ascent to the unnamed lake. In a stand of stunted pines, you will find trail signs and a junction for another trail that leads northwest to Kane Creek. Keep left at this junction. The trail is generally well marked, with one or two minor exceptions. When you reach the lake, you may notice a sign identifying it as "Washington Lake."

(2) Fall Creek Trailhead. The trailhead is located a little over 2.0 miles south of the Wildhorse GS, or about 3.0 miles south of the Copper Basin road. This road once ran east for 3.0 miles to Fall Creek but is now closed after 0.5 mile. At this point, the Forest Service has installed a good foot bridge across Fall Creek to mark the beginning of the Fall Creek trail system.

(a) Fall Creek Trails. From the end of the road, trails reach up the Left Fork, Main Fork and Right Fork of Fall Creek. The Moose Lakes are 4.0 miles up FST-045 and FST-068. FST-045 continues past the Moose Lakes junction and leads to Surprise Valley and Surprise Lake. A fisherman's trail leads up Fall Creek Valley to the base of a spectacular headwall.

(a.1) FST-059, Left Fork Trail. This trail runs due east to FS-138 [Approach: (C)(3)(a.1)] in 9.0 miles.

(3) FS-138, Star Hope Creek Road. This road leaves the main Copper Basin Road 13.0 miles from its junction with the Trail Creek Road. Turn south at the sign announcing "Starhope Canyon." The road creeps over 10.0 miles south toward Glide Mountain before turning north and returning to the Copper Basin road. Drive 8.0 miles and turn right to reach the Broad Canyon Trailhead

(a) Star Hope Trails. This road provides access to a number of trails that extend into the more remote Pioneer cirques. These trails vary in quality, but are generally in fair condition.

(a.1) FST-059, Left Fork Trail. FST-059 leads from FS-138 east to FS-136 [Approach: (C)(2)(a.1)] in a little over 9.0 miles. The trail, which begins as a primitive road designated FS-472, passes over the rugged northern slopes of Big

Black Dome on its way east.

(a.2) FST-060, Bellas Lake Trail. This trail starts 5.0 miles south of the beginning of FS-138 and leads to Bellas Lakes near Pyramid Peak in 3.0 miles. Look for the trailhead at the Bellas Canyon CG.

(a.3) FST-061, Betty Lake Trail. Access FST-061 8.0 miles from the beginning of FS-138. This trail leads to Betty Lake and the Standhope Peak area in 4.5 miles. The Forest Service map incorrectly shows FST-061 as continuing on to Surprise Valley. Instead, the trail crosses a saddle between Betty and Baptie lakes and then loops back on itself.

(a.4) FST-062, Bear Canyon Trail. This trail runs due west to join FST-176 [Approach: (D)(1)(a)], which leads north to the Little Wood River and south to the Garfield GS. Access from FS-138 is at the Star Hope CG.

(b) FST-064, Lake Creek Trail. Take FS-138 to the Lake Creek Campground. The trail leaves the campground and proceeds to several lakes in the upper basin.

(D) US-20 Access Points.

This major east/west highway connects with ID-75 just south of Ketchum and runs east to Carey and Arco.

(1) Carey Area Roads. From Carey, a good gravel road leads into the Muldoon area, which was an active mining site in the recent past.

(a) Muldoon Area Trails. A number of seldom-used trails are accessed from this area. The most prominent is FST-176, which climbs up to the Pioneer Crest and gives good access to Glide Mountain and the upper reaches of the Little Wood River. FST-179 and FST-160 are accessed from the end of FS-130, which is about 3.0 miles northwest of the Garfield GS. FS-130 is a rough road that usually requires a 4WD. Both of these trails, which traverse seldom-visited country, provide access to Swede Peak and Mandolin Peak.

4. The White Knob Mountains

The White Knob Mountains are a compact group of sedimentary mountains located west of Mackay. The crest of the range runs east to west and is about 30 miles in length and 10 miles in width. The East Fork of the Big Lost River and the Big Lost River almost completely encircle the White Knob Mountains, forming the range's southern, western, northern and eastern boundaries. Antelope Creek completes the circle along the range's southern boundary as it flows from Antelope Pass to the Big Lost River.

Geologists believe that the range was originally uplifted by forces associated with the creation of the Idaho Batholith. The range is composed of limestones capped in most places by Challis Volcanics deposits. Four peaks reach above 11,000 feet and three other named peaks are higher than 10,000 feet. Shelly Mountain, at 11,278 feet, is the highest White Knob peak. The White Knobs are in the Pioneer Mountains' rain shadow and are consequently dry and mostly treeless.

The range is administered by the Challis National Forest and the Idaho Falls District of the BLM, which administers a large section of the range in the vicinity of Sheep Mountain on the range's eastern end. Mining activity has taken place in the past in the area just west of Mackay; currently, cattle grazing and sheep grazing are the primary uses.

Although there are only three maintained hiking trails in the range, the terrain is open and conducive to easy cross-country travel. The major peaks are windswept rock piles that present attractive Class 2 goals to weekend scramblers. Recreational use of the range is limited, not because the White Knobs are unattractive, but rather because few people know about the scenic quality of these massive peaks.

Porphyry Peak *10,012 feet (Class 3)*
Porphyry Peak, the northern- and western-most of the range's named peaks, is a puzzle of different volcanic rocks, including andesite lava flows, ash flows and intrusions of dacite. These volcanic rock types were deposited by the Challis Volcanics over a base of limestone. The surest approach is by way of the Copper Basin Road [Approach: (B)(1)] where it crosses Castle Creek. From the road, hike up Castle Creek until you are at approximately 8,000 feet. Turn east and climb out of the drainage to the peak's south ridge. Once on the ridge, climb directly to the summit. USGS Copper Basin 15-minute

Castle Rock *8,781 feet (Class 3)*
Castle Rock is located 2.2 miles southwest of Porphyry Peak; it is also accessed from FS-135 and Castle Creek. Hike up Castle Creek until the drainage forks at roughly 7,500 feet. Follow the left-hand drainage past the base of Castle Rock until you can climb to the ridge on the rock's north side. From the ridge, it is possible to climb the north side of the rock [Approach: (B)(1)]. USGS Copper Basin 15-minute

Mackay Peak *10,273 feet (Class 2)*
Mackay Peak is located 4.0 miles west of Mackay. Both the town and mountain where named for George Mackay, a mining entrepre-

Castle Rock (left) and Porphyry Peak anchor the western end of the White Knob Mountains

neur, who built a railroad from Blackfoot, Idaho to present-day Mackay in 1901 to exploit the region's mining potential. Numerous old mine shafts are still found on the eastern slopes of this peak, which is the northernmost summit on an impressive north/south ridge line that extends 8.0 miles south to Antelope Pass. The Mackay summit ridge has three summits and numerous granite outcroppings. The southeasternmost summit is the highest (but just barely). Climb the peak by following the mining roads that lead from FS-207 [Approach: (A)(3)] in Rio Grande Canyon to the peak's north ridge. Once on the ridge, climb roughly 1.0 mile south to the eastern (and highest) summit. Bypass the lower northern and middle summits on their northeastern sides. USGS Mackay 15-minute

White Knob Mountain 10,835 feet (Class 2)

White Knob Mountain is located 2.2 miles southwest of Mackay Peak. The true summit is southwest of the "White Knob" label on the USGS quad. The peak has two almost identical summits; the northern sumit is 30 feet higher than the southern one. The mountain can be climbed from the ridge line which connects it with Mackay Peak by working up its northeast face, or from the Mammoth Canyon Jeep Trail, which is accessed from the Alder Creek Road [Approach: (A)(2)]. USGS Mackay 15-minute

Cabin Mountain 11,224 feet (Class 2)

Cabin Mountain is situated 10.0 miles southeast of Porphyry Peak, between the Cabin and Corral Creek drainages. It has two summits, of which the easternmost is the highest. The peak can be climbed from almost any direction. Based on approach considerations, climb it from either its northwest ridge which rises out of Corral Creek [Approach: (B)(2)(a)] or via the ridge which connects Cabin Mountain with Lime Mountain. USGS Copper Basin 15-minute

Lime Mountain 11,179 feet (Class 2)

Lime Mountain is located 2.5 miles southwest of White Knob Peak and 0.8 miles due east of Cabin Mountain. Climb this peak via its northeast ridge from the pass at the head of Corral Creek. The route is steep but without major obstacles [Approach: (A)(2)(a)] or [Approach: (B)(2)(a)]. USGS Mackay 15-minute

Redbird Mountain 11,273 feet (Class 2)

This summit sits just 1.0 mile southeast of Lime Mountain and 0.75 mile north of Shelly Mountain. The summit is an easy scramble by either its east or south ridges. It is best to climb this peak in conjunction with a climb of Shelly Mountain. To climb the east ridge, take FS-144 [Approach: (A)(2)] up Alder Creek to Sawmill Canyon, and then follow the old jeep trail up to its end. From

205

this point, climb north to the steep east ridge and follow it to the summit. USGS Mackay 15-minute

Shelly Mountain   *11,278 feet (Class 2)*
The highest White Knob summit is located 4.5 miles north of Antelope Pass and 0.75 mile south of Redbird Mountain. The most direct approach is from Antelope Pass [Approach: (B)(1)] across Lupine Mountain and along the ridge that leads to Shelly Mountain's northwest slopes. This is a long 5.0 miles up and down, including an ascent of Lupine Mountain, which is directly on the route. Take plenty of water. USGS Mackay 15-minute

Lupine Mountain   *9,554 feet (Class 2)*
Lupine Mountain is located 2.0 miles southwest of Shelly Mountain and 3.0 ridge miles north of Antelope Pass. Climb via the broad ridge line from Antelope Pass, which can be accessed from Copper Basin [Approach: (B)(1)] or Antelope Creek [Approach: (A)(1)]. USGS Mackay 15-minute

Sheep Mountain   *9,649 feet (Class 2)*
Sheep Mountain is located 8.5 miles east of Lupine Mountain. It is the distinctive-looking, jagged summit to the north of the Antelope Creek Road. From the Antelope Creek Road, take the rugged dirt road (across BLM land) up the right fork of Waddoups Canyon [Approach: (A)(1.1)] till you reach a saddle just north of Point 7521 on the USGS quad. From the saddle, climb due north towards Point 8907. At 8,500 feet, contour around the side of the point to the saddle on its west side. From the saddle, climb the peak's southeast ridge to the summit. USGS Mackay 15-minute

APPROACHES TO THE WHITE KNOB MOUNTAINS

Approach routes for this section are referenced in the text by bracketed entries [Approach:], which include appropriate letter and number references.

The vehicle access to these mountains can only be rated as poor. 4WDs are recommended everywhere, and required in some places. Primary approach begins at Arco, Mackay or Ketchum.

(A) East Side Access Routes.

Primary approach on the east side of the range is via US-93 from Arco north to the Big Lost River Road north of Mackay. The write-ups below are listed from south to north.

(1) Antelope Creek Road. The combination of county and Forest Service roads known as Antelope Creek Road lead up Antelope Creek, over Antelope Pass and into Copper Basin [Approach: (B)(1)], which are the primary approach corridors along the southern portion of the White Knob Mountains. Turn off of US-93 9.0 miles north of Arco. A number of primitive roads leave the main road and head north into the eastern end of the range. At the end of Antelope Valley, FS-135 heads north up Bear Creek and Cherry Creek, then reaches windswept Antelope Pass. The sections of this road which climb to Antelope Pass are narrow, winding, rutted, and can be very slick after a rain.

(1.1) Waddoups Road. This road leaves Antelope Creek at a signed junction midway between US-93 and the Antelope GS. In Section 14 the road forks. Though not shown on the Challis National Forest map, the right fork is a fairly good road. Turn right on this fork and follow it past a set of water troughs to a saddle just north of Point 7521. A 4WD is recommended.

(2) FS-144, Alder Creek Road. Access this road just south of Mackay by turning off of US-93 23.9 miles north of Arco, or 2.5 miles south of Mackay. Follow the county road for 6.8 miles south to Alder Creek and then turn southwest on the Alder Creek Road. In another 2.0 miles, there is a wire gate near an old ranch. (The road crosses private land at this point, but is open to the public. Leave the gate as you find it.) Once the road reaches the National Forest boundary, it deteriorates quickly and a 4WD is recommended.

(a) FST-070, White Knob Divide Trail. FST-070 leaves FS-144 12.4 miles from US-93 and leads west from Alder Creek at Stewart Canyon and quickly crosses the ridge line just north of Lime Mountain; it then drops down to Corral Creek [Approach: (B)(2)(a)].

(b) FST-069, Sawmill Canyon Trail. This trail begins where Sawmill Creek empties into Alder Creek (11.5 miles from US-93). The trail, an old mining road, leads west for roughly 3.0 miles to the base of Redbird Mountain.

(3) FS-207, Rio Grande Canyon Road. This road, which is accessed directly from Mackay, proceeds west to the numerous mines that occupy this region. Drive southwest on Mackay's main street, leave town and quickly cross the Big Lost River. In 2.4 miles you will pass a junction for FST-144 (which provides an alternative route to Alder Creek). The road crosses another road in 2.0 more miles—go straight. The road continues up and eventually dies out on Mackay Peak's north shoulder in 6.7 miles. A 4WD is required for the upper stretches of this route.

(B) West Side Access Routes.
The Trail Creek/Big Lost River Road runs between Ketchum and US-93. It is the primary approach road on the range's west side.
(1) FS-135, Copper Basin Road. This road leaves the Big Lost River Road roughly 22.0 miles east of Ketchum and 19.0 miles west of US-93 and follows the East Fork of the Big Lost River east into Copper Basin, eventually crosses Antelope Pass and descends into Antelope Creek [Approach: (A)(1)]. This is a good road for passenger cars until it reaches Copper Basin GS, from which point it deteriorates rapidly.
(2) FS-142, The Burma Road. From the Copper Basin Road, FS-142 climbs over the crest of the White Knob Mountains and then descends toward the Mackay Fish Hatchery.
(a) Corral Creek Trails. FST-070 is the most important trail in these mountains. The trail climbs up Corral Creek to a high pass at 10,000 feet and provides the hiker and peakbagger with access to most of the range's high peaks. From the start of the Burma Road, drive uphill for 4.0 miles and turn onto the primitive road that runs up Corral Creek. Park where the road ends, or becomes too rough. From the pass, the trail descends to Alder Creek [Approach: (A)(2)(a)].

5. The Lost River Range

The Lost River Range stretches 70 miles from north to south between Challis and Arco. The Big Lost River Valley and Salmon River flank the range on the west, and the Little Lost River and Pahsimeroi River are along its east side. The range contains not only the highest point in Idaho, 12,655-foot Borah Peak, but also seven of the state's nine 12,000-foot peaks. While the entire range is designated as the Lost River Range, the northern reaches are also identified as the Pahsimeroi Mountains; an eastern subsidiary ridge is known as the Hawley Mountains.

The Lost River Range is a textbook example of a fault block mountain range. The range began to form 46 million years ago, as the earth's crust was stretched apart and the Lost River block began to rise in relation to the valley floors. This impressive escarpment is steepest on its western side, but impressive when viewed from either side. On the west side, the range rises precipitously for 5,000 feet without foothills. Because of this intense vertical relief, there are few basins to catch water, and no dependable water sources. The east side is more gradual, with many foothills and glacially carved basins. It is wetter, and has a few alpine lakes and several permanent streams. The

Pass Creek Canyon, on the west side of the range, is one of the most striking gorges in the state. The heart of the gorge is over a mile in length and 2,000 feet in depth.

The Lost River Range is administered in part by the Challis National Forest, the Salmon District of the Bureau of Land Management, and the Idaho Falls District of the BLM. The Forest Service generally controls the high peaks and the BLM controls the foothills of the Lost River Range; however, the entire Hawley Mountain group is administered by the BLM.

Because of its remoteness and spectacular scenery, the Forest Service recommended 119,864 acres in the central Lost River Range for wilderness designation. The proposal is currently on hold, but has a better than even chance of some day succeeding. Hikers will find that there are only a few trails in the Lost River Range, and those that do exist usually require a 4WD to approach their trailheads. Experienced cross-country hikers can travel the area, but the going is always difficult.

Although climbers come from all over the west to scale Borah because of its "highest peak" status, most of the other peaks in the range are seldom climbed, due mainly to inaccessibility and bad crumbly rock. Technical climbing is limited to a few Class 4 routes and winter mountaineering. Nevertheless, climbing in the range is a tremendous experience, and the Lost River peaks are among the most demanding in the state. Above-average driving ability, route-finding skills, climbing experience and perseverance are needed to test this range—which, except for the standard route on Borah Peak, is not for beginners.

THE PAHSIMEROI RANGE

The northern end of the Lost River Range is known as the Pahsimeroi Range. (There is no physical reason for this distinction.) This guidebook includes three named summits which are part of the Pahsimeroi, including the highest point, Dickey Peak, which reaches 11,140 feet.

Grouse Creek Mountain *11,085 feet (Class 2)*
This peak, located directly south of Sheep Pen Basin, is the second highest point in the Lost River Range north of Doublespring Pass. To climb the mountain, hike toward Sheep Pen Basin from the east along Mill Creek [Approach: (A)(6)]. At the 8,000-foot contour, leave the trail and hike up the steep slopes to Point 10383. From this point, the route runs directly to the peak's northeast ridge. USGS Doublespring 15-minute

McGowan Peak* *10,716 feet (Class 3-4)*

McGowan Peak is an unnamed peak which was utilized by the USGS when they mapped the region. Located 3.0 miles southwest of Grouse Creek Peak, it is identified as the McGowan VAMB station on the USGS quad. The peak is composed of Challis volcanic rocks overlying older sedimentary rocks, a formation typical of the Lost River Range's northern peaks. The primary problem in climbing the peak is the loose rock. Approaches are fairly easy from both the east and the west. From the east, approach on FST-086, which runs up Grouse Creek [Approach: (A)(6)(a)]. From the 8,400-foot contour, leave the trail and climb up the drainage that goes into the basin southeast of the peak. Although several options exist from this point, the recommended route leaves the basin at roughly the 9,200-foot contour, runs up to the peak's east ridge, and then follows the ridge to the summit. The western approach is from the McGowan Creek Road, which leaves US-93 north of Willow Creek Summit. Reportedly, it is possible to hike into the upper McGowan Creek basin from the end of the road and climb the peak via its west face. This route information is, however, unconfirmed. USGS Doublespring 15-minute

Dickey Peak *11,141 feet (Class 3)*

Dickey Peak, located 9.5 miles southeast of McGowan Peak and 2.0 miles east of Doublespring Pass, is the highest point in the Lost River Range's Pahsimeroi Mountains subrange. Approach this peak from US-93 by turning off the highway 4.5 miles north of the junction for Doublespring Pass. Follow this road east to a water tank and park. From this point, hike north for 1.5 miles and enter the peak's southwest drainage. Follow this drainage east until it forks. Keep to the right-hand fork and follow it up until you spot a gully leading directly toward the summit. Take care in this gully; it is reportedly full of loose rock. USGS Dickey Peak

Borah Peak *12,655 feet*

The highest point in Idaho is located 8.0 miles southeast of Dickey Peak. It is climbed by 200 to 300 people each year, almost all of whom use the southwest ridge route. There have been three fatalities on the peak. Considering the number of inexperienced climbers who attempt this peak each year, this is a low number. The climbers who died were experienced but tempted fate by challenging adverse conditions. In November of 1977, two Idaho Falls climbers were swept away and killed by an avalanche on the southwest ridge

route. In the spring of 1987, a Boise climber died after losing control of his glissade and going over a cliff. USGS Borah Peak

Southwest Ridge. *(Class 2)*

Take the approach road [Approach: (B)(2)] to its end and follow the well-worn path up the gully. Soon this path makes a sharp left turn and climbs up the forest slope to the treeless upper slopes. The route works up a west-east-trending ridge to a point just south of the summit, at 11,898 feet. From here, the route climbs the south ridge of Borah peak. Although many inexperienced people climb this route each year, do not underestimate it. The route climbs over 5,200 feet in less than 3.5 miles and there is a knife-edged ridge crossing at the meeting point of east/west ridge and the main Lost River crest (just below Point 11898). This crossing, which is often covered with snow, is treacherous. The last 600 feet of the route climb the steep southwest ridge over blocky terrain that will bother many people. Take plenty of water and expect the ascent to take between three and twelve hours, depending on the abilities of your party.

North Face *(Snow Climb).*

The unsurpassed north face of Borah rises over 2,000 feet from the top of the Rock Creek drainage. The face, especially when covered with snow, looks more like it belongs in the Canadian Rockies than in Idaho. The north face can be reached by following Rock Creek from the Doublesprings Pass Road [Approach: (B)(1)]. The route follows the 50-degree slopes up to the base of the 300-foot gully that splits the upper portion of the face. The gully is usually filled with snow and ice late into the summer. The technical difficulty in the gully varies with the ice conditions. The first ascent was probably made by L. Dye in 1973, and the first winter ascent was in February of 1977 by F. Florence, A. Troutner and M. Weber.

East Face. *(YDS 5.2)*

Climb this face from the notch on the northeast ridge (between the summit and Point 12247). Climb to the notch from Rock Creek, which is just to the north. The crux of the climb is the first 90-foot pitch out of the notch. The angle decreases and the holds improve above the first pitch. The first ascent was made in 1962 by L. Dye.

Sacajawea Peak* *11,936 feet*

This is the first major summit south of Borah Peak. It is located 1.1 miles south of that peak on the main Lost River Crest. USGS Elkhorn Creek

Northwest Ridge. *(Class 4)*

Follow the route description for Borah's southwest ridge route to the main divide at the false

Borah Peak, Idaho's highest summit

summit marked 11898 on the USGS map. From this point, follow the ridge line south to Sacajawea's northwest ridge. The ridge line involves several short pitches of Class 4 climbing.

Mount Idaho* *12,065 feet*

Mount Idaho is located 1.5 miles northeast of Pass Lake and 2.0 miles south of Borah Peak on the main crest of the Lost River Range. This pyramid-shaped peak is the seventh highest summit in the state and especially impressive when viewed from Merrian Lake or from Borah Peak. USGS Elkhorn Creek

North Ridge. *(Class 4)*

The peak's north ridge can be gained from Merrian Lake [Approach: (A)(5)(a.1)] or by descending from the Sacajawea summit. Both routes involve short pitches of Class 4 climbing on rotten rock.

Southwest Face. *(Class 3-4)*

To reach the face, follow Elkhorn Creek northeast from US-93 [Approach: (B)(3.1)]. This face is split by a fairly obvious gully. The route goes up the lower half of the gully and then moves out onto the face. First ascent by D. Millsap in 1963.

Peak 11967 *11,967 feet (Class 2)*

This impressive, but seldom climbed, summit is located 0.8 mile south of Mount Idaho. It is best approached from Elkhorn Creek [Approach: (B)(3.1)]. Hike up Elkhorn Creek until you reach the spot indicated by the 8,200-foot contour line on your USGS map. Climb to Point 9887, turn northeast and follow the peak's broad western slopes up to the summit cap at roughly 11,400 feet. From this point, the route stays mostly on the ridge line, with a couple of detours onto the north slopes. USGS Elkhorn Creek

Mount Obsession* *11,899 feet (Class 2)*

Mount Obsession is located just west of Leatherman Pass and 0.5 mile west of Leatherman Peak. An impressive, steep-sided summit when viewed from almost any angle, it rises almost 2,000 feet above Pass Lake. The first winter ascent was by W. March and R. Albano in 1975; March rated the winter snow and rock climb Class 4. USGS Elkhorn Creek

March's route is the only reported route on the peak. It begins at Leatherman Pass [Approach: (A)(5)(a)] and runs up the peak's incredibly loose talus slopes to the summit. The route is straightforward, with no obstacles other than loose rock.

Mount Corruption* *11,857 feet (Class 3)*

Mount Corruption is located east of the main divide, 3.0 miles north of Mount Breitenbach. The peak's position on a subsidiary ridge makes this isolated summit seem even bigger than it actually is. The name is evidently derived from the peak's broken rock walls. The peak can be climbed from the East Fork of the Pahsimeroi [Approach: (A)(5)(b)]. Leave the East Fork Trail at approximately the 8,400-foot contour, cross the East Fork (difficult in early season) and ascend the wide gully that runs northeast directly to the summit. USGS Leatherman Peak

Leatherman Peak *12,228 feet*

This peak, the second highest mountain in the state, is located 4.5 miles southeast of Borah Peak. When viewed from ID-93, the summit is much more ostentatious than Mount Borah because its steep west face is closer to the road. Unlike Borah, it is impossible to find solid rock on Leatherman Peak. It is a 12,000-foot tower of crumbling Lost River rock. USGS Leatherman Peak

West Ridge. *(Class 3)*
Reach the west ridge from Leatherman Pass [Approach: (B)(5)(a)], which can be reached from the Pahsimeroi, Sawmill Gulch and Lone Cedar Creek drainages. The climb from the pass gains more than 1,600 feet over steep talus-covered slopes, over and around several fractured rock towers. Climbing without dislodging rock is difficult.

W. March and R. Albano made the first winter ascent in 1975 via the west ridge; they rated the climb YDS 5.3. This party descended via the east ridge.

Southwest Face. *(Class 3-4)*
From Lone Cedar Creek [Approach: (B)(3.2)], climb to the saddle between Leatherman Creek and Bad Rock Peak. From the saddle, climb up and across the face and aim for a point 100 feet below the summit. From this point, climb straight up on rotten Class 4 rock to the top. The first ascent was by L. Dye in 1962.

Bad Rock Peak* *11,953 feet (Class 3)*

This is the next peak south of Leatherman Peak on the main Lost River Crest. From Lone Cedar Creek [Approach: (B)(3.2)], climb to the saddle between Leatherman and Bad Rock, then follow the easy northwest ridge to the summit. USGS Leatherman Peak

Mount Church* *12,200+ feet (Class 3)*

This peak, unnamed on the USGS quad, is the third highest peak in Idaho. The summit is located 1.5 miles southeast of Leatherman Peak. Although the summit is not officially named, this is a very impressive mountain, which was probably first climbed in the 1920s. A rock cairn on the summit is graced with two summit registers and an axe handle, which has evidently been on the summit for many years. One register recorded a summit climb in 1951 and a climb by a large group from a Pocatello family in 1975. The 1975 group named the peak for their son—Ken Williams Peak. However, the name probably does not meet USGS naming criteria set up by the federal government for naming peaks (see the Introduction). The peak is unofficially named for the late Idaho Senator Frank Church. USGS Leatherman Peak

East Ridge. *(Class 3)*
The east ridge is mostly a scramble with the exception of two short steps that involve easy climbing—reaching the east ridge is the difficult proposition. Reaching the peak from either the east or west sides of the range first involves climbing nearly to the summit of Donaldson Peak. From the west, drive to the base of Jones Creek [Approach: (B)(3.3)] and then hike up the creek bottom (which has recently washed out) to the base of Donaldson Peak. Climb the steep talus slopes to the saddle just west of this peak and then contour around and up to the small pond in the cirque between the two peaks. Catch your breath as you marvel at how vertical the talus is in this eerie cirque, and then climb due east toward the large gully. To avoid Class 4 climbing in the gully, work around the base of the cliff to the east and climb a series of talus-filled ramps to the ridge line just west of Donaldson Peak. It's less than ten minutes to the top of Donaldson from this point—so, before continuing on to Mount Church, you might as well follow the ridge south to the top of Donaldson. From the east side of the range, make your approach via the East Fork of the Pahsimeroi River [Approach: (A)(5)(b)]. Follow the drainage up to its upper basin and Lake 9682. From Lake 9682, climb the steep slopes to Donaldson Peak's northeast ridge. Climb over Donaldson's summit and then follow the ridge line north to Church.

Northeast Face *(Snow Climb).*
This route is recommended only when stable snow conditions are present. In an average snow year, the northeast face holds snow late into the summer. This snow rarely forms into ice, but climbers should be prepared for that possibility. The approach is via the East Fork of the Pahsimeroi [Approach: (A)(5)(b)]. Begin at Lake 9682,

Mount Church, viewed from Donaldson Peak

northeast of the summit, and climb the 35- to 50-degree snowfield directly toward the summit. As you near the summit, there are several places where you can access the east ridge. To avoid loose rock, take the ridge and follow it to the summit.

Donaldson Peak* *12,023 feet*

Although the name has not yet shown up on the USGS quad, this peak, the eighth highest in Idaho, is officially named after the late Chief of the Idaho Supreme Court, Charles Russell Donaldson. The summit is located on the main crest, 0.7 mile east of Mount Church and 1.25 miles west of Mount Breitenbach. The peak a beautiful summit, with an extremely precipitous southwest ridge and south face. The first ascent of the peak is unknown, but the first winter ascent was made by W. March and R. Albano in 1975 via the west face and south ridge. They rated the climb YDS 5.3. USGS Leatherman Peak

West Ridge. *(Class 3)*

For approach directions, refer to the East Ridge route description for Mount Church. Once you gain the main Lost River crest, it is an easy walk up the east ridge of Donaldson to the summit. The route stays on the north side of the ridge for the first section of the ridge, then crosses to the south side for the last short approach to the summit.

No Regret Peak* *11,972 feet (Class 2)*

The main divide of the Lost River Range turns abruptly east on the summit of Donaldson Peak and runs east for 0.8 mile to the summit of No Regret Peak, where it once again turns southeast and runs for 0.75 mile to Mount Breitenbach. The only known approach to the summit is via its southwest ridge. Either follow the ridge over from Donaldson Peak or climb to the ridge line from Lake 9682, which is northwest of the peak [Approach: (A)(5)(b)]. USGS Leatherman Peak

Mount Breitenbach *12,140 feet*

The fifth highest point in Idaho is a massive summit that rests on the main crest at the heads of the Pahsimeroi River and Dry Creek. The peak was named for Jake Breitenbach, who died during the 1963 American Everest Expedition. Idaho mountaineer Lyman Dye, who learned his mountaineering skills from Jake in the Tetons in the early 1960s, successfully petitioned the Governor of Idaho and the USGS to officially adopt the name. USGS Leatherman Peak

USGS Peak, which sits between Shadow Lake Peak and Mount McCaleb, is one of the Lost River Range's most remote and most interesting summits.

South Ridge. *(Grade II, Class 3)*
The easiest route to the summit is from Pete Creek [Approach: (B)(3.3)]. Hike up the creek to the southern slopes. Climb the huge gully on the face and then climb to the east flange of the south ridge, which leads to the summit. Though not as difficult as the other routes, this is an extremely long and demanding route.

North Face. *(Class 6)*
As reported in the *American Alpine Journal*, the north face was climbed by B. Boyles, M. Weber and C. Olsen in 1982. The party used direct aid to overcome the crux. Given the steepness of the face and the fragility of the rock, this climb was quite an accomplishment. The north face is reached via Dry Creek [Approach: (A)(3)].

East Face. *(Class 3)*
Follow the Dry Creek drainage to its uppermost reaches [Approach: (A)(3)]. Turn east and climb into the east-facing cirque. Once within the cirque, climb the slopes to the northeast and gain the east summit. From the east summit, walk to the true summit.

Lost River Mountain* *12,078 feet*

This peak, the sixth highest summit in Idaho, is on the main Lost River Crest and is located 1.8 miles southeast of Mount Breitenbach. The peak has a long north/south summit ridge with two summits, both of which reach over 12,000 feet. The southern summit is slightly higher than the more difficult northern summit. USGS Leatherman Peak

South Face Super Gully. *(Grade II, Class 3)*
Access this climb from Upper Cedar Creek [Approach: (B)(3.41)] via the large, spectacular southeast-facing gully that cuts the peak's southeast face. Start the climb from the end of the road by climbing directly toward Point 8881. At 8,600 feet, traverse north across a gully to a large rib, which you can follow northeast to the base of a gully. Due to terrible loose rock and stonefall, this route is best climbed before the gully's snow melts (assuming that avalanche conditions are not present). The Super Gully is a bowling alley and the stonefall can be deadly. Plan your climb so that you are up and down the gully before it thaws out. Once you are on the summit ridge, it is an easy (although exposed) walk to the summit.

Northeast Ridge. *(Class 3-4)*
This ridge divides the two forks of Dry Creek. Hike up the easternmost fork of Dry Creek [Approach: (A)(3)]. Once above treeline, climb west to the ridge top. Follow the ridge to the top of the northernmost summit and then hike the summit ridge to reach the higher southern summit. This route gets steeper and more rugged as it

nears the northern summit. The route is passable, but hard to find.

Massacre Mountain *10,924 feet*

Massacre is a massive mountain with a long summit ridge, which separates its northern and southern summits by over 1.5 miles. The southern summit is the highest point but both summits are worthy goals. The long and strenuous ridge walk between the two summits is especially rewarding.

North Summit. *(Class 2)*
The north summit, which reaches 10,824 feet, can be reached by climbing up the peak's west slopes from Long Lost Creek [Approach: (A)(3)]. Leave the Long Lost Creek where the 8,040-foot contour line crosses Dry Creek. Cross the creek and climb up the intermittent creek drainage that flows into Long Lost Creek from the east. Once the drainage steepens, leave it and gain the ridge line to the south, which climbs to the summit. For those interested in making a ski ascent of the mountain, a second, but longer route begins in the Squaw Creek drainage far to the northeast [Approach: (A)(3.12)] and, via several 4WD roads, provides access to the broad saddle north of the summit. From this saddle, the route climbs through the trees at the base of Point 10382 and climbs to that point up steep but open slopes. Once Point 10382 is reached, the route follows the ridge line south over Point 10416 and makes a final climb up to the summit.

South Summit. *(Class 2)*
Climb the highest Massacre summit from Long Lost Creek [Approach: (A)(3)(a)] by following FST-194 and FST-092 to the 8,800-foot contour on the USGS map. From this point, leave the trail and climb through the trees to the north and the summit's west ridge. Once on the ridge, follow it directly to the summit.

Castle Peak *10,957 feet (Class 2)*

The point named Castle Peak on the Massacre Mountain USGS quad forms a walled promontory south of the deep, U-shaped pass that separates Upper Cedar Creek from Long Lost Creek. The summit, which is impressive from most sides, is actually a spur of a higher summit, USGS Peak, which is located just to the south. The peak is best climbed from the pass, which is reached via Upper Cedar Creek [Approach: (B)(3.4)] or Long Lost Creek [Approach: (A)(3)(a)]. There are no obstacles from the pass to the summit. USGS Massacre Mountain

USGS Peak* *11,982 feet (Class 3)*

This beautiful peak, which displays its sedimentary layering on a grand scale, is named to honor the United States Geological Survey. It is located 1.3 miles south of Castle Peak and is identified as the McCaleb triangulation station on the USGS quad. Hike up Lower Cedar Creek [Approach: (B)(3.5)(a)] to the base of a large gully that is almost directly southeast of the summit. Follow this gully up, avoiding the cliffs on its south side, into the upper cirque. The west wall of this cirque contains two large gully systems that lead southwest. Climb either of these to the south summit ridge and then follow the ridge to the summit. USGS Massacre Mountain

Shadow Lake Peak* *11,401 feet (Class 2)*
This large pyramid-shaped peak, which towers over the head of Dry Creek, is unnamed on the USGS quad. It is located 1.7 miles northeast of Castle Peak, and is sometimes referred to by the above name. Climb the peak by its southeast ridge from Shadow Lake [Approach: (A)(3)(b)]. The route, a long scramble, crosses long stretches of loose talus. The views from the summit are nothing short of spectacular. USGS Massacre Mountain

THE HAWLEY MOUNTAINS
The Hawley Mountains are a subrange of the Lost River Range formed by a ridge line that parallels the main Lost River Crest. Located east of the main crest in the Little Lost River Valley, this subsidiary ridge is roughly 10 miles long. Hawley Mountain, at 9,752 feet, is its highest point. The entire subrange is administered by the BLM, who studied it in 1982 for possible inclusion under the Wilderness Act. At this point, it is doubtful that the area will ever receive wilderness designation.

Hawley Mountain *9,752 feet*
Although not a high mountain by Lost River Range standards, Hawley Mountain dominates the Little Lost River Valley because it sits away from the main crest, almost in the center of the valley. The peak sits 22.0 miles due east of Mount Idaho and 5.0 miles southwest of Clyde. The name honors the Hawley family, who were among the first settlers in the Little Lost Area. USGS Hawley Mountain 15-minute

Northwest Ridge. *(Class 2)*
This route leaves from the point where the Wet Creek Road [Approach: (A)(2)] crosses Wet Creek. Climb the steep bluffs above Wet Creek until you reach the high rolling ridge which climbs to the west. Follow the ridge to the lower treeline, and then work your way up through the forest. From treeline, the route works up the large, unstable talus slopes to the summit.

Northeast Ridge. *(Class 2)*
This route is shorter, but requires a 4WD. Starting from the same point as the Northwest Ridge Route, drive east for 200 yards and take the first road south that climbs up the steep bank. At the top of the bank, the road forks; keep to the right and follow the road to its end. This will bring you to a water trough close to the lower treeline. Park here and hike to the Douglas fir stand to your left. Cross into the forest and climb up until you reach the ridge top. From here, follow the ridge until it brings you to treeline. From treeline, climb across the talus and block-covered slope to the main east ridge. From this point, take the east ridge to the summit.

Mount McCaleb *11,640+ feet*
This domineering peak was named after a teamster who was killed by Indians in the late 1800s. The peak's impressive south face, visible from US-93, is identified by a highway sign along the road just south of the Mackay town limits. The elevation given on the map is not for the summit, but for the USGS triangulation station, which was located on a point south of the true summit. USGS Mackay 15-minute

West Ridge. *(Class 2)*
Approach the peak from Mackay via the Lower Cedar Creek Road [Approach: (B)(3.5)]. When the road forks, turn left and follow the roadway along the Cedar Creek irrigation ditch. Leave the road due south of the summit and climb the north/south gully to the west ridge and follow the ridge to the summit.

East Face. *(Class 4)*
Approach via the Lower Cedar Creek Road [Approach: (B)(3.5) (a)] and lower Cedar Creek. Continue up the drainage until it is possible to traverse to the base of the first major gully (which cuts the peak's east face) is reached. Follow this steep gully, which is very brushy at first, up to the base of the face. The route on the face follows an obvious couloir up the face and involves several pitches of moderate Class 4 climbing. The couloir holds significant amounts of snow and ice into late June. First ascent by L. Dye, A. Barnes and W. Boyer.

East Ridge. *(Class 3)*
Use the same approach as listed for the East Face route. Instead of crossing to the face, continue on to the east ridge. As you follow the ridge toward the summit, it melds into the northeast side of the east face. The last 100 feet are quite steep. Early-summer climbs will require an ice axe to cut through the summit cornice.

Wet Peak* *11,309 feet (Class 3)*
Wet Peak is located 3.0 miles due east of Mount McCaleb and is identified on the USGS quad as the Wet triangulation station. The summit is accessed from Bear Creek Lake, which is reached from the Pass Creek Road [Approach: (B)(4)] or [Approach: (A)(2)]. From Bear Lake, climb due east into the upper basin, which contains a tarn. Continue on to the saddle, then turn south and climb the ridge line. Follow the ridge northwest to the summit. USGS Mackay 15-minute

Invisible Mountain *11,330 feet (Class 2-3)*
Invisible Mountain is located 2.25 miles southeast of Wet Peak. Access the route from Mahogany Gulch [Approach: (B)(3.6)]. Leave Mahogany Gulch at the point where it enters the mountains (at roughly the 6,800-foot contour) and gain the long south ridge of Invisible Mountain. It is 3.0 miles, with 4,600 feet of elevation gain, to the summit. USGS Mackay 15-minute

Sunset Peak *10,693 feet (Class 2)*
This peak is, perhaps, the most important southern summit in the Lost River Range, as it forms the headwaters of three major drainages. Although a dominant summit, the pyramid-shaped peak is not easily spotted from the valley floor. The peak, which is situated 7.0 miles east of Invisible Mountain, can be reached from almost any direction, but only the southern approach via Elbow Canyon is short enough to be practical [Approach: (B)(4.1)]. Follow the Mud Lake Road into the mountains until it forks and take the left (north) fork. When the road ends, continue up the drainage to the peak's west face. Climb up to the west ridge and follow it to the summit. USGS Sunset Peak

Jaggle Peak* *10,772 feet (Class 2)*
Jaggle Peak is identified on the USGS quad as a triangulation station. It is located 6.0 miles south of Sunset Peak. The summit forms one of the

Mount McCaleb's south face, a complex series of towers, faces, and gullies, has seen little climbing activity.

many seldom-visited high points in the southern stretches of the Lost River Range. Approach from the Little Lost River valley via Cabin Fork Creek [Approach: (A)(1)]. Follow the drainage to the north face of the peak and then turn west and climb to the saddle north of the summit. From the saddle, follow the ridge line to the summit. USGS Sunset Peak

King Mountain *10,612 feet (Class 3)*

King Mountain, the last major summit along the Lost River Crest, sits 8.5 miles south of Jaggle Peak. The peak is an easy walk from any number of directions, but is best approached from the west and the road in King Canyon [Approach: (B)(5)]. Follow the two-track road east for roughly 1.0 mile, park and hike cross country into King Canyon. Follow the canyon uphill until you are at 8,400 feet, and then climb to the top of the southwest ridge. Once on the ridge, follow it to the summit. USGS Ramshorn Canyon

APPROACHES TO THE LOST RIVER RANGE

Approach routes for this section are referenced in the text by bracketed entries [Approach:], which include appropriate letter and number references.

Lost River approaches are difficult and often require lots of time and a 4WD vehicle. The range can be reached from Idaho Falls, Idaho by taking US-20 to Arco. Hard-to-come-by BLM Planning Unit maps are the best guides available for traversing the many dirt roads that approach this range.

(A) East Side Approaches.

Just south of Arco, ID-33 leaves US-20 and runs east to Howe. At Howe, take the Pahsimeroi Highway north through the Little Lost and Pahsimeroi valleys. Most of the Little Lost Valley is managed by the BLM and is open to the public. From Howe to Clyde, the alluvial fans that stretch down from the mountains are crisscrossed by both gravel and primitive roads, which lead up to the bottoms of almost every Lost River canyon.

(1) FS-124 and FS-446, Cabin Fork/Cedarville Roads. This route leaves the Pahsimeroi Highway just north of Howe and climbs the broad alluvial fan toward Cedarville Canyon. The road splits at 12.5 miles; the north fork enters Cabin Fork canyon and the south fork climbs up Cedarville canyon.

(2) FS-122, Wet Creek Road. This road leaves the Pahsimeroi highway 28.0 miles north of Howe (at Clyde) and follows Wet Creek into the mountains. The road crosses the range at Pass Creek Summit and drops down to Mackay in 39.0 miles. [Approach: (B)(4)].

(3) FS-118, Dry Creek Road. To reach this road, take the Wet Creek Road west from Clyde. In 4.0 miles the road crosses Wet Creek. Just after the crossing, the road climbs a gravel bench. Go right at the junction; in 1.0 mile the road crosses the Dry Creek Canal. Just past this crossing, take the road that follows the canal into Dry Creek. At the end of the canal, take the road that climbs up the south side of the canyon and then follow it into the upper sections of Dry Creek. The road gets a little rugged after passing the ruins of the Dry Creek Dam (the collapse of which is responsible for the ravaged condition of the Dry Creek drainage).

(a) FST-194, Long Lost Creek Trail. Above the dam ruins, the road splits. Take the left fork to its end in 3.0 miles. FST-194 heads up the canyon and eventually crosses the divide and drops into Upper Cedar Creek. This trail is not maintained.

(b) FST-092, Shadow Lake Trail. This trail turns off FST-194 1.0 mile from the road's end. Shadow Lake is located in an grandiose box canyon.

(c) FST-091, Dry Creek Trail. Keep to the right when the road forks, crossing Dry Creek. From the road's end, this trail goes upstream and then climbs up to Swauger Lakes. Experienced cross-country travelers can follow the trail down into Long Lost Creek.

(3.1) Dry Creek Cutoff Road. This road turns off the Wet Creek Road 6.3 miles west of Clyde, just after that road crosses a cattle guard. Turn right, immediately cross a second cattle guard and follow the relatively smooth road into a narrow gulch. This road provides an alternative route into the upper reaches of Dry Creek as well as accessing the remote Buck Springs drainage. (This road should not be confused with the Dry Creek Road that follows the Dry Creek Flume and Dry Creek.)

(3.12) Buck Springs Road. This rough 4WD road should only be driven when it is thoroughly dried out. The road leaves the Dry Creek Cutoff Road 5.8 miles from Wet Creek and then descends to Buck Creek at a meadow with an old cabin. From the meadow, the road climbs up the drainage and eventually splits. Take the right fork and continue to follow it for a total of 4.5 miles to the saddle below the north peak of Massacre Mountain where it ends.

(4) FS-116, Doublespring Pass Road. At Goldberg, the Pahsimeroi Highway splits, each fork

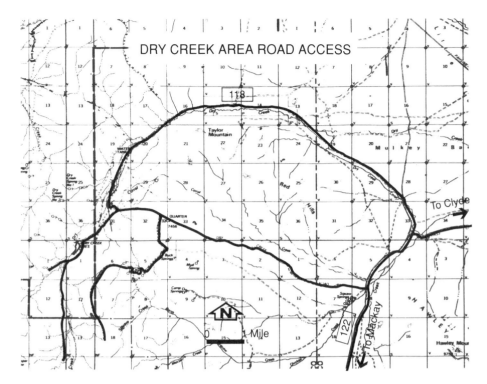

DRY CREEK AREA ROAD ACCESS

following its side of the valley northward. Take the west side fork to the signed junction. Doublespring Pass, 8,318 feet, is usually passable for passenger vehicles.

(5) FS-118, Pahsimeroi Headwaters Road. This road begins at the same point as the Doublespring Road. It runs up to the base of the range, where it splits. FS-117 travels north and joins the Doublespring Road, while FS-118 runs into the mountains containing the east and west forks of the Pahsimeroi River. This is a difficult road; a high-clearance vehicle is a necessity.

(a) FST-089, West Fork Trail. If you can get to the trailhead, this is a super trail which leads to two beautiful lakes, Pass Lake and Merrian Lake. It is also the best approach to Leatherman Peak and Mount Idaho. The trail, which is in good shape, runs to Leatherman Pass in 3.5 miles.

(a.1) FST-197, Merriam Lake Trail. This trail leaves FST-089 just past the trailhead and runs to the lake in 1.5 miles.

(a.2) FST-198, Pass Lake Trail. This trail leads from FST-089 to Pass Lake in about 1.0 mile. The trail's tread is only so-so, but the route is easy to follow.

(b) FST-090, East Fork Trail. This trail receives very little use, but does lead into the high basins below Mount Church and Donaldson Peak.

(6) FS-112, Grouse Creek/Mill Creek Road. This road connects the mountains to the south with the village of May. After entering the mountains, the road forks. The right fork climbs Grouse Creek, where it ends at a trailhead for FST-086. The left fork goes a short distance up Mill Creek. A livestock trail leads up this drainage to Sheep Pen Basin at the base of Grouse Creek Mountain.

(a) FST-086, Grouse Creek Trail. This trail is no longer shown on the newest Challis National Forest map. The trail, which is still passable, begins at the end of FS-112 and runs south for 6.0 miles to a small lake that sits between Grouse Creek Mountain and Mount McGowan.

(B) West Side Approaches.

US-93 runs north and south between Arco and Challis, on the west side of the range. The following roads are listed from north to south.

(1) FS-116, Doublespring Pass Road. This road leaves US-93 north of Mackay and runs due north to cross the Lost River Range at Doublespring Pass (8,318 feet). (Also see the write-up for [Approach: (A)(3)], above.)

(2) Mount Borah Trailhead. Access this trailhead from US-93 20.0 miles north of Mackay, just south of the Doublespring Road turn. The road is signed and well maintained, but rough.

(3) Mount Borah to Pass Creek Roads. This area is mostly BLM land and is crisscrossed by numerous roads that lead up to the mountains. A BLM land status map is helpful for finding your way. While a 4WD is not essential, the added security may be desirable. Here are descriptions of the most important of these access points.

(3.1) Elkhorn Creek. Access up Elkhorn Creek begins at US-93, roughly 0.3 miles south of where the Big Lost River Road runs east toward Ketchum. Park along the highway and follow the drainage up toward the base of the mountains to access the peaks between Borah and Leatherman Peak.

(3.2) Lone Cedar Creek Road. This road leaves US-93 11.0 miles north of Mackay and runs roughly 2.0 miles northeast at the base of the mountains. From the road's end, it is possible to hike the drainage up to Leatherman Pass, which is another 3.5 miles.

(3.3) Jones Creek/Pete Creek Road. This road leaves US-93 9.0 miles north of Mackay. Turn off the highway, go through the cattle guard and follow the road toward the base of the mountains. In 2.1 miles, turn east on an obvious road; follow this road for 0.4 mile and then once again turn toward the mountains. The main road goes to Jones Creek, where it ends. To reach Pete Creek, park just before the road ends and follow the base of the mountains toward the east. Pete Creek is the next major drainage in that direction.

(3.4) Upper Cedar Creek Road. This road leaves US-93 6.1 miles north of Mackay and runs northeast for 4.0 miles. The road starts out as a broad gravel road, but narrows considerably after it crosses through a fence line onto private property. Follow the road past an abandoned house to a second gate. Pass through this gate and you will soon encounter a broad irrigation ditch, which will be difficult to cross without a 4WD. Once past the ditch, the road leads directly to the mouth of Upper Cedar Creek. Once upon a time, a Forest Service trail ran up Cedar Creek, crossed over the Lost River crest and dropped into Long Lost Creek. Parts of this trail still exist, but those venturing into this country should have good cross-country travel skills.

(3.41) Lost River Mountain Access. Cross the irrigation ditch described in (3.4) and turn sharply left to follow the road that parallels the ditch for 0.1 mile. Turn right and follow the 4WD road until it ends, at the point where the 7,480-foot contour crosses the intermittent stream that drains the south face of Lost River Mountain.

(3.5) Lower Cedar Creek Road. Access this road directly from Mackay. From the center of town, drive east on the Bench Road for 1.85 miles, turn left toward the mountains and follow the

primitive two-track road due north to a fork in 0.9 mile. Go right at this fork, which leads around a private field. In roughly 3.0 miles, the road drops into the Lower Cedar Creek drainage and ends. A half mile before the end of the Cedar Creek Road, look for a road which forks very sharply to your left. This road climbs the bench to the west. Once on the bench, it follows the irrigation ditch to the west to gain access to the west side of Mount McCaleb.

(a) Lower Cedar Creek Cross-country Route. At the end of the Lower Cedar Creek Road, you must immediately wade a wide, deep canal. From the far bank, walk 25 feet to your right and then climb up the slope for roughly another 25 feet to an abandoned canal. Follow the course of this canal into the canyon until it ends near a stream-gauging device. From this point, the route follows the course of a dilapidated steel-wrapped wooden pipe upstream. The stream bottom is extremely difficult going in places—impossible during high water—and crosses some of the wildest terrain in the state. Expert cross-country skills are essential.

(3.6) Mahogany Gulch Road. Access this road from Mackay via the Bench Road; see (3.5) above. Turn left onto this road 2.0 miles from Mackay and follow it until it ends in Mahogany Gulch 2.0 miles ahead. Walk, or if you must drive, take a 4WD!

(4) FS-122, Pass Creek Road. Leave US-93 at Leslie, cross the railroad tracks and then turn north sharply. The road soon turns toward the mountains and enters Pass Creek Canyon and its rugged gorge. The road can also be accessed from Mackay via the Bench Road, which leaves town from the center of Mackay.

(a) FST-093, Bear Creek Trail. Follow the Pass Creek Road for 9.5 miles from US-93 to a small, signed road which leads up Bear Creek. Follow the road to its end. The trail leads 2.5 miles to Bear Creek Lake. This trail provides the best access to Wet Peak and passable access to Invisible Peak.

(4.1) Mud Lake Road. This road leaves Pass Creek just south of Bear Creek and climbs up to the divide. From a recent report, the road is better used as a trail. The road eventually climbs up to the crest of the range near Sunset Peak.

(5) King Canyon Road. Access this road from US-93 by turning east at Moore. Drive east nearly 2.0 miles to the gravel road that parallels US-93 along the base of the Lost River Range. Turn left (north) on this road and follow it for 1.25 miles to an intersection and a small gravel pit. Turn east and follow the two-track road uphill. Walk, or use a 4WD.

6. The Lemhi Range

The Lemhi Range is a linear mountain chain that runs from Salmon in a southeasterly direction for 100 miles to the Snake River plain. It varies in width from 10 to 15 miles. The Pahsimeroi and Little Lost River valleys border the range on its western side, and the Lemhi and Birch Creek valleys parallel its eastern side.

The Lemhis are a fault block range composed of hard dolomites, limestone and crumbling volcanic rocks. Glaciation along the crest has carved the relatively soft rock at will. While many peaks are nothing more than incredible piles of talus, others are solid blocks that present impressive faces to the valleys below. The crest of the range rises at least a mile above the broad alluvial valleys that flank it, staying above 10,000 feet in elevation. The northern section of the range is a wilderness (so far without official designation) of high peaks, remote valleys and many mountain lakes. The central sections of the Lemhis are narrower, steeper and drier than the north; they contain the range's most impressive peaks: 12,197-foot Diamond Peak and 11,618-foot Bell Mountain. The southern end of the Lemhi Range, south of Saddle Mountain, is a semi-desert region characterized by deep canyons and massive cliffs. The two most impressive of these canyons are Box and East canyons. Box Canyon is a winding canyon that has several archeological sites and some impressive cliffs. East Canyon, located north of Box Canyon, is most noted for its tremendous limestone cliffs, the largest of which is capped by a large natural bridge. These canyons were used extensively by early Indians; more than eighteen major archeological sites have been identified in this area.

The foothills and lower slopes of the Lemhi Range are administered in the north by the Salmon District of the BLM, and in the south by the Idaho Falls District of the BLM. Three national forests share the backbone of the range. The Salmon National Forest manages the entire northernmost 25 miles of the Lemhis and the eastern side of the crest south to Sheep Mountain. The Challis National Forest manages the remaining western side of the crest south to the Snake River Plain; the Targhee National Forest administers the southern half of the Lemhis east of the crest.

Hiking opportunities abound; in the northern part of the range, an extensive trail system features some of the best hiking in the state. The southern part of the range has few trails, but is open and conducive to cross-country travel. Recreational use of the range is limited because few Lemhi Range trailheads are accessible without a 4WD.

Climbing opportunities within the range, for the most part, fall within the Class 2 to 4 categories, with the majority of the routes rated Class 2. Technical climbing is limited due to the broken condition of the Lemhi limestone. Winter mountaineering will involve long approaches up to the bases of the mountains. While snowfall is not excessive on the alluvial fans, the wind generally blows the snow into drifts which prevent vehicle access and leave much of the ground bare and unsuitable for skiing. While there are no recorded winter ascents in the Lemhis, some have undoubtedly occurred.

Sal Mountain *9,592 feet (Class 1)*

This big peak in the northern Lemhi Range sits 11.0 miles south of Salmon, where it dominates the area between the Salmon River Valley and the Lemhi Valley. The peak was a Forest Service Lookout in the 1920s. A trail leads to the summit [Approach: (A)(8)]. Take the Withington Creek Road to its end and then follow the trail past the Harmony Mine to the summit. USGS Salmon 15-minute

Lem Peak *10,985 feet*

This impressive mountain is a jagged peak on the Lemhi crest 16.0 miles south of Sal Mountain. Lem Peak has four ridges, all of which are climbable. USGS Lem Peak

Northwest Ridge Route. *(Class 3)*
Gain the summit from the pass to the northwest. This is a relatively short scramble of 800 feet over loose, broken, and sometimes steep slopes. This pass can be reached via an old mining road up Allison Creek [Approach: (B)(2)] on the west side, or by the Bear Valley Creek Trail on the east side [Approach: (A)(7.1)(a)].

Long Mountain *10,696 feet (Class 2-3)*

Long Mountain is located 5.0 miles south of Lem Peak on the main Lemhi crest. There is no easy approach to this isolated summit. Approach via FST-071 [Approach: (C)(1)(a)], which runs northeast up the North Fork of Morgan Creek. When the trail ends, continue cross country to the top of the drainage. From a point 0.5 mile below the small lake at the top of the drainage, climb up to the large northwest-facing shelf that leads to the peak's south ridge and then follow the ridge to the summit. USGS May 15-minute

May Mountain *10,971 feet (Class 3-4)*

May Mountain is the sharp sedimentary summit that sits 2.5 miles due south of Long Mountain on the main Lemhi crest. The route to the summit

May Mountain

begins along the East Fork of Morgan Creek and FST-071 [Approach: (C)(1)(b)]. Leave the trail where it crosses the saddle southwest of the summit (and just east of Point 8140 on your USGS quad). Work your way northwest to the Lemhi crest 0.8 mile south of the summit. Follow this ridge north to the base of the summit pyramid and begin your climb on its western side, just below the ridge crest. This route climbs up for roughly 500 feet on loose talus and disintegrating ledges until a Class 4 wall in a V-shaped alcove blocks further progress. From this point, there are two options. The first climbs the Class 4 wall. Start on its south side and traverse to your left around a boulder into the center of the wall. From this point, climb straight up above the wall to the sloping ramp, which can be easily followed to the top of the summit ridge. The moves on the wall involve considerable exposure and loose holds. The second option begins at the base of the Class 4 wall and follows a ledge south to the ridge crest and a notch. From the notch, descend to a debris-covered ramp, which can be followed up the east side of the ridge under overhanging cliffs to a steep 50-foot-high mud- and rock-filled gully. Carefully climb the gully, which is slippery and subject to rockfall. At its top, turn left and climb up for 15 feet to the top of the summit ridge. Climbing the south ridge involves a 10.0-mile round trip with 4,500 feet of elevation gain. Set aside plenty of time and carry extra water. USGS May 15-minute

Mogg Mountain *10,573 feet (Class 2)*

Mogg Mountain sits 6.5 miles almost due east of May Mountain. The peak was named to honor Frederick W. Mogg, who lived in the Lemhi Valley in the early 1900s. Climb to the summit via the west ridge, which is accessed from Morse Creek on the peak's west side [Approach: (C)(2)(a)]. USGS Patterson 15-minute

Mill Mountain *10,792 feet (Class 2)*

Mill Mountain sits 2.5 miles northeast of Mogg Mountain on a subsidiary ridge. From the end of the East Fork Road [Approach: (A)(7.2)] contour around the ridge line to the north to Little Mill Creek. Follow the drainage up to the peak's southeast ridge. Climb to the ridge line and follow the ridge to the summit. USGS Patterson 15-minute

Gunsight Peak *10,853 feet (Class 2)*

Gunsight Peak sits east of the main Lemhi crest, 9.0 miles southeast of Mill Mountain. The name reportedly was given to this peak because from Big Eightmile Creek a notch in the summit looks like the rear sight of a rifle. From the highest lake in the North Fork of Little Timber Creek drainage, scramble to the ridge top and follow the ridge to the summit [Approach: (A)(6)]. USGS Patterson 15-minute

Yellow Peak *10,968 feet (Class 2)*

East of Leadore, the Lemhi Range is wider than at any other point; Yellow Peak is at the center of this vast roadless area. Although it is not the highest point in the area, it dominates the area due to its position at the head of three major drainages. The peak's distinctive yellow-tinted rock also adds to its prominence. It is located 4.0 miles due south of Gunsight Peak. Reach the summit by any of the peak's three ridges. The north and west ridges are very open and enjoyable scrambles [Approach: (A)(6)(b)]. USGS Patterson 15-minute

Junction Peak *10,608 feet (Class 2)*

Junction Peak is situated 1.0 mile southeast of Yellow Mountain. Climb this peak from Yellow Pass [Approach: (A)(6)(a)], or by traversing the connecting ridge line from Yellow Peak. The summit can also be reached from Big Timber Creek. There are a number of springs high on the peak's west side; elk and mountain goat are often seen in this area. USGS Leadore 15-minute

Inyo Peak *10,611 feet (Class 2)*

Inyo, a big, isolated peak, sits 5.0 miles west of Yellow Peak and the main Lemhi crest. It is designated as the Inyo triangulation station on the Patterson USGS quad. Although this peak can be climbed from any direction, it is most easily accessed from Big Creek [Approach: (B)(4)(a)]. Follow Big Creek north until you are directly east of the summit. At this point, a small tributary of Big Creek flows down into the main stream. Leave the trail at this point and follow the tributary up toward the peak. From the upper slopes, gain Inyo's east ridge at a point just after the ridge turns south. Follow the ridge to the summit. USGS Patterson 15-minute

Sheephorn Peak *10,665 feet (Class 2)*

Sheephorn Peak sits 4.5 miles east of the Lemhi crest and Junction Peak. Climb the northwest slopes from Big Timber Creek [Approach: (A)(6)(c)]. Total distance is 2.5 miles and 3,000 feet of elevation gain. USGS Leadore 15-minute

Big Creek Peak *11,350 feet*
Flatiron Mountain *11,019 feet (Class 3)*

These two giants are located on a subsidiary ridge west of the main crest, 3.5 miles south of Yellow Peak. Both peaks are good locations for sighting mountain goats. The recommended route begins on Yellow Pass [Approach: (A)(6)(b)]. From the pass, hike southwest past the small lake just below the pass and then traverse into the 9,600-foot saddle at the top of Big Timber Creek. From the saddle, follow the ridge line south across Point 10323 and then traverse around the west side of the next high point on the ridge. You will find a game trail which is three feet wide and as smooth as a groomed trail for the first part of the traverse. Unfortunately, the trail dies out before reaching the next saddle. From the next saddle, scramble up Big Creek Peak's northwest ridge. Big Creek Peak possesses one of the best views in the state. You can see the Beaverhead, Lost River, Pioneer, Boulder and Salmon River mountains, as well as the Lemhi Crest from Lem Peak to Diamond Peak. From the Big Creek Peak summit, drop down the southwest ridge to the saddle and then scramble up Flatiron's northwest ridge. Note that both summits can be reached by hiking up Fall Creek and then climbing to the intervening saddle. This route involves a short section of Class 3 climbing just below the saddle and difficult route-finding problems. USGS Donkey Hills 15-minute

Negro Peak *10,571 feet (Class 2)*
This remote summit is seldom climbed. It sits 5.0 miles northwest of Gilmore, between Deer Creek and Negro Green Creek. Hike up Deer Creek on the old jeep road designated FST-160 [Approach: (A)(5.1)(a)]. Follow the trail until the creek splits. Leave the trail at this point and follow the north fork of Deer Creek up the basin to the head of the creek. Climb directly through the forest to the saddle just west of the summit. Follow the ridge to the summit. USGS Gilmore 15-minute

Portland Mountain *10,820 feet (Class 2)*
Portland Mountain was named for the Portland Mining Company of Butte, Montana, which

The north slopes of Big Creek Peak

operated mines in the Gilmore area. It is located 2.5 miles south of Negro Mountain and 3.0 miles due west of the Gilmore. Drive to Meadow Lake [Approach: (A)(5)] and park. Hike north to the base of the peak's south ridge, and then climb up at a slight angle to the ridge top. Follow the ridge to the summit. An alternative route begins at the small unnamed lake on the peak's west side (approach is via FST-160 [Approach: (A)(5.1)(a)]). From this lake, climb directly to the saddle on the peak's south ridge and follow the ridge to the summit. USGS Gilmore 15-minute

Sheep Mountain *10,865 feet (Class 3)*
Sheep Mountain sits 5.0 miles south of Portland Mountain. Climb this peak from its east side via Lemhi Union Gulch [Approach: (A)(4)]. From the mining road in the gulch, climb north to gain the east ridge, which will take you to the summit. USGS Gilmore 15-minute

Big Windy Peak *10,400+ feet*
Trail Peak *10,533 feet (Class 2)*
These two peaks are located 3.5 and 4.0 miles

south of Sheep Mountain and are best climbed on the same excursion. Although the two peaks have been carved up by mining roads and digs, they offer exceptional views and easy access to the Lemhi Crest. From Hahn [Approach: (A)(4)], walk or drive (the roads are in poor condition; driving is not recommended) on the mining road that climbs up Spring Mountain canyon. This road eventually climbs onto the crest north of Big Windy and then continues on to the summit. The road then drops to the saddle between the two peaks and climbs nearly to Trail Peak's summit. USGS Gilmore 15-minute

Iron Creek Point   *10,736 feet (Class 1)*
This peak is situated west of the main Lemhi crest, 10.0 miles due west of Sheephorn Peak. A trail reaches to the summit. Approach on the Big Gulch Road, FS-099 [Approach: (C)(5)(a)]. From the road's end, FST-079 leads up to the saddle between Iron Creek Point and Bear Mountain. In the saddle, a trail forks off and leads to the summit. USGS Gilmore 15-minute

Bear Mountain   *10,744 feet (Class 2)*
Bear Mountain is a big dark mass that sits at the head of the Little Lost River valley, 2.0 miles southeast of Iron Creek Point. The summit can be reached by following the route for Iron Creek Point [Approach: (C)(5)(a)] to the saddle between the two peaks and then cutting cross country to the summit. It is 1.25 miles and about 1,000 feet of elevation gain from the saddle to the summit. USGS Gilmore 15-minute

Bell Mountain   *11,618 feet (Class 3)*
This peak, named after Robert Bell, Idaho's first state mining inspector, looks like a giant imitation of the Liberty Bell. It is located 7.5 miles south of Trail Peak. Its rugged summit block dominates both the Little Lost River and Birch Creek valleys. The summit block is composed of rock that varies in composition from solid and stable to broken and loose.

In 1980, an old tobacco can and several plastic bags formed a makeshift summit register. The Amy family of Howe had signed in on the register almost every year since the register was placed on the mountain. Lyman Dye has climbed the peak from every side and pioneered the four most difficult routes on the summit block. USGS Diamond Peak 15-minute

West Face. *(Class 3)*
Approach this route by driving to Baysinger Creek [Approach: (C)(7)], where you will find running water and several good campsites. The West Face route begins here, at about 6,400 feet,

and climbs south up a steep slope to the top of the west ridge, through aspens, sagebrush and into Douglas fir. Once on the main ridge, take its crest up to treeline at 10,000 feet. Traverse along this skyline portion of the ridge around two rock towers to the base of the summit dome. To reach the summit, climb the middle rib on the west face of the dome. This rib is steep, but the route moves from one small shelf to another and the exposure is minimal.

Southwest Gully. *(Class 4)*
This gully is located between the west face and southwest ridge; access it from Black Creek [Approach: (C)(7)]. The first ascent was accomplished by L. Dye, A. Barnes and W. Boyer, in 1963.

East Ridge. *(Class 3)*
Approach from ID-28 on the Charcoal Kiln Road [Approach: (A)(3)]. Hike up Bell Mountain Canyon and gain the east ridge, which leads to the summit.

Northeast Ridge. *(Class 4)*
This prominent ridge leads steeply to the summit, involving moderately difficult pitches with moderate exposure. Access from the Charcoal Kiln Road [Approach: (A)(3)]. The first ascent was by L. Dye in 1963.

North Couloir *(Snow Climb).*
This route offers an early season snow and ice climb of over 700 feet on 50-degree slopes. Gain the couloir from upper Bell Mountain Creek. The first ascent was by L. Dye in 1962.

Northwest Face. *(Class 4)*
Moderate Class 4 climbing leads to the top of this near-vertical face. First ascent by L. Dye, A. Barnes and W. Boyer, in 1973.

Foss Mountain   *9,182 feet (Class 1)*
Foss Mountain sits 2.5 miles due south of Bell Mountain. Its summit is reached by a 4WD mining road [Approach: (C)(8)] that is very rough. The road makes a good hiking route to this summit, which has great views of the Lemhi crest. USGS Diamond Peak 15-minute

Diamond Peak   *12,197 feet*
Diamond Peak sits 8.5 miles southeast of Bell Mountain. The fourth highest mountain in Idaho, it is shaped like a large pyramid, and is visible from the Idaho Falls area on clear days. On its eastern side, the peak rises almost 6,000 feet directly out of the Birch Creek valley without intervening foothills. The east ridge, though not technically difficult, is the most appealing line on the peak. The upper summit pyramid is a complex grouping of

The east face of Bell Mountain, as seen from the Birch Creek valley

tilted faces, which include a number of vertical walls. USGS Diamond Peak 15-minute

East Ridge. *(Class 3)*
This route climbs the prominent east ridge from the North Fork of Pass Creek [Approach: (A)(2)]. From ID-28, take the Pass Creek Road for 4.0 miles, crossing Pass Creek twice. Turn right along the North Fork of Pass Creek and follow the road until its end. Hike up the draw until you can

spot the peak, then move out onto the mountain. The upper reaches of the east ridge involve moderate Class 3 climbing, which can present some objective problems when the handholds are filled with snow.

Southwest Ridge. *(Class 3)*
Access this route from the Badger Creek Road [Approach: (C)(9)]. Follow Badger Creek up to its origin on the peak's western slopes and start

climbing from there. The route runs south to an east/west-trending buttress, which connects with the southwest ridge at 10,400 feet. From this point, it is reported that several routes will lead to the ridge top, but little detail was given by the people who climbed this route. Once on the ridge top, follow it north to the summit.

Northwest Ridge. *(Class 4)*
This ridge rises out of the Badger Creek [Approach: (C)(9)] drainage to the main divide and then turns southeast and connects with the summit dome. Follow the directions for the southwest ridge route above. The ridge is an easy scramble for most of its distance. There is one Class 4 pitch right above the prominent notch in the ridge. The first ascent was made by L. Dye, A. Barnes and W. Boyer, in 1962.

Tyler Peak   *10,740 feet*
This interesting summit sits high above Tyler Canyon, 12.0 miles south of Diamond Peak. From the mouth of Tyler Canyon, the peak's east side gains roughly 4,500 feet in less than 3.0 miles. USGS Tyler Peak

East Side. *(YDS 5.4)*
Follow Tyler Canyon until you can gain the east ridge line, which descends directly from the summit. This ridge is on the north side of Tyler Canyon [Approach: (A)(1)]. It is possible to climb the ridge without any difficulty except for the last 200 feet. The crux continues up a narrow snow gully that varies from six feet to two feet in width as it cuts through a rock band. The rock is reportedly good (remember, everything is relative) and the holds are more than adequate.

Northwest Face. *(Class 3)*
Drive as far as your 4WD vehicle will carry you on the North Creek Road [Approach: (C)(11)]. Then follow the creek bottom toward the crest, to a point just north of Point 10401. Continue up the northwest slope until you are about 300 feet below the summit. At this point, cut back to the west toward the west ridge. Gain the west ridge and scramble to the summit.

West Ridge. *(Class 2)*
Climb the west ridge directly from North Creek [Approach: (C)(11)]; there are no particular difficulties with this route.

Saddle Mountain   *10,810 feet*
This prominent peak, the last major summit at the south end of the Lemhi Range, is located 2.5 miles south of Tyler Peak. On clear days it is visible from Idaho Falls. The peak has two summits, which are about 0.5 mile apart. The lower

south summit is 10,248 feet high. Either summit can be reached from the west or the east. USGS Tyler Peak

West Side. *(Class 2)*
Drive to the end of the East Canyon Road [Approach: (B)(12)], then hike up to the main crest south of the summit and follow the ridge to the summit.

East Rib. *(Class 3)*
Access the east rib from Deer Canyon on the peak's east side [Approach: (A)(1)]. Deer Canyon is a box canyon, with the east face of Saddle Mountain closing the box. The rib descends from a point just south of the summit. Climb the rib, which is initially tree-covered, to the crest. The crux is an eight-foot rock band that presents no real problems. This is a long, grueling climb, which takes ten to twelve hours round trip.

Cedar Canyon/East Side. *(Class 2)*
This route is relatively straightforward. Follow the Cedar Canyon Road [Approach: (A)(1)] until the canyon splits. Park at this point and work up the north fork until you can gain the crest southeast of the south summit. Cross over the south summit, descend to the saddle and then climb up the southeast ridge of the higher north summit. This route is easy to follow but very long.

APPROACHES TO THE LEMHI RANGE

Approach routes for this section are referenced in the text by bracketed entries [Approach:], which include appropriate letter and number references.

Primary approach to the Lemhi Range is via ID-28 on the eastern side of the range, and via US-93 and the Pahsimeroi Highway on the western side of the range. ID-33 runs along the range's southern fringes and connects ID-28 and the Pahsimeroi Highway. The crest of the Lemhi Range is so rugged that it is only broken by one crude 4WD road. The quantity of roads that approach the base of the mountains is amazing, but you must note that the quality of side roads varies greatly from road to road and from year to year. A 4WD is invaluable in this country.

(A)   East Side Approaches/Blue Dome To Salmon.

The broad alluvial fans and foothills that are administered by the BLM are crisscrossed by roads. All of these roads are accessible from ID-

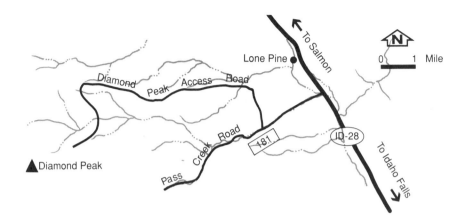

ACCESS TO THE EAST SIDE OF DIAMOND PEAK

28. The east side approach write-ups begin at the south end of range and move north toward Salmon.

(1) Eightmile Canyon to Pass Creek Access. To approach the southern end of the Lemhi Range, turn off of ID-28 just north of the Idaho National Engineering Laboratory (INEL) boundary. Please be aware that much of the land south of this road is administered by the INEL and is closed to the public. You could be arrested if you stray onto these lands. The turnoff is signed, and the road avoids INEL land.

The labyrinth of roads in this area requires a map and good map-reading skills, but if you possess both it is possible to gain access to all of the canyons in the southern end of the Lemhis. FS-531 runs up Cedar Canyon, FS-534 runs up Deer Canyon, FS-530 runs up Bartel Canyon, FS-540 runs up Tyler Canyon and FS-173 provides access to Eightmile Canyon. All of these roads require a high-clearance vehicle; a 4WD is recommended.

(a) FST-026, Eightmile Trail. FST-026 leaves FS-173 1.0 mile from its end and runs up the north fork of Eightmile Creek and then north to Pass Creek Lake in 2.5 miles.

(2) FS-173, Pass Creek Area. The Pass Creek Road, FS-181, leaves ID-28 just south of Lone Pine, where there is a small store and motel. Although there are numerous roads in this area, the Pass Creek Road is the only road which is numbered. At one time the road crossed the Lemhi Crest, but in the 1970s the Forest Service closed the road to prevent erosion. The main road and the feeder roads departing from it provide rugged wheeled access to the area around Diamond Peak.

(a) FST-025 and FST-045, Pass Creek Trails. Both of these trails leave the end of the FS-181 4.0 miles from ID-28. FST-025 runs up the

South Fork of Pass Creek, and FST-045 runs up the Middle Fork of Pass Creek. The two trails rejoin below Pass Creek Lakes and continue across the Lemhi Crest to connect with the Uncle Ike Road on the west side of the range [Approach: (C)(10)].

(3) FS-188, Charcoal Kilns Road. This road, located farther north along ID-28, is usually well graded and suitable for passenger cars. The main road leads up to the Charcoal Kilns historic site, while less well-maintained side roads leave this road and run toward Bell Mountain.

(4) FS-296, Hahn Area Roads. These roads are accessed from ID-28 5.0 bumpy miles south of Gilmore. A bumpy dirt road leads west to the old town site of Hahn and a junction 2.0 miles west of the highway. The road, which proceeds directly west, leads to South Mountain Canyon and an old mining road system that leads to the top of the Lemhi Crest and Big Windy and Trail peaks. Turning right at this junction and driving north 2.0 miles will bring you to a junction for Lemhi Union Gulch. Turning left on the Lemhi Union Gulch road and driving on it for 2.0 more miles will bring you within striking distance of Sheep Mountain.

(5) FS-002, Gilmore-Meadow Lake Campground Road. This washboard road leaves ID-28, passes through the ghost town of Gilmore and then continues to the Meadow Lake CG at 9,000 feet. The small campground is usually busy throughout the summer.

(5.1) FS-212, Gilmore to Deer Creek Road. From Gilmore, this road can be followed approximately 4.0 miles north to Deer Creek. A 4WD and a map are required.

(a) FST-160, Deer Creek Trail. FST-160 leaves the end of FS-212 and runs up Deer Creek for 5.0 miles to a small lake on the west side of Portland Mountain.

(6) Leadore Area Roads. From the village of Leadore, you can access a number of east side roads. Several of the drainages in this area have good hiking trails that provide access to several major peaks. Of particular note is the road up Little Timber Creek, FS-105. After 10.0 miles, this road leads to the Timber Creek drainage system, which in turn leads to a particularly windswept section of the Lemhis that includes Rocky, Yellow and Junction peaks.

(a) FST-187, Middle Fork Little Timber Creek. Take FS-105 to its end, past Timber Creek Reservoir. The trail follows the creek for 5.5 miles to Timber Pass (unnamed on the maps) on the main divide. From this point, the route splits into three. FS-184 invisibly crosses the meadow to the saddle northeast of Yellow Peak; FS-075 continues straight downhill across the meadow (also invisibly) into the trees where a good tread exists; and FS-195, which is signed, proceeds north to the Yellow Lake Basin.

(b) FST-075 to FST-183. From Timber Pass (described above), take FST-075 down the North Fork of Big Creek. The trail first passes through forest, then boggy forest and then a huge meadow. At the bottom of the meadow, 1.5 miles from the pass, is a tree with five directional signs on its trunk. Turn toward Yellow Peak, and you should see where the trail to Yellow Pass crosses a small creek. Take this trail, FST-183, which has a good tread, to the pass. South of the pass, there are several small ponds with excellent camping. FST-183 continues down into Big Timber Creek and eventually leads back to FS-105. Also note that a recently maintained trail turns off FST-183 3.0 miles below Yellow Pass and proceeds up Falls Creek to an unnamed and unmapped lake below Flatiron Mountain. This trail is shown on the latest Salmon National Forest map, but not on the USGS maps. The beginning of this trail is difficult to find, but once you are on it, the tread is very good. Good cross-country skills are invaluable in this area.

(c) FST-183, Big Timber Creek Trail. You can also access FST-183 from Leadore or FST-105. The trail, which sees little use, traverses the entire drainage, a distance of nearly 15.0 miles. Those who want to make a loop by combining this trail with FST-187 will need a shuttle or will have to walk for several miles on dirt roads.

(7) FS-008, Hayden Creek Road. Take ID-28 to a point 1.0 mile north of the Lemhi Post Office (27.0 miles south of Salmon) and turn onto a paved road, FS-008, which heads east into the mountains. At 3.5 miles the road turns to gravel, and then forks. The unnumbered right fork traverses BLM lands, leading toward Watson Peak; the left fork, FS-008, progresses up Hayden Creek. In the upper reaches of the Hayden Creek Valley and its tributaries, roads and trails provide access to Lem Peak and Long, May and Mogg mountains.

(a) FST-118, Carol Creek Trail. This trail leaves FS-008 roughly 20.0 miles from ID-28 and runs 6.0 miles south across the Lemhi crest to Morse Creek. This trail passes within 1.5 miles of Mogg Mountain's western slopes.

(7.1) FS-009, Bear Valley Creek Road. Access this road from FS-008, 10.0 miles from ID-28. Just after you pass a very narrow spot with caution signs, the Bear Valley Road winds away to your right.

(a) FST-179, Bear Valley Lake Trail. Drive 6.0 miles up FS-009 to its end, keeping right at Ford Creek. The trail starts here and proceeds to Bear Valley Lake in 5.5 miles. From the lake, the trail continues over the Lemhi crest to join with the Allison Creek Road [Approach: (C)(2)]. Look for a trail sign that indicates the way to Allison Creek and the Allison Creek Pass. The trail is sketchy in the meadow below the pass, but it is in good condition above the meadow.

HAHN AREA ACCESS POINTS

(7.2) FS-010, East Fork Road. FS-010 leaves FS-008 just past the point where FS-008 crosses Hayden Creek at 11.5 miles from ID-28. The road follows the East Fork of Hayden Creek for 4.0 miles and then leaves the creek, climbing out of the drainage to the north.

(a) FST-181, Mill Lake Trail. FST-181 leaves FS-010 where the road crosses the East Fork and follows the East Fork of Hayden Creek east, past Mill Mountain, to cross the East Fork/Mill Creek divide due south of Mill Mountain. From Mill Lake, the trail runs down along Mill Creek to meet FS-006.

(8) FS-031, Withington Creek Road. This road leaves ID-28 roughly 8.0 miles south of Salmon and leads towards the Harmony Mine. From the road's end, a trail goes the remaining distance to the mine and Sal Mountain.

(B) Westside Approaches/Salmon to Ellis.

You will find a relative abundance of good approach points on the west side of the Lemhi's. US-93 parallels the west side of the range for 42.0 miles between Salmon and Ellis. The following approaches are described from north to south.

(1) FS-017, Poison Creek Road. This road provides access to several trails in the area between Poison and Watson peaks. Take US-93 south from Salmon for 24.0 miles to reach this road.

(2) FS-019, Allison Creek Road. This road stretches high up into the Lemhis and nearly reaches the crest near Lem Peak, where it joins FST-179 [Approach: (A)(7.1)(a)]. Take-US 93 south from Salmon for roughly 34.0 miles to reach this road.

(C) West Side Approaches/Ellis To Howe.

The Pahsimeroi highway begins at US-93 42.0 miles south of Salmon and leads 60.0 miles southeast through the Pahsimeroi and then Little Lost River Valleys to Howe, Idaho. Much of this road is paved and the remainder is a high-quality gravel surface. The following road descriptions all leave the main thoroughfare and extend west into the mountains.

(1) FS-093, Morgan Creek Road. This road begins 7.2 miles south of Ellis. Turn off the Pahsimeroi Highway at a signed junction next to a private field. The road runs north and northeast to the mouth of Morgan Creek, crosses the creek in a stand of cottonwood trees and then continues into the canyon. Three miles from the highway, the road forks just below a large fenced meadow. Go left and follow the road around this private land. The road eventually recrosses Morgan Creek and ends shortly thereafter. A 4WD is required.

(a) FST-071, North Fork Morgan Creek Trail. FST-071 leaves the end of FS-093 and fol-

lows the North Fork of Morgan Creek toward Long Mountain. This poor trail completely dies out about 3.0 miles from the base of the peak, but it is possible to follow the drainage cross country to the Lemhi crest.

(b) FST-071, East Fork Morgan Creek Trail. This trail, which has the same trail number as the North Fork Trail described above, leaves FS-093 just after it crosses Morgan Creek for the second time and runs east for 7.5 miles to Morse Creek Road. This trail is rarely maintained; its beginning is difficult to locate, and it is hard to follow between the 7,000- and 7,600-foot contours on the USGS quad. FST-071 is a beautiful walk, and it provides the closest trail approach to May Mountain.

(2) FS-094, Morse Creek Road. This road leaves the Pahsimeroi Highway 10.3 miles south of US-93 at a small cemetary near the small village of May and heads due west into the mountains.

(a) FST-118, Carol Creek Trail. FST-118 leaves the end of the Morse Creek Road and crosses the Lemhi Crest west of Mogg Mountain. See [Approach: (A)(7.2)(a)], above.

(3) FS-096, Patterson Creek Road. This road is located 12.8 miles south of May (23.1 miles from US-93). The road turns off the main road at the former village of Patterson and leads past an old tungsten mine and through a large canyon. The upper reaches of the road are passable by 4WD only. This area contains no named summits for climbers but has an abundance of empty and wild country.

(a) FST-074, Devils Basin Trail. This trail leaves the end of FS-096 and climbs to the top of the Lemhi Crest, where it forks. One trail descends down to Big Eightmile Creek; the other follows the crest south to connect numerous trails in the Yellow Peak area (See [Approach: (A)(6)(b)] above.) These trails do not receive much use—you will need to use your route-finding skills.

(4) FS-097, Big Creek Area Road. This road turns off the Pahsimeroi Highway 6.0 miles south of Patterson (30.2 miles south of US-93). The road, which ends at a Forest Service CG, provides access to a large roadless area dominated by Big Creek Peak.

(a) FST-075, North Fork Big Creek Trail. This trail follows the North Fork of Big Creek north for 5.0 miles, then connects with FST-074 [Approach: (C)(3)(a)], which climbs into Devils Basin. The main trail continues up Park Fork Creek, connecting the many trails in the Yellow Peak area [Approach: (A)(6)(b)].

(b) FST-075, South Fork Big Creek Trail. FST-075 leaves FS-097 and runs south to the upper Little Lost River drainage, where it hooks up with FST-076, the Snowbank Trail, and other trails in the Iron Creek Point vicinity.

(5) FS-099, Big Gulch Road. This road leaves the Pahsimeroi Highway just north of Summit Reservoir. The road, which is signed, dead ends after 4.0 miles.

(a) FST-079, Iron Creek Point Trail. From the end of FS-099, this trail continues up to a subsidiary crest of the Lemhis to the summit of Iron Creek Point in 2.25 miles. You can approach Bear Mountain from where the trail crosses the saddle just north of that peak.

(6) FS-101, Sawmill Canyon Road. The Sawmill Canyon Road, is a major gravel artery, leaves the Pahsimeroi Highway roughly 9.0 miles north of the Clyde schoolhouse. The road heads due west into the Challis National Forest to the headwaters of the Little Lost River. There is an extensive trail system in the upper regions, as well as logging and mining operations.

(a) Mill Lake FST-082. This is a popular hike on the range's west side. The trail leaves the Sawmill Canyon Road 2.0 miles north of the Fairview GS just after the road crosses Mill Creek. Turn east and drive the short distance to the road's end at 7,200 feet. Mill Lake is 2.5 miles away, with 1,200 feet of elevation gain.

(b) Other Hikes. On the west side of the road, FST-078 and FST-076 provide good access to Iron Creek Point and Bear Mountain. A seldom-used trail follows Warm Creek east to the Lemhi Crest near Trail Peak. This trail, which is shown on the latest Challis National Forest map, does not have an official number.

(7) Bell Mountain Area Roads. These roads do not have number designations and can be quite rugged. A 4WD is recommended. The best approach to this area leaves the Pahsimeroi Highway 5.8 miles north of Clyde, where the road crosses the broad alluvial fan which descends out of the Lost River Range. At this point, you will notice an extensive set of sheep pens to the east. Take the road leading down to the pens (0.7 mile), drive through a wire gate, then turn right quickly and cross the bridge over the Little Lost River. In this general area, you will find roads leading up to almost every canyon in this stretch of the Lemhis. Access Bell Mountain from here either by going up Bell Mountain Creek or Black Creek.

(8) FST-126, Deep Creek/Foss Mountain Road. Cross the Little Lost River at Clyde by driving across the bridge in the BLM CG. From this point, drive north, paralleling the Little Lost River, through a gate. After about 1.0 mile, you will find this road, which leads up Deep Creek to the base of the Lemhis in 3.5 miles. The road then enters a gulch and runs to the summit of Foss Mountain at 9,182 feet. From the summit, it is a

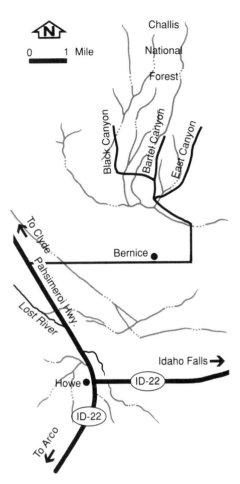

SOUTHERN LEMHI RANGE ACCESS

short cross-country hike to the midway point on the crest between Diamond and Bell mountains. This road, built by miners, requires a 4WD.

(9) Badger Creek Road. Leave the Pahsimeroi Highway 4.8 miles south of Clyde (23.2 miles north of Howe). The road begins where a gravel road forks off the highway at a small gravel pit. Turn into the gravel pit and follow a two-track road that leaves the back side of the gravel pit and continues due east along a fence line for 5.0 miles to the mouth of Badger Creek, where you will find several old mines and good access to the west side of Diamond Peak. A 4WD is recommended.

(10) Uncle Ike Road. This road is now closed to vehicles in its upper reaches. It is located midway between Clyde and Howe. The road leads up into the Challis National Forest in a scenic area without major peaks.

(a) FST-045, Pass Creek Lakes Trail. FST-045 leaves the Uncle Ike Road 8.0 miles from the Pahsimeroi Highway and runs across the Lemhi crest to the Pass Creek Road in 7.5 miles. See [Approach: (A)(2)(a)] above.

(11) North Creek Road. This route begins as a good gravel road that leads up to the base of the Lemhis. The turnoff is 12.8 miles north of Howe, just south of the Uncle Ike Road turnoff. At the top of the alluvial fan there is a small ranch and a fork in the road. Beyond the ranch, the left fork, which goes directly into the canyon, requires a 4WD. It leads to an old mine and eventually gets within striking distance of Tyler Peak.

(12) Southern Tip Roads. Access the southern end of the range, which is is managed by the BLM, via Howe on dirt roads. Drive north of Howe on the Pahsimeroi Highway for 3.0 miles and turn right on the road to Bernice. Drive through Bernice and then turn left in 1.0 mile. In another 1.0 mile, this road will bring you to BLM land and roads that lead into Black, Bartel and East canyons. All three of these canyons provide interesting hikes in the spring before it gets too hot.

7. The Beaverhead Range

The Beaverhead Range forms the Idaho/Montana border and the Continental Divide for nearly 150 miles, from Lost Trail Pass, north of Salmon, to Monida Pass, north of Dubois. The Beaverheads, like the Lost River and Lemhi ranges, were formed by fault blocking, which fractured, lifted and piled Paleozoic era limestone into a long, narrow mountain chain. The Beaverhead crest stays above 8,000 feet and reaches above 10,000 feet in two locations. The first location is east of Salmon, where a number of high ragged peaks surround 10,362-foot Freeman Peak. From Freeman Peak south the crest becomes lower in elevation and rolling in nature. Further south the crest once again gains altitude and tops out in an area known as the Italian Peaks. It is in this second area that the range reaches its high point on 11,393-foot Mount Scott. At the Italian Peaks, the crest turns eastward and once again loses elevation until it reaches its terminus at Monida Pass.

The Salmon National Forest manages the north sections of the range on the Idaho side, while the Beaverhead National Forest manages the Montana side of the range. The Salmon District of the BLM manages a great deal of the range's lower slopes and is, in places, responsible for the range right up to the crest. The southern sections of the range are administered by the Idaho Falls District of the BLM and the Targhee National Forest.

Congress has mandated that a Continental Divide Trail be constructed along the continental divide between Canada and Mexico. However, little money has been earmarked for this project and the trail is only partially complete. The BLM has designated a route and commenced some construction along the Beaverhead crest for the areas that it administers. The Forest Service has designated the general route, but has yet to start construction. Much of the trail will eventually be constructed on the Montana side of the border.

Hikers and climbers are, for the most part, unaware of the scenic and wilderness values offered by the Beaverhead Range. While the range has a relatively small trail system and road approach usually requires a 4WD, the open terrain and large vistas make cross-country travel worthwhile. The areas around Freeman Peak in the north and the Italian Peaks in the south offer the best climbing opportunities.

Perce Peak *8,266 feet (Class 1)*
Perce Peak is located 7.5 miles southeast of Lost Trail Pass. FST-124 leads to the summit from the Gibbonsville Road [Approach: (A)(1)(a)]. USGS Big Hole Pass

Sheep Mountain *9,858 feet (Class 2)*
Sheep Mountain sits 9.5 miles southeast of Perce Peak. The peak is best accessed from the Beaverhead National Forest in Montana. Climb the peak via Moose Creek and the southeast ridge. USGS Shewag Lake

Ajax Peak *10,028 feet (Class 2)*
Ajax Peak is located 10.0 miles due south of Sheep Mountain. Though the peak's south ridge is an easy Class 2 climb, it is difficult to approach the peak from Idaho. Instead, approach the peak from Montana via the Big Swamp Creek Trail, which leads to Ajax Lake. From the lake, climb due west to the top of the south ridge. USGS Homer Youngs Peak

Copperhead Peak *10,060 feet (Class 2)*
This peak sits west of the Continental Divide, totally in Idaho and 1.5 miles south of Ajax Peak. Climb the southeast ridge from Golway Creek. To reach Golway Creek drive up the Carmen Creek Road [Approach: (A)(3)] to Freeman Creek. Follow the road up Freeman Creek and then take the road's left fork, which climbs steeply up the ridge north of the creek. Continue up this ridge until the road crosses the 7,000-foot contour. Park at this point and contour into the Golway drainage to the north. Keep as high as possible and aim for the tiny pond in the upper drainage. Just below the pond, work up the steep southeast

ridge and boulder field to the summit. USGS Homer Youngs Peak

Freeman Peak *10,273 feet*

This eye-catching rock dominates the Salmon, Idaho skyline. The peak sits just west of the continental divide above Freeman Creek and the North Fork of Kirtley Creek, 2.5 miles south of Copperhead Peak. This prominent peak has been climbed via its three major ridges, and during the winter. The northeast and southeast ridges are the most accessible and the most difficult routes. The east ridge is reportedly the easiest route, but is difficult to access. USGS Homer Youngs Peak

East Ridge. *(Class 3)*
Follow the jeep road (hike it, instead of driving it) up Freeman Creek [Approach: (A)(3)(a)] to the vicinity of the Ore Cash Mine. (Remnants of the mining operation are still visible above the road.) Along the northern slopes of the peak, a faint trail descends from the road to the creek, crosses the creek and then climbs up into the boulder field that drops out of the peak's east face cirque. Climb into the cirque, hugging the east face, and then work your way up the couloir that leads to the top of the east ridge. The cirque contains snow late into the summer. From the top of the ridge, climb north to the summit. The route can be very slippery when wet or icy.

Monument Peak *10,323 feet (Class 3)*

Monument Peak, also known as McGarvey Peak, is situated 1.0 mile south of Freeman Peak. Climb this peak by its north ridge. Ascend Freeman Creek [Approach: (A)(3)(a)] on an old mining road and trail to the saddle east of Freeman Peak. From the saddle, cross into Montana, descend about 100 feet and then work the ledges back to the west, traversing around an impressive cirque that holds upper Miner Lake. This route eventually leads you to the saddle between Freeman Peak's southeast flank and Monument Peak. Climb the north ridge to the summit, an easy scramble. USGS Homer Youngs Peak

Peak 10390 *10,390 feet (Class 3)*

This unnamed summit is located 1.0 mile south of Monument Peak and can be climbed via its north ridge. Because of approach considerations, the easiest way to do the peak is in conjunction with a climb of Monument peak. USGS Homer Youngs Peak

Center Mountain *10,362 feet (Class 2)*

Center Mountain is located 3.0 miles east of Monument Peak. Climb this peak from Geerston Lake [Approach: (B)(1.2)] via the north ridge.

From the lake, hike directly to the north ridge and follow it to the summit. USGS Goldstone Mountain 15-minute

Horse Prairie Peak *10,194 feet (Class 2)*

Horse Prairie Peak is located 12.0 miles east of Leadore. Climb via the southeast ridge, which is accessed from the Cruikshank Creek Road and FST-191 [Approach: (B)(3.1)(a)]. USGS Deadman Pass

Baldy Mountain *10,773 feet (Class 2)*

Baldy Mountain is located 11.0 miles south of Horse Prairie Peak directly on the Continental Divide. Climb this peak via its west ridge, which is crossed by FST-222 [Approach: (B)(4)(a)]. USGS Morrison Lake 15-minute

Cottonwood Mountain *11,024 feet (Class 2)*

Cottonwood Mountain is located 10.0 miles south of Baldy Mountain and is identified as the Cottonwood triangulation station on the USGS quad. Climb this peak from Eighteenmile Creek [Approach: (B)(5)] by ascending the peak's western slopes from the point where the road ends. USGS Nicolia 15-minute

Jump Peak *10,941 feet (Class 3)*

Jump Peak sits 2.0 miles south of Cottonwood Peak and 1.0 miles west of the Continental Divide. This peak is also climbed from Eighteenmile Creek [Approach: (B)(5)]. The route starts from the point where the road ends and climbs directly up the west ridge and over Point 9975. This ridge presents no problems as it leads to the summit in 3.0 miles with 2,500 feet of elevation gain. This peak can also be climbed from the saddle between it and Eighteenmile Peak. USGS Nicolia 15-minute

Eighteenmile Peak *11,141 feet (Class 2)*

Eighteenmile Peak sits 1.5 miles south of Cottonwood Mountain and 1.0 mile east of Jump Peak. Climb from the saddle south of the peak, which is reached from Eighteenmile Creek [Approach: (B)(5)]. In 1978, there was a register on the summit. USGS Scott Peak 15-minute

Italian Peak *10,998 feet (Class 3)*

Italian Peak sits 9.0 miles southeast of Eighteenmile Peak and marks the southernmost point of the Continental Divide in Idaho. Climb to the northwest ridge from Italian Canyon [Approach: (B)(6.1)(a)] and scramble to the top. J. Kidd of Dubois has climbed the mountain from Italian Canyon, Scott Canyon and Crooked Creek. USGS Scott Peak 15-minute

Scott Peak *11,393 feet (Class 2)*
The highest Beaverhead peak is located 2.0 miles southeast of Italian Peak and just south of the Idaho/Montana border. Take the jeep road and then the trail up Scott Canyon [Approach: (B)(7)(a)]. From the end of the road, climb the southwest flanks of Peak 11291. At the summit of this subsidiary point, cross over to Scott Peak. USGS Scott Peak 15-minute

Webber Peak *11,223 feet (Class 2)*
This peak is the minor high point on the south ridge of Scott Peak. It reportedly can be accessed from Scott Peak via the 0.7-mile-long ridge that connects the two peaks, or via Scott Canyon [Approach: (B)(7)(a)] and the peak's southeast ridge. No details are known about either route. USGS Scott Peak 15-minute

Heart Mountain *10,442 feet (Class 2)*
Heart Mountain sits 4.0 miles southeast of Webber Peak, between Crooked Creek and Myers Creek. The easiest approach is from Myers Creek. Follow the Crooked Creek Road north until it forks. Take the left fork past the Ellis Ranch to Myers Creek. Follow the road up Myers Creek until it turns into a trail [Approach: (C)(2.11)(a)]. Follow this trail north to the top of the 9,200-foot Grouse Canyon/Webber Creek divide, on the north side of the peak. Climb the ridge from the point where the trail begins to descend into Webber Creek—a distance of 0.75 mile, with 1,200 feet of elevation gain. USGS Scott Peak/Edie Ranch 15-minute

Black Mountain* *8,860 feet (Class 2)*
Black Mountain is located 4.5 miles southeast of Heart Mountain and just west of Antelope Lakes. Climb the southeast slopes from Antelope Lakes. Access the lakes via the Crooked Creek Road system [Approach: (C)(2)]. USGS Edie Ranch 15-minute

Copper Mountain *10,303 feet (Class 2)*
Copper Mountain sits 12.0 miles due south of Scott Peak. This peak is an easy climb via its west ridge. The west ridge can be accessed from either Skull Canyon [Approach: (B)(8)] or from Long Canyon. An old mining road can be followed between the two canyons to the saddle on the west ridge. From this point, it is an easy walk to the top. USGS Copper Mountain

Gallagher Peak *9,825 feet (Class 2)*
This peak is located 2.0 miles east of Copper Mountain. The peak can be climbed easily (if you are in good shape) from the summit of Copper Mountain, from Blue Canyon [Approach: (C)(1.2)]

or from Gallagher Canyon [Approach: (C)(1.1)]. USGS Copper Mountain

Red Conglomerates Peak *10,150+ feet (Class 2)*
Red Conglomerate Peak is the easternmost Beaverhead Peak to reach above 10,000 feet. It is located 15.0 miles northeast of Scott Peak, at the head of Irving Creek. The USGS triangulation station was located on the lower north summit, directly on the Continental Divide. The true summit is 50 feet higher, and 0.25 mile to the south. The best ascent route follows Irving Creek [Approach: (C)(3.1)] and Red Canyon to its upper reaches. Continue on toward the divide and then follow the peak's west ridge to the summit. Other routes surely exist on this peak, but none have been reported. USGS Edie Ranch 15-minute

Horse Mountain *8,827 feet (Class 2)*
Horse Mountain is located between Irving Creek and Edie Creek, 3.5 miles southeast of Red Conglomerates Peak. This easy summit is surrounded by roads and jeep trails. Pick any route you like and enjoy the view. USGS Edie Ranch 15-minute

---

APPROACHES TO THE BEAVERHEAD RANGE

Approach routes for this section are referenced in the text by bracketed entries [Approach:], which include appropriate letter and number references.

(A) US-93 Access Points.
US-93 winds north out of Salmon and crosses Lost Trail Pass into Montana. At the pass, ID-43 cuts over to Chief Joseph Pass and leads east into Montana. The following approach points begin at Lost Trail Pass and are located successively south along the highway.

(1) FS-079, Gibbonsville Road. Eleven miles north of North Fork, this road leaves US-93 and climbs up and over the crest at Big Hole Pass on its way to Wisdom, Montana.

(a) FST-124, Perce Peak Trail. This trail begins just east of the confluence of Threemile Creek and Dohlonega Creek. (There is also a road junction at this point.) The trail climbs up the ridge that runs between Threemile Creek and the West Fork of Dahlonega Creek for about 6.0 miles to Perce Peak and the Idaho/Montana border.

(2) North Fork Trail System. These trails begin at the North Fork junction on US-93. FST-136 follows Silverlead Creek to the summit of Stein Mountain and connects with a number of other trails and primitive roads which offer good hiking opportunities.

(3) FS-069, Carmen Creek Road. Four miles north of Salmon, turn onto the Carmen Creek Road. Drive west until the road forks. The left hand fork follows Carmen Creek and eventually reaches FST-138, which climbs up to the crest and crosses into Montana. Take the right hand fork, which leads to Freeman Creek. Follow the road up Freeman Creek. After following the creek into the mountains, the road forks. The left fork switchbacks out onto the ridge, where it eventually ends. The right fork continues up the creek. A 4WD is needed for the last part of this road.

(a) FST-033, Freeman Creek Trail. This trail is an old mining road that leads to the Ore Cash Mine and then to the Continental Divide behind Freeman Peak.

(B) ID-28 Access Points.

This state highway follows the range south from Salmon to a junction with ID-22 in 109.0 miles.

(1) Salmon to Tendoy Access Points. A county-maintained dirt road can be accessed from the south end of Salmon. From this road, which parallels ID-28, a number of side roads climb toward the Beaverhead Crest.

(1.1) Kirtley Creek Road. This road leads east to the Monument Peak area.

(1.2) Geerston Creek Road. This road leads east to a trail which crosses BLM land and ends at Geerston Lake below Center Mountain.

(1.3) FS-185 to Lemhi Pass. This Forest Service road proceeds up Spring Creek to the crest and then follows the Idaho side of the border to Lemhi Pass.

(2) FS-013, Lemhi Pass Road. This good gravel road crosses into Montana from Tendoy via Lemhi Pass. From the pass, a road and trail system lead south to Bannock Pass.

(3) ID-29 to Bannock Pass. This paved and gravel road leads from ID-28 at Leadore into Montana at Bannock Pass.

(3.1) FS-130, Cruikshank Road. This road leaves ID-29 several miles below Bannock Pass and leads up Cruikshank Creek and then up Horse Prairie Peak.

(a) FST-191, Hall Creek Trail. FST-191 begins at the road's end and proceeds south, parallelling the range for 4.5 miles to Reservoir Creek.

(4) Powderhorn Gulch Road. Access this road by leaving ID-28 across the road from the ghost town of Gilmore. Take the good gravel road that leaves ID-28 and follow it out into the valley for 12.0 miles to the Powderhorn Gulch Road. Continue along this road toward the mountains. In 2.5 miles, FST-188 leads up Dry Canyon; at 4.4 miles, the road ends.

(a) FST-222, Powderhorn Gulch Trail. This trail leads up Powderhorn Gulch, then turns south and leads to Tenmile Creek, a total of 6.0 miles.

(5) Eighteenmile Creek. This road is best accessed from ID-28 across from Gilmore. Take the good gravel road northeast, cross Eighteenmile Creek and, after 0.5 mile, turn due east toward the mountains. Follow this rough road to its end to gain access to Cottonwood Mountain and Jump Peak.

(6) FS-189, Nicholia Area Roads. The road to Nicholia is well marked along ID-28. Both FS-174, which traverses Italian Canyon, and FS-190, which climbs up Scott Canyon, can be accessed from Nicholia. From the Nicholia townsite, drive west to Willow Creek and then follow the road up this drainage for a total of 7.0 miles to the road's end.

(a) FST-081, Willow Creek/Crooked Creek Trail. FST-081 leaves the end of FS-189, climbs up Willow Creek, crosses over into Italian Canyon (where it meets FST-057) and then climbs to the ridge line above Scott Canyon. From the top of Scott Canyon, the trail descends into Crooked Creek and meets FS-178. The total length of the trail is 14.0 miles.

(6.1) FS-174, Italian Canyon Road. Access this road from Nicolia by driving south on the Eighteenmile Creek road for 2.0 miles. The road enters Italian Canyon and ends after about 1.5 miles.

(a) FST-057, Italian Canyon Trail. This trail leaves the end of FS-174 and climbs 3.0 miles up the canyon to join FST-081 [Approach: (B)(6)(a)].

(7) FS-190, Scott Canyon Road. This road is best accessed from Nicholia by driving south past Italian Canyon for another 2.2 miles. The road follows the canyon east for 3.5 miles to a trailhead.

(a) FST-058, Scott Canyon Trail. FST-058 leaves FS-190 and climbs up Scott Canyon to join FST-081 [Approach: (B)(6)(a)] in a quick 2.0 miles.

(8) FS-298, Skull Canyon Road. This road is signed and leaves the old townsite of Blue Dome (no buildings are left). The road is open to the public but looks to be private because it goes right through a ranch yard and a closed gate. A 4WD is required.

(C) ID-22 Access Points.

This good state highway runs west from its junction with ID-28 to I-15 and Dubois.

(1) FS-202, Chandler Canyon Road. This road leaves ID-22 10.0 miles northeast of its junction with ID-28 and runs north into the southern tip of the Beaverhead Range. These roads are not suited for passenger cars.

(1.1) FS-201, Gallagher Canyon Road. Begins 6.25 miles north of ID-22 and proceeds west up Gallagher Canyon for 3.0 increasingly rough miles.

(1.2) FS-203, Blue Canyon Road Begins a couple of miles north of the Gallagher Canyon Road and then leads west up Blue Canyon for 2.0 more miles.

(2) FS-192, Antelope Lakes Road. This road leaves ID-22 13.0 miles northeast of its junction with ID-28 (1.5 miles southwest of Lidy Hot Springs) and runs north along the eastern edge of the Beaverhead Range for 20.0 miles to a junction with FS-196 [Approach: (C)(2.2)]. It connects with a road system that crosses much of the Beaverhead's southeastern canyons and provides access to Heart Mountain, Scott Peak and Webber Peak. Some of these roads are passable for autos—but most require a 4WD.

(2.1) FS-178, Crooked Creek Road. This road forks off FS-192 8.0 miles from ID-22 and runs northwest up Crooked Creek for 8.0 miles. This road is not well maintained and will be difficult for passenger cars.

(a) FST-081, Willow Creek/Crooked Creek Trail. This trail leaves the end of FS-178 and proceeds northwest. See [Approach: (B)(6)(a)] above.

(2.11) FS-191, Myers Creek Road. This road leaves FS-178 5.0 miles from its beginning and ends 3.0 miles up the drainage.

(a) FST-113, Myers Creek Trail. FST-113 leaves the end of FS-191 and climbs up the drainage and over the saddle on the east slopes of Heart Mountain to connect with FST-111 in the Webber Creek drainage in 5.5 miles.

(2.2) FS-196, Webber Creek Road. This road can be accessed from either FS-192 or FS-280. The road follows Webber Creek westward into the Beaverhead Range and ends at the Webber Creek CG.

(a) FST-111, Webber Creek Trail. FST-111 leaves from the end of FS-196 and follows the Webber Creek drainage west to the Continental Divide in 8.0 miles and then drops down into the Divide Creek drainage. It connects with FS-280 in another 6.0 miles.

(3) FS-280, Medicine Lodge Road. This road leaves ID-22 6.0 miles west of I-15 and proceeds 34.0 miles to the northwest to cross the Continental Divide and enter Montana.

(3.1) FS-187, Irving Creek Road. This road leaves the Medicine Lodge Road and follows Irving Creek northeast for 4.5 miles. A 4WD is recommended.

8. The Centennial Range

The Centennial Range forms the Idaho/Montana border for over 40 miles, from Red Rock Pass east of Yellowstone National Park to I-15 at Monida Pass. The range climbs abruptly out of the forested Island Park Caldera to form a high rugged crest that reaches its highest elevation at 10,196 feet on Mount Jefferson. The range continues due west, losing its sharp edge to become a series of high rolling ridges in the Monida Pass area.

The Idaho portions of this range are administered by the Targhee National Forest and the Idaho Falls District of the BLM. The Montana side of the range is administered by the Butte District of the BLM (and, in a small area, by the Beaverhead National Forest).

The Centennial Range's vehicle approach roads are plentiful, but road quality varies considerably. The range's trail system is widely disbursed, providing many day-hiking opportunities and a few overnight destinations. Climbing options are all in the Class 1 to Class 3 range.

Big Table Mountain   *9,083 feet (Class 1)*

This peak is located on the Continental Divide, 14.0 miles east of Monida Pass and 11.5 miles northwest of Kilgore. Its broad summit runs north to south, forming a major chunk of the divide. On the Idaho side of the divide, the summit can be reached by hiking up either the Bear Gulch Trail, FST-008 [Approach: (B)(1.2)(a)] or the Big Table Mountain Trail, FST-009 [Approach: (B)(2)(a)]. Both trails are readily accessible from Kilgore via good gravel roads. On the Montana side of the divide, the Price Pete Road leads to Pete Creek Divide; from this saddle, FST-004 follows the crest to the summit. USGS Big Table Mountain

Baldy Mountain   *9,889 feet (Class 2)*

Baldy Mountain is the most impressive summit at the western end of the Centennial Range. It is located 8.0 miles east of Big Table Mountain, directly on the Continental Divide. The peak has a north/south-trending summit ridge highest at the north end (just inside Montana). Climb the peak by following the ridge north from Slide Mountain, or by following the Ching Creek drainage from a point just south of Hancock Lake [Approach: (B)(3)(a)] to its highest point and then gaining the west ridge. USGS Lower Red Rock Lake 15-minute

Slide Mountain *9,805 feet (Class 2)*

Slide Mountain is directly on the Continental Divide, 1.5 miles southeast of Baldy Mountain. Take FST-039 [Approach: (B)(3)(a)] to Aldous and Hancock lakes. Hike north from the lake and ascend the peak's southwest ridge to a spot between the summit and Point 9163 by following a large, tree-filled gully. Once on the ridge top, hike northeast to the summit, which is another 700 feet above. It is roughly 1.7 miles from Hancock Lake to the summit. USGS Lower Red Rock Lake 15-minute

Dry Creek Peak *8,200+ feet (Class 2)*

This small summit is located just south of the Continental Divide above Dry Creek, 3.75 miles southeast of Slide Mountain. The summit is reached by hiking up FST-007/FST-171 [Approach: (A)(1)(a)] to the peak's south ridge and then by following that ridge to the top. USGS Lower Red Rock Lake 15-minute

Reas Peak *9,371 feet (Class 2)*

Reas Peak sits on the Continental Divide 14.0 miles east of Dry Creek Peak and 1.6 miles due south of Mount Jefferson. Climb this peak from the Kilgore Road via the Blue Creek Road system [Approach: (A)(2)]. Follow the road up until you can gain access to the peak's upper slopes. Reas is best known for its wide-open southern slope, which is excellent for March skiing. USGS Upper Red Rock Lake 15-minute

Mount Jefferson *10,196 feet (Class 2)*

Jefferson, the highest Centennial Range peak, is located 1.6 miles due north of Reas Peak. (The Continental Divide doubles back on itself—both Mount Jefferson and Reas Peak sit on the Divide, with Hell Roaring Creek in-between.) Jefferson is frequently climbed from the Sawtelle Peak Road [Approach: (C)]. Follow this road almost to the summit of Sawtelle Peak. Park at the last big curve before the road begins to switchback up the face of Sawtelle Peak. Look for an old jeep road that leads west; follow it until it ends near the eastern slopes of Jefferson. Hike to the east ridge and climb the peak by this broad, easy-to-follow ramp. The climb is an easy scramble. USGS Upper Red Rock Lake 15-minute

Red Rock Mountain *9,512 feet (Class 3)*

Red Rock Mountain is located 0.9 mile north of Mount Jefferson, to which it is connected by a snaking, jagged ridge. This peak can be climbed from Mount Jefferson. The descent to the saddle between the two peaks involves difficult Class 3

climbing in two places, but there is only minimal exposure. Descend to the west of Jefferson, going over a subsidiary peak. Continue down and north until reaching the saddle between the two peaks. USGS Upper Red Rock Lake 15-minute

Sawtelle Peak *9,902 feet*

This peak, the home of a Federal Aviation Administration radar station, sits just 3.0 miles east of Mount Jefferson. The radar dome on top of this imposing peak is plainly visible from the surrounding valleys. A good roadway [Approach: (C)] is kept open to the public throughout most of the summer. The sweeping view from the nearly 10,000-foot summit includes large parts of Idaho, Montana and Wyoming. USGS Sawtelle Peak

APPROACHES TO THE CENTENNIAL RANGE

Approach routes for this section are referenced in the text by bracketed entries [Approach:], which include appropriate letter and number references.

There are a number of good approach points into the range. Although few trails penetrate the area, good cross-country hiking conditions exist along the range's open and mostly rolling crest.

(A) The Yale/Kilgore Road Access Points.

This road is the primary approach route to the Centennial Range. Take I-15 to the Spencer exit to reach the west end of this road; take US-20/US-191, which runs between Idaho Falls and West Yellowstone, Montana, to reach the road's eastern end. From this road, any number of side roads will lead into the Centennials. The following roads are listed from west to east.

(1) Dry Creek Trailhead. The trailhead is located east of Kilgore on Dry Creek. To reach it, drive the Yale/Kilgore Road to a point 8.0 miles east of Kilgore and turn north. The trailhead is a short distance up the creek.

(a) FST-007 and FST-171, Dry Creek Trails. Follow Dry Creek directly to the Continental Divide. At roughly 1.5 miles north of the trailhead, FST-007 junctions with FST-171, which leads due west to climb over a ridge above Moose Creek, and then descends to Ching Creek, where it joins FST-014 (which climbs up to the divide above Aldous Lake). From this junction, FST-171 continues west to a trailhead on FS-027 [Approach: (B)(3)].

(2) FS-048, Blue Creek Road. This road is located along the Yale/Kilgore Road, 6.0 miles east of US-20. The road, which follows Blue Creek north, is connected to several other logging roads (which are not shown on the maps). This is the best winter approach to Reas Peak.

(B) Kilgore Area Roads.

Kilgore is a small village located just north of the Yale/Kilgore Road. (Gas and food are available there.) From Kilgore, three roads extend into the western end of the range.

(1) FS-006, West Camas Creek/Porcupine Pass Road. This road leads up West Camas Creek to Porcupine Pass, and then continues west to I-15. To reach this road, drive north from the Kilgore Post Office and turn left when the road ends. Drive west for 2.2 miles, turn right and drive 0.8 mile, then turn left—and you are on FS-006. Nine miles from Kilgore, the road crosses West Camas Creek. At this point, FS-006 continues upstream; FS-019 forks off and extends downstream.

(1.2) FS-019, Bear Gulch Road. This road leaves FS-006 just after it crosses West Camas Creek. FS-019 begins by running southeast along West Camas Creek, and then crosses over to Bear Gulch. Once in Bear Gulch, it proceeds north to a developed trailhead that has parking for 10 cars.

(a) FST-008. This trail follows Bear Gulch north and connects with FST-009, the Big Table Mountain Trail [Approach: (B)(2)(a)], in 2.0 miles.

(2) East Camas Creek/Cotton Wood Creek Roads. From the Kilgore Post Office, drive north. Turn left at the T-intersection at the north edge of town and then turn right at the next intersection. Follow this good gravel road north until it forks. This junction is the beginning of FS-026, a loop road that begins and ends here. Three major side roads and a number of trails are accessed from this road system. Only one trailhead has been developed.

(a) FST-009, Big Table Mountain Trail. This trail begins at Hirschi Flat. From the junction described above, take the left fork north for 3.0 miles and then turn left (west) onto a short feeder road. The road ends in 0.1 mile; find the trail on the south side. The trail quickly crosses East Camas Creek and works its way south to Larkspur Creek. In 3.0 miles, the trail meets the Bear Gulch Trail [Approach: (B)(1.2)(a)] and then continues uphill to the Continental Divide and Big Table Mountain.

(b) FST-004, Spruce Creek Trail. This is an alternate route to the area around Big Table Mountain. Take the west fork of FS-026 to the point where the road turns due east and FS-023 cuts off to the north. At this point, find FST-004 along the banks of Spruce Creek. Follow the trail

up the drainage until it reaches the Continental Divide. The trail runs east and west from here along the divide, providing many miles of excellent high ridge walking.

(3) FS-027, Aldous Lake Trailhead Road. Drive out of Kilgore on FS-026. When the road divides take the right (east) fork and continue on for 2.3 miles to a junction with FS-027. Turn right here and follow this road for 7.0 miles to the Aldous Lake Trailhead. There is parking available for 10 cars.

(a) Aldous Lake Trail. This short trail leads to Aldous and Hancock lakes in 2.0 short miles.

(b) FST-171. This trailhead is located 0.25 miles south of the end of FS-027. See [Approach: (A)(1)(a)] for further details.

(C) Sawtelle Peak Road.

This road leads to the summit of Sawtelle Peak from US-20. Turn east off US-20 8.0 miles north of Macks Inn and follow a very good gravel road to the top. (The road, maintained by the FAA, leads to a radar facility on the summit.) Passenger cars can negotiate the road, but be aware that it is steep—the descent will be hard on the brakes of cars equipped with automatic transmissions.

(D) Red Rocks Pass/Montana Access Points.

This road leads around the southern end of Henrys Lake and over Red Rocks Pass into Montana, providing access to the north side of the range all the way to I-15.

9. Henrys Lake Range

The Henrys Lake Range is located just south of West Yellowstone, Montana. The range forms a small arc of mountains, which run from the Centennial Range in the west to the Yellowstone Plateau in the east.

The sedimentary Henrys Lake Range is Idaho's northernmost segment of the Continental Divide. Its terrain, which is steep and abrupt in places, forms a transition zone between the drier mountains to the west and the wetter mountains to the east. Targhee Peak, at 10,280 feet, is the highest Idaho peak, while the highest Henrys Lake peak is unnamed Peak 10609, which lies north of the Continental Divide, in Montana.

The range, administered by the Targhee National Forest in Idaho and by the Gallatin National Forest in Montana, is managed as prime grizzly bear habitat. The bears found in the Henrys Lake Mountains are of two varieties—endemic and transplanted. The transplanted bears are, apparently, "troubled bears"—that is, bears unafraid of humans—which are captured in Yellow-

Targhee Peak, viewed from the east

stone National Park and "paroled" in the Henrys Lake Range. A word of warning: strictly observe all bear-country precautions.

Although this is a small mountain range, it provides a number of good hiking and climbing opportunities. Access is also good. The trail system has one excellent loop which includes the range's two mountain lakes—its peaks are well worth the effort. Recreational use, limited to the Targhee Creek area, is not very high because of the threat posed by the grizzly bears. Cross-country skiing, though, is exceptional; US-20, always plowed over Targhee Pass, leads to a number of good open slopes for backcountry skiers.

Black Mountain *10,237 feet (Class 2)*

Black Mountain is situated 3.0 miles due east of Raynolds Pass, directly on the Continental

Divide. Climb from either the east or the west via the Divide ridges. The shortest route begins on Raynolds Pass [Approach: (A)] and follows the Divide east to the summit in 3.0 miles. To approach the peak from the east, use FST-027 [Approach: (B)(1)(b)], which runs up Dry Fork. USGS Targhee Peak

Targhee Peak *10,280 feet*

The highest Idaho peak in the Henrys Lake Range is located 1.5 miles northeast of Black Mountain. Targhee Peak is a beautiful Rocky Mountain summit with trees, cliffs, meadows, and a boulder-strewn summit. It can be climbed via several routes. USGS Targhee Creek

West Ridge. *(Class 2)*

Take the Targhee Creek Trail [Approach: (B)(1)(a)] to the point where it crosses the west ridge, and follow the ridge to the top.

East Ridge. *(Class 2)*

Take FST-027 [Approach: (B)(1)(a)] to the point where it crosses to the south side of Targhee Creek for the second time. Climb up through the trees to the broad ridge and follow it to the summit.

West Fork Cliffs. *(Class 3)*

Follow the Targhee Creek Trail [Approach: (B)(1)(a)] to the point where the creek forks. Leave the trail and head up the West Fork. Look around and find a good game trail, which leads up the valley. Eventually the game trail reaches open terrain and you will be able to see the large sedimentary cliffs that tower over the valley—if a grizzly doesn't get you first. The route goes up the one large gully that splits the cliff. Route-finding is straightforward. From the top of the cliff, take the east ridge to the summit.

Bald Peak *10,180 feet (Class 2)*

Bald Mountain is located 2.0 miles due east of Targhee Peak. Climb this peak from FST-027 [Approach: (B)(1)(a)] by leaving the trail just below Clark Lake and traversing due east and up to the summit—a steep but straightforward approach. (Undoubtedly, this peak could be climbed from almost any direction.) USGS Targhee Pass

Lionhead Peak *9,574 feet (Class 2)*

This summit is located 1.25 miles east of Bald Mountain. Approach the summit from FST-027 [Approach: (B)(1)(a)]. Leave the trail where it crosses the East Fork of Targhee Creek and follow this drainage due north for 2.0 miles. At roughly 8,800 feet, climb northeast to the ridge, then follow the ridge line east to the summit. USGS Targhee Pass

APPROACHES TO THE HENRYS LAKE RANGE

Approach routes for this section are referenced in the text by bracketed entries [Approach:], which include appropriate letter and number references.

Exceptional access (by Idaho standards) leads into these mountains via US-20 and ID-87. Several Forest Service roads provide secondary access to the mountains from these paved highways. Although there are few trails into the Henrys Lake Mountains, access to the peaks is adequate, and much of the higher terrain is above treeline. There are no named peaks in the range between Red Rock Pass and Raynolds Pass. However, for your interest, it is noted that a jeep trail follows the divide between the passes.

(A) ID-87 Access Points.

This highway runs between US-20 and the Idaho/Montana border at Raynolds Pass. The only access point of interest is at Raynolds Pass, where there is good parking, access to Black Mountain and open slopes for skiing.

(B) US-20 Access Points.

This major north/south highway runs between Idaho Falls and West Yellowstone.

(1) Targhee Creek Trailhead. This trailhead can be reached by driving 2.0 miles north from the US-20/ID-87 junction to a signed turn for the Targhee Creek Road. Turn left and follow this road west into the mountains to the Targhee Creek trailhead in 2.5 miles. (Keep right at the only junction along this route.) The Targhee Creek trail system provides good hiking and access to all but one Henrys Lake Range peak.

(a) FST-027, Targhee Creek Trail. This trail climbs up Targhee Creek to the lake basin north of Targhee Peak. From the lake basin, a poorly maintained trail climbs up to the Continental Divide near Point 10130 west of Targhee Peak and then drops into the saddle between that peak and Black Peak, where it connects with the Dry Fork Trail.

(b) Dry Fork Trail. This trail begins as a logging road that turns off the Targhee Creek road just below the Targhee Creek trailhead. Follow the logging road until it turns into a trail. The trail (not shown on the Targhee Pass USGS quad and somewhat difficult to find) works its way up Dry Fork until it crosses over the ridge above the West Fork of Targhee Creek just east of two small ponds (which are shown on the quad). From the ponds, the trail eventually leads to the Continental Divide, where it joins the Targhee Creek Trail.

(2) Targhee Pass. At 7,072 feet, this pass offers the highest access point to the Henrys Lake Range's crest. This pass is a popular destination for cross-country skiers. The ski terrain at the higher elevations is suitable for advanced intermediates, while lower slopes are fine for beginners. From the pass, the western slopes are moderate and interspersed by forest and meadow. This route can be followed through alternating open and forested slopes to the crest of the range.

10. The Big Hole and the Snake River Mountains

These ranges are located east of Idaho Falls and north of the main fork of the Snake River. Although this group is designated as two separate ranges by the USGS map makers, the Big Hole and Snake River ranges are physically and geologically the same group of mountains. The Big Hole Mountains encompass the peaks west of Pine Creek Summit and ID-31. The peaks east of Pine Creek Summit are identified as the Snake River Range.

The mountains included in this group are a tangled web of ridges, streams, aspen thickets and meadows that rise out of the Snake River plain. They gradually gain elevation from east to west. Pine Peak, at 9,019 feet, is the highest point in the Big Hole group; Mount Baird, at 10,042 feet, is the highest point in the Snake River Range.

Geologically, the range has a limestone foundation and is part of the Overthrust Belt. Over the centuries the tilted limestone formations have proved to be very unstable, resulting in massive slope failures. Blowout Canyon, located at the eastern end of the range, is the most spectacular example of what happens when a lot of rock moves downhill rapidly. Although the extraordinary landslide that ravaged this canyon took place in prehistoric times, the canyon is still filled with rubble and debris that looks like it just recently came roaring down the mountain. Upper Palisades Lake is also the result of a slide, which dammed up the canyon. There are many high cirques, evidence of a history of glaciation. One other interesting feature is the presence of the largest coal deposit in Idaho, in the northwest end of the range.

The Targhee National Forest administers most of the range; cattle and sheep grazing are the main

commercial uses. But the range is still in a semi-wilderness condition in many places, and provides good habitat for a variety of wildlife. The Snake River Range has large populations of moose and mountain goats. When hiking at lower elevations, it is almost impossible to avoid seeing moose. The slopes around Mount Baird are thick with mountain goats, which were introduced in the 1970s. The range is threatened by those who want to explore for oil within its boundaries. So far, drilling activity has not taken place.

These mountains contain an extensive trail system, which is accessed by a better than average road system. The lower elevations are often cluttered with brush and aspen thickets, which make cross-country travel difficult, while the high country is composed of high bare ridges ideally suited for walking. Big Hole and Snake River peaks fall into the Class 1 to Class 3 range—and often the crux of a climb will be working your way through the low-level brush to get to the base of a climb.

BIG HOLE PEAKS

Garns Mountain *8,999 feet (Class 1)*
Garns Mountain, located 12.0 miles south of Driggs, Idaho, is a big bald mountain with the remains of an old fire lookout on the summit. The summit can be approached by several different trails. The most direct approach is via FST-056, the Elk Flat Trail [Approach: (C)(1)(a)], a well-maintained tread which passes through Elk Flat, a pleasing high-altitude meadow located on the peak's eastern flanks. USGS Garns Mountain 15-minute

Prospect Peak *8,023 feet (Class 2)*
Prospect Peak is 4.2 miles southwest of Garns Mountain. Take FST-068, the Burns Canyon Trail [Approach: (A)(1)(b)] northeast up Burns and Beartrap canyons to the point where the trail crosses over the peak's north ridge (in roughly 5.5 miles). Leave this little-used trail and walk south to the summit. USGS Garns Mountain 15-minute

Twin Peaks *7,761 feet (Class 2)*
Twin Peaks is situated 3.0 miles southwest of Prospect Peak, and although this peak offers a good view of the Snake River Plain, finding a human footprint on this summit would be about as likely as taking a trip to the moon. Hike up the Burns Canyon Trail [Approach: (A)(1)(b)] for 2.0 miles and then hike up the steep, forested east ridge of the peak. The high point is at the northwest end of the summit ridge, 1.5 miles away. USGS Garns Mountain 15-minute

Piney Peak *9,019 feet (Class 2)*
The highest point in the Big Hole Mountains can be approached most directly by the Black Canyon Trail, FST-073 [Approach: (A)(1)(c)], or from the West Pine Creek Trail, FST-078 [Approach: (B)(1)(a)]. Both trails provide access to the peak's south slopes, from which it is an easy 400-foot scramble to the summit. USGS Garns Mountain 15-minute

Red Mountain *8,715 feet (Class 1)*
Red Mountain is the prominent summit seen from the Teton Valley as you drive toward Pine Creek Summit from Victor. It is located 4.0 miles southeast of Garns Mountain. Several trails converge on the summit. The Big Horn Crest Trail [Approach: (B)(2)(b)] is the recommended approach during the summer. From Pine Creek Summit, it is roughly 6.0 miles to the point where the trail crosses over the peak's northwest ridge. Leave the trail at this point and hike southeast for 0.25 mile to the summit. Winter ski ascents are best made by following Patterson Creek. Be warned—high avalanche conditions can exist. USGS Garns Mountain 15-minute

Liars Peak *8,689 feet*
Chicken Peak *8,250 feet*
Black Mountain *8,796 feet (Class 2)*
These three summits are located on a ridge that extends south from Garns Mountain. A connecting trail, which has a number of different number designations, runs from north to south past each one of these peaks. (The shortest approach is from FST-078 [Approach: (B)(1)(a)], which runs up West Pine Creek from ID-31. However, you can approach the divide that contains these three peaks from the several other trails.) Climb Black Peak by leaving FST-078 on the peak's north slope and climbing the last 1,000 feet to the summit over steep forested ground. Climb Chicken Peak by leaving the trail on the peak's east side and climbing 150 feet to the summit. The northernmost of these three summits, Liars Peak, is 300 feet higher than the point where the trail crosses its southeast ridge. To climb it, leave the trail and hike up the southeast ridge. USGS Garns Mountain 15-minute

SNAKE RIVER MOUNTAINS
Fourth of July Peak *7,496 feet (Class 1)*
Fourth of July Peak is located 4.5 miles southeast of where ID-31 crosses Pine Creek Pass. From Pine Creek Pass, take FST-084 [Approach: (B)(2)(a)] to the summit. It is roughly 0.75 mile to the summit from the trailhead. USGS Fourth of July Peak

Thompson Peak *9,481 feet (Class 2)*
Thompson Peak sits 4.0 miles almost due south of Fourth of July Peak, on the high north/south divide that separates Rainey Creek from Palisades Creek. Take the FST-089, the Rainey Creek Trail [Approach: (A)(2)(a)] northeast to Dry Elk Canyon. Follow FST-091 [Approach: (A)(2)(a.2)] up Dry Elk Canyon to FST-091 [Approach: (A)(2)(a.21)]. Follow this trail to either the peak's southeast or north ridge and scramble up to the summit, which is a little over 600 feet above the trail. USGS Thompson Peak

Atkinson Peak *9,366 feet (Class 2)*
Atkinson Peak is located 1.75 miles southwest of Thompson Peak, on the same divide. Approach this peak via the Rainey Creek [Approach: (A)(2)(a)] or Palisades Creek [Approach: (A)(3)(a)] routes. From either of these routes, take FST-092 [Approach: (A)(2)(a.1)] or [Approach: (A)(3)(a.1)] to the peak's south ridge. Scramble up the ridge for 800 feet to the summit. USGS Thompson Peak

Mount Baldy *9,835 feet (Class 1)*
Mount Baldy is the very prominent peak that rises up east of the village of Swan Valley. It is located 4.5 miles southwest of Atkinson Peak and 4.5 miles north of Irwin, Idaho. The best route to the summit is via FST-092, the Cross Divide Trail, which begins in Rainey Creek [Approach: (A)(2)(a.1)] and Palisades Creek [Approach: (A)(3)(a.1)]. Follow FST-092 to the ridge line north of the peak. From this point, an unmaintained now-you-see-it, now-you-don't trail follows the peak's north ridge to the summit in 2.5 miles. USGS Thompson Peak

Sheep Mountain *9,680 feet (Class 2)*
Sheep Mountain sits between Palisades Creek and Sheep Creek, 4.0 miles southeast of Baldy Mountain. Climb this peak via its east slope from the point where FST-096 [Approach: (A)(4)(a)] crosses the ridge, 1.5 miles east of the summit. USGS Thompson Peak

Sheep Creek Peak *9,950 feet (Class 2)*
Sheep Creek Peak is located 2.0 miles southeast of Sheep Mountain, between Sheep Creek and Little Elk Creek. Climb this peak from Sheep Creek via FST-096 [Approach: (A)(4)(a)], which crosses its west ridge, or from FST-151 [Approach: (A)(5)(a)], which provides access to the peak's north ridge. Both routes are roughly 2.5 miles in length. Neither ridge presents any objective difficulty. USGS Palisades Dam

Palisades Peak   *9,778 feet (Class 2)*

Palisades Peak is located in the upper Palisades Creek drainage, just north of Upper Palisades Lake. Approach the summit from FST-97 [Approach: (A)(5)(a)], which crosses the saddle east of the peak. From the saddle, hike 0.5 mile due west to the summit. USGS Palisades Peak

Little Palisades Peak   *9,707 feet (Class 2)*

Little Palisades is located just east of Palisades Peak and is also accessed from FST-097 [Approach: (A)(3)(b)], which crosses the peak's southern slopes. From the trail, follow the south ridge to the summit. USGS Palisades Peak

Mount Baird   *10,025 feet (Class 3)*

The highest Snake River Range peak is situated on the high ridge that divides Big Elk and Little Elk Creeks. Its summit is reached via the Little Elk Creek trail [Approach: (A)(3)(b)]. Take the trail to the saddle west of the peak. (The summit is visible from the trail as you approach the saddle.) Climb the peak via its north ridge, a rewarding scramble on unstable terrain. The crux is a short gully just below the summit. The view north to the Grand Teton is memorable. USGS Mount Baird

The chiseled summit of Mount Baird, viewed from the top of Elkhorn Peak

Elkhorn Peak   9,988 feet (Class 2)

Elkhorn Peak sits 0.5 mile south of Mount Baird and can be climbed from Mount Baird by traversing down the south ridge to a saddle and then climbing up Elkhorn's north ridge. The summit can also be reached via a steep gully that climbs out of Little Elk Creek to the saddle north of the peak. USGS Mount Baird

Needles Peak   *9,449 feet (Class 2)*

Needles Peak sits 3.0 miles southeast of Elkhorn Peak, just west of the Idaho/Wyoming border. The USGS has attached the name Needles Peak to a high point on the peak's north ridge. The true summit is designated by the elevation numbers—9449. The peak is climbed from Quaker Flat, which can be reached from either the Blowout Canyon Trail [Approach: (A)(7)(a)] or from Big Elk Creek via FST-108 [Approach: (A)(6)(b)]. At the top of Quaker Flat, a sign located high up on a tree trunk marks the trail to the summit. The trail is no longer maintained, but is easy to follow to the summit's east ridge. Follow the ridge 0.5 mile east to the summit. USGS Mount Baird

APPROACHES TO THE BIG HOLE AND THE SNAKE RIVER MOUNTAINS

Approach routes for this section are referenced in the text by bracketed entries [Approach:], which include appropriate letter and number references.

The Forest Service maintains a substantial trail system within these mountains. Many of these trails, especially in the Big Hole Mountains, see little use and are a good place to get away from things. Road approach is generally suited for passenger cars, but can be quite rough.

(A) US-26 Access Points.

US-26 runs east from Idaho Falls through Swan Valley and on to Alpine Junction in Wyoming. The following approach points are described from west to east.

(1) Heise/Kelly Canyon Road. This road begins 17.0 miles east of Idaho Falls at a signed junction. From this point, it is roughly 8.0 miles to the Kelly Canyon Ski area. This road forks just before it enters Kelly Canyon. The right fork, FS-206 (a dirt road), leads east along the Snake River to Wolverine Creek, Big Burns Creek, and Black Canyon. The left fork, FS-218/FS-217, leads to the ski area and then continues into the mountains,

providing access to several nice spots, including the Table Rock CG, before rejoining FS-206 along the Snake River.

(a) FST-082, Wolverine Creek Trail. There are two major routes up Wolverine Creek. Neither are well maintained but both offer a good deal of solitude and are especially nice for early season day hikes. The east fork of Wolverine Canyon holds unique 40-foot-high rock "tepees." Look for these formations roughly 1.0 mile into the valley, in a stand of aspen on the west side of the trail.

(b) FST-068, Big Burns Creek Trail. This trail is located along the Snake River, roughly 4.5 miles east of the junction of FS-218/FS-217 and FS-206 (described above). Turn north off FS-206 and follow a bumpy road 0.5 mile to the trailhead. The trail accesses the entire Big Hole backcountry. From this trail and its many side trails the following peaks can be reached: Prospect Peak, Garns Mountain, Pine Peak, and Chicken Peak. The trail is maintained in reasonably good shape.

(b.1) FST-071, Little Burns Canyon Trail. This trail leaves FST-068 3.0 miles northeast of its trailhead and proceeds east to connect with FST-073 [Approach: (A)(1)(c)] just west of Chicken Peak.

(c) FST-073, Black Canyon Trail. This trail starts in the next major canyon east of Big Burns Creek. Access it by following FS-206 east for 2.0 miles. FS-073 links up with the Little Burns Creek Trail, FST-071 (described above), before continuing north to a junction with FST-072.

(2) FS-257, Rainey Creek Road. This road leaves US-26 just east of Swan Valley and works its way 5.0 miles northeast into the Rainey Creek canyon to a developed trailhead. This road can also be accessed from US-26, where a road leaves the small hamlet of Irwin and proceeds due north to the mouth of Rainey Creek.

(a) FST-089, Rainey Creek Trail. FST-089 begins at the end of FS-257 and follows Rainey Creek north to FS-253 [Approach: (B)(2)(a)] the top of the Snake River Range crest.

(a.1) FST-092, Cross Divide Trail. This trail leaves FST-089 2.0 miles northeast of its trailhead, then proceeds due east to the Palisades Creek drainage, crossing the divide between Atkinson Peak and Baldy Mountain in 6.5 scenic miles.

(a.2) FST-092, Dry Elk Canyon Trail. This trail leaves FST-089 at the confluence of the North and South forks of Rainey Creek and runs east to a junction with FST-191 [Approach: (A)(2)(a.21)] just south of Thompson Peak.

(a.21) FST-091, Thompson Divide Trail. This trail follows the Thompson Peak divide north from FST-092 to FST-050 [Approach: (B)(2)(a)].

(3) FS-255, Palisades Creek Access. Take US-26 10.0 miles east of Swan Valley to Irwin and Palisades Creek. FS-255 leads up the road to a trailhead and campground. This is the start of the Palisades Creek Trail.

(a) FST-084, Palisades Creek Trail. The trail gains roughly 600 feet in its first 4.0 miles, bringing the hiker to Lower Palisades Lake. There are a few camping spaces at the lake's southern end, along with pit toilets. The trail continues along the western side of the lake up the canyon toward upper Palisades Lake.

(a.1) FST-092, Cross Divide Trail. See [Approach: (A)(2)(a.1)] above.

(a.12) FST-091, Thompson Divide Trail. See [Approach: (A)(2)(a.21)] above.

(b) FST-099/FST-118/FST-097, Palisades Peak Loop Trail. These trails form a 12.0-mile loop through the Snake River Range high country. Begin this loop by leaving the Palisade Creek Trail 1.5 miles north of Lower Palisades Lake and hiking east to Upper Palisades Lake. Just above the lake, the trail forks into three routes. Stay left at these route junctions and follow the trail north to a saddle between Palisades and Little Palisades peaks. From this point, the trail descends northwest to rejoin Palisades Creek.

(c) FST-102. This trail leaves the Palisades Creek trail just south of Lower Palisades Lake and crosses east, over a divide to Sheep Creek. See [Approach: (A)(4)(a)] below.

(4) FS-260, Sheep Creek Access. This road is 3.0 miles east of Palisades Creek. The road stretches a short distance into the mountains and then turns into a seldom-used trail.

(a) FST-096/FST-102. The trail climbs out of Sheep Creek and crosses a divide east of Sheep Mountain, then drops into the Palisades drainage.

(5) FS-268, Little Elk Creek Access. Take US-26 2.5 miles east of Palisades Dam and turn left on the good gravel road, which leaves the highway just west of where a causeway leads across the reservoir. Follow this road to its end.

(a) FST-151, Little Elk Creek Trail. This steep, but well-maintained, trail runs up Little Elk Creek to a pass just east of Mount Baird in just over 3.0 miles. At the pass, the trail forks. FST-099 descends Waterfall Canyon to Upper Palisades Lake. FST-104 leads to a number of side trails that lead east into Wyoming and north to the far side of Palisades Peak.

(6) Big Elk Creek Access. Take US-26 4.5 miles east of Palisades Dam and turn onto the gravel road that leads up Big Elk Creek. Follow the road to its end in 2.4 miles.

(a) FST-097, Big Elk Creek Trail. This trail leaves the trailhead and ascends Big Elk Creek into Wyoming. In Wyoming, two feeder trails can be taken back into Idaho.

(b) FST-108, Quaker Flat Trail. This trail (not shown the Mount Baird USGS quad) leaves the trailhead and goes around a Boy Scout camp and then up a draw to the saddle between Big Elk Creek and Booth Canyon. At the saddle, the trail divides. The right fork descends Booth Canyon to US-26. The main trail cuts up the north sidehill (not well marked) and continues on to Quaker Flat and Blowout Canyon.

(7) FS-271, Blowout Canyon Road. This road leaves US-26 about 5.0 miles east of Palisades dam at a signed junction. The road is 2.0 miles long and passable to autos.

(a) Blowout Canyon Trail. This trail climbs up the canyon and over the rubble of the slide. Just 1.1 miles up the canyon, the trail forks; the right-hand fork goes into Wyoming, and the left-hand fork (FST-108) leads to Quaker Flat. (Quaker Flat is a beautiful high-altitude meadow, which is—unfortunately—often covered with domestic sheep.) Take the left fork toward Quaker Flat and Needle Peak. Another steep mile will bring you to the top of Quaker Flat. The left fork of the trail descends to Booth Canyon and Big Elk Creek [Approach: (A)(6)(b)]. The right fork (not shown on the Forest Service map, but which does appear on the Mount Baird USGS quad) is the Needle Peak Trail, which climbs up toward the summit of that peak and then drops into Wyoming.

(B) ID-31 Access Points.
If you continue along US-26 to Swan Valley, you can turn north on ID-31 and gain access to the Snake River Mountains' central and northeast sections.

(1) Pine Creek Access. Take ID-31 from Swan Valley north toward Driggs. 9.2 miles from Swan Valley, turn onto the Pine Creek Road and follow it to its end in 0.5 mile.

(a) FST-078, West Pine Creek Pass. This trail leaves ID-31 at a signed trailhead about 4.0 miles northeast of where the highway enters the mountains. The trail runs northwest up West Pine Creek to Trail Canyon. It then climbs up Trail Canyon and joins FST-072 [Approach: (A)(1)(c)] in a total of 5.0 miles from the trailhead.

(b) FST-050, Pine Creek Trail. This trail leaves from ID-31 where the North Fork of Pine Creek flows into Pine Creek. (Look for a turn signed for an organizational camp.) The trail follows the North Fork east to Elk Flat in 12.0 miles.

Over the course of this hike, the trail encounters a good cross-section of Big Hole terrain. It eventually joins up with the central Big Hole trail system.
(2) **Pine Creek Summit Area.** The summit, crossed by ID-31, is located on the Big Hole/Snake River crest between Swan Valley and Driggs. Good cross-country skiing is available on both the east and west side of the highway. To ski the west side, ski up the broad ridge through small stands of aspen to the open slopes above. The rolling ridge climbs steeply in only two places. Views from the ridge are superb and include the Tetons on clear days. On the east side of the pass, a snowbound road can be followed for several miles along the ridge line. The road accesses many long open slopes; from its end, you can descend into Swan Valley via Rainey Creek.
(a) **Snake River Range Crest Trail.** From Pine Creek Summit, follow the gravel road east to its end. FST-050 leaves the road's end, follows the crest over Fourth of July Peak and then continues on to the Big Elk drainage.

(b) **FST-053, Big Hole Crest Trail.** This seldom-used trail begins on Pine Creek Summit and quickly climbs west to the ridge top above. From here, the trail follows the undulating ridge west and, eventually, connects with the central trail system. Advanced cross-country skills are recommended.

(C) **ID-33 Access Points.**
From Driggs, a county road leads directly west for 12.0 miles to Horseshoe and Mahogany canyons.
(1) **Horseshoe Canyon and Mahogany Canyon Access Points.** Both of these canyons contain trails which lead into Big Hole backcountry near Garns Peak. The Mahogany Canyon trail system is the preferred route.
(a) **Central Big Hole Trail System.** From the Horseshoe Canyon trailhead, FST-056, the Elk Flat Trail proceeds south to the top of the Horseshoe drainage, where it connects with the central trail system. This system includes trails that connect with every other trailhead listed in this section.

IV

SOUTHERN IDAHO

From the Snake River
South to the Utah
and Nevada Borders

1. The Owyhee Mountains

The Owyhee Mountains are located in Idaho's southwest corner, extending more than 50 miles southeast from the Oregon border into Idaho. This range is bounded by the Oregon border on the west, the Nevada border in the south, the Snake River in the north and the barren plains of central Idaho to the east. Owyhee was the original name used by Captain Cook for the Hawaiian Islands. It was attached to these mountains when several Hawaiian trappers vanished in the area in 1818. The name Silver City Range is sometimes used to identify the mountains that surround Silver City; the southeastern extension of the range is often called the Ruby Mountains.

The Owyhee Mountains were forced up by the Owyhee Batholith 40 million years ago. The range is surrounded by the younger volcanic rocks of the Snake River Plain, and is still covered in places by extensive deposits of older sedimentary rock. Where Owyhee granite has been exposed to the surface, it has formed impressive outcroppings and an occasional dome. However, the granite is somewhat soft and has been plastered with various water-deposited materials, which makes it a poor climbing surface. Hayden Peak, at 8,403 feet, is the range's highest peak.

The formation of the batholith created zones of extensive mineralization, which were discovered during the Civil War. Soon after the discovery, Silver City was established. Today, the town does not have a single permanent resident—but midsummer finds the Silver City area thronging with sightseers and offroad vehicle enthusiasts, who congregate around the town like an encampment of modern-day gypsies. The popularity of this area with the offroaders significantly detracts from the quality of the superb self-propelled recreation opportunities available.

The entire range is administered by the Boise District of the Bureau of Land Management. While recreational use of the Owyhees is the current rage, the more traditional consumptive uses of mining and grazing still dictate the pulse of Owyhee life. Mining has historically dominated man's use of the range, and although it has ebbed and flowed in importance over the years, it is currently on the upswing. Delamar Mountain is the site of the world's largest open-pit silver mine as well as smaller-scale prospecting operations, all with the blessing of lackadaisical federal mining laws.

There are no officially maintained hiking trails within the range, but numerous trails and old mining roads do exist. Be forewarned: the entire range receives heavy use by offroad vehicles. If you go hiking in the range on a summer weekend, the noise may be very annoying. Climbing is limited to Class 1 and Class 2 ascents, but this write-up only scratches the surface of hiking and climbing opportunities in the Owyhees. The real joy of the Owyhee Mountains is not in its summits, but in its lower-elevation canyons and its vast southern stretches, which are still in a wilderness condition. See Sheldon Bluestein's *Exploring Idaho's High Desert* for information on several enjoyable Owyhee hikes.

Tennesse Mountain *7,114 feet (Class 2)*
Tennessee Mountain is located 3.5 miles northwest of Silver City. This mountain is composed of rhyolite that rests on top of Owyhee Batholith. Prospectors have dug up the slopes in places, but there are no large mines on the mountain's slopes. This peak is located near the headwaters of Cunningham Creek, which is a tributary of Jordan Creek. Drive 3.0 miles east of Delamar along Jordan Creek and park where the road widens out near the confluence of Cunningham Creek and Jordan Creek. A seldom-used trail leads up the west side of Cunningham Creek—if you can find it, follow it up to a point east of the mountain and then climb up to the summit. USGS Rooster Comb Peak 15-minute

Florida Mountain *7,784 feet (Class 2)*
Florida Mountain is located 3.0 miles south of Tennessee Mountain and 1.0 mile due west of Silver City. Its slopes are pitted by numerous mining digs, and the BLM is evaluating a proposal to create an open-pit mine on the very summit of this abused mountain. To hike to the summit from Silver City, utilize the old mining roads on the peak's northeast side [Approach: (A)(2)(b)]. USGS Rooster Comb Peak 15-minute

War Eagle Mountain *8,051 feet (Class 2)*
War Eagle Mountain sits 1.5 miles southeast of

245

This unnamed granite dome near Silver City is one of the many granite outcroppings that can be found throughout the Owyhee Mountains

Silver City. The summit of this peak, reached by a 4WD road, is covered by radio towers. The summit can be also reached on foot from Silver City via its juniper-covered western slopes [Approach: (A)(1)(a.1)]. Watch out for snakes! USGS Silver City 15-minute

Hayden Peak *8,403 feet (Class 2)*
The highest point in the Owyhees is a long but easy walk from Silver City. It is located 2.0 miles southeast of War Eagle Peak. Access the peak directly from the Silver City Road by turning south on the Linehan Flat Road, which is located midway between New York Summit and Jordan Creek. Follow this jeep trail south to the saddle between Hayden and War Eagle Peak in roughly 6.0 miles. From the saddle, another jeep trail leads

nearly to the summit [Approach: (A)(2)(a)]. USGS Triangle 15-minute

APPROACHES TO THE OWYHEE MOUNTAINS

Approach routes for this section are referenced in the text by bracketed entries [Approach:], which include appropriate letter and number references.

(A) Owyhee Mountain Access.
Primary access is via several major highways: I-84 runs to the north of the range, US-95 cuts

along the Owyhees western border, and state highways ID-78 and ID-51 run along the eastern fringes of the range. In addition to the major paved highways, Owyhee County maintains a number of unpaved roads. Although rough and winding, they do provide access to almost every corner of these mountains. Within the range, there is a large system of primitive roads and abandoned mining roads that makes the Owyhees easily accessible to 4WDs, motorcycles, mountain bikes, horses and hikers. The internal Owyhee roads are often open between April and November. During the winter months, all roads are closed by snow, with the exception of the Delamar Mine Road.

(1) Murphy/Silver City Road Access. Drive south from I-84 at Nampa on ID-78 to Murphy. Just south of Murphy, a well-signed dirt road leads south and crosses over New York Summit into the heart of the Owyhees. This winding and narrow road can be crowded on summer weekends, so be prepared for oncoming traffic on your side of the road. From the beginning of the road, it is 18.0 miles to Silver City, 21.0 miles to Dewey, 25.0 miles to Delamar and 53.0 miles to Jordan Valley, Oregon.

(a) Jordan Creek Area. Although there are no designated trails within the Owyhees, the old mining roads will allow you to penetrate the brushy lower slopes and reach the relatively open upper slopes, where no trails are needed. Within the Silver City area, the Jordan Creek drainage acts as a major conduit, which can be used to reach locations throughout the drainage. South of Silver City, the road quickly dwindles down to a jeep trail. The jeep trail follows the creek south and eventually climbs to the top of the drainage in 3.5 miles, where it joins a two-track road that leads east to the War Eagle/Hayden Peak area and west to a number of different destinations.

(a.1) War Eagle Mountain Jeep Trails. This area begins 0.25 mile south of Silver City, at a ford of Jordan Creek. Cross the creek and follow the well-worn jeep trail southeast and then due east to a saddle south of War Eagle Peak, where it joins the Linehan Flat Road.

(2) Linehan Flat Road. This road is accessed from the Silver City Road midway between New York Summit and Jordan Creek. The road proceeds south for 3.0 miles, where it joins the Jeep Trail which leads up from Silver City [Approach: (A)(1)(a.1)]. After this junction, the road continues south for another mile to a second junction. From this point, the left fork proceeds southeast to Pickett Creek Saddle.

(a) Hayden Peak Jeep Trail. This primitive road leaves the Linehan Flat Road on the northeast side of Hayden Peak and climbs to the summit of Hayden Peak in 1.5 miles. It is recommended that you walk this jeep trail.

(b) Florida Mountain Trail. The route to Florida begins in Silver City and follows Long Gulch southwest for roughly 1.5 miles, then runs due west to the vicinity of the old Venus Mine in another 0.5 mile. At this point, the Florida Mountain Jeep Trail runs due north across the summit of Florida Mountain. The northeast slopes of Florida Mountain are covered with digs and old mining trails, which can be utilized to return to Silver City.

(3) Delamar Silver Mine Road. Take US-95 south toward Jordan Valley, Oregon. Near Shearville, two routes lead east into the Silver City area. Both dirt roads are over 30 miles long. The road to the Delamar Silver Mine has recently been improved and is kept open to the mine throughout the winter.

2. The Goose Creek Mountains

This group of mountains, located south of Twin Falls and southwest of Burley, is also known as the South Hills. The Goose Creek Mountains stretch roughly 25 miles from north to south and 20 miles east to west. They form a group of complicated ridges and peaks; 8,050-foot Monument Peak is the highest summit. One of the most prominent features of the Goose Creek Mountains is a long north/south ridge line known as Deadline Ridge, which runs from Grand View Peak south into Utah.

The Goose Creek Mountains are administered by the Sawtooth National Forest, which maintains an extensive road system within its boundaries. Almost every valley and basin is penetrated by roadways, but there is only one designated hiking trail within the range. Nevertheless, the range has numerous open ridges conducive to cross-country travel. Although the range includes nineteen named summits ranging in elevation between 7,100 and 8,000 feet, there is little to interest hikers or climbers because of the many roads within the range.

Monument Peak *8,050 feet (Class 1)*
Monument Peak is located 18.0 miles southwest of Oakley in the central part of the Goose Creek Mountains. Take FS-515 south to the Porcupine CG. Turn onto FS-538 and follow it to FS-671. Follow FS-671 for 1.0 mile and then turn east on the short dirt road that leads to the summit. USGS Trapper Peak

APPROACHES TO THE GOOSE CREEK MOUNTAINS

Approach routes for this section are referenced in the text by bracketed entries [Approach:], which include appropriate letter and number references.

The Goose Creek Mountains are inundated by roads, many of which are quite good. Primary approach is either from Twin Falls or from Oakley. Beyond the primary approach into this area, scores of roadways offer secondary approach to every drainage within the range.

(A) Twin Falls Access.

Access from Twin Falls, one of Idaho's largest cities, is reached via I-84 and US-93. All necessary services are available.

(1) FS-515, Rock Creek Canyon Road. To access this road, which leads south from Twin Falls and into the Sawtooth National Forest (where it becomes FS-515), drive to the abandoned Magic Mountain Ski Area. From this road, numerous side roads penetrate the range in every direction.

(B) Oakley Access.

The small village of Oakley is accessed from I-84 and Burley by taking ID-27 south from Burley for 26.5 miles. Food and gas are available in Oakley.

(1) FS-500, Cottonwood Creek Road. This road runs from downtown Oakley due west into the Goose Creek Mountains and eventually links up with FST-515 south of Rock Creek CG.

3. The Albion Range

The Albion Range extends 25 miles north from the Idaho/Utah border to a point just southeast of Burley. The range varies in width from 10 to 25 miles and includes a parallel southwestern ridge line named Middle Mountain, and an eastern ridge line known as the Malta Range. On the main Albion crest, Cache Peak reaches an elevation of 10,339 feet, making it not only the highest Albion peak, but also the highest point in Idaho south of the Snake River.

The main Albion crest is composed of two large, rolling ridges with two high points separated by a low saddle. In the north, Mount Harrison reaches 9,265 feet; in the south, the high point is reached on 10,339-foot Cache Peak. The largest glacial cirque in southern Idaho is nestled into the northeast slopes of this mountain. It holds several mountain lakes, which is rare in the mostly dry mountains of southern Idaho.

The geology of the range is highlighted by the 40-square-mile Cassia Batholith, which pushed up into the earth's crust some 28 million years ago. It is exposed at the southern end of the range. While the Cassia Batholith is among Idaho's youngest granitic intrusions, the Albion Range also possesses large deposits of very old Precambrian rocks, which cover the granite throughout most of the range. The heart of the Cassia Batholith is exposed at the southern end of the range and is known as the City of Rocks. The City is best known for rock climbing, thanks to its assortment of towers, spires and faces of hard, clean and readily accessible granite. The variety of routes, both established and unclimbed, is unlimited. Most routes present one- to two-pitch problems, while longer, more demanding climbs could be pioneered on some of the larger domes. A very extensive climbing guide to The City of Rocks has been published (see Appendix D).

The majority of the Albion Range is managed by the Sawtooth National Forest. Many sections along the range's foothills and in the City of Rock are managed by the Burley District of the Bureau of Land Management. In 1988, the City was declared a Natural Preserve by the U.S. Congress. The Natural Preserve will be managed by the National Park Service, in conjunction with state and local officials as well as the private landowners, who control much of the surrounding area.

The Albion Range has an extensive road system and a small trail system. Beyond the City of Rocks, recreational use of the glacial cirque below Cache Peak is high but the rest of the area sees little use by hikers. The terrain is open and the spectacular vistas make it well worth your time to explore cross country.

Mount Harrison *9,265 feet (Class 2)*

Mount Harrison, named after President Benjamin Harrison, is located 16.0 miles southeast of Burley. The peak has an excellent view of the Snake River Plain and, on clear days, the mountains of central Idaho. To reach the summit from the north, hike up FS-549 [Approach: (A)(1)] from Cleveland Lake. For a more interesting and rewarding trip to the top of this peak, follow the ridge line north from FS-548 and Elba Pass [Approach: (A)(2)]. This journey covers roughly 7.0 miles of the Albion crest. USGS Mount Harrison

Mount Independence *9,950 feet (Class 2-3)*

Mount Independence is located 7.0 miles due south of Mount Harrison and 10.0 miles southeast of Oakley. It is a somewhat pointed peak that rises

The City of Rocks, with Graham Peak in the background

out of the rolling Albion Range crest and towers over the Independence Lakes cirque. Its east face, the most precipitous wall in southern Idaho, drops 900 feet in less than 0.25 mile. The summit can be approached from almost any direction. USGS Cache Peak

South Ridge. *(Class 2-3)*
The most interesting route leads up from the Independence Lakes [Approach: (A)(2.1)(a)] to the saddle between Cache Peak and Mount Independence. Hike to a point midway between the upper two Independence Lakes and look for a gully which splits the lower east end of the east face. This gully leads up to a point roughly 100 feet above the saddle. Climb to the south ridge and then hike up to the summit. If you run into any sections along the ridge which are beyond your abilities, move off the crest and onto the western slopes, which are much easier.

North Slopes. *(Class 2)*
The peak can also be climbed from almost anywhere along the Rangers Trail, FST-012

[Approach: (A)(2.1)(a)]. Hike FST-012 east from the trailhead until it enters a large meadow (the second clearing on the USGS quad). Leave the trail and hike due north. This route is filled with brush in its lower stretches, but despite this inconvenience, it does lead to the summit in only 2.0 miles.

Cache Peak *10,339 feet*
The highest Albion Range summit is located 1.1 miles southeast of Mount Independence. Cache Peak, like Mount Independence, can be approached from almost any direction; but because of approach considerations is best climbed from the Independence Lakes. USGS Cache Peak

Northwest Ridge. *(Class 2)*
From the saddle between Cache Peak and Mount Independence, the northwest ridge of Cache Peak provides a 0.5-mile route to the summit. (To reach the saddle, follow the South Ridge route for Mount Independence.) While there are no real obstacles along the peak's northwest ridge,

Dome-shaped Cache Peak, the highest Albion Range peak, as seen from Mount Independence

the trees are clumped so close together that progress is often difficult. The higher you get on this route, the easier the journey.

Graham Peak   *8,867 feet (Class 3)*
    Graham Peak is located 5.5 miles southwest of Cache Peak, due north of the City of Rocks. This peak is accessed from FS-562 [Approach: (A)(3.1)], which follows the Albion crest north and passes

along Graham's western slopes to within 200 feet of the summit. At the northwest end of the summit, an old road can be followed almost to the top of the peak. USGS Almo

THE MALTA RANGE

    The Idaho Encyclopedia identified the barren ridge that lies in the afternoon shadow of the Albion Range as the Malta Range. The USGS has since identified this group of mountains as the Cotterrel Mountains in the north and the Jim Sage Mountains in the south. This subrange, which is visible from I-84, looks like a high desert plateau. The rocks have a red tint and there are few trees other than junipers. On the eastern escarpment, the range rises precipitously above the town of Malta and the Raft River. On the west, the range merges into the Albion Range. The Jim Sage Mountains reach an elevation of 8,046 feet on a mountain top sometimes identified as Elba Peak. The range is a rugged piece of real estate dominated by rocky cliffs and ragged rock outcrops. Vegetation is limited to junipers, sagebrush and grasses. The range itself is administered by the Burley District of BLM, and the state of Idaho controls several thousand acres of land spread throughout the range.

APPROACHES TO THE ALBION RANGE

Approach routes for this section are referenced in the text by bracketed entries [Approach:], which include appropriate letter and number references.

(A) Albion Range Access.

ID-27 and ID-77 are on the range's west and east sides, respectively. A combination of county and Forest Service roads traverse the southern part of the range between Oakley, City of Rock, Almo, and Elba.

(1) FS-549, Cleveland Lake Road. This road leads to Lake Cleveland and Harrison Peak in the northern section of the range. To reach FS-549, take ID-77 south from Albion for 4.5 miles and turn west. The road is signed for the Pommerel Ski Area (downhill skiing).

(2) FS-548, Elba to Oakley Road. This road between Elba and Oakley crosses the range at Elba Pass, north of Cache Peak. The road is easily accessed directly from either village. This road is steep, narrow and can be difficult to drive when wet; a 4WD is not absolutely required, but is recommended. Passenger cars with automatic transmissions are not recommended because the steep grades are hard on brakes.

(2.1) FS-562, Pot Holes Road. At Elba Pass, take FS-562 south toward the Pot Holes. Drive past the Pot Holes and turn onto a rough road, which eventually merges into FS-728 and leads into the Dry Creek drainage to the trailhead for FST-012 at 4.7 miles from the pass.

(a) FST-012, The Rangers Trail. This trail circles Cache Peak. Although several roads are now infringing on the route, it is still a good trail to get away from it all. The trail begins in Dry Creek, where there is a well-developed trailhead, and runs east and then south around the fringes of Mount Independence. In 2.0 miles, it junctions with FST-035, which proceeds due west to Independence Lakes. From this junction, the Ranger Trail is signed but difficult to follow as it continues its course around Cache Peak.

(3) City of Rocks Access. To visit the City of Rocks, drive along I-84 to the Malta-Sublett exit. (This exit is located roughly 32.0 miles north of the Utah border.) Drive west from the exit through the villages of Malta, Elba, and Almo on a good paved road. From just south of Almo, you take a good gravel road another 6.0 miles until you reach the City of Rocks area.

(3.1) FS-562, Graham Peak Access. FS-562 is accessed just east of the City of Rocks. Follow the main road through the City to the west, cross over a low saddle and immediately look for FS-562, which leaves the main road in a large meadow. A 4WD is recommended to follow this road, which runs 3.0 miles north along the west side of the Albion crest to the northern slopes of Graham Peak.

(4) Malta Range Access. Roads penetrate into many parts of the Malta Range. Primary approach is via two state highways. ID-77 follows the perimeter of these mountains on their west and south sides. ID-81 provides main road access to the Raft River Valley on the east side of the range. There are no hiking trails at present.

4. The Black Pine Mountains

The Black Pine Mountains are located just north of the Utah border and west of I-84. Geographically, the range, which is 17 miles in length and 7 miles in width, is the most distinctly defined mountain range in Idaho; it is surrounded by wide, flat valleys, and rises steeply on all sides. Geologically, the range is a textbook example of a Great Basin mountain range. The fault block, which forms the entire range, rises to 9,395 feet on Black Peak and has eroded into a maze of ridges and deep canyons.

The Black Pine Mountains are managed by the Sawtooth National Forest and are seldom visited by hikers or climbers. A mining company is planning to open and operate an open-pit gold mine on the range's eastern side, which will cause significant environmental degradation. Unfortunately, because so few hikers know about this range, there was little public input into the Forest Service's permit process. Now it may be too late.

At present, the range offers exceptionally good hiking opportunities, which are truly away from the crowds. Despite the lack of a large, well-maintained trail system, hikers should place these isolated summits high on their lists of places to visit. The five major Black Pine peaks are all Class 2 climbs. The views of the Great Salt Lake from the southern end of the range are the biggest drawing card in this area.

Black Peak* 9,395 feet (Class 2)

Black Peak is the highest of the Black Pine Mountain summits. It is located at the north end of the range, between Pole Canyon to the east and Little Eightmile Canyon to the west. The USGS survey marker is located on a point about 10 feet lower than the true summit. The peak is identified only as the Black triangulation station on the USGS 15-inch quad. (Note: the USGS is now issuing a provisional 7.5-minute quad to replace the 30-year-old 15-minute quad.) Black Peak can be climbed from almost any direction, but because of approach considerations, it is suggested that you climb it either from Pole Canyon or from Black Pine Peak. The traverse over from Black Pine Peak involves roughly 1.25 miles of scenic ridge-walking on very easy terrain. USGS Strevell 15-minute

Black Pine Peak 9,385 feet (Class 2)

Black Pine Peak is located 1.25 miles south of Black Peak. Climb this summit from Kelsaw Canyon [Approach: (A)(3.1)(a)] or Pole Canyon [Approach: (A)(1.1)(a)] which are linked by FST-018. Follow the trail to the south side of War Eagle Peak. Leave the trail at this point and climb over War Eagle Peak and then traverse the connecting ridge line to Black Pine Peak. Total distance from the trail is about 1.5 miles, with an 800-foot elevation gain. USGS Strevell 15-minute

War Eagle Peak 8,720 feet (Class 2)

War Eagle Peak is a very minor summit. Actually, it is not even a true mountain summit, but rather a bump on the south ridge of Black Pine Peak. Access the peak via its south slopes from FST-018 [Approach: (A)(1.1)(a)] or [Approach: (A)(3.1)(a)]. USGS Strevell 15-minute

Black Pine Cone 8,008 feet (Class 2)

Black Pine Cone is a cone-shaped summit located 3.0 miles southeast of War Eagle Peak and just east of Black Pine Canyon. Climb from either Mineral Gulch [Approach (A)(1.2)] or Black Pine Canyon [Approach: (A)(2)]. USGS Strevell 15-minute

The high, windswept crest of the Black Pine Mountains is nearly uniform in height as it runs from north to south.

Gunnell Peak* *8,316 feet (Class 2)*

Gunnell Peak is identified as the Gunnel triangulation station on the USGS quad. It sits 2.5 miles southwest of War Eagle Peak and provides the best Idaho view of the Great Salt Lake. Climb to the summit of this peak via its northern slopes from Kelsaw Canyon [Approach: (A)(3.1)]. This route utilizes the peak's partially forested northeast ridge, which climbs to the summit in 1.0 mile with an elevation gain of 2,300 feet. USGS Strevell 15-minute

---

APPROACHES TO THE BLACK PINE MOUNTAINS

Approach routes for this section are referenced in the text by bracketed entries [Approach:], which include appropriate letter and number references.

(A) Black Pine Mountan Access.

Primary approach to this range is via ID-81 on the west side, I-84 on its east side and UT-42 (Utah) along the range's southern slopes.

(1) FS-187, East Side Road. This road parallels the Black Pine crest on the the east side of the range. To access this road, exit I-84 at the Juniper exit (13.0 miles north of the Utah border) and drive to the west side of the freeway. The dirt road immediately turns south, leading to the southern end of the range in 13.0 miles.

(1.1) FS-761, Pole Canyon Road. This road leaves FS-587 0.5 mile south of I-84 and proceeds due west into Pole Canyon, ending in 9.0 miles.

(a) FST-018, East/West Trail. FST-018 begins in Pole Canyon 0.5 mile before the end of FS-761 and continues up Pole Creek to climb onto the ridge east of the creek. The trail then follows the ridge up to the crest south of War Eagle Peak and then descends into Kelsaw Canyon [Approach: (A)(3.1)].

(1.2) FS-198, Mineral Gulch Road. Access this road by taking FS-587 south from I-84 for 4.0 miles. The road proceeds west up Mineral Gulch for 4.0 miles.

(2) Utah-42, Curlew Junction and Black Pine Canyon. Take UT-42 west from I-84 for 15.0 miles to Curlew Junction. FS-586 leaves the highway at this point and heads 10.0 miles north across the Idaho border to Black Pine Canyon.

(3) ID-81, West Side Canyons. The canyons on the western slopes of the Black Pine Mountains are accessed 13.0 miles south of Malta by turning east from ID-81 onto FS-588. This dirt road proceeds east toward the range. After 4.2 miles, the road reaches a junction, where FS-767 leads northeast to Eighteenmile and West canyons. At 5.2 miles, FS-588 makes a 90-degree turn and runs due south to rejoin ID-81 in another 7.0 miles.

(3.1) FS-589, Kelsaw Canyon Road. This is the most important access road on the west side of the Black Pine Mountains. The road leaves FS-588 just over 5.0 miles north of ID-81. It is passable to high-clearance vehicles.

(a) FST-018, East/West Divide Trail. This trail is in very poor condition on the west side of the range and difficult to follow after 1.0 mile. Consider this a cross-country route for now, and write the Forest Service and ask them to fix it [Approach: (A)(1)(a)].

5. The Sublett Mountains

The Sublett Mountains are named after trapper William Sublette. The range extends from the Snake River Plain south almost to Snowville on the Idaho/Utah border. From the surrounding valleys, the range resembles a rather low grouping of hills. The highest point in the range is an unnamed summit which reaches 7,492 feet; 7,464-foot Cedar Creek Peak is the highest named summit in the range.

The Sawtooth National Forest administers the northern sections of the range, and the Burley District of the BLM administers the southern expanses. While both agencies maintain extensive road networks within the range, there is only one designated hiking trail. Because the Subletts are mostly open, their grass- and sage-covered ridges provide good cross-country hiking opportunities. The range thaws out earlier than most Idaho mountain ranges, and in many years it is possible to hike this country by mid-May. All Sublett peaks are rated Class 2; the ability to navigate by map and compass is the only real requirement.

Cedar Creek Peak *7,464 feet (Class 2)*

Cedar Creek Peak is located at the northern end of the Sublett Range between North and South Helgar canyons. The best approach to this peak is from North Helgar Canyon [Approach: (A)(1)] via the Spring Canyon drainage. It is roughly 1.5 uneventful miles from the road to the top of Spring Canyon (and Point 7442 on the USGS quad). Once on the summit ridge of Cedar Creek Peak, hike north 0.5 mile to the summit. USGS Sublett 15-minute

APPROACHES TO THE SUBLETT MOUNTAINS

Approach routes for this section are referenced in the text by bracketed entries [Approach:], which include appropriate letter and number references.

(A) Sublett Mountain Access.

Primary approach to the Sublett Range is via I-84 on the range's western flanks and ID-37 on its eastern side. There are only two approach routes listed below. However, the range is covered with roads and those with 4WDs can access almost every nook and cranny of these mountains.

(1) Helgar Canyon Access. Turn off I-84 at the first exit south of its junction with I-86. Proceed west for 15.0 miles to where the road forks. The left fork leads to North Helgar Canyon; the right fork leads to South Helgar Canyon. These are good gravel roads, usually passable in dry conditions for two-wheel drive vehicles. Spring Canyon, the jumping-off point for Cedar Creek Peak, is located 8.0 miles southeast of the junction for North and South Helgar canyons.

(2) Sublett Reservoir Access. Leave I-84 at the Malta-Sublett exit and drive east toward the mountains. After passing through the village of Sublett, the road passes Sublett Reservoir and then forks. The left fork, FS-564, creeps north up Lake Fork Creek; the right fork, FS-578, goes east and northeast up Sublett Creek. Both of these roads cross saddles and join the Helgar Canyon Roads [Approach: (A)(1)].

6. The Deep Creek Mountains

The Deep Creek Mountains form a rolling, unbroken crest that begins near American Falls and runs south for 30 miles to a point near Holbrook. The Arbon Valley flanks the range on the east; the Rockland Valley on the west. Deep Creek Peak is the highest point in the range at 8,748 feet. The range includes several long, well-developed canyons, including Knox Canyon.

Geologists speculate that the crest of the Deep Creek Mountains was once the surface of an ancient peneplain (i.e., the surface of a former flat plain), which was uplifted roughly 40 million years ago. This ancient surface has been repeatedly eroded, leaving only the crest, a remnant of the high plain that once existed here.

The Burley District of the BLM administers much of the Deep Creek Mountains. The state of Idaho also controls a considerable amount of land in the range, and the Fort Hall Indian Reservation controls the northern end of the range, including the summit of Bannock Peak. Although the range is devoid of hiking trails, the mostly treeless terrain is suitable for cross-country hiking. Water, although not plentiful, is present in a number of canyons and springs. Road access is adequate. The best maps available for approach routes are the BLM's Pocatello and Malad City land status maps.

Bannock Peak *8,263 feet*

Bannock Peak is the most impressive of the Deep Creek Mountain peaks. It is located at the north end of the range, 14.0 miles southeast of American Falls, in the southwest corner of the Fort Hall Indian Reservation. Access to this peak is across the Fort Hall Indian Reservation; permission must be secured by writing or calling the reservation before attempting the peak. (See Addresses in the Introduction.) USGS Bannock Peak

Deep Creek Peak *8,748 feet (Class 2)*

Deep Creek Peak is located 9.0 miles south of Bannock Peak, east of the main Deep Creek crest. The highest point in the range rises steeply from the valley floor—a good conditioning climb in late spring. This peak can be climbed from almost any direction. Two routes have been suggested. The longest route begins at the Knox Canyon Road [Approach: (A)(2.1)] and ascends the peak's western slopes. This is reported to be a steep but easy hike. The second route begins at the point where the Knox Canyon Road [Approach: (A)(2.1)] and Big Canyon Road [Approach: (A)(1.1)] join on Deep Creek Peak's west ridge. From this point, it is a 2.5-mile ridge walk to the summit. USGS Deep Creek Peak

APPROACHES TO THE DEEP CREEK MOUNTAINS

Approach routes for this section are referenced in the text by bracketed entries [Approach:], which include appropriate letter and number references.

(A) Deep Creek Mountain Access.

Primary approach is via ID-31, which traverses the Rockland Valley on the range's west side, or

Deep Creek Peak, the highest Deep Creek summit

via the Arbon Valley Road, which parallels the range on the east.

(1) ID-37 Access Points. ID-37 is a good paved highway that runs through the Rockland Valley; it provides primary access to all west-side approaches to the Deep Creek Mountains (only one is listed in this guide).

(1.1) Big Creek Road. This road is accessed from ID-37 19.5 miles south of I-86. This good gravel road, which is signed, runs due east to the top of the Deep Creek crest in 9.5 miles. Under dry conditions, this road does not require a 4WD.

(2) Arbon Valley Road. This is a paved secondary road that runs the entire length of the Arbon Valley. Access this road, and the east side of the Deep Creek range, by taking Exit 52 on I-86 and following the Arbon Valley south.

(2.1) Knox Canyon Road. This road leaves the Arbon Valley Road 27.25 miles south of I-86, at a signed junction. It leads up into the Deep Creek Range to a divide above Knox, Bull and Big canyons. Roads descend from the pass through both Big [Approach: (A)(1.1)] and Bull canyons.

7. The Bannock Range

This range begins just west of Pocatello and then stretches southeast for 65 miles, ending north of Dayton near the Utah border. The range encompasses a group of small escarpments, which are loosely tied together and which include the North Promontory Range, the Blue Springs Hills, the Samaria Mountains and the Malad Range.

The main Bannock Range crest is broken into three distinct high sections linked together by fairly low passes. In the north, near Pocatello, the range reaches an elevation of 8,710 feet on Scout Mountain and then loses elevation as it runs south, dropping to 5,468 feet at Garden Creek Gap. It then rises again, this time to over 9,000 feet on Elkhorn Peak, then descends to Malad Summit, 5,615 feet. At Malad Summit, the range curves to the east and then to the southeast before climbing to the summit of Oxford Peak, at 9,282 feet the highest point in the range. The extreme southern end of the range is anchored by Old Baldy Peak, 8,356 feet. The majority of Bannock Range rock is composed of Cambrian age sedimentary rock, while some Precambrian rock is found on Scout Mountain. The Bannock peaks are high, but rolling in nature, with no prominent faces or large cirques.

The main Bannock Range crest is administered by the Caribou National Forest. The Burley District Office of the Bureau of Land Management controls the North Promontory Range and the Samaria Mountains. A good portion the land surrounding these mountains is in private ownership, so access quality varies. In the Pocatello area, paved roads lead to numerous locations, and trails are reasonably well maintained. The two southern sections of the range see few hikers, and the approach is not developed for passenger cars. Climbing opportunities are limited to Class 1 and Class 2.

Kingsport Peak *7,222 feet (Class 2)*
Kingsport Peak is located 4.0 miles southeast of Pocatello. Although it has a road to its summit, it makes a good early season conditioning hike. Climb this peak from downtown Pocatello by taking Lincoln Road South west from town [Approach: (A)(1)]. Park when the road becomes too rough for your vehicle and walk the road to the west side of the peak and then on to the summit in 2.5 miles. The road continues on to Wild Mountain, 7,160+ feet, which is 1.0 mile to the southeast. USGS Pocatello South

Slate Mountain *6,980 feet (Class 2)*
This peak is located 4.5 miles south of Kingsport Peak. The peak loses its snow cover early, making the summit a good place for spring conditioning. Follow the West Fork Trail [Approach: (A)(2)(a)] until you reach several beaver dams in roughly 2.5 miles. From this point, the peak is located due east. Hike up the peak's west ridge from the beaver dams to the summit. USGS Pocatello South

Scout Mountain *8,710 feet (Class 2)*
Scout Mountain is located 6.5 miles south of Slate Mountain. Because of its proximity to Pocatello it is probably the most popular summit in all of southeast Idaho. This peak can be reached from the Scout Mountain CG [Approach: (A)(2.1)]. At the south edge of the picnic area, a hiking trail leads off to the south. Follow the trail for 200 yards, until it breaks out of the aspens. Start up toward a saddle on the mountain's north shoulder. The route is steep and crosses some talus. From this saddle it is an easy walk to the summit. (Note: a road leads to the summit from the opposite side of the mountain.) USGS Scout Mountain

GARDEN CREEK GAP

Garden Creek Gap is a popular rock-climbing area that can be reached from Pocatello by driving 25.0 miles south on I-15. Take the Arimo exit and drive west for roughly 5.0 miles, to where limited parking is available. (The gap is visible from I-15.) The area is made up of mostly broken rock; however, there are a few good walls. Routes are multipitch and offer varying degrees of difficulty. The north-facing walls are the most difficult. Winter conditions produce good ice-climbing conditions in a prominent gully on the north wall.

Elkhorn Peak *9,095 feet (Class 2)*
Elkhorn Peak is located 5.25 miles due west of Malad Summit. The summit, known as Elkhorn Peak, is the high point on the 4.5-mile ridge known as Elkhorn Mountain. The summit of Elkhorn Peak is formed by a narrow promontory nearly 0.25 mile long. The peak can be climbed by either its north ridge or its eastern slopes. Access to the north ridge is via FST-133 [Approach: (B)(2)(a)]; to the eastern slopes is via FST-134 [Approach: (B)(2)(b)]. The recommended route is FST-133, which leads to the Bannock Range divide 1.5 miles north of the peak. From this point, follow the ridge line south to the summit in 1.0 mile with a 1,000-foot elevation gain. USGS Elkhorn Peak

Oxford Peak *9,282 feet (Class 2)*
Oxford Peak, the highest point in the Bannock Range, is located 4.0 miles west of the village of Oxford. Though the peak can be approached from a number of directions, the best approach begins at Oxford and follows Oxford Creek west towards Rockslide Canyon [Approach: (B)(4))(a)]. This road is gated shut after roughly 3.0 miles. From the gate, take the Forest Service trail west for 1.0 mile to the Oxford Ridge Trail [Approach: (B)(1)(a.1)]. Hike north on this trail for 0.5 mile

to the Gooseberry drainage. From this point, it is possible to leave the trail and climb southwest directly toward the ridge top and Point 8416, which is about 1,000 feet above. Once on the ridge line, climb Oxford Peak's north ridge to the summit in another 0.75 mile and another 800 feet of elevation gain. USGS Oxford Peak

Weston Peak *8,165 feet (Class 2)*

Weston Peak is situated 7.0 miles south of Oxford Peak and 4.0 miles southwest of Clifton. The summit is easily accessed from FST-122 [Approach: (B)(3)(a.1)], which passes along its southern and western slopes. Climb the peak from the trail by either its north or south ridge. Both ridges gain roughly 500 feet of elevation from the trail. USGS Clifton

Old Baldy Peak *8,356 feet (Class 2)*

Darn near every Idaho mountain range has a peak with the letters "bald" in its name, and the Bannock Range is no exception. This Old Baldy Peak is located 1.0 mile due south of Weston Peak. Make the easy ascent up this peak's north ridge from the point where FST-191 [Approach: (B)(3)(a)] crosses the ridge. Total distance up the ridge is about 0.5 mile, with a 700-foot elevation gain. USGS Clifton

THE MALAD RANGE

The Malad Range is tucked into the western slopes of the Bannock Range just east of I-15. The southern end of the range extends into Utah, where it reaches over 7,000 feet in elevation. The highest Idaho point is an unnamed 6,995-foot summit. The Malad range is geologically similar to the Bannock Range and is also administered by the Caribou National Forest.

THE SAMARIA MOUNTAINS

The Samaria Mountains are located on the Idaho/Utah border just west of I-15. The range's high point is on Samaria Mountain, which is 7,795 feet tall. The first Mormon settlers in this area adopted the name, which has its origins in Palestine. The Samaria Mountains are linked to the Bannock Range via a long spur ridge, known as the Blue Spring Hills, which runs north for nearly 30 miles to connect the two ranges. The range is administered by the Burley District of the BLM.

THE NORTH PROMONTORY RANGE

The North Promontory Range is an extension of the Bannock Range and, like the Samaria Mountains, is connected to the Bannock Range by the Blue Spring Hills. The range, which is also known as the North Hansel Range, is located south of Holbrook and just west of the Samaria Mountains. Only 12 miles of this range are on the Idaho side of the Idaho/Utah border. Its highest point, north of the Utah border, is an unnamed 6,986-foot summit. From Holbrook, these mountains look like a series of dry broken hills, with few trees other than junipers. The range is administered by the Burley District of the BLM. Limited access is available via dirt roads that leave the ID-37 in Holbrook area.

APPROACHES TO THE BANNOCK RANGE

Approach routes for this section are referenced in the text by bracketed entries [Approach:], which include appropriate letter and number references.

Primary access is gained from I-15, which parallels the range for almost its entire length and crosses it at Malad Summit. US-91 provides access to east-side approaches on the southern end of the range. Additionally, county roads cross Garden Creek Gap and Mink Creek Summit west of Pocatello. Unfortunately, almost every trail in the Bannock Road is open to motorcycles.

(A) Pocatello Area Access Points.

Pocatello is reached by both I-15 and I-86. It is a college town, with all necessary services including outdoor equipment stores.

(1) Lincoln Road South/City Creek Road. Access this road from downtown Pocatello. The road leaves town as Lincoln Road South, runs up the hill onto Pocatello's south bench, becomes City Creek Road, and proceeds southwest up City Creek. The road is paved for 2.0 miles and then turns into dirt, deteriorating rapidly as it climbs up the mountain.

(2) Bannock Highway Access Points. Bannock Highway leaves the south end of Pocatello, crosses Mink Creek Summit on the crest of the range and then descends to the Arbon Valley Road on the eastern flanks of the range. This paved highway provides access to several hiking areas and, in the winter, to a state-run Park 'n Ski trail system.

(a) West Fork Trail. Take the Bannock Highway for 11.7 miles to the West Fork turnoff. Turn right just past the Pocatello water system intake structure on the left. The trail is well maintained and closed to motorized vehicles.

(2.1) FS-001, East Fork Mink Creek Road. Take the Bannock Highway southwest from Pocatello for 10.0 miles and turn onto the East Fork of Mink Creek Road, which leads to Scout Mountain CG.

(B) Southern Bannock Range Access Points.
Access to the southern sections of the Bannock Range is a complex subject. This write-up includes only limited information, which is designed to get you to the peaks listed in the guide. If you have time to explore, you can find a lot of interesting country in this area.

(1) FS-047, Cherry Creek Road. This road is accessed from I-15 at Malad Summit or at Downey. The road that connects these two locations provides two different access points for Cherry Creek. Once on the Cherry Creek Road, follow it south for 5.0 miles to the Cherry Creek CG. Just past the CG, the road is gated shut.

(a) FST-181, Left Fork Trail. FST-181 leaves the end of FS-047 just beyond the Cherry Creek CG and follows the Left Fork of Cherry Creek east for 2.0 miles, where it meets FST-119/ FST-189.

(a.1) FST-119, Oxford Ridge Trail. This is the premier trail in this part of the Bannock Range. It begins in the north near Red Rock Pass and runs south for over 12.0 miles along the east side of the crest. The southern end of the trail traverses windswept Oxford Ridge. This trail intersects with seven trails and three roads.

(2) FS-041, Summit Guard Station Access. This road begins at the Malad Summit exit from I-15 and leads west to the GS in a little over 1.0 mile. There are a number of trails in this area besides the two listed below.

(a) FST-133, Elkhorn Mountain Trail. This trail is accessed at the end of FS-041. The trail follows Mill Creek west to its headwaters, crosses over Elkhorn Mountain and then descends west along Indian Mill Creek to FST-129.

(b) FST-134, Kents Canyon Trail. FST-134 leaves the end of FS-041 and proceeds 2.0 miles due south to the Bannock Range crest, then descends Kents Canyon to FST-129 in another 3.0 miles.

(3) FS-038, Deep Creek/Weston Creek Road. This road is accessed from the Malad area via either I-15 or the old highway which parallels it. Take the Malad exit and drive east on this road, which runs between the Bannock Range and its Malad subrange. The road eventually leads to Weston.

(a) FST-191, Old Baldy/Weston Peak Trail. Access this trail just south of Weston Creek Reservoir. This old jeep trail leaves FS-038, runs northeast past the western slopes of Baldy Peak and then joins FST-122 just south of Weston Peak.

(a.1) FST-122, Weston Mountain Trail. This trail is accessed by FST-191, which connects with it roughly midway between its two ends. The trail can also be accessed via FST-231, which begins near the Forest Service's Deep Creek Administrative Site.

(4) FS-230, Oxford Creek Road. This road is accessed from the village of Oxford. Oxford is located on the east side of the range, just south of Red Rock Pass, on US-91. Follow the signs from the highway to the village. The Oxford Creek Road leaves the county highway just north of the village and proceeds northeast along Oxford Creek for 2.0 miles and then climbs due west toward Rockslide Canyon for another 0.5 mile, where it is closed by a gate.

(a) Rockslide Canyon Cutoff Trail. This trail begins at the gate on the Oxford Creek Road and climbs up Rockslide Canyon for nearly 1.0 mile to join with FST-119 [Approach: (A)(1)(a.1)] just east of Oxford Peak.

(C) Malad Range Access.
This range is accessed from either Malad, via the old highway which parallels the freeway, or from FS-038, which begins at I-15 just north of Malad and follows Deep Creek and then Weston Creek along the eastern side of this subrange. From either of these roads, numerous roads lead into the mountains.

(D) Samaria Mountain Access.
To approach this small mountain range, you will need the BLM's Malad City land status map. The roads shown on that map are accurate. The only recommended approach route into this group is via the North Canyon Road, which is on the range's southern edge. This road, which can be approached by any number of roads from both Idaho and Utah, connects with almost all of the numerous roads serving the range. The Gardner Canyon Road is a more direct route into the range, but is not recommended because it requires a 4WD. (Actually, all of these roads will require 4WD when wet.) While there are no hiking trails at present, the open nature of the terrain makes for good hiking on the ridge lines.

(E) North Promontory Range Access.
This small group of mountains is shown on the BLM's Malad City land status map. All of the roads on the map are open to the public—but none of the roads have names. All will require 4WD when they are wet.

8. The Portneuf Range

The Portneuf Range begins east of Blackfoot and extends southeast for 60 miles. The range is broken by the Portneuf River, which cuts through it at Lava Hot Springs. The northern section of the range begins high above the Blackfoot River and gradually climbs up to the summits of North and South Putnam mountains, the first major peaks encountered in the north. Moving south, the crest undulates, reaching its highest elevation southeast of Pocatello on 9,278-foot Bonneville Peak. After being broken by the Portneuf River, the range once again climbs steeply, reaching high points at Sedgwick Peak, Baldy Mountain, and Cottonwood Peak. Sedgwick Peak, at 9,167 feet, is the highest point in the southern section, and the second highest point in the Portneuf Range. The range encompasses two minor subranges, the Pocatello Range and the Fish Creek Range.

Geologically, these mountains are composed of sedimentary and volcanic formations. Volcanic ash has been deposited in places over underlying layers of limestone, dolomite, shale and quartzite. The eastern slopes contain thick stands of Douglas fir, lodgepole, and limber pine. The drier western slopes of the range are covered by juniper and other mountain shrubs.

The Portneuf Range is administered by the Fort Hall Indian Reservation in the north, the Caribou National Forest in the central sections and by the State of Idaho and the Idaho Falls District of the Bureau of Land Management in the southern section, which also contains much private land.

The quality of vehicular access points varies considerably throughout the range. In general, there are lots of roads and only a few trails. The Forest Service is trying to improve hiking opportunities in the Pocatello area, but because of low use, much of the remaining range is ignored by government planners. A number of Portneuf peaks make enjoyable day hikes and scrambles. While none of the peaks present any technical difficulties, they tower over the surrounding valleys and are blessed with exceptional views. The walk to the top of any of these peaks will be strenuous.

South Putnam Mountain 8,949 feet (Class 2)

South Putnam Mountain is located 15.0 miles due east of Pocatello, at the north end of Portneuf Range. It is located inside the Fort Hall Indian Reservation and permission must be acquired before attempting the ascent (see Addresses in the Introduction). The peak is rated Class 2 via the south ridge, which can be accessed from Webb Creek [Approach: (S)(3)(a)] or Topance Creek [Approach: (B)(2)(a)]. On clear days, most of the region is visible from the summit, including the Pioneers to the northwest and the Tetons to the northeast. USGS South Putnam Mountain

THE POCATELLO RANGE

The Pocatello Range consists of a group of low peaks just east of Pocatello, which are connected to the western slopes of the main Portneuf crest. Chinks Peak, at 6,791 feet, is the highest summit in these mountains. The area is covered by the Moonlight Mountain quad. Access to the peaks is not difficult—if you have a 4WD. Much of this area is in private ownership, with several large blocks of BLM land clustered mostly in the southern end.

Moonlight Mountain 6,639 feet
Camelback Mountain 6,586 feet (Class 2)

These two Pocatello Range peaks are located directly east of Pocatello on land owned by the BLM. Neither peak has a road to its summit—but the Pocatello Creek Road system [Approach: (A)(1)] provides easy access to both summits. USGS Moonlight Mountain

---

Bonneville Peak 9,271 feet
Snow Peak 9,132 feet (Class 2)

Bonneville Peak is the highest point in the Portneuf Range. The peak can be accessed from almost any direction. Many people climb it from the Pebble Creek Ski Area by following the ski runs up toward the ridge line. Another route, recommended as more aesthetically pleasing, involves a long ridge walk and an ascent of 9,132-foot Snow Peak. Drive to the Robbers Roost trailhead [Approach: (A)(6)(a)] and then hike FST-073 east to the Portneuf divide. From the divide, hike the Class 2 ridge line north to Snow Peak, which is roughly 1.5 miles away. Descend that peak's north ridge toward Bonneville Peak, which is 1.0 mile to the north. If a car is left at the Pebble Creek trailhead, a descent to that point would save a re-ascent of Snow Peak. USGS Bonneville Peak

Haystack Mountain 9,033 feet (Class 2)

Haystack Mountain is the large rounded summit 3.0 miles south of Snow Peak. Climb to the summit from the pass between Snow Peak and Haystack Mountain. Leave FST-073 at the saddle and hike the ridge line south to the summit, which is less than 1.0 mile away [Approach: (A)(6)(a)]. USGS Haystack Mountain

THE FISH CREEK RANGE

The Fish Creek Range is centered just east of Lava Hot Springs. This small but rugged subrange is about 21 miles in length and 6 miles in width. Petticoat Peak is the highest peak in the range at 8,033 feet. The entire range is administered by the Idaho Falls District of the BLM.

Petticoat Peak   *8,033 feet (Class 2)*

Petticoat Peak, the only named summit in the Fish Creek Range, is located 4.0 miles northeast of Lava Hot Springs. Its summit is an easy Class 2 scramble from the roads on its west and north slopes. Climb the southeast ridge from US-30 where the highway crosses the Fish Creek Divide, just east of Soda Springs [Approach: (C)(1)]. Most of the range is administered by the Idaho Falls District Office of the BLM. USGS Bancroft 15-minute

APPROACHES TO THE PORTNEUF RANGE

Approach routes for this section are referenced in the text by bracketed entries [Approach:], which include appropriate letter and number references.

As with almost all areas administered by the Caribou National Forest, roads run all over the Portneuf Range—and all hiking trails are open for motorcycle use. Primary approach is from Pocatello via I-15, and from US-30, which runs east from I-15 to the town of Lava Hot Springs. The southern section, around Sedgwick Peak, is administered by the State of Idaho and has no hiking trails, but plenty of roads.

(A)   Pocatello Area Access.

Primary approach to Pocatello is via I-15 and I-86. All essential services are available in town.

(1) Pocatello Creek Roads. These roads are accessed from the first I-15 exit south (about 1.0 mile) of the I-15/I-86 junction. This road system proceeds due east from the freeway into the group of minor peaks known as the Pocatello Range. In addition to the main routes, a number of side roads traverse these canyons and ridges. One side road leads to the summit of Chinks Peak, the highest point in the Pocatello Range.

(2) Rapid Creek Road. This road is the main artery used to access the Webb Creek Road and Inman Creek Road. To reach the Rapid Creek

Road, drive south from Pocatello on I-15 to the Inkom exit (15.0 miles south of I-86). From the stop sign at the end of the exit, turn right and drive 50 yards and then turn left. Follow this road until you reach a stop sign. Turn left again, and you are on the Rapid Creek Road. The road goes under the Interstate and then north. It is 5.0 miles to the Webb Creek Road and 4.2 miles to the Inman Creek Road.

(3) FS-019, Webb Creek Road. From the I-15 Inkom exit, drive north up the Rapid Creek drainage to Webb Creek. Turn onto FS-019 and follow it up the Webb Creek drainage for 2.0 miles until this rough dirt road ends.

(a) FST-087, Webb Creek Trail. This trail climbs up along Webb Creek. About 1.75 miles from the trailhead, the trail forks. The right fork, FST-081, climbs to the Portneuf divide in another 0.75 mile, where it joins FS-018. The left fork continues up Webb Creek and reaches the Portneuf divide in another 3.0 miles (as the crow flies). Although this trail shows up on the maps, it is not well maintained; the upper portions of the canyon are, basically, a cross-country hike.

(4) FS-018, Inman Creek Road. Exit I-15 at Inkom and drive up along Rapid Creek to Inman Creek. FS-018 runs up the Inman Creek drainage and crosses the Portneuf divide to join with FS-013, which descends along the North Fork of Pebble Creek to the Big Springs CG.

(5) FS-210, Green Canyon Road. Access this road from the I-15 Inkom exit. Drive west from the freeway for a little over 1.0 mile and then follow the road south for a long mile to Green Canyon. The road turns east and climbs up to the Pebble Creek Ski Area. This approach is kept in excellent shape.

(a) FST-072, The Boundary Trail. This trail forms a 36.0-mile loop, which circles Bonneville Peak, Snow Peak and Haystack Mountain. There are several other ways to approach this trail, but none is on a better road. Access this trail just after the road crosses the national forest boundary.

(6) FS-035, Robbers Roost Road. Take I-15 to the Inkom exit. Exit and drive south through Inkom and under the freeway on US-91/US-191 for 7.0 miles to reach FS-035. Turn east onto FS-035 and drive 2.3 miles to its end.

(a) FST-073, Robbers Roost Creek Trail. From the road's end, it is 5.0 miles to the Portneuf divide between Haystack and Snow Peaks. The trail begins in the creek bottom and then climbs out of the trees to the steep dry ridges above. From the divide, FST-073 and FST-074 both descend to the east to the Big Springs area on Pebble Creek. The trails vary in quality but are passable.

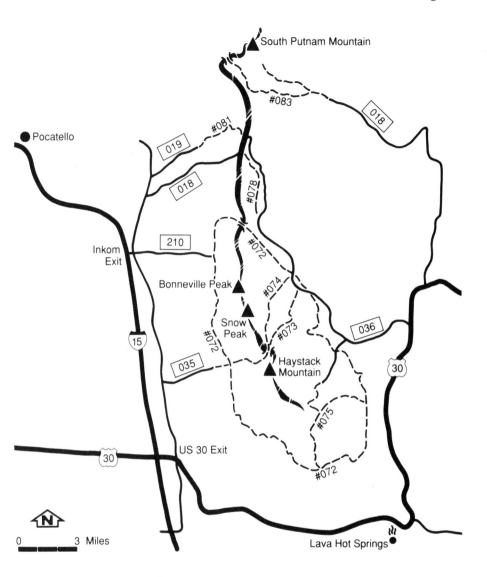

CENTRAL PORTNEUF RANGE
ROADS AND TRAILS

(B) East Side Access.

The following approach routes begin in Lava Hot Springs, a small resort town on US-30. Originally, US-30 left Lava Hot Springs and proceeded around the northern end of the Fish Creek Range on its journey to Soda Springs. The highway now runs straight across the Fish Creek Range just south of Petticoat Peak and proceeds directly east to Soda Springs. The old highway is referred to as US-30N in the following write-ups.

(1) FS-036, Pebble Creek Road. From Lava Hot Springs, follow US-30N north for 8.0 miles. Turn west on FS-036 and follow it to the Big Springs CG.

(a) Big Springs Area Trails. FST-072, FST-073 and FST-074 can all be accessed from the Big Springs area. See [Approach: (A)(6)(a)] above for more details.

(2) FS-018, Topance Creek Road. Take US-30N north from Lava Hot Springs for 9.0 miles to the point where the highway makes a sweeping turn to the east. Turn left off the highway and follow the gravel road that leads north up the Portneuf River. This road leads to Topance Creek in roughly 5.0 miles. Turn west on FS-018 and follow the road to its end.

(a) FST-083, Buckskin Trail. This primitive trail stretches from the end of the Topance Creek Road up the Middle Fork of Topance Creek to a point on the Portneuf divide south of South Putnam Mountain.

(C) Southern Portneuf Range Access.

Primary approach to the southern sections of the Portneuf Range is via US-30.

(1) Dempsey Creek Road. Turn south off US-30 just east of Lava Hot Springs onto the Dempsey Creek Road. This road provides direct access to the roads that crisscross the southern sections of the range, including the road that crosses Windy Pass and Baldy Mountain and leads to the summit of Sedgwick Peak.

(2) Fish Creek Range Access. The Fish Creek Range is surrounded by US-30N and US-30. US-30 crosses this range 3.0 miles southeast of Petticoat Peak. A second road leaves US-30N just north of Lava Hot Springs and crosses the range north of Petticoat Peak. Though its upper reaches are a crude jeep trail, it provides the best access to Petticoat Peak.

9. The Blackfoot Mountains

The Blackfoot Mountains and their two subranges, the Chesterfield and Ninety Percent ranges, form a group of barren ridges which trend from northwest to southeast for over 50 miles between Idaho Falls and Soda Springs. The range's western slopes climb roughly 2,400 feet above the Snake River, but the eastern slopes rise only 600 feet above the Willow Creek and Blackfoot River drainages. Taylor Mountain, at 7,414 feet, and Blackfoot Peak, 7,550 feet, are the range's highest points. Wolverine Canyon forms a scenic gorge on the western slope of the range; this canyon offers some rock climbing opportunities on impressive cliffs and weird rock formations.

Much of the land is in private ownership. There is no national forest land, but the Idaho Falls District of the BLM and the State of Idaho control some large tracts of land. This ownership pattern causes some access problems for the public. For example, the summit of Taylor Mountain is owned by the BLM, but the peak is completely surrounded by private land.

Access is via the numerous county and BLM roads that penetrate the entire range. Private land often blocks access to public land and complicates access considerations. There are no maintained trails within these mountains. Because of the low elevations within these ranges, they are usually free of snow a month earlier than more lofty mountains. Opportunities for early season cross-country hikes and ascents are plentiful.

Taylor Mountain 7,414 feet (Class 2)
Taylor Mountain sits southeast of Idaho Falls and 12.0 miles east of Firth. At one time, a small ski area was operated on its slopes. The summit is publicly owned, but the surrounding land is private. If you are interested in visiting the summit, contact the Idaho Falls District of the BLM to learn the current status of public access to this peak. Aesthetically, the best route is to climb the peak from Wolverine Canyon. USGS Ammon 15-minute

Blackfoot Peak 7,550 feet (Class 2)
Blackfoot Peak, the highest point in the Blackfoot Mountains, is located on Blue Ridge east of Blackfoot and 8.5 miles south of Taylor Mountain. The summit is located on BLM land and can be climbed from any direction; but because of access considerations, it is difficult to approach the peak, which is surrounded by private land. As with Taylor Mountain, discuss your approach route with the BLM beforehand. USGS Poison Creek

THE CHESTERFIELD RANGE

The Chesterfield Range, an extension of the Blackfoot Mountains, is located between the Blackfoot River and the Portneuf River. This minor escarpment is roughly 30 miles in length and is composed of a series of parallel ridges with no prominent peaks. Elevations reach above 7,000 feet on Reservoir Mountain, which is on the west shore of Blackfoot Reservoir.

Reservoir Mountain 7,000+ feet (Class 2)
Reservoir Mountain is located on the west shore of Blackfoot Reservoir. It is an easy climb from the road along the reservoir's west shore via the peak's east slopes [Approach: (A)(2.1)] or [Approach: (B)(1)]. The mountain is entirely owned by the state of Idaho, so access is no problem. USGS Henry 15-minute

NINETY PERCENT RANGE

The Ninety Percent Range is the southern-most extension of the Blackfoot Mountains. It extends southeast from the Chesterfield Range to Soda Springs. The smallest mountain range in Idaho, it is roughly 7 miles long and 3 miles wide. The highest point, 6,851 feet in altitude, is unnamed. Most of this mountain group is in private ownership; the Idaho Falls District of the BLM administers a few acres.

APPROACHES TO THE BLACKFOOT MOUNTAINS

Approach routes for this section are referenced in the text by bracketed entries [Approach:], which include appropriate letter and number references.

(A) West Side Access.

Primary approach is from Idaho Falls and US-91, which parallels I-15 between Idaho Falls and Blackfoot. Beyond the primary routes, these mountains are crisscrossed by gravel roads.

(1) Bone Road. This road leaves Idaho Falls and runs along the east side of the range. To access this road from downtown Idaho Falls, take West Yellowstone Avenue east to Lincoln Road. Turn right onto Lincoln Road, which leads out of town and eventually becomes the Bone Road.

(2) Wolverine Canyon Road. This road starts south of Firth and traverses the range south of Taylor Mountain before eventually meeting the Bone Road south of the tiny hamlet of Bone. This road also splits and follows the Blackfoot River along the southern portion of the range.

(2.1) Blackfoot Reservoir Road. This road leaves the Wolverine Canyon Road just before it enters the canyon and then runs east to Blackfoot Reservoir. This gravel road is well maintained.

(B) East Side Access.

Access for the eastern side of the Blackfoot Mountains begins along US-30 in Soda Springs.

(1) Chesterfield Range Access. The Chesterfield Range is covered with roads. The main public road follows along the west side of Blackfoot Reservoir from Soda Springs. It is advisable to use a BLM land status map on visits to this area because the public and private lands are difficult to differentiate.

(2) Ninety Percent Range Access. Access this range directly from Soda Springs via several dirt roads that leave from the townsite. There is very little public land to visit in this area. If you want to travel in this area, contact the Idaho Falls District of the BLM for up-to-date access information.

10. The Bear River Range

The Bear River Range is a northern extension of Utah's Wasatch Range. The Idaho portion of the range is 43 miles long, over 20 miles wide, and contains many peaks over 9,000 feet high. The name is derived from the Bear River, which loops around the range on its east, north, and west sides. The range ends abruptly at Soda Springs, where the Bear River makes a great curve, cutting the range off from its northern neighbors.

Sherman Peak is the highest point in the Bear River Range, reaching an elevation of 9,682 feet. For the most part, the Bear River crest is rolling, with a few large rounded summits reaching above treeline. Much of the range is composed of limestone, which has eroded to form sinkholes, ponds, disappearing streams, and many subsurface caves.

The Caribou National Forest administers the Bear River Range. Only a small section of the range, its extreme southwestern corner, is managed as roadless land. Most of the range is covered with roads—and where there are trails, they are open to motorcycles and all-terrain vehicles. If more hikers were to use these trails, it is likely that the Forest Service would attempt to close some of them to motor vehicles. The major peaks in the range offer hikers and peakbaggers interesting but non-technical climbing goals. All are rated as Class 2 climbs.

Sherman Peak *9,682 feet (Class 1)*

Sherman Peak, the highest Bear River Range peak, is located 12.0 miles south of Soda Springs. The Peak is accessed from FS-425, the Eight mile Creek Road and FST-317 [Approach: (A)(1)(a)]. It is roughly 3.0 miles to the summit via the trail. USGS North Canyon

Paris Peak *9,575 feet (Class 2)*

Paris Peak is situated 18.0 miles due south of Sherman Peak and just north of Bloomington Creek. The peak is accessed via FS-409, the Bloomington Creek Road. Follow this road west from Bloomington until it reaches the confluence of the North Fork, Middle Fork and South Fork of Bloomington Creek. From this point an old road (closed to 4WDs), FST-453, follows the North Fork [Approach: (A)(2)(a)]. After 1.0 mile, this route switchbacks out of the creek bottom and begins a climb up the south slopes of Paris Peak. The former jeep trail ends on the north side of the peak at 8,800 feet. To climb this peak, leave the road at its end and climb the peak's north ridge, or leave the road at the point where it crosses the peak's broad south ridge and hike that ridge to the summit. Neither ridge presents any objective problems. USGS Paris Peak

Bloomington Peak *9,311 feet (Class 2)*
Bloomington Peak sits at the head of the Bloomington Canyon, 3.0 miles southwest of Paris Peak. Bloomington Peak's north face is as steep and rugged as Bear River Range peaks get. Climb to the summit from almost any direction. (The north ridge, from the Middle Fork of Bloomington Creek, is recommended as the most enjoyable ascent route [Approach: (A)(2.1)].) USGS Paris Peak

Saint Charles Mountain* *9,245 feet (Class 2)*
This unnoffically named mountain rises up directly south of Bloomington Lake, 2.0 miles southeast of Bloomington Peak. The peak is a tri-summited mass, with the middle summit the most impressive point. The peak can be climbed from the High Line Trail [Approach: (A)(2)(b.1)], which intersects the western ridge, or from Bloomington Lake [Approach: (A)(2)(b)]. The route from the lake is more challenging, bordering on a Class 3 climb. From the lake, the route circles around the lake's east shore and climbs up the sloping terrace above the sedimentary cliffs that rise out of the lake. Above the cliffs are three couloirs. All three will lead to the upper slopes on the middle summit without significant difficulties. From the ridge line, follow the crest east to the highest summit. USGS Paris Peak

APPROACHES TO THE BEAR RIVER RANGE

Approach routes for this section are referenced in the text by bracketed entries [Approach:], which include appropriate letter and number references.

US-30 and US-89 provide primary access to the east side of the range; ID-34 is the primary access route on the west side. ID-36 crosses the range between Preston and Montpelier. Two other roads cross the range, one north of ID-36 and one south of ID-36. Only a few of the many roads and trails in this area are listed below.

(A) US-30 Access Points.
This two-lane highway is the main travel route between Soda Springs and Utah, on the range's western side.

(1) FS-425, Eight Mile Creek Road. This road is accessed from downtown Soda Springs. The road runs due south into the mountains to Cold

Springs CG in about 12.0 miles and then continues south, eventually connecting other Forest Sevice roads, which link up with ID-36.

(a) FST-317, Sherman Peak Trail. Access this trail from FS-425 0.5 mile south of Cold Springs CG. The trail runs from the road up Mill Fork Creek for nearly 2.0 miles and then begins an ascent of Sherman Peak, which is reached after 3.5 miles. This trail is not well maintained.

(2) FS-409, Bloomington Creek Road. Access this road from US-89 in Bloomington and take it west into the mountains. The road eventually divides into three routes. The south fork goes to the Bloomington Lake trailhead. The middle fork goes to the area north of Bloomington Peak; the north fork provides access to the Paris Peak area. Passenger cars are not recommended along the upper reaches of this road system.

(a) FST-453, Paris Peak Trail. This trail leaves FS-409 at the confluence of the North and Middle forks of Bloomington Creek and climbs to 8,800 feet on the north side of Paris Peak in 3.5 miles. This trail is an old road which is now closed to all but hikers, horses and (unfortunately) motorcyles.

(b) Bloomington Lake Trail. Take the south fork of the Bloomington Creek Road until it splits at Telegraph Park. Go left at this fork for roughly 1.0 mile. The road ends just below the lakes.

(b.1) High Line Trail Access. The South Fork of Bloomington Creek Road also provides access to the High Line trail, which follows the Bear River Range crest from north to south for over 45.0 miles. Although the trail does not cross any major summits along its route, it still constitutes the premier ridge walk in the Bear River Range. The trail crosses alpine meadows and hovers around the 9,000-foot contour for almost its entire distance.

(2.1) FS-456, Middle Fork of Bloomington Creek Road. This road follows the Middle Fork west for 2.5 miles. Passenger cars are not recommended.

11. The Peale Mountains

East of the Bear River Range, a scattered group of geologically related mountains fill Idaho's easternmost corner. The name "Peale Mountains" was adopted by the writers who compiled the Idaho Encyclopedia to identify this tangled web of ridges and peaks—and to honor the geologist A. C. Peale, who was the first to propose that this area was actually one group of mountains instead of many. However, the USGS ignored this recommendation in favor of naming each individual ridge as a separate mountain range. The primary USGS subdivisions of the Peale Mountains are: the Schmid Ridge, the Grays Range, the Aspen Range, Dry Ridge, the Pruess Range, and the Wooley Range. These ridges, in total, occupy an area roughly 65 miles in length and 25 miles in width. Meade Peak is the highest point in the Peale Mountains.

The Peale Mountains receive little more than 24 inches of precipitation per year and consequently are somewhat dry in appearance. Large stands of pine and fir are interspersed with thick aspen stands, while thick brush fills many creek bottoms. The high ridges are bare of trees. Valley-to-summit elevation differences can be substantial, and sections of the range are quite rugged.

The majority of the Peale Mountains are administered by the Caribou National Forest. The Idaho Falls District of the BLM has some holdings in the area, but they are minor. In addition, several large chemical companies hold the mineral rights to extensive deposits of phosphates found throughout the range. Several of these deposits are being exploited by large open-pit mining operations, which are causing significant environmental deterioration in some areas.

Mining and grazing have traditionally dominated the economic uses of these mountains. The area is lightly used by hikers for two reasons: there are only a few trails, few of which are maintained; and many people automatically assume the area is a wasteland because of the extensive mining operations. While in some areas the environment has been terribly damaged by the phosphate mining, many places are untouched and almost pristine in nature. Cross-country travel can be difficult due to brushy conditions. Still, many open slopes exist, and some peaks reach well above treeline.

Although few people in Idaho know anything about the Peale Mountains, make it your business to visit the range. The scenery is exceptional, access is adequate and, above all, the range needs friends. Hike the range and tell the Forest Service to consider your interests the next time they make a planning decision. At this time, mining and grazing interests are the only groups that make demands on the Forest Service. You can change that!

THE GRAYS RANGE

This Peale Mountain subrange forms the northernmost extension of the range. This group rises up south of Grays Lake and extends southeast for roughly 10 miles. The range contains two named peaks: Lanes Butte, 8,320 feet, and Henrys Peak, 8,300+ feet. Although no one has reported summiting on Lanes Butte, it is likely that many people

have ambled across its summit. This subrange is administered by the Caribou National Forest.

Henrys Peak* *8,300+ feet (Class 2)*
Henrys Peak sits 7.0 miles due east of Blackfoot Reservoir; it is the northernmost Peale Mountain peak covered by this guide. It is climbed from FS-191, which follows Gravel Creek [Approach: (A)(1)] on the peak's eastern slopes. Hike to the top from the end of FS-191. USGS Lanes Creek 15-minute

THE WOOLEY RANGE

The Wooley Range is located east of Blackfoot Reservoir and due south of the Grays Range. It is the smallest of the Peale Mountain subranges, extending only 7 miles from northwest to southeast. The range's highest point, unnamed, reaches 7,800 feet. USGS Lanes Creek 15-minute

THE WEBSTER RANGE

This Peale Mountain subrange forms the eastern boundary of these mountains. The range is located along the Idaho/Wyoming border, stretching 25 miles from north to south. Draney Peak, at 9,131 feet, is the highest point in this group. Draney Peak overlooks the Smoky Canyon phosphate mine; the summit is only recommended for those who wish (for some perverse reason) to watch mining operations from a great height.

Diamond Peak *8,697 feet (Class 2)*
Diamond Peak, the second highest peak in the Webster Range, is located 10.0 miles west of Auburn, Wyoming. The summit is accessed from Stump Creek to the east. From the road's end, follow FST-016 [Approach: (A)(2)(a)] up the Horse Creek drainage to the base of the peak's east ridge. From here, you can hike cross country up the east ridge to the summit. A second option is to continue on the trail until it intersects with another trail, which leads off to the north. From this junction, hike north to the top of the peak's west ridge and then follow the ridge to the top. USGS Freedom 15-minute

THE ASPEN RANGE

The Aspen Range forms the westernmost section of the Peale Mountains. This subrange extends south from the Blackfoot River for 23 miles, ending at the range's highest point, Harrington Peak. Sulphur Peak, 8,302 feet, is the only other named peak in the range. Its lower slopes are the sight of an active phosphate mine and an ascent of the peak is not recommended. The range is administered by the BLM in the north end (which also includes many private land holdings) and by the Caribou National Forest at its southern end.

Harrington Peak   *8,554 feet (Class 2)*
Harrington Peak is the highest Aspen Range Peak. It is located 8.0 miles northeast of Georgetown. The summit can be reached from the left fork of Georgetown Canyon by following the peak's southeast ridge north from Summit View CG [Approach: (A)(4)]. It is about 3.5 cross-country miles to the summit. USGS

THE PRUESS RANGE

The southern end of the Peale Mountains is known as the Pruess Range. This group is roughly 25 miles from north to south, and 12 miles east to west. The range, which was named for William Pruess (a topographer in John C. Freemont's 1842 expedition) contains three peaks worth climbing.

Hawks Peak   *9,079 feet (Class 2)*
This peak is located directly above the Georgetown Canyon Road [Approach: (A)(2)], due east of Snowdrift Mountain. The summit is a very steep Class 2 scramble from the road via its south ridge. USGS Harrington Peak

Snowdrift Mountain   *9,577 feet (Class 1)*
Snowdrift Mountain, situated east of Georgetown, is a Class 1 hike via the Snowdrift Mountain trail [Approach: (A)(3)(a)]. It is roughly 4.5 miles to the summit from Georgetown Saddle. The peak is a broad, high ridge, which has a north/south orientation. Water that falls onto the mountain's western slopes flows into the Great Basin; onto its eastern slopes, into the Columbia Basin via the Salt and Snake Rivers. The views from the top are terrific! USGS Snowdrift Mountain

Meade Peak   *9,957 feet (Class 3)*
Meade Peak is the highest point in the Peale Mountains, and the second highest Idaho peak south of the Snake River. The peak, which is located 7.0 miles east of Georgetown, was named for General George C. Meade of Civil War fame. The summit area can be accessed from two directions. The first approach follows the Snowdrift Mountain Trail [Approach: (A)(2)(a)] to Meade Basin--a long but enjoyable 7.0-mile hike. The second approach leaves the Georgetown Canyon Road just before the National Forest boundary line and proceeds up the Right Hand Fork Canyon [Approach: (A)(5)] until the road ends. From the road's end, you must go cross country up to the ridge line south of the peak and then cross into Meade Basin. The peak is a walkup via its north

ridge or east slopes. The south ridge and west slopes are Class 3 scrambles on rotten rock. USGS Meade Peak

APPROACHES TO THE PEALE MOUNTAINS

Approach routes for this section are referenced in the text by bracketed entries [Approach:], which include appropriate letter and number references.

(A) Peale Mountain Access Points.
Primary approach to these mountains is via US-30, which provides access to the western side. US-89, which traverses the southern and eastern reaches, and ID-34 provide northern access. Many secondary and Forest Service roads provide access to all parts of the range. The limited approach write-ups below are designed to direct you to the peaks listed in this guide—do not let the limited listing keep you from exploring.
   (1) Henrys Peak Access. This route begins along ID-34 at Wayan. Turn south off of the highway and drive south nearly 1.0 mile to a second junction, where you turn right. In just over another mile, turn left and drive south along Gravel Creek until the road ends.
   (2) Diamond Peak Access. Begin along US-89 4.0 miles north of Afton, Wyoming. Turn west off the highway and drive to Auburn, where the road jogs to the south for 0.5 mile. Turn west again on the Stump Creek Road and follow it for about 5.0 miles to the Stump Creek GS.
   (a) FST-016, Horse Creek Trail. This trail begins near the Stump Creek GS and runs due west up the drainage for 5.0 miles to a four-trail junction. Diamond Peak is just north of the trail near its western end.
   (3) FS-102, Georgetown Canyon Road. This is the major approach road in the center of the Peale Mountains. Access this road from US-30 at Georgetown. The road leads due east into the mountains. Just over 2.0 miles from US-30, a left turn leads north into the Left Fork of Georgetown Canyon. The main road continues into the mountains, crosses Georgetown Saddle and drops down into Diamond Creek. The Diamond Creek Road eventually connects with ID-34 many miles to the north. Georgetown Canyon was the sight of an active phosphate mine in the past—remnants are still visible today.
   (a) Snowdrift Mountain Trail. From the Georgetown Saddle, a good trail leads up the

ridge line to the south and crosses over Snowdrift Mountain, then drops into Meade Basin on the east side of Meade Peak. After steeply climbing for the first mile, the trail emerges on the top of Snowdrift Mountain ridge, where there is open hiking with spectacular views of the Bear River area and the Salt River Range in Wyoming. It is 7.0 miles to the basin from Georgetown Saddle.

(4) FS-095, Left Fork of Georgetown Canyon Road. This road leads north from the Georgetown Canyon Road between the Aspen Range and Schmid Ridge. Dozens of roads depart from this road.

(5) FS-225, Right Fork Georgetown Canyon Road. This road leaves FS-102 just west of the National Forest boundary and runs up the canyon for 3.0 miles. This road is not recommended for passenger cars.

12. The Caribou Range

This range is located just south of the Snake River on the Idaho/Wyoming border. Palisades Reservoir and the Snake River form the Caribou's northern boundary. The Salt River in Wyoming forms the eastern boundary of the range, the Peale Mountains the south, and Blackfoot Reservoir and Grays Lake form the western boundary.

The Caribou Range covers an area over 60 miles in length and 20 miles in width and reaches 9,805 feet on Caribou Mountain. The northern end of the range is composed of a number of parallel ridges that rise and fall in a wavelike succession, while the central portion of the range contains all of the major summits. The Caribou landscape is interspersed with rolling meadows, dense stands of pines and fir trees and compact quaking aspen groves. The geologic history is written in sedimentary rocks, which have been intruded by igneous rock. These intrusions produced gold deposits, and the area was mined in the late 1800s. In addition, there are phosphate deposits just waiting to be exploited.

The range is officially part of the Caribou National Forest, but is managed in a large part by the Targhee National Forest. Self-propelled recreational use of the range is minimal; a pity, because these mountains are among the most picturesque in the state. Access is better than average and the trail system, while not heavily used, is extensive. Climbing opportunities are limited to Class 1 and Class 2 hikes up dome-shaped summits.

Red Peak *8,720 feet (Class 1)*
Red Peak is located 6.0 miles due west of the Palisades Dam. It is the northernmost of the

Caribou peaks covered by this guidebook. The summit is reached by the Red Ridge Trail from Long Gulch [Approach: (A)(1.1)(a)]. The peak can be approached from a number of other directions, but all of these routes are considerably longer. USGS Red Ridge

Big Elk Mountain *9,476 feet*
Little Elk Mountain *8,760 feet (Class 1)*
Big Elk and Little Elk mountains are located roughly 7.5 miles south of Red Mountain. These two summits are separated by a snaking ridge line about 3.0 miles long. Trails lead to the summits of these two peaks from at least four directions. From the McCoy Creek Road, take FST-003 [Approach: (B)(1)(b)] up Box Canyon to the summit. (This is reportedly the most scenic route.) The shortest route is via FS-063 [Approach: (A)(2.1)(a)], which is accessed from the Bear Creek Road. Follow FS-063 to its end and then take the seldom-used trail east to the summit of Big Elk. (The Forest Service reports that this trail system was rebuilt in 1989.) Another alternative is to follow FST-041 [Approach: (B)(1)(d)] up Wolverine Canyon to the saddle east of Little Elk, and then follow the ridge trail east to Big Elk or west to Little Elk. The fourth alternative begins at the Bear Creek Trailhead and utilizes FST-044 [Approach: (A)(2)(b)], which follows Muddy and Currant creeks to the summit of Big Elk. USGS Big Elk Mountain

Poker Peak *8,720 feet (Class 2)*
Poker Peak is located 4.0 miles east of Big Elk Mountain, 6.0 miles south of the Palisades Dam. Just south of the Current Creek GS, FST-035 [Approach: (A)(2)(c)] climbs up Pine Creek and traverses nearly to the summit of this peak. From the trail, follow the easy slopes to the summit. USGS Poker Peak

Caribou Mountain *9,803 feet*
Caribou Mountain is situated 5.0 miles east of Bald Mountain. It is a unique-looking summit, with windswept upper ridges and glacial cirques nestled into its northern and eastern slopes. The mountain's summit ridge is almost 1.0 mile long and has two high points—the southern summit is 9,586 feet; the northern, 9,803 feet. The mountain can be climbed from the west or the east. USGS Caribou Mountain

West Side. *(Class 2)*
From FS-019, follow the old jeep trail (best accomplished on foot) [Approach: (B)(2.1)] that climbs up the North Fork of Eagle Creek to the Evergreen Mine at 8,400 feet. From the mine, gain the ridge line above by hiking due south to Point

8732. Once at this point, follow the ridge line northeast to the peak's lower southern summit, and then follow the summit ridge north to the north summit. Total distance from the mine is 1.5 miles, with a 1,200-foot elevation gain. (The peak's south slopes can be climbed from the mine, but that route is much steeper.)

East Side. *(Class 2)*
The east side route climbs the peak's northeast ridge from the jeep trail [Approach: (B)(1)(e)] that cuts across it at 8,400 feet. The northeast ridge provides straightforward access to the summit ridge as it climbs 1,200 feet in 0.6 mile. Once on the summit ridge, turn northeast and follow the ridge the last 0.3 mile to the north summit.

Old Baldy *8,325 feet*
Bald Mountain *8,488 feet (Class 1)*
Old Baldy and Bald Mountain are located on a large northwest/southwest-trending ridge line 8.0 miles south of Poker Peak. These two peaks are separated by 1.0 mile of ridge. Utilize FST-109 [Approach: (B)(1)(c)] from the McCoy Creek Road to reach the summits of both of these peaks. USGS Tincup Mountain

Black Mountain *8,920 feet (Class 1-2)*
Black Mountain sits 4.5 miles east of Bald Mountain on the next parallel ridge line. Black Mountain is formed by a ridge and has three high points, all of which reach above 8,900 feet. This mountain is accessed via FST-004 [Approach: (B)(1)(a)], which leads along the ridge almost to the top of all three summits. USGS Etna

Tincup Mountain *8,184 feet (Class 2)*
Tincup Mountain is situated 6.5 miles southeast of Caribou Mountain and just north of the Pinebar CG. Take FST-009 to FST-110 [Approach: (B)(2)(a)]. Follow FST-110 north for 1.0 mile and then (after a junction) southeast for 0.8 mile. At this point, a trail leads down the Tin Cup ridge toward the summit. USGS Tincup Mountain

APPROACHES TO THE CARIBOU RANGE

Approach routes for this section are referenced in the text by bracketed entries [Approach:], which include appropriate letter and number references.

Primary access to the Caribou Range is from US-26 in Idaho, US-89 in Wyoming, and ID-34 between Freedom, Wyoming, and Wayan, Idaho.

All other points in the range are reached by secondary Forest Service roads. There is a good selection of hiking trails in this range of mountains, most of which are seldom used. Despite the difficulties in reaching the trails, hikers will enjoy the exquisite hiking environment in the Caribous.

(A) US-26 Access Points.
(1) FS-058, Snake River Road. This road follows the south side of the Snake River between the point where US-26 crosses to the north side of the river (west of Swan Valley and Palisades Dam). This good gravel road is passable to passenger cars.
(1.1) FS-059, Long Gulch Road. This road leaves FS-058 at its midpoint and ascends Long Gulch to an organizational camp and a trailhead in about 3.0 miles.
(a) FST-035, Red Ridge Trail. This trail leaves the end of the Long Gulch road and climbs up to the top of Red Ridge in 2.0 miles. Once on the ridge, the trail proceeds southeast, just past the summit of Red Peak, and eventually leads to Palisades Dam in about 9.0 miles.
(2) FS-058, Bear Creek Road. This road leaves US-26 at the Palisades Dam, crosses the dam and proceeds along the reservoir, turns up Elk Creek and then down Jensen Creek where it meets McCoy Creek Road, FS-087 [Approach: (B)(1)]. When dry, this road is passable to passenger cars.
(a) FST-031, Bear Creek Trail System.
This trail system begins just south of the Bear Creek Arm of the Palisades Reservoir, at a trailhead with extensive parking. Bear Creek is the heart of an extensive roadless area that dominates the northern end of the range. Although the trails do not lead to any major peaks, the drainage offers exceptional hiking opportunities. A number of loop trips can be easily put together from the trailhead.
(b) FST-044, Big Elk Peak Trail. FST-044 is accessed from FST-031 just 1.0 mile west of its trailhead. The trail begins by following Muddy Creek and then climbs to the ridge line between Muddy and Currant creeks. After 3.0 miles, the trail reaches the north ridge of Big Elk, where it turns south and proceeds to that peak's summit in another mile. In this vicinity, it junctions with FST-153, which traverses the ridge line between Big Elk and Little Elk mountains.
(c) FST-035, Poker Peak Trail. This trail leaves FS-058 where it crosses Pine Creek. The trail climbs east to the Poker Peak ridge line. Once on the ridge, the trail turns south and leads to the eastern slopes of Poker Peak in 3.5 miles. One mile south of the peak, the trail junctions with several other trails that provide access to the

roadless area between the Bear Creek Road and Palisades Reservoir.

(2.1) FS-063, West Fork Road. This road is accessed from FS-058 a little over 2.0 miles south of where FS-058 leaves Bear Creek. This road runs up the West Fork of Elk Creek for 4.0 miles. It is a primitive road, and a 4WD is recommended.

(a) FST-153, Elk Mountain Trail. This trail begins east of Big Elk Mountain at the end of FS-063 and proceeds west to junction with FST-044 just south of Big Elk Mountain's summit. From this point, the trail continues west along a ridge line and junctions with FST-041 in roughly 2.0 miles. After this junction, the trail continues west to Little Elk Mountain and ends at FS-159 in another 3.0 miles.

(B) US-89 Access Points.

US-89 between Alpine Junction and Afton, Wyoming provides access to the western edge of the Caribou Range. It is a wide two-lane highway.

(1) FS-087, McCoy Creek Road. To reach this road, take US-89 south from Alpine, Wyoming for 8.0 miles and turn east. This road eventually traverses the range and ends at Grays Lake.

(a) FST-004, Black Mountain Trail. Follow the McCoy Creek Road south from Palisades Reservoir for 4.0 miles. The trailhead is on the east side of the road. This trail traverses the major north/south ridge line that has Black Mountain as its high point.

(b) FST-003, Canyon Creek Trail. This trail leaves FS-087 a little over 6.0 miles west of the McCoy Creek CG and follows Canyon Creek northwest to Big Elk Mountain in 6.5 miles.

(c) FST-109, Bald Mountain Trail. This trail leaves FS-087 and quickly climbs a ridge line,

then runs south to Old Baldy Peak in 3.0 miles and Bald Mountain in another mile.

(d) FST-041, Wolverine Creek Trail. Drive east of the Bald Mountain GS and turn north on a dirt road, which will cross Clear Creek and then bring you to Wolverine Creek. The trail follows the creek to the saddle between Big Elk and Little Elk mountains.

(e) Caribou Mountain Access. FS-188, a rocky, seldom-used road, leaves FS-087 at the site of Keenan City (just west of the Caribou Basin GS) and leads south toward Caribou Mountain. Near the headwaters of Barnes Creek, a 4WD road leaves FS-188 and runs south to a mine on the northeastern slope of Caribou Mountain. This jeep trail reaches Caribou Mountain's northeast ridge in 2.0 miles. It is suggested that you hike this road.

(2) ID-34, The Tin Cup Highway. ID-34 crosses the range from Freedom, Wyoming to Wayan, Idaho. This road is well maintained, but far from a major access route.

(a) FST-009 and FS-010, Tincup Mountain Trail. This trail leaves ID-34 1.5 miles west of Pinebar CG and heads north to the ridge line west of Tincup Mountain. From this point, the trail connects with a series of lonesome trails that traverse the roadless area between Black Mountain and Caribou Mountain.

(2.1) Evergreen Mine Access. Leave ID-34 on the east side of Grays Lake 2.5 miles northwest of Wayan by turning onto the county road that parallels the eastern shore of Grays Lake. Shortly after this road crosses Eagle Creek, turn east onto FS-119, which will end in a mile. From this point, a jeep road leads northeast up the North Fork of Eagle Creek to the Evergreen Mine in 3.2 miles. The jeep trail requires a 4WD.

Borah Peak, viewed from the south

APPENDICES

Appendix A: Named Idaho Peaks 10,000 Feet or Higher

Peak	Range	Elevation	USGS Quad
1. Borah Peak	Lost River	12,655	Borah Peak
2. Leatherman Peak	Lost River	12,228	Leatherman Pk
3. Mount Church*	Lost River	12,200+	Leatherman Pk
4. Diamond Peak	Lemhi	12,197	Diamond Peak
5. Mount Breitenbach	Lost River	12,140	Leatherman Pk
6. Lost River Mountain*	Lost River	12,078	Leatherman Pk
7. Mount Idaho*	Lost River	12,065	Elkhorn Creek
8. Donaldson Peak*	Lost River	12,023	Leatherman Pk
9. Hyndman Peak	Pioneer	12,009	Hyndman Peak
10. USGS Peak*	Lost River	11,982	Massacre Mtn
11. No Regret Peak*	Lost River	11,972	Leatherman Pk
12. Bad Rock Peak*	Lost River	11,953	Leatherman Pk
13. Falling Mountain*	Lost River	11,936	Elkhorn Creek
14. Goat Mountain*	Pioneer	11,913	Phi Kappa Mtn
15. McKinley Peak*	Lost River	11,899	Elkhorn Creek
16. Standhope Peak	Pioneer	11,878	Standhope Pk
17. Devils Bedstead East*	Pioneer	11,865	Phi Kappa Mtn
18. Mount Corruption*	Lost River	11,857	Leatherman Pk
19. Brocky Peak*	Pioneer	11,839	Standhope Peak
20. Castle Peak	White Cloud	11,815	Boulder Chain of Lakes
21. Old Hyndman Peak	Pioneer	11,775	Grays Peak
22. Duncans Peak*	Pioneer	11,755	Phi Kappa Mtn
23. Ryan Peak	Boulder	11,714	Ryan Peak
24. Angels Perch*	Pioneer	11,687	Standhope Pk
25. Kent Peak	Boulder	11,664	Ryan Peak
26. Cobb Peak	Pioneer	11,650	Hyndman Peak
27. Mount McCaleb	Lost River	11,640+	Mackay
28. Pyramid Peak	Pioneer	11,628	Copper Basin
29. Bell Mountain	Lemhi	11,618	Diamond Peak
30. Glassford Peak	Boulder	11,602	Ryan Peak
31. Salzburger Spitzl*	Pioneer	11,600+	Phi Kappa Mtn
32. Mount Deception*	Lemhi	11,598	Diamond Peak
33. Smiley Mountain	Pioneer	11,508	Muldoon Canyon
34. Caulkens Peak*	White Cloud	11,487	Boulder Chain of Lakes
35. Shadow Lake Peak*	Lost River	11,401	Massacre Mtn
36. Scott Peak	Beaverhead	11,393	Scott Peak
37. Black Dome	Pioneer	11,353	Copper Basin
38. Big Creek Peak	Lemhi	11,350	Donkey Hills
39. D. O. Lee Peak*	White Cloud	11,342	Washington Pk
40. Invisible Mountain	Lost River	11,330	Mackay
41. Wet Peak	Lost River	11,309	Mackay
42. Shelly Mountain	White Knob	11,278	Mackay
43. Redbird Mountain	White Knob	11,273	Mackay

Peak	Range	Elevation	USGS Quad
44. WCP-9*	White Cloud	11,263	Washington Pk
45. Cabin Mountain	White Knob	11,224	Copper Basin
46. Webber Peak	Beaverhead	11,223	Scott Peak
47. Lime Mountain	White Knob	11,179	Mackay
48. Galena Peak	Boulder	11,153	Galena Peak
49. Eighteenmile Peak	Beaverhead	11,141	Scott Peak
50. Dickey Peak	Lost River	11,141	Dickey Peak
51. Silver Peak	Boulder	11,112	Easley Hot Spr
52. Easley Peak	Boulder	11,108	Easley Hot Spr
53. WCP-10*	White Cloud	11,102	Boulder Chain of Lakes
54. Grouse Creek Mountain	Lost River	11,085	Doublesprings
55. Devils Bedstead West	Pioneer	11,051	Phi Kappa Mtn
56. Cottonwood Mountain	Beaverhead	11,024	Nicholia
57. Flatiron Mountain	Lemhi	11,019	Donkey Hills
58. Italian Peak	Beaverhead	10,998	Scott Peak
59. Lem Peak	Lemhi	10,985	Lem Peak
60. Boulder Peak	Boulder	10,981	Easley Hot Spr
61. May Mountain	Lemhi	10,971	May
62. Yellow Peak	Lemhi	10,968	Patterson
63. Castle Peak	Lost River	10,957	Massacre Mtn
64. Jump Peak	Beaverhead	10,941	Nicholia
65. Massacre Mountain	Lost River	10,924	Massacre Mtn
66. Merriam Peak*	White Cloud	10,920	Boulder Chain of Lakes
67. Sheep Mountain	Boulder	10,915	Rock Roll Canyon
68. Patterson Mountain	White Cloud	10,872	Boulder Chain of Lakes
69. Sheep Mountain	Lemhi	10,865	Gilmore
70. Bowery Peak	Boulder	10,861	Sheep Mountain
71. Gunsight Peak	Lemhi	10,853	Patterson
72. Handwerk Peak	Pioneer	10,840	Phi Kappa Mtn
73. White Knob Mountain	White Knob	10,835	Mackay
74. Portland Mountain	Lemhi	10,820	Gilmore
75. Saddle Mountain	Lemhi	10,810	Tyler Peak
76. Mill Mountain	Lemhi	10,792	Patterson
77. Baldy Mountain	Beaverhead	10,773	Morrison Lake
78. Copper Basin Knob	Pioneer	10,784	Copper Basin
79. WCP-7*	White Cloud	10,777	Washington Pk
80. Jaggle Peak*	Lost River	10,772	Sunset Peak
81. Bear Mountain	Lemhi	10,774	Gilmore
82. Thompson Peak	Sawtooth	10,751	Stanley Lake
83. Tyler Peak	Lemhi	10,740	Tyler Peak
84. Iron Creek Point	Lemhi	10,736	Gilmore
85. Mount Cramer	Sawtooth	10,716	Mount Cramer
86. McGowan Peak*	Lost River	10,716	Doublesprings
87. Decker Peak	Sawtooth	10,704	Mount Cramer
88. Long Mountain	Lemhi	10,696	May
89. Sunset Peak	Lost River	10,693	Sunset Peak
90. Mickeys Spire*	Sawtooth	10,680+	Stanley Lake
91. Sheephorn Peak	Lemhi	10,665	Leadore
92. Snowyside Peak	Sawtooth	10,651	Snowyside Peak
93. Williams Peak	Sawtooth	10,635	Stanley Lake
94. King Mountain	Lost River	10,612	Ramshorn Canyon
95. Inyo Peak	Lemhi	10,611	Patterson
96. Junction Peak	Lemhi	10,608	Leadore

Peak	Range	Elevation	USGS Quad
97. WCP-5*	White Cloud	10,597	Robinson Bar
98. Mount Carter*	Sawtooth	10,590	Stanley Lake
99. WCP-3*	White Cloud	10,588	Robinson Bar
100. Elk Peak	Sawtooth	10,582	Warbonnet Pk
101. Mogg Mountain	Lemhi	10,573	Patterson
102. Negro Peak	Lemhi	10,571	Gilmore
103. Grays Peak	Pioneer	10,563	Grays Peak
104. WCP-8*	White Cloud	10,577	Washington Pk
105. Rocky Peak	Lemhi	10,551	Leadore
106. Scorpion Mountain	Pioneer	10,545	Muldoon Canyon
107. Trail Peak	Lemhi	10,533	Gilmore
108. Washington Peak	White Cloud	10,519	Washington Pk
109. Phi Kappa Mountain	Pioneer	10,516	Phi Kappa Mtn
110. Mount Sevy*	Sawtooth	10,480+	Mount Cramer
111. Horstmann Peak	Sawtooth	10,470	Warbonnet Peak
112. Rock Roll Peak*	Boulder	10,458	Rock Roll Canyon
113. Watson Peak	White Cloud	10,453	Robinson Bar
114. WCP-4*	White Cloud	10,450	Robinson Bar
115. Heart Mountain	Beaverhead	10,442	Edie Ranch
116. Saviers Peak*	Smoky	10,441	Galena
117. Basils Peak*	Boulder	10,414	Amber Lakes
118. White Mountain	Salmon River	10,400+	Twin Peaks
119. Big Windy Peak	Lemhi	10,400+	Gilmore
120. Meridian Peak	Boulder	10,400+	Meridian Peak
121. Mount Limbert*	Sawtooth	10,385	Stanley Lake
122. Center Mountain	Beaverhead	10,362	Goldstone Mtn
123. WCP-1*	White Cloud	10,353	Robinson Bar
124. Braxon Peak	Sawtooth	10,353	Mount Cramer
125. Twin Peaks	Salmon River	10,340	Twin Peaks
126. Cache Peak	Albion	10,339	Independence Mtn
127. Norton Peak	Smoky	10,336	Galena
128. The General*	Salmon River	10,329	Mount Jordan
129. Mount Iowa*	Sawtooth	10,327	Mount Cramer
130. Mounument Peak	Beaverhead	10,323	Homer Young Pk
131. Croesus Peak*	White Cloud	10,322	Horton Peak
132. Merritt Peak*	Sawtooth	10,312	Stanley Lake
133. Bald Mountain	Salmon River	10,313	Bald Mountain
134. Copper Mountain	Beaverhead	10,303	Copper Mountain
135. Blackman Peak	White Cloud	10,300	Washington Pk
136. Baron Peak	Sawtooth	10,297	Warbonnet Peak
137. Parks Peak	Sawtooth	10,280	Snowyside Mtn
138. Targhee Peak	Henrys Lake	10,280	Henrys Lake
139. Mackay Peak	White Knob	10,273	Mackay
140. Freeman Peak	Beaverhead	10,273	Homer Youngs Pk
141. WCP-2*	White Cloud	10,271	Robinson Bar
142. Perfect Peak*	Sawtooth	10,269	Snowyside Peak
143. Glide Mountain	Pioneer	10,265	Muldoon Canyon
144. WCP-6*	White Cloud	10,256	Robinson Bar
145. Black Mountain	Henrys Lake	10,237	Henrys Lake
146. Bromaghin Peak	Smoky	10,225	Galena
147. Redfish Peak*	Sawtooth	10,212	Mount Cramer
148. Payette Peak	Sawtooth	10,211	Snowyside Mtn
149. Cirque Lake Peak*	Sawtooth	10,210	Warbonnet

Peak	Range	Elevation	USGS Quad
150. Goat Perch*	Sawtooth	10,200+	Mount Cramer
151. Warbonnet Peak	Sawtooth	10,200+	Warbonnet Peak
152. Mount Heyburn	Sawtooth	10,200+	Mount Cramer
153. Mount Jefferson	Centennial Lakes	10,196	Upper Red Rocks
154. Horse Prairie Peak	Beaverhead	10,194	Deadman Pass
155. Mount Regan	Sawtooth	10,190	Stanley Lake
156. Bald Peak	Henrys Lake	10,180	Henrys Lake
157. Baker Peak	Smoky	10,174	Baker Peak
158. Red Conglomerates Pk	Beaverhead	10,150+	Edie Ranch
159. Prairie Creek Peak*	Smoky	10,138	Baker Peak
160. Imogene Peak*	Sawtooth	10,125	Snowyside Mtn
161. Two Point Mountain	Boise	10,124	Newman Peak
162. Titus Peak*	Smoky Mts	10,110	Galena
163. Smoky Dome	Soldier	10,095	Fairfield
164. Redfish Point*	Sawtooth	10,095	Mount Cramer
165. Mount McGuire	Bighorn Crags	10,082	Mount Mcguire
166. Monte Verita	Sawtooth	10,080+	Warbonnet Peak
167. Eagle Perch*	Sawtooth	10,080+	Mount Cramer
168. Mayan Temple*	Sawtooth	10,080	Warbonnet Peak
169. Reward Peak	Sawtooth	10,074	Warbonnet Peak
170. McDonald Peak	Sawtooth	10,068	Snowyside Peak
171. Mount Jordan	Salmon River	10,063	Mount Jordan
172. Copperhead Peak	Beaverhead	10,060	Homer Youngs Pk
173. Glenns Peak	Sawtooth	10,053	Mount Everly
174. Big Peak	Smoky	10,047	Baker Peak
175. Tohobit Peak	Sawtooth	10,046	Warbonnet Peak
176. Ajax Peak	Beaverhead	10,028	Homer Youngs Pk
177. Mount Baird	Snake River	10,025	Mount Baird
178. Jerry Peak	Boulder	10,015	Jerry Peak
179. Porphyry Peak	White Knob	10,012	Copper Basin
180. Mount Loening*	Tango	10,012	Knapp Lakes

Appendix B: Highest Peak
in each Idaho Mountain Range
or Subrange

Range	Peak	Elevation	USGS Quad
Albion	Cache Peak	10,339	Independence Mtn
Aspen	Harrington Peak	8,554	Harrington Peak
Bannock	Oxford Peak	9,282	Oxford Peak
Bear River	Sherman Peak	9,682	North Canyon
Beaverhead	Scott Peak	11,393	Scott Peak
Big Hole	Piney Peak	9,019	Garns Mtn
Bighorn Crags	Mount McGuire	10,082	Mount McGuire
Bitterroot	Peak 9439	9,439	Mount Jerusalem
Blackfoot	Blackfoot Mtn	7,550	Poison Creek
Black Pine	Black Peak	9,395	Strevel
Boise	Two Point Mtn	10,214	Newman Peak
Boulder	Ryan Peak	11,714	Ryan Peak
Caribou	Caribou Mountain	9,803	Caribou Mtn.
Centenial	Mount Jefferson	10,196	Upper Red Rocks
Chesterfield	Reservoir Mtn	7,000+	Henry
Chilco	Chilco Mountain	5,685	Bayview
Clearwater	Stripe Mountain	9,001	Stripe Mountain
Coeur d'Alene	Grizzly Mountain	5,960	Kellog
Cotterrel	Peak 7718	7,718	Idahome
Craigs	Craigs Mountain	5,341	Frye Point
Cuddy	Cuddy Mountain	7,867	Copperfield
Danskin	Danskin Peak	6,694	Danskin Peak
Deep Creek	Deep Creek Peak	8,748	Deep Creek Peak
Fish Creek	Petticoat Peak	8,033	Bancroft
Goose Creek	Monument Peak	8,050	Trapper Peak
Grass	Granite Mtn	8,478	Hazzard
Grays	Lanes Butte	8,320	Lanes Creek
Hawley	Hawley Mountain	9,752	Hawley Mtn.
Henrys Lake	Targhee Peak	10,280	Henrys Lake
Hitt	Sturgill Peak	7,589	Sturghill Peak
Hoodoo	Bald Mountain	5,334	Emida
Jim Sage	Elba Peak	8,046	Elba
Lemhi	Diamond Peak	12,197	Diamond Peak
Lick Creek	Nick Peak	9,064	Fitsum Peak
Little Goat	Blackdome Peak	6,412	Boehls Butte
Lost River	Borah Peak	12,655	Borah Peak
Malad	Peak 6995	6,995	Henderson Creek
Moose	Moose Creek Butte	6,937	Moose Mtn.
Ninety Percent	Peak 6851	6,851	Soda Springs
North Fork	East Mountain	7,752	Boiling Springs
North Hansel	Peak 6986	6,986	Co-op Spring
Owyhee	Hayden Peak	8,403	Triangle
Pahsimerio	Dickey Peak	11,141	Dickey Peak
Palouse	Moscow Mountain	4,983	Moscow Mtn.
Pioneer	Hyndman Peak	12,009	Hyndman Peak
Pocatello	Chinks Mountain	6,791	Inkom
Portneuf	Mount Bonneville	9,271	Bonneville Peak
Preuss	Meade Peak	9,957	Meade Peak

Range	Peak	Elevation	USGS Quad
Purcell	Goat Mountain	6,641	Line Point
Saint Joe	Latour Peak	6,408	Saint Joe
Salmon River	White Mountain	10,400+	Twin Peaks
Samaria	Samaria Peak	7,795	Samaria
Sawtooth	Thompson Peak	10,776	Stanley Lake
Schmid	Peak 7923	7,293	Lanes Creek
Selkirk	Parker Peak	7,670	Pyramid Peak
Selway Crags	Fenn Mountain	8,021	Fenn Mtn.
Seven Devils	He Devil	9,393	He Devil
Sheep	Eagle Point	5,709	Sheep Mtn.
Shoshone	Bennett Peak	6,209	Taylor Peak
Silver City	Hayden Peak	8,403	Triangle
Smoky	Saviers Peak*	10,441	Galena
Snake River	Mount Baird	10,025	Mount Baird
Soldier	Smoky Dome	10,095	Fairfield
Sublet	Peak 7492	7,492	Sublet Trough
Tango Peaks	Mount Loening*	10,012	Knapp Lakes
Webster	Draney Peak	9,131	Stewart Flat
West	Snowbank Mtn	8,322	Smiths Ferry
White Cloud	Castle Peak	11,815	Boulder Chain Of Lakes
White Knob	Shelly Mountain	11,278	Mackay
Williams	Williams Peak	7,501	Cayuse Junction
Wooley	Peak 7800	7,800	Lanes Creek
Yellowjacket	Middle Fork Peak	9,127	Aparejo Point

Appendix C: First Ascents of Peaks and Major Formations

Only a peak's first ascent and first winter ascent are listed. First ascents by other routes are listed with route description in the main text. Many first ascents were probably completed by persons who are no longer living and the information is lost forever. However, the author welcomes any pertinent information regarding first ascents.

Season and Peak	Range	Year	Party
Annas Pinnacle	Sawtooth	Summer 1948	Iowa Mountaineers
Arrowhead	Sawtooth	Summer ?	G. Webster/J. Beaupre
Baron Peak	Sawtooth	Summer 1934	R. & M. Underhill/D. Williams
Big Baron Spire	Sawtooth	Summer 1949	F. Beckey/J. Schwabland /P. Schoening
Black Aiguille	Sawtooth	Summer 1960	H. Gmosser/R. Harris /Iowa Mountaineers
Braxon Peak	Sawtooth	Summer Winter 1975	Unknown W. Cove/L. Adkins
Breakfast Tower	Sawtooth	Summer 1961	E. Bjornstad/D. Davis
Cabin Creek Peak	Tango Peaks	Summer 1988	P. Bellamy/D. Lopez /T. Lopez
Castle Peak	White Cloud	Summer Winter 1971	Unknown R. Watters/I. Gayfield J. Hokum/H. Hilbert S. Schaffer/J. Elphinston
Cathedral Rock	Bighorn Creek North Summit	Summer 1924	
U.S. Forest Service	South Summit	Summer 1955	L. Hales/P. Schoening
Chimney Rock	Selkirk	Summer 1934	J. Carey/M. Chamberlain /F. Thieme/B. Ward
		Winter 1973	C. Kopczynski/W. Parks
The Chisel	Bighorn Creek	Summer 1955	L. Hales/P. Schoening
Chockstone Peak	Sawtooth	Summer 1960	Iowa Mountaineers
Cirque Lake Peak	Sawtooth	Summer 1954	Seattle Mountaineers
Cobb Peak	Pioneer	Summer Winter 1971	Unknown R. Watters/J. Lowry / R. Albano/D. McBride / J. Elphinston
Damocles	Sawtooth	Summer 1961	F. Beckey/S. Marts
Desert Tower	Sawtooth	Summer 1961	D. Davis
Devils Bedstd	W. Pioneer	Summer Winter ?	Unknown L. Stur/R. Kiesel B. Gorton/B. Bachman

Season and Peak	Range	Year	Party
Devils Throne	Seven Devil	Summer 1938	A. H. Marshall
Devils Tooth	Seven Devil	Summer 1963	D. Eastman/J. Angel
Dinner Tower	Sawtooth	Summer 1961	E. Bjornstad/D. Davis /S. Marts
Donaldson Peak	Lost River	Summer Winter 1975	Unknown W. March/R. Albano
Eagle Perch	Sawtooth	Summer 1960	H. Gmosser/Iowa Mountaineers
East Lions Head	Selkirk	Summer 196?	N. McAvoy/?
Ed-A-How Spire	Sawtooth	Summer 1973	L. Dye/Spring/Howard /Taylor/Bravance
Ede Peak	Sawtooth	Summer 1948	Iowa Mountaineers
El Capitan	Sawtooth	Summer 1935	R. & M. Underhill/D. Williams
Elephants Perch	Sawtooth	Summer 1960	Iowa Mountaineers
Elk Peak	Sawtooth	Summer 1934	R. Underhill/D. Williams
El Pima	Sawtooth	Summer 1947	F. Beckey/J. Schwabland /P. Schoening
Finger Of Fate	Sawtooth	Summer 1958	L. Stur/J. Fuller
Fishhook Spire	Sawtooth	Summer 1960	R. Maynard/F. Chappel /Iowa Mountaineers
Flat Rock Needle	Sawtooth	Summer 1960	H. Gmosser/B. Echo/D. Millsap/C. Brown
Goat Perch	Sawtooth	Summer 1960	H. Carter/Iowa Mountaineers
Goblin	Seven Devil	Summer 1935	A. H. Marshall/E. Hughes
Grand Aigille	Sawtooth	Summer 1946	J. Hieb/W. Grande/R. Widrig/W. Graham Mathews
Grand Mogul	Sawtooth	Summer 1948	F. Beckey/J. Fuller
He Devil	Seven Devil	Prior To 1938	B. Savage/C. Brown H. Barton /J. Ratcliff
Horstmann Peak	Sawtooth	Summer 1934	R. & M. Underhill/D. Williams
Hyndman Peak	Pioneer	Summer Winter	Unknown L. Stur/?
Knuckle Peak	Bighorn Creek	Summer 1955	L. Hales/P. Schoening
La Fiama	Sawtooth	Summer 1962	F. Beckey/S. Marts /D. Davis
Leaning Tower of Pisa	Sawtooth	Summer 1961	F. Beckey/D. Davis /S. Marts
Leatherman Peak	Lost River	Summer Winter 1975	Unknown W. March/R. Albano
Le Bec d'Aigle	Sawtooth	Summer 1954	H. Carter/G. Constan
Litner Peak	Bighorn Cr.	Summer 1955	L. Hales/P. Schoening
Lunch Tower	Sawtooth	Summer 1961	E. Bjorstad/D. Davis

Season and Peak	Range	Year	Party
McGown Peak	Sawtooth	Summer 1934	R. & M. Underhill
Mickeys Spire	Sawtooth	Summer 1934	R. & M. Underhill
Mount Belial	Seven Devil	Summer 1943	A. H. Marshall
Mount Bush	Sawtooth	Summer 1948	Iowa Mountaineers
Mount Carter	Sawtooth	Summer 1948	Iowa Mountaineers
Mount Ebert	Sawtooth	Summer 1957	Iowa Mountaineers
Mount Heyburn	Sawtooth		
West Summit		Summer 1935	R. & M. Underhill/D. Williams
		Winter 1975	W. Cove/L. Adkins
East Summit	Sawtooth	Summer 1927	B. Limbert
Mount Obsession	Lost River	Summer	Unknown
		Winter 1975	W. March/R. Albano
Mount Ogre	Seven Devil	Prior To 1940	Unknown
Mount Regan	Sawtooth	Summer 1934	R. & M. Underhill/D. Williams
		Winter 1971	R. Sargent/J. Leonard /N. Garrison/B. Weaver
Mount Underhill	Sawtooth	Summer 1935	R. & M. Underhill/D. Williams
North Raker	Sawtooth	Summer 1934	R. & M. Underhill
Packrat Peak	Sawtooth	Summer 1935	R. & M. Underhill/D. Williams
Painted Peak	Seven Devil	Summer 1963	Mazama Club
Parks Peak	Sawtooth	Summer 1960	D. Miller/T. Robertson /H. Wendling
Quartzite Peak	Sawtooth	Summer 1960	H. Gmosser/W. Joura /Iowa Mountaineers
Ramskull Peak	Bighorn Cr.	Summer 1955	L. Hales/P. Schoening
Red Bluff Peak	Sawtooth	Summer 1960	G. Vendor/E. Vendor
Redfish Peak	Sawtooth	Summer 1948	Iowa Mountaineers
Reward Peak	Sawtooth	Summer 1925	Unknown
Rothorn Spire	Sawtooth	Summer 1973	L. Dye/Spring/Howard /Taylor/Bravance
Rotten Monolith	Sawtooth	Summer 1961	F. Beckey/L. Stur
Salzburger Spitzl	Pioneer	Summer	Unknown
		Winter	C. Caldwell/D. Millsap /B. Echo
Schwartz Pinnacle	Sawtooth	Summer 1948	Iowa Mountaineers
She Devil	Seven Devil	Summer 1940	A. H. Marshall
Silicon Tower	Sawtooth	Summer 1961	H. T. Carter
Smiley Mountain	Pioneer	Summer	Unknown
		Winter 1957	C. Caldwell/D. Millsap /B. Echo
Snowyside Peak	Sawtooth	Prior To 1924	Unknown
South Raker	Sawtooth	Summer 1949	F. Beckey/P. Schoening
Pinnacle #3	Bighorn Crags	Summer 1963	B. Hammer/Idaho Alpine Club
Pinnacle #4	Bighorn Crags	Summer 1963	B. Hammer/Idaho Alpine Club

Season and Peak	Range	Year	Party
Splinter Tower	Sawtooth	Summer 1948	J. Holden/J. Schwabland
Season and Peak	Range	Year	Party
Split Tooth	Sawtooth	Summer 1960	B. Echo & Idaho Alpine Club
Steeple Tower	Sawtooth	Summer 1948	F. Beckey/H. King
Thimble Tower	Sawtooth	Summer 1948	F. Beckey/H. King
Thompson Peak	Sawtooth	Summer 1934	R. & M. Underhill/D. Williams
Tilted Slab	Sawtooth	Summer 1971	L. Dye Pinnacle
Twin Imps	Seven Devil		
North Summit		Summer 1963	Mazama Club
South Summit		Summer 1938	A. H. Marshall
Tower Of Babel	Seven Devil	Summer 1939	A. H. Marshall
Warbonnet Peak	Sawtooth	Summer 1947	P. Petzoldt/J. Speck / C. Wilson/B. Adams / C. Fish/B. Merrian
West Lions Head	Selkirk	Summer 196?	N. McAvoy/?
Williams Peak	Sawtooth	Summer 1934	R. & M. Underhill/D.

Appendix D: Selected References

GENERAL INTEREST

Conley, Cort. *Idaho for the Curious.* Cambridge, Idaho: Backeddy Books, 1981.
Federal Writers Project. *The Idaho Encyclopedia.* Caldwell, Idaho: Caxton Printers, 1938.
State of Idaho. *Idaho Almanac.* Boise, Idaho: 1977.

HIKING

Bluestein, Sheldon. *Exploring Idaho's High Desert.* Boise, Idaho: 1988.
_____. *Hiking Trails of Southern Idaho.* Caldwell, Idaho: Caxton Printers, 1981.
_____. *North Idaho Hiking Trails.* Boise, Idaho: 1982.
Fuller, Margaret. *Trails of the Sawtooth and White Cloud Mountains.* 2d ed. Edmonds, Washington: Signpost Books, 1989.
_____. *Trails of the Frank Church-River of No Return Wilderness.* Edmonds, Washington: Signpost Books, 1987.
_____. *Trails of Western Idaho.* Edmonds, Washington: Signpost Books, 1987.
Maughan, Jackie Johnson. *The Hikers Guide to Idaho.* Billings and Helena, Montana: Falcon Press Publishing Company, 1984.

CLIMBING GUIDES

Bingham, Dave. *City of Rocks, A Climber's Guide.* 2d ed. Ketchum, Idaho: 1988.
Caffrey, Pat. *Climber's Guide to Montana.* Missoula, Montana: Mountain Press Publishing Company, 1986.
Green, Randall. *Idaho Rock.* Seattle: The Mountaineers, 1988.

CROSS-COUNTRY SKIING

Watters, Ron. *Ski Trails and Old Timers' Tales in Idaho and Montana.* Moscow, Idaho: Solstice Press, 1978.

GEOLOGY

Maley, Terry. *Exploring Idaho Geology.* Boise, Idaho: Mineral Land Publications, 1987.

INDEX

Asterisks indicate unofficial peak names.

282

TOM LOPEZ, an attorney in Boise, Idaho, has lived and climbed in all four corners of the state. Other climbing trips have taken him across the nation and to Bolivia, New Zealand and Mexico. He has contributed articles to *Rock and Ice, Summit, Climbing* and *The Mountain Express.*